Introduction to Financial Accounting

A User Perspective

Kumen H. Jones
Arizona State University

Jean B. Price
Clemson University

Michael L. Werner
University of Miami

Martha S. Doran
Stephens College

Prentice Hall, Englewood Cliffs, New Jersey 07632

Library of Congress Cataloging–in–Publication Data

Introduction to financial accounting: a user perspective/Kumen H.
   Jones . . . [et al.].
     p. cm.
      Includes bibliographical references and index.
      ISBN 0-13-228768-4
      1. Accounting   2. Financial statements.   I. Jones, Kumen H.
   HF5635.I657 1996   95–6526
 657—dc20   CIP

Acquisitions Editor: *Rob Dewey*
Editor in Chief: *Richard Wohl*
Assistant Editor: *Diane DeCastro*
Development Editor: *David Cohen*
Editor in Chief, Development: *Stephen Deitmer*
Production Editor: *Edith Pullman*
Interior Design: *Delgado Design, Inc.*
Design Director: *Patricia H. Wosczyk*
Photo Research: *Teri Stratford*
Photo Coordinator: *Melinda Reo*
Prepress and Manufacturing Buyer: *Paul Smolenski*
Production Services Manager: *Lorraine Patsco*
Electronic Page Layout: *Christy Mahon*
Electronic Artist: *Warren Fischbach*
Cover Art: *Marjory Dressler/Photo-Graphics*

FASB Concepts Statements No. 1, *Objectives of Financial Reporting by Business Enterprises,* No. 2, *Qualitative Characteristics of Accounting Information,* and No. 6, *Elements of Financial Statements,* are copyrighted by the Financial Accounting Standards Board, 401 Merritt 7, P.O. Box 5116, Norwalk, Connecticut, 06856-5116, U.S.A. Portions are reprinted with permission. Copies of the complete documents are available from the FASB.

Quotations in Chapters 3, 10, and 13 from American Institute of Certified Public Accountants are Copyright ©1994 by American Institute of Certified Public Accountants, Inc. Reprinted with permission.

The authors dedicate this book
to their families.

Printed in the United States of America

10 9 8 7 6 5 4 3 2 1

ISBN 0-13-228768-4 (Student Edition)
ISBN 0-13-228776-5 (Instructor Edition)

Prentice-Hall International (UK) Limited, *London*
Prentice-Hall of Australia Pty. Limited, *Sydney*
Prentice-Hall Canada Inc., *Toronto*
Prentice-Hall Hispanoamericana, S.A., *Mexico*
Prentice-Hall of India Private Limited, *New Delhi*
Prentice-Hall of Japan, Inc., *Tokyo*
Simon & Schuster Asia Pte. Ltd., *Singapore*
Editora Prentice-Hall do Brasil, Ltda., *Rio de Janeiro*

Brief Contents

Contents

Chapter 5 The Balance Sheet (Continued): Additional Financing—Borrowing from Others   120

Chapter 6 Tools of the Trade, Part II Income Statement and Statement of Owners' Equity   150

Preface

As the twenty-first century approaches, we need to reassess the way we are preparing our students for the business world of tomorrow. Clearly, technological advances have changed the skills required in the business world, and advances we can not yet imagine will affect the skills required in the future. Although computers are taking over many of the more repetitive business tasks, business people must still do all the things only people can do — in particular, communicating, thinking, and making decisions. Decision making is *the* critical skill in today's business world, and *Introduction to Financial Accounting: A User Perspective* helps its users to better use accounting information and improve their decision-making skills.

This text provides an introduction to accounting within the context of business and business decisions. Readers will explore accounting information's role in the decision-making process, and learn how to use various types of accounting information found in financial statements and annual reports. Seeing how accounting information can be used to make better business decisions will benefit all students, regardless of their major course of study or chosen career.

We agree with the recommendations made by the Accounting Education Change Commission in its *Position Statement No. Two: The First Course In Accounting*. We believe the course should be a broad introduction *to* accounting, rather than introductory accounting as it has traditionally been taught, and it should be taught from the perspective of the user, not the preparer. It should emphasize *what* accounting information is, *why* it is important, and *how* it is used by economic decision makers.

As you work with this text, you will find it focuses heavily on the uses of accounting information rather than the preparation of the information. This, however is only one characteristic which distinguishes *Introduction to Financial Accounting: A User Perspective* from other texts you may have used in the past.

SUPPORT FOR THE INTERACTIVE CLASSROOM

We believe this text will help get students more involved in their learning process. The conversational tone of the text, its user perspective, and the logical presentation of topics all contribute to the ability of this text to meet that goal. However, several features are particularly important in developing a classroom atmosphere in which students share ideas, ask questions, and relate their learning to the world around them.

Throughout each chapter of the text, you will find *Discussion Questions (DQs)*. In most cases, answers to the DQs require thought beyond the surface of the written text. They are NOT review questions for which the students can scan a few pages of the text to locate an answer. Many of the DQs provide a starting point in relating students' own experiences to the knowledge they are gaining through the text.

The DQs will be very useful in the classroom because of their versatility. They can be used in several different ways:

- Many of the DQs will provide the basis for lively classroom discussions. Many of them require students to think about issues and formulate their own opinions.
- If your students are working in groups, some of the DQs may be used as group assignments (in or out of the classroom). This approach is a good initial step into cooperative learning.
- DQs may be assigned as individual written assignments to be collected and graded. Our students will certainly benefit from the opportunity to practice their writing skills.
- Often, a combination of individual and group work is best. When students come to class with their individual written responses to the DQs, have them get into groups, debate the issues, and come to an answer based on group consensus. When there is no "right" or "wrong" answer, group discussions will get *very* lively!
- Having students keep a journal of their responses to ALL the DQs (whether or not they are used in another way) is a good approach to take advantage of the questions which require solitary pondering.

The DQs are a critically important part of the text. Even if they are not formally used as part of the required work for your course, they should not be ignored. We have designed the DQs to emphasize important points that students may otherwise skim across in their reading. Students will gain a greater understanding of the issues discussed if they will take the time to ponder each question as they reach it in their reading.

Another way to open up your classroom and get students enthused about accounting is to relate topics to the real world. Rockwell International's 1994 annual report is shrink-wrapped with our text, providing your students with the "real thing." We have found that this feature of our text generates enthusiasm among the students, because they can immediately see the relevance of the knowledge they are gaining.

Chapter 13 introduces students to the two major outputs of financial reporting — the annual report and Form 10-K. The chapter walks students through the Rockwell annual report. After this guided tour through one annual report, your students will be better able to handle others. Chapter 14 focuses on ratio analysis, and uses the financial information from the Rockwell annual report in its examples. Although specific text reference to the Rockwell report is not made until Chapter 13, you may have your students explore it even earlier in their work.

Sara Lee Corporation's 1994 annual report is reproduced in the appendix of the text. End-of-chapter assignments related to this annual report and Rockwell's are included in Chapters 13 and 14.

Both Chapters 13 and 14 provide students with help in using library resources to learn about companies. You may find this feature particularly useful if you send your students out on the adventure of gathering and analyzing accounting information. Adventures into *real* information about *real* companies always raises student interest!

In addition to these features which help to foster an open, interactive environment in the classroom, a major distinction of this text is its total separation of the *use* of accounting information and its preparation.

SEPARATION OF ACCOUNTING AND BOOKKEEPING

Our text has no debits or credits whatsoever. Is this an indication we think a knowledge of bookkeeping skills is unnecessary? On the contrary, bookkeeping is the nuts and bolts that holds our accounting systems together. What we've learned, though, is that beginning accounting students can't digest the use of financial statements, the role of accounting information, the world of business, and the details of bookkeeping simultaneously. Once students have a basic knowledge of the other topics, however, details of the recording process are much easier for them to learn, and by that time they even know WHY they are learning it.

Separating accounting and bookkeeping makes both subjects easier to grasp and more enjoyable to learn. This approach also allows the timing and degree of coverage of the recording process to be at the discretion of individual instructors and institutions. Some schools may choose to have all students learn basic recording procedures; others may only require accounting majors to acquire these skills.

To facilitate the separation of accounting and bookkeeping, we have developed a separate short text. *Accounting Procedures: The Recording Process* offers a clear, concise introduction to the basic procedures of recording business transactions. This new, modular text covers the recording process in detail from debits and credits, through adjusting, closing, and reversing entries. Additionally, it covers journals, ledgers, and other accounting documents in detail. The modular format of *Accounting Procedures: The Recording Process* allows instructors to pick and choose the topics they wish to cover, and when.

Accounting Procedures: The Recording Process can be used in a variety of ways. Some schools have chosen to provide a one-hour class to accompany the second term of introductory accounting. In this setting, *Accounting Procedures: The Recording Process* and its optional software support is an ideal choice for teaching debits and credits to accounting majors, business majors, or all students in the introductory accounting course sequence.

In many cases, a separate class may not be feasible or desirable. In this situation, we suggest devoting three to four weeks of class time to accounting procedures. We have found that once students have a firm understanding of the financial statements and their use, grasping the "behind the scenes" process leading up to the production of that accounting information is made much easier. We would suggest that the recording process not be introduced before students have handled the income statement, statement of owners' equity, balance sheet and the concepts underlying accrual accounting. Therefore, *Accounting Procedures: The Recording Process* should be covered **sometime** after the students have worked through Chapter 7 of this text.

Some schools have chosen to end the first term of introductory accounting with this material. Other schools are setting aside three to four weeks during the second term to cover the recording process. Other approaches are to incorporate accounting procedures into a systems course or simply provide students the procedural knowledge they need during the first few weeks of the intermediate accounting course.

Regardless of the implementation scheme, *Accounting Procedures: The Recording Process* provides a well-written exploration of the accounting cycle from an accounting information preparer's point of view.

In addition to the decision to focus on the uses of accounting information rather than the details of accounting procedures in this text, we have made several other deliberate and important choices about topical coverage.

TOPICS COVERED

The decision to include or exclude a topic from this text was made in keeping with the overall goal of teaching students how to understand and use the accounting information found in financial statements and annual reports to make decisions. Because our focus is introducing students to accounting information and its uses in decision making, we could not simply follow the traditional coverage of topics. During the development of the book, we had no map to follow, no pattern to copy. This offered us a challenge and an opportunity. The challenge was to determine which topics should be included and how they should be presented. As we considered individual topics, we continually explored whether their inclusion would enhance a student's ability to interpret and use accounting information throughout his or her life — both professional and personal. The opportunity this gave us was to create a book that would provide students with more useful accounting knowledge and the skills to use that knowledge. The result is that *Introduction to Financial Accounting: A User Perspective* does not cover every topic that may be included in some traditional texts.

For example, we cover the calculations of only two depreciation methods — straight-line and double-declining-balance. By limiting the coverage of detailed calculations to these two depreciation methods, we can focus on the really important issues related to accounting for depreciable assets, and offer an interesting comparison between straight-line and accelerated methods. Students will not only know how to calculate depreciation expense, but also understand *why* they are calculating it and how to use those calculations in making business decisions. In the chapter, students learn how to properly interpret gains and losses. Most of them are surprised to find out that two companies buying identical assets for the same price can sell them later for exactly the same amount and have quite a difference in results—one company can have a gain and the other a loss.

Another example of the important choices made in topic coverage is in the subject of inventory and cost of goods sold. We describe both periodic and perpetual inventory systems, but we cover calculations of inventory values under the FIFO, LIFO, and average cost methods only for a perpetual system. Again, by limiting the attention given to detailed calculations, students can focus their attention on the issues crucial to their use of this accounting information. They can see the importance of inventory method choice, and the impact it has on financial statements. Again, our approach focuses on enhancing the students' skills in using accounting information to make wise business decisions.

Throughout the development process, we seriously considered not only what has traditionally been covered, but also many topics not usually included. The decisions made to include or exclude items were difficult at times, but we believe you will be pleased with the choices made. The topics we cover and our method of presentation help students to see the difference between reality and the measurement of reality!

In addition to the choices regarding the selection of topics to cover, we designed a sequence of these topics which helps to make them more understandable.

SEQUENCE OF COVERAGE

The sequence of topic presentation in this text is different than that of other books. We developed the chapters in a logical sequence that follows the students' need to know. The role of accounting information in the decision-making process is a theme carried throughout the book. As the chapters unfold, students see how to use each new piece of accounting information they learn about.

In writing this book, we set out to present accounting information in the context of how it is used: to make decisions. To effectively present the user perspective, we developed a more logical flow of topics so that each chapter builds on what the student has already learned. Students can easily understand how the topics fit together logically and how they are all used together to make good decisions. Moreover, students can see that accounting and the information it provides is not merely something that exists unto itself, but rather it is something developed in response to the needs of economic decision makers.

If you could read the entire text before using it in your classroom, you would have a very clear picture of the experience awaiting your students. However, even a short tour through the material covered in each chapter will show you how we have structured our presentation of the topics to maximize student learning:

Chapter 1 provides a brief overview of business, setting the stage for the introduction of accounting information. Without the world of business, there would be no need for accounting information or the accounting profession.

Chapter 2 presents an introduction to decision making. Because the stated purpose of financial accounting information is to provide information to be used in making decisions, we believe an understanding of the decision-making process is not only appropriate, but essential.

Chapter 3 extends the topic of decision making begun in Chapter 2 to focus on economic decisions. We explore the characteristics crucial to making accounting information useful in the decision-making process.

Chapter 4 introduces the balance sheet as the first of several financial tools developed to present accounting information in a useful form. In this chapter, we focus on how equity financing affects businesses and how its results are reflected on balance sheets.

Chapter 5 continues the exploration of the balance sheet, this time examining the impact of debt financing. We present notes and bonds as financing options for businesses.

Chapter 6 presents the income statement and statement of owners' equity as additional financial tools. Now that students have been introduced to the first three financial statements used by economic decision makers, they can see how the statements relate to one another.

Chapter 7 compares the cash basis and accrual basis of accounting. Basic knowledge of the cash basis is important for two reasons. First, students should realize that accrual accounting is *one* basis of measurement and not *the* measurement basis. Second, understanding the weaknesses of cash basis accounting makes the logic of accrual accounting much easier to grasp.

Chapter 8 explores issues surrounding the acquisition, depreciation, and disposal of long-lived tangible assets under accrual accounting. As previously mentioned, this chapter examines effects of depreciation method choice, using straight-line and double-declining-balance as examples. We also show students how to properly interpret gains and losses.

Chapter 9 explores another challenging issue arising from the use of accrual basis accounting — merchandise inventory and inventory cost flow methods. Students learn how to calculate amounts under LIFO, FIFO and average cost methods. More importantly, they learn how the choice of method affects the accounting information provided on income statements and balance sheets.

Chapter 10   returns to the balance sheet and income statement, taking a closer look at the way these two financial statements are organized. We explore the information provided in a classified balance sheet and an expanded multistep income statement in detail.

Chapter 11   introduces the statement of cash flows as another financial tool. After using the information provided by the other three financial statements, prepared under accrual accounting, students see the need to refocus their attention on cash. With an understanding of the purpose of the statement of cash flows in hand, students find its creation and use easier to understand.

Chapter 12   presents the basic concepts underlying generally accepted accounting principles (GAAP) and the types of outside assurance (audit, review, and compilation) available. GAAP provide a set of standards for the preparation of financial statements, and the audit function provides external decision makers with the assurance that these standards have been consistently applied.

Chapter 13   takes an in-depth look at the annual report to the stockholders and the Form 10-K required by the Securities and Exchange Commission. The 1994 annual report of Rockwell International Corporation, shrink-wrapped with this text, provides students with an example of a real annual report. Sara Lee Corporation's 1994 annual report is reproduced as an appendix in the text.

Chapter 14   explains the importance of gathering various types of information in order for the results of financial statement analysis to be most useful. Ratio analysis is the featured technique; information from Rockwell International's annual report is used to illustrate the computations, comparisons, and analyses throughout the chapter.

OTHER IMPORTANT FEATURES OF THIS TEXT

In addition to the DISCUSSION QUESTIONS and the inclusion of the ROCKWELL ANNUAL REPORT, discussed in detail above, our text offers other features which will enhance the learning process:

- LEARNING OBJECTIVES - Previewing each chapter with these objectives allows students to see what direction the chapter is taking, making the journey through the material a bit easier.

- MARGINAL GLOSSARY - Students often find learning accounting terminology to be a challenge. As each new key word is introduced in the text, it is shown in bold and also defined in the margin. This feature offers students an easy way to review the key terms and locate their introduction in the text.

- SUMMARY - This concise summary of each chapter provides an overview of the main points, but is in no way a substitute for reading the chapter.

- KEY TERMS - At the end of each chapter, a list of the new key words and their definitions is provided. This list also directs students to the page on which the key word or phrase was introduced.

- REVIEW THE FACTS - Students can use these basic, definitional questions to review the key points of each chapter. The questions are in a sequence reflecting the coverage of topics in the chapter.

- APPLY WHAT YOU HAVE LEARNED - Our end-of-chapter assignment materials include a mix of traditional types of homework problems, as well as innovative assignments requiring critical thinking and writing. Many of the requirements can be used as the basis for classroom discussions. You will find matching problems, short essay questions, and calculations. Assignments dealing directly with the use of financial statements are also included. Many of these applications also work well as group assignments.

SUPPLEMENTS FOR USE BY THE INSTRUCTOR

Additional support for your efforts in the classroom is provided by our group of supplements:

- INSTRUCTOR'S MANUAL - For each chapter, we provide: (1) a chapter overview, giving you a sense of how the chapter fits with your students' prior knowledge, and where we will be taking them in the chapter; (2) the learning objectives, to give you a set of goals for the skills you want your students to acquire; (3) a topical outline indicating the DQs and applications for each topic; (4) a more detailed chapter outline with teaching tips based on our experiences with the material; (5) a quick quiz, designed to indicate whether the student has read the chapter; (6) suggested solutions to the Discussion Questions, which may help guide your class discussions and anticipate some of the responses your students will offer.

- SOLUTIONS MANUAL - Solutions to the end-of-chapter applications are provided in a clear and easy-to-use format. Transparencies may be made from these pages, or from the disk version of the solutions manual.

- DISK COPY OF THE SOLUTIONS MANUAL - The entire solutions manual is available in an ASCII format which can be imported and converted for use within the word processing software of your choice. With this product, you can edit solutions to emphasize points or make variations to suit your presentation of the material. Then use the files to make handouts or transparencies.

- ■ TEST BANK - A variety of test questions is included. Multiple choice, short answer, and applications are the primary formats for the objective questions. Short essay questions are also included to give you the opportunity to test your students' critical thinking and written communication skills.

- ■ TEST MANAGER - Prentice Hall's *Test Manager 2.0* can be used to generate tests of up to 200 questions. The existing question bank can be edited on-screen, and instructors can create and insert their own questions as well. Instructors can select the questions they want to use or allow questions to be randomly selected. Tests can be previewed on-screen before printing, then saved to one of three word processing file formats: WordPerfect, Microsoft Word, or ASCII. A comprehensive, fully-indexed desktop reference guide is included.

We believe the approach we have taken will help students see how accounting fits into the "big picture" of business, and they should certainly see that what is in the introductory accounting class relates directly to them, no matter what their chosen career. We also think instructor and student alike are in for a rich and wonderful experience as they cover the material in this book. We have devised homework and classroom materials to stimulate robust and invigorating interchange between instructor and student as together they grapple with accounting issues.

Kumen H. Jones

Jean B. Price

Michael L. Werner

Martha S. Doran

1

Introduction to Business in the United States

Accounting touches each of us everyday—in both our personal and professional lives. To be used properly, accounting information must be studied in context. Therefore, to better understand accounting for business enterprises, we must first explore "business" in its many different forms.

The business of America is business.

—Calvin Coolidge
30th President of the United States

The word **business** means different things to different people. For some, the word conjures up a dream of excitement and opportunity; for others, it represents a nightmare of greed and exploitation. But whether our view of business is positive or negative, each of us is touched every day by what goes on in the world of business.

The dictionary gives several definitions of "business":

> **Busi-ness** (biz'niz) *n.* 1. One's work or occupation. 2. A special task or duty. 3. A matter or affair. 4. Commerce or trade. 5. A commercial or industrial establishment.

As you can see, not only do people have different impressions of "business," but the word itself means different things in different contexts. The last two definitions are particularly relevant for this book. It is important for you to understand that at times "business" is used to describe the entirety of commerce and trade, and at other times it is used to describe an individual company. In fact, in the economic world, and in books about the world of business (including this one), the words "company" and "business" are often used interchangeably. So, whenever you see the word "business," make sure you understand the context in which it is used.

This chapter is intended to serve as a brief introduction to business in general and the way in which it is conducted in the United States. The information in this chapter should provide you with the background necessary to put the accounting concepts presented throughout this text into the proper business context. After all, accounting information is the key ingredient for making wise business decisions.

After completing your work on this chapter, you should be able to do the following:

1. **Describe the four factors of production.**
2. **Distinguish between a planned economy and a market economy.**
3. **Explain the basic concepts of capitalism and how they relate to the profit motive.**
4. **Compare and contrast sympathetic and mercenary societies as described by Adam Smith.**
5. **Explain the basic issues involved in the debate over whether businesses have a social responsibility.**

6. Distinguish among the three basic forms of business organization—the proprietorship, the partnership, and the corporation—and describe the advantages and disadvantages of each.
7. Distinguish among the three major types of business activities and define hybrid-type businesses.
8. Explain the basic need for international business trade and the complications involved in this activity.

business Depending on the context, the area of commerce or trade, an individual company, or the process of producing and distributing goods and services.

factors of production The four major items needed to support economic activity: natural resources, labor, capital, and entrepreneurship.

natural resources Land and the materials that come from the land, such as timber, mineral deposits, oil deposits, and water. One of the factors of production.

labor The mental and physical efforts of all workers performing tasks required to produce and sell goods and services. This factor of production is also called the human resource factor.

human resource factor Equivalent to labor. One of the factors of production.

capital A factor of production that includes the buildings, machinery, and tools used to produce goods and services. Also, sometimes used to refer to the money used to buy those items.

entrepreneurship The factor of production that brings the other three factors—natural resources, labor, and capital—together to form a business.

entrepreneurs People willing to accept the opportunities and risks of starting and running businesses.

WHAT IS BUSINESS?

Essentially, **business** is the process of producing (manufacturing) goods (products) and services and then distributing (selling) them to those who desire or need them. This process sounds simple enough, but it is actually amazingly complex, and few people ever gain a complete understanding of all its aspects.

While we cannot even begin to present an in-depth study of the many aspects of business, there are a few basics we must talk about at the outset so that we can present accounting in its proper context. We begin with the factors of production.

Factors of Production

Several key ingredients are needed to support economic activity; these items are called the **factors of production**. (See Exhibit 1-1.) Economists have classified the factors of production into four categories:

1. **Natural resources**. These include land and the materials that come from the land, such as timber, mineral deposits, oil deposits, and water.

2. **Labor**. This is sometimes called the **human resource factor**. It encompasses the mental and physical efforts of all workers, regardless of their skill or education, who perform the many tasks required to produce and sell goods and services.

3. **Capital**. This factor includes the buildings, machinery, and tools used to produce goods and services. The word "capital," unfortunately, is often used rather loosely. Sometimes it refers to the *money* that buys the buildings, machinery, and tools used in production. This double usage can be confusing, so whenever you see the word, whether in this book or elsewhere, be careful to note the context in which it is being used.

4. **Entrepreneurship**. This is the factor of production that brings the first three factors together to form a business. **Entrepreneurs** are people willing to accept the opportunities and risks of starting and running businesses. They acquire the capital, assemble the labor force, and utilize available natural resources to produce and sell goods and services.

How these four factors of production are combined to produce goods and services depends on the type of economic system utilized by a society.

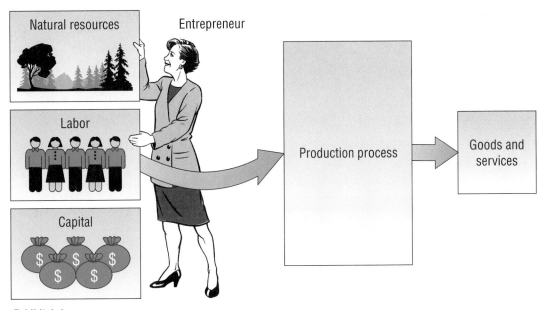

Exhibit 1-1
Factors of Production

Planned and Market Economies

In a **planned economy**, a strong, centralized government controls all or most of the natural resources, labor, and capital used to produce goods and services. In other words, the government replaces the entrepreneur as the fourth factor of production. **Communism** and, to a lesser extent, **socialism** are examples of planned economies. In both systems, private ownership of the resources is limited and government controls most business activity. However, there is a distinction between the two systems. Communism is generally characterized by totalitarian control by a dictator or a single political party. Some people argue that communism is dying out and soon will be nonexistent; however, this system is alive and well in Cuba and North Korea, at least for the time being. Socialism supports government control, but generally offers the people a voice in the political leadership of the country. Sweden operates under one of the purest forms of socialism.

A **market economy** relies on competition in the marketplace to determine the most efficient way to allocate the economy's resources. In a market economy, all or most of the factors of production are privately owned and controlled, and the government does not attempt to coordinate economic activity. **Capitalism** is an example of a market economy. Capitalism, also known as the *free enterprise, free market,* or *private enterprise system,* is the economic system used to conduct business in the United States.

The concept of capitalism is most often traced to the writings of Adam Smith (1723–1790). In his book *An Inquiry into the Nature and Causes of the Wealth of Nations* (usually referred to simply as *Wealth of Nations*),

The word "business" is used everyday in a variety of contexts. Each example provided here suggests a slightly different use of the word, but all the examples relate to what we think of as the "business world." Next time you hear, "It's none of your business!" consider what is meant.

Teri Stratford

published in 1776, Smith said that in societies where individuals are free to promote their own self-interests, an "invisible hand" of competition would lead to the production of the best possible products at the lowest possible prices. The market system guided by this invisible hand of competition, Smith believed, would not allow unsafe or poor-quality products to flourish because people would not buy them. And while the environment was not an issue in Smith's day, the market he envisioned would also presumably adjust to prevent environmental damage.

The Profit Motive

profit motive The motivational factor that drives a person to do something when the benefit derived from doing it is greater than the sacrifice required to do it.

The self-interests discussed by Adam Smith can be broadly summed up as the **profit motive**. The basic idea behind the profit motive is that a person will do something only if the benefit derived from doing it is greater than the sacrifice required to do it. A rational person desires to derive the greatest benefit with the least amount of sacrifice. When this natural desire in one person is pitted against the same desire in another person, the result is competition.

To illustrate the profit motive, let's say that Marty needs a new pair of shoes. Because he is a rational person, Marty desires the best pair of shoes he can get for the lowest possible price. Ralph owns a shoe store. Because he, too, is a rational person, Ralph desires to sell his shoes for the highest price he can get for them. Marty goes to Ralph's shoe store and looks at a pair of shoes Ralph has priced at $100. Assuming he likes the shoes and can afford to pay $100, Marty will buy them if he feels they provide him with the most benefit for the least sacrifice.

Now let's add one other ingredient to the situation—competition. Enter Elizabeth, who also owns a shoe store. She sells shoes identical to the pair Marty is considering buying at Ralph's. The difference is that she is selling them for $90.

DISCUSSION QUESTIONS

1-1. What do you think caused Ralph and Elizabeth to establish different selling prices for an identical pair of shoes?

1-2. Assuming Marty decides to buy the shoes, what do you think will determine where he buys them?

In this example, Marty's self-interest pits the self-interests of Ralph and Elizabeth against each other because Marty's desire to pay the lowest price possible for the shoes will make Ralph and Elizabeth compete for his business. If Ralph loses enough sales to Elizabeth because she is selling shoes for less than he is, he will be forced to lower his selling price. In fact, he may want to reduce his selling price for the shoes Marty liked to $85 in order to attract sales away from Elizabeth. She will then be forced to lower her selling price. This is Adam Smith's invisible hand at work. No one makes Ralph and Elizabeth lower their prices; the force comes from competition in the market. (See Exhibit 1-2.)

Exhibit 1-2
Invisible Hand at Work

There comes a point, of course, below which the selling price cannot go. If Ralph and Elizabeth pay $55 for the shoes they buy for resale, they obviously cannot sell those shoes for less than that. In order to make a profit, in fact, they must sell the shoes for more than they paid for them. **Profit** is the excess of benefit over sacrifice. Thus, if Marty buys the shoes from Ralph for $100, Ralph's profit can be calculated as:

profit The excess of benefit over sacrifice.

Amount received from Marty (BENEFIT) $100
Less what Ralph paid for the shoes (SACRIFICE) 55
Equals GROSS PROFIT on the sale of shoes .... $ 45

This $45 profit that Ralph earned on the sale of this one pair of shoes is usually called **gross profit**. However, it does not represent his actual profit from operating his shoe store. Besides the cost of the merchandise he buys to sell, he has other costs, such as rent on the store, utilities, and wages paid to employees. All these items must be taken into account before he can calculate his real profit, which is usually called **net profit** or **net income**.

gross profit The excess of benefit received over the sacrifice made to complete a sale. Gross profit considers only the cost of the item sold; it does not consider the other costs of operations.

net profit Actual profit; equivalent to net income.

net income The amount of profit that remains after all costs have been considered.

If Ralph does not earn a sufficient profit on his shoe store business, he will have to close it and go into another line of work. The same, of course, holds true for Elizabeth. And what is true for Ralph and Elizabeth in their shoe stores is true for the society as a whole if it operates within a capitalistic economy. If businesses do not earn profits, they cease to exist. Once again, this is Adam Smith's "invisible hand" at work. Only those companies that are profitable will be allowed by the market to stay in business; those that are not profitable will be forced out of business.

Profits Versus Social Responsibility

Some people feel that "profit" is a dirty word and that society would be better off if companies were motivated by something other than the "Almighty Dollar." These individuals feel that American business should strike a balance between profit and social responsibility. On the other side of this issue are those who believe that business has no obligation beyond earning profits. They deny that companies have any social responsibility.

We live in a society that seems to measure success by whether someone "beat" someone else. It's what has been described as a zero-sum game, meaning that for every winner there must be a loser. So the following quotation from Vince Lombardi, legendary coach of the Green Bay Packers, seems to more accurately capture the workings of our world than the one by the gentlemanly sportswriter Grantland Rice.

> **W**inning is not everything, it is the only thing!
>
> —Vince Lombardi
>
> **I**t matters not whether you win or lose, but how you play the game.
>
> —Grantland Rice

In recent years, however, there has been renewed concern over how the game of business is played. An increasing number of investors, creditors, and other economic decision makers have become interested not only in "the bottom line" (making money) but also in how companies conduct themselves as citizens in the community. In other words, business can be viewed as a win/win situation rather than a win/lose game.

Many people who are opposed to the profit motive have attacked Adam Smith's *Wealth of Nations* as nothing but formal justification for capitalism's greed and exploitation of people and the environment, while many proponents of capitalism seem to think the "invisible hand" Smith described will automatically protect society from unsafe or poor quality products. In truth, very few people have actually read *Wealth of Nations*. They talk about it, pro or con, and have read what others have written about the book, but they have not read it themselves. This is unfortunate because there is, in fact, nothing in Smith's book to support either of the extreme positions we just described. This is especially true if the work is placed in the context of Adam Smith's philosophy.

Seventeen years before he published *Wealth of Nations*, Smith wrote *The Theory of Moral Sentiments* (1759). In it, he describes what he calls the optimal society, one in which all affairs—social, economic, and political—are conducted with the love of others in mind:

> **I**t is thus that man, who can subsist only in society, was fitted by nature to that situation for which he was made. All the members of human society stand in need of each other's assistance, and are likewise exposed to mutual injuries. Where the necessary assistance is reciprocally afforded from love, from gratitude, from friendship,

and esteem, the society flourishes and is happy. All the different members of it are bound together by the agreeable bands of love and affection, and are, as it were, drawn to one common centre of mutual good offices.

This was the optimal society, also called the **sympathetic society**, as envisioned by Adam Smith, the "Father of Capitalism." Smith did, however, recognize that we often fail to act on that innate sympathy he attributed to human beings, the result being a suboptimal society:

> But though the necessary assistance should not be afforded from such generous and disinterested motives, though among the different members of the society there should be no mutual love and affection, the society, though less happy and agreeable, will not necessarily be dissolved. Society may subsist among different men, as among different merchants, from a sense of its utility, without any mutual love or affection; and though no man in it should owe any obligation, or be bound in gratitude to any other, it may still be upheld by a mercenary exchange of good offices according to an agreed valuation.

In this suboptimal society, also referred to as the **mercenary society**, the "invisible hand" still works, but all members must be constantly on their guard because each member is presumed to be trying to get ahead by taking advantage of everyone else. Basically, it is a society based on mutual distrust. A good example of self-interest run amok is the Major League Baseball players' strike that aborted the 1994 baseball season on August 12, 1994, canceling the World Series for the first time in 90 years. The owners and players totally distrusted each other, focused solely on their own pocketbooks, and seemed indifferent to the interest of the baseball fans, who actually pay all the bills.

The real questions we all must ask are: (1) What kind of society do we want? and (2) If we are living in a mercenary society and want to create a more sympathetic society, how do we go about making the necessary changes? These are questions that transcend this class—indeed, they transcend all the other courses you will take while you are in college.

DISCUSSION QUESTIONS

1-3. In what ways do you think the optimal (sympathetic) and the suboptimal (mercenary) societies differ?

1-4. Which of the two societies (sympathetic or mercenary) do you think best describes our own? Provide an example to support your position.

1-5. If you think that we are living in a mercenary society and that a sympathetic society would be better, what do you think is the best way to move from the one to the other?

Social Responsibility in Business Today

As we said earlier, there is interest today in the socially responsible conduct of business. A growing number of Americans are refusing to do business with companies they feel are insensitive to social and environmental concerns. In response to this concern, a great many U. S. companies are making an effort to communicate their commitment to responsible and ethical business practices.

The word coined in the past few years to describe anyone to whom a company owes a responsibility is **stakeholder**. A stakeholder is anyone who is affected by the way a company conducts its business. The idea is that many people and other companies are affected by the decisions a company makes and the manner in which it conducts its affairs. That is, they have a stake in the way a company is run. The trick is to determine exactly who a company's stakeholders are and just what the company's responsibilities are to each of them.

In the past couple of years, annual reports of certain companies have included information directed at parties the company deems to be stakeholders. This is an example of what we mean when we say many companies today are taking great pains to demonstrate their commitment to responsible conduct.

Whether this trend to publicize socially conscious business behavior is mere "public relations" or a real commitment, however, remains to be seen. In any event, the era when a company could conduct its business without regard to anything but making a profit is very likely gone forever. It could be said that Adam Smith's invisible hand is sweeping out of the marketplace companies that are unwilling to respond to public pressure to act responsibly. Some mutual funds—companies that pool investor funds to buy stocks and bonds— invest only in companies that the fund's managers consider socially responsible. For example, prior to the election of Nelson Mandela as president of

Ben and Jerry's prides itself on being socially responsible, but the company doesn't stop there. It urges its customers to be socially responsible as well. For example, not only does Ben and Jerry's support the 1% for Peace movement, which calls for taking 1 percent of the U.S. defense budget and spending it on peace projects, on the wrappers of its Peace Pops, the company also asks its customers to support 1% for Peace.

Teri Stratford

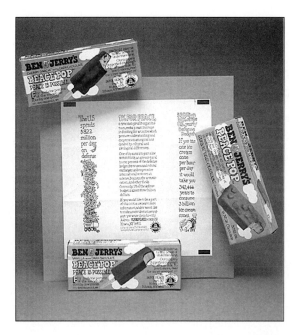

South Africa, there were U. S. mutual funds that would not invest in companies doing business in that country. Many investors today will not invest in alcohol or tobacco companies or in companies that are known polluters of the environment. So the marketplace is having an impact on companies that are not socially responsible because certain investors will not consider investing in them.

DISCUSSION QUESTIONS

1-6. Make a list of those to whom you think a company owes responsibility. What are the specific responsibilities it has to each of these stakeholders? How do you think it could best go about fulfilling each of those responsibilities?

1-7. Can you think of any companies that have fulfilled the responsibilities you outlined in your answer to Question 1-6 and yet managed to remain profitable?

FORMS OF BUSINESS ORGANIZATION

Generally speaking, there are three forms of business organization in the United States: sole proprietorships, partnerships, and corporations. Each of the three has certain advantages in relation to the others, and each has certain disadvantages.

Sole Proprietorships

sole proprietorship Equivalent to a proprietorship.

proprietorship A business that is owned by one individual.

A **sole proprietorship**, also called a **proprietorship**, is a business that is owned by a single individual. A common misconception about this form of business is that it is always small. While the vast majority of sole proprietorships *are* small, the classification has nothing to do with the size of the business, only with the fact that it has a single owner.

ADVANTAGES OF SOLE PROPRIETORSHIPS

1. *Easy and inexpensive to set up.* Except for obtaining the necessary government permits (all of which are state and local), there are no special legal requirements associated with starting a sole proprietorship. All a person has to do is decide what kind of business he or she wants to establish and obtain the necessary licenses and permits, and that person is in business.

2. *No sharing of profits.* When there is a single owner, there is no such thing as sharing of profits (except with the government, of course, in

the form of taxes). Whatever the business earns belongs solely to the owner.

3. *Owner has total control.* This is probably the number one reason people start their own business. Virtually everyone who works for someone else feels stifled by having to "answer to the boss." The sole proprietor answers to no one when making decisions about how to run the business (so long as it's legal).

4. *Independence.* This is closely related to having total control. We have listed it as a separate advantage because it has a broader meaning than simply being in control of how the company is run. Independence can be thought of as the freedom to choose one's lifestyle. There is no set number of "vacation days" for sole proprietors. Rather, they are free to take days off whenever they want to, if they feel they can spare the time from the business.

5. *Few government regulations.* We already touched on this advantage when we talked about how easy it is to start a sole proprietorship. Corporations face many government regulations once they are organized. This is not true for proprietorships. So long as the owner pays his or her taxes and does not engage in illegal activities, a proprietorship is reasonably free from government regulation.

6. *No special income taxes.* From a legal standpoint, a sole proprietorship is simply an extension of its owner. Therefore, a proprietorship pays no income tax. The earnings of the company are considered the earnings of the owner and become a part of his or her taxable income.

7. *Easy and inexpensive to dissolve.* Sole proprietorships are about as easy to end as they are to start. If the owner decides to shut the company down, all he or she must do is notify the appropriate licensing agent of the state and local governments and pay off remaining debts, and the business is no longer a business.

DISADVANTAGES OF SOLE PROPRIETORSHIPS

1. *Unlimited liability.* We stated earlier that from a legal standpoint, a sole proprietorship is simply an extension of its owner. For this reason, all obligations incurred by the business are considered legal obligations of the owner. What this means is that if the company goes into debt and cannot pay its bills (regardless of the reason), the folks to whom the business owes the money can sue for the owner's personal property, including his or her house, car, and boat.

2. *Limited access to capital (money).* All businesses, regardless of form (proprietorship, partnership, corporation), must have money to operate. This is often referred to as *capital*. The amount of capital available to a sole proprietorship is limited to the amount of his or her own money the owner can put into the business or the amount the owner can borrow on a personal loan. Remember, that legally this form of business is

the same as the owner; therefore, whenever the business borrows money, it is the owner who is actually borrowing.

3. *Limited management expertise.* Under advantages of the proprietorship form we listed "total control." While this can certainly be considered a positive factor, it does have a negative side to it. No one is an expert in everything (although we're sure you know people who think they are), and a sole proprietorship is limited to whatever management expertise the proprietor possesses. Many proprietorships get into trouble because the owner lacks skills in areas critical to the survival of the company.

4. *Personal time commitment.* Running a business is hard work, and most sole proprietors work very long hours—probably longer hours than they would have to if they were employees of someone else. However, because they are working for their own benefit and not someone else's, most sole proprietors consider the time well spent. But make no mistake about it, it takes a tremendous amount of time to run your own business.

5. *Often have limited lives.* As we shall see when we discuss the other two business forms, partnerships and corporations tend to have longer lives than sole proprietorships. The reason for this is fairly simple: Unless the company is sold to someone else (another sole proprietor) or is passed on to the owner's heirs, the life of the business is no longer than the life of the owner.

Notwithstanding the disadvantages of proprietorship, it is the dream of many Americans to own their own business, and nearly 71 percent of companies in the United States are sole proprietorships. Because most of them are small businesses, only about 6 percent of all business revenues come from this form of business.

Partnerships

partnership A business form similar to a proprietorship, but having two or more owners.

Think of a **partnership** as a proprietorship with two or more owners. This is a bit simplistic because there are actually several different types of partnerships; however, for our purposes here, thinking of a partnership as a proprietorship with two or more owners is appropriate. As with the sole proprietorship, there is a common misconception that all partnerships are small businesses. In fact, some partnerships are quite large. Most large public accounting firms, for instance, are partnerships, and some of them have as many as 1,500 partners and 20,000 employees.

ADVANTAGES OF PARTNERSHIPS

1. *Easy to form.* From a legal standpoint, partnerships are not much more complicated to form than are proprietorships. Once the appropriate licenses and permits are obtained, a partnership is in business.

2. *Increased management expertise.* Partnerships are often formed because one person has skills in one critical area of business and another person possesses expertise in a different critical area. Combining those

areas of expertise into a partnership enhances the business's chances of success.

3. *Access to more capital (money).* Having more than one person involved in the ownership of the business usually increases access to capital. In fact, many partnerships are formed for this very reason.

4. *Few government regulations.* Like sole proprietorships, partnerships are subject to relatively few government regulations. So long as the partners pay their taxes and the partnership does not engage in illegal activities, there is not much government interference.

5. *No special income taxes.* Partnerships are not legally separate from their owners. Therefore, partnerships do not pay income taxes. Rather, any profits earned by a partnership are considered personal income of the partners and the partners pay tax on these earnings as part of their personal tax returns.

6. *Greater business continuity.* Because there are more people involved, partnerships tend to have longer lives than do sole proprietorships. When a partner dies or withdraws from the partnership, the legal life of the partnership ends. For all practical purposes, however, the business generally does not need to stop its operations. The partnership agreement may allow the remaining partner or partners to either continue with one less partner or to admit another partner to the firm.

DISADVANTAGES OF PARTNERSHIPS

1. *Unlimited liability.* Because partnerships are legally no different from their owners, the partners are personally liable for all obligations of the business. In fact, in most instances, each partner is personally liable for *all* the obligations of the partnership. This means that if any partner makes a decision that obligates the partnership, all the other partners are also liable, even if they knew nothing about the decision.

2. *Must share profits.* When a partnership is formed, there is an agreement prepared outlining how any profits of the company are to be divided. Usually this is based on how much each partner has invested in the partnership. Regardless of whether such an agreement is fair and equitable, once a partnership is formed, there will be a sharing of profits with others.

3. *Potential conflicts between partners.* Suppose one partner wants the company to begin selling a new product and another partner disagrees. If the two partners have equal power, they have entered into what it has become fashionable to call "gridlock." The basis for conflicts among partners may range from personal habits to overall business philosophy, and there may be no other way to resolve them but to dissolve the partnership.

4. *Often difficult to dissolve.* Ending a partnership can be very nasty. When a partnership is formed, everybody is happy and the future looks bright. But people and circumstances change. So when someone has become

severely dissatisfied with the way the partnership is being run, the partnership may have to be dissolved. Unfortunately, the dissolution of a partnership under these circumstances often leads to accusations and counteraccusations, friends becoming enemies, and litigation (lawsuits). If they are wise, individuals forming a partnership will include provisions for dissolution in the original partnership agreement, while all the partners are still friendly. You might think of this as the business version of the prenuptial agreement: The parties forming the business agree on how the business marriage is to be ended.

Frankly, while there are advantages to the partnership form, many people feel those advantages are far outweighed by the disadvantages. Only about 1 percent of all businesses in the United States are partnerships, and they account for just about 4 percent of all business revenues.

Corporations

corporation One of the three forms of business organization. The only one that is legally considered to be an entity separate from its owners.

From a record-keeping and accounting standpoint, proprietorships, partnerships, and corporations are all considered to be completely separate from their owner or owners. This means that all information pertaining to the financial affairs of a company is carefully separated from information about the personal financial affairs of the owners, regardless of the organizational form of the company. This distinction between companies and their owners only holds true for accounting purposes. As we noted earlier, both proprietorships and partnerships are legally considered to be the same as their owners. Of the three forms of business organization, only the **corporation** is legally considered a separate entity from its owners.

Way back in 1819, Chief Justice John Marshall of the United States Supreme Court made this statement:

> **A** corporation is an artificial being, invisible, intangible, and existing only in contemplation of law.

This ruling changed the course of business in the United States forever. As a separate legal entity, a corporation has many of the rights and obligations of a person. These include the right to enter into contracts and the right to buy, own, and sell property. A corporation is required by law to discharge its obligations lawfully, and it can be sued if it does not. A corporation can be taken to court if it breaks the law, and it is obligated to pay taxes, just like an actual person. In addition to the legal obligations of corporations, the moral obligation of corporations to be socially responsible has been a topic of widespread discussion in recent years. The fact that corporations are separate legal entities leads to several distinct advantages and disadvantages of this business form.

ADVANTAGES OF CORPORATIONS

stockholder A person who owns shares of stock in a corporation.

1. *Limited liability.* Because a corporation is a separate legal entity from its owners (stockholders), the owners are not liable for the corporation's obligations. The maximum amount a **stockholder** can lose is the amount of his or her investment.

2. *Greater access to capital.* By dividing ownership into relatively low-cost shares of stock, corporations can attract a great number of investors. Some corporations in the United States have more than a million different stockholders.

3. *Easy transferability of ownership.* Because shares of ownership in corporations are usually relatively low in cost, they can be purchased or sold by individual investors much more easily than an ownership interest in either of the other two forms of business can.

4. *Continuity of life.* Because a corporation is legally separate and distinct from its owner or owners, it continues to exist even when there is a complete change in ownership. The transfer of shares of stock has no effect on a corporation.

DISADVANTAGES OF CORPORATIONS

double taxation The tax imposed on the after-tax profits of a corporation that have been distributed to the stockholders in the form of dividends.

1. *Greater tax burden.* All businesses, regardless of form, must pay property taxes and payroll taxes. In addition to these taxes, corporations must pay a federal income tax, and in many states, they are also required to pay state and even local income taxes. Part of the after-tax profit is distributed to the owners in the form of dividends. These dividends are considered personal income to the owners and are taxed again. This is what is referred to as **double taxation**, and it has been the subject of fierce debate for many years in the United States.

2. *Greater government regulation.* Corporations are subject to significantly more government control than are either sole proprietorships or partnerships. Some corporations are required to file reports with both federal and state regulatory bodies. Filing these reports is time-consuming and costly.

3. *Absentee ownership.* In almost all proprietorships and in most partnerships, the owners also manage the business. They are assured, therefore, that the company is being operated according to their wishes. In many corporations, the vast majority of the stockholders have no involvement in the day-to-day operation of the business. Professional managers sometimes operate the company in their own interests rather than for the benefit of the owners.

Although corporations represent a relatively small percentage of the total number of businesses in the United States, they transact roughly six times as much business as all proprietorships and partnerships combined. They also control the vast majority of business resources in the United States.

Exhibit 1-3
Advantages and Disadvantages of the Three Forms of Business Organization

Business Form	Advantages	Disadvantages
Proprietorship	1. Easy and inexpensive to set up. 2. No sharing of profits. 3. Owner has total control. 4. Independence. 5. Few government regulations. 6. No special income taxes. 7. Easy and inexpensive to dissolve.	1. Unlimited liability. 2. Limited access to capital. 3. Limited management expertise. 4. Personal time commitment. 5. Often have limited lives.
Partnership	1. Easy to form. 2. Increased management expertise. 3. Access to more capital. 4. Few government regulations. 5. No special income taxes. 6. Greater business continuity.	1. Unlimited liability. 2. Must share profits. 3. Potential conflicts with partners. 4. Often difficult to dissolve.
Corporation	1. Limited liability. 2. Greater access to capital. 3. Easy transferability of ownership. 4. Continuity of life.	1. Greater tax burden. 2. Greater government regulation. 3. Absentee ownership.

DISCUSSION QUESTIONS

1-8. Imagine that you have the opportunity to start a company. Would you prefer to be an owner (or part owner) of a proprietorship, partnership, or corporation? Cite specific reasons for your choice.

TYPES OF BUSINESSES

Companies in the United States are classified not only according to the organizational form (proprietorship, partnership, or corporation) they take, but also according to the type of business activity in which they are engaged. The three broad classifications are *manufacturing*, *merchandising*, and *service*. While a single company can be involved in all three of these business activities, usually one of the three constitutes the the company's major interest.

Manufacturing Companies

manufacturing The business activity that converts purchased raw materials into some tangible, physical product.

The standard definition of a **manufacturing** company is one that purchases raw materials and converts them into some tangible, physical product. We often think of these raw materials as the completely unprocessed natural resources discussed earlier as one of the factors of production. While these natural resources certainly describe raw materials used in the manufacture of some products, raw materials often include completely finished products manufactured by others. For example, a company that manufactures household appliances may purchase many items, such as coils and generators used in the production of refrigerators. These coils and generators, while raw materials to the refrigerator manufacturer, are manufactured finished products for another company.

The distinguishing characteristic of a manufacturing type business is that it takes the raw materials it purchases and creates essentially a different product from them. To see examples of manufactured products, all you need to do is look around you wherever you are as you read this. With the exception of the items provided by Mother Nature, all the tangible items you see were made by somebody. Examples of well-known manufacturing companies are Bethlehem Steel, Intel (producer of computer components), the Boeing Company, and McDonnell Douglas Corporation.

The economic might of the United States was built on a strong manufacturing base. For many years, the country enjoyed almost total domination of world manufacturing. While this situation has changed somewhat over the past 50 years, manufacturing is still an important part of the American economy. Roughly 22 percent of American jobs are offered by companies classified primarily as manufacturers.

Merchandising Companies

merchandising The business activity involving the selling of finished goods produced by other businesses.

wholesale merchandiser A company that buys its product from the manufacturer (or another wholesaler) and then sells the product to a retail merchandiser.

retail merchandiser A company that buys its product from a wholesaler or manufacturer and then sells the product to the end consumer.

Like manufacturers, **merchandising** companies sell tangible, physical products as their major business activity. The difference is they buy the product they sell in a finished form rather than manufacturing it. This tangible, physical product is called *merchandise*, hence the designation for this type of company.

There are two kinds of merchandisers:

- **Wholesale merchandiser.** A wholesaler is a company that buys its product from the manufacturer (or another wholesaler) and then sells that product to the company that eventually sells it to the end consumer. Examples of wholesale merchandisers are A. L. Lewis, a well-known grocery wholesaler, and W. W. Grainger, a major wholesale merchandiser of tools. These names may not be familiar to you because, as a consumer, you most often deal directly with a retailer rather than with a wholesaler.
- **Retail merchandiser.** A retailer is a company that buys its product from a wholesaler (or, in some instances, directly from the manufacturer of the product) and then sells the product to the end consumer. We are

all familiar with major national retail operations such as Sears, Wal-Mart, and Kmart. Other retail chains have focused on establishing themselves in specific regions of the country; companies such as Target and Rose's have taken this approach. Still other successful retailers are individual rather than chain operations. Gift shops, clothing stores, and shoe stores are often individually owned retail operations.

Wholesalers have traditionally been referred to as "middlemen" in American business. There are those who feel that wholesalers add nothing to the business process and that the economy would be better off without them. In fact, you will often see advertising in which some retailer claims to be able to sell you products for a lower price because the retailer has "cut out the middleman." This concept of reducing prices to end consumers by eliminating the middleman has spurred the growth of many popular factory outlets. Warehouse stores provide only limited customer service and sales assistance, but promise lower prices in exchange for customers' willingness to accept "no-frills shopping."

Tanger factory outlet centers are thriving as consumers seek lower prices without sacrificing quality. Outlet shopping offers consumers lower prices by allowing the manufacturer to serve as the retailer. This eliminates the wholesaler in the distribution of goods. Tanger's seventeen factory outlet centers offer a range of retailers from Calvin Klein and Ralph Lauren to Reebok and Tandy.

Wyatt McSpadden

The wholesale merchandiser serves an important purpose in the American economy. While there are surely instances in which eliminating the middleman enable these merchandisers to offer lower prices, it is more often the very high volume they deal in that gives wholesale merchandisers an important role in the distribution process and makes consumer products less expensive.

Exhibit 1-4 shows us how the manufacturing and distribution process works as we follow a pair of shoes that moves from the manufacturer, to the wholesaler, to the retailer, and ultimately into the hands of the consumer.

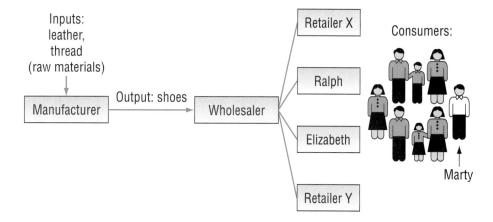

Exhibit 1-4
Manufacturing and Distribution

The manufacturer purchases leather, thread, and the other raw materials necessary to manufacture shoes. When these raw materials have been converted into a pair of shoes, the manufacturer sells them to a wholesaler for $30. In setting this selling price the manufacturer is allowing for all the costs associated with producing the shoes, plus a profit. The wholesaler then sells the pair of shoes to a retailer for $55. In setting this selling price the wholesaler is considering its cost for the shoes ($30), and the cost of running its own business, plus a profit.

We covered the part of the process in which the shoes go from the wholesaler to the retailer to the ultimate consumer when we discussed Marty, Ralph, and Elizabeth and the profit motive. Ralph or Elizabeth buys the pair of shoes for $55 from the wholesaler, and Marty buys the shoes from one of them for the price dictated by market pressure.

The whole manufacturing and distribution process is very simple in concept, but extremely complicated in application. It is not a process that was planned, but rather one that has evolved over several hundred years. Although there are many problems associated with this system, it has proved to be remarkably efficient. Merchandising operations provide approximately 28 percent of all jobs in the United States. This proportion has been stable since 1975 and is expected to remain so into the next century.

Service Companies

service A business activity that does not deal with tangible products, but rather provides some sort of service as its major operation.

The last of the three broad types of companies in the United States is the **service** company. These are companies that do not deal in tangible products, but rather, as their name implies, perform some sort of service as their major business activity. Doctors, lawyers, and accountants are examples of people who provide services instead of products. Another example would be the freight companies that transported the shoes in our previous example from the manufacturer to the wholesaler and from the wholesaler to the retailer.

The service industry is the fastest-growing part of the U. S. economy. From 1975 to 1989, the percentage of total jobs in the United States provided by companies classified primarily as service companies rose from 21 percent to 30 percent.

Hybrid Companies

hybrid companies Those companies involved in more than one type of activity (manufacturing, merchandising, service).

Earlier we stated that although businesses could be broadly classified by their type of operation (manufacturing, merchandising, service), some are involved in more than one type of activity. These are known as **hybrid companies**. For example, General Motors Corporation manufactures automobiles and trucks and is therefore classified as a manufacturer. In recent years, however, GM has become involved in activities that are classified as service. General Motors Acceptance Corporation (GMAC) was created specifically to provide financing for customers purchasing GM cars and trucks. Ford Motor Company has created the same kind of financing operation with its Ford Motor Credit Company. Even more recently, both companies have begun to issue credit cards (Visa and Master Card).

In the near future, we can expect the distinction among manufacturing, merchandising, and service companies to become even more blurred. As the struggle for survival in the world of business becomes even more intense, many companies will find it beneficial to involve themselves in a wide variety of business activities. This will be particularly true as the trend toward a global marketplace becomes more pronounced. American businesses simply must be prepared to view the world of business in a different light than ever before.

DISCUSSION QUESTIONS

1-9. In what type of business activity (manufacturing, merchandising, or service) would you like to be involved? Describe in detail the type of operation that most interests you. What characteristics of this type of business do you find appealing?

THE GLOBAL NATURE OF BUSINESS IN THE 1990s AND BEYOND

There are Americans who long for "the good old days," when nearly everything sold in the U.S.A. was made in the U.S.A. Well, those days are gone forever. American businesses simply cannot produce all the goods and services demanded in the American marketplace. On the other hand, there are certain items produced in the United States that either have no market here or that are produced in greater quantities than can be sold here. Both these facts result in international business. Ford Motor Company, for example, over the last five years, sold an average of 5,842,000 cars per year.

Of these cars, 41.7 percent were sold outside the United States. Clearly, international trade is important to the financial health of Ford.

When goods produced outside the United States are brought into the country and sold, they are called **imports**. When goods produced in the United States are sold in some other country, they are called **exports**. The importing and exporting of goods are critical components of most countries' economic health. However, there are complications caused by conducting business across national borders. While there are several specific complications we could discuss, they can all be thought of broadly as either *economic* or *political* complications (and even these two categories are not truly separate).

imports Goods that are produced outside the country in which they are sold.

exports Goods that are produced in one country and sold in another country.

Economic Complications

Earlier in the chapter we touched on the major economic systems existing in the world today (communism, socialism, and capitalism). Whenever a company located in a country that is under one of these economic systems does business with a company located in a country with a different economic system, there are bound to be difficulties. Companies in capitalistic economies are motivated by profits. This motivation is not the driving force behind companies in communistic and socialistic economies. Rather, the movement of goods and services in these types of economies is part of some social plan.

Another economic complication results from the use of different currencies by different countries: for example, the United States uses dollars, England uses pounds, France uses francs, Japan uses yen, and other countries have their own form of currency. When a company based in the United States conducts business with companies in other countries, the results of the business transactions must be translated into dollars before the American company can know if the transactions have been profitable. **Translation** means converting the currency of one country (pounds, for example) into its equivalent in another country's currency (dollars, for example). This process would be quite simple if it were not for one problem—the currency exchange rates change constantly. Banks and other financial institutions often operate using a daily quotation of the exchange rate. In reality, however, the rate of exchange between dollars and pounds, yen, or any other foreign currency may change from minute to minute, which makes international trading very complicated.

translation The conversion of the currency of one country into its equivalent in another country's currency.

Political Complications

The economic system employed by a particular country is usually an outgrowth of the political system employed by that country (or vice versa). Therefore, the type of political system used by a country has tremendous economic implications. The political complications of the international trade, however, go beyond the issue of type of economic system.

Even countries with the same type of economic system experience difficulties in economic dealings with each other because every country, regardless of its economic system, seeks to protect what it views as its own self-interest. In the area of international trade, this self-interest usually focuses on the comparison of import levels and export levels. It is usually considered bad for a country to import a larger quantity of products than it is exporting. As an extreme example of what we are talking about, assume that the merchandising businesses in a certain country begin to import all the products sold in that country because they cost less than the same products produced by manufacturing companies within the country. Before long, all the manufacturing companies in the country will be out of business, all the jobs associated with manufacturing will disappear, and an essential part of the country's economic base will cease to exist. To provide protection for their own economic bases, countries create trade agreements among themselves.

International trade is crucial to the well-being of American business. Trade agreements among countries are designed to control the levels of imports and exports. Each country uses quotas and tariffs to protect its products.

Copyright © 1994 by The New York Times Company. Reprinted by permission.

Trade agreements are formal treaties between two or more countries that are designed to control the relationship between imports and exports. These agreements generally establish quotas and/or tariffs on imported products. **Quotas** limit the quantities in which particular items can be imported. For example, a limit may be placed on the number of Japanese cars that can be brought into and sold in the United States. **Tariffs** are taxes that raise the price of imported products so they cost about the same as similar products produced within the country.

Trade agreements are usually very complicated and sometimes take years to negotiate. One of the largest modern trade treaties is the General Agreement on Tariffs and Trade (GATT), which was signed by 92 countries shortly after World War II. This agreement was renegotiated by President Clinton in 1994. Other treaties that have been in the news in recent years are the United States–Canada Free Trade Pact of 1989, which eliminated most trade barriers between those two countries, and the North American Free Trade Agreement (NAFTA) signed by the United States, Canada, and Mexico in 1993.

The problem with all these international trade agreements is the same as the problem with all treaties—getting the parties involved to abide by them. Even after the agreements have been formally ratified, compliance essentially depends on the good faith of the treaty members.

quotas Quantity limitation placed on imported goods.

tariffs Taxes that raise the price of imported products so they cost about the same as products produced within the country.

BUSINESS AND ACCOUNTING

Business is about making decisions: decisions about what business form to take (proprietorship, partnership, corporation); decisions about what type of business activity to engage in (manufacturing, merchandising, service); and decisions about whether or not to engage in international business. Accounting information, in one form or another, plays a significant role in all these decisions.

This is an accounting text. Its emphasis, however, is not so much on how accounting information is *prepared* as on how accounting information is *used*. To illustrate the relationship between accounting and business decisions, let's return to the example involving Ralph, Marty, and Elizabeth.

Remember that Ralph paid $55 for the pair of shoes he later sold to Marty for $100. We calculated the gross profit on the sale of these shoes as:

Amount received from Marty (BENEFIT) $100
Less what Ralph paid for the shoes (SACRIFICE)   55
Equals GROSS PROFIT on the sale of shoes .... $ 45

We pointed out that the $45 does not represent Ralph's real profit because he has other costs associated with his shoe store that must be taken into account before he can calculate his real profit. Think about the phrase "taken into account": this is accounting. The function of accounting is to provide information to Ralph, Elizabeth, and the shoe manufacturers so they can make sound business decisions.

1-10. If rent and other costs associated with his shoe store amount to $3,000 a month, how many pairs of shoes must Ralph sell at $100 a pair before he earns a profit?

1-11. What should Ralph do if his competitor, Elizabeth, begins to take sales away by selling identical pairs of shoes for $90?

1-12. What if Ralph finds out he can buy the identical pair of shoes from a manufacturer in Mexico for only $40 instead of the $55 he is paying the U. S. manufacturer?

1-13. What should the U. S. shoe manufacturer do if it begins to lose sales to the Mexican shoe manufacturer that is selling these identical shoes at the cheaper price?

We live in what is known as the *information age*. Advances in computer and telecommunication technology have given us access to a great deal of information about almost any subject of interest to us. Not only do we have access to more information; we can also obtain it quicker than was possible at any previous time in history. But every advancement has its price. One of the drawbacks of the information age is that we are now flooded with data. Trying to find the optimal amount of information specific to your needs sometimes feels like standing on the beach trying to catch the incoming tide with your mouth. Quite simply, it's easy to drown in all the information that hits you.

The purpose of this book is to provide you with the knowledge and skills you need to sift through and use the information available to you. Specifically, we will provide you with a set of tools you can use as you make decisions involving accounting information.

SUMMARY

"Business" has several different meanings, but in the context of this book, "business" means either commerce or trade as a whole or a specific company involved in commerce or trade. All economic activity revolves around the four factors of production: (1) natural resources, (2) labor, (3) capital, and (4) entrepreneurship. These four factors of production are handled differently in different types of economies. In a planned economy, a strong, centralized government controls most or all of the factors. In a market economy, most of the factors of production are privately owned.

Capitalism, the market economy within which American business operates, depends on each participant's concern about his or her self-interests to create competition. This system relies on the profit motive and its resulting competition to allocate resources and force businesses to operate efficiently.

Adam Smith described two basic types of societies: sympathetic and mercenary. One issue resulting from a study of his philosophy is whether business has a social responsibility to its stakeholders. Adam Smith's writings offer thought-provoking views of how societies operate and how they should operate.

The three basic forms of business organization are the proprietorship, the partnership, and the corporation. Each form has advantages and disadvantages compared to the other two.

Most business activity can be categorized as either manufacturing, merchandising, or service. Hybrid businesses are those that conduct more than one of these types of activities.

The global market is here to stay. Today's businesses must see the world as a global economy if they wish to survive. Conducting business with other countries involves two major types of complications. Economic complications from the interaction of countries with different types of currencies and, sometimes, different types of economies. Political complications result from the fact that each country is concerned about its own self-interests. Political complications are worsened when the trading countries have different types of economies.

This overview of American business was provided as a basis for understanding the context within which accounting operates. Accounting provides information critical to making business decisions, and this book will provide you with an understanding of how to use accounting information.

Key Terms

business Depending on the context, the area of commerce or trade, an individual company, or the process of producing and distributing goods and services. (p. 4)

capital A factor of production that includes the buildings, machinery, and tools used to produce goods and services. Also, sometimes used to refer to the money used to buy those items. (p. 4)

capitalism A type of market economy. The economic system in place in the United States. (p. 5)

communism A type of a planned economy, characterized by dictatorial government control. (p. 5)

corporation One of the three forms of business organization. The only one that is legally considered to be an entity separate from its owners. (p. 16)

double taxation The tax imposed on the after-tax profits of a corporation that have been distributed to the stockholders in the form of dividends. (p. 17)

entrepreneurs People willing to accept the opportunities and risks of starting and running businesses. (p. 4)

entrepreneurship The factor of production that brings the other three factors—natural resources, labor, and capital—together to form a business. (p. 4)

exports Goods that are produced in one country and sold in another country. (p. 23)

factors of production The four major items needed to support economic activity: natural resources, labor, capital, and entrepreneurship. (p. 4)

gross profit The excess of benefit received over the sacrifice made to complete a sale. Gross profit considers only the cost of the item sold; it does not consider the other costs of operations. (p. 8)

human resource factor Equivalent to labor. One of the factors of production. (p. 4)

hybrid companies Those companies involved in more than one type of activity (manufacturing, merchandising, service). (p. 22)

imports Goods that are produced outside the country in which they are sold. (p. 23)

labor The mental and physical efforts of all workers performing tasks required to produce and sell goods and services. This factor of production is also called the human resource factor. (p. 4)

manufacturing The business activity that converts purchased raw materials into some tangible, physical product. (p. 19)

market economy A type of economy in which al or most of the factors of production are privately owned and that relies on competition in the marketplace to determine the most efficient way to allocate the economy's resources. (p. 5)

mercenary society A society based on mutual distrust in which members must be constantly on their guard against being taken advantage of by others. (p. 10)

merchandising The business activity involving the selling of finished goods produced by other businesses. (p. 19)

natural resources Land and the materials that come from the land, such as timber, mineral deposits, oil deposits, and water. One of the factors of production. (p. 4)

net income The amount of profit that remains after all costs have been considered. The net reward for doing business for a specific time period. (p. 8)

net profit Actual profit; equivalent to net income. (p. 8)

partnership A business form similar to a proprietorship, but having two or more owners. (p. 14)

planned economy An economy in which a strong, centralized government controls all or most of the natural resources, labor, and capital used to produce goods and services. (p. 5)

profit The excess of benefit over sacrifice. A less formal name for net income. (p. 8)

profit motive The motivational factor that drives a person to do something when the benefit derived from doing it is greater than the sacrifice required to do it. (p. 7)

proprietorship A business that is owned by one individual. (p. 12)

quotas Quantity limitation placed on imported goods. (p. 25)

retail merchandiser A company that buys its product from a wholesaler or manufacturer and then sells the product to the end consumer. (p. 19)

service A business activity that does not deal with tangible products, but rather provides some sort of service as its major operation. (p. 21)

socialism A type of planned economy in which a government chosen by the people controls the resources of the society. (p. 5)

sole proprietorship Equivalent to a proprietorship. (p. 12)

stakeholder Anyone who is affected by the way a company conducts its business. (p. 11)

stockholder A person who owns shares of stock in a corporation. (p. 17)

sympathetic society A society in which all affairs are conducted with the love of others in mind. (p. 10)

tariffs Taxes that raise the price of imported products so they cost about the same as products produced within the country. (p. 25)

translation The conversion of the currency of one country into its equivalent in another country's currency. (p. 23)

wholesale merchandiser A company that buys its product from the manufacturer (or another wholesaler) and then sells the product to a retail merchandiser. (p. 19)

Review the Facts

A. What are the four factors of production? Define each.

B. Describe the primary difference between a planned economy and a market economy. Provide an example of systems that operate under each type of economy.

C. Explain what is meant by the profit motive.

D. Define gross profit and net profit.

E. Contrast the two societies described by Adam Smith—the sympathetic society and the mercenary society.

F. Explain the meaning of the word "stakeholder."

G. Name and describe the three basic forms of business organization.

H. Describe several advantages and disadvantages of each form of business organization referred to in Question G.

I. Name and describe the three major classifications of business activity.

J. What are the two types of merchandisers and how do they differ?

K. What is a hybrid company?

L. Give two examples of the complications that arise as a result of doing business with companies in other countries.

M. Define quotas and tariffs. Explain the purpose of each.

N. Describe the relationship between business and accounting.

APPLY WHAT YOU HAVE LEARNED

1-14 Presented below are the three basic forms of business in the United States, followed by some of the advantages relating to those forms of business:

a. Sole proprietorship   **b.** Partnership   **c.** Corporation

1. ___ Owner has total control
2. ___ Greater business continuity
3. ___ Easy transfer of ownership
4. ___ Limited liability
5. ___ Greater access to capital
6. ___ Easy and inexpensive to establish
7. ___ Few government regulations
8. ___ Easy to dissolve
9. ___ No special income taxes
10. ___ No sharing of profits
11. ___ Greater management expertise

REQUIRED:

Match the letter next to each form of business with the appropriate advantage. Note that each letter will be used more than once and it is possible that a particular advantage applies to more than one of the business forms.

1-15. Presented below are the three basic forms of business in the United States, followed by some of the disadvantages relating to those forms of business:

a. Sole proprietorship   **b.** Partnership   **c.** Corporation

1. ___ Usually has less access to capital than the other two forms
2. ___ Greater tax burden
3. ___ Limited management expertise
4. ___ Unlimited liability
5. ___ Absentee ownership
6. ___ Must share profits
7. ___ Greater government regulation
8. ___ Often difficult to dissolve
9. ___ Potential ownership conflicts

Match the letter next to each form of business with the appropriate disadvantage. Note that each letter will be used more than once and it is possible that a particular disadvantage applies to more than one of the business forms.

1-16. Suzanne Weiser owns and operates a jewelry store. During the past month, she sold a necklace to a customer for $1,500. Suzanne paid $1,000 for the necklace.

REQUIRED:

  a. What type of business does Suzanne own (manufacturer, wholesaler, retailer, etc.)? Explain how you determined your response.
  b. Calculate Suzanne's gross profit on the sale of the necklace.
  c. Identify four costs besides the $1,000 cost of the necklace that Suzanne might incur in the operation of her jewelry store.

1-17. Explain the concept behind the word "stakeholder" and contrast it with the definition of the word "stockholder."

1-18. The chapter discussed five types of business in the United States. They were:

1. Manufacturer   **4.** Service

2. Wholesale merchandiser   **5.** Hybrid

3. Retail merchandiser

REQUIRED:

  a. Explain in your own words the characteristics of each type of business.
  b. Discuss how each of these five types of business is different from the other four.
  c. Give two examples of each type of business (do not use any examples given in the chapter) and explain how you determined your answers.

1-19. Presented below are items relating to some of the concepts presented in this chapter, followed by the definitions of those items in scrambled order:

a. Entrepreneurship **f.** Manufacturing company

b. Capitalism **g.** Merchandising company

c. Planned economy **h.** Mercenary society

d. Exports **i.** Translation

e. Factors of production

1. ____ Goods produced in one country yet sold in another country.
2. ____ A business that converts purchased raw materials into some tangible, physical product.
3. ____ The factor of production that brings all the other factors of production together.
4. ____ Either a wholesaler or a retailer.
5. ____ A type of market economy.
6. ____ The four major items needed to support economic activity.
7. ____ The conversion of the currency of one country into its equivalent in another country's currency.
8. ____ A strong, centralized government controls all or most of the factors of production.
9. ____ Based on mutual distrust, so that all members must be constantly on their guard.

REQUIRED:

Match the letter next to each item on the list with the appropriate definition. Note that each letter will be used only once.

1-20. Consider the following statement made by Adam Smith and quoted in the chapter:

> It is thus that man, who can subsist only in society, was fitted by nature to that situation for which he was made. All the members of human society stand in need of each other's assistance, and are likewise exposed to mutual injuries. Where the necessary assistance is reciprocally afforded from love, from gratitude, from friendship, and esteem, the society flourishes and is happy. All the different members of it are bound together by the agreeable bands of love and affection, and are, as it were, drawn to one common centre of mutual good offices.

REQUIRED:

a. Find the definitions of the following words in the dictionary. If more than one definition is given for any of the words, select the one that seems to make sense in the context of Smith's statement.

1. Subsist
2. Reciprocal
3. Flourish
4. Bands
5. Offices

b. Reword Smith's statement into modern English.

c. Explain in your own words what you think Smith was attempting to say in this statement.

1-21. Consider the following statement made by Adam Smith and quoted in the chapter:

> But though the necessary assistance should not be afforded from such generous and disinterested motives, though among the different members of the society there should be no mutual love and affection, the society, though less happy and agreeable, will not necessarily be dissolved. Society may subsist among different men, as among different merchants, from a sense of its utility, without any mutual love or affection; and though no man in it should owe any obligation, or be bound in gratitude to any other, it may still be upheld by a mercenary exchange of good offices according to an agreed valuation.

REQUIRED:

a. Find the definitions of the following words in the dictionary. If more than one definition is given for any of the words, select the one that seems to make sense in the context of Smith's statement.

    1. Disinterested   4. Obligation

    2. Subsist   5. Offices

    3. Utility   6. Valuation

b. Reword Smith's statement into modern English.

c. Explain in your own words what you think Smith was attempting to say in this statement.

1-22. The chapter discussed two types of societies—mercenary and sympathetic— and two types of economies—market and planned. This question deals with the compatibility of the two types of societies and the two types of economies.

REQUIRED:

For each of the following, discuss how well suited the type of society is to the type of economy:

a. A mercenary society and a market economy

b. A mercenary society and a planned economy

c. A sympathetic society and a market economy

d. A sympathetic society and a planned economy

1-23. Besides the two types of societies—mercenary and sympathetic—the chapter discussed the topic of social responsibility.

REQUIRED:

Answer the following questions:

   a. Which of the two types of societies is more conducive to social responsibility? Explain your reasoning.

   b. Is social responsibility possible in the type of society not chosen as your response to part a of this question? Explain your reasoning.

   c. What role do you think the government plays in encouraging social responsibility in the following types of economy:

       1. Market?   2. Planned?

1-24. Professor Theano Korus is opening a publishing company to publish and distribute accounting textbooks throughout the United States. She feels this will be a successful venture because the textbooks will be based upon a revolutionary new format of accounting education. Korus has extended an invitation to all her students to invest in her new business. She is offering shares of stock for a mere $100 each.

REQUIRED:

   a. What form of business is Professor Korus proposing?

   b. Briefly explain four advantages of doing business in such a form.

2

Introduction
to Decision Making

Regardless of the form of organization or the business activity involved, success in the world of business—sometimes even survival—depends on making wise decisions. A key ingredient to wise decision making is an understanding of the decision-making process itself.

What time did you get up this morning? Why did you get up when you did? Did the time you went to bed last night influence what time you got up this morning? What time did you go to bed last night? Why did you go to bed when you did? How would you answer if we asked why you enrolled in this course? OK, it's required. But why did you take it this term and not next? What course did you not take because you decided to take this one?

As the questions posed above illustrate, life is a never-ending sequence of decisions, some very complex and others relatively simple. Most of these decisions then lead to, or at least influence, other decisions that must be made. The problem with making decisions, regardless of their complexity, is that they almost certainly must be made using incomplete information about the outcome. Because we cannot know the future, about the best we can hope for in any given decision situation is to reduce uncertainty by assembling as much information as we can before we have to make the decision.

The purpose of this chapter is to present the decision-making process in a way you may not have thought about it before. It has been designed to help your decision making become a more cognitive process. By "cognitive" we mean taking a logical, thinking approach to making decisions rather than just reacting to the pressures of the moment.

Decision making is usually considered a topic more appropriately covered in management or psychology classes. So why is it being presented in an accounting class? The answer can be found in the subtitle of this book, *A User Perspective*. What *is* accounting information used for? To make decisions, of course. In fact, accounting is of no use whatsoever unless it helps people make decisions. Therefore, it is appropriate, before we present how accounting information is used, to spend some time on the general subject of decision making.

After completing your work on this chapter, you should be able to do the following:

1. **Explain the concepts of extrinsic and intrinsic rewards, sacrifices, and opportunity costs as they pertain to decision making.**
2. **Differentiate between routine and nonroutine decision situations.**
3. **Describe the different information-processing styles used in making decisions.**
4. **Use a general problem-solving model to make decisions.**
5. **Explain the importance of creativity in the decision-making process.**
6. **Describe the role of values in decision making.**
7. **Differentiate between two distinctly different views of ethics.**
8. **Describe the advantages and disadvantages of individual and group decision making.**

WHAT IS DECISION MAKING ANYWAY?

decision making The process of identifying alternative courses of action and selecting an appropriate alternative in a given decision situation.

Decision making is the process of identifying alternative courses of action and selecting an appropriate alternative in a given decision situation. That's a good textbook definition, but there are a couple of things we should emphasize before we proceed. First, the phrase "identifying alternative courses of action" does not mean that the ideal solution will present itself if we just look hard enough. The ideal solution may not be apparent given the available information. In fact, the ideal solution may not even be possible given the circumstances at the time the decision must be made. Second, the phrase "selecting an appropriate alternative in a given decision situation" implies that there may be other appropriate alternatives and also that inappropriate alternatives were evaluated and rejected. Thus, judgment is fundamental to decision making.

Another concept implicit in our definition of decision making is that of choice. Without the ability to choose, there would be no decision to be made. Fortunately, we always have a choice. We may not like the alternatives available to us, but we are never left without choices.

DISCUSSION QUESTIONS

2-1. Do you believe that you always have a choice?

2-2. Can you identify any instances in your own life where you were truly powerless to make a choice?

Rewards and Sacrifices: The Trade-off

reward The benefit or benefits attained by selecting an alternative in a decision situation.

sacrifice Something given up in order to attain a desired reward.

In general, the aim of all decisions is to obtain some **reward**. That reward may be money or almost anything else, but there is always a desired reward. To obtain that reward, there will always be **sacrifice**. When you made the decision to attend college, for example, you certainly desired a reward for doing so. So what was the sacrifice? If you are paying for your own education, it won't take you long to answer that question. But what if your employer or your parents are paying the bills? What if you are on a full scholarship? Does that mean you have made no sacrifice? No, there are still sacrifices you are making.

Decision making is an integral but sometimes difficult part of life. One of the most important decisions you recently made was where to go to school. This was really a series of decisions. For example, first, you may have had to decide whether to attend college at all. Then you had to decide on which college and whether to attend full-time or part-time and so on. What are some other major decisions you've had to face recently?

Leduc/Monkmeyer Press

DISCUSSION QUESTIONS

2-3. What reward or rewards do you hope to obtain by attending college?

2-4. What sacrifices are you personally making to attend college?

opportunity cost The benefit or benefits forgone by not selecting a particular alternative. Once an alternative is selected in a decision situation, the benefits of all rejected alternatives become part of the opportunity cost of the alternative selected.

In answering the second of the two discussion questions above, you should have thought of some things you can't do because you are going to college. Some of these sacrifices cannot be measured in dollars (such as the major loss of sleep, the lack of home-cooked meals, and the loss of leisure time). Some, however, can be measured. Suppose that instead of attending college you could work full time and earn $15,000 a year. In a very real sense, then, it is costing you $15,000 a year to attend college, in addition to what it costs you for tuition, books, and so on. That $15,000 could be called an **opportunity cost** of making the decision to attend college. An opportunity cost is the cost of what is forgone (given up) because a particular alternative is chosen. It is the amount of benefit that *would* have been received if a different choice had been made. Opportunity costs are just one type of sacrifice that a decision may involve.

cost/benefit analysis Deals with the trade-off between the rewards of selecting a given alternative and the sacrifices required to obtain those rewards.

If every decision involves sacrifice, what we really desire as decision makers is that the reward (benefit) derived from making a decision be greater than the sacrifice (cost) required to attain it (see Exhibit 2-1). Examining the relationship between rewards and sacrifices is known as **cost/benefit analysis**. In a condition of absolute certainty, determining the cost/benefit of any decision is a breeze. Unfortunately, absolute certainty rarely, if ever, exists.

Exhibit 2-1
Cost versus Benefit

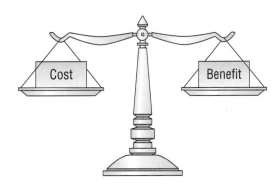

extrinsic reward Any reward that comes from outside the decision maker. The money earned for fulfilling job responsibilities is an example of an extrinsic reward.

intrinsic reward Any reward that comes from within the decision maker. The sense of satisfaction that comes from doing a job well is an example of an intrinsic reward.

The examples we use in describing the trade-off between rewards and sacrifices almost always involve money as the reward. However, money often is not the reward we truly desire. Money is what is known as an **extrinsic reward**, meaning simply that it comes from outside ourselves and is only a material object we may acquire. An **intrinsic reward**, on the other hand, is one that comes from "doing" rather than "getting." When you have worked hard and accomplished a difficult task, the sense of satisfaction you feel is an example of an intrinsic reward. The reward comes from within, and you feel the same sense of satisfaction whether or not you receive an extrinsic reward. While money may be very important, it is not necessarily the most important thing in life.

One final comment to consider about rewards and sacrifices is the old adage that says "the best things in life are free." Not so! Anything worth having requires sacrifice. What the saying really means is money cannot buy happiness, and most of us (once we get past our lust for toys) would agree. Even those who do not agree will very likely come to believe it at some point in their lives. While many of the best things in life do not involve money, all involve sacrifice.

ANYTHING WORTH HAVING WILL REQUIRE SACRIFICE.

Any reward (intrinsic or extrinsic) you seek will require some sort of sacrifice.

DISCUSSION QUESTIONS

2-5. Can you think of something you genuinely desire in life that will not require a sacrifice of some kind?

2-6. What is the one thing you desire most out of life? What sacrifices do you think will be required to obtain it?

Coping with Uncertainty and Risk

uncertainty A lack of complete information about the future. The greater the degree of uncertainty, the greater the risk of selecting unacceptable alternatives.

risk The probability that an alternative selected in a decision situation will yield unsatisfactory results.

Uncertainty in any given decision situation increases the chances of making the wrong choice. The higher the degree of uncertainty, the greater the **risk** of making the wrong choice. Unfortunately, because we cannot know the future, uncertainty will always exist. Therefore, good decision making does not lie in the elimination of uncertainty, but in learning how to cope with it.

It may surprise you to learn that there has been a significant amount of research into how people cope with uncertainty in decision situations. Most of it merely confirms what you probably already know: that as the uncertainty of the outcome increases, the confidence of the decision maker decreases.

So how do you cope with uncertainty, knowing that it can never be entirely eliminated? You compile as much relevant information as you can in a given decision situation, thereby reducing the amount of risk involved and increasing your level of comfort in making the decision. This is a valuable strategy no matter what type of decision you are facing.

Routine and Nonroutine Decisions

routine decisions Recurring decision situations in which an appropriate solution need be found only once. That decision becomes the rule, or standard, and whenever the situation recurs, the rule is implemented.

nonroutine decisions Decisions that must be made in new and unfamiliar circumstances.

The number of times a particular decision needs to be made varies greatly from situation to situation. Some situations recur so frequently that the decision alternative is selected automatically. These kinds of decisions are known as **routine decisions**. The basis of routine decision making is that recurring problems need only be solved once, and that decision then becomes a rule, or standard. Whenever the situation recurs, the rule is simply implemented.

It is too easy to fall into the trap of thinking that routine decisions arise only in simple situations. Whether or not a decision is routine depends not on its complexity, but rather on whether the situation recurs. In reality, some very complicated problems must be routinely faced.

Nonroutine decisions are those that must be made in new and unfamiliar circumstances. While the problems presented in these situations are often intricate, once again, decisions are determined to be nonroutine by their frequency—or, rather, their infrequency—not by their complexity.

All of us face both routine and nonroutine decision situations. It is important that we learn to identify which type of decision we are facing.

2-7. Think of a decision situation in your life that you consider to be routine. Can you remember the first time you had to make that particular decision? How did you go about making it?

2-8. Can you think of a situation in your life in which you faced a nonroutine decision? How did you go about making that decision?

2-9. Describe a situation in which you (or someone else) applied a decision rule developed for a routine decision to a nonroutine situation and experienced unexpected results.

HOW WE MAKE DECISIONS

Thinking is something we do constantly, yet we rarely stop to analyze our own thinking in a methodical, orderly way. It may sound silly, but we really should spend some time thinking about the way we think, because the quality of the decisions we make is directly related to the way we process information. It is very easy, if we are not careful, to allow our thinking to get into an unproductive rut. Our brains are amazing and will run on automatic pilot if we let them.

Information-Processing Styles

intuitive style A style of processing information in which decisions are based on hunches after considering the big picture and brainstorming to find possible solutions.

systematic style A style of processing information in which decisions are made after breaking a problem down into parts and methodically approaching each part.

As is the case with determining how people cope with uncertainty, there has been a great deal of research devoted to finding out how people use their brains to process information. This research has identified two general information processing styles, which we will refer to as the **intuitive style** and the **systematic style**.[1] (See Exhibit 2-2.)

People who possess the intuitive processing style prefer to solve problems by looking at the overall situation, exploring many possible solutions, and finally making a decision based on intuition (hunches). These people are not content with working on problems that arise repeatedly and require the same solution each time; they enjoy a rapidly changing environment, dealing with broad issues, and general policy options. These are "big-picture" people.

Conversely, people who possess the systematic style of information processing are more comfortable solving problems by breaking them down into parts and then approaching each part systematically. They prefer working in a

---

[1]Weston H. Agor, "Managing Brain Skills: The Last Frontier," *Personnel Administrator* (October 1987): 55–56.

Exhibit 2-2
Information Processing Styles

STYLE	Intuitive	Systematic
APPROACH	Hunches	Methodical
PEOPLE	"Big Picture"	"Detail"

slower-paced environment that allows them to be methodical in their problem solving. These are "detail" people.

One style of information processing is not per se better than the other. Sometimes the intuitive style is more effective in a given situation, and sometimes the systematic style is more effective. Also, nobody uses one style exclusively. We all use both styles to some degree, but everyone favors one style or the other. For example, some investment analysts use primarily an intuitive style and others tend to use a systematic style. The job of a Wall Street investment analyst is to pick good stocks—stocks that will go up in price rather than down. Some analysts systematically study every piece of data about a company, carefully sifting the numbers through a computer and analyzing statistics before making a decision. Other analysts do a little computer work, but their claim to fame is their intuitive approach. Many of the best stock pickers on Wall Street operate on a gut level. They can actually "feel" what is going to happen to the price of a particular stock.

DISCUSSION QUESTIONS

2-10. To which careers do you think people using the intuitive style are most attracted?

2-11. To which careers do you think people using the systematic style are most attracted?

2-12. Which of the two information processing styles do you believe you use most often?

2-13. What kinds of problems could arise when you are forced to work with someone using a different information-processing style? (It may help to recall a situation in your life in which you were forced to work with someone who used a processing style different your own.)

reasoned decision making
An approach to decision making in which the decision maker attempts to consider all aspects of a situation before deciding on a course of action.

Reasoned Decision Making

Reasoned decision making, also called *cognitive*, or *rational decision making*, involves considering various aspects of a situation before deciding on a course of action. This approach to decision making can be used with both intuitive and systematic information processing. The existence of reasoned choices implies there are *un*reasoned choices, as indeed there are.

Remember, the brain will run on automatic pilot if we allow it to, and this leads to unreasoned choices.

Reasoned decision making can be described as a seven-step process:

STEP 1 *Determine the real decision to be made.*

The key to reasoned decision making is determining what decision needs to be made. In other words, you must make sure you understand what the real problem is. Too often, when confronted with a decision situation, we concentrate on a symptom of the problem and not on the problem itself. It is critical that the real decision be identified, and that it be correctly defined as either a routine or nonroutine decision.

STEP 2 *Identify alternative courses of action.*

The approach to this step is determined by whether the situation is routine or nonroutine. If the decision to be made is routine, you simply apply the appropriate decision rule. In this case, Steps 2, 3 and 4 of this decision model can be skipped. If, however, the decision is nonroutine, identifying alternative solutions becomes an important part of the decision-making process. Some alternatives will emerge quickly, but these are rarely more than stopgap measures (meaning they treat symptoms, not problems). Good decision making requires creativity. We are much more comfortable choosing obvious courses of action, which explains why so few of us are really good at making difficult decisions. Sherlock Holmes, the great master sleuth, offered this explanation as to why Dr. Watson had been unable to unravel a particular mystery:

Once again, Watson, you have confused the impossible with the improbable.

creative decision making
Allowing, even forcing, oneself to consider more than just the obvious alternatives in a decision situation.

This quotation suggests what makes for **creative decision making**: Be sure you eliminate *only* the impossible as a potential solution and be willing to consider everything else, however improbable. This was easy for Holmes because he was a fictional character. He could make all the right decisions because the author (who knew how everything would turn out in the end) wanted him to. In real life, creative decision making is much easier said than done. However, our decision-making abilities greatly improve once we learn to open our eyes to more alternative solutions. Since creative decision making is an important topic, following this presentation of the decision-making process, we will discuss it in greater detail.

STEP 3 *Analyze each alternative critically.*

If anything, this step is even more difficult than the previous one because it requires the decision maker to attempt to trace the alternatives into the future and to consider all the possible outcomes of each. This is not really possible with any degree of accuracy because there are too many variables in the future. Instead, you must choose a very few (probably no more than two or three) critical factors to consider and then see how each of the alternatives under consideration affects those factors. The critical factors to consider will depend on the circumstances, but some examples are: (1) how much each alternative will cost, (2) how much time each alternative will require, and (3) how much risk is associated with each alternative.

STEP 4 *Select the best alternative in the circumstances.*

Russell Ackoff, a noted scholar in the field of problem solving, has identified three types of alternatives available in any given decision situation: those that will *resolve* the problem, those that will *solve* the problem, and those that will *dissolve* the problem.[2] Resolving a problem means finding an alternative that is acceptable. Solving means finding the absolutely best solution. Dissolving means changing the circumstances that caused the problem, thereby not only eliminating the problem, but also ensuring that it will not happen again. Ideally, the results of a decision-making process will produce an alternative that dissolves the problem, but realistically, that occurs only occasionally. In fact, Ackoff suggests that most decisions we make are of the first type, meaning we resolve problems by finding acceptable (usually stopgap) solutions. For this reason, one decision may eventually create the need to make other decisions.

STEP 5 *Implement the chosen alternative.*

On the surface, this appears to be the easiest of all the steps in this process. You might think that once an alternative has been selected, implementation would be a snap. Not so. Oftentimes activity stops after an alternative is chosen or a decision is made. The hesitation that occurs before the chosen alternative is implemented is caused by what is known as **cognitive dissonance**,[3] and even if you've never heard of it, you have probably experienced it. In common language, it is called "having second thoughts." It doesn't matter how methodical and analytical you have been in your approach to making a decision,

cognitive dissonance The hesitation that sets in after an alternative has been chosen, but before it has been implemented. In common language, having "second thoughts."

---

[2]Russell L. Ackoff, "The Art and Science of Mess Management," *Interfaces 11*, No. 1 (February 1981): 20-21.

[3]Leon Festinger, *A Theory of Cognitive Dissonance* (Stanford, Cal: Stanford University Press, 1975).

SEVEN STEPS OF DECISION MAKING

STEP 1

Determine the real decision to be made.

STEP 2

Identify alternative courses of action.

STEP 3

Analyze each alternative critically.

STEP 4

Select the best alternative under the circumstances.

STEP 5

Implement the chosen alternative.

STEP 6

Reevaluate the decision as new information becomes available.

STEP 7

Evaluate the final outcome.

you still feel you have not considered everything. Much that affects the outcome lies in the future and is unknown. Therefore, there is always at least some chance you have made a poor choice. When cognitive dissonance sets in, all the alternatives you have rejected begin to look better and better. There is no easy remedy for such hesitation except to remember that there does come a point when you must simply take a deep breath and charge ahead by implementing your chosen alternative.

STEP 6 *Reevaluate the decision as new information becomes available.*

This step is often skipped, because once you have overcome those "second thoughts" spoken of in Step 5, you will tend to become very committed to the decision you have made. In fact, most of us will go out of our way to avoid new information after we have begun implementing a decision. Why? Because it puts us back in the position of questioning the soundness of our decision—and that makes us extremely uncomfortable. It may sound crazy, but if you really want to become good at making tough decisions, you must become comfortable with being uncomfortable. You must not be afraid to continue analyzing your decision in the light of new and better information, even after your decision has been implemented.

STEP 7 *Evaluate the final outcome.*

This step is very difficult because it may be a long time before the results of a decision are known. Thus, it may be a long time before you can determine whether your decision was a good one. Moreover, you don't make decisions in a vacuum. The decisions of others, over which you have no control, may influence the outcome of the decision you have made. Nevertheless, this is an important step in the process if you are to continue refining your decision-making skills.

This basic decision model, in one form or another, is found in numerous texts for various classes. Our model is not the only "right" way to make decisions. However, it is important that you begin to take a reasoned, cognitive approach to decision making. By way of review, the steps of the decision making model are presented in the margin and illustrated in Exhibit 2-3.

Exhibit 2-3
The Seven-Step Decision Model

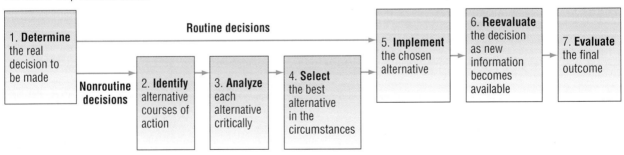

2-14. Some might argue that this seven-step process of decision making is too rigid. How would you respond?

2-15. Think back to your decision to choose the college you now attend. If you had used this decision model, would you have made the same choice? Explain.

2-16. Think again about your decision to attend your particular college. At what point will you be able to apply Step 7 to your decision-making process?

Creative Decision Making

The second step of the decision-making model outlined in the previous section stressed the importance of being creative in identifying possible courses of action. This means going beyond the obvious alternatives. By considering a greater number of possible alternatives, you reduce your chances of overlooking the best possible solution.

Anyone can become a more creative decision maker. While it has been traditionally thought (and therefore taught) that people are either inherently creative or not, there is convincing evidence that creativity is an art that can be learned. Sidney J. Parnes, a professor of creative studies at Buffalo State University, has stated that creativity is increased if the problem solver progresses from "what is" (meaning being aware of the facts surrounding the present situation), to "what might be" (implying a free-thinking consideration of many possible alternatives), to "what can be" (weeding out impossible and unacceptable alternatives), to "what will be" (choosing the best alternative in the circumstances), and finally to an action that creates a new "what is."[4]

For an example of this approach to creative decision making, consider the simple act of getting the oil in your car changed. There was a time when getting an oil change took at least a whole day (unless you changed it yourself, which many of us were either too lazy or too inept to do). You called the local garage and made an appointment (usually for two or three days later if the garage was busy). When the big day came, you dropped your car off at the garage and found some other way to get where you had to be that day. Late in the afternoon, you called to see if your car was ready. If it was, you found some way to get back to the garage and pick it up. If it wasn't (which was often the case), you were without your car for a second day. All this just to get your oil changed.

Do people go through all this inconvenience to get their oil changed today? Why not? Because somebody went through the creative problem-solving

---

[4]Sidney J. Parnes, "Learning Creative Behavior," *The Futurist* (August 1984): 30.

process. The result was a new "what is": oil changes in less than 30 minutes. In this case, the outcome of the creative problem-solving process has been the formation of a whole new type of business—service centers providing fast oil changes. Jiffy Lube International, Inc., a division of Pennzoil Company, is the world's largest franchiser of fast oil-change centers.

DISCUSSION QUESTIONS

2-17. Try to recreate the development of the 30-minute oil change using Professor Parnes' creative process. How many alternatives did you come up with under "what might be"? Was it difficult to think of any? If so, why do you think it was?

2-18. You have recently gone through the registration process at your school. That certainly qualifies as a "what is." What creative suggestions do you have to improve the process?

2-19. If you could change one other "what is" into a new "what is," what would it be? How would you do it?

A word of caution before we leave this section on creative decision making: Creativity is very hard for most of us, which often leads us to a very limited vision of the future. It has been suggested that we can soon expect "the arrival of that period when human improvement must end." Oddly enough, that observation was made back in 1844 by Henry Ellsworth, the first commissioner of patents. Wouldn't he be shocked by the human inventions and creations of the past 150 years! You may feel Mr. Ellsworth was extremely shortsighted, but in fact he was not all that different from the rest of us. What he lacked was the ability to envision better ways of doing things. The late Senator Robert Kennedy once said:

Some men see things as they are and ask, "Why?"; I dream of things that never were and ask, "Why not?"

What he meant was that we must constantly force ourselves to reevaluate the present "what is" and find creative ways to improve it.

If it weren't for creative decision making, it might still take all day for you to get your car's oil changed. Without the new "what is"of quick-service oil changes, Jiffy Lube International wouldn't even exist let alone be an industry leader. In 1993, consumers spent $539 million at the 1,071 U.S. Jiffy Lube stores.

Courtesy of Penzoil Co.

PERSONAL VALUES AND DECISION MAKING

personal values The system of beliefs that guides an individual in determining what is right and what is wrong in the decision-making process.

The most important influence on the decisions we make is the set of **personal values** we hold. Some of you are now saying to yourselves "Oh boy, here it comes. They're about to preach a sermon on what I should believe and how I should live my life." Well, we are not about to do any such thing. Personal values are just that, *personal*. Yours are different (even if only slightly) from those of every other person. We would not be so presumptuous as to try and tell you what is "right" and what is "wrong."

What is important in relation to personal values and decision making is that each of us examine critically what is truly important to ourselves.

> **A**n unexamined life is not worth living.
>
> —Socrates

Because life is so hectic, we all have a tendency to become complacent about defining those things we hold dear. If we do not stop periodically to take inventory of what we believe, we run the risk of waking up one day and realizing that the decisions we have made run counter to what we thought we valued. And this one thing is absolutely true:

THE COMPROMISE OF PERSONAL VALUES IS A PROCESS, NOT AN EVENT.

It happens a little bit here and a little bit there, until you have become a different person altogether. The halls of history are littered with the remains of men and women who spent a lifetime climbing a ladder only to find it was leaning in the wrong window.

So you should examine your life from time to time to determine what your priorities are.

> **I**t is better to be Socrates dissatisfied than a pig satisfied.
>
> —John Stuart Mill

You may not like what the examination reveals, but it is better to examine your life and be dissatisfied than to drift along and be satisfied. What you believe is not as important as knowing and understanding exactly what it is you believe and how those beliefs affect the decisions you make.

2-20. What has been the most important single influence in the development of your personal values?

2-21. Provide an example of conflicts that can arise when you deal with others whose personal values differ from your own.

2-22. Do you think it is possible to reach a compromise with someone who has different values without compromising your own values? Explain.

Ethics and Personal Values

ethics A system of standards of conduct and moral judgment.

There is no hotter topic in American business today than **ethics**. Universities across the country are experiencing an increased demand for courses in ethics. Major corporations are stepping up their training in this area in an attempt to improve the "ethical behavior" of their officers and managers. Virtually every new textbook in accounting, finance, marketing, and other business subjects comes with supplements and helpful hints on teaching students how to react to situations in which they might be tempted to act "unethically."

virtues ethics A system of ethics in which the individual decides what kind of person he or she desires to be, thereby establishing a code of conduct that can be applied to any situation. Also called character ethics.

character ethics Another name for virtues ethics. Sometimes called *classical ethics.*

There are two very different approaches to ethics.[5] The first is known as **virtues ethics** or **character ethics**. It is also sometimes called *classical ethics* because its historical roots are in ancient Greece, most notably in the teachings of Socrates, Plato, and Aristotle. This approach could be described as an "inward-out" approach, meaning that power and direction come from inside the individual and are manifested outward in dealings with others. It requires you to spend a good deal of time determining what kind of person you want to be. Once you have identified the virtues and character traits required to be that kind of person, they predetermine your reaction to *any* situation. Virtues ethics is the basis for the famous warning by William Shakespeare:

---

[5]Our treatment of this subject is light. If you are interested in in-depth coverage, begin by reading one or more of the following books: John Kekes, *The Examined Life* (Totowa, NJ: Rowan & Littlefield, 1988); Alasdair MacIntyre, *After Virtue* (South Bend, IN: University of Notre Dame Press, 1981); David L. Norton, *Personal Destinies* (Princeton, NJ: Princeton University Press, 1976); Edmund Pincoffs, *Quandaries and Virtues* (Lawrence, KS: University of Kansas Press, 1986); Richard Taylor, *Ethics, Faith, and Reason* (Englewood Cliffs, NJ: Prentice Hall, 1985).

> **T**his above all, to thine own self be true, And it must follow, as the night the day, Thou canst not then be false to any man.

rules ethics A system of ethics in which the rules of conduct come from outside the individual. When a situation occurs, the individual determines the appropriate rule of conduct and applies it to the decision required by the situation. Also called quandary ethics.

quandary ethics Another name for rules ethics. Sometimes called modern ethics.

The second approach is called **rules ethics** or **quandary ethics** (quandary means "predicament" or "dilemma"). This approach, sometimes referred to as *modern ethics*, has its roots in organized religion. Quandary ethics could be described as an "outward-in" approach, meaning that power and direction come from outside the individual in the form of rules that dictate how one should react to a given quandary or dilemma. Under this approach, when you are confronted by a difficult situation, you search until you find the appropriate rule and then apply it to the problem at hand. The key difference between rules ethics and character ethics is that the individual goes "outside himself" to find the rule.

Without suggesting that either of these approaches is superior to the other, we want to discuss the potential problems with each approach. First, virtues ethics can lead to disastrous results if a person confuses it with selfishness. The highest perversion of this approach is self-centered, egoistic greed. The necessary moral presumption behind virtues ethics is that the virtues and character traits the individual identifies as desirable will include respect for others. Rules ethics, on the other hand, is absolutely dependent on (1) the individual's ability to determine the appropriate rule in a given situation and (2) how much confidence the individual has in the rules (and those who establish them). An inability to determine the appropriate rule or a loss of respect for the rules (or rule makers) leads to moral confusion and uncertainty.

If we do not have our own sense of power and direction, we must get it from someone or something outside ourselves. The real danger lies in not being aware of where our power and direction are coming from. This concern brings us back to our original discussion of personal values and our statement that *what you believe is not nearly as important as knowing and understanding what it is that you believe*. More important still is the need to be alert and aware of how your personal values necessarily influence your decision making, so that whenever you make a decision, you will see it as supported by your values or in conflict with your values. The point is that as you make important decisions in your life, you should be able to determine whether each decision is in harmony with your personal values.

People who work in the business world constantly face ethical dilemmas. Should an American running-shoe manufacturer open a plant in Southeast Asia, where workers are paid only 35 cents an hour? One might argue that the company would be exploiting those workers. On the other hand, 35 cents an hour might be the going wage rate in that country, and by opening the plant the company might be providing employment for people who otherwise would not have a job. It's a tough decision, without any clear-cut "right" answer.

Kidder Dismisses 2d Trader, Saying He Concealed Loss
By STEVE LOHR

Tobacco Industry Tries A New Pitch: Openness
By MICHAEL JANOFSKY

Cigarette makers go public in an effort to win trust.

An Ad (Gasp!) in Cyberspace

Lawyer's Message Violates 'Netiquette'

By PETER H. LEWIS

Teledyne To Pay Big Fine to U.S.

Accusers to Get Part Of $112.5 Million

By CALVIN SIMS

Supreme Court Curbs Securities Fraud Suits

Once Again, U.S. Indicts Towers Financial Head
By DIANA B. HENRIQUES

Today's news is full of ethical problems in the business world. Managers and employees seem to have a hard time doing "what's right" when it clashes with what's profitable. Exploring your personal values and understanding rules ethics and virtues ethics is a good first step in preparing for the ethical dilemmas of business.

Copyright © 1994 by The New York Times Company. Reprinted by permission. Jeff Topping/NYT Pictures

DISCUSSION QUESTIONS

2-23. Ponder your own personal values. Are these values determined from outside yourself or from inside yourself? Have any of your values started as external and become internal?

2-24. How much do your personal values influence your decisions? Do you ever find yourself making a different decision if others will know of it than you would if no one would ever know what you have decided? What do you think this means in terms of "inward-out" versus "outward-in" ethics?

INDIVIDUAL VERSUS GROUP DECISION MAKING

individual decision making One person working alone to solve a problem.

group decision making Two or more persons working together to solve a problem.

Thus far we have discussed the problems in decision making caused by uncertainty, different information-processing styles, routine versus non-routine decision situations, the need for creativity, and the influence of personal values on the decision-making process. We will now complicate the process even further by considering **individual decision making** versus **group decision making**.

There is an old saying that two heads—or more—are better than one, meaning that the more people involved in the decision process, the better the chances of making the right decision. That is not always true. Some situations are so personal that no one outside of ourselves can be involved in the decision process, even if we would like them to be. On the other hand, there are times when we are required to work in groups, even though we might prefer to make decisions by ourselves. Thus it is essential that you understand the advantages and disadvantages of both individual and group decision making.[6]

Individual decision making has some distinct advantages over group decision making. For one thing, you don't have to find a time and place everyone in the group can meet. You also don't have to listen to group members make comments and suggestions you know for a fact are no good. Finally, compromise is unnecessary because your point of view is the only one you need to consider. However, your decision will be only as good as your individual judgment and grasp of the circumstances. Therein lies the single most significant drawback to making decisions by yourself. This limitation is the reason that when we make important, nonroutine decisions by ourselves, most of us desire to bounce the decision off someone else. We know—or at least fear—that we may have failed to consider some important factors.

Group decision making has several advantages over individual decision making. Groups bring a greater knowledge base to the process simply because more people are involved. The problem at hand will usually be viewed from more than one legitimate perspective, and viewing the problem from various perspectives almost certainly leads to more alternative solutions being considered. An additional advantage is that groups tend to be less apprehensive about whether the alternative chosen is at least reasonable; there seems to be safety in numbers.

On the surface, then, it would seem that group decision making is superior to individual decision making. There are, however, some serious problems associated with working in groups. Some of these have to do with the actual functioning of groups, and others with the quality of decisions made by groups.

---

[6]For a very interesting and enlightening discussion of individual versus group decision making, see Gayle W. Hill, "Group versus Individual Performance: Are N + 1 Heads Better Than One?" *Psychological Bulletin 91*, No. 3 (1982): 517–539.

- *Information-processing styles.* If all members of the group are intuitive types, the group may have a lot of grandiose ideas, but wind up short on specifics. If all members are systematic types, the group may never get past deciding on a seating arrangement at the first meeting. Ideally, there should be a mix of the two types. But they must be able to work together, utilizing the best aspects of each style, or the group can become paralyzed.
- *Domineering members.* The quality of group decision making usually suffers when some members of the group feel compelled to "cave in" to other members simply because those other members talk louder and longer.
- *Social pressure.* The pressure to conform to the views of other members of the group, coupled with the natural desire not to look foolish, can stifle an individual's creative contributions.
- *Goal replacement.* The goal of the group should always be to accomplish whatever it was formed to do. Secondary considerations, such as winning an argument, proving a point, or taking revenge on a fellow group member, sometimes become more important to some members of the group.
- *Differing personal values.* Each member of the group will bring a different set of personal values to the process. From time to time, those values may conflict, and resolution is often difficult and sometimes impossible.
- *Unequal effort.* For a group to succeed, all members must do their share of the work. If anyone slacks off, not only will the quality of work suffer, but the morale of other group members will probably be affected as well.
- *Groupthink.* This is considered by many to be the most dangerous threat to good group decision making. In a group setting, people are often tempted to ignore their own sound judgments in evaluating alternatives in order to achieve consensus. A group member may not feel good about the decision being made but thinks everyone else in the group does, and so he or she goes along with the decision. Remember, the fact that everybody agrees on an alternative does not mean it is a good or even an acceptable alternative.

DISCUSSION QUESTIONS

2-25. Which of the seven items listed as potential problems of group decision making would you consider least likely to occur in a group formed in a business environment? Why?

2-26. Which of the seven items listed as potential problems of group decision making would you consider the most serious in a group formed as part of a class at your school? Why?

2-27. If you were the instructor of this course, what policies would you institute to make certain all members of assigned groups worked for the common good of the group?

Decision making is important in many aspects of life. Now that you have a basic understanding of the decision making process, we can explore particular decisions involving the business world. Chapter 3 provides insight into economic decision making and useful accounting information.

Summary

Life is a sequence of decision situations, some complex, others simple. Regardless of their complexity, virtually all decisions must be made using incomplete information because they deal with the future, which is unknown.

In general, the aim of all decisions is to obtain some type of reward, either extrinsic or intrinsic. To obtain that reward, certain sacrifices must be made. Good decisions are made when a reasonable balance is found between the sacrifice and the reward in the context of uncertainty.

Decisions can be classified as either routine or nonroutine. Routine decisions are recurring, whereas nonroutine decisions are those that must be made in new and unfamiliar circumstances. A key to good decision making is the ability to distinguish between routine and nonroutine decisions.

Along with the uncertainty of the future, the way people process information has a great influence on their decision-making process. There are two general information-processing styles: the intuitive style and the systematic style. Each has some advantages over the other, and one is not necessarily better than the other.

Another key to good decision making is establishing some sort of reasoned (cognitive) approach to the decision process. A seven-step model for making decisions was presented as a guideline.

Still another key to making good decisions is the development of a more creative approach to the process. The most important factor for creative decision making is the ability to consider alternatives that are not readily apparent.

The personal values each of us holds exert a tremendous influence on the decisions we make. Erosion of our values is a process, not an event. To prevent this erosion, we must take stock of what we believe from time to time. The personal values we hold form the basis of our system of ethics.

There are two general approaches to ethics: virtues (character) ethics and rules (quandary) ethics. While these approaches are different, either of them can serve you well. The question is not which approach to take, but which approach you are taking.

Finally, we discussed individual versus group decision making. Each has distinct advantages and disadvantages, and all of us participate in both kinds of decision making in our lives.

Key Terms

character ethics Another name for virtues ethics. Sometimes called *classical ethics.* (p. 51)

cognitive dissonance The hesitation that sets in after an alternative has been chosen, but before it has been implemented. In common language, having "second thoughts." (p. 45)

cost/benefit analysis Deals with the trade-off between the rewards of selecting a given alternative and the sacrifices required to obtain those rewards. (p. 40)

creative decision making Allowing, even forcing, oneself to consider more than just the obvious alternatives in a decision situation. (p. 44)

decision making The process of identifying alternative courses of action and selecting an appropriate alternative in a given decision situation. (p. 38)

ethics A system of standards of conduct and moral judgment. (p. 51)

extrinsic reward Any reward that comes from outside the decision maker. The money earned for fulfilling job responsibilities is an example of an extrinsic reward. (p. 40)

group decision making Two or more persons working together to solve a problem. (p. 54)

individual decision making One person working alone to solve a problem. (p. 54)

intrinsic reward Any reward that comes from within the decision maker. The sense of satisfaction that comes from doing a job well is an example of an intrinsic reward. (p. 40)

intuitive style A style of processing information in which decisions are based on hunches after considering the big picture and brainstorming to find possible solutions. (p. 42)

nonroutine decisions Decisions that must be made in new and unfamiliar circumstances. (p. 41)

opportunity cost The benefit or benefits forgone by not selecting a particular alternative. Once an alternative is selected in a decision situation, the benefits of all rejected alternatives become part of the opportunity cost of the alternative selected. (p. 39)

personal values The system of beliefs that guides an individual in determining what is right and what is wrong in the decision-making process. (p. 49)

quandary ethics Another name for rules ethics. Sometimes called modern ethics. (p. 52)

reasoned decision making An approach to decision making in which the decision maker attempts to consider all aspects of a situation before deciding on a course of action. (p. 43)

reward The benefit or benefits attained by selecting an alternative in a decision situation. (p. 38)

risk The probability that an alternative selected in a decision situation will yield unsatisfactory results. (p. 41)

routine decisions Recurring decision situations in which an appropriate solution need be found only once. That decision becomes the rule, or standard, and whenever the situation recurs, the rule is implemented. (p. 41)

rules ethics A system of ethics in which the rules of conduct come from outside the individual. When a situation occurs, the individual determines the appropriate rule of conduct and applies it to the decision required by the situation. Also called quandary ethics. (p. 52)

sacrifice Something given up in order to attain a desired reward. (p. 38)

systematic style A style of processing information in which decisions are made after breaking a problem down into parts and methodically approaching each part. (p. 42)

uncertainty A lack of complete information about the future. The greater the degree of uncertainty, the greater the risk of selecting unacceptable alternatives. (p. 41)

virtues ethics A system of ethics in which the individual decides what kind of person he or she desires to be, thereby establishing a code of conduct that can be applied to any situation. Also called character ethics. (p. 51)

REVIEW THE FACTS

A. Provide two examples of rewards and sacrifices that may be involved when a decision is being made.

B. What is an opportunity cost?

C. Define cost/benefit analysis.

D. Describe the difference between an extrinsic reward and an intrinsic reward.

E. How are uncertainty and risk related?

F. What is the difference between routine and nonroutine decisions?

G. Describe the two major information-processing styles.

H. Explain the term *reasoned decision making*.

I. Describe the seven steps of the decision model presented in this chapter.

J. Why is creative decision making important?

K. What is the role of personal values in the decision-making process?

L. Name and describe the two different approaches to ethics.

M. Describe the advantages and disadvantages of both individual and group decision making.

APPLY WHAT YOU HAVE LEARNED

2-28. Listed below are the disadvantages of group decision making as presented in the chapter, followed by the definitions of those disadvantages in scrambled order:

a. Different information-processing styles

b. Domineering members of the group

c. Social pressure

d. Goal replacement

e. Differing personal values

f. Unequal effort

g. Groupthink

1. ___ Some members of the group may not work as hard as others.

2. ___ Not everyone believes the same way.

3. ___ The group may contain both intuitive types and systematic types.

4. ___ The natural desire not to look foolish may stifle a group member's creative contribution.

5. ___ Group members are often tempted to ignore their own judgment in order to achieve consensus.

6. ___ Winning an argument, proving a point, or taking revenge can become more important than accomplishing the task at hand.

7. ___ The work of the group suffers simply because some members can talk louder and longer than others.

REQUIRED:

Match the letter next to each disadvantage with the appropriate definition. Each letter will be used only once.

2-29. Bob Sturges, a college sophomore, has just gotten a job working with mentally handicapped children. He will make $5 per hour. Working with handicapped children is something Bob has always wanted to do. He even thinks he may pursue this work as a career.

REQUIRED:

a. From the facts given in the problem, what would you consider to be the extrinsic and intrinsic rewards Bob will receive from his new job?

b. Which do you think will be more valuable to Bob, the extrinsic rewards or the intrinsic rewards? Explain your reasoning.

2-30. Vicki Carlisle is in trouble! She has been in New York on business for the past week, and this morning she was supposed to fly to Los Angeles for a very important dinner meeting to be held at 6:00 P.M. Unfortunately, Vicki has overslept and missed her flight. As she hurries to shower and get dressed, she is trying to decide what to do next. "If only I had not slept through my alarm," she says to herself over and over, "that's the real problem."

REQUIRED:

a. Do you think Vicki has determined her real problem? If not, help her identify the real problem.

b. Now that the real problem has been determined, identify two alternative courses of action Vicki might take to solve her problem. Then analyze each of them critically for her.

2-31. Clarence Oddbody, an employee of Barnstorm, Inc., has been on business in Bedford Falls, New York, for the past two weeks. Bedford Falls happens to be his hometown, and Clarence has stayed the entire two weeks with his mother. Orville Potter (Clarence's boyhood chum) owns the local hotel and has offered to provide Clarence with receipts for a two-week stay at the hotel. Clarence would then submit the receipts and be reimbursed by his company. Barnstorm would really not be out anything, because it is company policy to reimburse employees for out-of-town lodging.

REQUIRED:

a. Explain how Clarence would approach this decision situation under virtues or character ethics.

b. Explain how Clarence would approach this decision situation under quandary or rules ethics.

c. Which approach do you think would serve Clarence better in all such decision situations? Explain your reasoning.

2-32. Presented below are items relating to concepts discussed in this chapter, followed by the definitions of those items in scrambled order:

a. Cost/benefit

b. Ethics

c. Intuitive information processing style

d. Opportunity cost

e. Systematic information processing style

f. Risk

g. Uncertainty

1. ___ Decisions are made after breaking a problem down into parts and methodically evaluating each part.

2. ___ Decisions are based on hunches after considering the big picture and brainstorming.

3. ___ The probability that an alternative selected will yield unsatisfactory results.

4. ___ The rewards of selecting a given alternative in relation to the sacrifices required to obtain those rewards.

5. ___ The benefit forgone by not selecting a particular alternative.

6. ___ A system of standards of conduct and moral judgment.

7. ___ Lack of complete information about the future.

REQUIRED:

Match the letter next to each item with the appropriate definition. Each letter will be used only once.

2-33. The Thanksgiving holiday is approaching and Reggie Wilkins, a college student, is trying to decide how he will spend the weekend. He has narrowed his options to these three:

Option 1: He can go to Steamboat Springs, Colorado and ski for the weekend (he is an avid skier). He estimates the total cost of the trip (airfare, lodging, food, and lift tickets) to be $350. If he selects this option, he will have to cut the last day of classes before the break. He will also have to take time off from his job at Fred's Burger Palace. He earns $5.00 per hour and could work as many as 40 hours over the long weekend.

Option 2: He can drive to his parents' house for the weekend. They live only 140 miles from Reggie's school, so he would not have to leave until after his last class the day before Thanksgiving. This option would require no out-of-pocket cost because he will be staying at his parents' house and his dad has offered to pay for the gas. He would, however, have to take time off from work, just as in Option 1.

Option 3: He can stay at school for the weekend and devote his time to studying and working at Fred's Burger Palace.

The final decision as to how to spend Thanksgiving weekend must be Reggie's. He has, however, come to you for advice because he believes you are a person of sound judgment.

REQUIRED:

a. Tell Reggie what you think are the most important factors he needs to consider when making his decision. These factors may or may not involve money. Identify the factor you consider to be *most* important, and explain why you think it is crucial.

b. Prepare an analysis for Reggie of what you perceive to be the potential benefits and costs of each of his three alternatives. Although economic benefits and costs are always important, do not restrict yourself to money considerations for either benefits or costs.

c. Assume Reggie decides to go skiing at Steamboat Springs over Thanksgiving weekend (Option 1). This decision was made on October 15 and Thanksgiving weekend is the last week in November. Identify *three* pieces of new information Reggie might receive before he leaves on his ski trip and explain how each of them might cause him to rethink his decision.

2-34. Today you received a letter from Pat Arvaseth. She has heard a lot of good things about you, and she wants you to quit school right away and come to work for her. Your salary would be only $15,000 per year, but you are sure you would find the work very rewarding. If you continue on in school and earn your degree in three years, you are almost guaranteed a job with a starting salary of $25,000 per year. You can only make one choice, to work for Pat or continue in school (assume no raises in either job in the near future).

REQUIRED:

Analyze the alternatives before you, using as many of the decision-making tools presented in the chapter as you think apply.

2-35. Explain the difference between an extrinsic reward and an intrinsic reward. Cite an example of each.

2-36. Briefly describe the intuitive and the systematic information-processing styles. Include in your answer ways in which these two styles are similar and ways in which they differ.

2-37. Explain in your own words the advantages and disadvantages of group decision making in relation to individual decision making.

2-38. The chapter states that the most important influence on the decisions we make are the personal values we hold.

REQUIRED:

a. Explain in your own words the relationship between personal values and ethics.

b. Explain what the phrase "the compromise of personal values is a process, not an event" means.

3

Economic Decision Making and Useful Accounting Information

Decision making is an important activity in the business world. Economic decision making relies heavily on accounting information. Therefore, it is crucial that the accounting information provided possesses the qualities necessary to be useful to economic decision makers.

economic decision making
Generally, the process of making decisions involving money; here, decision making that takes place in the course of business transactions.

In Chapter 1, we provided a brief introduction to business in the United States, and in Chapter 2, we discussed decision making in very general terms. In this chapter, we examine **economic decision making**, which will require you to draw upon what was learned in the first two chapters. Economic decision making refers generally to the process of making decisions involving money; for this class, that means business decisions involving money. Everything discussed in Chapter 2 about decision making applies to economic decision making.

All economic decisions of any consequence require the use of some sort of accounting information. Often that information is available in the form of financial reports. The relationship between financial reports and the decision makers who use them can be described this way:

Financial reporting should provide information that is useful to present and potential investors and creditors and other users in making rational investment, credit, and similar *decisions*. The information should be comprehensible to those who have a *reasonable understanding of business and economic activities and are willing to study the information with reasonable diligence*.

—Statement of Financial Accounting Concepts #1, Financial Accounting Standards Board, 1986, pp. 39–40 (emphasis added)

Anyone using accounting information to make economic decisions must understand the business and economic environment in which accounting information is generated, and they must also be willing to devote the necessary time and energy to make sense of the accounting reports. In this chapter, we will explore economic decision making and the role of useful accounting information in that process.

After completing your work on this chapter, you should be able to do the following:

1. Describe the two types of economic decision makers.
2. Explain the basic differences between management accounting and financial accounting.
3. List the three questions all economic decision makers attempt to answer and explain why these questions are so important.
4. Describe the concept of cash as the ultimate measurement of business success or failure.
5. Define accounting information and distinguish it from accounting data.
6. Name the primary characteristics of useful accounting information and describe each one in your own words.
7. Name the secondary characteristics of useful accounting information and describe each one in your own words.

ECONOMIC DECISION MAKING

internal decision makers
Economic decision makers within a company who make decisions for the company. They have access to much or all of the accounting information generated within the company.

external decision makers
Economic decision makers outside a company who make decisions about the company. The accounting information they use to make those decisions is limited to what the company provides them.

Much of human life revolves around economic issues. We will be better equipped to deal with these issues and their effects on our daily lives if we understand the economic decision-making process and the information that affects it. First, let's take a look at the people making economic decisions.

Economic decision makers can be divided into two broad categories: internal and external. **Internal decision makers** are individuals within a company who make decisions on behalf of the company, while **external decision makers** are individuals or organizations outside a company who make decisions that affect that company.

Internal Decision Makers

The first characteristic of internal decision makers is they make decisions *for* the company. In other words, they act on behalf of the company. They decide such things as whether the company should sell a particular product, whether it should enter a certain market, and whether it should hire or fire employees. Note that in all of these matters, the responsible internal decision maker is not making the decision for herself or himself, but rather for the company.

Internal decision makers are faced with a variety of business decisions about the company. One of the most basic business decisions is whether to take the plunge and open a new business.

Hazel Hankin/Stock Boston

The second characteristic of internal decision makers is that they have greater access to the financial information of the company than do people outside the company. Depending on their position within the company, internal decision makers may have access to much, or even all, of the company's financial information. Don't be misled: This does not mean that these people have *complete* information, for decisions always relate somehow to the future and therefore always involve unknowns.

External Decision Makers

The first characteristic of external decision makers is they make decisions *about* a company. In other words, their decisions are not made on behalf of the company, but they affect the company nonetheless. External decision makers decide such things as whether to invest in the company, whether to sell to or buy from the company, and whether to lend money to the company.

The second characteristic of external decision makers is they have limited financial information on which to base their decisions about the company. In fact, their information is limited to what the company gives them—which, in most cases, is not all the information it possesses.

Exhibit 3-1 illustrates the differences between the two categories of economic decision makers.

Exhibit 3-1
Economic Decision Makers

TYPES	INTERNAL	EXTERNAL
Decisions	Makes decisions *for* company	Makes decisions *about* company
Information	Available information limited only by user's position within the company	Available information limited to what the company supplies to the user

DISCUSSION QUESTIONS

3-1. Identify a particular company (large or small). Who do you think are considered internal economic decision makers of the company?

3-2. With regard to the company identified in Question 3-1, who do you think are considered external economic decision makers?

3-3. For what reasons do you think a company would withhold certain financial information from external parties?

The decisions made by internal and external decision makers are similar in some ways, but so different in other ways that two separate branches of accounting have developed to meet the needs of these two categories of user. The accounting information generated specifically for use by internal decision makers is the product of what is called **management accounting**, while that generated for use by external parties is the product of what is called **financial accounting**.

What All Economic Decision Makers Want To Know

Although internal and external parties face different decision situations, both are trying to predict the future, as are all decision makers. Specifically, all economic decision makers attempt to predict the future of **cash flow**—that is, the movement of cash in and out of a company. So one of the major objectives of financial reporting is to provide information that is helpful to those trying to predict cash flows.

> Thus, financial reporting should provide information to help investors, creditors, and others assess the *amounts, timing, and uncertainty* of prospective net cash inflows to the related enterprise.
>
> —Statement of Financial Accounting Concepts #1, Financial Accounting Standards Board, 1986, p.40 (emphasis added)

The difference between cash inflows and cash outflows is known as **net cash flow**. When we say a company has a *positive net cash flow*, we mean that the amount of cash flowing into the company exceeded the amount flowing out during a particular period. When we say a company has a *negative net cash flow*, we mean that the amount of cash flowing out of the company exceeded the amount flowing in during a particular period. (See Exhibit 3-2.)

management accounting The branch of accounting developed to meet the informational needs of internal decision makers.

financial accounting The branch of accounting developed to meet the informational needs of external decision makers.

cash flow The movement of cash in and out of a company.

net cash flow The difference between cash inflows and cash outflows; it can be either positive or negative.

Exhibit 3-2
Cash Flow

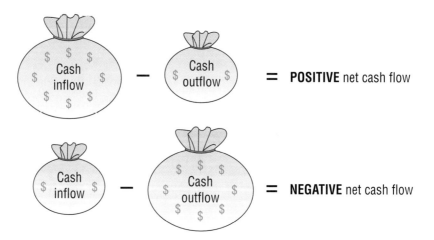

All economic decisions involve attempts to predict the future of cash flows by searching for the answers to the following three questions:

1. Will I be paid?
   This question refers to the *uncertainty* of cash flows.

2. When will I be paid?
   This question refers to the *timing* of cash flows.

3. How much will I be paid?
   This question refers to the *amounts* of cash flows.

A couple of things need to be made clear concerning the answers to these questions. First, we are talking about *cash!* Cash is not a word we have to define for you—you already know what it means (you may not have any cash, but you know it when you see it). Second, the answer to each question contains two parts: return *on* investment and return *of* investment. Exhibit 3-3 shows the conceptual link between the three major questions posed by economic decision makers and the resulting cash flows.

As an example, let's assume you are considering buying a $1,000 certificate of deposit (CD) at your bank, which will earn 10 percent interest annually over the course of two years (interest will be paid to you every three months). If you buy this CD, you must hold it for two years, after which the bank will return your $1,000. Before you make this economic decision, you must attempt to answer the three questions:

1. *Will you be paid?* Recall our discussion of the *uncertainty* of the future discussed in Chapter 2: Because it is impossible to know the future, there is *always* a risk in making an economic decision. However, assuming the economy doesn't collapse and the bank stays in business, you very likely will be paid both your return *on* investment and your return *of* investment.

2. *When will you be paid?* The answer to this question focuses on the *timing* of future cash flows. Assuming you will be paid (see answer to Question 1), you will receive an interest payment every three months for two years (return *on* investment), and then you will receive your initial $1,000 investment back (return *of* investment).

3. *How much will you be paid?* This question refers to the *amount* of future cash flows. The return *on* your investment is the $200 interest you receive ($1,000 X 10 percent X 2 years), and the return *of* your investment is the $1,000 the bank gives you back.

Don't get the wrong impression about the last two questions. In the simple example of a CD, the answers to Questions 2 and 3 were very explicit once you satisfied yourself concerning the first question. In the vast majority of economic decision situations, however, the answers to Questions 2 and 3 are much less certain. A major purpose of this text is to show how accounting information is used to answer the three questions in various economic decision situations.

Exhibit 3-3
Three Big Questions for Economic Decision Makers

Questions	Concepts	Cash Outcome
1. Will I be paid?	Uncertainty	Return *on* investment
2. When will I be paid?	Timing	*and*
3. How much will I be paid?	Amount	Return *of* investment

SEVEN STEPS OF DECISION MAKING

STEP 1

Determine the real decision to be made.

STEP 2

Identify alternative courses of action.

STEP 3

Analyze each alternative critically.

STEP 4

Select the best alternative under the circumstances.

STEP 5

Implement the chosen alternative.

STEP 6

Reevaluate the decision as new information becomes available.

STEP 7

Evaluate the final outcome.

DISCUSSION QUESTIONS

3-4. Consider the most recent economic decision you made. Show how the decision could be reduced to answering the three questions.

3-5. Can you think of any economic decision situation that cannot be reduced to answering the three questions? Explain.

3-6. Describe how to apply the seven-step decision model presented in Chapter 2 to the example of the certificate of deposit.

Cash Is the "Ball" of Business

This section head probably won't make sense to you immediately, but it will once you have grasped the concept we discuss here. Pay close attention because this concept is one of the most important you will learn in this or any other business class.

Let's talk for a minute about the game of golf and try to relate it to business. If you've ever played golf, you know it is impossible to play well consistently unless you keep your eye on the ball (Exhibit 3-4). You may hit a decent shot from time to time even if you do look up during your swing, but you'll never become a good player if you don't learn to keep your head down and your eye on the ball. The strange thing is that even when you know this and have trained yourself to keep your eye on the ball, you'll be tempted not to. Well, in business cash is the ball, and anyone who hopes to be successful at the game of business had better learn to keep an eye on cash. Unfortunately, because this game is so complex, it is very easy to become distracted and lose sight of cash. In your business classes in college and throughout your life, whether you become an investor or an entrepreneur, or take a position that involves responsibility for the financial situation of your company, you will hear a lot about the importance of various measures of performance such as profits, net income, net worth, and equity. Just remember: These items

Exhibit 3-4

are important measures of financial performance, *but they are not cash!* Never allow yourself to become so focused on any of them that you lose sight of cash.

There you have it: Cash is cash, and everything else is something else. It's a simple enough concept, but an amazing number of people never grasp it, and even those who do are tempted at times to divert their attention from cash. Make no mistake: Businesses die when they run out of cash, and many of them run out of cash because management became too concerned with something else, such as profits, net worth, net income, or other measures of performance.

The accounting profession has played a part in causing financial information users to take their eye off the ball. Some methods used to account for business and economic activity in the United States measure performance in something other than cash. While there are sound reasons for doing so, the accounting reports based on such measurement criteria can be misleading to

Performance measures make news! No wonder management can be distracted by them. Just remember, none of these performance measures indicate if the companies have enough cash to survive.

people who do not truly understand the reasons for, and the limitations of, those criteria. If you work hard to grasp the ideas presented in this text and in this class, you will understand how these limitations affect the usefulness of accounting information. Only then will you be a "street smart" user of accounting information.

What Exactly Is Accounting Information?

The dictionary defines *accounting* as a reckoning of financial matters, and *information* as knowledge or news. Putting the two together, we see that **accounting information** is knowledge or news about a reckoning of financial matters. The accounting profession's own definition of accounting is as follows:

> Accounting is a service activity. Its function is to provide *quantitative information, primarily financial in nature, about economic entities that is intended to be useful in making economic decisions.*
>
> —Statement of the Accounting Principles Board #4, 1970, p. 6
> (emphasis added)

accounting information Raw data concerning transactions that have been transformed into financial numbers that can be used by economic decision makers.

Quantitative refers to numbers, and *financial* means having to do with money. Thus, accounting information involves the numbers (primarily those dealing with money) used to make economic decisions.

What do these numbers represent and where do they come from? Whenever a company or person has a transaction involving money, accounting data are generated. Consider your own experience with transactions involving money. You may pay your rent, buy groceries, make car payments, lend money to a friend, and so on. For every one of these economic transactions, accounting data are generated. If you think about it, you have a tremendous number of monetary transactions. This is true for companies as well. In fact, the volume of business accounting data can be staggering.

Data versus Information

data The raw results of transactions and events. Data are of little use to decision makers because they do not differentiate among transactions of relatively different importance.

information Data that have been transformed so that they are useful in the decision-making process.

Note that in the previous paragraph we used the phrase accounting **data** rather than accounting **information**. The two terms are *not* interchangeable. Data are the raw results of transactions: data become information only when they are put into some useful form. Consider this example:

Carol Brown, vice president of sales for Balloo Industries, noticed that the amount spent by the sales force on gasoline for company cars over the last few months was extremely high. She suspected that salespersons were using the company cars for personal trips. When each car is brought in for monthly maintenance, odometer readings are made; therefore, Ms. Brown knew she could find out how many miles each member of the sales force put on each car on a monthly basis. She hoped that gathering this information would help her to determine if the salespeople were misusing the cars. Ms. Brown notified

Jack Parsons, the sales supervisor, of her concerns. He agreed to prepare a report to provide her with the necessary information.

The report compiled by Mr. Parsons consisted of six columns of data: (1) salesperson's name; (2) make and model of that salesperson's company car; (3) date the car was issued to the salesperson; (4) odometer reading on the date of issue; (5) date of most recent maintenance work; and (6) odometer reading at time of most recent maintenance.

When Ms. Brown reviewed the report, she quickly concluded that it contained very little useful information. Mr. Parsons was reminded of the purpose of the report: to help Ms. Brown determine if any members of the sales force were using company cars for personal activities. Mr. Parsons retreated to his office to try again.

The second version of Mr. Parsons' report consisted of all six columns he had included in the original report plus five additional columns: (7) sales region covered; (8) serial number of the vehicle; (9) how long the salesperson had been with the company; (10) total sales generated by the salesperson this year; and (11) current odometer reading of the vehicle.

Mr. Parsons had gone to considerable trouble to gather this additional data. Was Ms. Brown pleased? *No!* Mr. Parsons had provided additional *data*, but no additional *information*.

DISCUSSION QUESTIONS

3-7. Evaluate the usefulness of each column of data (1–11) offered by Mr. Parsons. Were any items of *no* value to Ms. Brown? For each item you found to be of no help to Ms. Brown, identify a different decision setting in which the item would be useful.

Clearly, the correct data items must be gathered and converted into useful information before they are of any help to economic decision makers. As an example, suppose you are considering investing in Safeway stock. You call your broker and she tells you the stock is currently selling at $30 per share. Do you want to buy it? Although your broker has given you a datum, this datum provides insufficient information upon which to base a buying decision. You need to know something about the company's current and historic earnings, the stock price behavior over the past year, the grocery industry's prospects, and so on. That's why brokerage firms such as Merrill Lynch, Morgan Stanley, and Dean Witter have research departments that extract such data and synthesize them into useful information for their clients.

3-8. Describe some of the economic transactions you have had in the past month that generated accounting data.

3-9. What criteria would you use to determine if an item should be classified as data or information?

Useful Accounting Information

In the first part of this chapter, we warned that users of accounting information must have an understanding of business and, further, that they must be willing to study the information if they hope to make sound economic decisions. Those are the user's obligations. It is the provider's obligation to present accounting information in such a way that economic decision makers can make sense of it. Accountants have been roundly criticized in recent years for failing to provide information that is understandable to anyone but other accountants.

This criticism is not without some merit. As business and economic activities have become more complex, the accounting profession has responded with increasingly complex rules, many of which serve to make accounting information incomprehensible to those who do not spend their lives studying those rules. But regardless of the complexity of accounting rules or the economic environment, there are certain characteristics accounting information must possess in order to be considered useful. Once you understand these characteristics, you will have a much easier time making sense of reports based on accounting information.

Who Decides What Is Useful Accounting Information?

There are two parties that decide what accounting information is useful and what is not. One is the *users*. It is a grave mistake for economic decision makers to leave this decision up to the "experts." If the accounting profession is not providing the information users need, or is not preparing it in a way that makes sense, the users must demand a change. The second party that decides what accounting information is useful and what is not is the *accounting profession*—but always with the proviso that the information should be tailored to the needs of users.

Currently, the organization that is principally responsible for establishing accounting guidelines and rules is the **Financial Accounting Standards Board (FASB)**. In 1976, it issued a three-part Discussion Memorandum entitled *Conceptual Framework for Financial Accounting and Reporting: Elements of Financial Statements and Their Measurement*. This mammoth

Financial Accounting Standards Board (FASB) The organization that is principally responsible for establishing accounting guidelines and rules in the United States at the present time.

memorandum was different from any statement previously issued by the U.S. accounting profession in that it described not only what accounting is but also what it should be. In the 19 years since the *Conceptual Framework* was published, the FASB has issued six *Statements of Financial Accounting Concepts* related to financial reporting. The remaining discussion in this section of the chapter is based on the *Conceptual Framework* and the six subsequent *Statements of Concepts*. We will focus on what the FASB called the **qualitative characteristics** of useful accounting information—those qualities accounting information must possess in order to be useful.

Before we proceed, however, one other matter needs to be addressed. Earlier we stated that separate branches of accounting have evolved to meet the needs of internal and external decision makers. Management accounting generates information specifically for internal users, while financial accounting provides information specifically for external parties. As its name implies, the Financial Accounting Standards Board is part of the financial accounting branch and thus does not concern itself directly with the needs of internal users. Therefore, the concepts and ideas contained in the *Conceptual Framework* and the six subsequent *Statements of Concepts* are intended to apply to financial accounting. Most of the characteristics of useful accounting information discussed in those statements, however, are equally important for generating useful management accounting information.

Remember that all economic decision makers are trying to determine whether they will be paid, when they will be paid, and how much they will be paid. In other words, they are attempting to predict the amounts and timing of future cash flows. To be of value in this decision process, accounting information must possess certain qualitative characteristics. These are divided into two categories: primary and secondary qualities.

PRIMARY QUALITIES OF USEFUL ACCOUNTING INFORMATION

The two primary qualities that distinguish useful accounting information are **relevance** and **reliability**. If either of these qualities is missing, accounting information will not be useful.

Relevance

To be considered relevant, accounting information must have a bearing on a particular decision situation. In other words: Does the information make a difference to decision makers in that situation? Does it relate to what they need to decide? The accuracy of information isn't important if the information does not matter to the decision being made.

Relevant accounting information possesses at least two characteristics:

■ **Timeliness.** The highest-quality accounting information is useless if it arrives too late to influence a decision. This may sound bizarre, but timeliness is more important than total accuracy. In an attempt to produce absolutely accurate reports, information providers often delay making information available until it is too late to be of any value. If accounting information is not timely, it has *no* value.

Timeliness alone, however, is not enough. In order for accounting information to be relevant, it must also possess at least one of the following characteristics:

predictive value A primary characteristic of relevance. To be useful, accounting must provide information to decision makers that can be used to predict the future and timing of cash flows.

feedback value A primary characteristic of relevance. To be useful, accounting must provide decision makers with information that allows them to assess the progress of an investment.

■ **Predictive Value.** Before economic decision makers commit resources to one alternative instead of another, they must be able to satisfy themselves that there is a reasonable expectation of a return on investment and a return of investment. Accounting information that helps reduce the uncertainty of that prediction is said to have predictive value.

or

■ **Feedback Value.** After an investment decision has been made, information must be available to assess the progress of that investment. Think back to the seven-step decision model presented in Chapter 2. Step 6 is a reevaluation of the decision as new information becomes available, and Step 7 is an evaluation of the final outcome of the decision. If accounting information provides input for those evaluations, it is said to have feedback value.

Reliability

To be considered reliable, accounting information must possess three qualities:

verifiability A primary characteristic of reliability. Information is considered verifiable if several individuals, working independently, would arrive at similar conclusions using the same data.

■ **Verifiability.** Accounting information is considered verifiable if several qualified persons, working independently of one another, would arrive at similar conclusions using the same data. In other words, if several individuals reach consensus about the measurement of an item, that measurement information would be considered verifiable. For example, if several people were asked to determine the amount of wages paid to George Roberts this year, they should all come to the same conclusion: A simple review of payroll records should provide verifiable information as to the amount. On the other hand, if those same people were all asked to determine how good a job Mr. Roberts is doing, they might each draw a different conclusion. Even if each individual were given the same performance reports and evaluations of Mr. Roberts, one person might say he was doing a fine job, while another might view his performance as marginally acceptable.

representational faithfulness A primary characteristic of reliability. To be useful, accounting information must reasonably report what actually happened.

neutrality A primary characteristic of reliability. To be useful, accounting information must be free of bias.

■ **Representational Faithfulness.** There must be agreement between what the accounting information says and what really happened. If a company's accounting information reports sales revenue of $1,000 and the company really had sales revenue of $1,000, the accounting information is representationally faithful. However, if a company's accounting information reports sales revenue of $1,000 and the company really had sales revenue of only $800, then the accounting information lacks representational faithfulness.

■ **Neutrality.** To be useful, accounting information must be free of bias. That means it should not leave things out simply because they are unpleasant.

We have stressed how difficult it is to make good decisions. The problem becomes even worse when information is suppressed or slanted, either positively or negatively. The need to remain neutral is one of the most difficult challenges facing the accounting profession. Accountants in both the management and the financial branches come under constant pressure by interested parties to "cook the books" or practice "creative accounting." In other words, they are often asked to make the accounting information present a more favorable picture than reality warrants.

There are those who feel that the importance of reliability (and its implied qualities of verifiability, representational faithfulness, and neutrality) pertains only to information provided to external users (financial accounting), not to information provided to internal parties (management accounting). They base their position on the essential difference between the information available to each type of user. Remember that internal parties may have access to all the accounting information available within the company, whereas external users are limited to whatever information the company is willing to provide to them. External users therefore, *must* have assurance that the information they receive is reliable. Although we do not disagree that reliability is extremely important to external users, we think it is just as important to internal decision makers.

DISCUSSION QUESTIONS

3-10. Think back to the seven-step decision model presented in Chapter 2 (reproduced on page 70). How would the absence of the primary qualities of useful accounting information affect Steps 3 and 4?

3-11. Do you think the primary qualities apply to information other than financial information? Explain.

SECONDARY QUALITIES OF USEFUL ACCOUNTING INFORMATION

"Secondary" does not mean that these characteristics are of lesser importance than the primary qualities we just discussed; in some decision-making settings, secondary characteristics are crucial. However, if a secondary characteristic is missing, the accounting information is not necessarily useless. This is the distinction between primary and secondary qualities. The secondary qualities of useful accounting information are comparability and consistency.

Comparability

Economic decision making involves the evaluation of alternatives. In order to be useful in such an evaluation, the accounting information for one alternative must be comparable to the accounting information for the other alternative(s). For example, assume you intend to make an investment and are considering two companies as investment alternatives. If the two companies use totally different accounting methods, you would find it very difficult to make a useful comparison. **Comparability** is an important quality of accounting information in many decision-making settings.

Let's look at comparability in a setting with which you are familiar. Joshua is a high school junior who always achieves 93 percent averages in his classes. For two and a half years, he attended a school that operates on a 10-point grading scale, where 90–100 percent earns an "A." Midway through Joshua's junior year, his mother received a job transfer and the family moved to another part of the state. In spite of the disruption caused by the move, Joshua maintained his 93 percent average in all his classes. However, the new school uses a 6-point scale, so only a performance of 94 percent and above earns students an "A." Thus, after being a straight-A student for two and a half years, Joshua received all B's on his report card.

To an outsider, it would appear that Joshua's performance dropped off in the middle of his junior year, but it had not: It was the grading system that changed. This is an example of the consequences of using information that is not comparable. The meaning of an "A" at the old school is not comparable to the meaning of that grade at the new school.

Consistency

We will examine the characteristic of **consistency** by extending the example of Joshua's grades. Suppose that Joshua's mother never received a job transfer and the family stayed put, with Joshua remaining at his original high school for all four years and maintaining his performance level at 93 percent. But after Joshua's junior year, the school's administrators instituted new policies to improve education. Beginning in Joshua's senior year, the school required students to reach a 94 percent level of performance to earn an "A." This resulted in Joshua receiving three years of straight A's and one year of B's. Is it fair to conclude from his academic record that Joshua's performance fell in his senior year? No, Joshua was a victim of information (an academic record) that lacks (rating) consistency.

Now consider the concept of consistency as it relates to economic decision making. Imagine how difficult it would be to assess the progress of an investment if, through the years, different accounting treatments were applied to similar events. Consistency in the application of measurement methods over periods of time increases the usefulness of the accounting information provided about a company or an investment alternative.

Comparability and consistency (or lack thereof) often have similar effects on the decision-making process. Basically, comparability relates to comparisons between information from different entities or alternatives. Consistency

comparability One of the two secondary qualitative characteristics of useful accounting information. It means reports generated for one entity may be usefully compared with the reports generated for other entities.

consistency One of the two secondary qualitative characteristics of useful accounting information. It means an entity consistently uses the same accounting methods and procedures from period to period.

relates to the use of information from the same source over time. Both factors are important and can have major impacts on economic decision making.

DISCUSSION QUESTIONS

3-12. Think back to the seven-step decision model (reproduced on page 70). How would the absence of the secondary qualities of useful accounting information affect Steps 4 and 6?

The following story reflects the frustration of some users of accounting information:

There was a guy who wanted more than anything to take a hot-air balloon ride. So he bought a balloon, filled it with hot air, and set out on a journey from Philadelphia to Pittsburgh to fulfill his lifelong dream. The trip was everything he had imagined it would be. From high in the air, he could look down and see people going about their business. The only time they stopped was to look up at him and his balloon floating gracefully through the sky. He knew how envious they were because he had felt that way many times himself.

Everything was going along smoothly until he had traveled about 75 miles. Then he ran into rough weather. He faced just a few clouds at first, but then came those awful winds. Next the brave balloonist faced rain, with thunder and lightning. Before long, he was hopelessly lost, having been blown way off course. To make matters worse, his balloon began to lose air, and for the first time, the man began to fear for his life. He did not crash, however, because as his balloon fell to earth, its ropes became caught in the branches of a huge tree—his fall had been broken.

So there he was, sitting in his balloon basket, hanging in a tree, without the slightest idea where he was. Just then, he spotted a man walking along the road below. "Pardon me," said the man in the tree, "can you tell me where I am?" "Certainly," said the man walking on the road, "you are in a basket, in a tree." The man in the tree thought about that for a moment and then said, "You must be an accountant!" The man on the road beamed with pride that his professionalism was showing. "Why yes, I am," he said, "but how did you know?" "Because," answered the guy in the tree, "your information is totally accurate and absolutely worthless."

Exhibit 3-5

As you work your way through this book, you should become comfortable with your ability to determine what information you need and how to get it so you can avoid the frustrating experience of the man in the tree.

DECISION MAKERS AND UNDERSTANDABILITY

Now that you know the qualities required to make accounting information useful, you can appreciate the fact that, as a decision maker and user of accounting information, you must evaluate the qualities of available information to assess its usefulness. In order to do this, you will need information that is, as the FASB said in *Statement of Financial Accounting Concepts #1*, understandable to those who have a reasonable understanding of business or are willing to devote the effort required to gain that understanding. There is persuasive evidence today of a real communication gap between those who prepare accounting information and those who use it.

The accounting profession itself is at least partially responsible for this problem. However, the users also bear some responsibility. We live in a complex world, and accounting for the events and transactions of that world is necessarily complex. To expect accountants to provide information that can be understood without effort is foolish. At a minimum, users must understand the basis upon which accounting information is prepared.

Economic decision makers must also recognize that the information they receive from accountants constitutes only a part of the information they need to make sound economic decisions. It is an important part, to be sure, but only a part. The reports generated from accounting information can be thought of as the tools of the accounting trade. Those attempting to use them must have a thorough understanding of what these tools can do and what they cannot be expected to do. As financial tools are introduced and discussed throughout the rest of this text, keep in mind that each tool has its limitations and imperfections. However, after working with the material provided, you should be able to use each financial tool to its fullest potential.

SUMMARY

E conomic decisions are those decisions involving money. For our purposes, they are decisions within the context of business transactions. These economic decisions are made by two distinctly different types of decision makers. Internal decision makers are individuals within a company. They have access to much, if not all, of the financial information available concerning the company, and they make decisions on behalf of the organization. External decision makers are individuals or organizations outside a company. They are limited to the information provided to them by the company, and they make decisions about the organization.

Because there are essential differences between the kinds of decisions made by internal and external parties, two separate branches of accounting have developed to provide information to the two types of users. Management accounting information is the information prepared for use by internal parties, and financial accounting information is the information prepared for use by external parties.

Both internal and external parties attempt to predict the future and timing of cash flows. Essentially, they are all trying to determine whether they will be paid, when they will be paid, and how much they will be paid.

As suggested by the concerns of economic decision makers, cash is of utmost importance. When evaluating business success or failure, cash is the ultimate measurement criterion.

Accounting information is a key ingredient of good decision making. Business activity produces data. These data are of no value to decision makers until they are put into a useful form. At that point, data become information.

To be useful to economic decision makers in their attempt to predict the future and timing of cash flows, accounting information must possess certain qualitative characteristics. The primary qualitative characteristics of useful accounting information are: (1) relevance, including timeliness and either predictive value or feedback value; and (2) reliability, including verifiability, representational faithfulness, and neutrality.

Useful accounting information should also possess the secondary characteristics of comparability and consistency. In addition, in order to be useful, accounting information must be understandable to economic decision makers.

Key Terms

accounting information Raw data concerning transactions that have been transformed into financial numbers that can be used by economic decision makers. (p. 72)

cash flow The movement of cash in and out of a company. (p. 68)

comparability One of the two secondary qualitative characteristics of useful accounting information. It means reports generated for one entity may be usefully compared with the reports generated for other entities. (p. 78)

consistency One of the two secondary qualitative characteristics of useful accounting information. It means an entity consistently uses the same accounting methods and procedures from period to period. (p. 78)

data The raw results of transactions and events. Data are of little use to decision makers because they do not differentiate among transactions of relatively different importance. (p. 72)

economic decision making Generally, the process of making decisions involving money; here, decision making that takes place in the course of business transactions. (p. 65)

external decision makers Economic decision makers outside a company who make decisions about the company. The accounting information they use to make those decisions is limited to what the company provides them. (p. 66)

feedback value A primary characteristic of relevance. To be useful,

accounting must provide decision makers with information that allows them to assess the progress of an investment. (p. 76)

financial accounting The branch of accounting developed to meet the informational needs of external decision makers. (p. 68)

Financial Accounting Standards Board (FASB) The organization that is principally responsible for establishing accounting guidelines and rules in the United States at the present time. (p. 74)

information Data that have been transformed so that they are useful in the decision-making process. (p. 72)

internal decision makers Economic decision makers within a company who make decisions for the company. They have access to much or all of the accounting information generated within the company. (p. 66)

management accounting The branch of accounting developed to meet the informational needs of internal decision makers. (p. 68)

net cash flow The difference between cash inflows and cash outflows; it can be either positive or negative. (p. 68)

neutrality A primary characteristic of reliability. To be useful, accounting information must be free of bias. (p. 76)

predictive value A primary characteristic of relevance. To be useful, accounting must provide information to decision makers that can be used to predict the future and timing of cash flows. (p. 76)

qualitative characteristics These are characteristics upon which an assessment of the usefulness of accounting information can be based. They include the primary characteristics of relevance (predictive value, feedback value, and timeliness) and reliability (verifiability, representational faithfulness, and neutrality), and the secondary characteristics of comparability and consistency. (p. 75)

relevance One of the two primary qualitative characteristics of useful accounting information. It means the information must have a bearing on a particular decision situation. (p. 75)

reliability One of the two primary qualitative characteristics of useful accounting information. It means the information must be reasonably accurate. (p. 75)

representational faithfulness A primary characteristic of reliability. To be useful, accounting information must reasonably report what actually happened. (p. 76)

timeliness A primary characteristic of relevance. To be useful, accounting information must be provided in time to influence a particular decision. (p. 75)

verifiability A primary characteristic of reliability. Information is considered verifiable if several individuals, working independently, would arrive at similar conclusions using the same data. (p. 76)

REVIEW THE FACTS

A. What is economic decision making?

B. There are two broad categories of economic decision makers. Name them and explain the differences between them.

C. What are the two major branches of accounting and how do they differ?

D. List the three major questions asked by economic decision makers.

E. What is accounting information?

F. Explain the difference between data and information.

G. What is the name of the organization principally responsible for the establishment of accounting guidelines?

H. Name the two primary qualitative characteristics of useful accounting information.

I. What characteristics are necessary for accounting information to be relevant?

J. List the characteristics necessary for accounting information to be reliable.

K. Explain the difference between the primary and secondary qualities of useful accounting information.

L. What are the secondary qualities of useful accounting information?

M. Explain the responsibility of both the accounting profession and the user for the understandability of accounting information.

3-13. Dave Cavazos is a commercial artist. His business entails painting signs of various types for businesses. He has received a $10,000 order from Steve Demmon and Company for 1,000 signs to be displayed in Demmon's retail outlets. While Dave is excited about the job, he is a little concerned because he estimates it will take him a month working full-time to complete the signs and Demmon proposes to pay him the contract amount 30 days after he delivers the signs. These are Demmon's standard payment terms, although Dave did a small job for the company last year ($500) and did not receive payment until 45 days after completing the work.

Dave figures the materials for the job (poster board, paint, brushes, etc.) will cost $5,500, which he can buy on credit from Long's Art Supply Company (30-day terms).

Having taken the accounting course in which you are now enrolled, Dave remembers that any economic decision entails attempting to answer the following three questions:

- Will I be paid?
- When will I be paid?
- How much will I be paid?

REQUIRED:

a. Presuming Dave can satisfy himself as to the first question (Will I be paid?), what are the answers to the other two questions? Remember the last question (How much?) has two parts.

b. The problem states that Dave is concerned. What do you think is troubling him about the order from Demmon and Company?

c. Based on your answer to the previous requirement, identify three things Dave could do to lessen his anxiety and explain how they might help him feel more at ease.

3-14. Presented below are the qualitative characteristics of useful accounting information as discussed in the chapter, followed by definitions of those items in scrambled order.

a. Relevance	**f.** Verifiability
b. Timeliness	**g.** Representational faithfulness
c. Predictive value	**h.** Neutrality
d. Feedback value	**i.** Comparability
e. Reliability	**j.** Consistency

1. ___ The same measurement application methods are used over time.
2. ___ The accounting information is free of bias.

3. ___ The information provides input to evaluate a previously made decision.

4. ___ The information allows the evaluation of one alternative against another alternative.

5. ___ In assessing the information, qualified persons working independently would arrive at similar conclusions.

6. ___ The information helps reduce the uncertainty of the future.

7. ___ The information has a bearing on a particular decision situation.

8. ___ The information is available soon enough to be of value.

9. ___ The information can be depended upon.

10. ___ There must be agreement between what the information says and what really happened.

REQUIRED:

Match the letter next to each item with the appropriate definition. Each letter will be used only once.

3-15. Claudia Peel is the controller (chief accountant) of Holesapple Company. She is trying to decide whether to extend credit to Mower Company, a new customer. Holesapple does most of its business on credit, but is very strict in granting credit terms. Mike Mower, the owner and president of Mower Company, has sent the following items for Claudia to look at as she performs her evaluation:

1. All company bank statements for the past five years (a total of 60 bank statements).

2. A detailed analysis showing the amount of sales the company expects to have in the coming year and its estimated profit.

3. Another, less detailed analysis outlining projected company growth over the next 20 years.

4. A biographical sketch of each of the company's officers and a description of the function each performs in the company.

5. Ten letters of reference from close friends and relatives of the company's officers.

6. A report of the company's credit history prepared by company employees on Mower Company letterhead.

7. A letter signed by all company officers expressing their willingness to personally guarantee the credit Holesapple extends to Mower. (You may assume this is a legally binding document.)

REQUIRED:

a. As she evaluates Mower Company's application for credit, is Claudia Peel an *internal* decision maker or an *external* decision maker? Explain your reasoning.

b. Analyze each item Mower sent in light of the primary qualitative characteristics of relevance (including timeliness, predictive value, and feedback value) and reliability (including verifiability, representational faithfulness, and neutrality). Explain how each item either possesses or does not possess these characteristics.

3-16. Presented below are items relating to the concepts discussed in this chapter, followed by the definitions of those items in scrambled order:

a. Cash flow   **e.** Information

b. Comparability   **f.** Management accounting

c. Data   **g.** Net cash flow

d. Financial accounting   **h.** Economic decision making.

1. ___ The raw results of transactions and events.
2. ___ Developed to meet the information needs of internal decision makers.
3. ___ Data transformed so they are useful in the decision-making process.
4. ___ The movement of cash in and out of a company.
5. ___ Decisions involving money.
6. ___ Reports generated for one entity may be compared with reports generated for other entities.
7. ___ The difference between the cash coming into a company and the cash going out of a company.
8. ___ Developed to meet the information needs of external decision makers.

REQUIRED:

Match the letter next to each item with the appropriate definition. Each letter will be used only once.

3-17. You are in the market for a used car. You notice a promising advertisement in the local newspaper and make an appointment to meet with the seller, whose name is Bob. During your meeting you obtain the following information:

1. The car is a 1992 model.
2. Bob said he has used the car only for commuting to and from work.

3. You notice the car has New York license plates.

4. The odometer reading is 50,286 miles.

5. Bob reports that he has had the oil changed every 3,000 miles since he bought the car new.

6. Bob says this is the best car he has ever owned.

7. The glove box contains a maintenance record prepared by a licensed mechanic.

REQUIRED:

    a. Evaluate each item from the list above in terms of its relevance (specifically, predictive value and timeliness) to your decision about whether to buy Bob's car.

    b. Evaluate each item from the list above in terms of its reliability (verifiability, representational faithfulness, and neutrality) for deciding whether to buy Bob's car.

3-18. Explain in your own words what the statement "Cash is the 'ball' of business" means.

3-19. The chapter states that to be useful, accounting information must possess the primary qualitative characteristics of relevance (timeliness and predictive value or feedback value) and reliability (verifiability, representational faithfulness, and neutrality). These characteristics are also applicable to other types of information.

    Suppose that prior to taking your midterm exam in this course, your instructor gives you two options:

    Option 1: One week before the midterm exam you will be given a rough idea of what is going to be on the exam.

or

    Option 2: On the day following the exam, you will be given a copy of the actual midterm exam with an answer key.

Assume further that you have two goals:

    Goal 1: To prepare for the midterm exam.

    Goal 2: To evaluate your performance on the midterm exam.

REQUIRED:

Within the context of *each* of your two goals, evaluate both options using the primary qualitative characteristics. Be sure to explain how the primary characteristics are present or absent and how such presence or absence affects you as a rational decision maker.

3-20. The chapter states that to be useful, accounting information must possess the primary qualitative characteristics of relevance and reliability. These characteristics are also applicable to other types of information.

Suppose you are about to buy a new car. The car you want is a Nissan Altima. You have $20,000 in the bank, ready to spend on the new car. You obtain the following items of information:

1. On your first visit to Quality Nissan, a salesperson casually tells you that the price of a new Nissan Altima is $15,500.
2. A friend tells you he heard that someone was selling a three-year-old Altima for $12,000.
3. Another friend just bought a new Chevy pickup truck for $22,000.
4. The sticker price of an Altima with the options you want is $16,200.
5. A Nissan dealer in the area is advertising a new Altima with the options you want for $15,200.
6. A friend tells you she heard that someone bought a new Altima a couple months ago for around $14,000.

Assume that you are about to visit a Nissan dealership and your goal is to buy a new Altima for the best price. You intend to use the above information to evaluate whether or not the price you get is a good deal.

REQUIRED:

a. Evaluate each item from the list above in terms of its relevance (feedback value, predictive value, and timeliness). Explain how the presence or absence of the characteristics affects your ability to use the information to determine if you are getting a good deal.

b. Evaluate each item from the list above in terms of its reliability (verifiability, representational faithfulness, and neutrality). Explain how the presence or absence of these characteristics affects your ability to use the information to determine if you are getting a good deal.

3-21. Exactly two weeks from today you must take the midterm exam for this class. You feel you are in trouble because you can't seem to grasp exactly how you should prepare for the exam. As you are walking across campus, you see the following notice pinned to a bulletin board:

WORRIED ABOUT THE ACCOUNTING MID-TERM???

I CAN HELP!!!

I GUARANTEE AN "A" OR "B"

WILL TUTOR FOR $10 PER HOUR

Qualifications:
1. Got an "A" in the course myself.
2. Have outlines of all chapters of the text.
3. Over 140 satisfied customers from previous semesters.
4. Know the Professor personally.
5. Know the authors of the text personally.
6. Working on a graduate degree in Biology.

CALL JOE DOKES AT 555-5555

REQUIRED:

Evaluate each of Joe's claimed qualifications in relation to the primary characteristics of:

a. Relevance (including timeliness and predictive value or feedback value).

b. Reliability (including verifiability, representational faithfulness and neutrality).

4

Tools of the Trade, Part I
The Balance Sheet:
Initial Financing—
Investments by Owners

As we examine various aspects of business activity, you will better appreciate how important economic decision making is. Regardless of the form of business chosen or the type of business activity engaged in, cash is needed to get the operation started. Usually, the first source of cash for a business is the owner(s) of the company. Once a business has been created, a balance sheet providing a picture of the company's financial position can be developed.

Tools are invented to solve problems. They are responses to specific needs. If a tool is adequate and properly used, it will produce satisfactory results; but if it is inadequate or improperly used, it will not, and disaster may result.

Consider the following:

THE PROBLEM developed. Somebody analyzed THE PROBLEM and having figured out what needed to be done to solve it, invented THE TOOL. Soon many people began using THE TOOL to solve THE PROBLEM. Eventually, no one would even consider using anything else.

For many years THE TOOL was used with great success. There came a time, however, when it no longer solved THE PROBLEM, but nobody realized it. Whenever confronted with THE PROBLEM, folks instinctively reached for THE TOOL. Even with people dying (THE PROBLEM was a very dangerous one), no one ever questioned the use of THE TOOL.

There are at least three possible explanations as to what happened in this situation:

1. The nature of THE PROBLEM had changed. If true, it was no wonder THE TOOL ceased to provide the desired results.

2. Those using THE TOOL only thought they were applying it to THE PROBLEM. In fact, they were using it to try to solve ANOTHER PROBLEM, which, on the surface, looked like THE PROBLEM.

3. THE TOOL never really did solve THE PROBLEM, but merely appeared to, and reality finally caught up with it.

What probably happened in this situation is that a routine solution was applied to a nonroutine situation. Recall that the key to reasoned decision making—step 1 of the decision-making process discussed in Chapter 2—is determining the real problem to be solved. Similarly, determining the real problem is of paramount importance in choosing a tool to apply. Only when the real problem has been determined can the appropriate tool be applied to solve it or, if no appropriate tool exists, can one be developed.

Financial statements should be thought of as tools for solving economic problems. Like all tools, these statements were developed in response to specific needs. If these financial tools are adequate and are properly used, they will produce satisfactory results. If they are inadequate or improperly used, they will not, and disaster may result. In this chapter, we will discuss only one financial statement—the balance sheet. There are several other kinds of financial statements, and they will be discussed as we proceed through this text.

After completing your work on this chapter, you should be able to do the following:

1. Identify and explain the accounting elements contained in the balance sheet.
2. State in your own words how the balance sheet provides information about the financial position of a business.
3. Compare and contrast the balance sheets of proprietorships, partnerships, and corporations.
4. Describe the basic organizational structure of a corporation.
5. Differentiate between common stock and preferred (preference) stock.
6. Describe the components of stockholders' equity and understand the meaning of treasury stock.
7. Explain what information is available on a corporate balance sheet and what information is not.
8. Explain the basic process operating in the primary and secondary stock markets.

THE FIRST TOOL: INTRODUCTION TO THE BALANCE SHEET

balance sheet A financial statement providing information about an entity's present condition. Reports what a company possesses (assets) and who has claim to those possessions (liabilities and owners' equity).

We took great pains in Chapter 3 to define the problems facing those who must make economic decisions. As these people evaluate alternative investment opportunities, they try to determine whether they will be paid, and if so, when the payment will occur and how much it will be. We also stated that this evaluation begins with an assessment of an alternative's present condition and its past performance. Keep in mind that the present and the past are useful only if they can be used to reasonably predict the future. Over time, financial tools have been developed to convey information about the present condition and past performance of an entity. The financial tool that focuses on the present condition of a business is the **balance sheet** (Exhibit 4-1).

Exhibit 4-1
First Tool of the Trade:
the Balance Sheet

4-1. When Aunt Hattie was alive, she was always a joker. Now she has passed on and left you and your cousin Igor (whom you can't stand) the two businesses she owned. You get first choice. Aunt Hattie's will stipulates that you may ask ten questions in order to determine the present condition of each company and that lawyers for the estate will provide the answers. Provide your list of ten questions.

4-2. You are locked in a room that has no windows and only one door. To get out of the room, you must request one tool and explain how you will use it to get through the door. You may not request a key or any lock-picking equipment. Choose the one tool you request and describe its features. Then explain in detail how you will use it to get out of the room.

The Accounting Elements

accounting elements The categories under which the results of all accounting transactions can be classified.

assets An accounting element that is one of the three components of a balance sheet. Assets are probable future economic benefits controlled by an entity as a result of previous transactions or events—that is, what a company has.

liabilities An accounting element that is one of the three components of a balance sheet. Liabilities are probable future sacrifices of assets arising from present obligations of an entity as a result of past transactions or events—that is, what a company owes.

Before we talk about the balance sheet, we need to explain the **accounting elements**. The dictionary defines the word "element" as a component, part, or ingredient. The results of every economic transaction or event experienced by a company can be classified into one or more accounting elements. In this chapter, we will introduce you to the accounting elements that are the components of a balance sheet. Other accounting elements will be presented later in the text, as circumstances warrant. As we discuss these elements, we will give you both the actual FASB definition in italics and a less technical explanation in roman type.

The three accounting elements that are major components of a balance sheet are:

1. **Assets**. *Probable future economic benefits obtained or controlled by a particular entity as a result of past transactions or events.* Assets are the "things" a company has. Cash is the item that most clearly fits the definition of an asset.

2. **Liabilities**. *Probable future sacrifices of economic benefits arising from present obligations of a particular entity to transfer assets or provide services to other entities in the future as a result of past transactions or events.* Liabilities are the debts a company has—what it owes. A company may have an obligation to transfer assets to someone (pay off a debt) or provide services (if the company received payment in advance). Liabilities are the result of past transactions and will require settlement some time in the future.

equity An accounting element that is one of the three components of a balance sheet. Equity is the residual interest in the assets of an entity that remains after deducting liabilities.

investments by owners That part of owners' equity generated by the receipt of cash (or other assets) from the owners.

earned equity The total amount a company has earned since its beginning, less any amounts distributed to the owner(s). In a corporation, this is called retained earnings.

3. **Equity**. *The residual interest in the assets of an entity that remains after deducting its liabilities*. Equity is the ownership interest in a company. Equity is calculated by adding up what a company has (assets) and subtracting what it owes on what it has (liabilities). The result is the portion of the assets that are owned free and clear by the owner(s) of the company.

The present financial position of an entity can be captured in these three elements: assets, liabilities, and equity. Equity in a company comes from two sources:

a. **Investments by owners**. This is another accounting element, representing the amount invested by the owner(s) of the company. It represents "seed money" put into the company to get it started or to finance its expansion.

b. **Earned equity**. This is the total amount a company has earned since it was first started, less any amounts that have been taken out by the owner(s). Earned equity comes from the profitable operation of the company over time.

Exhibit 4-2
Accounting Element:
Investments by Owners

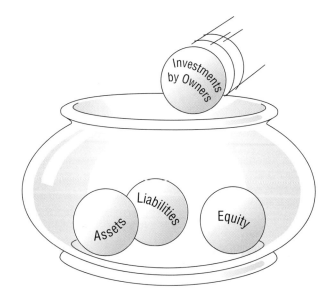

Organization of the Balance Sheet

A constant relationship exists among the three main elements on the balance sheet (assets, liabilities, and equity). Logically, what a company has (assets) will always be equal to the claims that are made on those assets. In other words, the assets of a company must be owned by someone. Either the creditors of the company have a claim to them (liabilities) or the owners own them free and clear (equity). In most cases, the assets of a company are claimed partly by creditors and partly by owners. This relationship can be stated as an equation:

$$\text{ASSETS} = \text{LIABILITIES} + \text{EQUITY}$$

accounting equation Assets = Liabilities + Owners' Equity. Also called the business equation.

business equation Assets = Liabilities + Owners' Equity. Also called the accounting equation.

owners' equity The owners' residual interest in the assets of a company after consideration of its liabilities.

statement of financial position Another name for the balance sheet.

statement of financial condition Another name for the balance sheet.

account form A common format of the balance sheet, in which assets are placed on the left side of the page and liabilities and owners' equity on the right side.

This is usually referred to as the **accounting equation**, but we think it is better termed the **business equation** because it sums up the reality of business. Accounting merely uses the equation to measure that reality. The business equation can also be presented as:

$$\text{ASSETS} - \text{LIABILITIES} = \text{EQUITY}$$

meaning that if you take what a company has and subtract what it owes on what it has, you find what it *really* has. This presentation of the equation shows equity for what it is: the owners' residual interest in the company. To make sure we don't forget whose equity we are talking about, we usually use the phrase **owners' equity** instead of the word "equity." Thus, the business (accounting) equation is usually presented as:

$$\text{ASSETS} = \text{LIABILITIES} + \text{OWNERS' EQUITY}$$

You should remember this equation because we will deal with it over and over again. Simple memorization, however, will not suffice, for in order to understand the balance sheet, you must understand the meaning of the equation.

The term "balance sheet" comes from this equation. It is a nickname only, and frankly is not very descriptive of the financial statement's purpose. The financial statement's formal name is the **statement of financial position** or **statement of financial condition**, either of which is more descriptive than "balance sheet." The informal title is firmly entrenched, however; it is the usual term for referring to this statement in the business world.

One of the most common formats of the balance sheet is called the **account form**. In this format, which we use throughout this chapter, assets are placed on the left side of the page and liabilities and owners' equity on the right. As you can see in Exhibit 4-3, the story told by the balance sheet is

$$\text{ASSETS} = \text{LIABILITIES} + \text{OWNERS' EQUITY.}$$

Exhibit 4-3
Account Form of the Balance Sheet

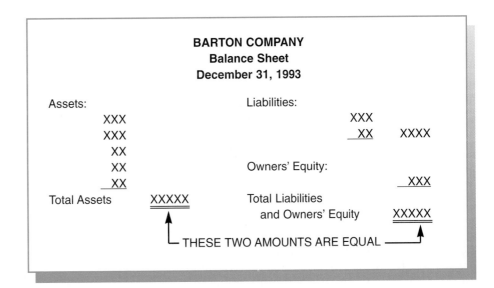

report form The vertical format of a balance sheet in which assets, liabilities, and owners' equity are shown one after another down the page.

The same information can be placed on the page in a vertical format called the **report form** (Exhibit 4-4).

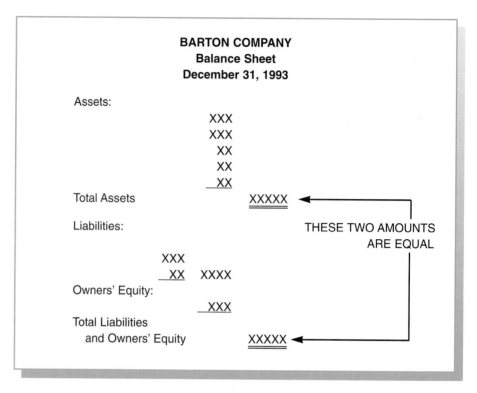

BARTON COMPANY
Balance Sheet
December 31, 1993

Assets:
| | |
| XXX |
| XXX |
| XX |
| XX |
| XX |

Total Assets   XXXXX ← THESE TWO AMOUNTS ARE EQUAL

Liabilities:
XXX
XX   XXXX

Owners' Equity:
XXX

Total Liabilities and Owners' Equity   XXXXX ←

Exhibit 4-4
Report Form of the Balance Sheet

Note that the balance sheet is a "financial snapshot" of a company. Like any snapshot, *it only shows what existed on the day it was taken*. It is not a valid representation of the day before it is taken, nor the day after. What it says is that on the day the financial snapshot was taken, these are the assets the company possessed and here's who had claim to those assets.

STARTING A BUSINESS—INVESTMENTS BY OWNERS

Let's imagine that a woman named Rosita is about to begin the operations of her new company. What does she need to do? Starting out *BIG* may require lots of things—hiring a secretary and/or other employees, getting a company car, or renting office space. Even if she plans to begin as a one-person operation, there are many things to consider, such as having stationery and/or business cards printed and taking out insurance to protect the company in case of lawsuits.

Even the smallest company will have startup costs. In other words, Rosita's new operation will need *cash*! In fact, usually the first activity in which a new company is involved is obtaining the cash to get started. The most logical source for this initial funding is the owner/owners themselves. As we develop the balance sheet in this chapter, we will assume that the new company will be initially financed with cash from owners.

Recall that we have discussed the three major forms of business organization in Chapter 1: proprietorships, partnerships, and corporations. Each form requires a slightly different presentation of the initial financing of a new company.

Balance Sheet for a Proprietorship

A proprietorship, a business entity with only one owner, must keep track of only that one owner's equity. If Rosita's proprietorship began operations on January 1, 1993, with an owner's investment of $5,000 cash, the first balance sheet of her company would look like Exhibit 4-5.

Exhibit 4-5
Balance Sheet
for a Proprietorship

ROSITA'S BUSINESS
Balance Sheet
January 1, 1993

Assets:		Liabilities:	$ 0
Cash	$5,000		
		Owner's Equity:	
		Rosita, Capital	5,000
Total Assets	$5,000	Total Liabilities and	
		Owner's Equity	$5,000

Notice that the business (accounting) equation still holds true:

$$\text{ASSETS} = \text{LIABILITIES} + \text{OWNERS' EQUITY}$$
$$\$5,000 = 0 + \$5,000$$

The owner's claim to the assets held by a sole proprietorship is represented by a capital account bearing the owner's name. In a proprietorship, there is only one owner; therefore, there will be only one capital account.

Balance Sheet for a Partnership

Partnerships, you recall, are organized like proprietorships, except that they have more than one owner. Assume that the new company is being started by two partners, Rosita and Caroline. If Rosita invested $3,000 and Caroline invested $2,000 to begin operations, the partnership's first balance sheet would look like Exhibit 4-6.

```
                    ROSITA and CAROLINE'S BUSINESS
                              Balance Sheet
                            January 1, 1993

        Assets:                      Liabilities:                    $    0
             Cash     $5,000
                                     Owners' Equity:
                                         Rosita, Capital   $3,000
                                         Caroline, Capital   2,000
                                     Total Owners' Equity          5,000

        Total Assets  $5,000         Total Liabilities and
                                         Owners' Equity           $5,000
```

Exhibit 4-6
Balance Sheet for a Partnership

Compare the balance sheet for this partnership with that for the proprietorship (Exhibit 4-5). Notice that the total assets, $5,000 in cash, are the same. Total owners' equity ($5,000) is also the same. The only difference is that we must keep track of each partner's claim to the assets in a separate capital account.

In our example, one partner—Rosita—provided 60 percent of the beginning capital ($3,000/$5,000 = 60 percent) and the other partner—Caroline—provided 40 percent of the initial capital ($2,000/$5,000 = 40 percent). The proportional size of a partner's initial investment is generally reflected by the proportional size of the beginning balance in the partner's capital account.

Partnership agreements may be simple or complex, but as long as the partners agree and understand clearly how their claims to the assets of the company (their capital balances) are being calculated, any rules can be adopted.

Balance Sheet for a Corporation

A corporation is a legal entity and that characteristic sets it apart from proprietorships and partnerships. With very few exceptions, such as national banks (which are incorporated under federal law), U.S. corporations are created by obtaining a **corporate charter** from one of the 50 states. This charter is a legal contract between the state and the corporation allowing the company to conduct business.

corporate charter A legal contract between a corporation and the state in which it is incorporated.

incorporators Individuals who make application to form a corporation.

articles of incorporation An application for a charter allowing the operation of a corporation.

To form a corporation, states require the **incorporators** to submit a formal application for the corporate charter and file it with the appropriate state agency. The application, called the **articles of incorporation**, generally must include: (1) basic information about the corporation and its purpose; (2) details concerning the types of stock to be issued; and (3) names of the individuals responsible for the corporation.

If the application is approved, a charter is issued and the corporation is legally entitled to begin operations. The incorporators then meet to formulate

bylaws The basic rules by which a corporation is operated.

the corporate **bylaws**. These bylaws serve as basic rules to be used by management in conducting the business of the corporation. Next, capital is raised by issuing stock, which means exchanging ownership interests in the corporation for cash. Once stock is issued, there are stockholders, and they elect a permanent board of directors. The directors then meet to appoint a president and such other officers as they deem necessary to manage the company.

CORPORATE ORGANIZATIONAL STRUCTURE

In the preceding section, we referred to several groups of people within the structure of the corporate form. Because these groups are critical to the successful operation of a corporation, we will now discuss each of them in greater detail.

The Stockholders

shareholders The owners of a corporation. Also called stockholders.

The stockholders are the owners of the corporation. They are also referred to as **shareholders** because they have provided cash or other assets to the corporation in exchange for ownership shares in the company. In most corporations, the stockholders are not involved in the daily management of the company, unless they have been elected to the board of directors or have been appointed as officers or managers.

Corporations issue stock certificates to their owners as evidence of the investment made by stockholders. This stock certificate represents one share of stock. Sometimes, however, a single certificate can represent thousands of shares.

stock certificate Document providing evidence of ownership of shares in a corporation.

When stockholders invest in the corporation they receive a **stock certificate**, a legal document providing evidence of ownership and containing the provisions of the stock ownership agreement. The stockholders usually meet once a year to elect members of the board of directors and conduct other business important to the corporation.

Board of Directors

The board of directors has ultimate responsibility for managing the corporation. In practice, however, most boards restrict themselves to formulating very broad corporate policy and appointing officers to conduct the daily operation of the corporation. The board serves as a link between the stockholders and the officers of the company. If the officers are not managing the corporation in the best interests of the stockholders, the board of directors, acting on behalf of the stockholders, can replace the officers.

chief executive officer (CEO) The person responsible for all activities of the corporation. This person is usually also the president.

controller The person in charge of all accounting functions of a corporation.

treasurer The person in charge of managing the cash of a corporation.

secretary The person who maintains the minutes of meetings of the board of directors and stockholders of a corporation. This person may also represent the corporation in legal proceedings.

Corporate Officers

A corporation's **chief executive officer (CEO)** is usually also the president, and this person is responsible for all activities of the company. In addition to the president, most corporations have one or more vice presidents who are responsible for specific functions of the company, such as marketing, finance, and production.

Other officer positions in many corporations include the **controller**, who is responsible for all accounting functions; the **treasurer**, who is responsible for managing the company's cash; and the **secretary**, who maintains the minutes of meetings of the board of directors and stockholders and may also represent the company in legal proceedings.

Exhibit 4-7 illustrates the relationship among the various groups in the corporate structure.

Exhibit 4-7
Corporate Organization

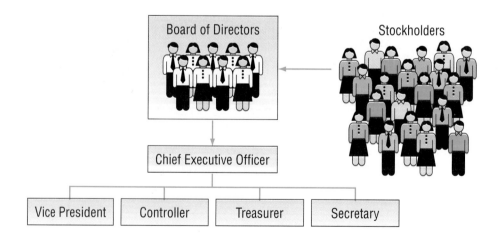

4-3. In his book *Short-Term America*, Michael Jacobs reports that "nearly 80 percent of the chief executives of U.S. companies also serve as chairman of the board" (1991, p. 82). In light of our discussion of the functions of corporate officers and the board of directors, express your views concerning this information. Is there cause for concern, or is this just "the way it is". Support your view with specific reasons.

4-4. Jacobs also reports that the practice of having CEOs serve as board chairman "is used by only 30 percent of British firms, 11 percent of Japanese companies, and never in Germany" (1991, p. 82). Why do you think there is such a difference in this practice between the United States and other countries? Does this new information affect your response to Discussion Question 4-3?

CORPORATE CAPITAL STRUCTURE

authorized shares The maximum number of shares of stock a corporation has been given permission to issue under its corporate charter.

issued shares Stock that has been distributed to the owners of the corporation in exchange for cash or other assets.

outstanding shares Shares of stock actually held by shareholders. The number may be different than that for issued shares because a corporation may reacquire its own stock (treasury stock).

treasury stock Corporate stock that has been issued and then reacquired by the corporation.

As part of the formal application to create a corporation, the incorporators must include details of their plans to sell shares of stock. They request the authority to issue (sell) a certain number of shares of stock. **Authorized shares** is the maximum number of shares that can legally be issued under the corporate charter. The shares do not exist until they are issued, however, and ownership in the corporation is based on issued, not authorized, shares. **Issued shares** refers to the number of shares of stock already distributed to stockholders in exchange for cash or other assets. **Outstanding shares** refers to shares of stock currently being held by stockholders. In many instances, issued shares and outstanding shares will be the same number. Occasionally, however, a corporation reacquires shares of stock it has previously issued. This reacquired stock, called **treasury stock**, will cause the issued shares and the outstanding shares to be different numbers. For example, assume a corporation issued 10,000 shares of its stock and then later reacquired 2,000 of those shares. The company still has 10,000 shares issued, but now has only 8,000 outstanding shares.

Previously, we referred to the owners' interest in a company as *owners' equity*. In the corporate form of business organization, owners' equity is called

stockholders' equity The corporate form of owners' equity. Stockholders' equity is divided into contributed capital and retained earnings.

stockholders' equity. There is no real difference between the two terms, because in the corporate form, the equity of the owners (stockholders) is the excess of assets over liabilities, just as it is in the proprietorship and partnership forms of business. There are, however, some differences in the way equity items are classified on the balance sheet.

In the corporate form, the owners' capital accounts are replaced by stock accounts. Most state corporation laws require stockholders' equity to be divided into the portion invested by the owners and the portion earned by the company and retained in the corporation. Amounts received by the corporation in exchange for shares of stock are called **contributed capital** or **paid-in capital**. A classification called **retained earnings** is used to reflect earnings reinvested in the company rather than distributed to the owners in the form of **dividends**. Total stockholders' equity is a combination of contributed capital and retained earnings.

As previously explained, the owners of a corporation are shareholders. If someone wants to have an ownership interest in a corporation, he or she must acquire shares of stock. The individual ownership interests of each shareholder are not disclosed on the face of the balance sheet. Instead, only totals of the ownership interests represented by each class of stock are shown. The two basic classes of stock are common stock and preferred stock.

contributed capital Total amount invested in a corporation by its shareholders. Also called paid-in capital.

paid-in capital The portion of stockholders' equity representing amounts invested by the owners of the corporation. Consists of common stock, preferred stock, and amounts received in excess of the par values of those stocks. Also called contributed capital.

retained earnings Earnings reinvested in a corporation. Equal to the total profits of the corporation since it was organized less amounts distributed to the stockholders in the form of dividends.

dividends A distribution of earnings from a corporation to its owners. Dividends are most commonly distributed in the form of cash.

common stock A share of ownership in a corporation. Each share represents one vote in the election of the board of directors and other pertinent corporate matters.

par value (for stock) An arbitrary amount assigned to each share of stock by the incorporators at the time of incorporation.

par value stock Stock with a par value printed on the stock certificate (see par value).

Common Stock

Common stock is the voting stock of the corporation. Each share of common stock represents an equal share in the ownership of the corporation; therefore, the owners' equity portion of a corporate balance sheet will show information about common stock.

Common stock may or may not have a **par value**. Par value is an arbitrary amount placed on the stock by the incorporators at the time they make application for the corporate charter, and has nothing to do with the actual value of the stock. There was a time when all states required common stock to carry a par value, but all 50 states have done away with the requirement. So why are we discussing par value if it is no longer required? Because most of the large corporations in the United States were formed before the requirement was done away with, so their stocks carry a par value. Also, many newly formed corporations elect to issue **par value stock**.

Most corporations set the par value of their stock considerably below its actual value because most states do not allow stock to be sold for less than its par value (see Exhibit 4-8 for a comparison of par and market values for some major corporations' stocks). It is not unusual to see par values of $1.00 per share or even lower. Disney Corporation, for example, has a par value on its stock of 10 cents per share.

To see what issuing par value common stock involves, assume that Rosita started her new company as a corporation and that Rosita Corporation began operations on January 1, 1993 by issuing (selling) 1,000 shares of its $1 par value stock for $5 per share. The business receives a total of $5,000 cash, so assets increase by that amount. The transaction also affects the other side of the accounting equation in stockholders' equity. Most states stipulate that only the par value of the stock multiplied by the number of shares issued can be

	Par Value	Market Value (March 6, 1995)
Exxon	$ 25.00	63¼
GM	$ 10.00	39⅞
IBM	$ 1.25	79⅞
GE	$ .63	53
Mobil Oil	$ 2.00	87¾
Philip Morris	$ 1.00	62
Chevron	$ 3.00	46⅞
Chrysler	$ 1.00	40¾
Boeing	$ 5.00	46¼
Pepsico	$ .01	38⅞

additional paid-in capital
The amount in excess of the
stock's par value received
by the corporation when par
value stock is issued.

classified as common stock. In the case of Rosita Corporation, that would be
$1,000 (1,000 shares × $1 par value). The remaining $4,000 ($5,000 cash
received less the $1,000 classified as common stock) is classified on the bal-
ance sheet as **additional paid-in capital** or some similarly descriptive title. A
balance sheet prepared immediately after the sale of the stock would look like
Exhibit 4-9.

Exhibit 4-9
Balance Sheet for a Corporation
That Issued Par Value Common
Stock

ROSITA CORPORATION
Balance Sheet
January 1, 1993

Assets:		Liabilities:		$ 0
Cash	$5,000			
		Owners' Equity:		
		Common Stock	$1,000	
		Additional Paid-in Capital	4,000	
		Total Shareholders' Equity		5,000
Total Assets	$5,000	Total Liabilities and		
		Owners' Equity		$5,000

Understand what this balance sheet *can* and *cannot* tell you. The $1,000
shown as common stock is the par value of the common stock multiplied by
the number of shares issued thus far by the corporation. Combining that
amount with the $4,000 additional paid-in capital tells you that the corpora-
tion received a total of $5,000 in return for the 1,000 shares of common stock
it issued. What is the value of those shares of common stock today? The answer
to that question cannot be found on the balance sheet. Amounts shown on the
corporate financial statements are intended to provide information about the
results of *past* activities of the corporation—not the current values of stock
already issued to shareholders.

4-5. If the balance sheet of a corporation does not show the current market value of the shares of stock, where do you think an investor could find this information?

No-Par Stock

no-par stock Stock that has no par value assigned to it.

Stock that does not have a par value is known as **no-par stock**. Choosing to issue no-par stock instead of stock with a par value has no effect on the market value of the shares. Procter and Gamble's stock has no par value and was selling for over $60 per share in 1995. No-par stock is considered by many to have at least two distinct advantages over par value stock:

- Accounting for stock transactions is less complicated for no-par stock than it is for par value stock.
- No-par stock prevents confusion as to the amount received from the sale of the stock. The relevant information is what shareholders were willing to pay for the stock, and an arbitrary par value may mislead some investors.

If the Rosita Corporation's common stock in the previous example had been no-par stock, the entire $5,000 proceeds from the sale of the stock would be classified as common stock and the balance sheet immediately after the sale would look like Exhibit 4-10.

Exhibit 4-10

Balance Sheet for a Corporation that Issued No-Par Common Stock

ROSITA CORPORATION
Balance Sheet
January 1, 1993

Assets:		Liabilities:		$ 0
Cash	$5,000			
		Owners' Equity:		
		Common Stock	$5,000	
		Total Shareholders' Equity		5,000
Total Assets	$5,000	Total Liabilities and		
		Owners' Equity		$5,000

Like Exhibit 4-9, this balance sheet can tell us how much was received from the sale of stock, but it does not tell us about the current market value of the stock.

DISCUSSION QUESTIONS

4-6. If you were setting up a new corporation, would you establish a par value for your common stock? Why or why not?

4-7. Michael Jacobs reports in *Short-Term America* that "Twenty-five years ago, shares of companies traded on the New York Stock Exchange were held an average of eight years; by 1987, the average holding period had declined to a little more than a year" (1991, p. 60). Some experts feel we are no longer a nation of investors, but rather a nation of speculators. What do you think that statement means? What influence do you think this shorter-term ownership is having on the way companies are run in the United States?

Preferred Stock

preferred (preference) stock A share of ownership in a corporation that has preference over common stock as to dividends and as to assets upon liquidation of the corporation. Usually nonvoting stock.

Preferred stock, also referred to as **preference stock**, is so named because it has certain preference features over common stock. Preferred stock is nonvoting stock. Although preferred shareholders do not have voting rights, they receive other types of benefits, which are outlined in the stock agreement. Two benefits of ownership that are found in virtually all preferred stock agreements are:

■ Owners of preferred stock must receive a dividend before any dividend is paid to owners of common stock.
■ In the event of a corporation's liquidation, preferred shareholders receive a distribution of assets before any assets can be distributed to common shareholders. *Liquidation* refers to the process of going out of business: The corporation is shut down, all assets are sold, and all liabilities are settled.

Preferred stock is almost always par value stock. While par value has become almost meaningless for common stock, the par value of preferred stock is important because dividends are usually stated as a percentage of this value. For example, if a corporation issued 8 percent preferred stock with a par value of $100 per share, the annual dividend would be $8.00 per share ($100 × 8% = $8). Most corporations must offer a reasonable dividend in order to encourage investors to buy their preferred stock. Because the dividends are stated as a percentage of par, the par value of preferred stock is normally much higher than is the par value of common stock.

To illustrate how preferred stock is issued, let us assume that Rosita Corporation, in addition to the common stock it issued as described in our previous discussion, issued (sold) 50 shares of $100 par value preferred stock for $150 per share on January 1, 1993. Then the total amount the business received from the sale of stock would be $12,500 (50 shares of preferred stock × $150 = $7,500 + $5,000 from the sale of the common stock). Under the laws of most states, only the par value of the preferred stock multiplied by the number of shares issued would be classified as preferred stock (50 shares × $100 par value = $5,000). The remaining $2,500 of the proceeds would be classified as additional paid-in capital. A balance sheet prepared immediately after the sale of the two classes of stock would look like Exhibit 4-11.

ROSITA CORPORATION
Balance Sheet
January 1, 1993

Assets:		Liabilities:		$ 0
Cash	$12,500			
		Owners' Equity:		
		Preferred Stock	$5,000	
		Additional Paid-in		
		Capital—Preferred Stock	2,500	
		Common Stock	1,000	
		Additional Paid-in		
		Capital—Common Stock	4,000	
		Total Shareholders' Equity		12,500
Total Assets	$12,500	Total Liabilities and		
		Owners' Equity		$12,500

Again, the balance sheet reveals the amounts received for issuing each class of stock ($5,000 for common and $7,500 for preferred), but the current market value of the stock is not shown.

The following information is a portion of the December 31, 1983, balance sheet of Investors Accumulation Plan, Inc. Look at it carefully, and then try to answer the questions below.

Common stock, $100 par value, authorized
      10,000 shares; issued 5,000 shares $500,000
Additional paid-in capital 533,000

1. What was the total amount the corporation received for the sale of its stock?

2. What was the average selling price per share?

3. If the corporation wanted to sell all the stock it could possibly sell, how many more shares could it offer for sale?

4. If all the stock mentioned in Question 3 were sold, how much money would the corporation receive?

Try to reason through each question, using what you have learned about stock from reading this chapter, before you look at the answers. Don't give up too easily!

Here are the answers.

1. In total, the corporation received $1,033,000 for its stock. That is the total of the par value and the additional paid-in capital ($500,000 + $533,000).

2. If the corporation received a total of $1,033,000 from the sale of its stock, the average selling price was $206.60.

$$(\$1,033,000 \ / \ 5,000 \ \text{shares} \ = \ \$206.60 \ \text{per share})$$

3. The corporation has been authorized to sell up to 10,000 shares. If 5,000 shares have already been issued, an additional 5,000 shares could be sold.

4. Based solely on the information provided, there is no way to determine the current market value of the stock. If the stock is traded on a public stock exchange, the current selling price is common knowledge. Business publications such as *The Wall Street Journal* and the business sections of many daily newspapers publish stock prices daily. We will provide more information about the trading of stock later in this chapter.

THE STOCK MARKET

In Chapter 1, we discussed the relative advantages and disadvantages of the three forms of business organization (sole proprietorship, partnership, corporation). One of the advantages we listed under corporations was greater access to capital (money). We stated that by dividing ownership into relatively low-cost shares, corporations could attract a great number of investors. We also mentioned that some corporations in the United States have more than a million different stockholders (owners).

Another advantage of the corporate form that we listed in Chapter 1 was easy transferability of ownership. We stated that because shares of ownership in corporations are relatively low in cost, they can usually be purchased and sold by individual investors much more easily than an ownership interest in either a proprietorship or a partnership.

In this chapter, we used the example of Rosita Corporation to demonstrate the sale of common (par and no-par) stock and preferred stock and how the sale of those classes of stock would be reflected in Rosita's balance sheet. But how would Rosita go about finding people interested in buying her company's stock? If she desires to raise a great deal of money by selling shares of stock in her corporation, she must find a way to contact many more people than she knows personally. Once investors have purchased stock in Rosita Corporation, how do they go about selling their shares if and when they decide they no longer desire to be stockholders?

If corporations are to have access to many potential investors, and if there is to be easy transferability of shares already owned by investors, there must be some mechanism to bring interested buyers and sellers of stock together. There is such a mechanism, and it is called the **stock market**. As with many business terms, this one is used rather loosely. Many people think of Wall Street when they hear the words "stock market," but that thinking is too narrow. While Wall Street is a very important part of the stock market, there is much more to it than that. For one thing, there is not one stock market in the United States, but several, including the New York Stock Exchange (NYSE), the American Stock Exchange (AMEX), and regional stock exchanges such as the Midwest Stock Exchange in Chicago and the Pacific Stock Exchange in Los Angeles and San Francisco. NASDAQ (National Association of Securities Dealers' Automated Quotations) is a relative newcomer to the business world, but this stock exchange prides itself on its ability to attract and support the growth of many of America's most successful and innovative companies, including Microsoft, MCI, Apple Computer, and Intel. In fact, in 1993, *Fortune* magazine reported that 65 of the nation's 100 fastest-growing companies chose to be listed with NASDAQ rather than with the older, more established stock exchanges.

A **stock exchange** is an organization created to provide a place where interested buyers and sellers of shares of stock can get together. As recently as 1980, the U.S. stock market (encompassing all the national and regional exchanges) accounted for better than half the stock trading in the world. By 1990, that figure was down to just over 34 percent, and the trend toward worldwide exchanges outside the United States is expected to continue into the next century. Already, stock exchanges in Tokyo, London, and several other foreign cities are as important to world stock trading as exchanges in the United States.

stock market A general term referring to activities in the secondary stock market.

stock exchange An organization that brings together buyers and sellers of stock.

From the time it opens each day until it closes each night, the New York Stock Exchange is the scene of incredible trading activity. It is not unusual for 150,000,000 shares of stock in U.S. corporations to change owners in a single day.

Edward C. Topple/The New York Stock Exchange

Primary and Secondary Markets

stock offering The process of announcing the issue of shares of stock.

When a corporation (such as Rosita Corporation) desires to raise capital (money) by selling shares of stock, it makes what is referred to as a **stock offering**. A stock offering gives investors the opportunity to purchase ownership shares in the company. The company announces the offering in such business publications as *The Wall Street Journal*. The announcement outlines the number of shares being offered and the anticipated selling price. If investors are interested in purchasing shares, the company is able to sell its stock and raise the money it needs.

investment bankers Intermediaries between the corporation issuing stock and the investors who ultimately purchase the shares. Also called underwriters.

underwriters Professionals in the field of investment banking. Also called investment bankers.

Although a company can market its stock directly to the public, most offerings are made through **investment bankers**. The function of investment bankers, also called **underwriters**, is to act as intermediaries between the company issuing the shares of stock and the investors who ultimately purchase those shares. An investment banker purchases all the shares of stock being offered, then resells the shares to other investors (for a higher price). Some well-known investment banking firms are Merrill Lynch, Salomon Brothers, and Morgan Stanley.

primary stock market The business activity involved in the initial issue of stock from a corporation.

What we have described in the preceding two paragraphs is known as the **primary stock market**. Primary means *first* or *initial* in this instance, not main or most important. Earlier in the chapter we illustrated the issuing (sale) of stock for Rosita Corporation and how the sale of that stock was reflected on the company's balance sheet. What we were demonstrating in that illustration was the primary or initial sale of the stock.

secondary stock market The business activity focusing on trades of stock among investors subsequent to the initial issue.

After a company has initially sold shares of its stock, all sales of those shares take place in what is called the **secondary stock market**. The company itself receives no money from the sale of its stock in the secondary market. It needs to be notified, of course, when shares of its stock are sold from one investor to another, because it must know to whom it should send dividend payments. But the company itself is not directly involved in the trading of its stock in the secondary market.

The daily reports we hear about fluctuations in the overall stock market and in the Dow Jones Industrial Average refer to the trading of previously issued shares of stock in the secondary stock market. Whether you someday own a corporation, work for one, or invest your money in one, you will find that a basic understanding of corporate structure and the operation of the stock market is very valuable.

Government Influence on the Stock Market

As the secondary stock market grew in importance during the early part of the twentieth century, there was little government interference in how the buying and selling of corporate stock were conducted. That all changed with the stock market crash of 1929, which led to the Great Depression.

Securities and Exchange Commission (SEC) The government agency empowered to regulate the buying and selling of stocks and bonds.

In the aftermath of the Crash, the U.S. Congress took steps to standardize Wall Street practices and regulate the buying and selling of corporate securities in the secondary stock market. Congress passed two very significant pieces of legislation: the Securities Act of 1933 and the Securities Exchange Act of 1934. The second of these two laws created the **Securities and Exchange Commission (SEC)**.

One of the express purposes of the SEC is to regulate the procedures involved in the buying and selling of corporate stock on the U.S. stock markets. Any company whose shares of stock are traded on one of the recognized national or regional stock markets in the United States is required by law to file periodic reports with the SEC. The influence of this government agency on the way stock markets operate has grown significantly since it was first created in 1934.

Despite its increased influence, however, the SEC could not prevent the stock market crash of October 19, 1987, when the Dow Jones Industrial Average fell

Exhibit 4-12
Notice of Stock Offering

Courtesy of William Blair & Company

This is not an offer to sell nor a solicitation of offers to buy any of these securities. This offer is made only by the Prospectus.

September 28, 1994

2,185,000 Shares

TESSCO TECHNOLOGIES

Common Stock

Price $12 Per Share

Copies of the Prospectus may be obtained within any State from any Underwriter who may lawfully offer these securities within such State.

William Blair & Company

Alex. Brown & Sons *Incorporated*	Dean Witter Reynolds Inc.	Dillon, Read & Co. Inc.
Donaldson, Lufkin & Jenrette *Securities Corporation*	A.G. Edwards & Sons, Inc.	Hambrecht & Quist *Incorporated*
Montgomery Securities	Oppenheimer & Co., Inc.	PaineWebber Incorporated
Prudential Securities Incorporated		Robertson, Stephens & Company
Salomon Brothers Inc	Smith Barney Inc.	Wertheim Schroder & Co. *Incorporated*
Robert W. Baird & Co. *Incorporated*	George K. Baum & Company	J.C. Bradford & Co.
The Chicago Corporation	Cowen & Company	Crowell, Weedon & Co.
Ferris, Baker Watts *Incorporated*	First of Michigan Corporation	Gabelli & Company, Inc.
Hanifen, Imhoff Inc.	Janney Montgomery Scott Inc.	Kemper Securities, Inc.
C.L. King & Associates, Inc.		Ladenburg, Thalmann & Co. Inc.
Legg Mason Wood Walker *Incorporated*	McDonald & Company *Securities, Inc.*	Mesirow Financial, Inc.
Morgan Keegan & Company, Inc.	Needham & Company, Inc.	The Ohio Company
Pennsylvania Merchant Group Ltd		Raymond James & Associates, Inc.
The Robinson-Humphrey Company, Inc.	Sutro & Co. Incorporated	Tucker Anthony *Incorporated*
Unterberg Harris	Wessels, Arnold & Henderson	Wheat First Butcher Singer

508 points, or 22.3 percent of its value, in one day. To prevent another drop of this magnitude, the stock exchanges created "circuit breakers" so that, in the future, trading would be halted when the market dropped more than a certain percentage. Fortunately, investors shrugged off the 1987 crash and started buying stocks again almost immediately. Within a few months, the Dow Jones Industrial Average had recovered all its losses, and by 1994, it had nearly doubled in value.

When companies issue stock, the lead investment bank often puts an ad, such as the one in Exhibit 4-12, in *The Wall Street Journal* and other papers to alert potential investors to the offering. This particular ad indicates that William Blair & Co. is the lead underwriter for 2,185,000 shares of Tessco Technologies stock, priced at $12 per share. The other securities firms helping to distribute the shares are also listed in the ad. Note that the ad's disclaimer directs interested investors to contact one of the brokers listed in order to obtain a *prospectus*, the legal document describing the offering in detail.

In addition to its authority to regulate the buying and selling of corporate stock, the SEC has the power to regulate the buying and selling of corporate bonds. Selling corporate bonds is a very sophisticated form of borrowing. It is one of the major topics addressed in the next chapter.

SUMMARY

The balance sheet is a financial tool that provides information about the present financial position of an entity. This financial statement shows the relationship of three accounting elements: assets, liabilities, and owners' equity. This relationship is known as the accounting equation or business equation:

ASSETS = LIABILITIES + OWNERS' EQUITY.

Basically, assets are what the company owns, liabilities are what the company owes to outsiders, and owners' equity is what is left when liabilities are subtracted from assets—the residual interest that the owners can claim. Regardless of the type of business, the balance sheet shows the relationship among the company's assets, liabilities, and owners' equity.

Generally, the first activity of a new company is acquiring the cash needed to begin operations. Most often, this cash comes from the owner or owners of the company. The balance sheet for each type of business organization presents the results of this investment by owners in a slightly different way. Proprietorships have a single capital account, representing the ownership interest of the sole proprietor. Partnerships generally show a separate capital account for each partner, because their levels of ownership interest may vary. Corporations are owned by their stockholders; therefore, ownership interests are shown in common stock and additional paid-in capital accounts.

Because it is a separate legal entity, a corporation has a more complex organizational structure than either of the other two business forms. After issuing ownership interests in the form of shares of stock, the corporation has owners, called shareholders or stockholders. Corporate stockholders elect a board of directors to oversee the management of the corporation. The board, how-ever, usually restricts itself to setting broad corporate policy; it appoints offi-cers to conduct the daily affairs of the corporation. Corporate officers nor-mally consist of a chief executive officer (usually the president), one or more vice presidents, a controller, a treasurer, and a secretary.

Corporations may issue both common stock and preferred stock. Common stock is voting stock, and the owners of common shares are the real owners of the business. Common stock may have a par value, or it may be no-par stock. Preferred (preference) stock is usually nonvoting stock that has certain pref-erences over common stock. The two primary preferences given to preferred shareholders relate to dividends (which are usually based on some percentage of the par value) and to a claim on the assets if the corporation is liquidated.

Corporate capital (stockholders' equity) is classified by source: paid-in (contributed) capital and retained earnings. Paid-in capital represents the cash or other assets acquired by the company from the owners, generally through the sale of stock. Retained earnings represents the amount of earnings rein-vested in the business rather than distributed to the owners in the form of div-idends. For a number of reasons, a corporation might reacquire shares of stock it previously issued. Reacquired stock is known as treasury stock. Treasury stock is still considered issued stock, but is no longer considered outstanding; it is shown on the balance sheet as a reduction of stockholders' equity.

The balance sheet is a representation of the financial position of the busi-ness on a particular date. The current market value of the corporation's stock cannot be determined from its balance sheet. Rather, the balance sheet pro-vides information about how much was received by the corporation for the stock when it was originally issued.

Corporate stock is initially issued in the primary stock market, either to individuals or to an investment banker (or underwriter), which resells the stock to individual investors. Secondary stock market activity includes all sub-sequent trading of the shares of stock. Although the corporation does not receive money from trades in the secondary market, since these trades deter-mine the market value of the stock, they are certainly important to the corpo-ration. Activity in both the primary and secondary stock markets is regulated by the Securities and Exchange Commission (SEC).

Key Terms

account form A common format of the balance sheet, in which assets are placed on the left side of the page and liabilities and owners' equity on the right side. (p. 95)

accounting elements The cate-gories under which the results of all accounting transactions can be classified. (p. 93)

accounting equation Assets = Liabilities + Owners' Equity. Also called the business equation. (p. 95)

additional paid-in capital The amount in excess of the stock's par value received by the corpora-tion when par value stock is issued. (p. 103)

articles of incorporation An application for a charter allowing the operation of a corporation. (p. 98)

assets An accounting element that is one of the three components of a balance sheet. Assets are probable future economic benefits controlled by an entity as a result of previous transactions or events—that is, what a company has. (p. 93)

authorized shares The maximum number of shares of stock a corporation has been given permission to issue under its corporate charter. (p. 101)

balance sheet A financial statement providing information about an entity's present condition. Reports what a company possesses (assets) and who has claim to those possessions (liabilities and owners' equity). (p. 92)

business equation Assets = Liabilities + Owners' Equity. Also called the accounting equation. (p. 95)

bylaws The basic rules by which a corporation is operated. (p. 99)

chief executive officer (CEO) The person responsible for all activities of the corporation. This person is usually also the president. (p. 100)

common stock A share of ownership in a corporation. Each share represents one vote in the election of the board of directors and other pertinent corporate matters. (p. 102)

contributed capital Total amount invested in a corporation by its shareholders. Also called paid-in capital. (p. 102)

controller The person in charge of all accounting functions of a corporation. (p. 100)

corporate charter A legal contract between a corporation and the state in which it is incorporated. (p. 98)

dividends A distribution of earnings from a corporation to its owners. Dividends are most commonly distributed in the form of cash. (p. 102)

earned equity The total amount a company has earned since its beginning, less any amounts distributed to the owner(s). In a corporation, this is called retained earnings. (p. 94)

equity An accounting element that is one of the three components of a balance sheet. Equity is the residual interest in the assets of an entity that remains after deducting liabilities. (p. 94)

incorporators Individuals who make application to form a corporation. (p. 98)

investment bankers Intermediaries between the corporation issuing stock and the investors who ultimately purchase the shares. Also called underwriters. (p. 109)

investments by owners That part of owners' equity generated by the receipt of cash (or other assets) from the owners. (p. 94)

issued shares Stock that has been distributed to the owners of the corporation in exchange for cash or other assets. (p. 101)

liabilities An accounting element that is one of the three components of a balance sheet. Liabilities are probable future sacrifices of assets arising from present obligations of an entity as a result of past transactions or events—that is, what a company owes. (p. 93)

no-par stock Stock that has no par value assigned to it. (p. 104)

outstanding shares Shares of stock actually held by shareholders. The number may be different than that for issued shares because a corporation may reacquire its own stock (treasury stock). (p. 101)

owners' equity The owners' residual interest in the assets of a company after consideration of its liabilities. (p. 95)

paid-in capital The portion of stockholders' equity representing amounts invested by the owners of the corporation. Consists of common stock, preferred stock, and amounts received in excess of the par values of those stocks. Also called contributed capital. (p. 102)

par value (for stocks) An arbitrary amount assigned to each share of stock by the incorporators at the time of incorporation. (p.102)

par value stock Stock with a par value printed on the stock certificate (see par value). (p. 102)

preferred (preference) stock A share of ownership in a corporation that has preference over common stock as to dividends and as to assets upon liquidation of the corporation. Usually nonvoting stock. (p. 105)

primary stock market The business activity involved in the initial issue of stock from a corporation. (p.109)

report form The vertical format of a balance sheet, in which assets, liabilities, and owners' equity are shown one after another down the page. (p. 96)

retained earnings Earnings reinvested in a corporation. Equal to the total profits of the corporation since it was organized less amounts distributed to the stockholders in the form of dividends. (p. 102)

secondary stock market The business activity focusing on trades of stock among investors subsequent to the initial issue. (p. 109)

secretary The person who maintains the minutes of meetings of the board of directors and stockholders of a corporation. This person may also represent the corporation in legal proceedings. (p. 100)

Securities and Exchange Commission (SEC) The government agency empowered to regulate the buying and selling of stocks and bonds. (p. 109)

shareholders The owners of a corporation. Also called stockholders. (p. 99)

statement of financial condition Another name for the balance sheet. (p. 95)

statement of financial position Another name for the balance sheet. (p. 95)

stock certificate Document providing evidence of ownership of shares in a corporation. (p. 100)

stock exchange An organization that brings together buyers and sellers of stock. (p. 108)

stock market A general term referring to activities in the secondary stock market. (p. 108)

stock offering The process of announcing the issue of shares of stock. (p. 109)

stockholders' equity The corporate form of owners' equity. Stockholders' equity is divided into contributed capital and retained earnings. (p. 102)

treasurer The person in charge of managing the cash of a corporation. (p.100)

treasury stock Corporate stock that has been issued and then reacquired by the corporation. (p. 101)

underwriters Professionals in the field of investment bankers. Also called investment bankers. (p. 109)

REVIEW THE FACTS

A. List and define the three accounting elements that are components of the balance sheet.

B. Describe the two sources from which a company builds equity.

C. State the business or accounting equation.

D. What is a more formal and descriptive name for the balance sheet?

E. Name and describe the two formats of the balance sheet.

F. How does the balance sheet for a proprietorship differ from that for a partnership?

G. In what ways does a stockholder of a corporation differ from a partner in a partnership?

H. Explain the differences among authorized, issued, and outstanding shares of stock.

I. Define treasury stock.

J. Name and describe the two major components of stockholders' equity.

K. What are the two major classes of stock and how do they differ?

L. What is meant by the par value of stock and what significance does it have?

M. Explain what a stock exchange and a stock offering are.

N. What is the role of underwriters or investment bankers?

O. Distinguish between the primary stock market and the secondary stock market.

P. What type of organization is the SEC and what is its function?

APPLY WHAT YOU HAVE LEARNED

4-8. On January 2, 1995, Marty McDermitt started a business.

REQUIRED:

a. Prepare a balance sheet as of January 2, 1995, assuming Marty's company is a sole proprietorship named Marty McDermitt Enterprises and that he invested $3,000 cash in the operation.

b. Now assume that the business organized on January 2, 1995, was a partnership started by Marty and his brother Barton, which they have named M&B Enterprises. Marty invested $2,000 and Barton invested $1,000. Prepare a balance sheet as of January 2, 1995, for the company to reflect the partners' investment.

c. Now assume that the business organized on January 2, 1995, was a corporation started by Marty and his brother Barton, which they have named M&B Enterprises, Inc. Marty invested $2,000 and received 200 shares of common stock. Barton invested $1,000 and received 100 shares of common stock. The common stock has a par value of $2 per share. Prepare a balance sheet as of January 2, 1995, for the company to reflect the stockholders' investment.

d. Assume the same facts as in Requirement c, except that the common stock is no-par stock. Prepare a balance sheet as of January 2, 1995, for the company to reflect the stockholders' investment.

4-9. Fisher Corporation began operations in 1972 by issuing 10,000 shares of its no-par common stock for $5 per share. The following details provide information about the company's stock in the years since that time:

1. In 1982, the company issued an additional 50,000 shares of common stock for $15 per share.

2. Fisher Corporation stock is traded on the New York Stock Exchange (NYSE). During an average year, about 25,000 shares of its common stock are sold by one set of investors to another.

3. On December 31, 1994, Fisher Corporation common stock was quoted on the NYSE at $38 per share.

4. On December 31, 1995, Fisher Corporation common stock was quoted on the NYSE at $55 per share.

REQUIRED:

a. Which of the stock transactions described above involved the primary stock market and which ones involved the secondary stock market?

b. How much money has Fisher Corporation received in total from the sales of its common stock since it was incorporated in 1972?

c. When Fisher Corporation prepares its balance sheet as of December 31, 1995, what dollar amount will it show in the owners' equity section for common stock?

d. What, if anything, can you infer about Fisher Corporation's performance during 1995 from the price of its common stock on December 31, 1994 and December 31, 1995?

4-10. Presented below is a list of items relating to the corporate form of business, followed by definitions of those items in scrambled order:

a. Incorporators   **f.** Board of directors

b. Charter   **g.** Corporate officers

c. Bylaws   **h.** Par value

d. Stockholders   **i.** Additional paid-in capital

e. Stock certificate

1. ____ An arbitrary value placed on either common stock or preferred stock at the time a corporation is formed.

2. ____ The group of men and women who have the ultimate responsibility for managing a corporation.

3. ____ The owners of a corporation.

4. ____ Any amount received by a corporation when it issues stock that is greater than the par value of the stock issued.

5. ____ The formal document that legally allows a corporation to begin operations.

6. ____ The group of men and women who manage the day-to-day operations of a corporation.

7. ____ The person or persons who submit a formal application with the appropriate government agencies to form a corporation.

8. ____ A legal document providing evidence of ownership in a corporation.

9. ____ Rules established to conduct the business of a corporation.

REQUIRED:

Match the letter next to each item on the list with the appropriate definition. Each letter will be used only once.

4-11. Atkinson Corporation began operations on July 10, 1995 by issuing 5,000 shares of $3 par value common stock and 500 shares of $100 par value preferred stock. The common stock sold for $10 per share and the preferred stock sold for $120 per share.

REQUIRED:

Prepare a balance sheet for Atkinson Corporation at July 10, 1995, immediately after the common stock and preferred stock were issued.

4-12. The questions below are based on this selected information from the balance sheet of E.I. duPont de Nemours and Company (commonly known as DuPont).

	(Dollars in millions)	
	December 31	
	1991	1990
Common Stock, $.60 par value; 900,000,000 shares authorized; issued at Dec. 31: 1991—671,242,137; 1990—669,847,961	$ 403	$ 402
Additional Paid-in Capital	4,418	4,342

a. What was the average selling price of the stock that had been issued as of December 31, 1990?

b. The par value of the outstanding shares of common stock as of December 31, 1991 is shown as $403 million. This is actually a rounded amount. What is the exact par value of the common stock outstanding as of that date?

c. How many shares of common stock were issued during 1991?

d. How many shares would DuPont be allowed to issue during 1992?

4-13. Martha Walton has always been known for making the best cookies in town. She is about to start a company called Martha's Home Made Cookies. On February 3, 1995, Martha invests $2,500 to form the company.

REQUIRED:

a. Prepare a balance sheet for Martha's Home Made Cookies as of February 3, 1995, assuming Martha decided to form a proprietorship.

b. Prepare a balance sheet for Martha's Home Made Cookies as of February 3, 1995, assuming Martha decided to form a partnership with her daughter Tracy, who invested $1,500.

c. Assume that Martha decided to form a corporation called Martha's Home Made Cookies, Inc. Martha invested $2,500 and received 250 shares of common stock, and her daughter Tracy invested $1,500 and received 150 shares of common stock. The common stock has a par value of $1 per share. Prepare a balance sheet as of February 3, 1995.

d. Assume the same facts as in Requirement c, except that the common stock is no-par stock. Prepare a balance sheet for the company as of February 3, 1995.

4-14. On January 2, 1988, Hellen Steinmann formed a company called Baby Covers, Inc., which sells expensive infant clothing. Originally, Hellen invested $50,000 in cash in exchange for 5,000 of the company's 50,000 authorized $1 par shares of common stock. By 1993, the company had grown from one store to three successful stores. In January of 1994, Hellen decided to finance further expansion of Baby Covers by selling additional stock.

REQUIRED:

a. Prepare a balance sheet for Baby Covers, Inc., as of January 2, 1988, that reflects Hellen's $50,000 initial investment.

b. How many additional shares can Baby Covers, Inc., issue during 1994?

c. If 20,000 additional shares were sold for $35 per share, what would the balance sheet show for common stock and additional paid-in capital—common stock?

d. If Hellen wanted to raise money for expansion of the company, what would be the advantage to issuing preferred stock instead of common stock?

4-15. Presented below is a list of three accounting elements, followed by partial definitions of those items in scrambled order:

a. Assets   **b.** Liabilities   **c.** Equity

    1. ___ Debts of the company.

    2. ___ Probable future economic benefits.

    3. ___ "Things" of value a company has.

    4. ___ The residual interest in the assets of an entity that remains after deducting its liabilities.

    5. ___ Probable future sacrifices of economic benefits.

    6. ___ What the company owes.

    7. ___ What the company has less what it owes.

    8. ___ The owner's interest in the company.

REQUIRED:

For each partial definition, identify the element (a, b, or c) to which it refers.

4-16. A corporation with both preferred stockholders and common stockholders is in the process of liquidating its assets. Which stockholders will receive a distribution first and why?

4-17. Assume you have $10,000 to invest and you are trying to decide between investing in the preferred stock of Company X and the common stock of Company X.

REQUIRED:

a. List and briefly explain at least two reasons why you would invest in the preferred stock rather than the common stock of Company X.

b. List and briefly explain at least two reasons why you would invest in the common stock rather than the preferred stock of Company X.

4-18. The chapter discusses the balance sheet presentations for each of the three forms of business organization.

REQUIRED:

Discuss the similarities and differences in the balance sheets of proprietorships, partnerships, and corporations.

5

The Balance Sheet (Continued): Additional Financing—Borrowing from Others

Businesses often need more funding than is available through investments by their owners. Additional cash to support day-to-day operations or expansion of the business is often acquired through borrowing. Results of borrowing are reflected on a company's balance sheet.

internal financing Providing funds for the operation of a company through the earnings process of that company.

external financing Acquiring funds from outside the company. Equity and debt financing are the two major types of external financing.

equity financing Acquiring funds for business operations by giving up ownership interest in the company. For a corporation, this means issuing capital stock. Equity financing is one type of external financing.

debt financing Acquiring funds for business operations by borrowing. Debt financing is one type of external financing.

No matter what organizational form a company takes (proprietorship, partnership, corporation), or what type of company it is (service, merchandise, manufacturing), all companies have one thing in common: They must obtain capital (money) to support operations. In the long run, a company must be financed by the profits from its operations. This is known as **internal financing**. However, either when just starting out or in a time of expansion, almost all companies find it necessary to obtain capital from sources other than their profits. This is called **external financing**.

The two external sources of capital are known as equity financing and debt financing. **Equity financing** involves offering ownership interest in the company in exchange for the needed cash. Most businesses begin their operations using cash invested by the owners. Chapter 4 illustrated the impact of this initial financing on the balance sheets of proprietorships, partnerships, and corporations. In many cases, however, more cash than the owners can come up with is needed to get the operation started. Almost all companies, at one time or another, need additional funds from outsiders. To obtain these funds, companies can sell more ownership shares or they can borrow funds. Borrowing funds for business operations is called **debt financing**.

> **N**either a borrower nor a lender be!
>
> **William Shakespeare**

Although Shakespeare's advice may serve you well in your personal life, many companies would not be able to survive if they didn't participate in the borrowing and lending that are integral to today's business world. In this chapter, you will learn about several different approaches to debt financing. As you will see, financial institutions function as primary lenders. The bond market also serves as a source of debt financing. Companies borrow funds for various reasons. Needing funds from external sources is *not* necessarily a sign of weakness. Often funds are needed for expansion because the company is growing even faster than expected.

After completing your work on this chapter, you should be able to do the following:

1. Describe how banks earn profits.
2. Explain the effects on a company's balance sheet when funds are borrowed from a bank.
3. Distinguish among notes, mortgages, and bonds.
4. Calculate interest payments for notes and bonds.
5. Explain the functions of underwriters in the process of issuing bonds.
6. Describe in your words the effect of market interest rates on bond selling prices.
7. Contrast the operations of the primary and secondary bond markets.
8. Compare and contrast two investment alternatives—equity investment and debt investment.

short-term financing Financing secured to support an operation's day-to-day activities. Repayment is usually required within five years.

long-term financing Any financing in which repayment extends beyond five years. This type of financing supports the long-range goals of the company.

The financing requirements of companies fall into two general categories. A company needs short-term financing to run its day-to-day operations and long-term financing to achieve its long-range goals. **Short-term financing** is generally defined as any financing that must be repaid within five years. **Long-term financing**, then, can be defined as any financing in which repayment extends past five years. However, don't consider those definitions as hard and fast. Understand that different people have different interpretations of what "short-term" and "long-term" mean. In any event, several sources have developed to provide these two types of financing to businesses.

Borrowing from Financial Institutions

At one time or another, almost everyone has had dealings with a bank. You may have had a savings account (time deposit), a checking account (demand deposit), or a loan to finance a car, a motorcycle, or some other purchase. Individuals borrow money from financial institutions every day, but this activity represents only one type of borrowing. Financial institutions must meet the needs of both individuals and companies. This demand leads to two distinct types of borrowing: consumer and commercial.

consumer borrowing Loans obtained by individuals to buy homes, cars, or other personal property.

Consumer borrowing refers to loans obtained by individuals to pay for such items as the car and motorcycle mentioned in the previous paragraph. While most of the loans classified as consumer loans are relatively small, the definition has to do with the purpose of the loan, not its amount. If an item is for personal use rather than for use in business, the loan obtained to finance it is classified as consumer borrowing. When a company obtains a loan to finance day-to-day operations or achieve long-term goals, that loan is referred to as **commercial borrowing**. The word "commercial" comes from the word "commerce," which was, as you will recall, listed in the dictionary as one of the definitions of the word "business."

commercial borrowing The process that businesses go through to obtain financing.

Banks are not the only places to go for a loan. Actually, there are several distinct types of financial institutions whose major business function is lending money. Although their functions have become somewhat blurred over the past several years, certain of the financial institutions discussed below were developed specifically to satisfy the need for consumer loans, while others came into being to meet the financing needs of companies.

- *Savings and Loan Associations (S&Ls) and Mutual Savings Banks (MSBs).* Savings and loan associations were created primarily to lend money for home mortgages. Over time, S&Ls began lending money for other consumer items. In the 1980s, many S&Ls ventured into still other lending arrangements, such as real estate speculation, and in many instances the results were disastrous. Mutual savings banks are somewhat different from S&Ls in that they are owned by their depositors and any profits earned are divided proportionately among those depositors. Like S&Ls, MSBs began as consumer lending institutions (particularly for home mortgages), but over time they broadened their lending activities. And, as was the case with S&Ls, many have experienced financial difficulties in the last decade.

- *Credit Unions (CUs).* Credit unions are typically formed by a company, labor union, or professional group. They accept deposits and lend money only to their members. To become a member of a credit union, a person must meet a specific set of qualifications. This usually means working for a particular employer or belonging to the organization that formed the credit union. Traditionally, CUs have concentrated on short-term consumer loans (financing cars and stereos, for example) and savings deposits for their members. In recent years, many credit unions have developed checking accounts for their members (called *share draft accounts*), but their lending activities are still mostly for consumer purchases by members rather than for financing business activities.

- *Commercial Banks.* This is what most people think of when they think of a bank. As the name implies, commercial banks are heavily involved in commercial lending. In fact, while they have ventured into the area of consumer lending, the vast majority of lending by these institutions is to companies, for commercial purposes. There are roughly 13,000 commercial banks in the United States today. Exhibit 5-1 is a list of the ten largest American banks.

Exhibit 5-1
The 10 Largest Banks
in the United States

	Location	Assets (in $ billions)
Citicorp	New York	$217.4
BankAmerica	San Francisco	193.6
Chemical Bank	New York	135.4
NationsBank	Charlotte, NC	118.2
Chase Manhattan	New York	98.5
J. P. Morgan	New York	96.9
Bankers Trust	New York	58.9
Wells Fargo	San Francisco	54.4
First Interstate Bancorp	Los Angeles	50.3
Banc One	Columbus, Ohio	49.3

This book deals primarily with business and how accounting information is used in making business decisions. Therefore, whenever we refer to "the bank," we are referring to a commercial bank.

How Banks Earn Profits

Think back to our discussion of Ralph and his shoe store in Chapter 1. In order to stay in business, Ralph must be profitable. He must sell shoes for enough money to recover what the shoes cost him, plus pay all other expenses associated with running his store. Whatever is left after all those costs have been covered is his profit. Well, banks are companies, too, and in order to stay in business, a bank must be profitable. Most of a bank's income comes from the **interest** paid on loans by borrowers.

Think of interest as rent paid on borrowed money. The bank rents money from its depositors and then rents it out to others. Logic dictates that the rent (interest) the bank pays must be less than the rent (interest) it receives if it is to be profitable. For example, let's say you open a savings account at the bank by depositing $100. The bank agrees to pay you 5 percent annual interest on the amount you have deposited. This means if you leave the $100 in the bank for a full year, you will earn $5 interest.

Let's say further that nine other people did exactly as you did and opened savings accounts at the bank by depositing $100 each. The bank has agreed to pay them 5 percent annual interest on their deposits as well. The bank now has $1,000 ($100 X 10 depositors), and the interest the bank must pay on this $1,000 is $50 ($5 to each of the ten depositors).

The bank can now take the $1,000 and lend it to someone. Obviously, it must charge something greater than 5 percent interest on the loan (or loans) it makes with the $1,000 or it will lose on the exchange. So let's say the bank lends the $1,000 to someone for one year and that person agrees to pay the bank 9 percent annual interest on the loan.

At the end of the year, the person who borrowed the $1,000 repays the loan, plus $90 interest ($1,000 × 9%). The bank then adds $5 to the account of each of the ten depositors, and the bank has earned a gross profit of $40, calculated as follows:

Interest the bank received on the loan	$90
Less the interest paid to the ten depositors	50
Equals gross profit on the loan	$40

It's a simple enough process, right? Wrong! In fact, there are a number of possible complications in this process. Two that immediately come to mind are:

1. The person who borrowed the $1,000 may fail to repay the loan. Failure to repay is known as **defaulting** on the loan.
2. One or more of the ten depositors may decide not to leave their $100 deposit in the bank for the full year.

---

interest The cost to the borrower of using someone else's money. Also, what can be earned by lending money to someone else.

defaulting Failing to repay a loan as agreed.

5-1. In addition to the two complications described in the text, what other factors complicate the process whereby banks earn their profits by making loans?

5-2. What steps would you suggest to the bank to overcome the two complications we listed in the text plus the ones you thought of in your response to Discussion Question 5-1?

By the way, the $40 profit we calculated for the bank on the loan does not constitute the bank's real profit. Just as was the case with Ralph selling a pair of shoes to Marty in Chapter 1, the profit we calculated above represents *gross profit* (see Exhibit 5-2). All other costs involved in running the bank must be deducted before the *net profit* (real profit) can be calculated.

Exhibit 5-2
How Banks Earn Profits

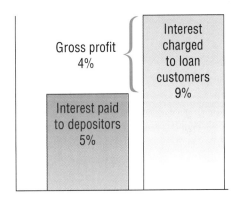

Notes Payable

note payable An agreement between a lender and borrower that creates a liability for the borrower.

If a company needs to borrow funds for only a short time (usually five years or less), a bank may lend it money and require it to sign a **note payable**. The amount of money lent and the term (length) of the loan will be determined by the bank's policies and the judgment of the lending officer. Borrowing funds by signing a note payable adds to the assets of the company, but at the same time creates a liability. Building upon the example introduced in the previous chapter, we illustrate the effects of borrowing funds in Exhibit 5-3.

Exhibit 5-3
The Effects of Borrowing Funds on a Corporation's Balance Sheet

ROSITA CORPORATION
Balance Sheet
January 1, 1993

Assets:		Liabilities:		
		Notes Payable	$1,000	
Cash	$6,000	Total Liabilities		$1,000
		Owners' Equity:		
		Common Stock	$1,000	
		Additional Paid-in Capital	4,000	
		Total Shareholders' Equity		5,000
Total Assets	$6,000	Total Liabilities and Owners' Equity		$6,000

The information provided in this balance sheet indicates that the company borrowed $1,000 by signing a note payable. This transaction provided the company with $1,000 additional cash, so total assets rose to $6,000. Because the additional asset amount is claimed by someone external to the business (probably a bank), it counts as a liability. Notice that the business equation still holds true:

ASSETS	=	LIABILITIES	+	OWNERS' EQUITY
$6,000	=	$1,000	+	$5,000

collateral Something of value that will be forfeited if a borrower fails to make payments as agreed.

A note payable generally requires the signing of a legal "promise to repay." In addition, the lender may require the use of **collateral** to secure the loan. Collateral is something of value that is forfeited to the lender if the borrower fails to make payments as agreed. For example, if you borrow money from BankAmerica to buy a new car, the car generally serves as collateral. That is, if you fail to make the payments, the bank may repossess the car and sell it to get its money back.

mortgage A document that states the agreement between a lender and a borrower who has secured the loan by offering something of value as collateral.

By offering collateral, companies may be able to borrow more funds for a greater length of time. This type of larger, longer-term debt that identifies a specific item as collateral is called a **mortgage**. For instance, a company can mortgage a piece of property it owns by allowing it to serve as collateral for a loan. In this case, the lender (bank) has the right to seize the property if the borrower defaults (fails to repay the loan).

Calculating Interest

The cost of borrowing these funds can be determined using information about the note payable. You should become familiar with the terminology used when funds are borrowed. Here's an example:

Boston Brothers borrowed $5,000 on January 2, 1993 by signing an 8 percent, three-year note. The lender requires interest payments to be made each year.

First of all, the amount of interest involved is always stated in annual terms. Therefore, 8 percent refers to the amount of interest the lender expects each year. Interest is based on the amount borrowed, the **principal**. The formula to determine annual interest is:

Principal × Rate = Annual Interest

In our example of the Boston Brothers' note, the amount of interest due each year is calculated as:

$5,000 × .08 = $400

Notice that for purposes of calculations, the percentage rates can be converted to numbers. The lender would expect $400 payment of interest on January 1, 1994, and on January 1, 1995. On January 1, 1996, the lender expects another $400 interest payment as well as the principal, because this was a three-year note. The payment that Boston Brothers is required to make to the bank on January 1, 1996, then, is $5,400. This amount reflects both the interest due ($400) and the return of the principal amount ($5,000).

The term (length) of notes payable varies. If Boston Brothers needed to borrow the funds from the bank for only a short time, the note may have been described as a

$5,000, 8 percent, 90-day note

This terminology suggests that the $5,000 must be repaid 90 days (3 months) from the day the funds were borrowed. On that day, Boston Brothers would pay the lender the principal ($5,000) and the interest due. Recall that interest rates are stated in annual terms, so 8 percent indicates the amount of interest that would be due if the funds were held for one year. If the funds are held for three months, only a portion of the year's interest would be due. Now we can use a formula that considers the length of time that the funds are held:

$$\text{Principal} \times \text{Rate} \times \text{Time} = \text{Interest}$$
$$P \times R \times T = I$$

The calculation to determine the interest owed by the Boston Brothers is:

$5,000 × .08 × 3/12 = $100

Because the interest rate is annual, the time factor in the calculation is a proportion of the year. If the funds are borrowed for three months, time is represented by 3/12, indicating three months out of the total twelve in a year.

In calculations such as this one, the time factor may be represented by the number of days involved as a proportion of the number of days in a year. When this method is used, the number of days in a year is generally rounded to 360. Thus, the calculation above could be presented as:

$5,000 × .08 × 90/360 = $100

When the time period involved is a number of whole months, either approach will work. If the funds are borrowed for some other time period, such as 45 days, using 360 as the number of days per year is much clearer.

5-3. In the example given in the text of the Boston Brothers' three-month loan, what is the lender's return *of* investment and return *on* investment?

> ***Note:*** The next two Discussion Questions require that you go to the business section of your local newspaper and look up current interest rates.

5-4. List the different rates a local bank is paying on various certificates of deposit (CDs). Explain why the bank is offering these various rates.

5-5. What are the current rates banks are charging for mortgages in your area? What are the current credit card rates? Why are there differences between these two rates?

Interest costs are an important factor in the decision whether or not to borrow funds. Businesspersons in various capacities (e.g., CEOs, regional managers, store managers) are frequently faced with financing decisions. We began our discussion of how companies are financed by saying that companies require both short-term financing to run day-to-day operations and long-term financing to achieve long-range goals. While the use of collateral may allow a company to secure financing for a longer term, the commercial banks discussed in the previous section are ideally suited to provide short-term financing. At the end of 1991, the total dollar amount of loans outstanding from banks was nearly $1.5 trillion. Most of these loans were to companies, and most of them fell under the definition we used for short-term financing (repayment within five years).

While there is no law preventing banks from lending money to companies for very long periods of time, there are a couple of factors that make this type of lending arrangement unfeasible for most banks. First, many companies are looking for financing for as long as 40 years, and most banks are not interested in making loans of that duration. Second, and perhaps more importantly, the amount of money required for long-term financing in many large companies is more than a single bank can accommodate. Even very large banks are unwilling or unable to address the borrowing needs of these large companies. For this reason, another source of financing is available for corporations.

BORROWING BY ISSUING BONDS

bond An interest-bearing debt instrument that allows corporations to borrow large amounts of funds for long periods of time and creates a liability for the borrower.

A **bond** is similar to a note payable in that it is an interest-bearing debt instrument. The main differences between the two are the length of time the debt will be outstanding and the amount of money borrowed. Notes payable are usually up to five years in duration and are limited to the amount of money a single lender is willing to lend. Bonds payable can be as long as 40 years in duration, and because they are sold to many different parties, the amount of money borrowed can usually be much greater.

Corporate debt in the form of bonds is a major factor in our economy. In 1980, $412 billion worth of corporate bonds were outstanding, and this figure has risen steadily each year since. By the end of 1988, the figure had topped $1 trillion. As Exhibit 5-4 indicates, the amount of corporate bonds outstanding is approaching $1.5 trillion. In 1993, this figure represented 53.5 percent of total corporate debt, indicating that bonds are a major source of funds for American business. It is typical for large industrial American companies to have billions in long-term debt on their balance sheets. For example, International Paper had long-term debt of $3.6 billion as of December 31, 1993.

Bonds are issued in some set denomination, generally $1,000 for each bond. The **par value** of such bonds is then $1,000. This indicates that when the borrower pays back the debt, $1,000 will be repaid. Par value is also called the **face value**.

The **nominal interest rate** is the specified annual interest paid on a bond and is a percentage of the par value of the bond. In other words, it is the rate of interest that the issuing company (borrower) has agreed to pay. The nominal rate is also called the **contract rate**, **coupon rate**, or **stated rate**, and these terms are used interchangeably.

Information such as the par value and the nominal interest rate is included in the bond **indenture**. This legal document details the agreement between the company issuing the bonds (the borrower) and the buyers of the bonds (the lenders). Information concerning timing of the interest payments and timing of total repayment (retirement) of the bonds is also included in the indenture.

In contrast to the nominal interest rate, which is set at the time bonds are issued and remains constant, the **effective interest rate** fluctuates with market conditions. The effective interest rate is the actual interest rate that will be earned by the bondholder over the life of the bond. Unlike the nominal rate,

par value (for bonds) The amount that must be paid back upon maturity of a bond. Also called **face value**.

nominal interest rate The interest rate set by the issuers of bonds, stated as a percentage of the par value of the bonds. Also called the **contract rate** or **coupon rate**, or **stated rate**.

indenture The legal agreement made between a bond issuer and a bondholder that states repayment terms and other details.

effective interest rate The rate of interest actually earned by a bondholder. This amount will be different from the nominal interest rate if the bond is bought at a discount or premium. Also called yield rate or market interest rate.

Exhibit 5-4
Growth of Corporate Bonds

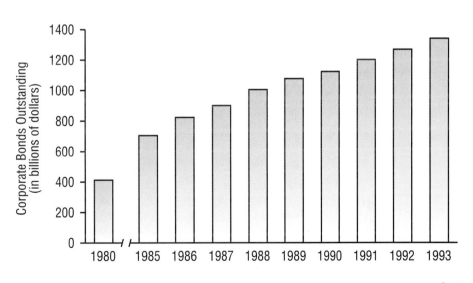

which is determined by the issuing company, the effective rate is determined by the financial markets and may cause a bond to sell for more or less than its par value. The effective rate is also called the **yield rate** or **market interest rate**; these terms are used interchangeably.

The **selling price** is the amount for which a bond actually sells and is also called the **market price**. As we stated, it is determined by the effective or market interest rate. If the effective interest rate and the nominal interest rate are the same, a bond is said to be selling at 100, meaning at 100 percent of its face or par value. Bonds may sell for less than par value. For instance, a selling price of 95 means the bond is selling at 95 percent of its par value. This situation occurs when the stated rate is less than the market rate. If you think about it, you will realize why, if you are trying to sell a bond that pays a rate lower than the market rate, you will be forced to lower the price. Only then will you attract the investors (buyers) you need. Bonds may also sell for more than their par value. This happens when a bond's stated rate of interest is more than the market interest rate. A bond with a sale price of 106 is selling for 106 percent of its par value.

Issuing Bonds Sold at Par

To illustrate the impact of issuing bonds at par value, assume Rosita Corporation issued $300,000 worth of ten-year, 8 percent bonds on January 1, 1993. From our previous use of this example, we know that Rosita Corporation has also sold $5,000 worth of common stock and borrowed $1,000 from the bank. Exhibit 5-5 shows results of all three of these activities.

Exhibit 5-5
Balance Sheet for a Corporation That Has Issued Both Stock and Bonds and Borrowed from a Bank

ROSITA CORPORATION
Balance Sheet
January 1, 1993

Assets:			Liabilities:		
			Notes Payable	$ 1,000	
			Bonds Payable	300,000	
Cash	$306,000		Total Liabilities		$301,000
			Owners' Equity:		
			Common Stock	$1,000	
			Additional Paid-in Capital	4,000	
			Total Shareholders' Equity		5,000
Total Assets	$306,000		Total Liabilities and Owners' Equity		$306,000

On January 1, 1993 (the day the bonds were sold), Rosita Corporation would record the sale of the bonds. Assets (cash) would increase by $300,000, and liabilities (bonds payable) would increase by the same amount. The business equation remains in balance:

$$\text{ASSETS} = \text{LIABILITIES} + \text{OWNERS' EQUITY}$$
$$\$306,000 = \$301,000 + \$5,000$$

As stated earlier, most bonds are issued in denominations of $1,000; Rosita sold 300 of these $1,000 bonds, agreeing to pay 8 percent of the par value per year in interest. Therefore, the nominal rate on the bonds is 8 percent. If other opportunities for investors offer 8 percent per year for using their money, the market interest rate is said to be 8 percent. When the market interest rate and the nominal interest rate are the same, investors are generally indifferent between buying the bonds and choosing other investment opportunities. This indifference results in these bonds being sold at 100, meaning 100 percent of their par value.

Interest payments on corporate bonds are generally paid semiannually (twice each year). In the case of Rosita Corporation, interest would be paid each June 30 and December 31. As we did for the examples of notes payable, we can calculate the annual interest due on the corporate bonds issued by Rosita Corporation:

$$\$300,000 \times .08 = \$24,000$$

This indicates that $24,000 is the annual interest the corporation owes to its bondholders. If interest payments are made every six months, Rosita Corporation would send a total of $12,000 to its bondholders on each interest payment date. The semiannual interest payments are to be made throughout the ten-year life of the bonds. At the end of ten years, Rosita Corporation must pay back the principal amount borrowed, $300,000.

Corporate bonds, as we noted earlier, were developed to accommodate companies' long-term financing needs. Bonds also facilitate borrowing larger sums of money than any single lender is either willing or able to handle. If businesses are to have access to large sums of money, there must be some mechanism for bringing together companies that want to issue bonds and investors who are interested in buying them. That mechanism is the bond market, and it is similar to the stock market.

Initial Offerings—The Primary Bond Market

As with the stock market, there is both a primary bond market and a secondary bond market. The initial sale of bonds by the issuing corporation is the focus of the primary bond market. Most corporations are not equipped to handle the details of the actual sale of their bonds to individual investors. For this reason, most large bond offerings are made through an intermediary investment banker or a group of such bankers called a **syndicate**. The bankers, serving as underwriters, buy all the bonds available in the offering and then resell them to interested investors at a higher price. The underwriters' basic fee is known as

syndicate A group of underwriters working together to get a large bond issue sold to the public.

the spread, the difference between the price paid to the issuer and the price at which securities are sold to the public....In debt issues, the price spread typically ranges from a low of 0.5 percent to as high as 2 percent, with typical spreads in the 1 percent to 1.5 percent range.

—Dennis E. Logue, ed. *Handbook of Modern Finance*, 1994, p. A2-18

Underwriting is a primary source of income for investment banking firms. A list of the major underwriters is shown in Exhibit 5-6. Many of the firms' names are probably familiar to you.

Exhibit 5-6
Top Global Underwriters of Debt and Equity (in billions of dollars for January, February, March-1994)

	Amount (in billions)	1994 Market Share
Merrill Lynch & Co., Inc.	$48.99	13.2%
Goldman, Sachs & Co.	31.61	8.5%
Shearson Lehman Brothers Inc.	31.57	8.5%
The First Boston Corporation	30.78	8.3%
Kidder, Peabody & Co. Incorporated	29.86	8.0%
Salomon Brothers Inc.	25.94	7.0%
Morgan Stanley Group Inc.	22.63	6.1%
Bear, Stearns & Co. Inc.	15.17	4.1%
J.P. Morgan Securities Inc.	9.69	2.6%
Prudential Securities Incorporated	7.99	2.1%
Top 10	$254.23	68.4%
Industry total	$371.91	100.0%

Source: Securities Data Company, Inc.

prospectus A description of an upcoming bond issue that is provided as information for potential investors.

The underwriter assists the corporation in completing all the necessary steps for a successful bond issue. One of the most important steps in the process is preparation of the **prospectus**. This document provides important information to prospective buyers of the bonds, including information about the issuing corporation as well as about the bond issue itself. The preliminary prospectus is just one of the documents that must be filed with the Securities and Exchange Commission. This preliminary version of the prospectus contains no selling price information and no offering date. While the SEC is reviewing the documents filed by the corporation, no sale of the bonds may take place. Clearly, the preliminary prospectus does not provide all the information a potential buyer should want; in particular, it does not give the actual selling price of the bonds.

discount If a bond's selling price is below its par value, the bond is being sold at a discount.

premium If a bond's selling price is above its par value, the bond is being sold at a premium.

The final selling price of the bonds is a result of negotiations between the underwriter and the corporation and is not determined until the very last minute. A crucial meeting takes place after SEC approval has been obtained, and often just one day prior to offering the bonds for sale. At that meeting, the final coupon rate and selling price of the bonds are negotiated. Bond selling prices are stated in relation to their par value. That is, if a bond sells below its par value, it is said to be selling at a **discount**. Bonds with prices above par value are said to be selling at a **premium**. Most underwriters hope to be able to sell bonds for par value or at a slight dis-

Corporations issue bond certificates to their bond-holders just as they issue stock certificates to their stockholders. The bond certificate serves as evidence of the investment made by those who purchase the bonds. A bond certificate looks very much like the stock certificate we looked at in Chapter 4.

Four by Five, Inc.

count. Psychologically, it is easier to sell a bond that is priced at or below par value than it is to sell one at a premium. For this reason, new issues are rarely sold at a premium.

When the bonds are ready to be sold to the public, the underwriter makes a bond offering, which is similar to the stock offering discussed in Chapter 4. The offering is announced in business publications, such as *The Wall Street Journal*, and in major newspapers across the country. The announcement includes information about the number of bonds being offered, the denomination of each bond, the interest rate being offered, the term of the bonds (how long before the debt is to be repaid), and other features of the bonds. If the underwriter has negotiated well, investors will buy all the bonds within a few days, and the risk originally taken by the underwriter will be quickly eliminated. At that point, the agreement is between the issuing corporation and the investors. Any subsequent trades are part of the secondary bond market.

Interest Rates and the Secondary Bond Market

Once the bonds have been issued, those who purchased them are free to sell the bonds to other investors. There is, then, a secondary bond market, just as there is a secondary stock market, and the process works the same way. After a company initially sells its bonds, it receives no money when those bonds are resold. It needs to be notified, of course, when the bonds pass from one investor to another, because it must know to whom it should send the interest payments and who should receive the repayment amount when the bonds are retired (paid off).

During the life of a bond (20, 30, 40 years), the investment may be traded many times. Remember that the coupon rate was fixed prior to the original sale of the bonds. However, the market rate of interest—what investors expect as a return on their investments—fluctuates considerably. For this reason, during the life of a bond, its price on the secondary market may fluctuate considerably as well.

If the investors can get more than 10 percent interest on their money in other areas of investment, bonds with a coupon rate of 10 percent will trade at a discount. By paying less than the face value for the bonds, the investor can actually realize a return greater than the coupon rate. Let's look at an example from an investor's point of view.

If a $1,000 bond paying 10 percent interest is bought for par, the investor has spent $1,000 to receive $100 ($1,000 X 10%) each year. His annual effective interest rate is 10 percent. Common sense may tell you that, but the annual effective interest rate can be calculated by dividing the annual return on investment by the invested amount. In this case:

$100 / $1,000 = 10%

If the investor is able to buy the bond for only $980 (sale price is 98), his effective interest rate will be greater than 10 percent. He will still receive $100 each year from the corporation that issued the bonds because the interest paid is based on the coupon rate, but since he bought the bond at a discount, he will be receiving a rate that is higher than the coupon rate. To determine the investor's annual effective interest rate, we once again divide the annual return on his investment by the amount invested:

$100 / $980 = 10.2%

Again, it is important to understand that market pressure and competing opportunities for investors will affect the price of a bond selling in the secondary market. Also, be sure to remember that the obligation on the part of the corporation is set by the coupon rate, and is unaffected by the current selling price of the bonds.

Business publications offer daily information about bonds traded in the secondary market. In the first column, we find the stated interest rate and year of maturity. The current yield indicates the effective interest rate. Notice how each bond's price at the end of the business day (close) determines whether the current yield is above or below the stated interest rate.

Bonds	Cur Yld	Vol	Close	Net Chg.
NCNB 8⅜99	8.4	4	99⅝	...
NJBTI 7¼11	8.2	5	88⅜	...
NMed 12⅛95	12.1	50	100 9/32	-1/16
Navstr 9s04	9.6	22	94	+1
NETelTel 6⅜08	7.9	5	81	-1½
NETelTel 8⅝01	8.5	32	102	-1¼
NETelTel 6¼97	6.6	10	94½	-1
NYTel 3⅜96	3.6	5	94½	+⅛
NYTel 4⅞06	6.6	8	73½	+¼
NYTel 7¾06	8.3	5	93¾	...
NYTel 7⅜11	8.4	3	88¼	+⅛
NYTel 7⅞17	8.7	19	90¾	-1
NYTel 6½00	7.4	10	87⅞	+⅞
NYTel 7¼24	8.5	20	85	-⅜

5-6. Think about the effects of premiums on the effective interest rate. What annual effective interest rate is an investor earning on a $1,000 bond that pays 12.5% interest if he pays 105 to buy it?

5-7. What if an investor with more funds bought $10,000 of the bonds described in Discussion Question 5-6? What annual effective interest rate would he earn?

The bond market receives much less attention from the media than the stock market. Nevertheless, it plays a significant role in the way corporations finance their long-term capital needs. As Exhibit 5-7 shows, businesses use both internal and external financing to support their operations. The two types of external financing provide investment opportunities for those with excess funds. From an investor's point of view, the stock market and the bond market offer two distinct choices.

Exhibit 5-7
Financing a Business

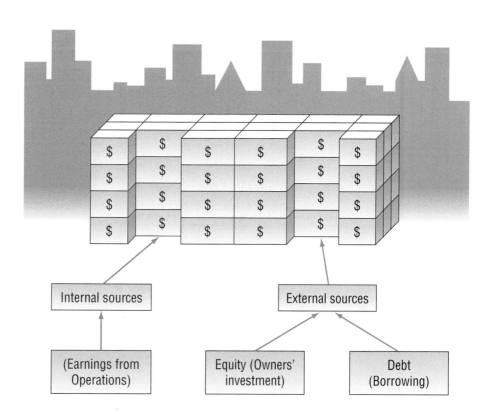

Internal sources

External sources

(Earnings from Operations)

Equity (Owners' investment)

Debt (Borrowing)

Equity and Debt Investments Compared

Our presentation of equity and debt financing in this and the preceding chapter was from the standpoint of the company receiving the proceeds from the sale of stocks and bonds. We will now look at the same subject from the standpoint of the investor. Consider the following:

Charlene's Aunt Tillie (whom she had met only once, at a family reunion) recently passed away and left Charlene $1,000,000. (Charlene saved Aunt Tillie's cat from Uncle Fred's pit bull at the reunion.) After all the inheritance taxes were paid, Charlene received $750,000. Upon mature reflection, she decides to blow $250,000 on cars, world cruises, and other such extravagant items. She plans to invest the remaining $500,000 on January 2, 1996, and has narrowed the list of possible investments to the following two. Both alternatives involve Fotheringap Corporation, a large company with an impressive track record over the past 35 years.

- Charlene can purchase shares of Fotheringap's no-par common stock. On January 2, 1996, the stock will be selling for about $50 per share, so Charlene would be able to purchase 10,000 shares. Fotheringap has a million shares of common stock outstanding, so Charlene would own only 1 percent of the company.
- Charlene can purchase 500 of Fotheringap's $1,000, five-year, 8 percent bonds. Interest is to be paid semiannually on June 30 and December 31. The bonds will be issued on January 2, 1996, and will mature on December 31, 2000. The first interest payment will be made on June 30, 1996.

Does it make more sense for Charlene to buy stock in Fotheringap (equity investment) or to buy the company's corporate bonds (debt investment)? Before we can decide that question, we need to ask how the two investment alternatives answer the three questions that should be posed by all economic decision makers:

1. Will I be paid?
2. When will I be paid?
3. How much will I be paid?

Remember that inherent in these three questions is a consideration of return on the investment and return of the investment.

Equity Investments

QUESTION 1 *Will Charlene be paid?*

There is no way to answer this question with absolute certainty; it is dependent on how Fotheringap performs in the future. If it is a solid company with a good market for its products and/or services, if the economy is (and stays) strong, and if the industry is (and stays) healthy, she will probably receive both a return on and a return of her investment. She should be aware, however, that with only a 1 percent ownership interest, Charlene will be able to exert little influence on how the company is run.

QUESTION 2 *When will Charlene be paid?*

There is no way to answer this question with absolute certainty either. Payment on a stock investment is of two types. First, Charlene may receive a periodic dividend on each share of stock she owns. Remember, however, that corporations are not required to pay dividends. Fotheringap may or may not pay dividends to its stockholders. The second form of payment Charlene may receive would be from the sale of the stock she owns. This would be on the secondary stock market and is dependent on whether there are investors willing to buy Fotheringap common stock. In any event, the company itself is under no obligation whatever to return Charlene's $500,000. She has contributed that amount to the company and must find some third person if she desires to sell her shares.

QUESTION 3 *How much will Charlene be paid?*

Like the first two questions, this one cannot be answered with absolute certainty. To answer it at all, we need to explain the two components of return on investment for an equity investment:

a. *Dividends*. This component is pretty easy to understand. Charlene pays $50 for each of the 10,000 shares she buys. If Fotheringap pays an annual dividend of $1.50 per share, Charlene will receive $15,000 (10,000 shares × $1.50). This constitutes a part of the return on her $500,000 investment.

b. *Stock Appreciation*. In most instances, this component represents the greater part of return on investment. If Fotheringap performs well in the future, the price of each share of its common stock will go up in the secondary stock market. This happens because as the company does well, more and more investors will desire to own its shares of stock. They will, in effect, bid up the price. For example, let's say the company is very profitable and within two years its common stock is selling for $125 per share. If Charlene sells her 10,000 shares, she will have earned a return on investment of $75 per share, or a total of $750,000, calculated as follows:

	Per Share	Total
What Charlene sold the stock for	$125	$1,250,000
What Charlene paid for the stock	50	500,000
Charlene's return on investment	$ 75	$ 750,000

Note that when Charlene sold the stock, she received not only a return *on* her investment, but also a return *of* her investment. Also note that we talked about "stock appreciation" and "sale" as if they had already happened. But as Charlene ponders whether or not to buy Fotheringap's common stock, she has no way of knowing for sure if the corporation will perform well enough to drive the stock price to the level we used (or even if the company will be profitable at all).

In the final analysis, the equity investment alternative yields rather vague answers to the three questions. Now let's see how the debt investment alternative answers the same three questions.

Debt Investments

QUESTION 1 *Will Charlene be paid?*

The answer to this first question is essentially the same for the debt investment alternative as it was for the equity investment alternative. That is, it is dependent on how Fotheringap performs in the future. Again, if it is a solid company with a good market for its products and/or services, if the economy is (and stays) strong, and if the industry is (and stays) healthy, Charlene will probably receive both a return on and a return of her investment.

As a creditor of the company rather than a stockholder, Charlene will have absolutely no voice in how Fotheringap conducts its business, so long as it makes the periodic interest payments on the bonds and accumulates a sufficient amount of cash to retire the bonds when they mature.

Charlene must also consider that the investors who purchase the bonds will be paid the periodic interest before any dividends are paid to the investors who purchase the shares of common stock.

QUESTION 2 *When will Charlene be paid?*

Assuming Fotheringap performs well enough to make the interest payments on the bonds and retire them upon maturity, the answer to this question is absolutely certain. Charlene will be paid interest every June 30 and December 31 throughout the life of the bonds. On December 31, 2000, in addition to the final interest payment, Charlene will receive her initial investment back.

QUESTION 3 *How much will Charlene be paid?*

The answer to this question, too, is absolutely certain assuming Fotheringap performs well enough to meet the financial obligations created by issuing the bonds. Over the life of the bonds, Charlene will earn a return on her investment of $200,000 ($20,000 X 10 semiannual interest payments). On December 31, 2000, she will receive $500,000, which represents the return of her investment.

In the final analysis, if Charlene satisfies herself as to Question 1, the answers to the last two questions are very certain for the debt investment alternative.

Which Is Better, Equity Investment or Debt Investment?

Take a few minutes to ponder the way the two investment alternatives answered the three questions. If you were advising Charlene, which investment would you suggest she make? If you were the one with the $500,000 to invest, which alternative would you choose?

On the surface, it appears to be no contest. While the answer to Question 1 was essentially the same for both alternatives, the debt investment alternative is much more certain in its answers to Questions 2 and 3 than is the equity investment alternative. So why would Charlene (or anyone, for that matter) even consider the equity investment as an alternative? There is a one-word answer to that question: POTENTIAL!

Although there is risk associated with any investment, equity investments are inherently riskier than debt investments. Along with the additional risk, however, comes the potential for greater reward.

Let's return now to Charlene's two investment alternatives in Fotheringap Corporation. Assume the company has net income each year of $10 million for the next five years. If Charlene chooses the bond alternative, she will receive $20,000 interest every six months for five years and then will receive her $500,000 back. But what if Fotheringap's net income turns out to be $100 million each year for the next five years, or even $1 billion each year? How will that affect Charlene's return if she purchases the bonds? The answer is that it doesn't matter how profitable Fotheringap is, Charlene will only receive the $20,000 every six months, plus the return of her $500,000 when the bonds mature after five years.

If Charlene chooses to buy the 10,000 shares of stock, however, the return on her $500,000 investment will be very different if Fotheringap earns $1 billion profit each year than it will be if the company earns $10 million or $100 million each year. For one thing, the more profitable the company is, the higher its dividends are likely to be. For another, the market price of Fotheringap's stock in the stock market will almost certainly increase as the company's profits increase, thereby increasing Charlene's return. In other words, the potential associated with the equity investment alternative is theoretically unlimited.

Whether a person chooses an equity investment or a debt investment depends upon how that person feels about the trade-off between the amount of risk involved and the potential reward. The real key to evaluating any investment alternative is reducing the uncertainty surrounding the question: *Will I be paid?* In attempting to predict an alternative's future cash flow potential, economic decision makers must consider the past performance and present condition of that alternative. Most big-name public companies have issued both debt and equity—they need both sources of funds to grow and prosper. But a few are so successful that they can grow rapidly without any debt financing. One example is Microsoft, the big software developer. Between 1992 and 1994, the company's sales rose from $2.8 billion to $4.6 billion. Its long-term debt: $0.

Chapters 4 and 5 have introduced you to the balance sheet, a financial tool that provides information about the present condition of a company. Chapter 6 will introduce you to two additional financial tools—the income statement and the statement of owners' equity.

SUMMARY

Companies often need more funds than they can get from their owners. The other major source of external financing is debt financing, or borrowing. Banks earn their profits by charging borrowers interest. Therefore, at agreed-upon intervals or when the loan is repaid, the company will pay interest in addition to the original amount borrowed.

If a company makes a bank loan, it incurs a liability—commonly called notes payable—and it receives cash. Loans from commercial banks usually meet companies' needs for short-term financing (five years or less).

A company may be required to provide collateral for its loan. If a particular asset is identified as collateral in the loan agreement, the note is generally referred to as a mortgage. Bank loans are generally suitable only for short-term financing; if a company needs long-term financing (up to 40 years or more), the alternative is to issue bonds. Bonds are similar to notes payable in that (1) both are liabilities and (2) both require repayment of the borrowed amount plus interest. Bonds are issued in set denominations, generally $1,000, and are sold to many different investors. Corporations can issue bonds for very large amounts.

Regardless of the type of borrowing involved, the amount of interest being charged can be calculated using the formula Principal × Rate × Time = Interest. In this calculation, "principal" refers to the amount owed, "rate" refers to the annual interest rate, and "time" reflects how much of the year is being considered in this particular borrowing situation.

Most corporations do not have the expertise necessary to tend to all the details involved in issuing bonds. Documents must be filed with regulatory agencies, and the actual transactions of issuing bonds to a large number of investors may be quite involved. For this reason, corporations usually use underwriters, or investment bankers, who for a fee assist the corporation to prepare the bond issue. The underwriters assume all the risk of the debt issuance by buying the entire bond issue. They then immediately resell the bonds to individual investors.

The face value or par value of a bond is the principal amount that must be repaid (generally in denominations of $1,000). If a bond is said to be selling at par, it is sold for $1,000. In order to entice investors, bond issuers usually have to sell their bonds at a discount (below par value) when the market rate of interest is higher than the rate paid on the bond.

The buying and selling of bonds is the focus of the bond market. Like the stock market, the bond market consists of activity in both a primary and secondary market. The activity of the primary bond market is centered around the initial issuance of corporate bonds. In the secondary bond market, the debt investments are traded. If the market rate of interest is lower than the nominal rate, investors will pay a premium (a sale price above par value) for the bonds. Conversely, if the market rate of interest (the return available to investors through other investments) is higher than the rate paid by a bond, that bond will sell below its par value (at a discount).

Activity in the bond market is very similar to activity in the stock market, even though these two markets represent the activity of investors with regard to two different investment alternatives. Investors may purchase bonds (make a debt investment) or purchase stock (make an equity investment). Each type of investment has its own advantages and disadvantages. Debt investment and equity investment were compared in light of the three questions asked by economic decision makers:

1. Will I be paid?
2. When will I be paid?
3. How much will I be paid?

Key Terms

bond An interest-bearing debt instrument that allows corporations to borrow large amounts of funds for long periods of time and creates a liability for the borrower. (p. 128)

collateral Something of value that will be forfeited if a borrower fails to make payments as agreed. (p. 126)

commercial borrowing The process that businesses go through to obtain financing. (p. 122)

consumer borrowing Loans obtained by individuals to buy homes, cars, or other personal property. (p. 122)

contract rate Another name for nominal interest rate. (p. 129)

coupon rate Another name for nominal interest rate. (p. 129)

debt financing Acquiring funds for business operations by borrowing. Debt financing is one type of external financing. (p. 121)

defaulting Failing to repay a loan as agreed. (p. 124)

discount If a bond's selling price is below its par value, the bond is being sold at a discount. (p. 132)

effective interest rate The rate of interest actually earned by a bondholder. This amount will be different from the nominal interest rate if the bond is bought at a discount or premium. Also called yield rate or market interest rate. (p. 129)

equity financing Acquiring funds for business operations by giving up ownership interest in the company. For a corporation, this means issuing capital stock. Equity financing is one type of external financing. (p. 121)

external financing Acquiring funds from outside the company. Equity and debt financing are the two major types of external financing. (p. 121)

face value Another name for par value of a bond. (p. 129)

indenture The legal agreement made between a bond issuer and a bondholder that states repayment terms and other details. (p. 129)

interest The cost to the borrower of using someone else's money. Also, what can be earned by lending money to someone else. (p. 124)

internal financing Providing funds for the operation of a company through the earnings process of that company. (p. 121)

long-term financing Any financing in which repayment extends beyond five years. This type of financing supports the long-range goals of the company. (p. 122)

market interest rate Another name for the effective interest rate. (p. 130)

market price Another name for the selling price of a bond. (p. 130)

mortgage A document that states the agreement between a lender and a borrower who has secured the loan by offering something of value as collateral. (p. 126)

nominal interest rate The interest rate set by the issuers of bonds, stated as a percentage of the par value of the bonds. Also called the contract rate or coupon rate, or stated rate. (p. 129)

note payable An agreement between a lender and borrower that creates a liability for the borrower. (p. 125)

par value (for bonds) The amount that must be paid back upon maturity of a bond. Also called face value. (p. 129)

premium If a bond's selling price is above its par value, the bond is being sold at a premium. (p. 132)

principal In the case of notes and mortgages, the amount of funds actually borrowed. (p. 127)

prospectus A description of an upcoming bond issue that is provided as information for potential investors. (p. 132)

selling price The amount received when bonds are issued or sold. This amount is affected by the difference between the nominal interest rate and the market rate. Selling price is usually stated as a percentage of the bond's par value. (p. 130)

short-term financing Financing secured to support an operation's day-to-day activities. Repayment is usually required within five years. (p. 122)

stated rate Another name for nominal interest rate. (p. 129)

syndicate A group of underwriters working together to get a large bond issue sold to the public. (p. 131)

yield rate Another name for the effective interest rate. (p. 130)

REVIEW THE FACTS

A. Explain the difference between internal and external financing.

B. What are the two major sources of external financing?

C. Contrast consumer borrowing and commercial borrowing.

D. What are the three major types of financial institutions providing financing in the United States today?

E. What is interest?

F. Describe the effects of borrowing on the balance sheet of a business.

G. Explain the formula used to determine the amount of interest owed for a particular time period.

H. What is collateral? How can it help a borrower?

I. What is a mortgage, and how is it different from a note payable?

J. Why are bonds sometimes necessary to meet the borrowing needs of businesses?

K. Explain the terms "par value" and "stated rate" as they pertain to bonds.

L. How do the nominal rate and the market rate of bonds differ?

M. What is the relationship between the selling price of a bond and its face value?

N. What is the primary function of underwriters?

O. Explain what causes a bond to sell for either a premium or a discount.

P. How do the primary and secondary bond markets differ?

Q. Explain the calculation used to determine the annual effective interest rate earned by an investor.

R. On what basis do investors choose between equity investments and debt investments?

APPLY WHAT YOU HAVE LEARNED

5-8. Marty and Barton McDermitt formed M&B Enterprises, Inc., on January 2, 1995. Marty invested $2,000 and received 200 shares of common stock. Barton invested $1,000 and received 100 shares of common stock. The common stock has a par value of $2 per share. A balance sheet prepared immediately after the corporation was formed was as follows:

<table>
<tr><td colspan="4" align="center">**M&B ENTERPRISES, INC.**</td></tr>
<tr><td colspan="4" align="center">**Balance Sheet**</td></tr>
<tr><td colspan="4" align="center">**January 2, 1995**</td></tr>
<tr><td>Assets:</td><td>Liabilities:</td><td></td><td>$ -0-</td></tr>
<tr><td>Cash $3,000</td><td>Owners' Equity:</td><td></td><td></td></tr>
<tr><td></td><td>Common Stock</td><td>$ 600</td><td></td></tr>
<tr><td>Total Assets $3,000</td><td>Additional Paid-in Capital</td><td>2,400</td><td></td></tr>
<tr><td></td><td>Total Owners' Equity</td><td></td><td>3,000</td></tr>
<tr><td></td><td>Total Liabilities and Owners' Equity</td><td></td><td>$3,000</td></tr>
</table>

On January 3, 1995, M&B Enterprises borrowed $10,000 from the 2nd National Bank by signing a one-year, 8 percent note. The principal and interest on the note must be paid to the bank on January 2, 1996.

REQUIRED:

a. Prepare a balance sheet for M&B Enterprises, Inc., at January 3, 1995, to reflect the $10,000 note payable.

b. Calculate the amount of interest M&B Enterprises must pay on January 2, 1996.

c. Think about the three questions all economic decision makers are trying to answer (Will I be paid? When? How much?). Assuming 2nd National Bank has satisfied itself as to the first question, how would the bank answer the second and third questions regarding the loan to M&B?

5-9. Assume the same facts as in preceding application question, except that the note is for three months rather than one year, so it must be repaid on April 2, 1995.

REQUIRED:

a. Prepare a balance sheet for M&B Enterprises, Inc., at January 3, 1995, to reflect the $10,000 note payable.

b. Calculate the amount of interest M&B Enterprises must pay on April 2, 1995.

c. Think about the three questions all economic decision makers are trying to answer (Will I be paid? When? How much?). Assuming the bank has satisfied itself as to the first question, how would it answer the second and third questions regarding the loan to M&B?

5-10. Marty and Barton McDermitt formed M&B Enterprises, Inc., on January 2, 1995. Marty invested $2,000 and received 200 shares of common stock. Barton invested $1,000 and received 100 shares of common stock. The common stock has a par value of $2 per share. A balance sheet prepared immediately after the corporation was formed was as follows:

M&B ENTERPRISES, INC.
Balance Sheet
January 2, 1995

Assets:		Liabilities:		$ -0-
Cash	$3,000	Owners' Equity:		
		Common Stock	$ 600	
Total Assets	$3,000	Additional Paid-in Capital	2,400	
		Total Owners' Equity		3,000
		Total Liabilities and Owners' Equity		$3,000

On January 3, 1995, M&B Enterprises sold 100 of its $1,000, five-year, 10 percent bonds. Interest is to be paid semiannually on June 2 and January 2. The bonds mature (must be repaid) on January 2, 2000.

REQUIRED:

a. Prepare a balance sheet for M&B Enterprises, Inc., at January 3, 1995, to reflect the sale of the bonds, assuming they sold at their par value.

b. Calculate the amount of interest M&B must pay each June 2 and January 2.

c. How much would M&B Enterprises, Inc., have received from the sale of the bonds on January 3, 1995, assuming they sold at 98 (a discount)?

d. How much would M&B Enterprises, Inc., have received from the sale of the bonds on January 3, 1995, assuming they sold at 103 (a premium)?

5-11. Presented below are some items related to notes payable and bonds payable followed by definitions of those items in scrambled order:

a. Interest	**f.** Premium
b. Nominal interest rate	**g.** Principal
c. Effective interest rate	**h.** Defaulting
d. Maturity value	**i.** Note payable
e. Discount	**j.** Bond payable

1. ____ The amount above par value for which a bond is sold.
2. ____ The amount of funds actually borrowed.
3. ____ The rate of interest actually earned by a bondholder.
4. ____ Failing to repay a loan as agreed.
5. ____ Liabilities that allow corporations to borrow large amounts of money for long periods of time.
6. ____ The cost of using someone else's money.
7. ____ The amount below par value for which a bond is sold.
8. ____ An agreement between a lender (usually a bank) and borrower that creates a liability for the borrower.
9. ____ The interest rate set by the issuers of bonds, stated as a percentage of the par value of the bonds.
10. ____ The amount that is payable at the end of a borrowing arrangement.

REQUIRED:

Match the letter next to each item on the list with the appropriate definition. Each letter will be used only once.

5-12. Assume a five-year, $1,000 bond paying 8 percent interest is bought for $970 (sale price is 97).

REQUIRED:

a. How much cash will the person buying the bond receive each year as interest?

b. Calculate the effective interest rate on the $1,000 bond.

5-13. Assume a five-year, $1,000 bond paying 9 percent interest is bought for $960 (sale price is 96).

REQUIRED:

  a. How much cash will the person buying the bond receive each year as interest?
  b. Calculate the effective interest rate on the $1,000 bond.
  c. Calculate the return on investment and the return of investment over the life of the bond.

5-14. John Kenyon formed Kenyon Engines, Inc., on January 2, 1995. John invested $12,000 and received 600 shares of common stock. The common stock has a par value of $1 per share. On January 3, 1995, Kenyon Engines, Inc., borrowed $6,000 from Miami National Bank by signing a one-year, 9 percent note. The principal and interest on the note must be paid to the bank on January 2, 1996.

REQUIRED:

  a. Prepare a balance sheet as of January 2, 1995, immediately following John's investment of $12,000.
  b. Prepare a balance sheet as of January 3, 1995, that reflects both John's investment of $12,000 and the $6,000 borrowed from the bank.
  c. Calculate the amount of interest Kenyon Engines, Inc., must pay on January 2, 1996.
  d. Assume that the note was for six months rather than one year, so it must be repaid on July 2, 1995. Calculate the amount of interest Kenyon Engines, Inc., must pay on July 2, 1995.

5-15. Bobbye Miller formed Miller Public Relations, Inc. on January 2, 1995. Bobbye invested $15,000 cash and received 1,500 shares of common stock. The common stock has a par value of $5 per share. On January 3, 1995, Miller Public Relations, Inc., sold 50 of its $1,000, five-year, 8 percent bonds. Interest is to be paid semiannually on June 2 and January 2. The bonds mature (must be repaid) on January 2, 2000.

  a. Prepare a balance sheet for Miller Public Relations, Inc., at January 2, 1995 to reflect Bobbye Miller's investment of $15,000.
  b. Prepare a balance sheet for Miller Public Relations, Inc., at January 3, 1995, to reflect both Bobbye Miller's investment of $15,000 and the sale of the bonds, assuming they sold at their par value.
  c. Calculate the amount of interest Miller Public Relations, Inc., must pay each June 2 and January 2.

d. How much would Miller Public Relations, Inc., have received from the sale of the bonds on January 3, 1995, if they had sold at 99 (a discount)?

e. How much would Miller Public Relations, Inc., have received from the sale of the bonds on January 3, 1995, if they had sold at 105 (a premium)?

5-16. Presented below are two definitions of items related to interest on bonds payable, followed by a list of terms used to describe bond interest.

a. The rate of interest actually earned by the bondholder.

b. The interest rate set by the issuer of the bond, stated as a percentage of the par value of the bond.

1. ____ Nominal interest rate
2. ____ Effective interest rate
3. ____ Stated interest rate
4. ____ Coupon rate
5. ____ The interest rate printed on the actual bond
6. ____ Market interest rate
7. ____ Contract rate
8. ____ Yield rate

REQUIRED:

For each of the eight items above, indicate to which definition (a or b) it refers.

5-17. Assume 6,500 five-year, $1,000 bonds paying 9 percent interest are sold at 95.

REQUIRED:

a. How much cash will the company selling the bonds receive from the sale?

b. How much cash will the person buying the bonds receive each year as interest?

c. Calculate the effective interest rate on the bonds.

d. Determine the return on investment and the return of investment for each $1,000 bond over its life.

5-18. Assume 2,500 five-year, $1,000 bonds paying 11 percent interest are sold at 105.

REQUIRED:

a. How much cash will the company selling the bonds receive from the sale?

b. How much cash will the person buying the bonds receive each year as interest?

c. Calculate the effective interest rate on the bonds.

d. Determine the return on investment and the return of investment for each $1,000 bond over its life.

5-19. Bob's Corporation had the following balance sheet at December 31, 1995:

BOB'S CORPORATION
Balance Sheet
December 31, 1995

ASSETS:	LIABILITIES AND STOCKHOLDERS' EQUITY:
	Liabilities...$ -0-
Cash............. $200,000	Stockholders' Equity:
	Common Stock.................................. 200,000
Total Assets.. $200,000	Total Liabilities and Stockholders'
	Equity... $200,000

On January 2, 1996, Bob's Corporation issued $300,000 worth of ten-year, 10 percent bonds at their par value.

REQUIRED:

Prepare a new balance sheet for Bob's Corporation reflecting the sale of the bonds on January 2, 1996.

5-20. Chapters 4 and 5 of the text discuss two very different forms of financing available to corporations: debt and equity.

REQUIRED:

a. Explain why a corporation would prefer to issue bonds rather than shares of common stock.

b. Explain why an investor would prefer to purchase shares of a company's common stock rather than a company's corporate bonds.

5-21. Define nominal interest rates and market interest rates for a bond, and briefly explain how these rates affect a bond's selling price.

5-22. The two main instruments of debt financing are bonds and notes. Explain under what circumstances each instrument is generally used.

5-23. Ted Nuggent has $20,000 to invest. His options are:

Option 1: Huge Company's five-year, $1,000 par value, 8 percent bonds, which are selling for 98 on the secondary bond market.

Option 2: Small Company's initial offering of no-par common stock, which is selling for $20 per share. While there is no formal requirement to pay dividends, it is anticipated that Small Company will pay an annual dividend of $.80 per share on its common stock.

REQUIRED:

a. How much cash will Ted receive from Huge Company each year if he buys 20 of the bonds?

b. How much will Ted pay for the Huge Company bonds if he purchases 20 bonds?

c. Using the technique presented in Chapter 5, determine the effective annual interest rate Ted will earn if he buys 20 of Huge Company's bonds.

d. How many shares of Small Company's common stock can Ted purchase with his $20,000?

e. Assuming Small does pay the anticipated annual dividend on its common stock, how much will Ted receive each year if he invests his $20,000 in the stock?

f. Based on your answer to (e) what is the effective rate of return Ted would earn on his investment in Small's stock?

5-24. XYZ, Inc. borrowed $12,000 on July 1, 1996, by signing a 10 percent note due December 31, 1996.

REQUIRED:

Determine the total amount XYZ will have to pay (principal and interest) on December 31, 1996.

6

Tools of the Trade, Part II Income Statement and Statement of Owners' Equity

Accounting information, in the form of financial statements, is a major source of information provided to economic decision makers. The balance sheet is a financial tool that helps decision makers evaluate the present financial condition of a business. Two other financial tools, the income statement and the statement of owners' equity, help decision makers evaluate companies' past performance.

In Chapters 4 and 5, you encountered the first financial tool—the balance sheet. This financial statement provides information that helps economic decision makers evaluate the present condition of a company. The balance sheet tells what the company owns (assets), what it owes (liabilities), and what claim the owners have to the remaining resources (owners' equity). This picture of the financial position of a company is an important item of information. It is *not*, however, enough information to support the decision-making process.

To make wise decisions, economic decision makers must gather all the information they need to assess the future timing and amounts of cash flows. Economic decision makers rely on several financial tools to provide all pieces of the "information puzzle." Accurate prediction of the future performance of a company depends on quality assessment of both the present condition and the past performance of the firm.

We have seen that the balance sheet provides information pertaining to a company's present condition. However, to assess the past performance of a company, decision makers rely on another financial tool—the income statement. The income statement provides information about the business activities of a company during a particular period.

In addition to the income statement, this chapter will introduce you to one other financial tool—the statement of owners' equity. This third financial statement provides a bridge between the information provided by the income statement and that provided by the balance sheet.

By the time you have finished this chapter, you will have explored three financial statements. Remember that these are tools for economic decision makers. The importance of these statements lies in their usefulness and contribution to the decision-making process.

After completing your work on this chapter, you should be able to do the following:

1. Describe in your own words how the income statement provides information about the past performance of a business.
2. Distinguish between single-step and multistep income statements.
3. Explain the impact of net income or net loss on owners' equity.
4. Construct statements of capital for proprietorships and partnerships.
5. Identify the differences between statements of stockholders' equity and statements of retained earnings for corporations.
6. Compare and contrast the impact of drawings on statements of capital and the impact of dividends on statements of stockholders' equity and statements of retained earnings.
7. Explain why dividends are paid and under what circumstances they can be paid.
8. Describe in your own words the articulation of income statements, balance sheets, and statements of owners' equity.

INTRODUCTION TO THE INCOME STATEMENT

income statement A financial statement providing information about an entity's past performance. Its purpose is to measure the results of the entity's operations for some specific time period.

The **income statement** is a financial tool that provides information about a company's past performance (see Exhibit 6-1). Recall that the balance sheet, the previous financial tool we studied in detail, is comprised of assets, liabilities, and owners' equity—three accounting elements described by the FASB in Statements of Accounting Concepts. The income statement is also comprised of accounting elements (see Exhibit 6-2). The italicized definitions below are those provided by the Financial Accounting Standards Board. A less formal definition of each element follows the words of the FASB.

Exhibit 6-1
Tools of the Trade:
The Income Statement

revenues An accounting element representing the inflows of assets as a result of an entity's ongoing major or central operations. These are the rewards of doing business.

expenses An accounting element representing the outflow of assets resulting from an entity's ongoing major or central operations. These are the sacrifices required to attain the rewards (revenues) of doing business.

net income The amount of profit that remains after all costs have been considered. The net reward of doing business for a specific time period.

earnings Another name for net income.

net earnings Another name for net income.

profit The excess of benefit over sacrifice. A less formal name for net income.

net loss The difference between revenues and expenses of a period in which expenses are greater than revenues.

1. **Revenues.** *Inflows of assets to an entity from delivering or producing goods, rendering services, or carrying out other activities.* Revenue represents what a company's customers pay for its goods or services. Revenues are the reward of doing business.

2. **Expenses.** *Outflows or other using up of assets from delivering or producing goods, rendering services, or carrying out other activities.* Expenses are the sacrifices required to attain revenues.

The difference between the rewards (revenues) and the sacrifices (expenses) for a given period of activity is the net reward of doing business, which we call **net income**. Accountants also call net income **earnings, net earnings**, or **profit**. If the expenses for the period are greater than the revenues for the period, the result is a **net loss**. The relationship between revenues, expenses, and either net income or net loss can be represented by the following equation:

REVENUES – EXPENSES = NET INCOME (or NET LOSS)

Just as you were advised to do with the balance sheet equation, you should memorize the income statement equation and fix its meaning in your mind because we will deal with it over and over again.

Exhibit 6-2
Accounting Elements:
Revenues and Expenses

DISCUSSION QUESTIONS

6-1. Identify the transactions in your personal finances during the last month. Which transactions resulted in revenues and which resulted in expenses?

6-2. Use the equation in the text above, and your responses to Discussion Question 6-1 to determine if you had a net income or net loss for the month.

Construction of the Income Statement

period Length of time (usually a month, quarter, or year) for which activity is being reported on an income statement.

The basic format of an income statement is shown in Exhibit 6-3. The heading for an income statement must include the name of the business, the name of the statement, and the **period** for which activity is being reported. As you will recall, the heading for the balance sheet must include the precise date for which the information is being presented. If the balance sheet is, as we said, a snapshot of a business at a particular point in time, then the income statement is something of a "home movie" of a company for a period of time (usually a month, quarter, or year). For that reason, the heading includes the period of time described—not just a single date. The income statement says that during this specific time period, the company earned so much revenue, incurred so much expense, and produced either a net income or net loss, depending on whether the revenues were greater than the expenses or vice versa. Income statements may be produced annually, quarterly, monthly, or at whatever interval deemed necessary to provide useful accounting information.

statement of results of operations The formal name of the income statement.

statement of earnings Another name for the income statement.

The term "income statement" is only a nickname, and as was the case with the term "balance sheet," it is not very descriptive of the statement's purpose. The statement's formal name is the **statement of results of operations**, which is a far better description of its function. It is also sometimes called the **statement of earnings**. However, the informal title "Income Statement" is more widely used than the others. The authors of *Accounting Trends and Techniques* report that of 600 companies surveyed, about half of them used "income" as a key word in the headings of their 1993 financial statements—though when the financial statements showed a net loss, the title "Statement of Operations" was frequently chosen. When a net loss must be shown, the title "Income Statement" does seem a bit peculiar. Nevertheless, IBM used the title "Statement of Earnings" when its net losses were nearly $5 billion in 1992 and nearly $3 billion in 1991.

Exhibit 6-3

Basic Format of the Income Statement

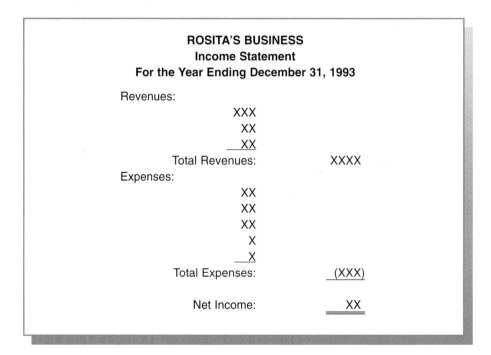

ROSITA'S BUSINESS
Income Statement
For the Year Ending December 31, 1993

Revenues:		
	XXX	
	XX	
	XX	
Total Revenues:		XXXX
Expenses:		
	XX	
	XX	
	XX	
	X	
	X	
Total Expenses:		(XXX)
Net Income:		XX

Notice that the basic format of the income statement illustrated in Exhibit 6-3 suggests that a company may have more than one type of revenue. Revenues are the inflows of the company, and these inflows may come from a variety of earnings activities. A business may be a service organization, producing service revenues, often called *professional fees*. Law firms, lawn service companies, and accounting firms are examples of service organizations. If a business is involved in merchandising or manufacturing, its major revenue will be sales of tangible units of product.

In addition to the revenues from its major operations, a company may produce revenues through other activities. For example, it may rent out portions of the office building it owns; that activity would produce rent revenue. If the company has invested some of its cash, interest revenue may be produced.

The income statement format in Exhibit 6-3 also allows for several different types of expenses. Expenses are the outflows of the company, and they, too, may take many different forms. For example, if a company has employees, the income statement will show salaries or wages expense. If a company is responsible for maintaining vehicles, the income statement may show gas expense and/or maintenance expense, or if the building a company uses is not owned by it, the company may have rent expense. These are just a few examples of the numerous expenses a company might face.

cost of goods sold The cost of the product sold as the primary business activity of a company.

cost of sales Another name for cost of goods sold.

Merchandising operations and manufacturers sell goods for their primary revenue. Costs associated with these goods comprise the expense called the **cost of goods sold**, or sometimes **cost of sales** or cost of products sold. For many companies, cost of goods sold is the major expense of doing business.

6-5. Think of a fast-food restaurant, such as McDonald's. Make a list of the costs you think the restaurant incurs in its day-to-day operations. Which of these costs do you think should be included in the cost of goods sold and which ones are other expenses? Explain.

Single-Step Format of the Income Statement

single-step income statement A format of the income statement that gathers all revenues into "total revenues" and all expenses into "total expenses." Net income is calculated as a subtraction of total expenses from total revenues.

In the basic form of the income statement, all revenues are added to provide "total revenues," and all expenses are added to create "total expenses." This format is called the **single-step income statement** because in one step, total expenses are subtracted from total revenues to determine net income (or net loss).

We can use Rosita's Business to illustrate the single-step format of the income statement. Assume that Rosita's Business had $2,690 in sales revenue and $990 in rent revenue during 1993. Also assume that the company's expenses for the period were $955 for cost of goods sold, $675 for wages, $310 for utilities, and $120 for interest payments. Based on that information, the company's 1993 income statement, prepared in a single-step format, would be as shown in Exhibit 6-4.

Unlike the balance sheet, the income statement is not directly affected by the type of business organization involved. Income statements for proprietorships, partnerships, and corporations all take the same general form. The only

Exhibit 6-4
Single-Step Format
of the Income Statement

ROSITA'S BUSINESS
Income Statement
For the Year Ending December 31, 1993

Revenues:		
Sales	$2,690	
Rent Revenue	990	
Total Revenues:		$3,680
Expenses:		
Cost of Goods Sold	$ 955	
Wages Expense	675	
Utilities Expense	310	
Interest Expense	120	
Total Expenses:		(2,060)
Net Income		$1,620

difference is in the name of the company included in the heading of the statement. Companies do, however, have the option of using either of the basic formats—the single-step format we have been discussing or the multistep format.

Multistep Format of the Income Statement

The **multistep income statement** provides two items of information not presented in income statements using the single-step format: (1) **gross margin** or **gross profit** and (2) **operating income** or **income from operations**. Each of these items is discussed in detail below.

The "bottom line," or net income, is not affected by the choice of format. However, the information provided within the income statement *is* different from format to format. The single-step income statement format gathers all revenues together to form "total revenues." All expenses are gathered together to form "total expenses." No special treatment is given to any specific revenue or expense. In contrast, the multistep format highlights the relationships among various items of accounting information.

Gross margin is one piece of information not shown on a single-step income statement. This item highlights the relationship between sales revenue and cost of goods sold. **Sales revenue** (often referred to simply as **sales**) is the revenue produced by the primary activity of the firm, which for a merchandiser or manufacturer comes from selling tangible units of product. Cost of goods sold is the cost of the tangible units of product sold and is very often the largest expense relating to sales. The difference between sales revenue and cost of goods sold is the gross margin or gross profit.

For example, sales of running shoes is the revenue produced by Nike, Inc. Cost of goods sold is the cost of the shoes to Nike. The difference between these amounts represents Nike's gross margin.

multistep income statement An income statement format that highlights gross margin and operating income.

gross margin An item shown on a multistep income statement, calculated as: Sales − Cost of Goods Sold.

gross profit Another name for gross margin.

operating income Income produced by the major business activity of the company. An item shown on the multistep income statement.

income from operations Another name for operating income, shown on the multistep income statement.

sales revenue The revenue generated from the sale of a tangible product as a major business activity.

sales Another term for sales revenue.

Nike, Inc. sells millions of pairs of running shoes each year. The cost of every piece of material you see in this shoe is included in Nike's cost of goods sold. For 1994, Nike reported sales of $3.8 billion and cost of goods sold totalling $2.3 billion. The company's 1994 gross margin, therefore, was $1.5 billion.

Eric Sander/Gamma-Liaison, Inc.

6-6. For Nike, Inc., what specific costs do you think are included in the cost of goods sold related to the running shoes?

6-7. Identify two additional companies and describe the source of their sales revenues and the components of their costs of goods sold.

A merchandiser or manufacturer cannot possibly be profitable unless it sells its product for more than what it paid for that product. Gross margin represents how much more a company received from the sale of its products than what the products cost the company. It also represents the amount available from sales to cover all other expenses the company has. For example, assume Magill Company (a merchandiser) sells its product for $20 per unit. Each unit of product costs Magill $14. If the company sold 5,000 units of product in January, it would have a gross margin of $30,000, calculated as follows:

Sales (5,000 X $20)	$100,000
LESS: Cost of goods sold (5,000 X $14)	70,000
Gross margin	$ 30,000

This $30,000 is what Magill has remaining from sales to cover all the other expenses of the company for the month of January. Assuming the company had no revenues other than sales, if those other expenses were less than $30,000, the company had a net income for the month; if they were greater than $30,000, the company experienced a net loss.

Economic decision makers frequently use gross margin in evaluating the performance of a manufacturing or merchandising company. Examining gross margin allows financial statement readers to quickly see the relationship among revenue produced by selling product, the cost of the product, and all the other expenses the company incurs.

6-8. Consider the following simplified multistep income statement for Early Company:

Sales (1,000 units)..............................$275,000
LESS: Cost of Goods Sold...................(280,000)
    Gross margin................................($ 5,000)
LESS: Other Expenses.........................(42,000)
    Net Income (Loss).......................($47,000)

a. What can you learn about Early Company from its gross margin?

b. How many units must the company sell in order to earn a profit?

    In addition to highlighting the relationship between sales and cost of goods sold, the multistep income statement separates income generated from the ongoing major activity of the firm from the revenues and expenses produced by other business activities. "Operating income" or "income from operations" denotes the results of the merchandising or manufacturing activity that is the company's primary business activity. This income can be expected to continue, while some of the revenues and expenses associated with secondary activities of the company may not be repeated. When economic decision makers are attempting to use the past performance of a company as presented on the income statement to predict the future, operating income may be more useful than final net income as an indicator of performance. Therefore, multistep income statements, which show both net income and operating income, may often be more useful to users of accounting information than single-step income statements, which show only net income.

    Exhibit 6-5 depicts Rosita's income statement for 1993 in the multistep format. As you can see, the net income reported is the same as that shown in Exhibit 6-4, using the single-step format. Notice, though, the multistep format makes two important stops before arriving at the "bottom line": gross margin and operating income (thus the term "multistep").

Exhibit 6-5
Multistep Format of the Income Statement

Net Income as an Increase in Owners' Equity

Net income represents an increase in the owners' interest in the business. As you'll recall from our discussion of the elements found in a balance sheet, one of the two sources of owners' equity is earned equity. Earned equity is directly affected by net income because each revenue is an asset received (increasing earned equity) and each expense is an asset sacrificed (decreasing earned equity). A net profit, therefore, increases earned equity, while a net loss decreases earned equity.

If a company's earned equity increases, it follows that its owners' equity also increases. Net income, or profit, is thus a particular period's addition to the owners' equity in the company and links the information on the income statement with the information on the balance sheet. This link is very logical when you realize that the past performance of a company is at least partially responsible for the present condition of that company.

statement of owners' equity
The financial statement that reports activity in the capital accounts of proprietorships and partnerships and in the stockholders' equity accounts of corporations. The statement of owners' equity serves as a bridge between the income statement and the balance sheet.

INTRODUCTION TO THE STATEMENT OF OWNERS' EQUITY

Some companies prepare only an income statement and balance sheet. There is a third financial statement, however, which is actually a "bridge statement" showing how the income statement and balance sheet are related (Exhibit 6-6). It is called the **statement of owners' equity**. Basically, this tool of the trade (Exhibit 6-7) shows how the owners' equity, as reported

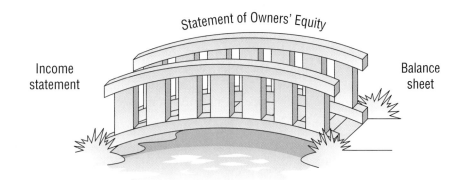

Statement of Owners' Equity

Income statement

Balance sheet

Exhibit 6-6
Statement of Owners' Equity:
The Bridge Statement

Exhibit 6-7
Tool of the Trade:
Statement of Owners' Equity

on the balance sheet, moved from its balance at the beginning of the period to its balance at the end of the period. Although the specifics of the statement vary according to the organizational form of the company, the basic format of this financial statement is as presented in Exhibit 6-8.

Proprietorships—Statement of Capital

Earned equity goes by various names, depending on the form of the business. For proprietorships and partnerships, there is usually no distinction

Exhibit 6-8
Basic Format of the Statement
of Owners' Equity

ROSITA'S BUSINESS
Statement of Owners' Equity
For the Year Ending December 31, 1993

Beginning Owners' Equity	XXX	
ADD: Net Income	X	
Ending Balance in Owners' Equity		XXX

made between the equity from owners' investment and earned equity. Because those forms of business are legally considered to be extensions of the owner or owners, the two types of equity are normally lumped together under the title "owners' equity" or "owners' capital," and the statement of owners' equity is generally called the *statement of capital*. Exhibit 6-9 shows the format of a statement of owner's equity prepared for a proprietorship.

Exhibit 6-9
Statement of Owner's Equity
(Capital) for a Proprietorship

ROSITA'S BUSINESS
Statement of Capital
For the Year Ending December 31, 1993

Rosita, Capital, January 1, 1993	$5,000	
ADD: Net Income	1,620	
Rosita, Capital, December 31, 1993		$6,620

You will notice from the heading that, like the income statement, the statement of owners' equity deals with business activity during a particular time period. For this reason, the heading of a statement of owners' equity includes the designation of the time period covered rather than just a specific date. The beginning balance used in Exhibit 6-9 is actually the ending balance from the previous period. The net income amount is drawn directly from the income statement, and the ending balance is calculated as shown. This ending balance appears not only on the statement of capital but also in the owners' equity section of the balance sheet. Earlier we referred to the statement of owners' equity as a bridge statement because it uses the net income figure from the income statement for the period and shows the calculation of the ending owners' equity amount that appears on the balance sheet.

Partnerships—Statement of Capital

A similar statement produced for a partnership would follow the same general outline. Of course, there would be a capital balance for each partner, and the net income for the period ($1,620) would be shared by the partners according to the rules stated in their partnership agreement. Using Rosita and Caroline's Business for our example, a statement of capital for this type of business form would look like Exhibit 6-10.

Exhibit 6-10 assumes that the partners, Rosita and Caroline, have agreed to share the net income in the same proportion as their initial investments. Thus, Rosita's capital balance is increased by 60 percent of the total net income for the period, and Caroline's capital balance is increased by 40 percent of the net income.

Exhibit 6-10
Statement of Owners' Equity
(Capital) for a Partnership

ROSITA and CAROLINE'S BUSINESS
Statement of Capital
For the Year Ending December 31, 1993

Rosita, Capital, January 1, 1993	$3,000	
ADD: Net Income	972	
Rosita, Capital, December 31, 1993		$3,972
Caroline, Capital, January 1, 1993	$2,000	
ADD: Net Income	648	
Caroline, Capital, December 31, 1993		2,648
Total Capital, December 31, 1993		$6,620

Corporations—Statement of Stockholders' Equity

Because a corporation is a legal entity separate from its owner or owners, keeping the equity from owners' investment and the earned equity separated is a legal requirement. In corporations, you will recall, the investment by owners is called *contributed capital* and earned equity is called *retained earnings*. A statement providing information about a corporation would use a format similar to that shown in Exhibit 6-11.

ROSITA CORPORATION
Statement of Stockholders' Equity
For the Year Ending December 31, 1993

	Common Stock	Additional Paid-in Capital	Retained Earnings	Total Stockholders' Equity
Balance, January 1	$1,000	$4,000	$ 0	$5,000
Net Income			1,620	1,620
Balance, December 31	$1,000	$4,000	$1,620	$6,620

Again, note that the beginning balances are the previous period's ending balances, the net income figure comes from the income statement, and the ending balance is calculated as shown. Also notice that the statement of stockholders' equity reflects activity in both parts of total owners' equity—contributed capital and earned equity. Common stock and additional paid-in capital are components of contributed capital, while retained earnings represents the earned equity portion of stockholders' equity. The four totals at the bottom of the statement of stockholders' equity would all be shown in the stockholders' equity section of the balance sheet prepared at the end of the period.

If additional shares of stock had been issued during 1993, the activity would have been reported in the contributed capital section (common stock and additional paid-in capital) of Rosita Corporation's statement of stockholders' equity. The activity in retained earnings is not affected by such changes in the contributed capital sections. The amount of retained earnings is increased by net income each period and decreased by net loss. Thus, if the beginning balance of retained earnings is 0, as it is in Exhibit 6-11, it can be assumed that this statement describes activity during the first year of operations for the company. In addition to net income and net loss, owners' equity is affected by the distribution of assets to the owners.

Exhibit 6-12 outlines the differences among owners' equity for the three business forms as we examined them for Rosita's business.

Exhibit 6-12
Owners' Equity by Business
Organizational Form

Organizational Form	Proprietorship	Partnership	Corporation
Name of Statement	Statement of Capital	Statement of Capital	Statement of Stockholders' Equity
Statement Section	Capital	Capital	Contributed Capital and Retained Earnings
Equity Account Titles	Rosita, Capital	Rosita, Capital Caroline, Capital	Common Stock Additional Paid-in Capital Retained Earnings

DISCUSSION QUESTIONS

6-9. How would it be possible for Rosita Corporation to have a zero balance in retained earnings on January 1, 1993, if 1993 were not the company's first year of business?

DISTRIBUTIONS TO OWNERS

With time, if the operations of a company are successful, owners' equity will increase. Eventually, the owner, or owners, will expect some type of distribution of this equity. Distributions to owners is another accounting element shown in Exhibit 6-13. Just as net income increases owners' equity, distributions to owners decrease owners' equity.

Do not interpret these distributions as being some sort of salary paid to the owners. These distributions are not considered expenses of the company and thus are not shown on the income statement. Rather, they are payments to owners representing a return on the investment they have made. Distributions to owners are handled in different ways, depending on the organizational form of the company. However, in each case, these distributions reduce total owners' equity.

Exhibit 6-13
Accounting Element:
Distributions to Owners

Drawings—Proprietorships and Partnerships

drawings Distributions to the owners of proprietorships and partnerships. Also called withdrawals.

withdrawals Another name for drawings.

In the case of a proprietorship, there is very little to restrict the owner from taking funds out of the company. If the cash is there, the owner may take it for his or her personal use. In this case, the distributions to the owner are called **drawings** or **withdrawals**. If Rosita chose to take $500 in cash from her proprietorship, the drawing would be reflected on the statement of capital as shown in Exhibit 6-14.

Exhibit 6-14
Distributions to Owners
in a Proprietorship: Drawings

ROSITA'S BUSINESS
Statement of Capital
For the Year Ending December 31, 1993

Rosita, Capital, January 1, 1993	$5,000
ADD: Net Income	1,620
	$6,620
LESS: Drawings	(500)
Rosita, Capital, December 31, 1993	$6,120

Partnership agreements may state explicitly when and in what amounts partners may take drawings or withdrawals. Clearly, the partnership must have sufficient cash to support the actions of its owners. When thinking of making a withdrawal of cash from the company, a partner must consider the impact of this action on his or her capital account. Using the partnership of Rosita and Caroline, let's examine the impact of a withdrawal made by only one of the partners. Assume that Caroline has found herself in a personal cash bind. Since there is no restriction on withdrawals in the partnership agreement and there is sufficient cash on hand, she decides to withdraw $500. This action reduces Caroline's capital account and the total amount of owners' equity, but has no impact on Rosita's capital balance. Exhibit 6-15 shows the resulting statement of capital for the partnership.

Exhibit 6-15
Distributions to Owners in a
Partnership: Drawings

ROSITA and CAROLINE'S BUSINESS
Statement of Capital
For the Year Ending December 31, 1993

Rosita, Capital, January 1, 1993	$3,000	
ADD: Net Income	972	
Rosita, Capital, December 31, 1993		$3,972
Caroline, Capital, January 1, 1993	$2,000	
ADD: Net Income	648	
	$2,648	
LESS: Drawings	(500)	
Caroline, Capital, December 31, 1993		2,148
Total Owners' Equity, December 31, 1993		$6,120

Distributions to Owners—Corporate Form

Owners of corporations (shareholders) have much less control over when and in what amount they receive a distribution than do owners of a proprietorship or partnership. This is particularly true in large corporations. Distributions to owners in a corporate setting are called *dividends*. Although they are not legally required to, virtually all corporations pay dividends at some point in their existence.

Why do corporations pay dividends if they are not legally required to do so? The reason is that, in the long run, investors (those who buy the corporation's stock) demand this distribution. A number of factors cause a company's stock to either go up or go down in value, but probably the most important factor is whether or not the company is profitable. Profitability is best demonstrated by the payment of dividends. Corporations that are profitable, then, periodically (usually every three months) pay a dividend to their stockholders as a demonstration of their ability and willingness to reward the stockholders for investing in the company.

If a corporation is not profitable and therefore cannot afford to pay dividends, or if it decides for some reason not to pay dividends even though it is profitable, investors and potential investors may become nervous or unhappy at the lack of return on their investment. This unhappiness may translate into a decline in demand for shares of that company's stock, which will result in a fall in the stock's price. When this happens, the corporation may find it difficult to obtain funds necessary to support its operations. Opportunities for both major types of external funding—issuing stock and borrowing funds—may disappear. Eventually, if enough people lose faith in the company, it will run out of cash and cease to exist.

In the long run, a company must pay dividends as a reward to the stockholders for investing in the company. Corporations that pay dividends usually make the declaration of a dividend a media event.

Microsoft CEO Bill Gates has something to smile about. Over the five-year period ending November 30, 1994, Microsoft stock has risen in price an average of 45.4% a year. Yet the company doesn't pay dividends. Instead, it reinvests its money in new products. Do you think Microsoft stockholders have suffered?

Bettmann

Some successful companies resist the pressure to pay dividends in order to reinvest profits in research and development. Microsoft is one such company. Investors have accepted Microsoft's reinvestment policy as a wise business strategy, and the company's stock price has not suffered. Ben and Jerry's is another successful company that does not pay dividends on its stock. By publicizing the corporate philosophy of using profits to keep the company healthy and growing, Ben and Jerry's has avoided any misinterpretation of its actions. Shareholders are well aware of the company's business strategy and have demonstrated their confidence in it by holding the stocks.

All decisions associated with dividends are made by the corporation's board of directors. These decisions include whether or not to pay a dividend, the type of dividend to be paid, and when the dividend will be paid. Companies can choose to distribute additional shares of their stock as a dividend. It is, however, much more common for companies to distribute cash dividends. Of the 600 companies surveyed by *Accounting Trends and Techniques*, 74 percent issued a cash dividend in 1993.

Cash Dividends on Common Stock   A cash payment is what most of us think of when we hear the word "dividend." In order to be able to pay a cash dividend, a corporation must possess two things: sufficient retained earnings and sufficient cash.

1. *Sufficient Retained Earnings.* Dividends are distributions of earnings; however, corporations are not restricted to the current year's earnings to cover the distribution. While it may be desirable for a company to pay dividends out of the current year's earnings, dividends are actually paid out of retained earnings. Remember, net income is only this period's addition to retained earnings; thus, it is not necessary that current net income be greater than the dividend amount. The real requirement is that there be a sufficient balance in retained earnings to cover the dividend.

Retained earnings represents the portion of a corporation's earnings that has not been distributed to the owners in the form of dividends. A more descriptive name might be *reinvested earnings*, because it is the portion of total corporate earnings reinvested (plowed back) into the company. This portion may have gone to purchase new plant and equipment, inventory, and other items necessary for the continued operation of the company. Exhibit 6-16 shows how retained earnings are created over time and how they are affected by net income, losses, and dividends.

Exhibit 6-16
How Retained Earnings
Are Created

	1991	1992	1993	1994	1995
Beginning Balance	$ -0-	$ 800	$1,300	$ 700	$1,150
Net Income (Loss)	800	1,000	(100)	950	400
Dividends	-0-	(500)	(500)	(500)	(500)
Ending Balance	$ 800	$1,300	$ 700	$1,150	$1,050

There are two things you should note as you look at this exhibit. First, the ending balance of one period (in this case, a year) becomes the beginning balance of the next period. Second, the payment of dividends is not directly related to profits in a given period. In 1993, this company paid dividends even though it experienced a net loss for the year, and in 1995, it paid out more in dividends than it earned for the year. This company appears to have adopted a policy of paying $500 per year in total dividends, regardless of its net income or loss for a particular year. This policy is perfectly acceptable, as long as the company has both sufficient retained earnings and sufficient cash each year to cover the dividend amount.

2. *Sufficient Cash.* "Retained earnings" is not cash. It is simply an amount representing all the profits a corporation has not yet distributed to its owners in the form of dividends. In general, the amount of retained earnings a corporation has and the amount of cash it has at a given time will be different. A corporation must make certain it has sufficient cash to pay the dividend. Some companies feel it so important to pay a regular cash dividend that they will actually borrow money if they have insufficient cash to cover their usual dividend amount.

The Rosita Corporation has sufficient retained earnings and sufficient cash to pay a dividend to its shareholders. Recall that the corporation has 1,000 shares of $1 par value common stock outstanding. If the corporation declared a $.50 per share dividend, the total dividend amount would be $500. In a sense, this is very similar to the $500 owner withdrawal in the proprietorship and partnership examples. However, remember that corporate owners' equity is divided between contributed capital and retained earnings. The funds received from the sale of ownership interests in the corporation are reflected in the stock and additional paid-in capital accounts. These funds are considered contributed capital and they do *not* increase retained earnings. The dividends are a reduction of retained earnings; thus, the Rosita Corporation's statement of stockholders' equity after the payment of a $500 dividend is as shown in Exhibit 6-17 on page 170.

Notice that, once again, the only section of stockholders' equity to reflect the results of activity is retained earnings. Both net income and dividends change the balance in retained earnings, but neither affects any portion of contributed capital.

Exhibit 6-17
Distribution to Owners
in a Corporation: Dividends

ROSITA CORPORATION
Statement of Stockholders' Equity
For the Year Ending December 31, 1993

	Common Stock	Additional Paid-in Capital	Retained Earnings	Total Stockholders' Equity
Balance, January 1	$1,000	$4,000	$ 0	$5,000
Net Income			1,620	1,620
Dividends			(500)	(500)
Balance, December 31	$1,000	$4,000	$1,120	$6,120

statement of retained earnings A corporate financial statement that shows the changes in retained earnings during a particular period.

Statement of Retained Earnings   If a corporation has not issued stock or engaged in any other activity that would affect contributed capital, it may issue a **statement of retained earnings** instead of the more comprehensive statement of stockholders' equity. A statement of retained earnings is very similar in form to the statement of capital for proprietorships and partnerships. Exhibit 6-18 is a statement of retained earnings for Rosita Corporation.

Exhibit 6-18
Statement of Retained Earnings
for a Corporation

ROSITA CORPORATION
Statement of Retained Earnings
For the Year Ending December 31, 1993

Retained Earnings, January 1, 1993	$ 0
ADD: Net Income	1,620
	$1,620
LESS: Dividends	(500)
Retained Earnings, December 31, 1993	$1,120

This simpler statement is an acceptable substitute for the statement of stockholders' equity only if no changes have been made in a corporation's contributed capital. However, because most corporations are frequently involved in activities affecting their stock accounts or other parts of their contributed capital, the statement of stockholders' equity is more widely used than the statement of retained earnings. Of the 600 companies surveyed in *Accounting Trends and Techniques*, 80 percent used the statement of stockholders' equity in 1993. Only 12 percent of the corporations presented a statement of retained earnings. The remaining group chose not to present either form of this "bridge statement."

Dividend Dates   The ownership shares of most large corporations are held by many different people, and these shares of stock trade hands constantly. Because their shares of stock are widely traded, most corporations do not know exactly who their stockholders are on any given day. For this reason, most corporations do not declare and pay a dividend on the same day.

Three important dates are associated with the payment of a cash dividend:

date of declaration The date upon which a corporation announces plans to distribute a dividend. At this point, the corporation becomes legally obligated to make the distribution: A liability is created.

1. **Date of Declaration.** As stated earlier, the board of directors decides if and when a cash dividend is to be paid. The day the board votes to pay a dividend is known as the date of declaration. The date of declaration marks the creation of a legal liability for the corporation.

date of record Owners of the shares of stock on this day are the ones who will receive the dividend announced on the date of declaration.

2. **Date of Record.** This date may follow the date of declaration by several weeks. Whoever owns shares of stock on the date of record will receive the dividend. Every time a company's stock changes hands, the company is notified, though that notification, especially in large corporations, may take several days or even weeks.

date of payment The date a corporate dividend is actually paid. The payment date is generally announced on the date of declaration.

3. **Date of Payment.** This is the date the dividend is actually paid. Payment of the dividend is made to whoever owned shares of stock on the date of record, even though some of those people have sold their shares of stock between the date of record and the date of payment. When the cash dividend is paid, the liability for the dividend is removed from the company's records.

Generally, on the date the board of directors declares a dividend, the date of record and the date of payment are announced as shown in Exhibit 6-19.

Exhibit 6-19
Example of Dividends Reported in the Business Press

Dividends Reported February 3				
Company	Period	Amt.	Payable date	Record date
ACE Limited	Q	.11	4-19-95	3-31
Aktlebol Svensk pf	Q	.4609	3-1-95	2-15
AlliedHlthcareProd	Q	.07	4-14-95	3-31
Arnold Industries	Q	.11	3-1-95	2-17
Atlanta Gas Light	Q	.52	3-1-95	2-17
Atlanta Gas Lt dep	Q	.48	3-1-95	2-17
BkTrustNY PfdPurch	Q	.534	3-1-95	2-15
BearStrnEpics8%pfA	M	.1666	2-28-95	2-21
Bird5%pf	Q	1.25	3-1-95	2-17
BoiseCascade depG	Q	.39	4-15-95	4-1
BoiseCascade	Q	.15	4-15-95	4-1
BoiseCascade depF	Q	.58	4-15-95	4-1
CPI Corp	Q	.14	2-27-95	2-13
Coastal Corp	Q	.10	4-1-95	2-28
Coastal Corp pfA	Q	.29	3-15-95	2-28
Coastal Corp pfB	Q	.45	3-15-95	2-28
Coastal Corp pfH	Q	.53	3-15-95	2-28
Cousins Properties	Q	.24	2-22-95	2-13
Daniel Industries	Q	.04	3-24-95	3-3
General Binding	Q	.10	3-20-95	2-21
Greenfield Indust	Q	.03	3-30-95	3-10
Harley Davidson	Q	.04	3-5-95	2-17
Interstate Power	Q	.52	3-20-95	2-21
Interstate/Johnson	Q	.03	3-2-95	2-10
Jefferies Group	Q	.05	3-15-95	2-15
LCI Intl pfd	Q	.31	2-28-95	2-10
Lee Enterprises	Q	.22	4-3-95	3-1

Assume today is February 3, 1995 and use the information in Exhibit 6-19 to answer the following:

6-10. If you own 100 shares of General Binding stock, how much is the next dividend you expect to receive and when would you expect to receive it?

6-11. If you are considering selling your shares of Arnold Industries stock in the next few weeks, what should you consider?

6-12. If you own 200 shares of Harley Davidson stock, how much would you expect to receive in dividends during the next year?

6-13. Which of the stocks listed has a dividend rate per share nearest to that of BearStrnEpics?

Cash Dividends on Preferred Stock The procedures associated with the payment of dividends on preferred stock are exactly the same as those for common stock. The distinctions between these two classes of stock are based on the preference features of preferred stock. As discussed in Chapter 4, one of those preferences involves dividends. If a corporation has preferred stock and elects to pay dividends, the preferred stockholders receive their dividend before the common stockholders can be paid.

6-14. As you listened to a broadcast of consumer news on public radio, you heard an angry consumer advocate, Ms. Nadia Ralphino, accuse large corporations of taking advantage of the small stockholder. As part of her angry attack, she cited the following example:

Mega-Millions, Incorporated, pays only $.62 per share dividend each year on its common stock, even though its retained earnings balance is now in excess of $7 billion.

She then went on to accuse Mega-Millions of hoarding profits. How would you respond to Ms. Ralphino's accusation if you were the spokesperson for Mega-Millions, Incorporated?

ARTICULATION

articulation The relationships (links) among the financial statements.

Earlier in this chapter, we referred to the link between income and owners' equity. This link is an example of what is called **articulation** of the financial statements. The three financial statements we have discussed thus far are definitely linked. This linkage, or articulation, is an important concept for you to understand. The income statement tells the story of the company's earnings activity for this period, and the balance sheet presents a picture of the company's current financial position. The third statement we introduced, the statement of owners' equity, provides a bridge between the other two. Now, let's take a closer look at how the three tools we have learned about thus far fit together.

Financial Statements of a Proprietorship

For a proprietorship, the set of these statements would look as shown in Exhibit 6-20 on page 174.

This exhibit is a visual representation of articulation. The arrows connecting items from the three financial statements show the relationships that should always exist. Net income is calculated on the income statement and used on the statement of capital. The ending balance shown on the statement of capital is used on the balance sheet. The accounting equation below the balance sheet shows that this important relationship still holds true.

Exhibit 6-20 illustrates each of the three statements in a very simplistic form. Notice that Rosita's Business has only one asset—cash—the presumption being that all activities recorded in these three statements involved cash. If only accounting statements really *were* so simple! Make sure you know how to use the information provided on this simple set of statements before we move on to investigate more complex sets of statements. Also, be sure you can explain in your own words how the information provided on each statement is affected by the information shown on the others.

Exhibit 6-20
Income Statement, Statement
of Capital, and Balance Sheet
for a Proprietorship

ROSITA'S BUSINESS
Income Statement
For the Year Ending December 31, 1993

Sales	$2,690	
Less:		
Cost of Goods Sold	955	
Gross Margin		$1,735
Wages Expense	$ 675	
Utilities Expense	310	
Total Operating Expenses		(985)
Operating Income		$ 750
Other Revenues:		
Rent Revenue		990
Other Expenses:		
Interest Expense		(120)
Net Income		$1,620

ROSITA'S BUSINESS
Statement of Capital
For the Year Ending December 31, 1993

Rosita, Capital, January 1, 1993	$5,000
ADD: Net Income	1,620
	$6,620
LESS: Drawings	(500)
Rosita, Capital, December 31, 1993	$6,120

ROSITA'S BUSINESS
Balance Sheet
December 31, 1993

Assets:		Liabilities:	
		Notes Payable	$1,000
Cash	$7,120		
		Owner's Equity:	
		Rosita, Capital	6,120
Total Assets	$7,120	Total Liabilities and	
		Owner's Equity	$7,120

$$A \ = \ L \ + \ OE$$
$$\$7,120 \ = \ \$1,000 \ + \ \$6,120$$

6-15. If a clerk in Rosita's Business decided to slip the cash from a sale into his pocket and not record the sale, how would each of the statements in Exhibit 6-20 be affected?

Financial Statements of a Partnership

By now it should be clear that the formats of the financial statements of partnerships are only slightly different from those for proprietorships. However, in order to provide a complete set of examples, we present the articulated statements of Rosita and Caroline's partnership in Exhibit 6-21.

Again, the arrows show the articulation between statements. The major difference between this set of statements and the set prepared for a proprietorship (Exhibit 6-20) is that these provide information about the activity in each partner's capital account.

As we explained in Chapter 1, not all partnerships are small organizations. The Arthur Andersen Worldwide Organization, for example, is one of the largest accounting firms in America; it operates over 300 offices and has more than 2,000 partners. With an organizational structure of that size, the financial statements of Arthur Andersen could not possibly offer details of each partner's holdings. Instead, figures are presented in terms of amounts "per partner."

Financial Statements of a Corporation

Financial statements providing information about corporate activities differ from those based on the activities of proprietorships or partnerships. Income statements for the three business forms generally use the same format. The differences occur in the other two financial statements. To illustrate these differences, let's examine Exhibit 6-22, which shows the full set of three financial statements for Rosita Corporation.

Once again, the arrows demonstrate the articulation of these corporate statements. As you can see, the income statement is exactly like that in Exhibits 6-20 and 6-21, because the form of business organization does not affect that statement. The information from the income statement is used on the statement of stockholders' equity in Exhibit 6-22. Note that the balance sheet, although different from that for a proprietorship or partnership, still reflects the ending balance shown on the statement of stockholders' equity.

Exhibit 6-21
Income Statement, Statement
of Capital, and Balance Sheet
for a Partnership

ROSITA and CAROLINE'S BUSINESS
Income Statement
For the Year Ending December 31, 1993

Sales		$2,690
Less:		
Cost of Goods Sold		955
Gross Margin		$1,735
Wages Expense	$ 675	
Utilities Expense	310	
Total Operating Expenses		(985)
Operating Income		$ 750
Other Revenues:		
Rent Revenue		990
Other Expenses:		
Interest Expense		(120)
Net Income		$1,620

ROSITA and CAROLINE'S BUSINESS
Statement of Capital
For the Year Ending December 31, 1993

Rosita, Capital, January 1, 1993	$3,000	
ADD: Net Income	972	
Rosita, Capital, December 31, 1993		$3,972
Caroline, Capital, January 1, 1993	$2,000	
ADD: Net Income	648	
	$2,648	
LESS: Drawings	(500)	
Caroline, Capital, December 31, 1993		2,148
Total Owners' Equity, December 31, 1993		$6,120

ROSITA and CAROLINE'S BUSINESS
Balance Sheet
December 31, 1993

Assets:		Liabilities:		
		Notes Payable		$1,000
Cash	$7,120			
		Owners' Equity:		
		Rosita, Capital	$3,972	
		Caroline, Capital	2,148	
		Total Owners' Equity		6,120
Total Assets	$7,120	Total Liabilities and		
		Owners' Equity		$7,120

Exhibit 6-22
Income Statement, Statement
of Stockholders' Equity, and
Balance Sheet for a Corporation

ROSITA CORPORATION
Income Statement
For the Year Ending December 31, 1993

Sales		$2,690
Less:		
Cost of Goods Sold		955
Gross Margin		$1,735
Wages Expense	$ 675	
Utilities Expense	310	
Total Operating Expenses		(985)
Operating Income		$ 750
Other Revenues:		
Rent Revenue		990
Other Expenses:		
Interest Expense		(120)
Net Income		$1,620

ROSITA CORPORATION
Statement of Stockholders' Equity
For the Year Ending December 31, 1993

	Common Stock	Additional Paid-in Capital	Retained Earnings	Total Stockholders' Equity
Balance, January 1	$1,000	$4,000	$ 0	$5,000
Net Income			1,620	1,620
Dividends			(500)	(500)
Balance, December 31	$1,000	$4,000	$1,120	$6,120

ROSITA CORPORATION
Balance Sheet
December 31, 1993

Assets:		Liabilities:		
		Notes Payable		$1,000
Cash	$7,120			
		Owners' Equity:		
		Common Stock	$1,000	
		Additional Paid-in Capital	4,000	
		Total Contributed Capital	$5,000	
		Retained Earnings	1,120	
		Total Shareholders' Equity		6,120
Total Assets	$7,120	Total Liabilities and Owners' Equity		$7,120

Exhibit 6-23
Income Statement, Statement
of Retained Earnings, and
Balance Sheet for a Corporation

ROSITA CORPORATION
Income Statement
For the Year Ending December 31, 1993

Sales	$2,690	
LESS:		
Cost of Goods Sold	955	
Gross Margin		$1,735
Wages Expense	$ 675	
Utilities Expense	310	
Total Operating Expenses		(985)
Operating Income		$ 750
Other Revenues:		
Rent Revenue		990
Other Expenses:		
Interest Expense		(120)
Net Income		$1,620

ROSITA CORPORATION
Statement of Retained Earnings
For the Year Ending December 31, 1993

Retained Earnings, January 1, 1993	$ 0	
ADD: Net Income	1,620	
	$1,620	
LESS: Dividends	(500)	
Retained Earnings, December 31, 1993		$1,120

ROSITA CORPORATION
Balance Sheet
December 31, 1993

Assets:		Liabilities:		
		Notes Payable		$1,000
Cash	$7,120			
		Owners' Equity:		
		Common Stock	$1,000	
		Additional Paid-in Capital	4,000	
		Total Contributed Capital	$5,000	
		Retained Earnings	1,120	
		Total Shareholders' Equity		6,120
Total Assets	$7,120	Total Liabilities and		
		Owners' Equity		$7,120

Exhibit 6-23 completes our demonstration of articulation. Here Rosita Corporation uses a statement of retained earnings instead of the statement of stockholders' equity. Note that the same relationships among the statements hold true.

Now that you have been introduced to the first three major financial statements and have seen how they fit together, you may be wondering when you can begin using them to make economic decisions. Do you feel you are ready to use these tools to predict future cash flows? We sincerely hope not, because without an understanding of the basis upon which these financial statements are prepared, it is impossible to use them effectively. At this point, then, it is premature to talk about how to use the tools. We must first discuss the way the items included in the financial statements are measured. Chapter 7 introduces and discusses two different measurement bases. After you complete your work on that chapter, you will be better prepared to use the income statement, statement of owners' equity, and balance sheet to predict future cash flows.

SUMMARY

The income statement is a financial statement providing information about the past performance of a company during a particular period of time. It consists of information about the rewards (revenues) and sacrifices (expenses) of doing business. The income statement shows the result of subtracting expenses from revenues. If revenues are greater than expenses, the result is net income; if expenses are larger than revenues for the period, the result is net loss.

Income statements may be prepared following either the single-step or multistep format. In the single-step income statement format, all revenues are gathered together to form "total revenues." Then all expenses are listed and totaled to form "total expenses." In one step, expenses are subtracted from revenues, and the resulting net income or net loss is presented. The multistep format begins with one special revenue—sales. From that revenue, cost of goods sold is subtracted to determine gross margin. All remaining operating expenses are then subtracted to determine income from operations. Any other revenues or expenses are then presented to arrive at the final "net income" or "loss." The bottom line (net income or loss) of the two formats of income statements is the same, but the presentation of the revenues and expenses for the period is different.

Whatever the income statement format chosen, net income results in an increase in owners' equity and net losses result in a decrease in owners' equity. The effect of net income or net loss on owners' equity is shown on the statement of owners' equity. This financial statement shows the beginning balance in owners' equity at a particular point in time and how that balance was affected during the period to arrive at the ending balance.

The statement of owners' equity will take one of several forms, depending on the organizational form of the company. The owners' equity sections of proprietorships and partnerships consist of capital accounts for each owner. Therefore, statements for these business forms are called "statements of capital."

Corporations prepare statements of stockholders' equity. These statements can show changes in all parts of owners' equity—stock accounts, additional paid-in capital accounts, and retained earnings. Net income or loss affects retained earnings, and if this portion of stockholders' equity is the only one having activity during the period, a corporation may simply prepare a statement of retained earnings.

In addition to net income or net loss, another item that affects the balance of owners' equity is distributions to owners. For proprietorships and partnerships, these distributions are called "drawings" or "withdrawals." In a corporate setting, distributions to owners are called "dividends," and cause a reduction of retained earnings. Both dividends and drawings reduce total owners' equity.

Dividends are paid to provide investors a return on their investment and also to indicate the corporation's financial well-being. Two criteria must be met before a corporation can pay a dividend: (1) there must be sufficient cash available to actually make the payment; and (2) the corporation's balance in retained earnings must be large enough to cover the dividend amount.

The income statement, statement of owners' equity, and balance sheet are all connected. The way in which these three financial statements fit together is known as "articulation." The net income (or net loss) reported on the income statement is shown as an increase (or decrease) to owners' equity on the statement of capital, statement of stockholders' equity, or statement of retained earnings. The ending balance shown on this "bridge statement" is reported on the balance sheet. Articulation exists among the financial statements of a company, whatever its form of business organization.

Key Terms

articulation The relationships (links) among the financial statements. (p. 173)

cost of goods sold The cost of the product sold as the primary business activity of a company. (p. 155)

cost of products sold Another name for cost of goods sold. (p. 155)

cost of sales Another name for cost of goods sold. (p. 155)

date of declaration The date upon which a corporation announces plans to distribute a dividend. At this point, the corporation becomes legally obligated to make the distribution: A liability is created. (p. 171)

date of payment The date a corporate dividend is actually paid. The payment date is generally announced on the date of declaration. (p. 171)

date of record Owners of the shares of stock on this day are the ones who will receive the dividend announced on the date of declaration. (p. 171)

drawings Distributions to the owners of proprietorships and partnerships. Also called withdrawals. (p. 165)

earnings Another name for net income. (p. 152)

expenses An accounting element representing the outflow of assets resulting from an entity's ongoing major or central operations. These are the sacrifices required to attain the rewards (revenues) of doing business. (p. 152)

gross margin An item shown on a multistep income statement, calculated as: Sales – Cost of Goods Sold. (p. 157)

gross profit Another name for gross margin. (p. 157)

income from operations Another name for operating income, shown on the multistep income statement. (p. 157)

income statement A financial statement providing information about an entity's past performance. Its purpose is to measure the results of the entity's operations for some specific time period. (p. 152)

multistep income statement An income statement format that highlights gross margin and operating income. (p. 157)

net earnings Another name for net income. (p. 152)

net income The amount of profit that remains after all costs have been considered. The net reward of doing business for a specific time period. (p. 152)

net loss The difference between revenues and expenses of a period in which expenses are greater than revenues. (p. 152)

operating income Income produced by the major business activity of the company. An item shown on the multistep income statement. (p. 157)

period Length of time (usually a month, quarter, or year) for which activity is being reported on an income statement. (p. 153)

profit The excess of benefit over sacrifice. A less formal name for net income. (p. 152)

revenues An accounting element representing the inflows of assets as a result of an entity's ongoing major or central operations. These are the rewards of doing business. (p. 152)

sales Another term for sales revenue. (p. 157)

sales revenue The revenue generated from the sale of a tangible product as a major business activity. (p. 157)

single-step income statement A format of the income statement that gathers all revenues into "total revenues" and all expenses into "total expenses." Net income is calculated as a subtraction of total expenses from total revenues. (p. 156)

statement of earnings Another name for the income statement. (p. 154)

statement of owners' equity The financial statement that reports activity in the capital accounts of proprietorships and partnerships and in the stockholders' equity accounts of corporations. The statement of owners' equity serves as a bridge between the income statement and the balance sheet. (p. 160)

statement of results of operations The formal name of the income statement. (p. 154)

statement of retained earnings A corporate financial statement that shows the changes in retained earnings during a particular period. (p. 170)

withdrawals Another name for drawings. (p. 165)

REVIEW THE FACTS

A. Name and define in your own words the accounting elements used to determine net income.

B. What is the primary expense associated with the products sold by merchandisers and manufacturers?

C. Name the two formats of the income statement and describe the differences between them.

D. What item is responsible for the primary increase in the capital account?

E. What is the difference between a statement of stockholders' equity and a statement of retained earnings?

F. What is the effect of owners' drawings, and on what financial statement is this information reported?

G. Under what circumstances is a corporation able to pay a dividend?

H. How is a corporation's financial position affected by the payment of a dividend?

I. Explain the following terms: date of declaration, date of record, and date of payment.

J. Describe the meaning of articulation as it is used in accounting.

6-17. George Adams and Company had $56,412 in sales revenue during 1995. In addition to the regular sales revenue, Adams rented out a small building it owned and received $3,600 for the year. Cost of goods sold for the year totaled $31,812. Other expenses for the year were as follows:

Rent	$12,500
Utilities	2,140
Advertising	3,265
Wages	10,619
Interest	856

REQUIRED:

a. Prepare a 1995 income statement for George Adams and Company using a single-step format.

b. Prepare a 1995 income statement for George Adams and Company using a multistep format.

6-18. Cederloff Company was organized on January 3, 1995. While many companies are not profitable in their first year, Cederloff experienced a modest net income of $7,500 in 1995.

REQUIRED:

a. Prepare a statement of capital for Cederloff Company for the year ending December 31, 1995, assuming Karen Cederloff began the company as a sole proprietorship by investing $10,000 of her own money.

b. Prepare a statement of capital for Cederloff Company for the year ending December 31, 1995, assuming Karen Cederloff, Stephen Sommers, and Barry Figgins began the company as a partnership. The three partners have agreed to share any income or loss in the same proportion as their initial investments, which were as follows:

Cederloff	$ 5,000
Sommers	3,000
Figgins	2,000
Total	$10,000

c. Prepare a statement of stockholders' equity for Cederloff Company for the year ending December 31, 1995, assuming Karen Cederloff, Stephen Sommers, and Barry Figgins organized the company as a corporation. The corporate charter authorized 50,000 shares of $2 par value common stock. The following shares were issued on January 3, 1995 (all at $10 per share):

500 shares to Cederloff......	$	5,000
300 shares to Sommers.....		3,000
200 shares to Figgins.........		2,000
Total..................................		$10,000

6-19. This is a continuation of the previous problem (6-18). It is now December 31, 1996 and it is time to prepare the statement of owners' equity for Cederloff Company. Net income for the year ending December 31, 1996, was $12,000, and there were no additional owner investments during the year.

REQUIRED:

a. Prepare a statement of capital for Cederloff Company for the year ending December 31, 1996, assuming the business was a proprietorship and that Karen Cederloff took drawings totaling $8,000 during 1996.

b. Prepare a statement of capital for Cederloff Company for the year ending December 31, 1996, assuming the partnership form. Recall from the previous problem that the partners share income in the same proportion as their initial investment. Drawings by the three partners during 1996 were as follows:

Cederloff......................	$4,000
Sommers.....................	2,500
Figgins.........................	1,500
Total............................	$8,000

c. Prepare a statement of stockholders' equity for Cederloff Company for the year ending December 31, 1996, assuming the corporate form. Recall from the previous problem that 1,000 shares of common stock were issued at the time of incorporation. Dividends paid during the year were $8.00 per share.

d. Prepare a statement of retained earnings for Cederloff Company, assuming the same information given in (c).

6-20. Use the set of financial statements on page 185 to meet the requirements below.

REQUIRED:

a. Is Hernandez a sole proprietorship, a partnership, or a corporation? Explain how you arrived at your answer.

b. Is Hernandez Company's income statement in the single-step or multistep format? Explain how you determined your answer.

c. Explain the term *articulation*, and describe how the financial statements of Hernandez Company articulate.

BEN HERNANDEZ COMPANY
Income Statement
For the Year Ending December 31, 1995

Sales	$88,722	
LESS: Cost of Goods Sold	41,912	
Gross Margin		$46,810
Rent	$17,500	
Wages	14,408	
Advertising	7,345	
Utilities	1,640	
Total Operating Expenses		(40,893)
Operating Income		$ 5,917
Other Revenues:		
Rent Revenue		2,700
Other Expenses:		
Interest Expense		(1,166)
Net Income		$ 7,451

BEN HERNANDEZ COMPANY
Statement of Capital
For the Year Ending December 31, 1995

Hernandez, Capital, January 1, 1995	$33,806	
ADD: Net Income	7,451	
	$41,257	
LESS: Drawings	(9,000)	
Hernandez, Capital, December 31, 1995		$32,257

BEN HERNANDEZ COMPANY
Balance Sheet
December 31, 1995

Assets:		Liabilities:	
Cash	$57,257	Notes Payable	$25,000
		Owner's Equity:	
		Hernandez, Capital	32,257
Total Assets	$57,257	Total Liabilities and	
		Owner's Equity	$57,257

6-21. Presented below is a list of items relating to the concepts discussed in this chapter, followed by definitions of those items in scrambled order:

a. Revenues

b. Expenses

c. Income statement

d. Statement of owners' equity

e. Dividends

f. Drawings

g. Date of declaration

h. Date of record

i. Date of payment

j. Articulation.

1. ____ The date distributions of earnings to owners of a corporation are actually paid.

2. ____ Inflows of assets from delivering or producing goods, rendering services, or other activities.

3. ____ Distribution of earnings to the owners of a corporation.

4. ____ The link between the income statement and the balance sheet.

5. ____ A bridge statement showing how the income statement and balance sheet are related.

6. ____ Distribution of earnings to the owners of proprietorships and partnerships.

7. ____ Outflows or other using up of assets from delivering or producing goods, rendering services, or carrying out other activities.

8. ____ The date a corporation announces it will make a distribution of earnings to its owners.

9. ____ A financial tool providing information about an entity's past performance.

10. ____ Whoever owns shares of stock on this date will receive the distribution of earnings previously declared.

REQUIRED:

Match the letter next to each item on the list with the appropriate definition. Each letter will be used only once.

6-22. Pam Powers and Company had $156,000 in sales revenue during 1995. In addition, Powers had interest revenue of $5,200 for the year. Cost of goods sold for the year totaled $92,000. Other expenses for the year were:

Rent	$18,000
Wages	14,600
Advertising	3,200
Utilities	2,400

REQUIRED:

a. Prepare a 1995 income statement for Pam Powers and Company using a single-step format.

b. Prepare a 1995 income statement for Pam Powers and Company using a multistep format.

6-23. Wayne's Camera and Video, Inc., had sales revenue of $580,000 during 1995. Expenses for the year were:

Wages	$ 92,000
Rent	24,000
Advertising	6,400
Cost of goods sold	450,000
Utilities	12,400

REQUIRED

a. Prepare a 1995 income statement for Wayne's Camera and Video, Inc., using a single-step format.
b. Prepare a 1995 income statement for Wayne's Camera and Video, Inc., using a multistep format.

6-24. The following information is taken from the accounting records of Alonso's Frame Shop for 1995:

Sales	$540,000
Wages	120,000
Store rent	36,000
Interest expense	21,000
Advertising	14,200
Electricity	3,400
Telephone	1,400
Cost of goods sold	380,000
Rent revenue	18,000

REQUIRED:

a. Prepare a 1995 income statement for Alonso's Frame Shop using a single-step format.
b. Prepare a 1995 income statement for Alonso's Frame Shop using a multistep format.
c. If you were the owner of the company, which format of income statement would you prefer to use? Why?

6-25. The following information is taken from the accounting records of Bonnie's Pet Shop for 1995:

Sales	$930,000
Cost of goods sold	540,000
Wages	220,000
Utilities	24,000
Rent	48,000
Advertising	12,000
Interest revenue	6,000

REQUIRED:

a. Prepare a 1995 income statement for Bonnie's Pet Shop using a single-step format.
b. Prepare a 1995 income statement for Bonnie's Pet Shop using a multistep format.

6-26. Use the following set of financial statements to meet the requirements below:

THE CHRISTOPHER STEINMANN COMPANY
Income Statement
For the Year Ending December 31, 1995

Sales		$688,250
LESS: Cost of Goods Sold		422,745
Gross Margin		$265,505
Rent	$ 38,456	
Wages	112,144	
Advertising	7,345	
Utilities	24,000	
Total Operating Expenses		(181,945)
Operating Income		$ 83,560
Other Revenues:		
Rent Revenue		24,600
Other Expenses:		
Interest Expense		(3,246)
Net Income		$104,914

THE CHRISTOPHER STEINMANN COMPANY
Statement of Capital
For the Year Ending December 31, 1995

Steinmann, Capital, January 1, 1995	$388,560
ADD: Net Income	104,914
	$493,474
LESS: Drawings	(38,000)
Steinmann, Capital, December 31, 1995	$455,474

THE CHRISTOPHER STEINMANN COMPANY
Balance Sheet
December 31, 1995

Assets:		Liabilities:	
Cash	$705,474	Notes Payable	$250,000
		Owner's Equity:	
		Steinmann, Capital	455,474
Total Assets	$705,474	Total Liabilities and	
		Owner's Equity	$705,474

REQUIRED:

a. Is The Christopher Steinmann Company a sole proprietorship, a partnership, or a corporation? Explain how you arrived at your answer.

b. Prepare a single-step income statement for The Christopher Steinmann Company.

c. Explain the term *articulation*, and describe how the financial statements of The Christopher Steinmann Company articulate.

6-27. Presented below is a list of items relating to the concepts discussed in this chapter, followed by definitions and examples of those items in scrambled order:

a. Assets   **d.** Revenues

b. Liabilities   **e.** Expenses

c. Equity

1. ___ Debts of the company.
2. ___ Sales.
3. ___ Probable future economic benefits.
4. ___ Inflows of assets from delivering or producing goods, rendering services, or other activities.
5. ___ "Things" of value a company has.
6. ___ The residual interest in the assets of an entity that remains after deducting its liabilities.
7. ___ Probable future sacrifices of economic benefits.
8. ___ Outflows or other using up of assets from delivering or producing goods, rendering services, or carrying out other activities.
9. ___ Costs that have no future value.
10. ___ What the company owes.
11. ___ What the company has less what it owes.
12. ___ The owner's interest in the company.

REQUIRED:

Match the letter next to each item on the list with the appropriate definition.

7

Keeping Score: Bases of Economic Measurement

The three financial statements introduced thus far provide information about a company's present condition and past performance. Before relying on information contained in financial statements, decision makers must understand the measurement criteria used to capture the information.

Thus far we have explored the development of three financial tools—the income statement, the statement of owners' equity, and the balance sheet. Each of these statements provides accounting information designed to assist in the decision-making process. Economic decision makers rely heavily on the information contained in the financial statements provided by companies.

All three of the financial statements examined thus far are composed of measurements of economic activity. Before decision makers can use this accounting information with confidence, however, they must answer one basic question: *From what perspective have the measurements been made?* Unless decision makers know what basis of economic measurement was used to prepare the financial statements, the information provided will be of little value to them.

There are two general bases of economic measurement—the cash basis and the accrual basis—and it is important that you understand the distinctions between them. In this chapter, we will consider these two approaches to measuring revenue and expense for a particular time period.

After completing your work on this chapter, you should be able to do the following:

1. **Explain the difference between reality and the measurement of reality.**
2. **Apply the criteria for revenue and expense recognition under the cash basis of accounting to determine periodic net income.**
3. **Determine periodic net income applying the rules of revenue and expense recognition required by accrual accounting.**
4. **Explain the concept of matching and describe how it relates to depreciation.**
5. **Describe the difference between accruals and deferrals and provide examples of each.**
6. **Contrast the cash basis and accrual basis of economic measurement, describing the relative strengths and weaknesses of each.**

REALITY VERSUS THE MEASUREMENT OF REALITY

There are two things going on in every company. First, there is reality. A company makes purchases, sells goods, provides services, pays employees, and performs a thousand other activities. These activities constitute the reality of being in business and doing business. Second, there is the measurement of that reality. As transactions and events occur in the company, their effects are recorded in an attempt to measure that reality. But remember this: *No matter how accurately the measurement of reality reflects reality, it is not reality.* In other words:

Reality is what reality is!

—Anonymous

As an example of what we're talking about, assume Rosita's Business purchased some office supplies and wrote a check for $480. In recording the check in the check register, the accountant read the amount of the check incorrectly and entered $48. After deducting the $48, the check register indicated a balance of $1,127. The fact that the accountant entered the wrong amount for the check in no way changes the reality of how much money was spent and how much is actually in the company's checking account.

DISCUSSION QUESTIONS

7-1. Assuming there are no other errors in the check register, what is the actual cash balance in Rosita's checking account?

7-2. In what ways could this incorrect measurement of reality have an effect on reality? Explain.

The concept that errors may cause differences between reality and the measurement of reality is relatively easy to grasp. However, many people find it difficult to believe that there might be perfectly legitimate reasons for a difference between reality and its measure. This discrepancy is best demonstrated in the measurement of the revenues and expenses to be reported in the income statement of a company for a particular time period.

The Problems of Periodic Measurement

Most discrepancies between reality and its measure occur when earnings activities are measured for a *specific period of time* (Exhibit 7-1). Regardless of the time period (month, quarter, year, etc.), it is not always readily apparent which revenues and which expenses should be included in determining the earnings (net income) of that period. In fact, the only true measure of net income for a company is a comparison between revenues and expenses over the entire life of that company.

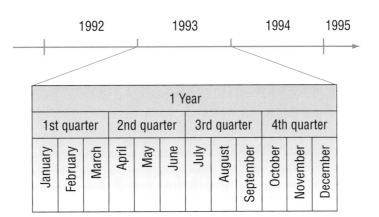

Exhibit 7-1
Periodic Measurement

DISCUSSION QUESTIONS

7-3. **Checker Business Systems sells computer equipment to small businesses. During 1994, the sales activity was as follows:**

February: Sold $6,000 of equipment on account. The customers paid in full on March 15.
March: Sold $4,500 of equipment on account. Customers paid in full on April 15.

Describe the impact of different periodic measurements. That is, what activity would be included in each period if the business activity is measured

a. **each month?**
b. **each quarter?**
c. **each year?**

In some ways, determining net income in the fifteenth century was easier and more precise than it is today. In the era of Christopher Columbus, if an entrepreneur planned to sail to the New World and bring back goods to sell, the net income for that particular venture could be measured. The entrepreneur began with a pile of money. With that, he bought a ship and supplies and hired men to help with the expedition. The group would set sail, gather up treasures and commodities from the New World, return, and sell the goods. Then the workers could be paid off, the ship could be sold, and the entrepreneur would end up, once again, with a pile of money. If the pile of money he had at the end of his venture was greater than the pile of money he had begun with, the difference would be net income. If the amount of money he ended up with was smaller than the amount he started with, the entrepreneur suffered a loss on the venture.

In today's world, it is unrealistic to expect companies to stop operations and sell off all their assets in order to determine their "true" net income. So although lifetime net income is the only truly precise measurement of an operation's success or failure, users of accounting information demand current information every year, or quarter, or month. It is this need to artificially break the company's operations into various time periods that requires us to make decisions about when revenues and expenses should be reported.

Revenue and Expense Recognition

recognition The process of recording an event in your records and reporting it on your financial statements.

In accounting, the word **recognition** has a very specific meaning. It refers to the process of

1. recording in the books

    and

2. reporting on the financial statements.

The problem of when to recognize an item applies to all of the accounting elements we have discussed so far, as well as to the ones we have yet to discuss. The greatest difficulties, however, concern when to recognize revenues and expenses.

When should a revenue be recognized? When should an expense be recognized? These are two *very* difficult questions, for which there are no "right" answers. A set of criteria must be established to determine when accounting elements, particularly revenues and expenses, are recognized. Over time, several different systems have been developed, each attempting to find some rational basis for the measurement of revenue and expense in a particular time period.

Those of you who have taken another accounting class may have been taught a particular set of criteria for revenue and expense recognition. We are *not* asking you to forget what you learned. What we *are* asking you to do is slide those criteria to the back of your mind, for what you learned in that other accounting class is a set of criteria, not *the* set of criteria.

DISCUSSION QUESTIONS

7-4. If a revenue is defined as the reward of doing business, at what point do you think it should be recognized? Explain.

7-5. If an expense is defined as the sacrifice necessary to obtain a revenue, at what point do you think it should be recognized? Explain.

Bases of Economic Measurement

There are two basic approaches to recording economic activity. As they are discussed, you will see that each has certain advantages over the other. Neither of them is "correct" in the sense of being in accordance with some natural law of finance and accounting. They are simply different approaches to the measurement of revenues, expenses, assets, liabilities, and owners' equity.

We will use a single set of data to illustrate the two bases of measurement. Consider the following information concerning Wooster Company (a proprietorship) for January 1993:

1. Bertie Wooster started the company on January 2, by investing $200,000.

2. Wooster Company borrowed $100,000 from the Friendly Bank on January 2, by signing a one-year, 12 percent note payable. Although the $100,000 does not have to be repaid until January 2, 1994, the interest charge must be paid each month, beginning on February 2, 1993.

3. The company purchased a vehicle on January 2 for $14,000 cash. Bertie's best guess is that the vehicle will fill the company's needs for four years, after which he estimates the vehicle can be sold for $2,000.

4. The company paid cash for $75,000 of merchandise inventory on January 8.

5. On January 15, the company sold $42,000 of the merchandise inventory for a total selling price of $78,000 and collected the cash the same day.

6. On January 22, the company sold $15,000 of the merchandise inventory for a total selling price of $32,000 on account (a credit sale). The terms of the sale were 30 days, meaning Wooster can expect to receive payment by February 22.

7. Cash payments for operating expenses in January totaled $22,500.

8. Besides the bank loan, the only amounts owed by the company at the end of the month were:

    a. $2,000 to employees of the company for work performed in January. They will be paid on February 3.

    b. A $700 utility bill that was received on January 26 and will be paid on February 15.

The above information is the reality of what happened in the Wooster Company during the month of January 1993. The measurement of that reality will be different, depending on the basis of accounting used to recognize the transactions. Remember, both treatments are based on exactly the same reality. *They are simply different methods of measuring reality.*

cash basis accounting A basis of accounting in which cash is the sole criterion used in measuring revenue and expense for a given income statement period. Revenue is recognized when the associated cash is received, and expense is recognized when the associated cash is paid.

CASH BASIS OF ECONOMIC MEASUREMENT

The first approach to measuring economic activity is **cash basis accounting**. This is the simpler of the two bases. Everyone understands what cash is and can therefore readily grasp the measurement criterion of this method. Its greatest strength, however, lies in the fact that it keeps the user's eye on the ball. As its name implies, the cash basis has only one measurement criterion: *CASH!*

Under cash basis accounting, economic activity is recognized only when the associated cash is received or paid. Thus, a revenue is recognized as such only when the associated cash is received by the company. Also understand that only cash received as a result of the earnings process is considered to be revenue. Cash received from the owners of the company, for example, is considered an investment by those owners rather than revenue. Also, cash received when a company borrows money is considered a liability rather than revenue.

Similarly, not all cash paid out is considered an expense in cash basis accounting. If a company pays a dividend to its owners, for example, the cash paid out is not an expense to the company. Such a payment is considered to be a distribution of profits or a return on the owners' original investment. Transactions such as these, which involve cash but are not considered revenues or expenses, are reported on the statement of owners' equity and/or on the balance sheet, but not on the income statement.

There are two keys to revenue and expense recognition under the cash basis. First, cash must be involved in the transaction. Second, the receipt or disbursement must relate to *delivering or producing goods, rendering services, or other activities*. If a transaction meets *both* of these requirements, it is a revenue or expense transaction (depending on whether the cash is received or paid), and will be reported on the income statement.

Cash Basis Financial Statements

In preparing the income statement, statement of capital, and balance sheet using the cash basis, you must first isolate the events and transactions involving cash. For our example of the Wooster Company, only the following meet that requirement:

1. Bertie Wooster started the company on January 2, by investing $200,000.

2. Wooster Company borrowed $100,000 from the Friendly Bank on January 2, by signing a one-year, 12 percent note payable. Although the $100,000 does not have to be repaid until January 2, 1994, the interest charge must be paid each month, beginning on February 2, 1993.

3. The company purchased a vehicle on January 2 for $14,000 cash. Bertie's best guess is that the vehicle will fill the company's needs for four years, after which he estimates the vehicle can be sold for $2,000.

4. The company paid cash for $75,000 of merchandise inventory on January 8.

5. On January 15, the company sold $42,000 of the merchandise inventory for a total selling price of $78,000 and collected the cash the same day.

7. Cash payments for operating expenses in January totaled $22,500.

These transactions, then, will be recorded in Wooster's books and reported on one or more of the financial statements: the income statement, statement of owners' equity, or balance sheet.

In order to determine which of the transactions should be reported on the income statement, we must determine which are directly related to Wooster's major or central operation (which appears to be the buying and selling of some product). Transactions 3, 4, 5, and 7 meet that criterion. Using the cash basis of accounting, the income statement for the month of January 1993, based on those transactions, would look like Exhibit 7-2.

Exhibit 7-2
Cash Basis Income Statement

WOOSTER COMPANY
Income Statement
For the Month Ended January 31, 1993

Sales Revenue...	$78,000	
Cost of Goods Sold..	75,000	
Gross Margin		$ 3,000
Expenses:		
Cost of Vehicle..	$14,000	
Cash Operating Expenses...................................	22,500	
Total Operating Expenses..		(36,500)
Net Loss...		$(33,500)

■ *Sales Revenue.* Because only $78,000 in cash was received from sales in the month of January, that is the amount shown as revenue.
■ *Cost of Goods Sold.* Wooster paid $75,000 in cash for merchandise inventory during January. Thus, this is the amount recognized as cost of goods sold.
■ *Expenses.* The cash expenses of $22,500 plus the entire $14,000 for the vehicle purchased were recognized as expenses in January. Other expenses will be recognized as the cash is paid by the company.

Transaction 1 reflects an inflow of cash, so the cash basis of measurement requires that it be recognized. This transaction represents an investment by the owner, Bertie Wooster. This investment by the owner would be an increase in the capital account, while the net loss determined in Exhibit 7-2 would be a decrease. Exhibit 7-3 is the statement of owner's equity prepared using the cash basis of measurement.

Exhibit 7-3
Cash Basis Statement of Owner's
Equity

WOOSTER COMPANY
Statement of Owner's Equity
For the Month Ended January 31, 1993

B. Wooster, Capital, January 1, 1993.........................	$ 0
Investment by owner..	200,000
Net Loss...	(33,500)
B. Wooster, Capital, January 31, 1993.......................	$166,500

The remaining cash transaction of the Wooster Company during January 1993 is Transaction 2, the $100,000 bank loan. Borrowing money creates a liability that would appear on the balance sheet. Exhibit 7-4 shows Wooster Company's balance sheet at January 31, 1993, under cash basis accounting.

Exhibit 7-4
Cash Basis Balance Sheet

WOOSTER COMPANY
Balance Sheet
January 31, 1993

ASSETS:		LIABILITIES:	
Cash.............	$266,500	Note Payable.....................................	$100,000
		OWNER'S EQUITY:	
		B. Wooster, Capital............................	166,500
Total Assets...	$266,500	Total Liabilities and Owner's Equity....	$266,500

Notice the articulation of the financial statements for the Wooster Company. The net loss from the income statement is shown on the statement of owner's equity, and the ending balance in the capital account from the statement of owner's equity is used on the balance sheet. The cash amount showing on the balance sheet is simply the $200,000 the owner invested in the company plus the $100,000 borrowed from the bank less the $33,500 net loss for the month of January.

DISCUSSION QUESTIONS

7-6. Assume for a moment that you are Wooster's loan officer at the bank. How would you evaluate the income statement and balance sheet presented in Exhibits 7-2 and 7-4 in terms of the primary qualitative characteristic of relevance, including predictive value and feedback value? (*Hint:* See Chapter 3.)

7-7. If your response to Question 7-6 led you to the conclusion that there is a problem in terms of predictive value and feedback value, what item or items do you feel caused the problem? How do you think the company could account for the item or items to better relate costs to the revenues they generate?

Strengths and Weaknesses of Cash Basis Accounting

Besides its relative simplicity, the greatest strength of the cash basis of accounting is its objectivity. Because cash is the only measurement criterion, less subjective judgment is required than with the other measurement basis we will discuss. This is not to say that cash basis accounting is totally objective. For example, a company can manipulate the expenses reported in a particular income statement period simply by delaying the payment of amounts owed. The greatest weakness of the cash basis is that it makes no attempt to recognize expenses in the same period as the revenues they helped generate. This makes the cash basis income statement very difficult to use either for predicting future profitability or for assessing past performance in cases where cash is not immediately received when earned or paid when owed.

DISCUSSION QUESTIONS

7-8. Provide two examples of situations in which your checkbook balance did not provide relevant information.

ACCRUAL BASIS OF ECONOMIC MEASUREMENT

accrual basis accounting A method of accounting in which revenues are recognized when they are earned, regardless of when the associated cash is collected. The expenses incurred in generating the revenue are recognized when the benefit is derived rather than when the associated cash is paid.

accrue As used in accounting, to come into being as a legally enforceable claim.

The second basis of economic measurement we will discuss is **accrual basis accounting**. This system does not rely on the receipt or payment of cash to determine when revenues and expenses should be recognized. The key to understanding accrual basis accounting is to understand the word **accrue**. To accrue means:

To come into being as a legally enforceable claim.

Essentially, in accrual basis accounting, sales, purchases, and all other business transactions are recognized whenever a legally enforceable claim to the associated cash is established. The main focus of accrual accounting is determining when a legally enforceable claim to cash has been established between the parties involved in the transaction.

Revenue Recognition

Revenue is recognized under accrual accounting when it is deemed to be earned—that is, revenue is recognized when the company has a legally enforceable claim to the cash associated with that revenue. Under accrual accounting, then, the recognition of revenue is completely unrelated to when the cash is received.

There are three possible relationships between the timing of the cash movement and the recognition of the revenue:

1. Cash is received *at the time* the revenue is earned. An example of this is when you pay cash for a pair of jeans at The Gap. Cash is received by The Gap at the same time as the store recognizes revenue from the sale.

2. Cash is received *after* the revenue has been earned. An example of this is a sale of merchandise on account (a credit sale). Napa Auto Parts records revenue for sales made to their regular customers in January, but the cash is not collected until February.

3. Cash is received *before* the revenue has been earned. An example of this is the payment received from a customer for a year's subscription to *Time* magazine.

Remember that under accrual accounting, the trigger mechanism for determining when revenue should be recognized is the earning process, *not* when the cash is received. In Examples 1 and 2, the revenue is recorded in the books and shown on the financial statements at the time the sale is made. The fact that in Example 2 the company did not receive cash at that time does not affect recognition of the revenue. In Example 3, the receipt of cash does not cause revenue to be recognized because, under accrual accounting, the revenue is not recognized until it is earned (when the magazines have been sent to the customer).

Exhibit 7-5
Earning As a Trigger to Accrual
Revenue Recognition

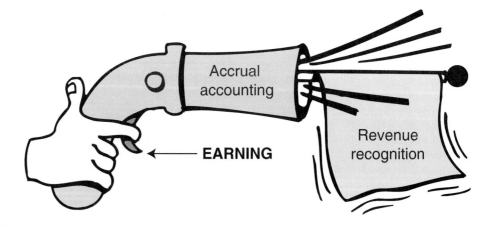

Identifying the point in time when a revenue is earned is not always a simple matter. There are three questions accountants try to answer in determining when revenue has been earned and should therefore be recognized. To emphasize that these questions are in no way related to the three examples, we are using letters to list them.

title Proof of legal ownership of an item.

a. *Has* **title** (legal ownership) *to whatever was sold been transferred to the customer?* If the answer to this question is yes, the revenue should definitely be recognized. This question can be applied more easily to the sale of tangible products than to the sale of services.

b. *Has an exchange taken place?* In other words, has the customer taken receipt of whatever he or she purchased? If the answer to this question is yes, the revenue will likely be recognized. This question, too, is more applicable to the sale of tangible products than it is to the sale of services.

c. *Is the earnings process virtually complete?* This is the toughest of the three questions to answer and applies better to the sale of services than it does to the sale of tangible products. Let's say that you have contracted with Joe Dokes to have your kitchen remodeled. It's a two-week job, and midway through the second week, Joe decides that he doesn't want to be a remodeler anymore. Are you obligated to pay him for removing your old cabinets, stripping the wallpaper, and making a hole in the wall for the new window? Probably not. He cannot recognize revenue until the job is "virtually" complete.

It is not necessary for all three questions to be answered "yes" for revenue to be recognized. In most cases, a positive answer to any one of them is persuasive evidence that revenue has been earned and should be recognized.

Presuming this man actually buys this copy of *Forbes* magazine, the magazine shop will receive the cash at the time the revenue is recognized. The magazine distribution company very likely sold the magazine to the magazine stand on a credit basis, meaning the distributor received the cash after the revenue was recognized. Had this man purchased and paid for a year's subscription of *Forbes* (rather than treating the magazine stand like a public library), the publisher would have received the cash before the revenue had been earned.

Liane Enkelis/Stock Boston

7-9. On Saturday morning, you finally decide which model of IBM computer to buy. The salesperson has agreed to have all the software you need installed and have the machine delivered to you by Tuesday afternoon. Because you purchased your last computer at Carl's Computer Shop, the store has agreed to extend credit to you as an established customer. You have 30 days to pay for your new computer. As of Monday,

   a. has title passed?
   b. has an exchange taken place?
   c. is the earnings process complete?

7-10. When should Carl's Computer Shop recognize revenue

   a. under the cash basis?
   b. under the accrual basis?

Expense Recognition

Under accrual accounting, expenses are recognized when the benefit from the expense is received. As with revenue recognition, the recognition of expense under accrual accounting is completely unrelated to the movement of cash.

Again, there are three possible relationships between the timing of the cash movement and the recognition of the transaction:

1. Cash is paid *at the time* the expense is incurred. An example of this is a cash purchase of the food served at the company Christmas party held that same day.

2. Cash is paid *after* the expense has been incurred. An example of this is Napa Auto Part's payment of a utility bill in February that was for electricity used in January.

3. Cash is paid *before* the expense has been incurred. An example of this is insurance. *Time* magazine buys insurance coverage for a full year and pays the entire premium when the policy is purchased.

matching Relating the expenses to the revenues of a particular income statement period. Once it is determined in which period a revenue should be recognized, the expenses that helped to generate the revenue are matched to that same period.

The key to expense recognition under accrual accounting is revenue recognition. That's right—*revenue recognition*. Remember that to be useful for predicting future profitability and cash flow, an income statement should measure revenues for a specific period of time as well as the expenses required to obtain those revenues. Thus, accrual accounting attempts to establish a relationship between revenues and expenses. This relationship is referred to as **matching**.

The Concept of Matching

The first step in the accrual matching process is to determine in which income statement period to recognize a particular revenue. The second step is to determine which expenses helped to generate that revenue. Those expenses are then recognized in that same financial statement period. This approach makes the income statement for that time period more reflective of true earnings results, and therefore more relevant for predicting future potential. It is important to note that it can be very difficult to determine which expenses are responsible for generating which revenue, so a significant amount of judgment is required in recognizing expenses under the accrual basis of accounting.

There are two possible relationships between revenues and expenses, and these determine when expenses are recognized:

1. *Direct cause and effect.* This situation, in which a direct link can be found between an expense and the revenue it helped generate, is the more desirable of the two relationships. An example is sales commissions. If Prudential Insurance Company pays a 10 percent sales commission to its salespersons, and a salesman makes a sale of $1,000, the company incurs a $100 expense. Once it is determined in which income statement period the $1,000 revenue should be recognized, the $100 expense is recognized in that same period. Unfortunately, relatively few expenses can be linked directly to the revenues they help generate.

2. *No direct cause and effect.* This is the more common relationship. In this case, there are two possible treatments:

   a. ALLOCATION TO THE PERIODS BENEFITED. If a purchased item has discernible benefit to future income statement periods and the periods can be reasonably estimated, the item is recorded as an asset when purchased. The cost of that item is then systematically converted to expense in the periods benefited. An example of this is insurance. If a premium for two years of insurance coverage is paid, there is no question that a benefit to future periods exists. Further, the estimate of those periods is clear—benefits will be derived for two years. As time passes during the two years, the cost of the insurance coverage is allocated to expense.

   b. IMMEDIATE RECOGNITION. There are two situations in which recording the expense immediately is the most appropriate action. First, if a purchased item has no discernible future benefit, or the periods benefited cannot be reasonably estimated, the cost of the item is recognized as an expense immediately. A good example of an expense requiring immediate recognition is Ford Motors' television advertising intended to increase the sales of the Taurus. The future benefit of this type of advertising is not discernible. Television ads purchased and presented to the public in one period almost certainly benefit future periods, but how many periods and how much in each of those periods cannot be reasonably estimated. Thus, the cost of television advertising is usually recognized as an expense in the periods when the ads are presented to consumers.

The second situation requiring the immediate recognition of an expense is when allocation of the cost of a purchased item provides no additional useful information. An example of this situation is the purchase of a $10 item such as a stapler. Even if the stapler will be used in the office for five years, allocation of the $10 cost over the five-year period serves no useful purpose. Remember, the purpose of accounting is to provide information useful to decision makers. Will allocating this minor cost over a five-year period provide useful accounting information? Since most decision makers would be unaffected by the treatment of a $10 item, the answer is no. The record-keeping cost of recording the stapler as an asset on the balance sheet and then allocating $2 per year as an expense on the income statement for five years far outweighs the benefit of doing so. Recognizing the $10 cost as an immediate expense makes more sense.

The concept of "allocation to the periods benefited" has a more widely used application than the one just described. When assets that will benefit the company for several periods (often many years) are acquired, the cost is recorded as an asset amount on the balance sheet. As time passes, the cost is transferred to expense on the income statement (Exhibit 7-6). This form of "allocation to the periods benefited" is a process known as *depreciation*. Depreciation is applied to a variety of long-lived assets such as machinery, buildings, and equipment. One asset that has a long life, but is *not* depreciated, is land.

What Depreciation Is (and What It Is Not)

depreciation The systematic and rational conversion of a long-lived asset's cost from asset to expense in the income statement periods benefited.

Depreciation is defined as *a systematic (methodical) and rational (reasoned) allocation of the cost of a long-lived item from asset to expense.* You should recall that under cash basis accounting, Wooster Company's purchase of a $14,000 vehicle resulted in a $14,000 expense because that amount of cash was spent. The real question is whether this asset has been "used up" (has the company received the benefit from the vehicle?) or does the asset still have a future benefit? The answer to the question is clearly that the asset (vehicle)

Exhibit 7-6
Conversion of Assets
to Expenses

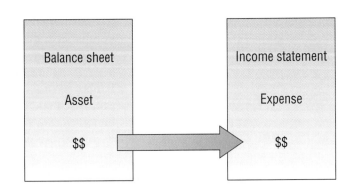

has not been used up, nor has the company received all the benefit from it. The accrual basis of measurement takes the position that this cash payment of $14,000 should not be considered an expense at the time the cash is paid. Rather than recognize the cost of the vehicle as an expense immediately, under the accrual basis it is recorded as an asset because it has probable future benefit. Over time, the cost of the vehicle will be converted from asset to expense as the benefit is derived from the use of the vehicle. The resulting expense is called **depreciation expense** (see Exhibit 7-6).

There is probably nothing in all of accounting as misunderstood as the concept of depreciation. The confusion is caused by the difference between the meaning of "depreciation" in accounting and in ordinary speech. In virtually every context except accounting, depreciation means the lowering of value. In accounting, it simply means the allocation of cost to the periods benefited. This allocation requires two highly subjective estimates: (1) the useful life of the asset and (2) the residual value of the asset.

The *useful life of an asset* is the length of time that asset will be of use to the company (not the length of time the asset will exist). Notice that in the case of the Wooster Company, Bertie Wooster feels that the vehicle will fill the company's needs for four years. This is not the same thing as saying the vehicle will last four years. There is an important distinction.

If the estimated useful life of an asset is less than the physical life of that asset, it follows that the asset will probably be sold at the end of its useful life. The estimated amount for which the asset can be sold at the end of its useful life is known as its **residual value**. It is also sometimes referred to as **salvage value** or **scrap value.**

In calculating depreciation, any estimated residual value is subtracted from the cost of an asset to arrive at what is called the **depreciable base** or **depreciable amount**. In the case of the Wooster Company, the cost of the vehicle was $14,000, and the company estimated that at the end of its useful life, the vehicle could be sold for $2,000. The depreciable amount, therefore, is $12,000 ($14,000 – $2,000). In one sense, then, the true cost of the vehicle to Wooster is $12,000, because the company expects to recoup $2,000 of the purchase price when the vehicle is sold.

depreciation expense The amount of cost associated with a long-lived asset converted to expense in a given income statement period.

residual value The estimated value of an asset when it has reached the end of its useful life. Also called salvage or scrap value.

salvage value Another name for residual value.

scrap value Another name for salvage or residual value.

depreciable base The total amount of depreciation expense that is allowed to be claimed for an asset during its useful life. The depreciable base is the cost of the asset less its residual value.

depreciable amount Another name for depreciable base.

Both the paving machine and the hand shovels shown in this photo are items that will likely provide benefit for several years to the paving company that purchased them. The cost of the paving machine was recorded as an asset when it was purchased. That cost is now being systematically and rationally allocated to the income statement periods expected to be benefited (depreciation). The cost of the hand shovels, on the other hand, was recorded as an expense for the income statement period in which they were purchased. The cost of recording a hand shovel as an asset and then depreciating it far outweighs any benefit.

Gary Walts/The Image Works

straight-line depreciation
One of several acceptable methods of calculating periodic depreciation. The depreciable base of an asset is divided by its estimated useful life. The result is the amount of depreciation expense to be recognized in each year of the item's estimated useful life: (Cost – residual value)/N = annual depreciation expense.

Once the useful life and residual value of the asset have been estimated, a method of depreciation must be selected. Several have been developed over the years. The simplest method is **straight-line depreciation**, and we will use it to demonstrate how depreciation expense is calculated.

The straight-line approach allocates an equal amount of depreciation expense to each period of the asset's estimated useful life. The amount of expense is calculated by dividing the estimated useful life of the asset into the depreciable amount of the asset. In the case of Wooster's vehicle, which cost $14,000 and has a four-year estimated useful life and a $2,000 residual value, the amount of expense works out to $3,000 per year ($12,000/4). Each year of the four-year estimated useful life, Wooster will transfer $3,000 of the asset "vehicle" on the balance sheet into the expense "depreciation" on the income statement. At the end of the four years, the entire cost of the vehicle (except the $2,000 residual value) will have been recognized as expense.

Depreciation is an important process that is based upon accrual accounting's attempt to recognize expenses in the periods in which they help to generate revenue. Even though all of the $14,000 in cash was spent during January for the Wooster Company's vehicle, the entire benefit expected from the asset has not been received. Because the company expects the asset to help generate revenues in future periods, part of the cost will be allocated to depreciation expense in those periods. The depreciation process is just one result of accrual accounting's attempt to match expenses and revenues. Additional examples are the other adjustments we explore next.

DISCUSSION QUESTIONS

7-11. Recall the scenario, introduced in Discussion Question 7-9, involving your purchase of a computer from Carl's Computer Shop. If the computer is to be used in the business you operate from your home, how should the purchase be treated

a. under the cash basis?
b. under the accrual basis?

Accruals and Deferrals

adjustments Changes made in recorded amounts of revenues and expenses in order to follow the guidelines of accrual accounting.

Because accrual accounting attempts to recognize revenues in the income statement period they are earned, and attempts to match the expenses that generated the revenue to the same income statement period, **adjustments** must be made each period to ensure that these guidelines have been followed. The adjustment process takes place at the end of the financial statement period, but before the financial statements are prepared. This process involves reviewing the financial records to be sure that all items that should be recognized in the current period have been recorded. In addition, during the adjustment process, it is ascertained that no items that should be recognized in future periods appear in the current period's records.

The two basic types of adjustments that are necessary are accruals and deferrals.

accruals Adjustments made to record items that should be included on the income statement, but have not yet been recorded.

1. **Accruals**. These adjustments are made to recognize items that should be included in the income statement period, but have not yet been recorded. Accrual adjustments recognize revenue or expense *before* the associated cash is received or paid. In other words, this type of adjustment comes before the cash flow takes place. There are two types of accruals:

accrued revenues Revenues appropriately recognized under accrual accounting in one income statement period although the associated cash will be received in a later income statement period.

   a. **Accrued revenues**. These are revenues considered earned during the financial statement period because they met the criteria (answered yes to Questions a, b, or c on pages 200-201), but which have not yet been recognized. Consider Warner Management Consulting Services, Inc. For the clients that use its services on an ongoing basis, the company sends bills on the 2nd of each month for work done during the previous month. Warner has a legal claim at the end of December to what was earned in that month. Revenues recognized (recorded) should reflect the amount earned in December, even though the clients will not be billed until January 2 of the next year.

accrued expenses Expenses appropriately recognized under accrual accounting in one income statement period although the associated cash will be paid in a later income statement period.

   b. **Accrued expenses**. These are expenses deemed to have been incurred during the financial statement period, but which have not yet been recognized. An example of this is accrued wages for employees. Assume Pellum Company pays its employees every two weeks for work performed in the previous two weeks. If part of the two-week pay period is in 1991 and part is in 1992, Pellum must make an adjustment at the end of 1991 to recognize the portion of wages expense incurred during that period. Even though the company will not spend any money until payday in January of 1992, part of that pay period's wages are 1991 expenses.

deferrals Situations in which cash is either received or paid, but the income statement effect is delayed until some later period. Deferred revenues are recorded as liabilities, and deferred expenses are recorded as assets.

2. **Deferrals**. These are postponements of the recognition of revenue or expense even though the cash has been received or paid. Deferrals are adjustments of revenues for which the cash has been collected but not yet earned, and of expenses for which cash has been paid but no benefit has yet been received.

deferred revenues Revenues created when cash is received before the revenue is earned. Because the cash received has not yet been earned, an obligation is created and a liability is recorded. Later, when the cash is deemed to have been earned, it will be recognized as a revenue.

   a. **Deferred revenues**. These are created when cash is received before it is earned. For example, Larry's Lawn Service provides lawn care to many wealthy Miami families. On June 1, the Weatherby family sends Larry's Lawn Service $450 for the cost of three months' lawn service. As of June 1, Larry's Lawn Service has not earned any revenue, even though it has received cash. In fact, at that point, a liability has been created. The company *owes* the Weatherby family either three months of lawn service or their money back. The key here is who has legal claim to the cash. Because Larry's Lawn Service has no legal claim to the cash, it cannot rightly account for it as earned. By the time financial statements are prepared at the end of June, however, one month's worth of lawn service was performed, and $150 should be recognized as revenue. The remaining $300, representing two months of service, is a deferred revenue. This amount represents a liability for Larry's Lawn Service, and will remain so until the company either performs the services required to attain a legal claim to the cash or returns the cash to the Weatherby family.

deferred expenses
Expenses created when cash is paid before any benefit is received. Because the benefit to be derived is in the future, the item is recorded as an asset. Later, when the benefit is received from the item, it will be recognized as an expense.

b. **Deferred expenses**. These are created when cash is paid before an expense has been incurred. On January 2, 1992, Crockett Cookie Company purchased a three-year insurance policy for $2,175. By December 31, 1992, one-third of the insurance coverage has expired (one-third of the benefit has been received). Financial statements prepared for 1992 should reflect the fact that one-third of the cost of the policy ($725) is an expense for that year. The remaining portion of the policy, two years' worth of coverage, is an asset providing future benefits to the company. Even though the entire $2,175 was spent in 1992, two-thirds of the cost is a deferred expense, an asset that will be recognized as an expense in future periods.

Accruals and deferrals are adjustments made to be sure that the financial statements reflect the guidelines of accrual accounting. Accruals occur in situations where the cash flow has not yet taken place, but the revenue or expense should be recognized. Deferrals are necessary in cases when the cash flow has already taken place, but the associated revenue or expense should not be recognized. Understand, too, that the original transaction (the receipt or payment of cash) is not an adjustment, but rather creates a situation where an adjustment will be necessary later.

Whether they reflect expenses or revenues, accruals and deferrals will always possess the following three characteristics:

1. *A revenue item or an expense item will always be affected.* This is logical because the whole purpose of the adjustment process is to make certain that revenues and expenses associated with a given financial statement period are recognized in that period. Clearly, adjustments will always affect the income statement.

2. *An asset item or a liability item will always be affected.* This means the balance sheet will also be affected by the adjustment process.

3. *Cash is never affected by accruals or deferrals.* Remember, adjustments are made to properly recognize accounting elements. It is assumed that inflows and outflows of cash were properly recorded at the time they occurred.

Accrual Basis Financial Statements

Let us once again turn to the transactions of the Wooster Company for the month of January 1993. For your convenience, the descriptions of the company's transactions are presented again:

1. Bertie Wooster started the company on January 2, by investing $200,000.

2. Wooster Company borrowed $100,000 from the Friendly Bank on January 2, by signing a one-year, 12 percent note payable. Although the $100,000 does not have to be repaid until January 2, 1994, the interest charge must be paid each month, beginning on February 2, 1993.

3. The company purchased a vehicle on January 2 for $14,000 cash. Bertie's best guess is that the vehicle will fill the company's needs for four years, after which he estimates the vehicle can be sold for $2,000.

4. The company paid cash for $75,000 of merchandise inventory on January 8.

5. On January 15, the company sold $42,000 of the merchandise inventory for a total selling price of $78,000 and collected the cash the same day.

6. On January 22, the company sold $15,000 of the merchandise inventory for a total selling price of $32,000 on account (a credit sale). The terms of the sale were 30 days, meaning Wooster can expect to receive payment by February 22.

7. Cash payments for operating expenses in January totaled $22,500.

8. Besides the bank loan, the only amounts owed by the company at the end of the month were:

   a. $2,000 to employees of the company for work performed in January. They will be paid on February 3.

   b. A $700 utility bill that was received on January 26 and will be paid on February 15.

All eight transactions will affect the income statement and/or the balance sheet and statement of owners' equity under the accrual basis of accounting. The income statement for January 1993 looks like Exhibit 7-7.

Exhibit 7-7
Accrual Basis Income Statement

WOOSTER COMPANY
Income Statement
For the Month Ended January 31, 1993

Sales Revenue	$110,000	
Cost of Goods Sold	57,000	
Gross Margin		$ 53,000
Expenses:		
Cash Operating Expenses	$ 22,500	
Wages Expense	2,000	
Utilities Expense	700	
Interest Expense	1,000	
Depreciation Expense	250	
Total Operating Expenses		(26,450)
Net Income		$ 26,550

Most of the items on this income statement differ from those on the income statement prepared under the cash basis (Exhibit 7-2). Let's discuss each item:

- *Sales Revenue.* Under the accrual basis, revenue is recognized when it is earned, regardless of when the associated cash is received. Transaction 6 says the company made a $32,000 sale on January 22. The fact that the cash is not expected to be received until February 22 is irrelevant. Therefore, total sales revenue for the month using accrual accounting is $110,000 ($78,000 cash sale + $32,000 credit sale).
- *Cost of Goods Sold.* Under accrual accounting, there is an attempt to match all expenses to the same income statement period as the revenues they help generate. In the case of merchandise inventory, it is relatively easy to establish a direct cause and effect between the revenue (sale of the inventory) and the expense (cost of the inventory sold). Transaction 5 says $42,000 of merchandise inventory was sold on January 15, and transaction 6 says $15,000 of merchandise inventory was sold on January 22. The total cost of this merchandise is $57,000, so this is the amount shown on the accrual basis income statement as cost of goods sold. This means, of course, that there is $18,000 of merchandise inventory not yet accounted for ($75,000 purchased − $57,000 sold). We will discuss this remaining inventory when we talk about the balance sheet.
- *Cash Operating Expenses.* This is the clearest and most understandable expense figure on the Wooster Company's income statement. Under both cash basis and accrual basis measurement, expenses paid in cash this period to support operations during this period are considered to be expenses for this period.
- *Wages Expense of $2,000.* Because these wages were earned by employees during January, Wooster has a legal liability at January 31 for this amount. Further, since the benefit derived from the employees' work was in January, the expense should be recognized in January regardless of when the employees will actually be paid.
- *Utilities Expense of $700.* Since the bill was received in January, let us assume that it was for utilities purchased and used during January. In that case, the expense should be recognized in January.
- *Interest Expense of $1,000.* The cost of the $100,000 loan is the interest Wooster must pay. Because the company had the $100,000 throughout the month of January, the interest cost for the month should be recognized as an expense even though it will not be paid until February 2. The amount is calculated using the formula explained in Chapter 5:

Principal	x	Rate	x	Time
$100,000	x	12%	x	1/12

- *Depreciation Expense of $250.* Under cash accounting, the cost of the vehicle was considered an expense the day it was paid for. But as explained earlier, under accrual accounting, only a portion of the cost is recognized as expense each period. Using straight-line depreciation, the amount of depreciation is calculated as ($14,000 − $2,000)/4 = $3,000. This $3,000 represents the amount of depreciation expense that should be recognized during each year of the asset's useful life. Because the financial statements we are using in the Wooster Company example are only for the month of January 1993, the amount of depreciation expense would be only $250 ($3,000/12) for the month.

7-12. Reexamine each item on Wooster Company's accrual basis income statement. Identify the items that are a result of the adjustment process.

7-13. Consider the following statement as it relates to the accrual basis of economic measurement: "Net income is an opinion, cash is a fact." What do you think this means?

Now that we have discussed the effect of accrual accounting on the income statement, we can look at what effects this system has on the statement of owners' equity. The $200,000 investment by the owner is treated just as it was under the cash basis. However, the results presented on the income statement under accrual accounting will be different, so the statement of owners' equity (Exhibit 7-8) will also be different under the accrual basis of measurement.

Exhibit 7-8
Accrual Basis Statement
of Owner's Equity

WOOSTER COMPANY
Statement of Owner's Equity
For the Month Ended January 31, 1993

B. Wooster, Capital, January 1, 1993................... $	0
Investment by Owner...	200,000
Net Income..	26,550
B. Wooster, Capital, January 31, 1993.................	$226,550

The balance sheet for Wooster Company at January 31, 1993, using the accrual basis of accounting is presented in Exhibit 7-9 on page 212. You will note that the items we discussed for the income statement have had an effect on the balance sheet as well.

```
                          WOOSTER COMPANY
                            Balance Sheet
                          January 31, 1993

  ASSETS:                              LIABILITIES:
  Cash ................................. $266,500    Accounts Payable ......... $      700
  Accounts Receivable............    32,000    Wages Payable .............    2,000
  Inventory...............................    18,000    Interest Payable ............    1,000
  Vehicle ...................$14,000              Note Payable.................   100,000
  Less: Accumulated                          Total Liabilities..............  $103,700
     Depreciation .......( 250)
  Vehicle, Net ..........................    13,750    OWNER'S EQUITY:
  Total Assets .........................  $330,250    B. Wooster, Capital .......  226,550
                                              Total Liabilities
                                              and Owner's Equity.......  $330,250
```

Exhibit 7-9
Accrual Basis Balance Sheet

Again, many items on this balance sheet differ from those on the balance sheet prepared under the cash basis (Exhibit 7-4). Each item on the statement will be discussed in turn.

- *Cash of $266,500.* The amount of cash is counted and reported. The basis of economic measurement in place cannot change the amount of cash on hand. Note, however, that under the accrual basis, net income is affected by several items not directly related to cash. Therefore, net income is not equal to the increase in cash.
- *Accounts Receivable of $32,000.* This asset was created by Transaction 6. Wooster recognized the sale because an exchange had taken place and title to the merchandise inventory had passed to the customer. When that transaction occurred, Wooster had a legal claim to the $32,000. This is certainly an item that has probable future benefit to the business; it is therefore shown as an asset. It will remain classified as an asset until such time as the customer pays Wooster the cash.
- *Inventory of $18,000.* This is the remaining amount of merchandise inventory not recognized as cost of goods sold on the income statement. It is classified on the balance sheet as an asset because Wooster has not yet sacrificed it to generate revenue (it has probable future benefit). It will remain classified as an asset until such time as it is sold.
- *Vehicle of $14,000.* The original cost of the vehicle still shows on the balance sheet.
- *Accumulated Depreciation of $250.* To show that a portion of the original cost of the vehicle has been converted to expense, an amount called **accumulated depreciation** has been deducted to arrive at what is called the *net amount of the asset.* This figure, $13,750, is also called the **book value** of the vehicle. In future periods, as more depreciation expense is recorded, the total amount recorded since the asset was acquired is shown

accumulated depreciation The total amount of cost that has been systematically converted to expense since a long-lived asset was first purchased.

book value The original cost of a long-lived asset less its accumulated depreciation. This item is often shown on the balance sheet.

as accumulated depreciation. Therefore, as time passes, accumulated depreciation increases and the book value of the asset decreases. This method of presentation tells decision makers what the assets originally cost and the amount not yet converted to expense (depreciated).

■ *Accounts Payable of $700.* This is for the utilities; the liability was created when Wooster recorded receiving the bill. Wooster has recognized the utilities expense, but the bill has not yet been paid. It is properly classified as a liability because it is an amount owed by the company and will require the sacrifice of assets (in this case, cash) in the future. It will remain classified as a liability until such time as Wooster pays the bill.

■ *Wages Payable of $2,000.* This is the amount Wooster owes its employees at the balance sheet date; the liability was created in the adjustment process.

■ *Interest Payable of $1,000.* This is the amount of interest Wooster owes the bank at the balance sheet date. Again, this liability was created in the adjustment process.

■ *Note Payable of $100,000.* This is a liability representing the amount Wooster Company owes to Friendly Bank.

■ *Capital of $226,550.* This is the ending balance shown on the accrual basis statement of capital. This amount is different from the capital balance shown on the cash basis balance sheet because of the difference in net income.

Strengths and Weaknesses of Accrual Basis Accounting

The strength of the accrual basis is that it attempts to establish a relationship between revenues and the expenses incurred in generating the revenue. This is helpful to economic decision makers as they assess the past performance of a company and as they attempt to predict a company's future profitability.

Accrual accounting's most glaring weakness is that it takes the user's eye off cash. Decision makers are provided no information about inflows or outflows of cash when looking at the income statement. Because revenue and expense recognition under the accrual basis are *totally* unrelated to the receipt or payment of cash, net income does not represent an increase in cash for the period covered by the income statement. Neither does a net loss represent a decrease in cash.

DISCUSSION QUESTIONS

7-14. What complications can you see if a revenue is recognized in December of 1991, but the cash is not collected until January of 1992?

COMPARING THE TWO BASES OF ECONOMIC MEASUREMENT

In Exhibits 7-10 and 7-11, you will find two sets of financial statements prepared for the Wooster Company. The first set used the cash basis of economic measurement, and the second set used the accrual basis.

Each set illustrates the articulation of financial statements. The net loss presented on the cash basis income statement results in a reduction of the owner's capital account. The accrual basis income statement shows a net income of $26,550, which increases the owner's capital account. In both sets of statements, the ending balance in the capital account, shown on the statement of owner's equity, is used on the balance sheet.

Exhibit 7-10
Set of Financial Statements
Prepared Using the Cash Basis
of Economic Measurement

WOOSTER COMPANY
Income Statement
For the Month Ended January 31, 1993

Sales Revenue	$78,000	
Cost of Goods Sold	75,000	
Gross Margin		$ 3,000
Expenses:		
Cost of Vehicle	$14,000	
Cash Operating Expenses	22,500	
Total Operating Expenses		(36,500)
Net Loss		$(33,500)

WOOSTER COMPANY
Statement of Owner's Equity
For the Month Ended January 31, 1993

B. Wooster, Capital, January 1, 1993	$ 0
Investment by Owner	200,000
Net Loss	(33,500)
B. Wooster, Capital, January 31, 1993	$166,500

WOOSTER COMPANY
Balance Sheet
January 31, 1993

ASSETS:		LIABILITIES:	
Cash	$266,500	Note Payable	$100,000
		OWNER'S EQUITY:	
		B. Wooster, Capital	166,500
		Total Liabilities and	
Total Assets	$266,500	Owner's Equity	$266,500

WOOSTER COMPANY
Income Statement
For the Month Ended January 31, 1993

Sales Revenue....................................	$110,000	
Cost of Goods Sold.............................	57,000	
Gross Margin...		$53,000
Expenses:		
Cash Operating Expenses.....................	$22,500	
Wages Expense....................................	2,000	
Utilities Expense	700	
Interest Expense..................................	1,000	
Depreciation Expense............................	250	
Total Operating Expenses..................................		(26,450)
Net Income..		$26,550

WOOSTER COMPANY
Statement of Owner's Equity
For the Month Ended January 31, 1993

B. Wooster, Capital, January 1, 1993.....................	$ 0
Investment by owner...	200,000
Net Income...	26,550
B. Wooster, Capital, January 31, 1993...................	$226,550

WOOSTER COMPANY
Balance Sheet
January 31, 1993

ASSETS:		LIABILITIES:	
Cash...............................	$266,500	Accounts Payable.......... $	700
Accounts Receivable......	32,000	Wages Payable..............	2,000
Inventory.........................	18,000	Interest Payable............	1,000
Vehicle.....................$14,000		Note Payable.................	100,000
Less: Accumulated		Total Liabilities...............	$103,700
Depreciation......... (250)			
Vehicle, Net	13,750	OWNER'S EQUITY:	
Total Assets...................	$330,250	B. Wooster, Capital....	226,550
		Total Liabilities	
		and Owner's Equity........	$330,250

Exhibit 7-11
Set of Financial Statements
Prepared Using the Accrual Basis
of Economic Measurement

Remember that both sets of statements were prepared using exactly the same transactions and events. The differences are caused, not by the reality of what happened in Wooster Company during January 1993, but by the different measurement criteria used by the cash and accrual bases of accounting.

7-15. Which of the two sets of financial statements do you think more closely relates the measurement of reality to reality? In other words, which set do you think is the better presentation of what actually happened during January 1993? Explain.

7-16. Which of the two sets of financial statements do you think better reflects Wooster Company's future profit potential? Explain.

7-17. Are you coming to the conclusion that accounting lacks the exactness you once thought it possessed? Explain.

So, which of the bases is better? Neither. Each has strengths and weaknesses in relation to the other, and each is appropriate for certain entities in certain situations.

However, having two valid bases of economic measurement does present a problem to economic decision makers, who often evaluate choices among various companies. If one company uses cash basis accounting and another uses accrual accounting, what are decision makers to do?

We have seen what different outcomes result when the two different measurement bases are used to measure the same reality. Imagine how difficult it would be to evaluate two sets of financial statements if they were developed using different measurement bases and they were based on different business activities! Even if the companies being compared both use accrual basis measurement, a number of factors could complicate the comparison.

Chapters 8 and 9 explore areas in which flexibility in the recognition of revenues and expenses is allowed. These variations reduce the comparability of financial statement information between companies. However, in order to make the best use of accounting information, you should be aware of the variations.

SUMMARY

There are two things going on in business. First, there is the reality of business transactions and events. Second, there is the attempt to measure that reality in the accounting records and reports. For a number of reasons, the measurement of reality may not precisely reflect reality. Some of the differences between reality and the measurement of reality are a result of the basis selected to recognize revenues and expenses in a particular time period. This chapter presented two distinct bases: the cash basis and the accrual basis.

The cash basis of accounting is fairly simple and straightforward. Under this basis, revenue is recognized when the cash associated with it is received, and expense is recognized when the cash associated with it is paid. Periodic net income (or loss) under the cash basis is simply the difference between revenues and expenses.

Under accrual accounting, periodic net income (or loss) is determined as it is under the cash basis—as a difference between revenues and expenses. However, the two bases differ as to the criteria necessary to record revenues and expenses. Under accrual accounting, revenue is recognized when it is earned (when the company has a legal claim to the associated cash). Expenses are recognized when their benefit is deemed to have been received, regardless of when the associated cash is paid. Further, accrual accounting attempts to recognize expenses in the same income statement period as the revenues they helped generate.

Accrual accounting's attempt to match expenses to the same income statement period as the revenues they helped to generate is the key to a concept called *matching*. This concept provides the foundation for accrual accounting's treatment of long-lived assets whose benefit to the company extends beyond a single income statement period. The cost of these items is recorded as an asset because the benefit lies in the future. Then the cost is systematically and rationally converted from asset to expense in the income statement periods benefited. This conversion process is known as *depreciation*.

In addition to depreciation, other adjustments to the accounting records are required to ensure that accrual accounting's revenue and expense recognition guidelines have been met before financial statements are prepared. The two basic types of adjustments are accruals and deferrals. Accruals are adjustments made prior to any cash flow taking place. These adjustments record revenues for which the cash has not yet been received and expenses for which the cash has not yet been spent. Deferrals are adjustments made for situations in which the cash flow has already occurred. Revenues that have not yet been earned, but for which cash has already been received, require a deferral adjustment. Cases in which cash has already been spent, but the related expense has not yet been incurred, also result in deferral adjustments.

The greatest strength of accrual accounting is its attempt to show the relationship between expenses and the revenues they help generate. Doing so makes the income statement and balance sheet more useful as predictive and feedback tools than financial statements prepared under the cash basis. The cash basis does a poor job of relating expenses to the revenues they generate in a given income statement period. For this reason, financial statements prepared using the cash basis of accounting make the prediction of future profitability (and therefore cash flow) very difficult. The greatest strength of the cash basis method (besides its simplicity) is that it keeps the financial statement user's eye on cash. Accrual accounting's greatest weakness is that it takes the financial statement user's eye off cash because recognition of revenue and expense is not related to cash flow. Neither accrual accounting nor cash basis accounting is "right" or "correct." They are simply different methods of recognizing revenues and expenses.

Key Terms

accrual basis accounting A method of accounting in which revenues are recognized when they are earned, regardless of when the associated cash is collected. The expenses incurred in generating the revenue are recognized when the benefit is derived rather than when the associated cash is paid. (p. 199)

accruals Adjustments made to record items that should be included on the income statement, but have not yet been recorded. (p. 207)

accrue As used in accounting, to come into being as a legally enforceable claim. (p. 199)

accrued expenses Expenses appropriately recognized under accrual accounting in one income statement period although the associated cash will be paid in a later income statement period. (p. 207)

accrued revenues Revenues appropriately recognized under accrual accounting in one income statement period although the associated cash will be received in a later income statement period. (p. 207)

accumulated depreciation The total amount of cost that has been systematically converted to expense since a long-lived asset was first purchased. (p. 212)

adjustments Changes made in recorded amounts of revenues and expenses in order to follow the guidelines of accrual accounting. (p. 206)

book value The original cost of a long-lived asset less its accumulated depreciation. This item is often shown on the balance sheet. (p. 212)

cash basis accounting A basis of accounting in which cash is the sole criterion used in measuring revenue and expense for a given income statement period. Revenue is recognized when the associated cash is received, and expense is recognized when the associated cash is paid. (p. 195)

deferrals Situations in which cash is either received or paid, but the income statement effect is delayed until some later period. Deferred revenues are recorded as liabilities, and deferred expenses are recorded as assets. (p. 207)

deferred expenses Expenses created when cash is paid before any benefit is received. Because the benefit to be derived is in the future, the item is recorded as an asset. Later, when the benefit is received from the item, it will be recognized as an expense. (p. 208)

deferred revenues Revenues created when cash is received before the revenue is earned. Because the cash received has not yet been earned, an obligation is created and a liability is recorded. Later, when the cash is deemed to have been earned, it will be recognized as a revenue. (p. 207)

depreciable amount Another name for depreciable base. (p. 205)

depreciable base The total amount of depreciation expense that is allowed to be claimed for an asset during its useful life. The depreciable base is the cost of the asset less its residual value. (p. 205)

depreciation The systematic and rational conversion of a long-lived asset's cost from asset to expense in the income statement periods benefited. (p. 204)

depreciation expense The amount of cost associated with a long-lived asset converted to expense in a given income statement period. (p. 205)

matching Relating the expenses to the revenues of a particular income statement period. Once it is determined in which period a revenue should be recognized, the expenses that helped to generate the revenue are matched to that same period. (p. 202)

recognition The process of recording an event in your records and reporting it on your financial statements. (p. 194)

residual value The estimated value of an asset when it has reached the end of its useful life.

Also called salvage or scrap value. (p. 205)

salvage value Another name for residual value. (p. 205)

scrap value Another name for salvage or residual value. (p. 205)

straight-line depreciation One of several acceptable methods of calculating periodic depreciation. The depreciable base of an asset is divided by its estimated useful life. The result is the amount of depreciation expense to be recognized in each year of the item's estimated useful life: (Cost – residual value)/N = annual depreciation expense. (p. 206)

title Proof of legal ownership of an item. (p. 200)

REVIEW THE FACTS

A. Explain the difference between reality and the measurement of reality, and provide an example of each.

B. How does periodic measurement create complications?

C. In accounting, what does it mean for an item to be "recognized"?

D. Under the cash basis of measurement, when does revenue recognition occur?

E. Under the cash basis, when are expenses recognized?

F. What is the greatest strength of the cash basis?

G. What is the greatest weakness of the cash basis?

H. Under the accrual basis of measurement, when does revenue recognition occur?

I. Under the accrual basis, when are expenses recognized?

J. Explain the concept of matching.

K. What is depreciation and why is it necessary in accrual accounting?

L. Compare and contrast accruals and deferrals.

M. What is the greatest strength of the accrual basis?

N. What is the greatest weakness of the accrual basis?

APPLY WHAT YOU HAVE LEARNED

7-18. Vicki Wright Company began operation on January 2, 1996. During its first month of operation, the company had the following transactions:

- Purchased $35,000 of merchandise inventory on January 2. The amount due is payable on February 2.
- Paid January office rent of $3,000 on January 3.
- Purchased $10,000 of merchandise inventory on January 5. Paid cash at the time of purchase.
- Sold $18,000 of merchandise inventory for $30,000 to a customer on January 10 and received the cash on that date.
- Sold $5,000 of merchandise inventory for $9,000 to a customer on January 20. The sale was on account and the customer has until February 20 to pay.
- Paid cash expenses during January of $7,500.
- Received bills for utilities, advertising, and phone service totaling $1,500. All these bills were for services received in January. They will all be paid the first week in February.

REQUIRED:

a. Prepare a January 1996 multistep income statement for Vicki Wright Company using the *cash basis* of accounting.

b. Do you think the income statement you prepared for the previous requirement provides a good measure of the reality of the company's performance during January? Explain your reasoning.

7-19. Vicki Wright Company began operation on January 2, 1996. During its first month of operation, the company had the same seven transactions as noted in 7-18.

REQUIRED:

a. Prepare a January 1996 multistep income statement for Vicki Wright Company using the *accrual basis* of accounting.

b. Do you think the income statement you prepared for the previous requirement provides a good measure of the reality of the company's performance during January? Explain your reasoning.

7-20. Fire & Cracker Company began operation on June 1, 1994. During its first month of operation, the company had the following transactions:

- Purchased $40,000 of merchandise inventory on June 1. The amount due is payable on August 1.

- Paid June office rent of $2,000 on June 3.
- Purchased $20,000 of merchandise inventory on June 4. Paid cash at the time of purchase.
- Sold $30,000 of merchandise inventory for $42,000 to a customer on June 10 and received the cash on that date.
- Sold $10,000 of merchandise inventory for $14,000 to a customer on June 20. The sale was on account and the customer has until July 20 to pay.
- Paid cash expenses during June of $9,500.
- Received bills for utilities, advertising, and phone service totaling $3,500. All these bills were for services received in June. They will all be paid the first week in July.

REQUIRED:

  a. Prepare a June 1994 multistep income statement for Fire & Cracker Company using the *cash basis* of accounting.
  b. Do you think the income statement you prepared for the previous requirement provides a good measure of the reality of the company's performance during June? Explain your reasoning.

7-21. Fire & Cracker Company began operation on June 1, 1994. During its first month of operation, the company had the same seven transactions as noted in 7-20.

REQUIRED:

  a. Prepare a June 1994 multistep income statement for Fire & Cracker Company using the *accrual basis* of accounting.
  b. Do you think the income statement you prepared for the previous requirement provides a good measure of the reality of the company's performance during June? Explain your reasoning.

7-22. Phil Galor and Company began operation on January 2, 1996. During its first month of operation, the company had the following transactions:

- Paid January office rent of $2,000 on January 2.
- Purchased $25,000 of merchandise inventory on January 5. The amount due is payable on February 5.
- Purchased $15,000 of merchandise inventory on January 8. Paid cash at the time of purchase.
- Sold $12,000 of merchandise inventory for $18,000 to a customer on January 16 and received the cash on that date.

- Sold $9,000 of merchandise inventory for $13,500 to a customer on January 26. The sale was on account and the customer has until February 26 to pay.
- Paid February office rent of $2,000 on January 31.

REQUIRED:

a. Prepare a January 1996 multistep income statement for Phil Galor and Company using the *cash basis* of accounting.

b. Prepare a January 1996 multistep income statement for Phil Galor and Company using the *accrual basis* of accounting.

c. Explain in your own words what caused the differences between the income statement prepared under the cash basis and the one prepared under the accrual basis.

d. Which of the two income statement presentations do you think:

(1) provides better information as to cash flow for the month of January?

(2) provides better information as to what Galor earned during the month of January?

(3) better reflects Galor's ability to generate future earnings and cash flow?

7-23. This is a continuation of the Phil Galor and Company problem begun in 7-22. During the month of February 1996, the company had the following transactions:

- Sold all the merchandise inventory it had on hand at the beginning of February for $28,500 cash on February 2.
- On February 5, the company paid the $25,000 it owed for the merchandise inventory it purchased on January 5.
- Purchased $20,000 of merchandise inventory on February 11. Paid cash at the time of purchase.
- Sold the $20,000 of merchandise inventory it had purchased on February 11 for $30,000 to a customer on February 21 and received the cash on that date.
- On February 26, Galor collected the $13,500 from the sale of January 26.

REQUIRED:

a. Prepare a February 1996 multistep income statement for Phil Galor and Company using the *cash basis* of accounting.

b. Prepare a February 1996 multistep income statement for Phil Galor and Company using the *accrual basis* of accounting.

c. Explain in your own words what caused the differences between the income statement prepared under the cash basis and the one prepared under the accrual basis.

d. Which of the two income statement presentations do you think:

   (1) provides better information as to cash flow for the month of February?

   (2) provides better information as to what Galor earned during the month of February?

   (3) better reflects Galor's ability to generate future earnings and cash flow?

7-24. This is a further continuation of the Phil Galor and Company problem. During the months of January and February 1996, the company (which began operations on January 2, 1996) had the following transactions:

- Paid January office rent of $2,000 on January 2.
- Purchased $25,000 of merchandise inventory on January 5. The amount due is payable on February 5.
- Purchased $15,000 of merchandise inventory on January 8. Paid cash at the time of purchase.
- Sold $12,000 of merchandise inventory for $18,000 to a customer on January 16 and received the cash on that date.
- Sold $9,000 of merchandise inventory for $13,500 to a customer on January 26. The sale was on account and the customer has until February 26 to pay.
- Paid February office rent of $2,000 on January 31.
- Sold all the merchandise inventory it had on hand at the beginning of February for $28,500 cash on February 2.
- On February 5, the company paid the $25,000 it owed for the merchandise inventory it purchased on January 5.
- Purchased $20,000 of merchandise inventory on February 11. Paid cash at the time of purchase.
- Sold the $20,000 of merchandise inventory it had purchased on February 11 for $30,000 to a customer on February 21 and received the cash on that date.
- On February 26, Galor collected the $13,500 from the sale of January 26.

REQUIRED:

a. Prepare a multistep income statement for Phil Galor and Company using the *cash basis* of accounting for the two-month period ending February 28, 1996.

b. Prepare a multistep income statement for Phil Galor and Company using the *accrual basis* of accounting for the two-month period ending February 28, 1996.

c. Explain in your own words what caused the differences between the income statement prepared under the cash basis and the one prepared under the accrual basis.

7-25. Baldorama and Company began operation on August 2, 1996. During its first month of operation, the company had the following transactions:

- Paid August office rent of $3,000 on August 2.
- Purchased $35,000 of merchandise inventory on August 5. The amount due is payable on September 5.
- Purchased $25,000 of merchandise inventory on August 8. Paid cash at the time of purchase.
- Sold $22,000 of merchandise inventory for $33,000 to a customer on August 16 and received the cash on that date.
- Sold $10,000 of merchandise inventory for $15,000 to a customer on August 26. The sale was on account and the customer has until September 26 to pay.
- Paid September office rent of $3,000 on August 31.

REQUIRED:

a. Prepare an August 1996 multistep income statement for Baldorama and Company using the *cash basis* of accounting.
b. Prepare an August 1996 multistep income statement for Baldorama and Company using the *accrual basis* of accounting.
c. Explain in your own words what caused the differences between the income statement prepared under the cash basis and the one prepared under the accrual basis.
d. Which of the two income statement presentations do you think
   (1) provides better information as to cash flow for the month of August?
   (2) provides better information as to what Baldorama earned during the month of August?
   (3) better reflects Baldorama's ability to generate future earnings and cash flow?

7-26. This is a continuation of the Baldorama and Company problem begun in 7-25. During the month of September 1996, the company had the following transactions:

- Sold all the merchandise inventory it had on hand at the beginning of September for $42,000 cash on September 2.

- On September 5, the company paid the $35,000 it owed for the merchandise inventory it purchased on August 5.
- Purchased $30,000 of merchandise inventory on September 11. Paid cash at the time of purchase.
- Sold the $30,000 of merchandise inventory it had purchased on September 11 for $45,000 to a customer on September 21 and received the cash on that date.
- On September 26, Baldorama collected the $15,000 from the sale of August 26.

REQUIRED:

a. Prepare a September 1996 multistep income statement for Baldorama and Company using the *cash basis* of accounting.

b. Prepare a September 1996 multistep income statement for Baldorama and Company using the *accrual basis* of accounting.

c. Explain in your own words what caused the differences between the income statement prepared under the cash basis and the one prepared under the accrual basis.

d. Which of the two income statement presentations do you think

   (1) provides better information as to cash flow for the month of September?

   (2) provides better information as to what Baldorama earned during the month of September?

   (3) better reflects Baldorama's ability to generate future earnings and cash flow?

7-27. This is a continuation of the Baldorama and Company problem. During the months of August and September 1996, the company (which began operations on August 2, 1996) had the following transactions:

- Paid August office rent of $3,000 on August 2.
- Purchased $35,000 of merchandise inventory on August 5. The amount due is payable on September 5.
- Purchased $25,000 of merchandise inventory on August 8. Paid cash at the time of purchase.
- Sold $22,000 of merchandise inventory for $33,000 to a customer on August 16 and received the cash on that date.
- Sold $10,000 of merchandise inventory for $15,000 to a customer on August 26. The sale was on account and the customer has until September 26 to pay.
- Paid September office rent of $3,000 on August 31.

- Sold all the merchandise inventory it had on hand at the beginning of September for $42,000 cash on September 2.
- On September 5, the company paid the $35,000 it owed for the merchandise inventory it purchased on August 5.
- Purchased $30,000 of merchandise inventory on September 11. Paid cash at the time of purchase.
- Sold the $30,000 of merchandise inventory it had purchased on September 11 for $45,000 to a customer on September 21 and received the cash on that date.
- On September 26, Baldorama collected the $15,000 from the sale of August 26.

REQUIRED:

a. Prepare a multistep income statement for Baldorama and Company using the *cash basis* of accounting for the two-month period ending September 30, 1996.

b. Prepare a multistep income statement for Baldorama and Company using the *accrual basis* of accounting for the two-month period ending September 30, 1996.

c. Explain in your own words what caused the differences between the income statement prepared under the cash basis and the one prepared under the accrual basis.

7-28. Presented below is a list of items relating to the concepts discussed in this chapter, followed by definitions of those items in scrambled order:

a. Cash basis revenues

b. Accrual basis expenses

c. Immediate recognition

d. Matching concept

e. Title passes to customer

f. Depreciation

g. No direct cause and effect between costs and revenues

h. Cash basis expenses

i. Residual value

j. Accrual basis revenues

1. ____ The amount of the cost of a long-lived asset that is never allocated to the periods supposed benefited.

2. ____ Recognized when cash associated with a sale is received.

3. ____ The situation that causes costs to be either recognized immediately as an expense or allocated to the income statement periods supposed benefited.

4. ____ One of the three evidences that revenue has been earned under accrual accounting.

5. ____ Recognized when the cash associated with a cost is paid.

6. ___ Recognized when there is a legal claim to the cash associated with a sale.

7. ___ An attempt to recognize expenses in the same income statement period as the revenues they generate.

8. ___ Recognized when the benefit is received rather than when the cash is paid.

9. ___ The process of converting the cost of a long-lived item from asset to expense.

10. ___ The treatment for costs where no future benefit can be determined or allocation to future periods serves no useful purpose.

REQUIRED:

Match the letter next to each item on the list with the appropriate definition. Each letter will be used only once.

7-29. Explain the difference between a deferred expense and an accrued expense. A simple definition of these items will not suffice. You should concentrate on what these items *really* mean. Include in your answer at least one example of a deferred expense and one example of an accrued expense.

7-30. Explain why accruals and deferrals are necessary under accrual basis accounting but not cash basis accounting. Your answer should include a discussion of accruals and deferrals as they apply to both revenues and expenses.

7-31. Jumbo Potential, Inc., sold some merchandise inventory for cash during the current month. Unfortunately, the company's accounting clerk simply slipped the cash from the sale into his pocket and did not even record the sale. Jumbo uses accrual accounting.

REQUIRED:

a. Explain how each of the following financial statements would be affected by the accounting clerk's despicable behavior. It will not be sufficient for you to simply use words like "understated" and "overstated." You should approach this requirement as if you were explaining the effects to someone with no knowledge of accounting or financial statements.

   (1) Income statement

   (2) Statement of stockholders' equity

   (3) Balance sheet

b. Briefly explain how your answer would differ if Jumbo used the cash basis of accounting.

8

Challenging Issues Under Accrual Accounting: Long-Lived Depreciable Assets—A Closer Look

Under accrual basis accounting, expenses are recognized in the same income statement period as the revenues they helped generate. This matching principle results in several matters requiring special treatment under accrual accounting. One such matter is the allocation of costs of long-lived assets.

We saw in Chapter 7 that accrual accounting has the disadvantage of being less objective than the cash basis of accounting. Because it recognizes revenues in the periods in which they were earned, and it tries to record expenses in the same periods as the revenues that they helped earn, accrual accounting requires more judgment and estimation than cash accounting does. One of the best examples of the effects of estimates in accrual accounting is the depreciation of long-lived assets.

In this chapter, we will extend our discussion of depreciation by considering several issues that further complicate the depreciation process. First, we will consider the impacts of the estimates made by management. You will recall from the discussion in Chapter 7 that management's estimates of an asset's useful life and its residual value are integral components of the depreciation process.

Second, we will examine the issue of depreciation method choice. Various methods of calculating depreciation are used by different companies. We will explore the effects of these different methods and the impact of management's decision to use one rather than another.

The third major topic of this chapter is the effects of asset disposal. Generally, when a company gets rid of an asset, the transaction results in the recognition of either a gain or a loss. As we will see, the estimates made and the depreciation method chosen will have effects on the determination of gains and losses. Our discussion of this topic will help you learn how to interpret the meanings of gains and losses properly.

The coverage in this chapter is not intended to be an exhaustive treatment of the complex measurement issues surrounding the depreciation process. Instead, it is designed to help you understand the nature of these complexities and how they influence the financial statements prepared using the accrual basis of accounting.

After completing your work on this chapter, you should be able to do the following:

1. Explain the process of depreciating long-lived assets as it pertains to accrual accounting.
2. Determine depreciation expense amounts using both straight-line and double-declining-balance depreciation methods.
3. Describe in your own words the effects on the income statement and balance sheet of using different methods of depreciation.
4. Compare and contrast gains and losses with revenues and expenses.
5. Calculate a gain or loss on the disposal of a long-lived depreciable asset.
6. Explain the effects on a company's financial statements when management disposes of a depreciable asset.
7. Draw appropriate conclusions when presented with gains or losses on an income statement.

DEPRECIATION

As you recall from our discussion in Chapter 7, depreciation is defined as a systematic (methodical) and rational (reasoned) allocation of the cost of a long-lived asset. Over time, the cost of the item is transferred from asset on the balance sheet to expense on the income statement. The purpose of this process is to more closely match the expenses with the revenues they help produce.

If when an item is purchased it is determined that the item will be used to produce revenues in more than one income statement period, the item is not recognized as an expense in the period in which it is purchased. Instead, it is recorded as an asset on the balance sheet. Then, in each year of the asset's *useful* life—useful because the asset is producing revenues—some portion of the cost of the item is recognized as an expense on the income statement for that year. Just how much is recognized as expense in a given year depends on several factors, including the estimates made and the depreciation method used.

The Effect of Estimates

Estimates of the length of the asset's useful life and the amount of its residual value directly affect the amount of depreciation expense recognized each year. For example, assume Marconi-Bozeman, a law firm, purchases a new copy machine for $20,000. If management estimates that the copier has a residual value of $4,000, the asset has a depreciable base of $16,000 (cost less residual value). The amount of depreciation expense recognized each year will be different if the useful life is estimated to be four years than it would be if the useful life is estimated to be three years or five years. By the same token, the depreciable base will be different if the residual value is estimated to be $3,000 rather than $4,000. Exhibit 8-1 shows how different depreciable bases result in different amounts of depreciation expense being recognized each year of the useful life of the machine.

You may have gotten the impression from our brief introduction in Chapter 7 that only machinery, buildings, and equipment are recorded as assets and then depreciated. In fact, in addition to the computer shown in this picture, the cost of the books that make up this law library would very likely be recorded as an asset when purchased and then systematically and rationally allocated (depreciated) to the income statement periods expected to be benefited by their use.

Arthur Tilley/Uniphoto

Exhibit 8-1
Marconi-Bozeman's New $20,000
Copier

Option	Details	Depreciable Base	Annual Expense
Decision 1	Residual value: $4,000 Useful life: 4 years	$16,000	$4,000
Decision 2	Residual value: $4,000 Useful life: 5 years	$16,000	$3,200
Decision 3	Residual value: $3,000 Useful life: 4 years	$17,000	$4,250
Decision 4	Residual value: $3,000 Useful life: 5 years	$17,000	$3,400

DISCUSSION QUESTIONS

8-1. What factors do you think a company should consider in determining the estimated useful life of a long-lived asset?

8-2. How do you think a company would go about determining the estimated residual value of a long-lived asset?

8-3. Consider a long-lived asset with a cost of $30,000. How would net income be affected by using an estimated useful life of four years and an estimated residual value of $5,000 rather than a five-year estimated useful life and a residual value of $5,000? Explain.

The Effect of Different Depreciation Methods

Several different depreciation methods are available to companies. Most companies have more than one depreciable asset, and they are free to choose one method for one type of asset and a totally different method for another. This situation results in many companies using more than one depreciation method. As users of the financial accounting information provided by these companies, it is important that you understand the impact of depreciation method choice on financial statements. To illustrate these effects, we will explore in detail the two most commonly used depreciation methods.

The first method we will explore is straight-line depreciation. Not only is this the simplest method of depreciation, it is also the one most widely used by companies in the United States. Of the 600 companies surveyed by the authors of *Accounting Trends and Techniques*, 95 percent used the straight-line method to calculate depreciation expense reported in their financial statements for the year 1993.

Even though straight-line depreciation is the method of choice in the vast majority of companies, other methods of calculating depreciation expense are used, and it is important for you to see how an alternative method works. Several depreciation methods record a larger amount of depreciation expense

accelerated depreciation methods Those methods that record more depreciation expense in the early years of an asset's life and less in the later years.

in the early years of an asset's life than in the later years. These methods are known collectively as **accelerated depreciation methods**. During 1993, 15 percent of the companies surveyed by the authors of *Accounting Trends and Techniques* used some type of accelerated depreciation. (Remember, some companies use more than one type of method.)

How do companies make the choice between using straight-line depreciation and an accelerated depreciation method? Recall that a basic premise of accrual accounting is that expenses should be matched to the revenues they help produce. Theoretically, then, straight-line depreciation should be used for assets that produce the same amount of revenue in each period of their useful lives, and, conversely, accelerated depreciation methods should be chosen for assets that produce more revenue in the early years and a lesser amount as time goes by. However, the choice of depreciation method is more likely to be made on more practical grounds. Often a depreciation method is chosen for its ease of implementation. This explains the widespread use of the straight-line method. The other major reason for management's choice of one type of depreciation method over another is the anticipated effect on the financial statements during the asset's useful life. Exhibit 8-2 contrasts depreciation expense recorded under the straight-line method to the amount recorded if an accelerated method is used. As we explore the consequences of depreciation method choice, you will become aware of the significant impact this decision can have on the accounting information offered to economic decision makers.

To illustrate the impact of depreciation method choice on a company's financial statements, we will contrast the results of straight-line depreciation with those of an accelerated depreciation method—the double-declining-balance method, which is the most widely used of the accelerated methods. We will explore the application of this method not simply so you can learn the mechanics of how to use it, but more importantly to demonstrate the impact the choice of depreciation method can have on depreciation expense (and therefore reported net income).

Straight-Line Depreciation In Chapter 7, we introduced the concept of depreciation with an example of the straight-line method. To review how straight-line depreciation is calculated, assume Barlow Corporation purchased an asphalt paving machine on January 2, 1995 for a total price of $300,000. Barlow's management estimates the useful life of this machine to be five years, at the end of

Exhibit 8-2
Straight-Line Depreciation versus
Accelerated Depreciation

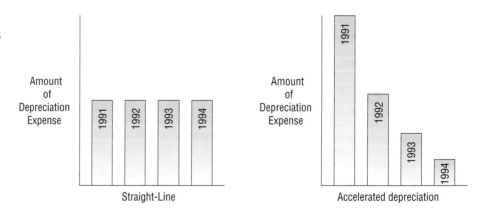

which the machine will be sold for an estimated $25,000. For simplicity, we will assume here that this machine is the only long-lived asset Barlow owns.

Using the straight-line method, Barlow's yearly depreciation expense is $55,000. This amount was calculated by determining the depreciable base of $275,000 ($300,000 cost less the $25,000 estimated residual value) and dividing that base by the five-year estimated useful life ($275,000/5 years = $55,000 per year).

In each of the five years of the asset's useful life, $55,000 of the original cost of the asset will be removed from the asset total on the balance sheet and shown as depreciation expense on the income statement. To illustrate this point, Barlow Corporation's income statements and balance sheets for the years 1995 through 1999 are presented in Exhibit 8-3. For ease of interpreta-

Exhibit 8-3
Barlow Corporation's
Financial Statements
Using Straight-Line
Depreciation

Income Statements

	1995	1996	1997	1998	1999
Sales	$755,000	$755,000	$755,000	$755,000	$755,000
Cost of Goods Sold	422,000	422,000	422,000	422,000	422,000
Gross Margin	$333,000	$333,000	$333,000	$333,000	$333,000
Operating Expenses Other than Depreciation	(236,000)	(236,000)	(236,000)	(236,000)	(236,000)
Depreciation Expense	(55,000)	(55,000)	(55,000)	(55,000)	(55,000)
Net Income	$ 42,000	$ 42,000	$ 42,000	$ 42,000	$ 42,000

Balance Sheets

	1995	1996	1997	1998	1999
ASSETS:					
Cash	$ 50,000	$ 96,000	$157,000	$213,000	$289,000
Accounts Receivable	206,000	257,000	293,000	334,000	355,000
Inventory	77,000	77,000	77,000	77,000	77,000
Machine	300,000	300,000	300,000	300,000	300,000
LESS: Accumulated Depreciation	(55,000)	(110,000)	(165,000)	(220,000)	(275,000)
Total Assets	$578,000	$620,000	$662,000	$704,000	$746,000
LIABILITIES AND STOCKHOLDERS' EQUITY:					
Accounts Payable	$206,000	$206,000	$206,000	$206,000	$206,000
Notes Payable	170,000	170,000	170,000	170,000	170,000
Common Stock	100,000	100,000	100,000	100,000	100,000
Additional Paid-in Capital	10,000	10,000	10,000	10,000	10,000
Retained Earnings	92,000	134,000	176,000	218,000	260,000
Total Liabilities and Stockholders' Equity	$578,000	$620,000	$662,000	$704,000	$746,000

tion, we have held constant most of the items not affected by the depreciation process applied to the machine.

Note that regardless of what else happened in Barlow's operations for the years 1995 through 1999, the amount of depreciation expense each year did not change. This constant depreciation expense is one of the main characteristics of straight-line depreciation. You should also note that there is a direct correlation between the yearly depreciation expense shown on the income statements and the book value of the machine on the balance sheets. You will recall from Chapter 7 that book value is the cost of a long-lived asset less all the depreciation expense recognized since the asset was placed in service (Exhibit 8-4). The total depreciation expense recognized since the asset was put in service is reflected in the balance of accumulated depreciation. Therefore,

Cost − Accumulated Depreciation = Book Value

Each year, as $55,000 of depreciation expense is recognized, the balance in accumulated depreciation increases by that amount, reducing the book value of the machine by that same $55,000. This example illustrates that *straight-line depreciation causes the book value of assets to decline by the same amount each year*. The book value at the end of 1999 is $25,000 ($300,000 − $275,000), which is equal to the estimated residual value. A total of $275,000 depreciation expense has been recorded. That is the amount of the depreciable base, and is therefore the maximum amount of allowable depreciation expense. At this point, the asset is considered to be fully depreciated.

Exhibit 8-4
Book Value

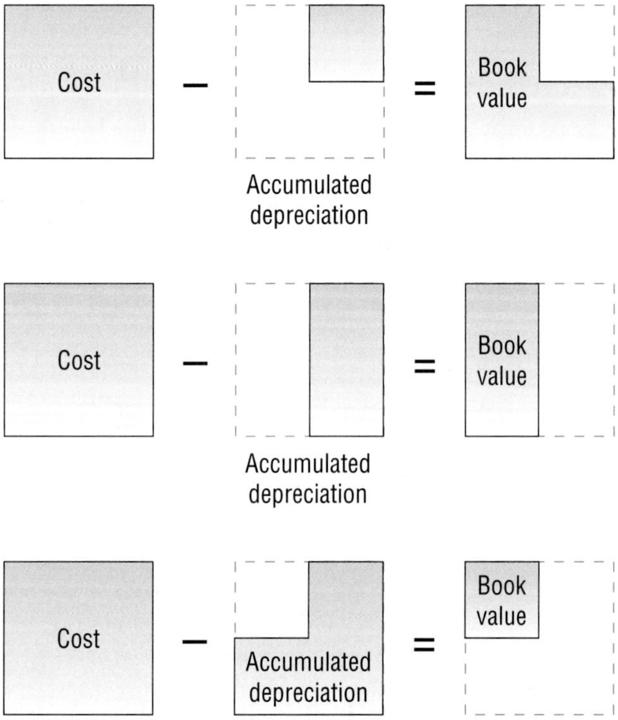

8-4. Refer back to Exhibit 8-1, which illustrates Marconi-Bozeman's four possible sets of estimates relating to its new copy machine. For each decision setting, determine the book value of the asset after three years of depreciation had been recorded.

Obviously, a different estimated useful life or a different estimated residual value would change the amount of yearly depreciation expense. So, too, would the selection of a different method of calculating yearly depreciation expense. To demonstrate how the choice of depreciation method can affect depreciation expense, we will now explore the most widely used accelerated depreciation method.

double-declining-balance method An accelerated depreciation method in which depreciation expense is twice the straight-line percentage multiplied by the book value of the asset.

Double-Declining-Balance Depreciation The **double-declining-balance method** got its name because it calculates depreciation expense at twice the straight-line rate. Rather than using the depreciable base to calculate yearly depreciation expense, as the straight-line method does, double-declining-balance calculates depreciation expense for a given year by applying the percentage rate to the book value of the asset. As a result, the double-declining-balance method ignores the estimated residual value in the depreciation calculation—though, as we will see, companies using this method must be careful not to depreciate an asset beyond its residual value.

There are three simple steps to calculating depreciation using the double-declining-balance method:

1. Figure the straight-line rate in percentages.

   (100% / N, where N = number of years in the asset's useful life.)

2. Double the straight-line percentage.

3. Apply that percentage to the book value of the asset.

As an example, let's apply this method to Barlow's asphalt paving machine. Each step below follows the directions above:

1. 100% / 5 = 20% (per year)

2. 20% X 2 = 40% (per year)

3. 40% X $300,000 = $120,000 (for the first year)

For 1995, Barlow Corporation would record $120,000 depreciation expense. Step 3 of this process uses the book value of the asset. Note that in the first year of the asset's useful life, before any depreciation has been recorded, the book value of the asset equals the cost of the asset.

Exhibit 8-5 shows how yearly depreciation expense would be calculated on Barlow's $300,000 machine using double-declining-balance depreciation and a five-year estimated useful life:

Year	Book Value at the Beginning of the Year		Depreciation Percentage		Yearly Depreciation Expense
1995	$300,000	X	40%	=	$120,000
1996	$180,000	X	40%	=	$ 72,000
1997	$108,000	X	40%	=	$ 43,200
1998	$ 64,800	X	40%	=	$ 25,920
1999	$ 38,880				$ 13,880
Total Depreciation..					$275,000

As you examine the calculations in the exhibit, you should note several points.

First, the book value of the machine declines each year by the amount of depreciation expense recognized that year. For example, the book value at the beginning of 1995 is the full $300,000 cost of the machine. At the beginning of 1996, the book value has dropped to $180,000 ($300,000 cost less $120,000 depreciation for 1995). The book value of the machine continues to drop until, at the beginning of 1999, it is $38,880.

Second, depreciation expense for 1999 ($13,880) is not 40 percent of the book value at the beginning of the year. The amount of depreciation expense in 1999 has been limited to $13,880 because companies are not allowed to depreciate assets beyond the point at which the book value of the asset is equal to its estimated residual value. In other words, the book value of an asset may never be lower than its residual value. This limitation is the same as stating that depreciation expense over the life of the asset cannot exceed the depreciable base (cost – residual value). As shown in Exhibit 8-5, total depreciation over the five-year life of the asset is $275,000. Recall, this amount is the asset's depreciable base.

As the book value declines toward the residual value and the accumulated depreciation rises toward the maximum allowed, we must be careful not to exceed the limits. Since the double-declining-balance method does not take into consideration the residual value as depreciation expense is calculated, this method does not automatically depreciate exactly the allowable amount of depreciation over the life of the asset. In 1999, the depreciation expense recorded is not the amount provided by the calculation using the double-declining-balance method; rather, it is the amount required to reduce the book value of the asset to its estimated residual value. This is the maximum depreciation expense allowed in that period. At that point, the asset is fully depreciated.

The third point you should note about calculations based on the double-declining-balance method is that during an asset's useful life, depreciation expenses start out high but quickly decrease. This rapid decrease is characteristic of all accelerated depreciation methods and has a profound effect on the financial statements of companies using accelerated depreciation methods. Barlow Corporation's income statements for the years 1995 through 1999 and its balance sheets at the end of each of those years using the double-declining-balance method of calculating depreciation are shown in Exhibit 8-6 to illustrate this point. Again, many items not affected by the company's choice of depreciation method have been held constant from year to year.

Exhibit 8-6
Barlow Corporation's Financial Statements Using Double-Declining-Balance Depreciation

Income Statements

	1995	1996	1997	1998	1999
Sales	$755,000	$755,000	$755,000	$755,000	$755,000
Cost of Goods Sold	422,000	422,000	422,000	422,000	422,000
Gross Margin	$333,000	$333,000	$333,000	$333,000	$333,000
Operating Expenses Other than Depreciation	(236,000)	(236,000)	(236,000)	(236,000)	(236,000)
Depreciation Expense	(120,000)	(72,000)	(43,200)	(25,920)	(13,880)
Net Income (Loss)	($ 23,000)	$ 25,000	$ 53,800	$ 71,080	$ 83,120

Balance Sheets

	1995	1996	1997	1998	1999
ASSETS:					
Cash	$ 50,000	$ 96,000	$157,000	$213,000	$289,000
Accounts Receivable	206,000	257,000	293,000	334,000	355,000
Inventory	77,000	77,000	77,000	77,000	77,000
Machine	300,000	300,000	300,000	300,000	300,000
LESS: Accumulated Depreciation	(120,000)	(192,000)	(235,200)	(261,120)	(275,000)
Total Assets	$513,000	$538,000	$591,800	$662,880	$746,000
LIABILITIES AND STOCKHOLDERS' EQUITY:					
Accounts Payable	$206,000	$206,000	$206,000	$206,000	$206,000
Notes Payable	170,000	170,000	170,000	170,000	170,000
Common Stock	100,000	100,000	100,000	100,000	100,000
Additional Paid-in Capital	10,000	10,000	10,000	10,000	10,000
Retained Earnings	27,000	52,000	105,800	176,880	260,000
Total Liabilities and Stockholders' Equity	$513,000	$538,000	$591,800	$662,880	$746,000

8-5. Based on the financial statements of Barlow Corporation presented in Exhibit 8-6, and assuming no dividends were declared during 1995, what was the balance in retained earnings at the beginning of 1995?

8-6. Construct the 1995 statement of retained earnings if Barlow Corporation had not recorded *any* depreciation on its asphalt paving machine.

Understanding the Impact of Depreciation Method Choice When you compare Barlow Corporation's income statements and balance sheets prepared using straight-line depreciation (Exhibit 8-3) with those same statements prepared using double-declining-balance depreciation (Exhibit 8-6), you should notice several differences and similarities:

- There are significant differences in the reported depreciation expense in each of the five years.
- There are significant differences in the reported net income in each of the five years.
- *Total* depreciation expense and *total* net income over the five-year period are exactly the same regardless of which depreciation method is used. The differences occur in the individual years, not over the total five-year period.
- There are significant differences in the amounts of accumulated depreciation on the balance sheets for years 1995 through 1998. The 1999 balance sheet, however, shows exactly the same amount of accumulated depreciation in both presentations. In fact, the 1999 balance sheets in the two presentations are identical.

Neither the straight-line method nor the double-declining-balance method is better than the other. Our purpose in presenting a comparison between them is to make the point that the choice of depreciation method can have a substantial effect on reported net income and on portions of the balance sheet.

8-7. Explain why the 1999 balance sheets for Barlow Corporation, using the two different depreciation methods, are identical, while all five income statements and the first four years' balance sheets are different.

8-8. Compare the amount of cash shown on the Barlow Corporation balance sheets using straight-line depreciation and double-declining-balance depreciation for each given year. Explain your findings.

We have now seen how Barlow's machine would be depreciated using both the straight-line method and the double-declining-balance method. Exhibit 8-7 summarizes the results by presenting a comparison of the depreciation expense, net income, and book value of the machine resulting from use of the two different methods.

Exhibit 8-7

Comparison of Depreciation Expense, Net Income, and Book Value of Barlow's Machine Under the Two Depreciation Methods

	Straight-Line			Double-Declining-Balance		
Year	Depreciation Expense	Net Income	Book Value of Machine	Depreciation Expense	Net Income	Book Value of Machine
1995	$ 55,000	$ 42,000	$245,000	$120,000	($ 23,000)	$180,000
1996	$ 55,000	$ 42,000	$190,000	$ 72,000	$ 25,000	$108,000
1997	$ 55,000	$ 42,000	$135,000	$ 43,200	$ 53,800	$ 64,800
1998	$ 55,000	$ 42,000	$ 80,000	$ 25,920	$ 71,080	$ 38,880
1999	$ 55,000	$ 42,000	$ 25,000	$ 13,880	$ 83,120	$ 25,000
Total	$275,000	$210,000		$275,000	$210,000	

8-9. Assume that Exhibit 8-7 depicts information from two different companies, and you are making an investment decision in 1996, when only the 1995 accounting information in the exhibit is available. How would you make a decision based on the given information?

DISPOSAL OF DEPRECIABLE ASSETS

I deally a long-lived asset would be used for exactly the time originally estimated, after which it would be sold for exactly the residual value originally estimated. In reality, this rarely happens. The actual useful life of an asset may differ greatly from its estimated useful life. In fact, a company may dispose of an asset at any time. There is no law that forces a company to keep an asset, whatever the estimates made of its useful life at the time it was acquired. Conversely, there is nothing that requires a company to dispose of an asset at the end of its depreciable life. There is also no guarantee that a company will receive the estimated residual amount when it does sell the asset. The decision to keep or dispose of an asset should be based on the needs of the business, not on accounting considerations.

As a general rule, disposing of depreciable assets is not an ongoing major or central activity in a company. Rather, this type of transaction is incidental or peripheral to the day-to-day operation of the business. For this reason, any increase in equity from the disposal of depreciable assets is not normally considered revenue, and any decrease in equity associated with this type of trans-

When IBM built its headquarters in Armonk, New York, the cost of the building was recorded as an asset. At the time, the company estimated the building's useful life and its residual value. As the building has been used, the calculated amount of depreciation expense has been recognized on the income statement each year. If IBM sells the building, there will almost certainly be a gain or loss.

Gamma-Liaison, Inc.

action is not normally considered expense. They are considered accounting elements, however, and are reported on the income statement as gains (inflows) and losses (outflows).

Gains and Losses—Important Accounting Elements

In *Statement of Concepts #6*, the FASB defined these two elements as follows:

gains Net inflows resulting from peripheral activities of a company. An example is the sale of an asset for more than its book value.

1. **Gains**. *Increases in equity from peripheral or incidental transactions of an entity and from all other transactions and other events and circumstances affecting the entity except those that result from revenues or investments by owners.* The characteristics of gains are very similar to those of revenues. Both of these elements represent inflows of assets. The distinction between these two elements results from the source of the inflows. Revenues are generated from the major business activity of the company. Gains result from other types of activity.

losses Net outflows resulting from peripheral activities of a company. An example is the sale of an asset for less than its book value.

2. **Losses**. *Decreases in equity from peripheral or incidental transactions of an entity and from all other transactions and other events and circumstances affecting the entity except those that result from expenses or distributions to owners.* Losses are very similar to expenses; both are outflows of assets. As was the case with gains and revenues, losses and expenses differ by source. Expenses are the results of the company's major business activity, whereas losses are incurred as a result of other activities.

Exhibit 8-8
Accounting Elements:
Gains and Losses

Remember that the purpose of the income statement is to provide information about the past performance of a company so that decision makers can better predict the company's future performance. Because gains and losses are incidental to a company's central operations and are usually one-time events, they should not be depended upon to predict the future success of a company's operations. To allow decision makers to evaluate the inflows of assets generated by the major or central operations of a business (revenues) differently from the inflows of assets generated by incidental activities (gains), the two are reported separately on the income statement. The same holds true for the outflow of assets: The outflows required for the major or central operations of a business (expenses) are reported separately from outflows associated with incidental activities (losses) on the income statement.

Although they are reported separately on the income statement, gains affect reported net income in exactly the same way that revenues do, and the effect of losses is exactly the same as that of expenses. The income statement equation introduced in Chapter 6 can be expanded, then, as follows:

$$REVENUES + GAINS - EXPENSES - LOSSES = NET INCOME$$

Calculating Gains and Losses

Calculating gains and losses that result from the disposal of long-lived depreciable assets is straightforward. When a company records this activity, the difference between what the company receives (most often cash) and the book value of the asset sold will be the amount of gain or loss on the sale. Let's return once again to the Barlow Corporation and its $300,000 asphalt paving machine. Assume Barlow depreciated this machine using the straight-line method over a five-year estimated useful life, with an estimated residual value of $25,000 (Exhibit 8-3).

It is now January 2, 2000, and Barlow has decided to sell the machine because it is of no further use to the operation of the company. The machine has a $25,000 book value at the end of 1999 ($300,000 cost – $275,000 accumulated depreciation). How much will Barlow be able to sell it for, do you think? If your answer is $25,000, you should reconsider. $25,000 is the book value of the machine—not its market value. The book value is based on an estimate made way back in 1995. In truth, most potential buyers will neither know nor care about the book value as reflected in Barlow's records. A buyer will pay what she or he thinks the item is worth. This amount will depend on a number of factors, such as the condition of the machine, the state of technology, and what comparable used machines are selling for. It's highly unlikely that Barlow will receive exactly $25,000, but it's hard to say whether it will receive more or less.

Gain on Disposal   Assume Barlow is able to sell the machine for a cash price of $32,000. Because the company has received more than the book value of the machine, there is a gain, which can be calculated as $32,000 cash received – $25,000 book value = a $7,000 gain. The $7,000 will be reported as a gain on the income statement for the year 2000. Shown in Exhibit 8-9 are Barlow's income statements for the years 1999 and 2000 and its balance sheets at the end of each of those years, reflecting a $7,000 gain on the disposal of its machine.

Exhibit 8-9

Barlow Corporation's Financial
Statements for 1999 and 2000
Reflecting a Gain on the Sale
of Its Machine

BARLOW CORPORATION
Income Statements

	1999	2000
Sales	$755,000	$941,000
Cost of Goods Sold	422,000	525,000
Gross Margin	$333,000	$416,000
Operating Expenses		
Other Than Depreciation	(236,000)	(319,000)
Depreciation Expense	(55,000)	-0-
Operating Income	$ 42,000	$ 97,000
Gain on Sale of Machine	-0-	7,000
Net Income	$ 42,000	$104,000

Balance Sheets

	1999	2000
ASSETS:		
Cash	$289,000	$225,000
Accounts Receivable	355,000	313,000
Inventory	77,000	172,000
Machine	300,000	-0-
LESS: Accumulated Depreciation	(275,000)	-0-
Total Assets	$746,000	$710,000
LIABILITIES AND		
STOCKHOLDERS' EQUITY:		
Accounts Payable	$206,000	$216,000
Notes Payable	170,000	20,000
Common Stock	100,000	100,000
Additional Paid-in Capital	10,000	10,000
Retained Earnings	260,000	364,000
Total Liabilities and Stockholders' Equity	$746,000	$710,000

As you examine these financial statements, there are several points you should note:

■ On the income statement for the year 2000, the $7,000 gain is shown in a different place than revenues from Barlow's ongoing major operations.

■ The $7,000 gain has exactly the same effect on net income as the revenues from Barlow's ongoing major operations on the income statement for the year 2000.

■ Both the cost of the machine ($300,000) and the accumulated depreciation ($275,000) have been removed from the balance sheet at the end of the year 2000.

8-10. Note that Barlow Corporation's income statements are presented in a multistep format in Exhibit 8-9. What specific items on the income statements are unique to this format and would not appear on a single-step statement?

Loss on Disposal   Now assume Barlow is able to sell the machine for a cash price of only $19,000. Because the company received less than the book value of the machine, there is a loss, which can be calculated as $19,000 cash received – $25,000 book value = a $6,000 loss. The $6,000 will be reported as a loss on the income statement for the year 2000. Exhibit 8-10 shows Barlow's income statements for the years 1999 and 2000 and its balance sheets at the end of each of those years, reflecting a $6,000 loss on the disposal of its machine.

As you study these financial statements, there are several points you should note:

■ On the income statement for the year 2000, the $6,000 loss is shown in a different place than expenses required to support Barlow's ongoing major operations.

■ The $6,000 loss has exactly the same effect on net income as the expenses required to support Barlow's ongoing major operations on the income statement for the year 2000.

■ Both the cost of the machine ($300,000) and the accumulated depreciation ($275,000) have been removed from the balance sheet at the end of the year 2000.

In our examples of both a gain and a loss, we have assumed that Barlow was able to sell its machine for some amount of cash. However, there are times when an asset has no market value and must simply be abandoned. If this were the case with the Barlow machine, it would result in a loss of $25,000 ($0 cash received – $25,000 book value = a $25,000 loss).

Exhibit 8-10
Barlow Corporation's Financial
Statements for 1999 and 2000
Reflecting a Loss on the Sale
of Its Machine

BARLOW CORPORATION
Income Statements

	1999	2000
Sales	$755,000	$941,000
Cost of Goods Sold	422,000	525,000
Gross Margin	$333,000	$416,000
Operating Expenses		
Other Than Depreciation	(236,000)	(319,000)
Depreciation Expense	(55,000)	-0-
Operating Income	$ 42,000	$ 97,000
Loss on Sale of Machine	-0-	(6,000)
Net Income	$ 42,000	$ 91,000

Balance Sheets

	1999	2000
ASSETS:		
Cash	$289,000	$212,000
Accounts Receivable	355,000	313,000
Inventory	77,000	172,000
Machine	300,000	-0-
LESS: Accumulated Depreciation	(275,000)	-0-
Total Assets	$746,000	$697,000
LIABILITIES AND		
STOCKHOLDERS' EQUITY:		
Accounts Payable	$206,000	$216,000
Notes Payable	170,000	20,000
Common Stock	100,000	100,000
Additional Paid-in Capital	10,000	10,000
Retained Earnings	260,000	351,000
Total Liabilities and Stockholders' Equity	$746,000	$697,000

DISCUSSION QUESTIONS

8-11. Look again at Barlow Corporation's income statements and balance sheets in Exhibit 8-10. What
items on the financial statements for the year 2000
would be different (and by how much) if Barlow had
simply abandoned the machine?

Disposal with No Gain or Loss   Now let's assume Barlow is able to sell the machine for a cash price of $25,000. Because the company received exactly the book value of the machine, there is neither a gain nor a loss ($25,000 cash received − $25,000 book value = $0 gain or loss). As Exhibit 8-11 shows, the sale of the machine will not directly affect the income statement for the year 2000, but it will affect the balance sheet.

As you examine these statements, there are two points you should note:

■ There is no gain or loss from the disposal of the machine on the income statement for the year 2000.
■ Both the cost of the machine ($300,000) and the accumulated depreciation ($275,000) have been removed from the balance sheet at the end of the year 2000.

Exhibit 8-11

Barlow Corporation's Financial Statements for 1999 and 2000 Reflecting the Sale of Its Machine for Book Value

BARLOW CORPORATION
Income Statements

	1999	2000
Sales	$755,000	$941,000
Cost of Goods Sold	422,000	525,000
Gross Margin	$333,000	$416,000
Operating Expenses		
Other than Depreciation	(236,000)	(319,000)
Depreciation Expense	(55,000)	-0-
Operating Income	$ 42,000	$ 97,000
Gain (Loss) on Sale of Machine	-0-	-0-
Net Income	$ 42,000	$ 97,000

Balance Sheets

	1999	2000
ASSETS:		
Cash	$289,000	$218,000
Accounts Receivable	355,000	313,000
Inventory	77,000	172,000
Machine	300,000	-0-
LESS: Accumulated Depreciation	(275,000)	-0-
Total Assets	$746,000	$703,000
LIABILITIES AND		
STOCKHOLDERS' EQUITY:		
Accounts Payable	$206,000	$216,000
Notes Payable	170,000	20,000
Common Stock	100,000	100,000
Additional Paid-in Capital	10,000	10,000
Retained Earnings	260,000	357,000
Total Liabilities and Stockholders' Equity	$746,000	$703,000

Thus far you have seen how to calculate gains and losses, as well as how these elements impact a company's financial statements. It is now time for you to learn how to properly interpret gains and losses when they are a part of the accounting information made available during the decision-making process.

UNDERSTANDING THE TRUE MEANING OF GAINS AND LOSSES

Let's assume there are two companies whose business activities are identical in almost all respects. The companies have the exact same sales for the year, and all their operating expenses (except depreciation) are the same.

We'll call the two companies in this example Straight-Line Movers and Accelerated Movers. Both companies purchased a fleet of trucks for $228,000 on January 2, 1994. In addition, both companies estimated a useful life of four years and a residual value of $92,000 for the trucks. Because Straight-Line Movers uses—you guessed it—straight-line depreciation and Accelerated Movers uses the double-declining-balance (accelerated) method, we would expect to see differences in their financial statements. The 1994 income statement and balance sheet for each company appear in Exhibit 8-12 on page 248.

DISCUSSION QUESTIONS

Refer to Exhibit 8-12 to answer the following questions:

8-12. The amount of depreciation expense recorded by each company is given. Provide computations to explain how these amounts were determined.

8-13. The financial statements indicate four items on the income statements that differ between the companies. There are six items on the balance sheets that differ between the companies. Identify each item and explain the cause of the difference.

8-14. Assuming that no dividends were paid by either company, what was the balance in retained earnings on January 1, 1994, for each company?

8-15. What are the depreciation expense and accumulated depreciation for each company? Are these two items always the same?

8-16. What are the accumulated depreciation and book value of the trucks for each company? Why are Accelerated Mover's figures the same, while Straight-Line's figures differ?

Exhibit 8-12
1994 Financial Statements of Straight-Line Movers and Accelerated Movers

Income Statements
For the Year Ending December 31, 1994

	Straight-Line Movers		Accelerated Movers	
Sales	$769,000		$769,000	
LESS: Cost of Goods Sold	295,500		295,500	
Gross Margin		$473,500		$473,500
Wages Expense	$ 67,500		$ 67,500	
Utilities Expense	31,000		31,000	
Depreciation Expense	34,000		114,000	
Total Operating Expenses		(132,500)		(212,500)
Operating Income		$341,000		$261,000
Other Revenues and Expenses:				
Interest Expense		(120,000)		(120,000)
Net Income		$221,000		$141,000

Balance Sheets
December 31, 1994

	Straight-Line Movers		Accelerated Movers	
Assets:				
Cash		$226,000		$226,000
Accounts Receivable		198,000		198,000
Inventory		223,000		223,000
Trucks	$228,000		$228,000	
Accumulated Depreciation	(34,000)		(114,000)	
Trucks, Net		194,000		114,000
TOTAL ASSETS		$841,000		$761,000
Liabilities:				
Accounts Payable	$ 22,000		$ 22,000	
Notes Payable	61,000		61,000	
Total Liabilities		$ 83,000		$ 83,000
Owners' Equity:				
Common Stock	$200,000		$200,000	
Additional Paid-in Capital	194,000		194,000	
Contributed Capital	$394,000		$394,000	
Retained Earnings	364,000		284,000	
Total Shareholders' Equity		758,000		678,000
TOTAL LIABILITIES				
AND OWNERS' EQUITY		$841,000		$761,000

The impact of the choice of depreciation method becomes even more evident over time. Exhibit 8-13, on page 250, shows the income statements and balance sheets of Straight-Line Movers and Accelerated Movers at the end of 1995. Again, we have held constant the items that are not affected by the use of different depreciation methods.

DISCUSSION QUESTIONS

8-17. Provide computations and an explanation to show how Accelerated Movers' depreciation expense amount of $22,000 was determined. (Exhibit 8-13)

A more profound effect of depreciation method differences than the differences occurring on the financial statements as the companies record depreciation can be shown. Suppose that Straight-Line Movers and Accelerated Movers both decide to sell their trucks on December 31, 1995. The assets being sold are identical in age, condition, and market value. Each company receives $150,000 cash in exchange for its trucks. The $150,000 is the market value of the trucks on the day of the sale. This transaction would still require the companies to record depreciation for the year, just as it was reflected in the previous statements.

DISCUSSION QUESTIONS

8-18. Were the companies wise to sell the assets? Did they get "a good deal"? What information might you want before deciding whether the companies made a smart move?

Even though the actual business activity performed by Straight-Line Movers and Accelerated Movers is identical, the presentation of the results of the sale on their financial statements would be quite different, as is shown in Exhibit 8-14 on page 251.

Exhibit 8-13
1995 Financial Statements of Straight-Line Movers and Accelerated Movers

Income Statements
For the Year Ending December 31, 1995

	Straight-Line Movers		Accelerated Movers	
Sales	$769,000		$769,000	
LESS: Cost of Goods Sold	295,500		295,500	
Gross Margin		$473,500		$473,500
Wages Expense	$ 67,500		$ 67,500	
Utilities Expense	31,000		31,000	
Depreciation Expense	34,000		22,000	
Total Operating Expenses		(132,500)		(120,500)
Operating Income		$341,000		$353,000
Other Revenues and Expenses:				
Interest Expense		(120,000)		(120,000)
Net Income		$221,000		$233,000

Balance Sheets
December 31, 1995

	Straight-Line Movers		Accelerated Movers	
Assets:				
Cash		$ 426,000		$426,000
Accounts Receivable		253,000		253,000
Inventory		223,000		223,000
Trucks	$228,000		$228,000	
Accumulated Depreciation	(68,000)		(136,000)	
Trucks, Net		160,000		92,000
TOTAL ASSETS		$1,062,000		$994,000
Liabilities:				
Accounts Payable	$ 22,000		$ 22,000	
Notes Payable	61,000		61,000	
Total Liabilities		$ 83,000		$ 83,000
Owners' Equity:				
Common Stock	$200,000		$200,000	
Additional Paid-in Capital	194,000		194,000	
Contributed Capital	$394,000		$394,000	
Retained Earnings	585,000		517,000	
Total Shareholders' Equity		979,000		911,000
TOTAL LIABILITIES AND OWNERS' EQUITY		$1,062,000		$994,000

Exhibit 8-14
Impact of the Sale of Trucks at the End of 1995 on the Financial Statements of Straight-Line
Movers and Accelerated Movers

Income Statements
For the Year Ending December 31, 1995

	Straight-Line Movers		Accelerated Movers	
Sales	$769,000		$769,000	
LESS: Cost of Goods Sold	295,500		295,500	
Gross Margin		$473,500		$473,500
Wages Expense	$ 67,500		$ 67,500	
Utilities Expense	31,000		31,000	
Depreciation Expense	34,000		22,000	
Total Operating Expenses		(132,500)		(120,500)
Operating Income		$341,000		$353,000
Other Revenues and Expenses:				
Gain on Sale of Trucks				58,000
Loss on Sale of Trucks		(10,000)		
Interest Expense		(120,000)		(120,000)
Net Income		$211,000		$291,000

Balance Sheets
December 31, 1995

	Straight-Line Movers		Accelerated Movers	
Assets:				
Cash	$576,000		$576,000	
Accounts Receivable	253,000		253,000	
Inventory	223,000		223,000	
TOTAL ASSETS		$1,052,000		$1,052,000
Liabilities:				
Accounts Payable	$ 22,000		$ 22,000	
Notes Payable	61,000		61,000	
Total Liabilities		$ 83,000		$ 83,000
Owners' Equity:				
Common Stock	$200,000		$200,000	
Additional Paid-in Capital	194,000		194,000	
Contributed Capital	$394,000		$394,000	
Retained Earnings	575,000		575,000	
Total Shareholders' Equity		969,000		969,000
TOTAL LIABILITIES				
AND OWNERS' EQUITY		$1,052,000		$1,052,000

The most obvious impact of depreciation method choice shown on the companies' income statements and balance sheets above is the result of the sale. Note that Straight-Line Movers recorded a $10,000 loss, but the same activity resulted in a $58,000 gain for Accelerated Movers. The moral of the story? Smart financial statement users are not overly impressed by gains or overly alarmed by losses. Remember, these elements are merely a result of the difference between the book value and the market value of assets sold. Don't assume that if a gain is shown on the income statement, the sale was "good for business," or that if a loss is shown, management made a bad move. In our example, there is not enough information available to determine whether the sale of the trucks for $150,000 was a wise business decision or a poor one. Clearly, though, the sale was no wiser for one company than for the other.

Also note that the retained earnings balance shown by Straight-Line Movers and Accelerated Movers in Exhibit 8-14 is the same—$575,000. As you know, over the time that a long-lived asset is owned, its cost is transferred from asset on the balance sheet to expense on the income statement through the process of depreciation. By claiming a large amount of depreciation in the early years of the asset's life—as happens when using an accelerated method of calculating depreciation—a company lowers its net income for those years. In this way, the company also lowers the asset's book value, which then may be much lower than the asset's market value. In our example, the book value of Accelerated's trucks was so low that the company registered quite a large gain on their sale. Conversely, if a company claims a smaller amount of depreciation—as happens when using the straight-line method—the asset's book value will be higher. In our example, the book value of Straight-Line Mover's trucks was so high at the time of sale that the company incurred a loss.

Exhibit 8-15 illustrates how the method of depreciation affects net income in our example. Note that in a specific period, the two companies experience differences, but over the entire period of ownership for the trucks, the method of depreciation used has no effect.

Exhibit 8-15

Impact of Method of Depreciation on the Net Income of Straight-Line Movers and Accelerated Movers

		Straight-Line Movers	Accelerated Movers
1994	Depreciation Expense (Reduction of Net Income)	($ 34,000)	($114,000)
1995	Depreciation Expense (Reduction of Net Income)	(34,000)	(22,000)
1995	Result of Sale (Gain or Loss)	(10,000)	58,000
	TOTAL IMPACT OF ASSET OWNERSHIP	($ 78,000)	($ 78,000)

Exhibit 8-15 illustrates why it isn't wise for decision makers to focus solely on the impact of gains and losses. Clearly, the result of the sale of an asset is only one component of the overall impact that ownership of that asset has had on the company over time.

As you can see from our discussion of the items presented in this chapter, the depreciation and disposal of long-lived depreciable assets can have a significant impact on a company's reported net income for a given year during the useful life of an asset. The issues surrounding depreciation are complex, and users of financial statements must have some understanding of them if they hope to be able to use financial statements for predicting a company's future or assessing its past performance.

Many issues besides depreciation have complicating effects under the accrual basis of accounting. We will continue our discussion of these complications in Chapter 9, where we consider issues surrounding the sale of merchandise inventory.

SUMMARY

Depreciation is the process of allocating the cost of long-lived assets to the periods in which they help to earn revenues. When an asset is purchased, its cost is recorded on the balance sheet. As time passes, the cost is transferred from an asset on the balance sheet to an expense on the income statement. The recording of depreciation expense accomplishes this transfer. The amount of accumulated depreciation for an asset represents all the depreciation expense related to that asset that has been recognized thus far. Accumulated depreciation is reported on the balance sheet as a reduction of the asset cost.

There are several acceptable depreciation methods. Calculating depreciation expense is easiest using the straight-line method. This method allocates depreciation expense evenly over the useful life of the asset. Accelerated depreciation methods recognize a greater amount of depreciation expense in the early years of an asset's life and a smaller amount in the later years. One such method is double-declining-balance.

The choice of depreciation methods affects companies' financial statements. In total, over the useful life of an asset, straight-line and double-declining-balance depreciation methods record the same amount of depreciation expense. However, in any particular period, different depreciation methods usually result in different amounts of depreciation expense, and this causes a difference in reported net income. Because the amount of depreciation expense affects accumulated depreciation, the balance sheets of companies using different depreciation methods will also be different during most of the life of the assets.

From time to time, companies sell some of their depreciable assets, and these transactions often result in gains or losses. Gains and losses affect net income in a manner similar to that of revenues and expenses, but they are shown as separate items on the income statement. Gains and losses result from activities peripheral to the major activity of the company; revenues and expenses are direct results of the company's primary business activity.

An asset's book value is its cost less the amount of its accumulated depreciation. If an asset is sold for more than its book value, the transaction results in a gain. Conversely, selling an asset for less than its book value results in a loss.

If the disposal of an asset results in a gain or loss, that outcome is reported on the income statement. If, however, an asset is sold for exactly its book value, the transaction results in no gain or loss. In any case, when a company disposes of an asset, both the asset and its corresponding accumulated depreciation account are removed from the balance sheet.

If the sale of an asset results in a gain, it cannot be assumed that this was a "wise move" or that management received a good price for the asset. A gain simply indicates that the asset was sold for more than its book value. Conversely, disposing of an asset at a loss is not necessarily an indication of poor management. Losses result when less than the book value is received for the asset. Book values of assets are affected by depreciation method choice and estimates of the useful life and residual value of the asset. Selling price is determined by what the buyer is willing to pay for the asset. Gains and losses are merely an indication of the relationship between book value and selling price. They should not be interpreted as anything more than that.

Key Terms

accelerated depreciation methods Those methods that record more depreciation expense in the early years of an asset's life and less in the later years. (p. 232)

double-declining-balance method An accelerated depreciation method in which depreciation expense is twice the straight-line percentage multiplied by the book value of the asset. (p. 235)

gains Net inflows resulting from peripheral activities of a company. An example is the sale of an asset for more than its book value. (p. 241)

losses Net outflows resulting from peripheral activities of a company. An example is the sale of an asset for less than its book value. (p. 241)

Review the Facts

A. Provide three examples of long-lived depreciable assets.

B. In your own words, describe the depreciation process.

C. What two estimates made by management will affect the amount of depreciation recorded each period?

D. What is the depreciable base of an asset?

E. Explain what is meant by an accelerated depreciation method.

F. Theoretically, in what situation is an accelerated depreciation method the appropriate choice?

G. Explain how the amount of depreciation expense is calculated using straight-line depreciation.

H. What is meant by an asset's book value?

I. What does the amount of accumulated depreciation represent?

J. In your own words, describe the process of determining depreciation expense using the double-declining-balance method.

K. Compared to straight-line depreciation, what is the effect of an accelerated depreciation method on the balance sheet? On the income statement?

L. Regardless of what depreciation method is used, at what point is an asset considered "fully depreciated"?

M. On what financial statement do gains and losses appear?

N. What is the difference between a revenue and a gain? A loss and an expense?

O. How is a gain or loss calculated?

P. What effect does the disposal of an asset that results in no gain or loss have on the income statement? On the balance sheet?

APPLY WHAT YOU HAVE LEARNED

8-19. Pat Garcia and Company has just purchased a lathe for use in its manufacturing operation. The machine cost $50,000, has a five-year estimated useful life, and will be depreciated using the straight-line method. The only thing remaining to be determined before yearly depreciation expense can be calculated is the estimated residual value. The alternatives are:

1. $5,000 estimated residual value.

2. $10,000 estimated residual value.

3. $15,000 estimated residual value.

REQUIRED:

a. Calculate the yearly depreciation expense for the new lathe under each of the alternatives given.

b. Which of the three alternatives will result in the highest net income?

c. How long will the new lathe be useful to Garcia and Company?

8-20. Winken, Blinken & Nod, Inc. has just purchased a minicomputer for use in its manufacturing operation. The machine cost $75,000, has a four-year estimated useful life, and will be depreciated using the straight-line method. The only thing remaining to be determined before yearly depreciation expense can be calculated is the estimated residual value. The alternatives are:

1. $7,500 estimated residual value.

2. $12,500 estimated residual value.

3. $17,500 estimated residual value.

REQUIRED:

   a. Calculate the yearly depreciation expense for the new minicomputer under each of the alternatives given.

   b. Which of the three alternatives will result in the highest net income?

   c. How long will the new minicomputer be useful to Winken, Blinken, and Nod, Inc.?

8-21. Brent Bird Publishing Company purchased a new printing press for a total installed cost of $350,000. The printing press will be depreciated straight-line, in accordance with corporate policy. Roberta Swensen, the corporate controller, is trying to decide on an estimated useful life and an estimated residual value for the asset. The alternatives are:

1. A six-year estimated useful life with a $20,000 estimated residual value.

2. A five-year estimated useful life with a $50,000 estimated residual value.

3. A four-year estimated useful life with a $70,000 estimated residual value.

REQUIRED:

   a. Calculate the yearly depreciation expense for the new printing press under each of the alternatives given.

   b. Which of the three alternatives will result in the lowest yearly net income?

   c. What should be the deciding factor in selecting among the three alternatives?

8-22. Taco and The Chiefs Restaurant Company purchased a new walk-in freezer for a total installed cost of $250,000. The walk-in freezer will be depreciated straight-line, in accordance with corporate policy. Joey Mountain, the corporate controller, is trying to decide on an estimated useful life and an estimated residual value for the asset. The alternatives are:

1. A five-year estimated useful life with a $10,000 estimated residual value.

2. A four-year estimated useful life with a $25,000 estimated residual value.

3. A three-year estimated useful life with a $50,000 estimated residual value.

REQUIRED:

a. Calculate the yearly depreciation expense for the new printing press under each of the alternatives given.

b. Which of the three alternatives will result in the lowest yearly net income?

c. What should be the deciding factor in selecting among the three alternatives?

8-23. Anatole Company purchased a high-tech assembler on January 2, 1995, for a total cost of $600,000. The assembler has an estimated useful life to the company of five years. Anatole thinks it will be able to sell the used assembler for $50,000. The company has decided to depreciate the new assembler using the double-declining-balance method.

REQUIRED:

a. Prepare a schedule showing the amount of depreciation expense for each of the five years of the estimated useful life.

b. What will be the book value of the assembler at the end of the five-year estimated useful life?

c. What does book value represent?

8-24. GADO Company purchased an earth-moving machine on January 2, 1996, for a total cost of $450,000. The earth-mover has an estimated useful life to the company of five years. GADO thinks it will be able to sell the used earth-mover for $40,000. The company has decided to depreciate the new earth-mover using the double-declining-balance method.

REQUIRED:

a. Prepare a schedule showing the amount of depreciation expense for each of the five years of the estimated useful life.

b. What will be the book value of the assembler at the end of the five-year estimated useful life?

c. What does book value represent?

8-25. Wanda Company purchased a very sophisticated stamping machine on January 2, 1996, for $480,000. The estimated useful life of the stamping machine is five years. The machine has an estimated residual value of $40,000.

REQUIRED:

a. Calculate the yearly depreciation expense for the stamping machine assuming the company uses the straight-line depreciation method.

b. Prepare a schedule showing the amount of depreciation expense for each of the five years of the estimated useful life assuming the company uses the double-declining-balance depreciation method.

8-26. WebCo Company purchased a very sophisticated pasteurizing machine on January 2, 1996, for $375,000. The estimated useful life of the machine is four years. The machine has an estimated residual value of $40,000.

REQUIRED:

a. Calculate the yearly depreciation expense for the machine assuming the company uses the straight-line depreciation method.

b. Prepare a schedule showing the amount of depreciation expense for each of the four years of the estimated useful life assuming the company uses the double-declining-balance depreciation method.

8-27. Bandicoot, Inc., purchased a fleet of delivery trucks on January 2, 1996, for $350,000. The estimated useful life of the vehicles is four years, after which Bandicoot thinks it will be able to sell the entire fleet for $25,000.

REQUIRED:

a. Calculate the yearly depreciation expense for the fleet of vehicles assuming the company uses the straight-line depreciation method.

b. Prepare a schedule showing the amount of depreciation expense for each of the four years of the estimated useful life assuming the company uses the double-declining balance depreciation method.

c. Address the following questions:

   (1) Double-declining-balance calculates depreciation at twice the straight-line rate. Why is the amount of depreciation expense in 1996 under double-declining-balance not exactly twice the amount under straight-line for 1996?

   (2) Over the four-year estimated useful life of the vehicles, how much depreciation expense will be charged against income using the straight-line method? How much will be charged against income using the double-declining-balance method?

8-28. Harry and Harriet, Inc., purchased a fleet of delivery trucks on January 2, 1996, for $500,000. The estimated useful life of the vehicles is three years, after which Harry and Harriet, Inc., thinks it will be able to sell the entire fleet for $35,000.

a. Calculate the yearly depreciation expense for the fleet of vehicles assuming the company uses the straight-line depreciation method.

b. Prepare a schedule showing the amount of depreciation expense for each of the three years of the estimated useful life assuming the company uses the double-declining-balance depreciation method.

c. Address the following questions:

   (1) Double-declining-balance calculates depreciation at twice the straight-line rate. Why is the amount of depreciation expense in 1996 under double-declining-balance not exactly twice the amount under straight-line for 1996?

   (2) Over the three-year estimated useful life of the vehicles, how much depreciation expense will be charged against income using the straight-line method? How much will be charged against income using the double-declining-balance method?

8-29. Shubert Company purchased a machine in January of 1993 and paid $200,000 for it. When originally purchased, the machine had an estimated useful life of five years and an estimated residual value of $25,000. The company uses straight-line depreciation. It is now January 2, 1996, and the company has decided to dispose of the machine.

REQUIRED:

a. Calculate the book value of the machine as of December 31, 1995.

b. Calculate the gain or loss on the sale of the machine assuming Shubert sells it for $102,000.

c. Calculate the gain or loss on the sale of the machine assuming Shubert sells it for $25,000.

8-30. Munn Company purchased a machine in January of 1994 and paid $300,000 for it. When originally purchased, the machine had an estimated useful life of four years and an estimated residual value of $20,000. The company uses straight-line depreciation. It is now January 2, 1996, and the company has decided to dispose of the machine.

REQUIRED:

a. Calculate the book value of the machine as of December 31, 1995.

b. Calculate the gain or loss on the sale of the machine assuming Munn sells it for $172,000.

c. Calculate the gain or loss on the sale of the machine assuming Munn sells it for $25,000.

8-31. Lydia and Lynette are twin sisters. Each of them has her own company. Three years ago, on the same day, they each purchased copy machines for use by their companies. The machines were identical in every way and cost exactly the same amount ($28,000). The copiers had the same estimated useful life (five years) and the same estimated residual value ($3,000). The only difference was the depreciation method chosen. Lydia chose to depreciate her copier using straight-line, while Lynette selected an accelerated depreciation method.

Owing to rapid technological developments in copiers, Lydia decided at the end of two years to sell her old copier and buy a new one. Lynette decided to do the same thing. In fact, they each received exactly the same amount when they sold their machines ($16,500). Later, while they were having lunch together, Lynette mentioned that when she old her copier, she had a gain of more than $6,000 on the sale. Lydia didn't say anything, but she thought something was fishy because she knew she had sold her copier for exactly the same amount Lynette had, yet the sale of her copier had resulted in a loss of $1,500.

REQUIRED:

Explain how Lydia could have had a loss of $1,500 on the sale of her copier, while Lynette had a sizable gain.

8-32. Presented below is a list of items relating to the concepts discussed in this chapter, followed by definitions of those items in scrambled order.

a. Accelerated depreciation   **f.** Straight-line depreciation

b. Book value   **g.** Gains

c. Gain on sale of asset   **h.** Loss on sale of asset

d. Losses   **i.** Depreciable base

e. Estimated useful life

1. ____ One of the factors determining how much of an asset's cost will be allocated to the periods supposed benefited.

2. ____ Net outflows resulting from peripheral activities.

3. ____ More of the cost of a long-lived asset is converted to expense in the early years of its life than in later years.

4. ____ The cost of a long-lived asset less the estimated residual value.

5. ____ Results when a depreciable asset is sold for more than its book value.

6. ___ An equal amount of a long-lived asset's cost is converted to expense in each year of its useful life.

7. ___ Net inflows resulting from peripheral activities.

8. ___ The cost of a long-lived depreciable asset less its accumulated depreciation.

9. ___ Results when a depreciable asset is sold for less than its book value.

REQUIRED:

Match the letter next to each item on the list with the appropriate definition. Each letter will be used only once.

8-33. In Exhibit 8-6 (on page 237), Barlow Corporation's financial statements based on the company's use of double-declining-balance depreciation are shown. Use the income statements and balance sheets presented in the exhibit as a basis for completing the following requirements:

REQUIRED:

a. Prepare statements of retained earnings for Barlow Corporation as of the end of 1996, 1997, 1998, and 1999.

b. What can you conclude about the dividend policy of Barlow Corporation from the information provided and your response to Requirement a?

c. If no depreciation had been recorded, how would the statements of retained earnings been different?

8-34. Cathie Barker Company opened for business on January 2, 1996. During its first month of operation, the company had the following transactions:

Jan 2:   Purchased a truck for $10,000 and paid cash. The truck has an estimated useful life of three years. The company estimates the truck's residual value to be $1,000, and uses straight-line depreciation.

Jan 2:   Purchased $40,000 of merchandise inventory on account. Payment in full is due February 2.

Jan 3:   Paid January office rent of $2,500.

Jan 5:   Purchased $15,000 of merchandise inventory and paid cash on that date.

Jan 10: Sold $12,000 of merchandise inventory for $25,000 to a customer and received the cash on that date.

Jan 20: Sold $7,000 of merchandise inventory for $11,000. The sale was on account and the customer has until February 20 to pay.

Jan 24: Paid miscellaneous January operating expenses totaling $8,000.

Jan 31: Received bills for utilities, advertising, and phone service totaling $1,200. All these bills were for services performed in January. They will all be paid the first week in February.

Use the January 1996 income statements for Barker Company prepared under the cash and accrual bases of accounting (page 263) to complete the following requirements:

REQUIRED:

a. Why are the cost-of-goods-sold amounts on the two income statements different? Explain your reasoning.

b. Reality is that Barker purchased $55,000 of merchandise inventory during January 1996. Under the accrual basis of accounting, the company has properly expensed $19,000 of that inventory as cost of goods sold for the month. Where (if anywhere) would the company show the remaining $36,000 of merchandise inventory? Explain your reasoning.

c. Reality is that Barker purchased $55,000 of merchandise inventory during January 1996. Under the cash basis of accounting, the company has properly expensed $15,000 of that inventory as cost of goods sold for the month. Where (if anywhere) would the company show the remaining $40,000 of merchandise inventory? Explain your reasoning.

d. Both income statements show an expense related to the truck purchased on January 2, 1996. How were the amounts on each income statement determined? Include in your answer what the amounts represent and why the cost of the truck is treated as it is.

BARKER COMPANY
Income Statement
For the Month Ending January 31, 1996
Cash Basis

Sales	$25,000	
LESS: Cost of Goods Sold	15,000	
Gross Margin		$10,000
Operating Expenses:		
Truck	$10,000	
Rent	2,500	
Miscellaneous Expenses	8,000	
Total Operating Expenses		(20,500)
Net Income (Loss)		($10,500)

BARKER COMPANY
Income Statement
For the Month Ending January 31, 1996
Accrual Basis

Sales	$36,000	
LESS:		
Cost of Goods Sold	19,000	
Gross Margin		$17,000
Operating Expenses:		
Rent	$ 2,500	
Depreciation—Truck	250	
Miscellaneous Expenses	8,000	
Accrued Expenses	1,200	
Total Operating Expenses		(11,950)
Net Income (Loss)		$ 5,050

e. What will be the book value of the truck on the December 31, 1996, balance sheet under

   1. cash basis accounting?

   2. accrual basis accounting?

f. What will be the book value of the truck on the December 31, 1998, balance sheet under

   1. cash basis accounting?

   2. accrual basis accounting?

g. Comment generally on why the net income (loss) amounts on the two income statements are so different.

9

Challenging Issues Under Accrual Accounting: Merchandise Inventory and Cost of Goods Sold

In addition to the variations allowed with regard to accounting for long-lived depreciable assets, accrual accounting allows several different methods for tracking the costs of merchandise inventory. The methods available under accrual accounting for the treatment of merchandise inventory and cost of goods sold can have a serious impact on financial statements.

In Chapter 8, we explored one source of variation across companies' financial statements—choice of depreciation method. Recall that this issue results from accrual accounting's attempt to recognize revenue in the period earned and match the expenses to the revenue they helped to generate. This characteristic of accrual accounting results in other differences among the financial statements of various companies. One such difference occurs as companies keep track of the movement of the products they buy and sell.

Cash basis accounting recognizes revenue from sales only when cash is received. In contrast, accrual accounting requires that sales revenue be recognized when earned, regardless of whether or not cash is received. Cash basis accounting recognizes the expenses related to the products as the cash is spent. Under cash basis accounting, whether or not the products have been sold is irrelevant. In contrast, accrual accounting focuses on matching the expenses—in this case, the cost of the product—with the revenue generated by the sale. A method must be developed to determine the amount of expense to recognize in a given period. Actually, several methods are available, and companies may use whichever method they prefer—another example of ways in which the financial statements of several companies using accrual accounting can vary. In fact, the way merchandise inventory purchases and sales are accounted for can have a direct and significant impact on a company's reported net income.

After completing your work on this chapter, you should be able to do the following:

1. **Explain goods available for sale (GAFS) and name its components.**
2. **Describe in your own words the relationship between ending inventory and cost of goods sold.**
3. **Differentiate between the physical flow of merchandise and the cost flow of merchandise.**
4. **Explain the differences between periodic and perpetual inventory systems.**
5. **List three different inventory cost flow assumptions and contrast how the use of each affects reported net income on the income statement.**
6. **Calculate cost of goods sold and ending inventory using FIFO, LIFO, and average cost inventory cost flow assumptions.**

TRACKING INVENTORY COSTS

In Chapter 1, you were introduced to the three major types of business activity—manufacturing, merchandising, and service. As you will recall, manufacturers make products to sell, merchandisers buy products to sell, and service companies sell services rather than tangible products. The tangible products that merchandisers sell are referred to as **merchandise inventory**, or simply **inventory**. For example, Walmart Corporation has inventory consisting of tubes of toothpaste, lawnmowers, clothing, and thousands of other products. Bassett Furniture Company's inventory includes beds, dressers, tables, desks and chairs. General Motors owns desks and chairs, too. But these

merchandise inventory The physical units (goods) a company buys to resell as part of its business operation.

inventory Another term for merchandise inventory.

desks and chairs are *not* inventory. Rather, they are items used in the offices of General Motors, and are assets, probably referred to simply as "furniture." Inventory items are items held by a company for resale. The inventory of General Motors includes cars, trucks, vans and a wide variety of auto parts.

Unfortunately, the terms "merchandise inventory" and "inventory" are often used to describe the *cost* of the items as well as the items themselves. Therefore, when you see merchandise inventory, you must analyze the context in which the term is used to determine whether it is describing the actual physical units of inventory or the cost of that inventory.

The amount of merchandise inventory on hand at the beginning of the income statement period is usually called **beginning inventory**, and the amount of merchandise inventory purchased during the period is usually called **purchases**. Again, both of these terms can be used to refer to the cost of the units as well as to the units themselves. The total amount of merchandise inventory a company *could* sell in a given income statement period is the amount the company started with (beginning inventory) plus the amount it bought (purchases). This total is referred to as **goods available for sale**. Once again, "goods available for sale" is used to describe both the physical amount of merchandise inventory available for sale and the cost of that inventory. Whether referring to the physical amount of inventory or its cost, the following relationship between beginning inventory (BI), purchases (Purch), and goods available for sale (GAFS) holds true:

$$\text{Beginning Inventory} + \text{Purchases} = \text{Goods Available for Sale}$$
$$BI + Purch = GAFS$$

beginning inventory The amount of merchandise inventory (units or dollars) on hand at the beginning of the income statement period.

purchases The amount of merchandise inventory bought during the income statement period.

goods available for sale The total amount of merchandise inventory a company has available to sell in a given income statement period.

Under the accrual basis of accounting, merchandise inventory is reported as an asset when it is purchased because it has probable future benefit (it should generate future revenues). As the merchandise is sold and revenues are generated, the cost of the merchandise is converted from an asset on the balance sheet to an expense on the income statement. This expense is known as **cost of goods sold**, or **cost of sales**, and was discussed briefly in Chapter 6. The cost of goods sold (COGS) can be determined by subtracting the amount of inventory on hand at the end of the period—called **ending inventory**—from goods available for sale. In other words, the total amount that we *could* have sold (GAFS) minus the amount we still had at the end of the period (EI) equals the amount we must have sold (COGS):

$$GAFS - EI = COGS$$

cost of goods sold The cost of the merchandise inventory no longer on hand, and assumed sold during the period.

cost of sales Another name for cost of goods sold.

ending inventory The amount of inventory (in units or dollars) still on hand at the end of an accounting period.

Conversely, if we know cost of goods sold, we can determine a company's ending merchandise inventory for a given period. The total amount we *could* have sold (GAFS) less the amount we *did* sell (COGS) is the amount we have left at the end of the period (EI):

$$GAFS - COGS = EI$$

These relationships hold true whether we are considering the amount of inventory (physical units) or the cost of that inventory.

Exhibit 9-1 shows examples of these relationships in terms of both units and dollar amounts.

Exhibit 9-1

Relationships Among BI, Purch, GAFS, EI, and COGS

	Units	Cost	
Beginning Inventory	20	$200	BI
+ Purchases	70	700	+ Purch
= Goods Available for Sale	90	$900	GAFS
− Ending Inventory	15	150	− EI
= Cost of Goods Sold	75	$750	COGS

Or

	Units	Cost	
Beginning Inventory	20	$200	BI
+ Purchases	70	700	+ Purch
= Goods Available for Sale	90	$900	GAFS
− Cost of Goods Sold	75	750	− COGS
= Ending Inventory	15	$150	EI

In the first table in the exhibit, ending inventory is used to calculate cost of goods sold and in the second table, cost of goods sold is used to calculate ending inventory. It is important to learn from these two calculations that *the total of ending inventory and cost of goods sold will always equal goods available for sale (in units and in dollars).*

To see this, consider your local Tower Record Store. All the records and CDs in the store on the first of the month (BI) plus any new records or CDs the store receives during the month (Purch) are the total of what the store could sell (GAFS). The products (GAFS) are either gone or still in the store at the end of the month. If items are gone, we presume they were sold, and consider them part of cost of goods sold. (*NOTE:* Some of the items could have been broken or stolen.) What's still in the store at the end of the period is the store's ending inventory.

REMEMBER: ALL GAFS BECOME EITHER COGS OR EI.

The movement of costs through a merchandising operation may be best understood by examining Exhibit 9-2 on page 268. Beginning inventory and purchases comprise cost of goods available for sale. By the end of the period, cost of goods available for sale become either cost of goods sold or ending inventory.

Exhibit 9-2
The Flow of Inventory and its Cost

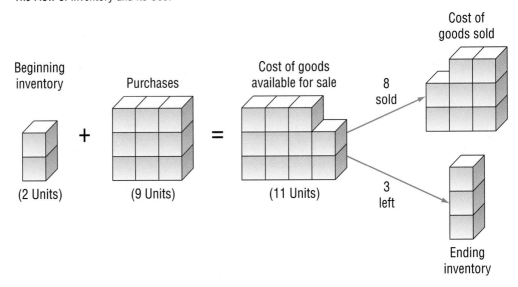

Beginning inventory + Purchases = Cost of goods available for sale → 8 sold → Cost of goods sold; → 3 left → Ending inventory

(2 Units)   (9 Units)   (11 Units)

DISCUSSION QUESTIONS

9-1. You decide to throw a weekend party, and begin to plan for it by checking out what's in the house. You find you have some hot dogs, buns, and pretzels. That stuff's a good start, but you dash to the store to buy soda, chips, dip, peanuts, and ice cream. The party is a *great hit*. Your guests devoured all the food and drinks, except for the ice cream—it was never touched! As you relax and enjoy the memories of the party's finest moments, you decide to figure out what the event cost you. What was your

   a. beginning inventory?
   b. purchases?
   c. goods available?
   d. ending inventory?
   e. "cost" of the party?

Now, let's look closer at the process of tracking a company's inventory and its cost as items are bought and sold.

Computers like this one comprise the inventory of Computer Exchange, Inc.

Courtesy of AST Research.

The Physical Movement of Inventory (Reality)

The photo above shows a computer similar to the one purchased by Computer Exchange, Inc., a retail merchandiser, from a wholesaler on January 17, 1995, for $800, and then moved to Computer Exchange's warehouse. The computer was purchased for the purpose of resale and was, in fact, sold and delivered to a customer on February 6, 1995, for $1,500.

Because the computer was purchased for the purpose of resale, it was considered merchandise inventory by Computer Exchange. Had the company bought the computer for its own use, the item would not have been considered inventory, but rather, a long-lived asset and would have been depreciated. Exhibit 9-3 illustrates the physical movement of the computer from the time it was purchased from the wholesaler until it was sold and delivered to the customer.

Exhibit 9-3
Physical Movement
of a Computer Purchased
by Computer Exchange

Wholesaler ——Purchase 1/17/95——▶ Warehouse ——Sale 2/6/95——▶ Customer

FIFO (first in, first out) The inventory flow concept based on the assumption that the first units of inventory purchased are the first ones sold.

Merchandise inventory is one of the most costly assets for many companies. Accordingly, the physical flow of merchandise from the time of purchase to the time of sale is a critical operation that must work efficiently.

For some companies, it is important that the oldest merchandise be sold before newer inventory—that is, that the first units in be the first units taken out and sold. This inventory flow concept, whereby the **First In** is the **First Out**, is often called **FIFO**.

9-2. For what products would it be important for the first units of merchandise purchased to be the first ones sold? Explain.

LIFO (last in, first out) The inventory flow concept based on the assumption that the last units of inventory purchased are the first ones sold.

For other companies, it is unimportant or impractical to sell the first units first. In such cases, goods may be sold in random order, or perhaps the merchandise is sold from the top of the pile so that the last units in are the first units taken out of inventory and sold. This inventory flow concept, whereby the **Last In** is the **First Out**, is called **LIFO**.

DISCUSSION QUESTIONS

9-3. If you owned a nursery and bought potting soil by the truckload to resell to customers in smaller quantities, what possible reasons would you have for insisting that potting soil from the first truckload of the season be sold before selling soil from the second truckload you purchased?

9-4. If you owned a retail camera shop, what possible reasons would you have for insisting that your employees sell the first Nikon 35mm cameras received before the ones that arrived at the store later?

Thus far, we have been discussing the physical flow of units in and out of inventory. But what about the cost of these units? As inventory is purchased, the physical units enter the warehouse and their cost is added to inventory in the accounting records. Likewise, as merchandise is sold, its cost is removed from inventory and added to cost of goods sold. The cost flows through accounting records much as the physical units flow through the warehouse.

You might suppose that accounting rules require that the flow of costs through a company's accounting records reflect the reality of how the physical units flow through the company's inventory. For example, if a company sells bread and its physical inventory flows in a FIFO fashion to ensure product freshness, it seems logical to expect that the company would be required to record the flow of inventory costs in a FIFO fashion as well. However, accounting rules do *not* require that the cost flow for inventory mirror the flow of physical units. That is, a company's physical inventory may flow in a FIFO fashion, but accounting rules permit the company to show cost information *as if* the inventory flowed in a LIFO fashion.

Regardless of how physical units flow through inventory, then, a company is permitted to use any cost flow assumption it chooses. This is yet another example of how reality and the measurement of reality may differ.

The Flow of Inventory Cost (Measurement of Reality)

Under accrual accounting, Computer Exchange would attempt to match expenses to the same income statement period as the revenues they help generate. For this reason, the company would not recognize the cost of the computer as an expense when it was purchased. Instead, the computer (and its $800 cost) would be considered an asset.

As of January 31, 1995, the computer had not been sold and was in the company's warehouse. Therefore, its cost would be shown on the balance sheet prepared at the end of January as merchandise inventory (an asset). Nothing related to the computer would be reported on the income statement. Exhibit 9-4 shows the calculation of cost of goods sold and ending inventory for Computer Exchange, Inc., as of January 31, 1995.

Exhibit 9-4
COGS and EI for Computer Exchange as of January 31, 1995

	Units	Cost	
Beginning Inventory, January 1.	0	$ -0-	BI
+ Purchases	1	800	+ Purch
= Goods Available for Sale	1	$800	GAFS
− Cost of Goods Sold	0	-0-	− COGS
= Ending Inventory, January 31	1	$800	EI

Assuming Computer Exchange had no business transactions during January except those related to the computer and the payment of warehouse rent, the company's income statement for the month of January 1995 and its balance sheet at January 31, 1995, would be as shown in Exhibit 9-5 on page 272.

COMPUTER EXCHANGE, INC.
Income Statement
For the Month Ended January 31, 1995

Sales	$	-0-
LESS: Cost of Goods Sold		-0-
Gross Margin	$	-0-
Operating Expenses:		
Warehouse Rent	$	(200)
Net Income (Loss)	$	(200)

COMPUTER EXCHANGE, INC.
Balance Sheet
January 31, 1995

ASSETS:
Cash	$22,000
Merchandise Inventory	800
Total Assets	$22,800

LIABILITIES AND
STOCKHOLDERS' EQUITY:
Common Stock	$15,000
Additional Paid-in Capital	8,000
Retained Earnings	(200)
Total Liabilities and Stockholders' Equity	$22,800

DISCUSSION QUESTIONS

9-5. Can you tell how long Computer Exchange, Inc., has been in business by looking at the income statement and balance sheet in Exhibit 9-5? Explain.

As you will recall, Computer Exchange sold the computer on February 6, 1995, and delivered it to the customer on that day. Exhibit 9-6 calculates the cost of goods sold that should be reported on February's income statement and the amount of ending inventory to be shown on the February 28 balance sheet.

	Units	Cost	
Beginning Inventory, January 1	1	$800	BI
+ Purchases...	0	-0-	+ Purch
= Goods Available for Sale	1	$800	GAFS
− Cost of Goods Sold	1	800	− COGS
= Ending Inventory, January 31	0	$-0-	EI

Assuming Computer Exchange had no business transactions during February except those related to the computer and the payment of rent, the company's income statement for the month of February 1995 and its balance sheets at January 31, 1995, and February 28, 1995, would be as shown in Exhibit 9-7.

We have included the (presale) January 31 balance sheet as well as the (postsale) February 28 balance sheet in Exhibit 9-7 to demonstrate how the $800 cost of the computer flowed through the financial statements. The $800 was reported as an asset (merchandise inventory) on the January 31

COMPUTER EXCHANGE, INC.
Income Statement
For the Month Ended February 28, 1995

Sales...	$ 1,500
LESS: Cost of Goods Sold...............................	800
Gross Margin..	$ 700
Operating Expenses:	
Warehouse Rent...	$ (200)
Net Income (Loss)	$ 500

COMPUTER EXCHANGE, INC.
Balance Sheets
January 31, 1995, and February 28, 1995

ASSETS:	January 31	February 28
Cash..	$22,000	$21,800
Accounts Receivable...	-0-	1,500
Merchandise Inventory...	800	-0-
Total Assets	$22,800	$23,300
LIABILITIES AND STOCKHOLDERS' EQUITY:		
Common Stock...	$15,000	$15,000
Additional Paid-in Capital.....................................	8,000	8,000
Retained Earnings..	(200)	300
Total Liabilities and Stockholders' Equity	$22,800	$23,300

balance sheet. Because the computer was sold during February, no merchandise inventory is listed on the February 28 balance sheet. Instead, the $800 cost has been converted to an expense and is reported on the February income statement as cost of goods sold. Cost of goods sold affects the gross margin, and thus the net income as well. The $500 net income is reflected in the February 28 balance sheet as an increase both in the total assets and in total liabilities and stockholders' equity. Total assets increase by $500 because while the company sacrificed $1,000 of assets during February ($800 cost of goods sold and $200 rent on the warehouse), those sacrifices generated a $1,500 asset (accounts receivable). As the arrow in Exhibit 9-7 shows, stockholders' equity increases by $500 as a result of the net income figure being combined with the previous retained earnings balance (which in this case was negative) to arrive at the updated retained earnings balance of $300.

DISCUSSION QUESTIONS

9-6. Can you tell by looking at the income statement and balance sheets in Exhibit 9-7 whether the customer who purchased the computer from Computer Exchange has paid for it by the end of February 1995? Explain.

Exhibit 9-3 illustrated the physical movement of the computer from the time it was purchased by Computer Exchange to the time it was sold to the customer. Exhibit 9-8 shows both the physical flow of the computer and the flow of the cost associated with the computer.

Computer Exchange purchased a computer, which was delivered to the company's warehouse. This is reality. Computer Exchange sold the computer and delivered it to its customer. This, too, is reality. The $800 cost of the computer was initially reported on the balance sheet as an asset; when the com-

Exhibit 9-8
Physical Movement (Reality) and
Cost Flow (Measurement of
Reality) for the Computer

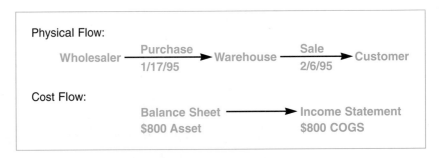

puter was sold, the $800 was transferred to an expense (COGS) on the income statement. This is the measurement of reality. As Exhibit 9-8 shows, in this simple example involving only one unit of inventory, the physical flow of the merchandise inventory and the flow of the cost associated with the merchandise inventory coincide. However, when a company has many units of inventory, the physical flow of merchandise (reality) and the cost flow of that merchandise (measurement of reality) do not usually coincide. This situation is another source of variation among companies' accounting information. To some degree, the differences are influenced by the type of inventory system a company chooses to use.

INVENTORY SYSTEMS

In our previous example, Computer Exchange transferred the $800 cost of the computer from an asset to an expense when the item was sold on February 6, 1995. This type of conversion, however, is not always immediate. The timing of the conversion of this cost depends on what kind of inventory system a company employs. Over time, two major inventory systems have been developed. As we will see, each has advantages and disadvantages in comparison to the other.

Periodic Inventory System

periodic inventory system
An inventory system in which all inventory and cost of goods sold calculations are done at the end of the income statement period.

Under a **periodic inventory system**, all inventory and cost of goods sold calculations are done at the end of the income statement period. Detailed inventory records are not updated during the period; companies using this system do not know which products have been sold until the end of period, when the company prepares its financial statements. The cost of the inventory sold is then reported as cost of goods sold on the income statement for the period, and the cost of the inventory still on hand is reported as an asset on the balance sheet at the end of the period.

The strength of the periodic inventory system is that it involves relatively little record keeping. Its greatest weakness is that it does not provide the company with any day-to-day information about the status of its inventory.

Prior to the computer age, virtually all companies with even a moderate volume of inventory employed the periodic inventory system because keeping detailed inventory records manually was too time-consuming. Now, however, rapid advances in computer technology have made the task of keeping daily records of inventory transactions a reasonably efficient process. For this reason, the perpetual inventory system has grown in popularity. Therefore, all of the examples we will use in the remainder of this chapter will be based on the perpetual inventory system.

Perpetual Inventory System

perpetual inventory system
An inventory system in which both the physical count of inventory units and the cost classification (asset or expense) are updated whenever there is a transaction involving inventory.

Under a **perpetual inventory system**, both the physical count of inventory units and the cost classification (asset or expense) are updated whenever there is a transaction involving inventory. To illustrate, let's return to our original example of Computer Exchange and its $800 computer.

Under a perpetual system, Computer Exchange would have an inventory control report similar to the one shown in Exhibit 9-9.

Exhibit 9-9
Inventory Control Report Under Perpetual Inventory System

		Purchases			Cost of Goods Sold			Merchandise Inventory Balance		
Date	Explanation	Units	Unit Cost	Total Cost	Units	Unit Cost	Total Cost	Units	Unit Cost	Total Cost
1/17	Purchase	1	$800	$800				1	$800	$800
2/06	Sale				1	$800	$800	0		$ -0-

This report shows the purchase of the computer on January 17, 1995, and the sale of the computer on February 6, 1995. At the end of the income statement period (February, in this case), the total cost column in the cost of goods sold section would be added up to determine the amount of cost to report as COGS on the income statement. The last amount showing in the total cost column of the merchandise inventory balance section at the end of February would be the amount of merchandise inventory to appear on the balance sheet.

Since a running balance of merchandise inventory on hand is kept (the far right side of the report), the company can tell the number of physical units it has on hand at any time. This report can also be used to determine the dollar amount that has been transferred from asset (merchandise inventory) on the balance sheet to expense (cost of goods sold) on the income statement.

Computer Exchange uses a computerized accounting system to generate its inventory control reports automatically. Purchases and sales of inventory are registered either by keyboard entries or, more commonly, by a scanning device. Retailers use scanners to read bar codes—formally known as *Universal Product Codes*, or *UPCs*—printed on their inventory. The computer can be programmed to assign a given cost to a given inventory item, and thus can perform the necessary calculations to update inventory records.

Chances are, when you purchased this book, the clerk in the bookstore either ran a stylus over the UPC on the back of the book or ran the back of the book over a little window on the checkout counter.

Besides ringing up the sales price of the book, the use of the UPC also updated the bookstore's inventory records. The number of physical units on hand was changed, and the transfer of the cost of the book from merchandise inventory to cost of goods sold was recorded. By utilizing this technology, the bookstore employees can determine the number of books sold and the number of books remaining on the shelf without physically counting them. Whenever they want, the employees can review an inventory control report similar to the one presented in Exhibit 9-9. Such reports help managers, or other employees, decide when to reorder inventory.

Virtually everything you see in this picture has a Universal Product Code somewhere on the item itself. For this sales clerk, recording the sale of any of these items is as simple as pointing the stylus at the UPC and pulling the trigger.

Frank Labua

9-7. Assume the inventory control report on this textbook shows 25 books remaining on the shelf. Just to make sure, the bookstore manager goes over to the shelf, counts the remaining books, and finds there are only 22. What might explain the discrepancy?

The Necessity of a Physical Inventory Count

book inventory The amount of ending inventory (units and dollars) resulting from transactions recorded by a perpetual inventory system.

The amount of ending inventory (units and dollars) generated by a perpetual inventory system is called **book inventory**. Book inventory may or may not coincide with the merchandise inventory actually on hand at the end of the period. Errors in recording inventory transactions and theft of inventory are two potential causes of differences between book inventory and actual inventory. Others are damaged and discarded inventory and, in the case of perishable inventory, spoilage. Because of these sources of discrepancies between the inventory records of a perpetual inventory system and the reality of the inventory on hand, physical inventory counts must be made from time to time.

Results of the physical inventory count take precedence over the book inventory generated by the inventory records. Cost of goods sold for the period is adjusted for any differences between the physical count and the book count. To illustrate, Exhibit 9-10 on page 278 shows the calculation of cost of goods sold and ending inventory.

The figures in this exhibit came from the company's records. The ending inventory of 15 units and $150 is the book inventory. However, a physical count reveals that there are only 13 units on hand. In this case, an adjustment of the

Another tremendous application of the Universal Product Code technology is periodically counting physical inventory. Here the person simply runs the stylus over the UPC, inputs the number of pairs of jeans into the hand-held computer, and the physical inventory count for this item is automatically updated.

Courtesy of Levi Strauss & Co.

Exhibit 9-10
Record of Ending Inventory Based on Book Inventory

		Units	Cost	
	Beginning Inventory, January 1.	20	$200	BI
+	Purchases..	70	700	+ Purch
=	Goods Available for Sale	90	$900	GAFS
−	Cost of Goods Sold	75	750	− COGS
=	Ending Inventory, January 31	15	$150	EI

records is necessary to reflect reality: The amount shown on the balance sheet as ending inventory must be the amount actually on hand. Since we know that cost of goods available for sale ($900 in this example) will end up as either cost of goods sold or ending inventory, a change in the amount shown as ending inventory will cause a change in the amount shown as cost of goods sold. After the necessary adjustments, the company's records would look like Exhibit 9-11.

Exhibit 9-11
Adjusted Record of Ending Inventory After Physical Count

		Units	Cost
	Beginning Inventory, January 1.	20	$200
+	Purchases..	70	700
=	Goods Available for Sale	90	$900
−	Cost of Goods Sold	77	770
=	Ending Inventory, January 31	13	$130

The cost of goods sold reported as an expense on the income statement for the period would be $770. The merchandise inventory reported as an asset on the balance sheet would be $130, which reflects the reality of the number of units actually on hand at the end of the period. With this adjustment of the records, Computer Exchange's financial statement amounts will more accurately reflect reality.

9-8. If careless employees break inventory items and discard them, or dishonest employees steal inventory items, how is a company's income statement affected?

COST FLOW ASSUMPTIONS

Inventory costs, as we explained earlier, may not flow through the system the same way that the physical units of merchandise inventory flow through the warehouse. The result is another situation in which the difference between reality and the measurement of reality leads to some complexities in accrual accounting. As financial statement users, you need to understand the way in which companies track their inventory costs and how they arrive at the amounts presented on their financial statements. We will now explore three different cost flow assumptions that take different approaches to measuring the flow of inventory costs through a perpetual inventory system.

If each product included in beginning inventory and each item purchased (or made) during the period cost exactly the same amount (per unit), the three approaches would result in identical measurements of reality. However, the cost of products rarely remains constant. For some products, prices rise regularly; wholesalers often warn the retailers to whom they sell goods of price increases months in advance. Products based on technology often fall in price as the "newness" of the technology wears off; more and more companies offer the products and competition drives prices down. (This is another example of the work of the "invisible hand" described by Adam Smith.) Prices may rise or fall over time, or they may fluctuate in unexpected patterns, but rarely will they remain constant for long periods.

Changes in the cost of inventory items over time cause cost flow assumptions to result in different amounts for cost of goods sold and ending inventory. To illustrate, we will examine the effect of three different cost flow assumptions on a very special product: PHIPs (pronounced "fips"). A PHIP is a *Product Having Increasing Prices*, and PHIPs 'R' Us is a major retailer of the product.

PHIPs 'R' Us began March with only one PHIP in stock. This item cost the company $800. As you can see from Exhibit 9-12 on page 280, the PHIPs purchased by the company during March certainly *did* have increasing prices, even though the five PHIPs purchased that month are identical in every way to the one purchased earlier.

Exhibit 9-12

Changes in Purchase Price
of PHIPs for PHIPs 'R' Us in
March 1995.

Date	Number Purchased	Cost per Unit
March 3	2	$1,000
March 17	1	$1,200
March 26	1	$1,300
March 29	1	$1,400

PHIPs 'R' Us sold one PHIP on March 22 and another on March 30. Because of competition from nearby stores, PHIPs 'R' Us was unable to raise the price it charges its customers for these items, so the selling price remained $1,500 per PHIP.

Considering what you know about when the PHIPs were purchased and the dates of the two sales, which one would you say was sold on March 22 and which do you think was sold on March 30? Different answers are possible, but the PHIPs sold were probably the ones most conveniently located in the warehouse (that is, those closest to the door). Remember, these are identical products: One PHIP is no more special than another, so it doesn't matter to the customer which PHIP he or she receives. About the only thing you can determine is that the PHIP sold on March 22 was either the $800 one, one of the $1,000 ones, or the $1,200 one; and that the one sold on March 30 was one of the five still in the warehouse on that day.

DISCUSSION QUESTIONS

9-9. Why must the PHIP sold on March 22 have been one costing either $800, $1,000, or $1,200?

9-10. In what type of business would it be impossible to identify individual units of inventory, as we did with the PHIPs?

Because the purchase prices of the PHIPs varied, it is impossible for us to determine the cost of goods sold when we don't know which PHIPs were sold. What we need is a method of determining cost flow that will allow us to calcultate COGS regardless of which specific products were sold.

In the sections that follow, we discuss three inventory cost flow methods that have been developed over time. Before we do so, however, we want to make two points:

1. None of the three methods we discuss attempts to reflect the physical movement of the actual units of merchandise inventory.

2. Our discussions of the three methods are not intended to be exhaustive. Our aim is to give you a basic understanding of these methods so that you will see how the choice of a particular inventory cost flow assumption can have a significant effect on a company's financial statements.

Our illustrations of cost flow methods assume a perpetual inventory system is in place. In that case, the amount recorded for inventory on hand and the amount considered cost of goods sold is recalculated each time inventory items come in or go out. The number of items purchased, when they were purchased, and how much they cost are facts. The number of items sold and when they were sold are also facts. The cost flow assumption in place cannot change these facts. What *can* be changed is the *assumption* of *which* items were sold. This, in turn, affects the amount recorded as cost of goods sold and also the amount shown as ending inventory—for, regardless of the cost flow assumption being used, the total cost of goods available for sale each period must end up as either cost of goods sold or ending inventory.

Cost of goods available for sale (COGAS) is the total cost of all inventory items on hand at the beginning of the period and all the items purchased during the period. Cost of goods available for sale for PHIPs 'R' Us for March 1995 can be calculated as shown in Exhibit 9-13:

Exhibit 9-13
Cost of Goods Available for Sale by PHIPs 'R' US in March 1995

	Date	Number of Items	Cost per Unit	Total
Beginning Inventory	March 1	1	$ 800	$ 800
Purchase	March 3	2	$1,000	$2,000
Purchase	March 17	1	$1,200	$1,200
Purchase	March 26	1	$1,300	$1,300
Purchase	March 29	1	$1,400	$1,400
			Total Cost of Goods Available for Sale	$6,700

The various cost flow assumptions applied to this information from PHIPs 'R' Us will separate the $6,700 into the portion assumed to be associated with the two PHIPs sold (cost of goods sold) and the cost associated with the four PHIPs still on hand at the end of March (ending inventory). Each cost flow method will take a different approach to determining which items were sold on March 22 and March 30, and thus to determining the cost of goods sold. Because these methods are being used in a perpetual inventory system, the cost of goods sold will be determined at the time of each sale. The portion of the cost of goods available for sale not recorded as cost of goods sold, then, must be the cost of ending inventory.

First-In, First-Out Method (FIFO)

The first-in, first-out method (FIFO) is so named because it assumes that the first units placed in inventory are the first units sold. Let's apply the FIFO logic to our example.

The first sale took place on March 22. One PHIP was sold, but which one? What inventory items were available on the sale date?

Exhibit 9-14 answers that question. Then, applying FIFO logic, we assume that the PHIP sold on March 22 must have been the one from beginning inventory. That is, the first PHIP in was the first one out. Therefore, cost of goods sold for the March 22 sale was $800.

Exhibit 9-14

Inventory Items Available for Sale on March 22

	Date	Number of Items	Cost per Unit	Total
Beginning Inventory	March 1	1	$ 800	$ 800
Purchase	March 3	2	$1,000	$2,000
Purchase	March 17	1	$1,200	$1,200

The next sale took place on March 30. What inventory items were on hand at the time of the sale? Exhibit 9-15 answers that question.

Exhibit 9-15

Inventory Items Available for Sale on March 30 Under FIFO Assumption

	Date	Number of Items	Cost per Unit	Total
Purchase	March 3	2	$1,000	$2,000
Purchase	March 17	1	$1,200	$1,200
Purchase	March 26	1	$1,300	$1,300
Purchase	March 29	1	$1,400	$1,400

Under FIFO, which of the PHIPs should we assume was sold on March 30? The first one into inventory was one of the PHIPs purchased on March 3, so we assume one of those was sold. Therefore, cost of goods sold for the March 30 sale is $1,000.

We can now calculate the cost of goods sold that should be reported on the March income statement for PHIPs 'R' Us. Since cost of goods sold for the month is the total of the cost of goods sold for each sale, the cost of goods sold to be reported on the income statement is $1,800 ($800 + $1,000).

Let's look again at the approach taken under the FIFO cost flow assumption used in a perpetual inventory system. Exhibit 9-16 summarizes the two sales of PHIPs.

Exhibit 9-16
Inventory Items Sold on March 22 and 30 Under FIFO Assumption

	Date	Number of Items	Cost per Unit
Beginning Inventory	March 1	1 SOLD	$800
Purchase	March 3	I LEFT 2 I SOLD	$1,000
Purchase	March 17	1	$1,200
SALE of 1	MARCH 22		COGS = $ 800
Purchase	March 26	1	$1,300
Purchase	March 29	1	$1,400
SALE of 1	MARCH 30		COGS = $1,000
			Total Cost of Goods Sold = $1,800

At the time of each sale, cost of goods sold is determined using the assumption that the first items into inventory are the first ones to be sold. As the exhibit indicates, it was assumed that it was the PHIP from beginning inventory that was sold on March 22 and one of the PHIPs purchased on March 3 that was sold on March 30. The items remaining in ending inventory are: one of the PHIPs purchased on March 3, and the ones purchased on March 17, 26, and 29. By adding up the costs of these four PHIPs, we can determine the cost of the company's ending inventory for March, which is shown in Exhibit 9-17:

Exhibit 9-17
Ending Inventory for March
Under FIFO Assumption

	Date	Number of Items	Cost per Unit	Total
Purchase	March 3	1	$1,000	$1,000
Purchase	March 17	1	$1,200	$1,200
Purchase	March 26	1	$1,300	$1,300
Purchase	March 29	1	$1,400	$1,400
			Total Cost of Ending Inventory	$4,900

DISCUSSION QUESTIONS

9-11. If PHIPs 'R' Us sells two more PHIPs before purchasing any more of the item, which two will be assumed sold under FIFO?

Even if we didn't specifically identify the items left in ending inventory, we could calculate their total cost. Knowing the amount of cost of goods available for sale ($6,700, as calculated in Exhibit 9-13) and the cost of goods sold ($1,800), we can determine the cost of the company's ending inventory for March 1995:

$$
\begin{array}{lr}
\text{COGAS} & \$6,700 \\
-\ \text{COGS} & \underline{1,800} \\
=\ \ \text{EI} & \underline{\$4,900}
\end{array}
$$

This $4,900 is the amount of ending inventory to be shown on the March 31 balance sheet, assuming none of the inventory was stolen or otherwise lost.

Note that cost of goods available for sale ($6,700) is separated into cost of goods sold ($1,800) and cost of ending inventory ($4,900). Cost of goods sold is shown as an expense on the income statement, and ending inventory is shown as an asset on the balance sheet.

Assuming PHIPs 'R' Us had no business transactions during March except those related to the PHIPs and the payment of rent, the company's income statement for the month of March 1995 and its balance sheets at February 28, 1995, and March 31, 1995, based on the FIFO cost flow method would be as shown in Exhibit 9-18:

Exhibit 9-18
PHIPs 'R' Us's Financial Statements Showing Effects of March Sales Under FIFO Assumption

PHIPS 'R' US
Income Statement
For the Month Ended March 31, 1995

Sales	$ 3,000
LESS: Cost of Goods Sold	1,800
Gross Margin	$ 1,200
Operating Expenses:	
Warehouse Rent	(200)
Net Income	$ 1,000

PHIPS 'R' US
Balance Sheets
February 28, 1995, and March 31, 1995

ASSETS:	February 28	March 31
Cash	$21,000	$22,300
Accounts Receivable	1,500	3,000
Merchandise Inventory	800	4,900
Total Assets	$23,300	$30,200
LIABILITIES AND STOCKHOLDERS' EQUITY:		
Accounts Payable	$ -0-	$ 5,900
Common Stock	15,000	15,000
Additional Paid-in Capital	8,000	8,000
Retained Earnings	300	1,300
Total Liabilities and Stockholders' Equity	$23,300	$30,200

We have included both the February 28 balance sheet and the March 31 balance sheet in the exhibit to demonstrate how the cost of inventory items flows through the financial statements. PHIPs 'R' Us had only $800 in merchandise inventory on February 28, as reflected on the balance sheet. This was the beginning inventory for March. During March, the company purchased $5,900 of PHIPs. The cost of goods available for sale ($6,700) can be seen in the merchandise inventory on the March balance sheet and the cost of goods sold on the March income statement. The $4,900 of merchandise inventory listed on the March 31 balance sheet represents the unsold PHIPs, while the $1,800 cost of goods sold represents the two PHIPs that were sold in March. The cost of goods sold affects the gross margin and thus the net income as well. The $1,000 net income has been combined with the previous retained earnings balance ($300) to arrive at the updated retained earnings balance of $1,300.

DISCUSSION QUESTIONS

9-12. Can you tell by looking at the financial statements of PHIPs 'R' Us in Exhibit 9-18 whether, as of March 31, the company had paid for the five PHIPs purchased during March 1995? Explain.

The next cost flow assumption we will explore is no less logical than FIFO, but it will result in different amounts for cost of goods sold and ending inventory.

Last-In, First-Out Method (LIFO)

The last-in, first-out method (LIFO) is so named because it assumes that the last units placed in inventory are the first units sold. In other words, at the time of each sale, a LIFO cost flow assumption requires that the unit of product that was most recently purchased is the one assumed to be sold. As we apply the LIFO logic to our example, look at Exhibit 9-19, which shows the inventory items on hand to be sold by PHIPs 'R' Us on March 22.

Exhibit 9-19
Inventory Items Available for Sale on March 22

	Date	Number of Items	Cost per Unit	Total
Beginning Inventory	March 1	1	$ 800	$ 800
Purchase	March 3	2	$1,000	$2,000
Purchase	March 17	1	$1,200	$1,200

Applying LIFO logic, we assume that the PHIP sold on March 22 was the one purchased on March 17. That is, the last one in was the first one out. Therefore, cost of goods sold for the March 22 sale was $1,200.

The next sale took place on March 30. Exhibit 9-20 shows what inventory items were on hand at the time of the sale.

Exhibit 9-20

Inventory Items Available for Sale on March 30 Under LIFO Assumption

	Date	Number of Items	Cost per Unit	Total
Beginning Inventory	March 1	1	$ 800	$ 800
Purchase	March 3	2	$1,000	$2,000
Purchase	March 26	1	$1,300	$1,300
Purchase	March 29	1	$1,400	$1,400

Under LIFO, we assume that the PHIP sold on March 30 was the last one into inventory—that is, the PHIP purchased on March 29. Therefore, cost of goods sold for the March 30 sale is $1,400.

We can now calculate the cost of goods sold that should be reported on the March income statement for PHIPs 'R' Us. Cost of goods sold for the month is the total of the cost of goods sold for each sale. Therefore, cost of goods sold is $2,600 ($1,200 + $1,400).

Let's take another look at the LIFO approach when the perpetual inventory system is used. Exhibit 9-21 summarizes the two PHIPs sales.

Exhibit 9-21

Inventory Items Sold on March 22 and 30 Under LIFO Assumption

	Date	Number of Items	Cost per Unit
Beginning Inventory	March 1	1	$ 800
Purchase	March 3	2	$1,000
Purchase	March 17	1	SOLD $1,200
SALE of 1	MARCH 22		COGS = $1,200
Purchase	March 26	1	$1,300
Purchase	March 29	1	SOLD $1,400
SALE of 1	MARCH 30		COGS = $1,400
			Total Cost of Goods Sold = $2,600

At the time of each sale, cost of goods sold is determined, assuming the last items into inventory are the first ones to be sold. As the exhibit indicates, it was assumed that it was the PHIP purchased on March 17 that was sold on March 22 and the PHIP that was purchased on March 29 that was sold on March 30. The items remaining in ending inventory are: the PHIP from beginning inventory, the two PHIPs purchased on March 3, and the one purchased on March 26. By adding up the costs of these four PHIPs, we can determine the cost of the company's ending inventory for March, which is shown in Exhibit 9-22.

Exhibit 9-22
Ending Inventory for March
Under LIFO Assumption

	Date	Number of Items	Cost per Unit	Total
Beginning Inventory	March 1	1	$ 800	$ 800
Purchase	March 3	2	$1,000	$2,000
Purchase	March 26	1	$1,300	$1,300
			Total Cost of Ending Inventory	$4,100

DISCUSSION QUESTIONS

9-13. If PHIPs 'R' Us sells two more PHIPs before purchasing any more of the item, which two will be assumed sold under LIFO?

Even if we didn't specifically identify the items left in ending inventory, we could calculate their total cost. Knowing the amount of cost of goods available for sale ($6,700, as calculated in Exhibit 9-13), and the cost of goods sold ($2,600), we can determine the cost of the company's ending inventory for March 1995:

$$
\begin{array}{ll}
\text{COGAS} & \$6,700 \\
- \text{ COGS} & \underline{2,600} \\
= \quad \text{EI} & \underline{\underline{\$4,100}}
\end{array}
$$

This $4,100 is the amount of ending inventory to be shown on the March 31 balance sheet, assuming none of the inventory was stolen or otherwise lost.

Note that cost of goods available for sale ($6,700) is separated into cost of goods sold ($2,600) and cost of ending inventory ($4,100). Cost of goods sold is shown as an expense on the income statement and ending inventory is shown as an asset on the balance sheet.

Assuming PHIPs 'R' Us had no business transactions during March except those related to the PHIPs and the payment of rent, the company's income statement for the month of March 1995 and its balance sheets at February 28, 1995, and March 31, 1995, based on the LIFO cost flow method, would be as shown in Exhibit 9-23 on page 288.

As with the FIFO presentation, we have included both the February 28 balance sheet and the March 31 balance sheet in the exhibit to demonstrate how the cost of inventory items flows through the financial statements. PHIPs 'R' Us had only $800 in merchandise inventory on February 28, as reflected on the balance

PHIPS 'R' US
Income Statement
For the Month Ended March 31, 1995

Sales	$ 3,000
LESS: Cost of Goods Sold	2,600
Gross Margin	$ 400
Operating Expenses:	
Warehouse Rent	(200)
Net Income...	$ 200

PHIPS 'R' US
Balance Sheets
February 28, 1995, and March 31, 1995

ASSETS:	February 28	March 31
Cash	$21,000	$22,300
Accounts Receivable.............................	1,500	3,000
Merchandise Inventory	800	4,100
Total Assets	$23,300	$29,400
LIABILITIES AND STOCKHOLDERS' EQUITY:		
Accounts Payable..................................	$ -0-	$ 5,900
Common Stock......................................	15,000	15,000
Additional Paid-in Capital	8,000	8,000
Retained Earnings.................................	300	500
Total Liabilities and Stockholders' Equity	$23,300	$29,400

Exhibit 9-23
PHIPs 'R' Us's Financial Statements Showing Effects of March Sales Under LIFO Assumption

sheet. This was the beginning inventory for March. During March, the company purchased $5,900 of PHIPs. The cost of goods available for sale ($6,700) can be seen in the merchandise inventory on the March 31 balance sheet and the cost of goods sold on the March income statement. The $4,100 of merchandise inventory listed on the March 31 balance sheet represents the unsold PHIPs, while the $2,400 cost of goods sold represents the two PHIPs that were sold in March. The cost of goods sold affects the gross margin, and thus the net income as well. The $200 net income has been combined with the previous retained earnings balance ($300) to arrive at the updated retained earnings balance of $500.

Now let's compare the financial statements prepared for PHIPs 'R' Us using FIFO (Exhibit 9-18) with those prepared using LIFO (Exhibit 9-23). Remember, these two sets of financial statements are based on exactly the same facts. Yet, applying the FIFO inventory method, the company shows net income of $1,000, whereas under the LIFO inventory method, the company reports net income of $200. Moreover, using FIFO results in total assets on the March 31 balance sheet of $30,200, while using LIFO results in total assets on the March 31 balance sheet of $29,400. Keep in mind a company may use either LIFO or FIFO, regardless of the physical flow of its inventory items.

9-14. The financial statements prepared using FIFO (Exhibit 9-18) show PHIPs 'R' Us to be more profitable than do the financial statements prepared using LIFO (Exhibit 9-23). Is the company really more profitable if it uses the FIFO method rather than the LIFO method? Explain.

9-15. How would you explain the differences between these two sets of financial statements to someone who did not know the facts behind them?

9-16. In a time of rising prices, which method (LIFO or FIFO) would reflect a higher cost of ending inventory? Which method would result in a higher expense amount? A higher net income?

LIFO's assumption of a last-in, first-out approach is just as logical as the FIFO assumption of first in, first out. However, in times of changing prices, the two methods will provide different financial statement amounts for cost of goods sold and ending inventory.

The third cost flow assumption we discuss will, in most cases, result in financial statement numbers different from those produced using either LIFO or FIFO.

Average Cost Method

average cost method The inventory cost flow method that assigns an average cost to the units of inventory on hand at the time of each sale.

The **average cost method** is so named because it averages the cost of all of the units of inventory on hand. That is, at the time of each sale, the inventory items on hand are assigned a per unit cost that is a weighted average of their actual costs. As we apply the average cost approach to our example, look at Exhibit 9-24, which shows the inventory items on hand on March 22.

Applying average cost logic, we don't identify a specific PHIP to be assumed sold on that date. Rather, we assign all units on hand an average cost and assume that one of the units at that cost was sold. At the time of the sale, the total cost of the PHIPs on hand was

$$\$800 + \$2,000 + \$1,200 = \underline{\$4,000}$$

Exhibit 9-24
Inventory Items Available for Sale on March 22

	Date	Number of Items	Cost per Unit	Total
Beginning Inventory	March 1	1	$ 800	$ 800
Purchase	March 3	2	$1,000	$2,000
Purchase	March 17	1	$1,200	$1,200

The total number of PHIPs on hand was four. The weighted-average cost of the units on hand is calculated by dividing the total cost by the total number of units. In this case,

$$\$4,000 \ / \ 4 \ = \ \$1,000$$

At this point, all four PHIPs are reassigned a new cost of $1,000.

What is the effect of assigning a new weighted-average to the inventory items? It may help you to imagine the application of a weighted-average cost this way: Pretend that each inventory item's "cost tag" showing its actual cost is removed and replaced with a new "cost tag" reflecting the weighted-average cost. In reallity, the actual items are unaffected. The "cost tags" are not real, but they should help you understand the application of weighted-average costs. Now, back to our example…

One PHIP was sold on March 22, and we now know that all four PHIPs on hand at the time of the sale were assigned an average cost of $1,000. We simply assume that one of them was sold. Therefore, cost of goods sold for the March 22 sale was $1,000.

The next sale took place on March 30. Exhibit 9-25 shows what inventory items were on hand at the time of the sale.

Exhibit 9-25

Inventory Items Available for Sale on March 30 Under Average Cost Assumption

	Date	Number of Items	Cost per Unit	Total
Inventory on Hand	March 22	3	$1,000	$3,000
Purchase	March 26	1	$1,300	$1,300
Purchase	March 29	1	$1,400	$1,400

Notice that the items left after the first sale now carry the weighted-average cost of $1,000. In addition, PHIPs 'R' Us purchased two more PHIPs after March 22, so before we can determine cost of goods sold for the March 30 sale, we must calculate a new weighted-average cost. Total cost of inventory on hand is

$$\$3,000 \ + \ \$1,300 \ + \ \$1,400 \ = \ \$5,700$$

The number of PHIPs on hand is five. Therefore, each one will be assigned a weighted-average cost of:

$$\$5,700 \ / \ 5 \ = \ \$1,140$$

So if one PHIP was sold on March 30, cost of goods sold for the sale is $1,140.

We can now calculate the cost of goods sold that should be reported on the March income statement for PHIPs 'R' Us. Cost of goods sold for the month is the total of the cost of goods sold for each sale. Therefore, cost of goods sold is

$$\$1,000 \ + \ \$1,140 \ = \ \$2,140$$

Let's take another look at the average cost approach when the perpetual inventory system is used. Exhibit 9-26 summarizes the two PHIPs sales.

Exhibit 9-26
Inventory Items Sold on March 22 and 30 Under Average Cost Assumption

	Date	Number of Items	Cost per Unit	Total	
Beginning Inventory	March 1	1	$ 800	$ 800	Average cost
Purchase	March 3	2	$1,000	$2,000	per unit
Purchase	March 17	1	$1,200	$1,200	= $1,000
SALE of 1	MARCH 22		ISOLD → COGS = $1,000		
Inventory on Hand	March 22	3 ← 3 LEFT	$1,000	$3,000	Average cost
Purchase	March 26	1	$1,300	$1,300	per unit
Purchase	March 29	1	$1,400	$1,400	= $1,140
SALE of 1	MARCH 30		COGS = $1,140		ISOLD
			Total Cost of Goods Sold = $2,140		4 LEFT

At the time of each sale, cost of goods sold is determined, using the assumption that the inventory items on hand are assigned a weighted-average cost. This newly assigned cost stays with each item until it is sold or another average cost is calculated and assigned. As Exhibit 9-26 indicates, the March 22 sale assumed one of the PHIPs with an assigned cost of $1,000 was sold. The three PHIPs left after the March 22 sale kept the $1,000 cost until they were combined with other inventory items to determine a new weighted-average cost. Recalculation of the weighted average cost was necessary to determine the cost of goods sold for the March 30 sale. On March 30, a new average cost of $1,140 was calculated and assigned to the five PHIPs on hand. Then, one was assumed sold and four were left. These four PHIPs constitute ending inventory. Therefore, the cost of the company's ending inventory for March is

$$4 \text{ units} \times \$1,140 = \underline{\$4,560}$$

There is an alternative to this calculation. By knowing the amount of cost of goods available for sale ($6,700, as calculated in Exhibit 9-13), and the cost of goods sold ($2,140), we can determine the cost of the company's ending inventory for March 1995:

COGAS	$6,700
− COGS	2,140
= EI	$4,560

This $4,560 is the amount of ending inventory to be shown on the March 31 balance sheet, assuming none of the inventory was stolen or otherwise lost.

Note the cost of goods available for sale ($6,700) is separated into cost of goods sold ($2,140) and cost of ending inventory ($4,560). Cost of goods sold is shown as an expense on the income statement and ending inventory is shown as an asset on the balance sheet.

9-17. If PHIPs 'R' Us sells two more PHIPs before purchasing any more of the item, which two will be assumed sold under the average cost method?

Assuming PHIPs 'R' Us had no business transactions during March except those related to the PHIPs and the payment of rent, the company's income statement for the month of March 1995 and its balance sheets at February 28, 1995, and March 31, 1995, based on the average cost flow method, would be as shown in Exhibit 9-27.

Exhibit 9-27

PHIP's 'R' Us's Financial Statements Showing Effects of March Sales Under Average Cost Assumption

PHIPS 'R' US
Income Statement
For the Month Ended March 31, 1995

Sales	$3,000
LESS: Cost of Goods Sold	2,140
Gross Margin	$ 860
Operating Expenses:	
Warehouse Rent	(200)
Net Income	$ 660

PHIPS 'R' US
Balance Sheets
February 28, 1995, and March 31, 1995

ASSETS:	February 28	March 31
Cash	$21,000	$22,300
Accounts Receivable	1,500	3,000
Merchandise Inventory	800	4,560
Total Assets	$23,300	$29,860
LIABILITIES AND STOCKHOLDERS' EQUITY:		
Accounts Payable	$ -0-	$ 5,900
Common Stock	15,000	15,000
Additional Paid-in Capital	8,000	8,000
Retained Earnings	300	960
Total Liabilities and Stockholders' Equity	$23,300	$29,860

As with the FIFO and LIFO presentations, we have included both the February 28 balance sheet and the March 31 balance sheet in the exhibit to demonstrate how the cost of inventory items flows through the financial statements. PHIPs 'R' Us had only $800 in merchandise inventory on February 28, as reflected on the balance sheet. This was the beginning inventory for March. During March, the company purchased $5,900 of PHIPs. The cost of goods available for sale ($6,700) can be seen in the merchandise inventory on the March 31 balance sheet and the cost of goods sold on the March income statement. The $4,560 of merchandise inventory listed on the March 31 balance sheet represents the unsold PHIPs, while the $2,140 cost of goods sold represents the two PHIPs that were sold in March. The cost of goods sold affects the gross margin, and thus the net income as well. The $660 net income has been combined with the previous retained earnings balance ($300) to arrive at the updated retained earnings balance of $960.

Companies may choose from a variety of inventory cost flow assumptions. We have explored the three approaches most commonly used and have seen how these different cost flow assumptions result in different amounts for the cost of goods sold and ending inventory shown on the income statement and balance sheet of PHIPs 'R' Us. Now we will further explore how the inventory cost flow method chosen by a company can affect its financial statements.

The Effects of Inventory Cost Flow Method Choice

The March 1995 financial statements for PHIPs 'R' Us prepared using the average cost method (Exhibit 9-27) are based on exactly the same set of facts as the financial statements prepared using FIFO (Exhibit 9-18) and LIFO (Exhibit 9-23). That is, the reality is the same. What differs is the measurement of that reality. The differences resulting from use of the three different cost flow assumptions treated in this chapter are summarized in Exhibit 9-28 on page 294.

	FIFO	LIFO	Average Cost
Goods Available for Sale	$6,700	$6,700	$6,700
Income Statement:			
Cost of Goods Sold	$1,800	$2,600	$2,140
Net Income	$1,000	$ 200	$ 660
Balance Sheet:			
Ending Inventory	$4,900	$4,100	$4,560
Retained Earnings	$1,300	$ 500	$ 960

It appears that PHIPs 'R' Us is most profitable if it employs the FIFO method and least profitable if it uses the LIFO method. The average cost method produces results somewhere between FIFO and LIFO. Actually, the company is no "better off" by selecting one cost flow method over another. To illustrate, let's extend our example to April.

PHIPs 'R' Us purchased no PHIPs in April but did sell the four it had remaining at the end of March, each for $1,500. Once again, assuming the company had no business transactions in April except those related to the PHIPs and the payment of rent, the cost of goods sold and ending inventory under the three cost flow methods would be calculated as in Exhibit 9-29:

	Units	Cost Flow Method		
		FIFO	LIFO	Average Cost
Beginning Inventory, April 1	4	$4,900	$4,100	$4,560
+ Purchases	0	-0-	-0-	-0-
= Goods Available for Sale	4	$4,900	$4,100	$4,560
− Cost of Goods Sold	4	4,900	4,100	4,560
= Ending Inventory, April 30	0	$ -0-	$ -0-	$ -0-

Ending inventory amounts for one period become the beginning inventory of the next period. Therefore, the beginning inventory for April for each cost flow method is the amount that had been calculated as ending inventory for March. If all items on hand are sold, cost of goods sold will equal cost of goods available for sale. No PHIPs are left in ending inventory at the end of April.

Using the COGS and EI calculations in Exhibit 9-29, we can develop the company's income statement for the month of April 1995 and its balance sheet at April 30 under each of the three cost flow methods. These are shown in Exhibit 9-30. Note that, while the income statements for April are different under the three methods (as they were for March), the balance sheet at April 30 is identical under the three methods.

PHIPS 'R' US
Income Statement
For the Month Ended April 30, 1995

	Cost Flow Method		
	FIFO	LIFO	Average Cost
Sales	$ 6,000	$ 6,000	$ 6,000
LESS: Cost of Goods Sold	4,900	4,100	4,560
Gross Margin	$ 1,100	$ 1,900	$ 1,440
Operating Expenses:			
Warehouse Rent	$ (200)	$ (200)	$ (200)
Net Income.................................	$ 900	$ 1,700	$ 1,240

PHIPS 'R' US
Balance Sheet
April 30, 1995

	Cost Flow Method		
	FIFO	LIFO	Average Cost
ASSETS:			
Cash..	$19,200	$19,200	$19,200
Accounts Receivable	6,000	6,000	6,000
Merchandise Inventory...............	-0-	-0-	-0-
Total Assets...............................	$25,200	$25,200	$25,200
LIABILITIES AND			
STOCKHOLDERS' EQUITY:			
Accounts Payable	$ -0-	$ -0-	$ -0-
Common Stock	15,000	15,000	15,000
Additional Paid-in Capital...........	8,000	8,000	8,000
Retained Earnings	2,200*	2,200†	2,200‡
Total Liabilities and			
Stockholders' Equity...............	$25,200	$25,200	$25,200

* $1,300 balance at April 1 + $ 900 April net income = $2,200.

† $ 500 balance at April 1 + $1,700 April net income = $2,200.

‡ $ 960 balance at April 1 + $1,240 April net income = $2,200.

9-19. Because the balance sheet is affected by the income statement, how can the balance sheet at the end of April be identical under the three inventory cost flow methods when the income statements for April were different (Exhibit 9-30)?

No one method of determining cost flow is better than another because, in the long run, they all produce the same results. Any differences, such as those we saw on the financial statements of PHIPs 'R' Us, are the effects of attempting to measure earnings activities (revenues and expenses) for relatively short periods of time (one month, three months, one year). These differences will be important to you as you explore the financial statements of companies.

When the authors of *Accounting Trends and Techniques* surveyed 600 companies to determine which inventory cost flow method they used for the year 1993, this was the response:

FIFO:	417
LIFO:	348
Average Cost:	189
Other:	42
Total:	996

The total of 996 far exceeds the number of companies surveyed because many companies use one method for one type of merchandise inventory and another method for a different type of merchandise. PHIPs 'R' Us, for example, might use the average cost method on its PHIPs, but FIFO on the accessories it sells. Clearly, FIFO, LIFO, and average cost are the most widely used inventory cost flow assumptions, so as financial statement readers, you are most likely to see these three methods.

9-20. Which method (FIFO, LIFO, or average cost) matches the most recent cost to current revenues?

As was the case with accounting for depreciation of long-lived assets, discussed in Chapter 8, accounting for the cost of merchandise inventory has a significant impact on a company's reported net income for a given income statement period. The amount reported as inventory on the balance sheet is also greatly affected. Informed users of financial statements must have an understanding of the impact of inventory cost flow method choice if they hope to be able to use the accounting information to the fullest extent possible.

Now that you have an understanding of some of the issues and situations that impact financial statements, we will explore in more detail the construction of the balance sheet and income statement in Chapter 10.

SUMMARY

The term "merchandise inventory" (or just "inventory") refers to the physical units of goods that a company plans to sell. Inventory on hand at the beginning of a given income statement period (beginning inventory) and the inventory bought during the period (purchases) constitute the total amount of goods the company *could* sell (goods available for sale). Goods available for sale will either be on hand at the end of the period or be assumed sold.

Under accrual accounting, when inventory is purchased, its cost is considered an asset to the company and is listed as such on the balance sheet. As inventory is sold, its cost is converted from an asset to an expense, which is listed on the income statement as cost of goods sold. It follows, then, that the total cost of goods available for sale will end up either as ending inventory (an asset on the balance sheet) or as cost of goods sold (an expense on the income statement).

Two types of systems have been developed to track the cost of inventory. The periodic system counts inventory and traces costs only at the end of each income statement period, while the perpetual system updates inventory counts and costs each time a sale or purchase is made. Perpetual inventory systems usually make use of computer technology and scanners that read UPC codes. Even though inventory records are updated often when a perpetual system is in place, physical inventory counts are still necessary. Determining the actual amount of inventory on hand may uncover theft, damage, or spoilage of inventory.

The physical flow of inventory is quite different from the flow of inventory costs. Several methods have been developed to trace inventory costs as they move from the balance sheet to the income statement. All of these methods are cost flow *assumptions* that prescribe which inventory items are assumed to be the ones sold. The first-in, first-out (FIFO) method assumes that the first units of inventory purchased are the first ones sold. Conversely, the last-in, first-out (LIFO) method assumes that the last units of inventory purchased are the first sold. The average cost method assigns an average cost to the units of inventory on hand at the time of each sale. Companies may choose to use any of these cost flow assumptions. If the price they pay for inventory items varies during the period, the choice will impact several amounts reported on the company's financial statements.

Key Terms

average cost method The inventory cost flow method that assigns an average cost to the units of inventory on hand at the time of each sale. (p. 289)

beginning inventory The amount of merchandise inventory (units or dollars) on hand at the beginning of the income statement period. (p. 266)

book inventory The amount of ending inventory (units and dollars) resulting from transactions recorded by a perpetual inventory system. (p. 277)

cost of goods sold The cost of the merchandise inventory no longer on hand, and assumed sold during the period. (p. 266)

cost of sales Another name for cost of goods sold. (p. 266)

ending inventory The amount of inventory (in units or dollars) still on hand at the end of an accounting period. (p. 266)

FIFO (first in, first out) The inventory flow concept based on the assumption that the first units of inventory purchased are the first ones sold. (p. 269)

goods available for sale The total amount of merchandise inventory a company has available to sell in a given income statement period. (p. 266)

inventory Another term for merchandise inventory. (p. 265)

LIFO (last in, first out) The inventory flow concept based on the assumption that the last units of inventory purchased are the first ones sold. (p. 270)

merchandise inventory The physical units (goods) a company buys to resell as part of its business operation. (p. 265)

periodic inventory system An inventory system in which all inventory and cost of goods sold calculations are done at the end of the income statement period. (p. 275)

perpetual inventory system An inventory system in which both the physical count of inventory units and the cost classification (asset or expense) are updated whenever there is a transaction involving inventory. (p. 275)

purchases The amount of merchandise inventory bought during the income statement period. (p. 266)

REVIEW THE FACTS

A. Define the terms "inventory" and "merchandise inventory."

B. What two amounts are added to determine goods available for sale (GAFS)?

C. GAFS is allocated to two places in financial statements. Name them.

D. Under accrual accounting, the cost of inventory still on hand at the end of the period is shown on which financial statement?

E. Under accrual accounting, the cost of inventory no longer on hand at the end of the period is shown on which financial statement?

F. Explain the difference between the physical flow of merchandise and the cost flow of merchandise.

G. What are the two types of inventory systems? Explain the differences between them.

H. List three causes of differences between book inventory and the results of a physical inventory count.

I. Why are FIFO, LIFO, and average cost referred to as "assumptions"?

J. Describe in your own words the differences among the FIFO, LIFO, and average cost methods.

APPLY WHAT YOU HAVE LEARNED

9-21. Nathlee Flandro Company began the month of March 1996 with 152 units of product on hand at a total cost of $1,824. During the month, the company purchased an additional 409 units at $15 per unit. Sales for March were 366 units at a total cost of $5,034.

REQUIRED:

From the information provided, complete the following schedule:

	Units	Cost
Beginning Inventory		
+ Purchases	_____	_____
= Goods Available for Sale		
− Cost of Goods Sold	_____	_____
= Ending Inventory	_____	_____

9-22. Chris G Company began the month of June 1996 with 75 units of product on hand at a total cost of $1,500. During the month, the company purchased an additional 280 units at $20 per unit. Sales for June were 255 units at a total cost of $5,100.

From the information provided, complete the following schedule:

	Units	Cost
Beginning Inventory		
+ Purchases..	_____	_____
= Goods Available for Sale		
− Cost of Goods Sold	_____	_____
= Ending Inventory..............................	_____	_____

9-23. Robert Randolph Company began the month of April 1996 with 226 units of product on hand at a cost of $27 per unit. During the month, the company purchased an additional 750 units at a total cost of $20,250. At the end of April, there were 308 units still on hand.

REQUIRED:

From the information provided, complete the following schedule:

	Units	Cost
Beginning Inventory		
+ Purchases..	_____	_____
= Goods Available for Sale		
− Ending Inventory..............................	_____	_____
= Cost of Goods Sold	_____	_____

9-24. Bennett and Mason Company began the month of July 1996 with 206 units of product on hand at a cost of $17 per unit. During the month, the company purchased an additional 650 units at a total cost of $11,050. At the end of July, there were 356 units still on hand.

REQUIRED:

From the information provided, complete the following schedule:

	Units	Cost
Beginning Inventory		
+ Purchases..	_____	_____
= Goods Available for Sale		
− Ending Inventory..............................	_____	_____
= Cost of Goods Sold	_____	_____

9-25. Paul Jackson and Company began the month of February 1996 with 325 units of product on hand at a total cost of $5,525. During the month, the company purchased an additional 942 units at $18 per unit. Sales for February were 867 units at $32 per unit. The total cost of the units sold was $15,406 and operating expenses totaled $9,450.

REQUIRED:

a. From the information provided, complete the following schedule:

	Units	Cost
Beginning Inventory............................		
+ Purchases..	_____	_____
= Goods Available for Sale		
− Cost of Goods Sold	_____	_____
= Ending Inventory................................	_____	_____

b. Prepare Jackson and Company's income statement for the month ended February 28, 1996.

9-26. Larry Allen and Company began the month of October 1996 with 235 units of product on hand at a total cost of $3,760. During the month, the company purchased an additional 622 units at $17 per unit. Sales for October were 640 units at $30 per unit. The total cost of the units sold was $10,645 and operating expenses totaled $5,650.

REQUIRED:

a. From the information provided, complete the following schedule:

	Units	Cost
Beginning Inventory............................		
+ Purchases..	_____	_____
= Goods Available for Sale		
− Cost of Goods Sold	_____	_____
= Ending Inventory................................	_____	_____

b. Prepare Larry Allen and Company's income statement for the month ended October 31, 1996.

9-27. Connie Borg TV Sales and Service began the month of March with two identical TV sets in inventory. During the month, six additional TV sets (identical to the two in beginning inventory) were purchased as follows:

2 on March 9
1 on March 13
3 on March 24

The company sold two of the TV sets on March 12, another one on March 17, and two more on March 28.

REQUIRED:

a. Assuming the company uses a perpetual inventory system and the first-in, first-out cost flow method:

(1) Which two TV sets were sold on March 12?

(2) Which one was sold on March 17?

(3) Which two TV sets were sold on March 28?

(4) The cost of which three TV sets will be included in Borg's inventory at the end of March?

b. If the company uses a perpetual inventory system and the last-in, first-out cost flow method, the cost of which three TV sets will be included in Borg's inventory at the end of March?

9-28. Penny's Piano Sales & Service began the month of February with two identical pianos in inventory. During the month, six additional pianos (identical to the two in beginning inventory) were purchased as follows:

2 on February 10
1 on February 20
3 on February 26

The company sold two of the pianos on February 12, another one on February 17, and two more on February 28.

REQUIRED:

a. Assuming the company uses a perpetual inventory system and the first-in, first-out cost flow method:

(1) Which two pianos were sold on February 12?

(2) Which one was sold on February 17?

(3) Which two pianos were sold on February 28?

(4) The cost of which three pianos will be included in Penny's inventory at the end of February?

b. If the company uses a perpetual inventory system and the last-in, first-out cost flow method, the cost of which three pianos will be included in Penny's inventory at the end of February?

9-29. Edmunds Company buys and then resells a single product as its primary business activity. This product is called the Do-Daw and is subject to rather severe cost fluctuations. Following is information concerning Edmunds' inventory activity for the Do-Daw product during the month of July 1996:

July 1:   431 units on hand, $3,017.
July 2:   Sold 220 units.
July 9:   Purchased 500 units @ $11 per unit.
July 12:   Purchased 200 units @ $9 per unit.
July 16:   Sold 300 units.
July 21:   Purchased 150 units @ $6 per unit.
July 24:   Purchased 50 units @ $8 per unit.
July 29:   Sold 500 units.

REQUIRED:

Assuming Edmunds employs a perpetual inventory system, calculate cost of goods sold (units and cost) for the month of July 1996 and ending inventory (units and cost) at July 31, 1996, using the following:
  a. First-in, First-out method.
  b. Last-in, First-out method.
  c. Average Cost method (round all unit cost calculations to the nearest penny).
  d. Which of the three methods resulted in the highest cost of goods sold for July? Which one will provide the highest ending inventory value for Edmunds' balance sheet?
  e. How would the differences among the three methods affect Edmunds' income statement and balance sheet for the month?

9-30. Dana Condie Company buys and then resells a single product as its primary business activity. This product is called the PHIP (Product Having Increasing Prices). Following is information concerning Condie's inventory activity for the PHIP product during the month of October 1996:

October 1:   216 units on hand @ $4 per unit.
October 5:   Sold 80 units.
October 7:   Purchased 150 units @ $7 per unit.
October 11:   Purchased 100 units @ $11 per unit.
October 15:   Sold 200 units.
October 21:   Purchased 300 units @ $13 per unit.
October 25:   Purchased 50 units @ $18 per unit.
October 29:   Sold 350 units.

REQUIRED:

   a. Assuming Condie employs a perpetual inventory system, calculate cost of goods sold (units and cost) for the month of October, using the following:

      (1) First-in, First-out method.

      (2) Last-in, First-out method.

      (3) Average Cost method (round all unit cost calculations to the nearest penny).

   b. Which of the three methods resulted in the highest cost of goods sold for October? Which one will provide the highest ending inventory value for Condie's balance sheet?

   c. How would the differences among the three methods affect Condie's income statement and balance sheet for the month?

9-31. David Buehner Company buys and then resells a single product as its primary business activity. This product is called the PHDP (Product Having Declining Prices). Following is information concerning Buehner's inventory activity for the PHDP product during the month of August, 1996:

August 1:   216 units on hand @ $18 per unit.

August 5:   Sold 80 units.

August 7:   Purchased 150 units @ $13 per unit.

August 11: Purchased 100 units @ $11 per unit.

August 15: Sold 200 units.

August 21: Purchascd 300 units @ $7 per unit.

August 25: Purchased 50 units @ $4 per unit.

August 29: Sold 350 units.

REQUIRED:

   a. Assuming Buehner employs a perpetual inventory system, calculate cost of goods sold (units and cost) for the month of August, using the following:

      (1) First-in, First-out method.

      (2) Last-in, First-out method.

      (3) Average Cost method (round all unit cost calculations to the nearest penny).

   b. Which of the three methods resulted in the highest inventory amount for Beuhner's August 31 balance sheet?

   c. How would the differences among the three methods affect Beuhner's income statement and balance sheet for the month?

9-32. Joylene Ellis Company buys and then resells a single product as its primary business activity. This product is called the PHSP (Product Having Stable Prices). Following is information concerning Ellis' inventory activity for the PHSP product during the month of July 1996:

July 1:   216 units on hand @ $4 per unit.

July 5:   Sold 80 units.

July 7:   Purchased 150 units @ $4 per unit.

July 11:   Purchased 100 units @ $4 per unit.

July 15:   Sold 200 units.

July 21:   Purchased 300 units @ $4 per unit.

July 25:   Purchased 50 units @ $4 per unit.

July 29:   Sold 350 units.

REQUIRED:

a. Assuming Ellis employs a perpetual inventory system, calculate cost of goods sold (units and cost) for the month of July, using the following:

   (1) First-in, First-out method.

   (2) Last-in, First-out method.

   (3) Average Cost method (round all unit cost calculations to the nearest penny).

b. Which of the three methods resulted in the highest cost of goods sold for July?

c. Describe the differences among income statements and balance sheets prepared under the three cost flow assumptions.

9-33. Presented below is a list of items relating to the concepts presented in this chapter, followed by definitions of those items in scrambled order:

a. Periodic inventory system   e. Merchandise inventory

b. Perpetual inventory system   f. First-in, First-out method

c. Goods available for sale   g. Last-in, First-out method

d. Cost of goods sold   h. Average cost method

1. ___ The total amount of merchandise inventory a company can sell during a particular income statement period.

2. ___ All inventory and cost of goods sold calculations are done at the end of the period.

3. ___ Cost of goods sold is determined based on the assumption that the first units acquired are the first ones sold.

4. ___ Updates both the physical count of inventory units and the cost classification of those units whenever there is a transaction involving inventory.

5. ___ The physical units of product a company buys and then resells as part of its business operation.

6. ___ Cost of goods sold is based on the assumption that the last units acquired are the first ones sold.

7. ___ Cost of goods sold is determined based on the total cost of inventory units divided by the number of units.

8. ___ The cost of merchandise inventory that has been converted from an asset on the balance sheet to an expense on the income statement.

REQUIRED:

Match the letter next to each item on the list with the appropriate definition. Each letter will be used only once.

9-34. Barbara Bitner Company and Mike Bordeaux Company both began operation on January 2, 1996. Both companies experienced exactly the same reality during 1996: They purchased exactly the same number of units of merchandise inventory during the year at exactly the same cost, and they sold exactly the same number of inventory units at exactly the same selling price during the year. They also purchased exactly the same type and amount of property, plant, and equipment and paid exactly the same amount for those purchases.

At the end of 1996, the two companies prepared income statements for the year. Bitner reported net income of $92,000 and Bordeaux reported net income of $55,000.

REQUIRED:

List and discuss all items you can think of that might have caused the reported net income for the two companies to be different. (*Note:* Do not restrict yourself to items covered in Chapter 9.)

9-35. Pete Ligeros and Company is a merchandiser. The company uses a perpetual inventory system, so both the physical count of inventory units and the cost classification (asset or expense) are updated whenever there is a transaction involving inventory. The company's accounting records yielded the following schedule for the month of October 1995:

	Units	Cost
Beginning Inventory, October 1 ...	200	$ 600
+ Purchases During October	1,700	5,100
= Goods Available for Sale	1,900	$5,700
− Cost of Goods Sold	1,500	4,500
= Ending Inventory, October 31	400	$1,200

On October 31, 1995, Ligeros conducted a physical count of its inventory and discovered there were only 375 units of inventory actually on hand.

REQUIRED:

a. Show Ligeros' schedule of cost of goods sold and ending inventory as it should be, to reflect the results of the physical inventory count on October 31.

b. Explain in your own words how the company's income statement and balance sheet will be affected by the results of the physical inventory count on October 31.

c. What are some possible causes of the difference between the inventory amounts in Ligeros' accounting records and the inventory amounts from the physical count?

10

The Balance Sheet and Income Statement: A Closer Look

Balance sheets and income statements are generally more complex than the ones we have explored so far. An understanding of the organization of these two financial statements is crucial, particularly when very detailed information is included. Even complex balance sheets and income statements are organized in a manner which serves to clarify rather than complicate the information provided.

I n the previous chapters of this book, we have introduced you to several financial statements economic decision makers use as tools to predict a company's future ability to generate positive cash flow. In this chapter, we return to the balance sheet and income statement.

To refresh your memory, we will briefly reiterate the purpose of each of these financial statements. The *balance sheet*, introduced in Chapters 4 and 5, is probably the best presentation of a company's current condition. It discloses what a business possesses (assets) and who has claim to those assets (liabilities and owners' equity). The balance sheet offers a snapshot of the financial position of a company as of a particular date. The *income statement*, introduced in Chapter 6, is probably the best presentation of a company's most recent past performance. It discloses a company's net income for a specific period of time (e.g., month, quarter, year). Information about the company's inflows (revenues and gains) and outflows (expenses and losses) is provided.

In this chapter, we will explore in further detail the construction of the balance sheet and income statement. Understanding why these two financial statements are organized as they are will help you to better comprehend the information provided by them. After all, the primary purpose of these and other financial statements is to provide information useful to economic decision makers. In addition, understanding the construction of the income statement and balance sheet is necessary to do financial statement analysis, which we will discuss in later chapters.

After completing your work on this chapter, you should be able to do the following:

1. **Describe in your own words how the balance sheet and income statement were developed as financial statements.**
2. **Explain the organization and purpose of the classified balance sheet.**
3. **Explain why recurring and nonrecurring items are presented separately on the income statement.**
4. **Interpret the net of tax disclosure of extraordinary items, discontinued operations, and accounting changes.**
5. **Describe in your own words the additional information provided by comparative financial statements.**

HISTORY AND DEVELOPMENT OF THE BALANCE SHEET AND INCOME STATEMENT

E ver since human beings began living in organized societies, they have kept track of their business affairs by "accounting" for economic events and transactions. Throughout history this has been done by recording these events and transactions on stone or clay tablets, papyrus, paper, or whatever writing material was available.

Originally, accounting records were not maintained for the purpose of preparing periodic financial statements. Books were kept to assist in conducting a company's operation rather than to report on the operation of a company. Amounts owed to suppliers, for example, were recorded so a company could keep track of what had and had not been paid, not so the company could show the proper amount of accounts payable on its balance sheet. Eventually, however, records were kept for the specific purpose of preparing financial statements. In *A History of Accounting Thought*, Michael Chatfield describes this transition as follows:

> More than most accounting tools, financial statements are the result of cumulative historical influences. Before the Industrial Revolution they were usually prepared as arithmetic checks of ledger balances. Afterward the roles were reversed and it was account books which were reorganized to facilitate statement preparation. As statements became communication devices rather than simple bookkeeping summaries, the journal and ledger evolved from narratives to tabulations of figures from which balances could easily be taken. (p. 64)

Financial statements, as we know them, are a relatively recent phenomenon. While accounting has been with us since long before the birth of Christ, the balance sheet, designated as a financial statement, only emerged around A.D. 1600. This statement was the primary output of the accounting process for several hundred years. In fact, the income statement, as a separate financial statement, was not developed until the late 1800s, and even then, the information it provided was not considered nearly as important as the balance sheet figures. In his landmark work *Accounting Evolution to 1900*, A. C. Littleton makes the following observation:

> It seems that the primary motive for separate financial statements was to obtain information regarding capital; this was the center of the interest of partners, shareholders, lenders, and the basis of the calculation of early property taxes. Thus balance-sheet data were stressed and refined in various ways, while expense and income data were incidental—in fact, the latter in the seventeenth century were presented merely as a "proof of estate"—to demonstrate by another route the correctness of the balance sheet. (p. 153)

At the beginning of the twentieth century, the income statement still had not attained the status of an important financial statement in its own right. Borrowing from banks was then the chief form of external financing available to companies in the United States. For this reason, creditors were the primary audience for whom financial statements were prepared. Since creditors' chief concern was whether a company would be able to repay its debts, the balance sheet—which focuses on the relationships among assets, liabilities, and owners' equity—was of prime importance.

During the first two decades of the twentieth century, there was a shift in the way U.S. companies financed expansion. They began to rely less on debt financing and more on equity financing, meaning they borrowed less from banks and sold more stock. When selling stock became the major source of external financing, stockholders became the primary users of financial statements. Stockholders are interested in the performance of the company and its impact on dividend payments and the value of the company's stock. Net income, therefore, became a primary focus of financial statement users, so the income statement came to be considered more important than the balance sheet. Over time even long-term creditors realized that earning power was crucial to debt repayment, so they also began to rely more on the income statement than on the balance sheet.

Late in the century, it became apparent that the balance sheet and the income statement are best used together. Neither is more important than the other. Each of these statements provides valuable information for economic decision makers. By learning more about the detailed structure of the balance sheet and income statement, you can make the best use of the information provided by each statement.

Financial statements, we have stressed, must be constructed for the benefit of the economic decision makers who use them. The more complex the company and its activities, the more complex its financial statements will be. This complexity can be confusing to those who do not understand the reasons the statements are organized the way they are. Users who do understand the reasons, however, find the manner in which the balance sheet and income statement are organized extremely helpful in assessing a company's present condition and past performance.

ORGANIZATION OF THE BALANCE SHEET

In introducing the balance sheet in Chapter 4, we used this simple equation:

ASSETS = LIABILITIES + OWNERS' EQUITY

We made no attempt to distinguish one asset from another or one liability from another. So long as we were using the cash basis of accounting, this did not present any serious problems—particularly on the asset side, because cash is the only asset under this basis of measurement. Even under the accrual basis, a balance sheet using this basic format could be presented.

A balance sheet prepared for Louise Eliason and Company at December 31, 1995, using the basic format would look like Exhibit 10-1.

Exhibit 10-1
Basic Format Balance Sheet

LOUISE ELIASON and COMPANY
Balance Sheet
December 31, 1995

Total Assets	$1,516,800
Liabilities .... $ 851,000	
Stockholders' Equity........ 665,800	
Total Liabilities and Stockholders' Equity	$1,516,800

This balance sheet gives economic decision makers very little useful information about the financial position of Eliason and Company at December 31, 1995. Even if the company uses the cash basis of accounting (meaning the $1,516,800 of assets is cash), there is no indication of how soon the $851,000 of liabilities must be paid or how much of the $665,800 of stockholders' equity is contributed capital and how much is retained earnings.

Why does any of this matter? What difference does it make to those who use the balance sheet? The answer is obvious if you remember that economic decision makers are attempting to predict the future and timing of cash flows by looking at the balance sheet. In response to this need for additional information, a more detailed balance sheet format was developed.

The Classified Balance Sheet

classified balance sheet
A balance sheet showing assets and liabilities categorized into current and long-term items.

A **classified balance sheet** prepared for Louise Eliason and Company at December 31, 1995, would look like Exhibit 10-2.

This balance sheet bears little resemblance to the one presented in Exhibit 10-1, but in fact, assets still total $1,516,800; total liabilities are still $851,000; and stockholders' equity is still $665,800. The only difference in the two balance sheet presentations is the amount of detail disclosed.

As we explain why the classified balance sheet is organized as it is, we will make reference to the Eliason and Company classified balance sheet in Exhibit 10-2.

DISCUSSION QUESTIONS

10-1. Which of the two balance sheet presentations for Eliason and Company do you think would be more useful in predicting the future and timing of the company's cash flow? Provide three specific examples to support your position.

Like many people, you may be intimidated and confused by the amount of detail in a classified balance sheet. This is certainly understandable, because it is much more complex than the basic format balance sheet. Your confusion will disappear, however, once you understand the rationale behind the different classifications.

The accrual accounting basis of measurement creates a need to segregate, or classify, assets on the balance sheet because, under this basis, items besides cash are considered assets. Two classifications of assets are identified on the balance sheet: current and long-term. **Current assets** are defined as assets that are either cash already or are expected to become cash within one year. As you can see from

current assets Assets that are either cash or will become cash within one year.

Exhibit 10-2
Classified Balance Sheet

LOUISE ELIASON and COMPANY
Balance Sheet
December 31, 1995

ASSETS:
Current Assets:

Cash... $	100	
Accounts Receivable...	251,000	
Inventory...	298,900	
Prepaid Expenses	50,000	
Total Current Assets		$ 600,000

Long-Term Assets:

Land...$	125,000	
Plant and Equipment.................... $1,075,000		
LESS: Accumulated Depreciation .... (283,200)		
Plant and Equipment, Net	791,800	
Total Long-Term Assets		916,800
Total Assets...		$1,516,800

LIABILITIES:
Current Liabilities:

Accounts Payable .... $ 501,000		
Short-Term Note Payable.............. 50,000		
Total Current Liabilities.....................................		$ 551,000

Long-Term Liabilities:

Bonds Payable	300,000	
Total Liabilities		$ 851,000

STOCKHOLDERS' EQUITY:
Common Stock, No Par Value,

10,000 Shares Issued and Outstanding.............. $ 400,000		
Retained Earnings... 265,800		
Total Stockholders' Equity...		665,800
Total Liabilities and Stockholders' Equity.......................................		$1,516,800

long-term assets Assets that are expected to benefit the company for longer than one year.

liquidity An item's "nearness to cash."

Exhibit 10-2, accounts receivable and inventory are examples of current assets. **Long-term assets** are defined as those assets that are expected to last longer than a year. That is, it is not anticipated that they will become cash within one year. Depreciable assets such as buildings, equipment, and vehicles are examples of long-term assets. Because of the way the classified balance sheet is organized, users can tell in a quick glance just which assets (and their dollar amount) the company thinks will be turned into cash within the next year (current assets) and which ones are not expected to be converted into cash (long-term assets).

Assets are listed on a classified balance sheet in order of decreasing liquidity. **Liquidity** means "nearness to cash." The further you read down the asset section of a classified balance sheet, the less likelihood there is of an item being converted to cash in the near future. In the case of Eliason and Company, current assets total $600,000 and long-term assets total $916,800.

DISCUSSION QUESTIONS

10-2. Are there any items listed as current assets on Eliason's December 31, 1995, classified balance sheet (Exhibit 10-2) that you think will never be converted into cash? If there are, why do you think they are classified as current assets?

10-3. Eliason has classified plant and equipment as long-term assets in 1995. Does this mean the company cannot sell one of its buildings in 1996? Explain your reasoning.

Almost all companies, certainly those that manufacture tangible products, have both current assets and long-term assets on their balance sheets. This photo of Veryfine's production process shows some of each type of asset. The machinery shown is surely classified as a long-term asset. Over its estimated useful life, its cost will be systematically converted to expense for the periods benefited by its use. The bottles of apple juice are classified as current assets (inventory) until they are sold, whereupon their cost is converted to expense (cost of goods sold).

Peter Vandermark/Stock Boston

current liabilities Liabilities that must be paid within one year.

long-term liabilities Amounts that are not due for repayment until at least one year from now.

The other sections of a classified balance sheet are constructed applying a system similar to that used to list assets. That is, liabilities and items constituting owners' equity are listed in order of how quickly they must be paid. This is why liabilities on the balance sheet are listed before stockholders' equity: If a company goes out of business, obligations to creditors must be paid before funds can be distributed to the owners.

Within the liabilities section of the classified balance sheet, amounts owed by a company are separated into categories reflecting how soon they must be repaid. The **current liabilities** are those debts that require payment within one year. Certainly, the suppliers to whom Eliason and Company owes a total of $501,000 (accounts payable) expect repayment within the year. Debts not requiring repayment within the next year are classified as **long-term liabilities**. Once again, the reason for this separation is obvious if you remember what the balance sheet is supposed to tell economic decision makers. Because of the way the balance sheet is organized, users know at a quick glance which liabilities are expected to be retired within the next year (current liabilities) and which ones are not (long-term liabilities). In the case of Eliason and Company, current liabilities total $551,000 and long-term liabilities total $300,000.

Exhibit 10-3 illustrates the current and long-term classifications of assets and liabilities.

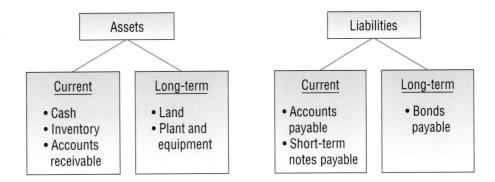

Exhibit 10-3
Examples of Current and Long-Term Assets and Liabilities

Assets		Liabilities	
Current	**Long-term**	**Current**	**Long-term**
• Cash	• Land	• Accounts payable	• Bonds payable
• Inventory	• Plant and equipment	• Short-term notes payable	
• Accounts receivable			

DISCUSSION QUESTIONS

10-4. Provide three examples of current liabilities and three examples of long-term liabilities not shown on the Eliason and Company balance sheet in Exhibit 10-2.

10-5. Eliason shows $600,000 of current assets and $551,000 of current liabilities. Who might be interested in these amounts, and why?

The stockholders' equity section of a classified balance sheet is also separated into two classifications. The first of these reflects the amount invested by the owners of the business. In the case of Eliason and Company, this is the $400,000 classified as no-par common stock. The second classification in this section, retained earnings, discloses the equity built by the company through profitable operations. At December 31, 1995, Eliason and Company had a retained earnings balance of $265,800.

DISCUSSION QUESTIONS

10-6. Some people prefer to call the second of the stockholders' equity classifications *reinvested* earnings rather than *retained* earnings. Why do you think that is so?

10-7. On average, how much did Eliason and Company receive for each share of stock sold?

10-8. What is the total current market value of the Eliason and Company stock?

ORGANIZATION OF THE INCOME STATEMENT

hen we introduced the income statement in Chapter 6, we used the following simple equation:

REVENUES – EXPENSES = NET INCOME

An income statement prepared for Louise Eliason and Company for the year ended December 31, 1995, using this simple format, would look like Exhibit 10-4.

Exhibit 10-4
Basic Format Income Statement

LOUISE ELIASON and COMPANY
Income Statement
For the Year Ended December 31, 1995

Revenue..	$752,500
LESS: Expenses.................................	(840,400)
Net Loss...	$ (87,900)

Net income—or net loss—is, of course, "the bottom line," and discloses whether or not a company has been profitable for a given period. This *is* important, and we would never suggest otherwise. However, there is more to the story of Eliason and Company's performance for 1995 than "net loss of $87,900."

To furnish a more complete picture of what happened to a business during a particular income statement period, income statement presentation guidelines have been developed. Income statements prepared following these guidelines provide more detail than given in the basic format shown in Exhibit 10-4, as well as important information about the characteristics of the revenues and expenses. Exhibit 10-5 is an income statement for Eliason and Company for the year ended December 31, 1995, prepared using the expanded format.

Although this income statement bears little resemblance to the one presented earlier in our discussion, revenues still total $752,500; total deductions from revenues still total $840,400; and the net loss is still $87,900. By this time the format should look familiar to you. In fact, only the last few lines should be new.

Exhibit 10-5
Expanded Format Income
Statement

LOUISE ELIASON and COMPANY
Income Statement
For the Year Ended December 31, 1995

Sales Revenue		$ 752,500
LESS: Cost of Goods Sold		352,800
Gross Profit on Sales		$ 399,700
LESS: Operating Expenses:		
Selling	$ 60,250	
General and Administrative	96,250	
Total Operating Expenses		(156,500)
Operating Income		$ 243,200
LESS: Interest Expense		(30,650)
Income Before Taxes		$ 212,550
LESS: Income Taxes		(64,660)
Income Before Extraordinary Item		$ 147,890
Extraordinary Loss (LESS: Income Taxes of $87,420)		(235,790)
Net Loss		$ (87,900)

10-9. Is Exhibit 10-5 a single-step or multistep income statement? How can you tell?

10-10. If you were considering some kind of economic involvement with Eliason and Company, which number on the expanded income statement would you consider most reliable in predicting the company's future profitability? Explain.

Recurring and Nonrecurring Items

Besides presenting more detail concerning Eliason and Company's regular revenues and expenses for 1995, the income statement in Exhibit 10-5 shows an extraordinary loss of $235,790, which is separated from the company's regular, recurring revenues and expenses. An extraordinary loss (or gain) is one of the items the accounting profession has determined should be shown separately as a nonrecurring item on the income statement.

A **nonrecurring item** can be broadly defined as any item (either positive or negative) that should not be considered a normal part of continuing operations because it is not expected to recur. Let's explore the logic of separating recurring and nonrecurring items on the income statement.

nonrecurring item Results of activities that cannot be expected to occur again, and therefore should not be used to predict future performance.

Suppose something happened to a company during the income statement period that was not expected to recur. This "something" might have been good or bad, but whatever it was, it is not expected to happen again. The company must report it because it happened. On the other hand, suppose you were looking at the company's income statement for the purpose of attempting to predict the company's ability to generate future profits (and therefore cash flows). If the company lumped this one-time "something" in with revenues and expenses that happen over and over again, you could be misled. Therefore, if nonrecurring items are deemed to *not* be representative of the ongoing results of a company's operations, it makes sense to report them separately from what *is* representative of the continuing operations.

If the extraordinary loss is truly a nonrecurring item for Eliason, then the net loss of $87,900 for 1995 is not a good predictor of future profitability and cash flow. In fact, the best predictive number on this income statement is probably $147,890 listed as the income before extraordinary item. Extraordinary losses are one type of nonrecurring item.

In this section, we will more fully explain the presentation and interpretation of information about nonrecurring items on the income statement. Throughout our discussion, we will use the Ogata, Inc., income statement for the year ended December 31, 1995, that is presented in Exhibit 10-6.

Income statements such as Ogata's (Exhibit 10-6) separate reported activities broadly into those that are expected to recur and those that are not. The first half of Ogata's income statement reflects results of activities that will probably continue in the future. The income tax amount shown ($64,760) relates to the ongoing activities of the company. Notice the item identified as "Income from Continuing Operations." The $95,890 represents the net results of Ogata's ongoing operations. Information provided on the income statement below this point relates to nonrecurring items.

The point on an income statement separating recurring from nonrecurring activities is always just below the presentation of income taxes. The amount remaining after taxes have been considered is often referred to as income from continuing operations, but the line on the income statement is not always titled as such. For instance, if the only item Ogata needed to report below the $95,890 had been the extraordinary gain, the line referring to the $95,890 would have been identified as "income before extraordinary item." In other words, the line representing the net result of a company's ongoing operations may be titled in various ways depending on the nonrecurring items that will be reported below it. The important thing here is that you be able to identify the results of a company's ongoing operations, indicated by the amount remaining after income taxes have been considered. Don't let the specific title of that line concern you. It should reflect what items are being reported below, in the section of the income statement dealing with nonrecurring items.

Recall that a nonrecurring item is any item (positive or negative) that should not be considered a normal part of continuing operations because it is not expected to recur. Proper classifications of items as recurring or nonrecurring is critical to the usefulness of the accounting information. A company might be tempted to treat an item as nonrecurring because it would make the income statement "look bad" to include it with its regular expenses. Or, in

OGATA, INC.
Income Statement
For the Year Ended December 31, 1995

Sales..		$ 858,600
LESS: Cost of Goods Sold..		456,800
Gross Profit on Sales...		$ 401,800
LESS: Operating Expenses:		
Selling	$ 94,450	
General and Administrative.....................................	116,050	
Total Operating Expenses		(210,500)
Operating Income		$ 191,300
LESS: Interest Expense		(30,650)
Income from Continuing Operations before Taxes........................		$ 160,650
LESS: Income Taxes		(64,760)
Income from Continuing Operations...		$ 95,890
Discontinued Operations:		
Income from Discontinued Operations		
(LESS: Income Taxes of $27,400)	$ 71,300	
Loss on Disposal of Discontinued Operation		
(LESS: Income Taxes of $16,300)	(54,000)	17,300
Income Before Extraordinary Item and Cumulative		
Effect of a Change in Accounting Principle..........................		$ 113,190
Extraordinary Gain (LESS: Income Taxes of $70,000)		131,470
Cumulative Effect of a Change in Accounting		
Principle (LESS: Income Taxes of $13,440)..........................		(38,400)
Net Income		$ 206,260

order to make the income statement "look good," it might want to include an item with its regular recurring revenues even though it is probably a nonrecurring item. To prevent companies from confusing the users of financial statements this way, the accounting profession is very restrictive as to what items may be considered nonrecurring.

The only three items normally reported on the income statement after income taxes from the business' normal operations are: (1) discontinued operations; (2) extraordinary items; and (3) changes in accounting principle. We will consider the criteria for each of these items after we discuss the income tax effects of these nonrecurring items.

Income Tax Disclosure

On Ogata's income statement there is an income tax amount shown in the income from continuing operations section ($64,760). This is the amount of tax expense associated with the ongoing, recurring operation of the business. So far, so good. But how should the company disclose the income tax effect of the non-recurring items shown on the income statement? These things happened, there will certainly be income tax consequences, and those consequences must be disclosed.

Since the three major types of nonrecurring items are presented in a section of the income statement separate from continuing operations, lumping their tax effect with the tax expense shown for continuing operations would distort the information. On the other hand, to show two different income tax expense amounts on the income statement (one for recurring items and one for nonrecurring items) would be confusing to statement users. The accounting profession has decided that the only tax expense shown on the income statement as a separate line item will be the amount associated with continuing operations. Therefore, the three major types of nonrecurring items included on the income statement are shown "less income tax," or "net of tax."

net of tax The proper presentation format for nonrecurring items shown below income from continuing operations on the income statement.

Net of tax means the amount shown for an item has been adjusted for any income tax effect. The treatment relates specifically to the nonrecurring items presented below income tax expense on the income statement.

Let's think about the effect of a gain experienced by a business on the taxes it must pay. The total amount a business earns is more because of a gain. Therefore, the Internal Revenue Service will require more taxes. The effect of a gain, then, is to increase the amount of taxes owed. *The actual amount of a gain is reduced by the increased tax caused by the gain* (see Exhibit 10-7).

Now let's consider the impact of a loss incurred by a business on the taxes it must pay. The total amount a business earns is less because of a loss. Therefore, the Internal Revenue Service will require less taxes. The effect of a loss, then, is to reduce the amount of taxes owed. *The actual amount of a loss is reduced by the tax savings caused by the loss* (see Exhibit 10-7).

Exhibit 10-7
Effect of Tax on Gains and Losses

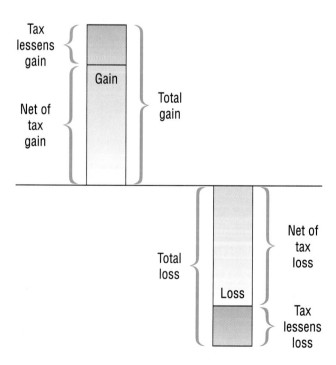

Current accounting rules require that on the face of the income statement the tax effect on each of these nonrecurring items, and the amount of that item *after* the tax effect, be shown. With this information, financial statement users can determine the actual amount of the item *before* any tax effect.

Now look again at the income statement for Ogata, Inc. (Exhibit 10-6 on page 319). Notice that the statement includes examples of the three major types of nonrecurring items, and all receive the same general presentation: Each is shown below "Income from Continuing Operations," and each is shown "net of tax."

Now it is time to explore the criteria for and specific presentation of each of these types of nonrecurring item.

Discontinued Operations

business segment A portion of the business for which assets, results of operations, and activities can be separately identified.

discontinued operations The disposal of a business segment. One of the nonrecurring items shown net of tax on the income statement.

If a company disposes of a major segment of its business, the results of operations for the segment of the company sold *and* any gain or loss from the actual disposal of the **business segment** are reported as nonrecurring items on the income statement. A business segment may be a portion of an entity representing either a separate major line of business or class of customer. In either case, specific criteria must be met in order for the **discontinued operations** to qualify as the disposal of a business segment. The part of the business being eliminated is considered a business segment

P rovided that its assets, results of operations, and activities can be clearly distinguished, physically and operationally and for financial reporting purposes, from the other assets, results of operations, and activities of the entity.

(APB Opinion No. 30, paragraph 13)

The following examples of situations meeting the criteria for disposal of a business segment may help you understand the application of these criteria:

1. A sale by a diversified company of a major division which represents the company's only activities in the electronics industry...
2. A sale by a meat packing company of a 25% interest in a professional football team...
3. A sale by a communications company of all its radio stations which represent 30% of gross revenues. The company's remaining activities are three television stations and a publishing company....
4. A food distributor disposes of one of its two divisions. One division sells food wholesale primarily to supermarket chains and the other division sells food through its chain of fast food restaurants, some of which are franchised and some of which are company-owned.

(AICPA Accounting Interpretations, AIN-APB30, #1)

Ryder is best known as a truck rental company. However, for many years it was also involved in aviation services. When Ryder disposed of its aviation services operation, results of the transaction were reported as discontinued operations. For 1992, Ryder reported a $6 million gain (net of tax) on the disposal of the aviation business segment. The net earnings generated by the segment during 1992 (before its sale) were also reported net of tax.

Merrim/Monkmeyer Press

10-11. The following examples do *not* qualify as disposals of business segments. For each one, explain specifically what criterion/criteria have not been met.

(a) The sale, by a mining company, of a major foreign subsidiary engaged in silver mining, which represents all of that company's interests in that particular country....

(b) The sale by a petrochemical company of a 25% interest in a petrochemical plant that was accounted for as an investment....

(c) A manufacturer of children's wear discontinues all of its operations in Italy which were composed of designing and selling children's wear for the Italian market....

(d) A diversified company sells a subsidiary which manufactures furniture. The company has retained its other furniture manufacturing subsidiary....

(e) The sale of all the assets (including the plant) related to the manufacture of men's woolen suits by an apparel manufacturer in order to concentrate activities in the manufacture of men's suits from synthetic products....

(AICPA Accounting Interpretations, AIN-APB30, #1)

Once a judgment has been made that the discontinued operations should be considered the disposal of a business segment, specific disclosures on the income statement are required. To illustrate, let's look back at Exhibit 10-6, the income statement for Ogata, Inc., for the year ended December 31, 1995.

Ogata is a merchandising company that buys and sells toys. Many years ago (for reasons no one at the company can remember), Ogata purchased a company that manufactured hats. While this portion of the business has always been profitable, current management did not feel the hat business fit into the corporation's strategic plans and sold it during 1995. Two items presented on Ogata's 1995 income statement reflect the disposal of the hat operation.

Ogata reported income from discontinued operations of $71,300. In 1995, prior to being sold, the hat operation had revenues of $200,000 and expenses of $101,300. So its pretax income for the time Ogata owned it during the year was $98,700 ($200,000 revenues – $101,300 expenses). Income taxes on the results of discontinued operations totaled $27,400, so the amount shown for income from discontinued operations on the income statement is $71,300 ($98,700 – $27,400). Because the hat operation is gone by the end of the year and can no longer be expected to generate income, the results for that part of the business are reported separately, net of tax.

Ogata also shows a $54,000 loss on the disposal of discontinued operations. When the company sold the hat operation, it incurred a $70,300 pretax loss on the sale. This loss resulted in a reduction of $16,300 in income taxes for the year. The after-tax loss was $54,000 ($70,300 – $16,300).

After each component of the results of discontinued operations is reported, the two amounts can be combined. The $71,300 income from discontinued operations and the $54,000 loss on disposal of the discontinued operation are netted, resulting in a total of $17,300 under discontinued operations as a non-recurring item on Ogata's income statement for 1995.

This example illustrates the proper income statement presentation of the disposal of a business segment, one of the three types of nonrecurring items requiring net of tax disclosure.

Extraordinary Items

extraordinary item A gain or loss that is both unusual in nature and infrequent in occurrence. One of the nonrecurring items shown net of tax on the income statement.

When used in financial statements, the word "extraordinary" has a very specific meaning. In order for an event to result in an **extraordinary item**, the event must be both *unusual* in nature and *infrequent* in occurrence. It can't be simply one or the other; it must be both. Judgment must be exercised in deciding whether or not to classify the result of an event as an extraordinary item.

When applying the criterion of "unusual in nature," the operating environment of the business entity must be considered.

> The environment of an entity includes such factors as the characteristics of the industry or industries in which it operates, the geographical location of its operations, and the nature and extent of government regulation. Thus, an event or transaction may be unusual in nature for one entity but not for another because of differences in their respective environments.
>
> (APB Opinion No. 30, paragraph 21)

So, a gain or loss that would be considered extraordinary for one company might not be considered extraordinary for another company.

This building was completely destroyed by a flood. Whether the loss associated with this catastrophe would be considered an extraordinary item depends on whether the loss is considered both unusual in nature and infrequent in occurrence. If the building is located in an area where floods often occur, the loss would likely not be considered extraordinary. If, on the other hand, floods are unusual and infrequent in this geographical area, the loss probably would be considered extraordinary. Each case where an item might be considered extraordinary must be considered separately within the operating environment of the business entity.

Grant/Monkmeyer Press

The operating environment of the entity must also be considered when applying the criterion of "infrequent in occurrence." In order to be considered infrequent, an event must not be expected to recur in the foreseeable future.

As you use financial statement information, a basic appreciation of how these criteria are applied will enhance your ability to interpret the impact of extraordinary items. The following are examples of events or transactions that would meet the criteria of unusual and infrequent, and should therefore be presented as extraordinary items on the income statement:

1. A large portion of a tobacco manufacturer's crops are destroyed by a hailstorm. Severe damage from hailstorms in the locality where the manufacturer grows tobacco is rare.

2. A steel fabricating company sells the only land it owns. The land was acquired ten years ago for future expansion, but shortly thereafter the company abandoned all plans for expansion and held the land for appreciation in value instead.

3. A company sells a block of common stock of a publicly traded company. The block of shares, which represents less than 10 percent of the publicly held company, is the only security investment the company has ever made.

4. An earthquake destroys one of the oil refineries owned by a large multinational oil company.

10-12. The following examples do *not* qualify as extraordinary items. For each one, explain specifically what criterion/criteria have not been met.

a. A citrus grower's Florida crop is damaged by frost....

b. A company which operates a chain of warehouses sells the excess land around one of its warehouses. When the company buys land to establish a new warehouse, it usually buys more land than it expects to use for the warehouse with the expectation that the land will appreciate in value....

c. A large diversified company sells a block of shares from its portfolio which it has acquired for investment purposes. This is the first sale from its portfolio of securities....

d. A textile manufacturer with only one plant moves to another location. It has not relocated a plant in twenty years and has no plans to do so in the foreseeable future....

(AICPA Accounting Interpretations, AIN-APB30, #1)

When the criteria of unusual in nature and infrequent in occurrence are deemed to have been met, an extraordinary item is presented on the income statement net of tax. Accounting rules specify (1) instances in which the criteria may be ignored and (2) certain types of events that *always* result in extraordinary items. However, rather than have you focus on those guidelines, we believe it is more important that you learn how to properly interpret the information provided by companies reporting extraordinary items. Let's return to the income statement for Ogata, Inc. (Exhibit 10-6 on page 319).

Ogata has reported an extraordinary gain of $131,470 ($201,470 less income taxes of $70,000). This gain resulted from the city government's purchase of land owned by the company. The property was located adjacent to the municipal airport, and the government needed it to complete an airport expansion project. Ogata's land was taken as a result of government expropriation. In other words, the company had no choice but to sell the property to the government.

The type of transaction that led to the gain has never happened before and is not likely to happen again. It is unusual in nature and infrequent in occurrence, both for Ogata and for its industry. Therefore it should be reported as an extraordinary item; a user of Ogata's financial statement information should not assume that this gain is repeatable.

One last point: We mentioned earlier that in order to be considered extraordinary (and therefore be presented net of tax) an item must be *both* unusual in nature and infrequent in occurrence. If an item is unusual in nature *or* infrequent in occurrence, it is shown as a separate component of continuing operations. That is, it warrants a separate line on the income statement, but will still be shown in the continuing operations section (above income tax expense) and will not be shown net of tax. Items that meet one but not both criteria of extraordinary items are generally identified as "special" or "unusual" items on the income statement. It is also acceptable for the term "nonrecurring" to be used in the presentation of these items.

Changes in Accounting Principles

One important factor in the usefulness of accounting information is consistency. Earlier, in Chapter 3, we discussed how the need for this quality discourages companies from changing their accounting methods. However, from time to time, business entities do find it necessary to make changes. In fact, the Financial Accounting Standards Board views changes in accounting principles or standards as part of accounting's natural progression.

> C onsistent use of accounting principles from one accounting period to another, if pushed too far, can inhibit accounting progress. No change to a preferred accounting method can be made without sacrificing consistency, yet there is no way that accounting can develop without change. Fortunately, it is possible to make the transition from a less preferred to a more preferred method of accounting and still retain the capacity to compare the periods before and after the change if the effects of the change of method are disclosed.
>
> (Statement of Accounting Concepts #2, paragraph 122)

cumulative effect of a change in accounting principle Results of adopting a new accounting standard or changing from one acceptable method of accounting to another. One of the nonrecurring items shown net of tax on the income statement.

Disclosure of the effects of these changes results in the third major type of nonrecurring item that is shown on the income statement net of tax: **cumulative effect of a change in accounting principle**. This nonrecurring item can result from either of two scenarios. Bear in mind, however, that in both cases the company must be changing from one *acceptable* accounting treatment to another *acceptable* treatment.

The first scenario involves the adoption of a newly required accounting standard. When a company applies a new accounting method required by the implementation of a new standard, net income is often adversely affected. This effect on net income must be reported in the year of implementation of the new rule. However, often the impact of a new standard is actually a cumulative effect, so the presentation represents how the new standard would have impacted income if it had been in place throughout the life of the company. Whenever a new standard is implemented, the effect is considered to be a nonrecurring item and is presented net of tax on the income statement.

The second scenario springs from the fact that there are many acceptable choices as to the methods used to account for a company's transactions and events. A company may choose to change from one acceptable method of accounting for an item to another acceptable method. For instance, in Chapter 8 we discussed two different methods for calculating periodic depreciation expense—straight-line and double-declining-balance—and in Chapter 9 we presented three different methods of accounting for the flow of inventory costs—FIFO, LIFO, and average cost. These are examples of the areas in which various accounting methods are allowed. However, as we emphasized in our earlier presentations, the choice of method can have a significant impact on reported net income for a period. Therefore, changes among these methods require proper presentation of the effect of the change on the income statement.

The required presentation for a cumulative effect of a change in accounting principle is the same whether the change was caused by a new accounting rule or was a discretionary choice. To illustrate this presentation, let's return once again to the example of Ogata, Inc. This company began operation in 1971, and from the beginning used the average cost method to account for its inventory transactions. Then, in 1995, Ogata decided to change to the FIFO method. The effect of this change was a significant reduction in the company's net income. This amount, however, is not related entirely to 1995. Rather, it relates to the years from 1971 to 1995. That is, if Ogata went all the way back to when it first began using the average cost method and recalculated all its inventory transactions using the FIFO method, cost of goods sold would have been higher for the 25-year period, and therefore, net income would have been lower over that same time span.

The change happened in 1995, so the effect must be reported in 1995. But to report the entire amount as an effect on cost of goods sold in 1995 would be misleading to those who use Ogata's 1995 income statement to try to predict future results. So, instead, the *cumulative* effect of this change from average cost to FIFO is shown as a nonrecurring item on the 1995 income statement (Exhibit 10-6 on page 319).

DISCUSSION QUESTIONS

10-13. What was the pretax amount of the effect of Ogata's change from the average cost method to FIFO?

Changes in accounting principles, the third major category of nonrecurring items that are presented net of tax, is the category most often used. On the 1993 income statements of the 600 companies surveyed by *Accounting Trends and Techniques*, 517 accounting changes resulting from the adoption of newly enacted standards, and 275 accounting changes resulting from discretionary changes were reported. Extraordinary items were presented on 1993 income statements by 91 of the 600 surveyed companies. Less than 10 percent of the companies reported discontinued operations in 1993. In total, these statistics suggest that in a review of income statements from 600 companies, 928 nonrecurring items shown net of tax were encountered. Clearly, these are important items of accounting information.

The income statement, like the balance sheet, is constructed as it is for a purpose. That purpose is to provide financial statement users with better information with which to predict the future and timing of a company's cash flows. Understanding the details of the information provided in an income statement will make you a wiser financial statement user.

The financial statements presented to external parties are prepared for a one-year period. A year is a relatively short period of time—too short to be used in making many economic decisions, particularly those of a long-term nature. For this reason, serious analysis of income statement and balance sheet information requires financial statements for more than one accounting period.

comparative financial statements Financial statements showing results from two or more consecutive periods.

COMPARATIVE FINANCIAL STATEMENTS

Comparative financial statements are statements showing results for two or more consecutive periods—usually years or quarters. The reasoning behind the use of comparative financial statements is simple: An economic decision maker who has only one year's financial statements sees the small picture. With two, three, or more years of statements, the user gets a bigger picture of how a company is performing over time (see Exhibit 10-8). The more periods presented, the more complete the pic-

Exhibit 10-8
Comparative Financial Statements

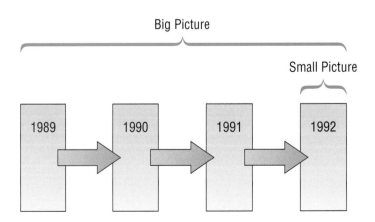

ture of how the company has been performing. The Committee on Accounting Procedure described the importance of comparative financial statements this way:

> S uch presentation emphasizes the fact that statements for a series of periods are far more significant than those for a single period and that the accounts for one period are but an installment of what is essentially a continuous history.

(ARB 43, Chapter 2, paragraph 1)

To illustrate the presentation of comparative financial statements, we provide the 1995 and 1996 income statements and balance sheets for Flores, Inc. in Exhibit 10-9.

DISCUSSION QUESTIONS

10-14. Using the comparative income statements and balance sheets of Flores, Inc., presented in Exhibit 10-9, prepare the company's 1996 statement of retained earnings.

10-15. What specific information that was not apparent from Flores' income statements or balance sheets did the statement of retained earnings you developed for Discussion Question 10-14 provide?

Exhibit 10-9
1996 and 1995 Financial
Statements for Flores, Inc.

FLORES, INC.
Income Statements
For the Years Ended December 31, 1996, and 1995
(in thousands)

		1996		1995
Sales		$14,745		$12,908
LESS: Cost of Goods Sold		10,213		8,761
Gross Profit on Sales		$ 4,532		$ 4,147
LESS: Operating Expenses				
Selling	$ 1,022		$ 546	
General and Administrative	2,721		2,451	
Total Operating Expenses		(3,743)		(2,997)
Operating Income		$ 789		$ 1,150
LESS: Interest Expense		(172)		(137)
Income Before Taxes		$ 617		$ 1,013
LESS: Income Taxes		(123)		(355)
Net Income		$ 494		$ 658

(continued on page 330)

Exhibit 10-9
(continued)

FLORES, INC.
Balance Sheets
December 31, 1996, and December 31, 1995
(in thousands)

ASSETS:		1996		1995
Current Assets:				
Cash		$ 2,240		$ 1,936
Accounts Receivable		2,340		2,490
Merchandise Inventory		776		693
Prepaid Expenses		200		160
Total Current Assets		$ 5,556		$ 5,279
Plant and Equipment:				
Buildings	$ 7,723		$ 6,423	
LESS: Accumulated Depreciation	(3,677)		(3,534)	
Buildings, Net		$ 4,046		$ 2,889
Equipment	$ 2,687		$ 2,387	
LESS: Accumulated Depreciation	(1,564)		(1,523)	
Equipment, Net		1,123		864
Total Plant and Equipment		$ 5,169		$ 3,753
Total Assets		$10,725		$ 9,032
LIABILITIES:				
Current Liabilities:				
Accounts Payable	$ 1,616		$ 1,080	
Notes Payable	2,720		2,920	
Total Current Liabilities		$ 4,336		$ 4,000
Long-Term Liabilities		2,000		1,600
Total Liabilities		$ 6,336		$ 5,600
STOCKHOLDERS' EQUITY:				
Common Stock, No Par Value		$ 3,000		$ 2,400
Retained Earnings		1,389		1,032
Total Stockholders' Equity		$ 4,389		$ 3,432
Total Liabilities and Stockholders' Equity		$10,725		$ 9,032

Comparative financial statements enhance the user's ability to analyze a company's past performance and present condition. They also make it possible to perform several analytical techniques, which we will explore in later chapters. Financial statement analysis, in fact, begins with the use of the statement of cash flows—the fourth financial statement, which is introduced in the next chapter.

SUMMARY

The two primary financial statements we have explored thus far, the balance sheet and the income statement, provide important information for economic decision makers. The balance sheet provides a picture of a company's financial position on a given day. This statement outlines what the company owns (assets), what it owes (liabilities) and the residual amount which can be claimed by the owner(s) (equity). The income statement provides a report of the results of business activity during a specific period. Its disclosures of revenues, expenses, gains and losses for the period are used to measure a company's past performance.

Both the balance sheet and income statement are useful tools. By learning more about the construction and organization of these statements, users of balance sheet and income statement information are able to use the information contained in the statements more effectively.

The classified balance sheet separates assets into two major categories: current and long-term. Liabilities on a classified balance sheet are similarly separated into current and long-term. These classifications provide additional information to users of the information.

Income statements often include items that are not part of the company's normal operations and are not expected to recur. Inflows or outflows of this type must be separated from results of activities that are expected to recur as part of the company's normal, ongoing operations. Reporting recurring items and nonrecurring items separately offers financial statement users additional useful information. Three major types of nonrecurring item (discontinued operations, extraordinary items, and changes in accounting principles) are presented below income from continuing operations and are shown net of tax. The other most common type of nonrecurring item, one that is unusual or infrequent but not both, is shown within the section of the income statement related to continuing operations, but is identified as a special item.

Even with the additional detail offered by a classified balance sheet or an expanded format income statement, economic decision makers are not getting the "big picture" if they consider financial statement information from only one period. Comparative financial statements, providing information for two or more consecutive periods, offer a clearer view of a company's performance and financial position.

Key Terms

business segment A portion of the business for which assets, results of operations, and activities can be separately identified. (p. 321)

classified balance sheet A balance sheet showing assets and liabilities categorized into current and long-term items. (p. 312)

comparative financial statements Financial statements showing results from two or more consecutive periods. (p. 328)

cumulative effect of a change in accounting principle Results of adopting a new accounting standard or changing from one acceptable method of accounting to another. One of the nonrecurring items shown net of tax on the income statement. (p. 326)

current assets Assets that are either cash or will become cash within one year. (p. 312)

current liabilities Liabilities that must be paid within one year. (p. 314)

discontinued operations The disposal of a business segment. One of the nonrecurring items shown net of tax on the income statement. (p. 321)

extraordinary item A gain or loss that is both unusual in nature and infrequent in occurrence. One of the nonrecurring items shown net of tax on the income statement. (p. 323)

liquidity An item's "nearness to cash." (p. 313)

long-term assets Assets that are expected to benefit the company for longer than one year. (p. 313)

long-term liabilities Amounts that are not due for repayment until at least one year from now. (p. 314)

net of tax The proper presentation format for nonrecurring items shown below income from continuing operations on the income statement. (p. 320)

non-recurring item Results of activities that cannot be expected to occur again, and therefore should not be used to predict future performance. (p. 317)

REVIEW THE FACTS

A. What was the original purpose of accounting records?

B. What caused the shift in attention from the balance sheet to the income statement?

C. Explain why a decision maker may prefer a classified balance sheet to one using the simplest possible format.

D. What is the difference between current and long-term assets? Offer two examples of each.

E. In what order are assets presented on a classified balance sheet?

F. Describe the difference between current and long-term liabilities and provide two examples of each.

G. Explain the difference between recurring and nonrecurring items on an income statement. Why are these items reported separately?

H. Identify the three major types of nonrecurring items that are shown net of tax on the income statement.

I. Explain the effect of taxes on both gains and losses.

J. What is a business segment?

K. What criteria must be met for an item to be considered extraordinary?

L. What does the cumulative effect of a change in accounting principle represent?

M. Describe comparative financial statements and explain their benefits to economic decision makers.

10-16. Presented below are some items related to the organization of the classified balance sheet, followed by the definitions of those items in scrambled order.

a. Liquidity

b. Current assets

c. Long-term assets

d. Current liabilities

e. Long-term liabilities

f. Stockholders' equity

g. Total liabilities and stockholders' equity

h. Plant and equipment, net

1. ____ Obligations not requiring payment within the next year

2. ____ Items controlled by a company that are not expected to become cash within the next year

3. ____ Describes an item's nearness to cash

4. ____ The owners' residual interest in a corporation

5. ____ Long-lived tangible assets less all the depreciation expense ever recognized on those assets

6. ____ Obligations that must be retired within the next year

7. ____ Equal to total assets

8. ____ Items controlled by a company that are expected to become cash within the next year

REQUIRED:

Match the letter next to each item with the appropriate definition. Each letter will be used only once.

10-17. Presented below are some items related to the multistep income statement as discussed in this chapter, followed by the definitions of those items in scrambled order.

a. Gross profit on sales

b. Operating expenses

c. Income from continuing operations

d. Discontinued operation

e. Extraordinary item

f. Change in accounting principle

g. Recurring item

h. Nonrecurring item

1. ____ A material gain or loss that is both unusual in nature and infrequent in occurrence

2. ____ Generally, the difference between normal ongoing revenues and normal ongoing expenses

3. ____ The difference between sales and cost of goods sold

4. ____ Any item that should not be considered a normal part of continuing operations because it is not expected to happen again

5. ___ Sacrifices incurred in the normal day-to-day running of a business

6. ___ Any item considered a normal part of continuing operations because it is expected to happen on an ongoing basis

7. ___ A change from a less preferred to a more preferred method of accounting

8. ___ The disposal of a business segment

REQUIRED:

Match the letter next to each item with the appropriate definition. Each letter will be used only once.

10-18. Presented below are the major sections of the classified balance sheet, followed by a list of items normally shown on the balance sheet.

a. Current assets   **d.** Long-term liabilities

b. Long-term assets   **e.** Contributed capital

c. Current liabilities   **f.** Retained earnings

1. ___ Accounts payable

2. ___ Common stock

3. ___ Buildings

4. ___ Accounts receivable

5. ___ Note payable due within one year

6. ___ Prepaid expenses

7. ___ Preferred stock

8. ___ Note payable due in two years

9. ___ Amounts earned by the company but not yet distributed to the owners of the business

10. ___ Amounts received in excess of par value on the sale of stock

11. ___ Bonds payable

12. ___ Land

13. ___ Cash

14. ___ Wages payable

15. ___ Vehicles

REQUIRED:

Indicate where each item on the list should be shown on the classified balance sheet by placing the letter of the appropriate balance sheet section in the space provided. The letters may be used more than once.

10-19. Presented below are several sections of the multistep income statement, followed by several independent situations or transactions.

a. Sales

b. Cost of goods sold

c. Income from continuing operations

d. Discontinued operation

e. Extraordinary item

f. Change in accounting principle

1. _____ A manufacturing company sells a warehouse with a book value of $20,000 for $20,000

2. _____ A company changed from the FIFO method to the average cost method of accounting for inventory cost flows

3. _____ A company sells units of inventory in the normal course of its business operation

4. _____ A company located in San Francisco, California, experiences a loss from earthquake damage. This loss is determined to be a "special" item

5. _____ A company disposes of a major segment of its business

6. _____ A company pays wages, rent, utilities, and so forth

7. _____ A company located in Columbia, South Carolina, experiences a loss from earthquake damage. This loss is determined to be both unusual in nature and infrequent in occurrence

8. _____ A company adopts a newly required accounting standard for accounting for postretirement benefits other than pensions. As a result, net income for the year is adversely affected

REQUIRED:

Indicate where the result of each situation or transaction should be shown on the multistep income statement by placing the letter of the appropriate income statement section in the space provided. The letters may be used more than once. Note: The results of some situations or transactions may not be shown on the income statement. If so, place the letter "n" in the space provided.

10-20. The following items relate to Hennekas Corporation at December 31, 1995:

Land	$210,000
Cash	14,600
Accounts Receivable	92,300
Accounts Payable	74,000
Common Stock (75,000 Shares Outstanding)	150,000
Bonds Payable	200,000
Additional Paid-in Capital—Common Stock	60,000
Inventory	118,000
Prepaid Expenses	11,200
Taxes Payable	17,000
Short-Term Note Payable	50,000

Buildings and Equipment..	400,000
Retained Earnings...	117,300
Wages Payable	35,800

Accumulated Depreciation (which is not reflected in the totals above) is $142,000 on the Buildings and Equipment.

REQUIRED:

a. What is the par value of Hennekas Corporation's common stock? Explain how you determined your answer.

b. How much cash did Hennekas Corporation receive from the sale of its common stock? Explain how you determined your answer.

c. Prepare a classified balance sheet for Hennekas Corporation at December 31, 1995.

10-21. The following items relate to Corbridge and Company at December 31, 1995:

Accounts Payable..	$172,000
Common Stock ($3.00 Par Value)................................	300,000
Bonds Payable	307,700
Prepaid Expenses	9,800
Taxes Payable	47,000
Short-Term Note Payable	70,000
Buildings and Equipment...	875,000
Additional Paid-in Capital—Common Stock.................	340,000
Land...	490,000
Cash	124,200
Accounts Receivable..	212,000
Inventory..	338,000
Retained Earnings...	463,700
Wages Payable	77,600

Accumulated Depreciation (which is not reflected in the totals above) is $271,000 on the Buildings and Equipment.

REQUIRED:

a. How many shares of Corbridge and Company's common stock are outstanding at December 31, 1995? Explain how you determined your answer.

b. How much cash did Corbridge and Company receive from the sale of its common stock? Explain how you determined your answer.

c. Prepare a classified balance sheet for Corbridge and Company at December 31, 1995.

10-22. The following items relate to Bob Devitt, Inc., for the year ended December 31, 1996:

- Sales for the year totaled $865,000.
- Cost of goods sold for the year totaled $471,000.
- Regular operating expenses for the year were $145,000.
- Interest expense for the year was $27,000.
- On February 18, 1996, one of Devitt's warehouses burned to the ground. The company's loss (after the insurance settlement) was $106,000 before any tax effect. This loss was determined to be both unusual in nature and infrequent in occurrence.
- During 1996, Devitt changed the way it depreciated its property, plant, and equipment from an accelerated method to the straight-line method. The cumulative effect of this change was a $93,000 increase in net income before any tax effect.
- Devitt's income tax rate is 40 percent on all items.

REQUIRED:

Prepare Devitt's income statement for the year ended December 31, 1996, using the expanded multistep format presented in this chapter.

10-23. The following items relate to Linda Chidister and Company for the year ended December 31, 1996:

- Sales for the year totaled $675,000.
- Cost of goods sold for the year totaled $472,500.
- Regular operating expenses for the year were $119,500.
- Interest expense for the year was $16,000.
- On September 5, 1996, Chidister sold the only land it owned at a pretax gain of $150,000. The land was acquired in 1986 for future expansion, but shortly thereafter the company abandoned all plans for expansion and held the land for appreciation.
- During 1996, Chidister changed the way it accounted for inventory from the FIFO method to the average cost method. The cumulative effect of this change was an $80,000 decrease in net income before any tax effect.
- Chidister's income tax rate is 30 percent on all items.

REQUIRED:

Prepare Chidister's income statement for the year ended December 31, 1996, using the expanded multistep format presented in this chapter.

10-24. The following items relate to Marsden Blanch Company for the year ended December 31, 1996:

- Sales for the year totaled $1,275,000.
- Cost of goods sold for the year totaled $867,000.
- Operating expenses for the year were $202,500.
- Interest expense for the year was $43,000.
- On June 30, 1996, Blanch sold a major segment of its business at a loss of $95,000 before any tax effects. This segment of the company represented a major line of business that was totally separate from the rest of Blanch's operation.
- Prior to being sold, the business segment had sales during 1996 of $150,000, cost of goods sold of $90,000 and operating expenses of $45,000. These amounts are *not* included in the previous information provided.
- Blanch's income tax rate is 40 percent on all items.

REQUIRED:

Prepare Blanch's income statement for the year ended December 31, 1996, using the expanded multistep format presented in this chapter.

10-25. The following items relate to Rollene Bradshaw, Inc., for the year ended December 31, 1996:

- Sales for the year totaled $565,000.
- Cost of goods sold for the year totaled $339,000.
- Operating expenses for the year were $103,200.
- Interest expense for the year was $11,000.
- On July 16, 1996, Bradshaw sold a major segment of its business at a gain of $50,000 before any tax effects. This segment of the company represented a major line of business that was totally separate from the rest of Bradshaw's operation.
- Prior to being sold, the business segment had sales during 1996 of $60,000, cost of goods sold of $40,000, and operating expenses of $35,000. These amounts are *not* included in the previous information provided.
- Bradshaw's income tax rate is 30 percent on all items.

REQUIRED:

Prepare Bradshaw's income statement for the year ended December 31, 1996, using the expanded multistep format presented in this chapter.

10-26. Assets on the classified balance sheet are identified as either current or long-term. Liabilities on the classified balance sheet are also identified as either current or long-term.

REQUIRED:

a. What criterion is used to determine whether an asset or liability is classified as current or long-term?

b. Explain in your own words why the following parties would be interested in the separation of current and long-term assets and liabilities on a company's balance sheet:

    (1) Short-term creditors (other businesses from whom the company buys inventory, supplies, etc.).

    (2) Long-term creditors (banks and others from whom the company borrows money on a long-term basis).

    (3) The company's stockholders.

    (4) The company's management.

10-27. Stockholders' equity on the classified balance sheet of a corporation is divided into two major categories: contributed capital and retained (reinvested) earnings.

REQUIRED:

a. Explain in your own words what each of the two major categories under stockholders' equity represents.

b. Explain in your own words why the following parties would be interested in the relative amounts of contributed capital and retained earnings in the stockholders' equity section of a company's balance sheet:

    (1) Short-term creditors (other businesses from whom the company buys inventory, supplies, etc.).

    (2) Long-term creditors (banks and others from whom the company borrows money on a long-term basis).

    (3) The company's stockholders.

    (4) The company's management.

10-28. The multistep income statement as presented in this chapter separates recurring items from nonrecurring items. Further, three major types of nonrecurring item are shown on the income statement net of tax.

REQUIRED:

a. Explain in your own words the rationale behind showing recurring and nonrecurring items separately on the multistep income statement.

b. Explain in your own words what the phrase "net of tax" means and why three major types of nonrecurring item are shown in this manner on the income statement.

11

Tools of the Trade, Part III The Statement of Cash Flows: Bringing the Focus Back to Cash

Thus far, we have explored three financial statements developed in response to the needs of economic decision makers. We have examined financial information produced using accrual accounting to measure results of business activity. As we have noted, the most striking weakness of accrual accounting is that it takes the information user's eye off cash. Another financial statement, the statement of cash flows, has been developed to bring the user's focus back to cash.

We have so far explored three major financial statements: the income statement, the statement of owners' equity, and the balance sheet. Our focus has been on information produced under the accrual basis of measurement. Recall that accrual accounting is affected by a number of items, which we have discussed:

■ The difficulties in determining when revenue should be recognized under accrual accounting.

■ The difficulties in matching expenses to the same income statement period as the revenues they helped generate.

■ The estimates of useful life and residual value required for depreciation.

■ Choices of inventory cost flow assumption (e.g., FIFO, LIFO) and depreciation method (e.g., straight-line, double-declining-balance).

These are just a few of the items that cause net income under accrual accounting to be different from the change in cash.

Net income is an opinion; cash is a fact.

—Anonymous

In a very real sense, this statement is true, particularly when the accrual basis of accounting is used to measure periodic earnings. And while accrual accounting has much to recommend it, it does have the weakness of taking the financial statement user's eye off cash. To address this problem and bring the financial statement user's focus back to cash, a fourth financial statement tool has been developed: the statement of cash flows. When information from this additional source is combined with the information contained in the other three financial statements, decision makers have a more complete picture of a company's financial health.

After completing your work on this chapter, you should be able to do the following:

1. Explain the purpose of the statement of cash flows.
2. Describe the three types of activities that can either generate or use cash in any business.
3. Reconcile accrual net income to the change in cash.
4. Determine where a company obtains its financing by examining its statement of cash flows.

INTRODUCTION TO THE STATEMENT OF CASH FLOWS

statement of cash flows
A financial statement that provides information about the causes of a change in a company's cash balance from the beginning to the end of a specific period.

I n its present format, the **statement of cash flows** has existed only since 1988. However, other forms of the statement have been in existence for a very long time. These earlier forms were known by such names as the "Where-Got and Where-Gone Statement," "The Funds Statement," the "Statement of Source and Application of Funds," and the "Statement of Changes in Financial Position."

All of these earlier versions had the same objectives as today's statement of cash flows. That is, their main purpose was to provide information about a company's cash receipts and cash payments during a specific period, for the balance sheet, income statement, and statement of owners' equity were not giving economic decision makers all the information they needed.

However, most earlier versions of this financial statement included items other than cash in their analyses. So while they helped users interpret the impact of accrual accounting procedures, they did not bring the financial statement user's focus firmly back to cash.

DISCUSSION QUESTIONS

11-1. How do revenue recognition and expense recognition criteria under accrual accounting take the focus off cash?

The statement of changes in financial position (SCFP) is the form of the statement that immediately preceded the currently used statement of cash flows. When the SCFP was introduced in 1971, the vast majority of companies prepared their SCFPs using the working capital format. This format was based on the assumption that **working capital**, which is defined as current assets less current liabilities, is a good approximation of cash. By examining items other than cash, the working capital format presented a broader picture of the changes experienced by a company. Statements using this format provided useful information to economic decision makers throughout the 1970s.

working capital The difference between current capital and current liabilities.

In the early 1980s, however, the financial environment changed significantly. Many companies became concerned about their cash flows as they took on increasing amounts of debt. The financial community also became more concerned about companies' cash flows, and therefore steadily more dissatisfied with the working capital format of the SCFP. After years of growing pressure on companies to provide more detailed information about the

sources and uses of their cash, the new statement of cash flows was introduced in 1988.

In addition to providing information about a company's cash receipts and cash payments during a specific period, the statement of cash flows helps investors, creditors, and other external parties to:

1. Assess a company's ability to generate positive future net cash flows.

2. Assess a company's need for external financing and its ability to pay its debts and pay dividends.

3. Reconcile the differences between net income and the change in cash.

The statement of cash flows is another tool of the trade to add to your repertoire (Exhibit 11-1).

Direct Method versus Indirect Method

There are two methods of preparing the statement of cash flows: the direct method and the indirect method. Both arrive at the same "bottom line."

direct method The format of a statement of cash flows that provides detail about the individual sources and uses of cash associated with operating activities.

The **direct method** involves a series of calculations to determine the amount of cash inflow (from customers, interest earned on loans, etc.) and cash outflow (to suppliers, employees, creditors, etc.). In addition, accounting rules require that if the direct method is used, a reconciliation must be shown to provide information about the relationship between the company's accrual net income and the cash used by or generated from the company's operations for the period. This information is very similar to that contained in the first section of the statement of cash flows that uses the other approach, the indirect method.

indirect method The more widely used format of the statement of cash flows. This approach begins with a reconciliation of accrual net income to the cash provided by or used by operating activities.

The **indirect method** is more closely tied to accrual accounting than is the direct method. Unlike the direct method, it does not attempt to provide any detail about the individual sources and uses of cash associated with the operating activities of a company. When the indirect method is used, the statement of cash flows begins with the accrual net income for the period. Then adjustments are made for all items included in the calculation of net income that did not either generate or use cash.

The detail concerning individual sources and uses of cash associated with the operating activities of a company that is provided under the direct method may be useful, but very few companies employ the direct approach. *Accounting Trends and Techniques* reports that of the 600 companies it surveyed, only 15 used the direct method for preparation of the statement of cash flows (Exhibit 11-2). Since the vast majority of firms use the indirect method, this is the method we will concentrate on in this chapter.

Exhibit 11-2
Users of the Direct and Indirect Methods of Preparing the Statement of Cash Flows

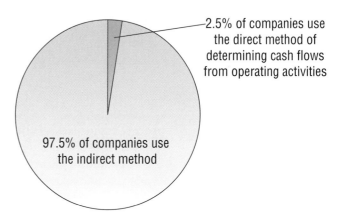

2.5% of companies use the direct method of determining cash flows from operating activities

97.5% of companies use the indirect method

Basic Organization of the Statement of Cash Flows

We have discussed the purpose of the statement of cash flows and how it attained its present form, but how does the statement go about fulfilling its purpose? The process begins by comparing the cash balance at the beginning of the period to the cash balance at the end of the period. The statement of cash flows discloses exactly what caused the cash balance to change from the beginning of the period to the end of the period.

Exhibit 11-3 shows the basic format of a statement of cash flows. Notice that the bottom line of the statement is the increase or decrease in cash during the period.

The statement of cash flows is organized around the three major types of business activities that can either generate or use cash: operating, investing, and financing. The total effect of these three categories of activities results in either a net increase or decrease in cash.

Exhibit 11-3
Basic Format of the Statement
of Cash Flows

Statement of Cash Flows
for the Year Ended December 31, 1996

Cash Flows from Operating Activities:

Net Income		$ XXXX
Adjustments to Reconcile Net Income to Net Cash Provided by Operating Activities:		
	XXX	
	XX	
Net Cash Provided (Used) by Operating Activities		?
Cash Flows from Investing Activities:		
	XX	
	XX	
Net Cash Provided (Used) by Investing Activities		?
Cash Flows from Financing Activities:		
	XXXX	
	XX	
Net Cash Provided (Used) by Financing Activities		?
Net Increase (Decrease) in Cash During 1996		$ XXX

Exhibit 11-3
Basic Format of the Statement
of Cash Flows

DISCUSSION QUESTIONS

11-2. **If you owned a small bookstore, what do you think would be your**

   a. operating activities?
   b. investing activities?
   c. financing activities?

   Explain your reasons for the classifications you made.

One of the most important tasks when developing a statement of cash flows, then, is to identify the business activities that took place during the period and to categorize them as operating, investing, or financing activities. We will describe each type of activity in turn.

Operating Activities

operating activities
Activities that result in cash inflows and outflows generated from the normal course of business.

Operating activities are those centered around the actual day-to-day business transactions of the company. A variety of transactions either generate or use cash. Cash is received (inflow) from the sale of goods or services. For example, McDonald's receives cash when its customers buy hamburgers. Cash is also received when a company earns interest on loans it has made to others, or when it receives dividends on investments it owns in other companies. Cash is paid (outflow) to suppliers for inventory, to employees for wages, to the government for taxes, to lenders for interest on loans, and to other parties for the expenses of running the company.

DISCUSSION QUESTIONS

11-3. Where would you look for the information to determine net cash flow from operations if your business used the cash basis of accounting?

If you think about the items listed in the previous paragraph, you will see they are all items that are reported on the income statement. Therefore, when attempting to determine the cash inflow and cash outflow from operating activities, the place to start is the income statement for the period. If Bart's Beanery uses the cash basis of accounting, net income for the period will equal the net cash inflow (or outflow) for the period from operating activities. If, however, Bart's uses the accrual basis of accounting, the net income figure must be adjusted for any revenue item that did not provide cash during this income statement period and any expense item that did not use cash during this income statement period. If this is not totally clear to you at this point, don't fret; we will show you how it works a little later in the chapter.

11-4. Think back to the situation in which you owned a small bookstore. If one of your customers purchased a large book order on account and had 30 days after she received the books to pay for them, how would this credit sale be reported for your company

    a. on a cash basis?

    b. on an accrual basis?

11-5. Continuing the scenario above, for your company's statement of cash flows, how would you determine the net cash flow from operations on an accrual basis?

Investing Activities

investing activities
Business activities related to long-term assets. Examples are the purchase and sale of property, plant, and equipment.

Investing activities are those centered on support of the operations. This support may take the form either of investments in assets necessary to the operation or of investments outside the company to wisely use any excess funds. For example, Campbell's Soup Company can use cash (outflow) to invest in machinery to can its soup, and it can later obtain cash (inflow) if it sells this machinery. Major assets used in a company's operations are often reported on the balance sheet in a category called "property, plant, and equipment." This classification includes the buildings, vehicles, furniture, equipment, and so on that a business needs to run its operations.

J.R. Simplot is the potato-processing company responsible for making billions of french fries for McDonald's each year. The company can generate cash from its machinery in two ways. The machinery can be used to produce potato products which can then be sold. Results of this activity would be reflected in net income, shown in the operating activities section of the statement of cash flows. Alternatively, the company could sell the machine. Cash inflows from the sale would be shown in the investing activities section of the statement of cash flows.

Courtesy of Simplot.

Companies normally sell these types of assets from time to time, as they are no longer needed. However, a company cannot afford to sell off assets it needs to run its operations for the obvious reason that, before long the cash generated through operating activities would be adversely affected. An airline, for example, could generate cash by selling all its airplanes, but if it did so, it would no longer be able to transport passengers and would go out of business. Instead of selling its property, plant, and equipment to generate cash, a growing and healthy company will likely use cash to acquire additional assets it can use in its operations. For this reason, the net cash flow from investing activities may very well be negative (net outflow) for companies that are experiencing healthy growth.

Besides investing in property, plant, and equipment, a company can purchase the stock of other companies or lend other companies money (both outflows). Cash is generated (inflow) when a company sells equity or debt investments (stocks or bonds of other companies). These are all examples of investing activities. Logically, it would seem that the interest earned on loans to others and the dividends received from investments in the stock of other companies would be classified under investing activities. However, because the amounts are reported on the income statement of the period, cash received from interest and dividends is almost always reported as results of operating activities.

If you think about the examples of investing activities mentioned in the previous two paragraphs, you will see they all involve items that are reported in the long-term asset section of the balance sheet. Therefore, when attempting to determine the cash inflow and cash outflow from investing activities, you must analyze the long-term asset section of the balance sheets at the start of the period and the end of the period. Once again, do not be concerned if this is not totally clear to you at this point. We will demonstrate the process a little later in the chapter.

Financing Activities

financing activities
Business activities, such as the issuance of debt or equity and the payment of dividends, that focus on the external financing of the company.

Because internal financing is accomplished through operating activities, **financing activities** reported on the statement of cash flows deal only with external financing. Companies can obtain cash (inflow) from two external sources. First, they can sell shares of stock (common or preferred). This subject was discussed in Chapter 4. Second, they can borrow, either by obtaining loans from banks or through issuing corporate bonds. This subject was presented in Chapter 5.

Under the financing activity category, companies report uses (outflows) of cash resulting from repaying loans and bonds, paying dividends to shareholders, and reacquiring shares of capital stock from their stockholders. Logically, the interest paid on borrowings might be classified under financing activities. However, because interest expense is reported on the income statement of the period, cash paid for interest is almost always reported as an operating activity.

If you think about the examples of financing activities mentioned in this section, you will see that they all involve items that are reported in the long-term liability or owners' equity section of the balance sheet. Therefore, when users are attempting to determine the cash inflow and cash outflow from financing activities, they must analyze those sections of the balance sheets at the start of the period and the end of the period. Once again, do not be concerned if this is not totally clear to you at this point. We will demonstrate the process a little later in the chapter.

Exhibit 11-4 summarizes what we have said so far about the three types of business activities as they are reported in the statement of cash flows. You should refer to this exhibit often as we discuss the construction and uses of the statement.

Although companies can have some fairly exotic variations on what is listed in Exhibit 11-4, every inflow and outflow of cash can be classified as a result of either operating, investing, or financing activities.

Exhibit 11-4

Summary of the Three Types of Business Activities Reported on the Statement of Cash Flows

---

Operating Activities (Income Statement Items)
    Cash inflows:
        From customers as a result of the sale of goods or services.
        From interest earned on loans to others.
        From dividends received from investment in the stock of other companies.

    Cash outflows:
        To suppliers for the purchase of inventory.
        To employees for salaries and wages.
        To governments for taxes.
        To creditors for interest on loans.
        To others for operating expenses.

Investing Activities (Long-Term Asset Items)
    Cash inflows:
        From the sale of property, plant, and equipment.
        From the sale of investments in debt or equity securities of other companies.

    Cash outflows:
        To purchase property, plant, and equipment.
        To purchase debt and equity investments in other companies.

Financing Activities (Long-Term Liability and Owners' Equity Items)
    Cash inflows:
        From selling shares of common stock or preferred stock.
        From bank loans or the sale of corporate bonds.

    Cash outflows:
        To pay dividends to stockholders.
        To reacquire shares of capital stock from stockholders.
        To repay loans or redeem corporate bonds.

CONSTRUCTION OF THE STATEMENT OF CASH FLOWS

We are now going to demonstrate how the statement of cash flows is constructed. Basically, we will be using an analysis of the changes in various other accounts to explain the overall change in cash. The necessary information can be found by examining balance sheets prepared in two consecutive periods. As you recall from Chapter 10, financial statements presented with two or more consecutive periods shown together are called *comparative financial statements*. For our example, we will use the information provided by the comparative balance sheets of Sanguine Company for 1996 and 1995 (Exhibit 11-5) and assume Sanguine uses accrual accounting. Be sure you understand that the balances in the asset, liability, and owners' equity accounts at the end of one period become the beginning balances in the next period. Thus, Exhibit 11-5 provides beginning and ending balances for all of Sanguine Company's balance sheet accounts for the year 1996—necessary information for the preparation of the company's statement of cash flows for 1996.

Exhibit 11-5

Comparative Balance Sheets for Sanguine Company for 1996 and 1995

SANGUINE COMPANY
Balance Sheets
December 31, 1996 and December 31, 1995
(in thousands)

ASSETS:		1996		1995
Current Assets:				
Cash		$ 2,800		$ 2,420
Accounts Receivable		2,925		3,112
Merchandise Inventory		970		866
Prepaid Expenses		250		200
Total Current Assets		$ 6,945		$ 6,598
Plant and Equipment:				
Buildings	$9,654		$8,029	
LESS: Accumulated Depreciation	(4,597)		(4,417)	
Buildings, Net		$ 5,057		$ 3,612
Equipment	$3,359		$2,984	
LESS: Accumulated Depreciation	(1,955)		(1,904)	
Equipment, Net		1,404		1,080
Total Plant and Equipment		$ 6,461		$ 4,692
Total Assets		$13,406		$11,290
LIABILITIES:				
Current Liabilities:				
Accounts Payable	$2,020		$1,816	
Notes Payable	3,400		2,700	
Total Current Liabilities		$ 5,420		$ 4,516
Long-Term Liabilities		2,500		2,000
Total Liabilities		$ 7,920		$ 6,516
STOCKHOLDERS' EQUITY:				
Common Stock, No Par Value		$ 3,400		$ 3,000
Retained Earnings		2,086		1,774
Total Stockholders' Equity		$ 5,486		$ 4,774
Total Liabilities and Stockholders' Equity		$13,406		$11,290

Refer to Exhibit 11-5 to answer the following questions:

11-6. What was Sanguine Company's balance in accounts receivable on January 1, 1996? Did accounts receivable increase or decrease during 1996?

11-7. What was Sanguine Company's balance in retained earnings on January 1, 1996? What do you think caused the increase from the beginning of 1996 to the end of the year?

In addition to information gathered from balance sheets, preparation of a statement of cash flows requires information from the company's income statement for the period. Remember, the starting point for figuring net inflows or outflows from operating activities is the net income of the period. Sanguine Company's income statement for the year ended December 31, 1996, is provided in Exhibit 11-6.

Before we tackle the preparation of the statement of cash flows, let's take a few minutes to review Sanguine's balance sheets and income statement. There are a couple of things you should note about the financial statements. First, if you look at the cash balances on the two balance sheets in Exhibit 11-5,

Exhibit 11-6
Income Statement for Sanguine
Company for 1996

SANGUINE COMPANY
Income Statement
For the Year Ended December 31, 1996
(in thousands)

Sales		$15,158
LESS: Cost of Goods Sold		11,151
Gross Margin		$ 4,007
LESS: Operating Expenses:		
Depreciation—Buildings	$ 180	
Depreciation—Equipment	51	
Other Selling and Administration	3,047	
Total Operating Expenses		(3,278)
Operating Income		$ 729
Less: Interest Expense		(160)
Income Before Taxes		$ 569
Income Taxes		(120)
Net Income		$ 449

you will see that cash increased from the start of 1996 to the end of 1996 ($2,800 - $2,420 = $380). Note that the Sanguine Company's financial statements are presented "in thousands." This implies that the $380 increase in cash is really $380,000. What caused the increase?

If you look at the net income figure on the income statement in Exhibit 11-6, you will see that net income for the year ended December 31, 1996, was $449,000.

Since Sanguine Company uses accrual accounting, you know that net income is certainly not the same as the change in cash. (Even if Sanguine used the cash basis of accounting, net income would not necessarily tell the whole story, because even in a cash basis system, some cash flows are not reflected in net income.) The statement of cash flows, if properly prepared and analyzed, will disclose exactly what caused cash to change by the amount it did, and will reconcile the net income figure with that change in cash.

DISCUSSION QUESTIONS

11-8. Back to the scenario in which you own a small book-store... What cash flows could you receive or pay out in your book business that *would not* show up in cash basis net income?

A few other bits of information besides the company's financial statements will be helpful as we create Sanguine's statement of cash flows:

- During 1996, Sanguine purchased a building for a total cost of $1,625,000 and equipment for a total cost of $375,000. These purchases were paid in cash.
- During 1996, Sanguine paid cash dividends to its stockholders of $137,000.

Now we have all the necessary information to prepare Sanguine Company's statement of cash flows. This detailed explanation of the construction of this statement is not intended to make you an expert *preparer*, but rather to help you become a wiser *user* of this financial tool. Knowing how the amounts on a statement of cash flows were determined will help you to assess their usefulness and impact on your decision-making process.

We begin by creating a format for Sanguine's statement of cash flows in Exhibit 11-7.

Exhibit 11-7

Basic Format of the Statement
of Cash Flows for Sanguine
Company

SANGUINE COMPANY
Statement of Cash Flows
For the Year Ended December 31, 1996
(in thousands)

Cash Flows from Operating Activities:	
Net Income	$ 449
Adjustments to Reconcile Net Income to Net Cash Provided by Operating Activities:	
Net Cash Provided (Used) by Operating Activities	?
Cash Flows from Investing Activities:	
Net Cash Provided (Used) by Investing Activities	?
Cash Flows from Financing Activities:	
Net Cash Provided (Used) by Financing Activities	?
Net Increase (Decrease) In Cash During 1996	$ 380

There are two things you should note about this format. First, it is divided into the three broad types of activities that can either generate or use cash (operating, investing, and financing). Second, we have already put two amounts into the statement (the $449,000 net income and the $380,000 increase in cash from the end of 1995 to the end of 1996). One of the nifty things about this statement is that we know the answer before we begin. In the case of Sanguine Company, we determined the change in cash by looking at the comparative balance sheets (Exhibit 11-5). *Remember, the more important purpose of the statement of cash flows is not to disclose what the change in cash was, but to disclose what caused the change.*

Determining Cash Flow from Operating Activities

We begin with net income in determining cash flow from operating activities because most items involved in net income are either already cash or are expected to eventually become cash. Even if some components of net income do not involve cash *this* period, most will eventually. Revenues will eventually become cash inflows, and most expenses will eventually become cash outflows. Over time, net income will be the same as the change in cash. Because of the way accrual accounting recognizes revenues and expenses, however, net income for a particular income statement period does not equate to the change in cash for that same period. For that reason, *we must adjust the net income figure for any revenues that did not generate cash (during this period) and any expenses that did not use cash (during this period).* This is a crucial concept, so read it again if you need to and make sure you understand it before you proceed.

11-9. Why is retained earnings not equal to cash?

The first adjustment we will make to Sanguine's net income figure is for depreciation expense because depreciation is a noncash expense. To fully grasp why, you must understand what depreciation is. It is an accrual accounting process of converting the cost of long-lived items (buildings and equipment in Sanguine's case) from asset to expense. Remember, it is totally unrelated to when the buildings and equipment were paid for (cash outflow). Therefore, if we are to determine the cash flow from Sanguine's operating activities, one of the things we must do is add the depreciation expense for the period to net income. We do this because depreciation is an expense that did not use cash, but which was included in the net income figure. If you look at Sanguine's income statement (Exhibit 11-6), you will see that the company had depreciation expense for the year of $231,000 ($180,000 on buildings and $51,000 on equipment).

The adjustment for depreciation expense for Sanguine's statement of cash flows is as shown in Exhibit 11-8. Any other adjustments to the net income figure will come from analyzing the current asset and current liability sections of the balance sheets.

Since current assets and current liabilities are associated with the day-to-day operation of the company, they are related to the revenues and expenses

Exhibit 11-8
Adjustment for Depreciation Expense for Sanguine Company's Statement of Cash Flows

SANGUINE COMPANY **Partial Statement of Cash Flows** **For the Year Ended December 31, 1996** **(in thousands)**		
Cash Flows from Operating Activities:		
Net Income		$ 449
Adjustments to Reconcile Net Income		
to Net Cash Provided by Operating Activities:		
Depreciation Expense	$ 231	
Net Cash Provided (Used) by Operating Activities		?

that make up the income statement. The current asset and current liability sections from Sanguine Company's comparative balance sheets are shown in Exhibit 11-9. We have added a column that calculates how each item changed from the end of 1995 to the end of 1996.

The only one of these items we will not consider as an adjustment on the statement of cash flows is cash. (After all, the change in cash is the object of the entire statement of cash flows.) A change in any of the other items listed will require an adjustment to net income in determining the net cash provided by operating activities. The adjustments, however, will be exactly opposite of what you probably think they should be. *An increase in any current asset item (except cash) is considered a **use** of cash, and a decrease in any current asset item (except cash) is considered a **source** of cash. An increase in any current liability item is considered a **source** of cash, and a decrease in any current liability item is considered a **use** of cash.*

While this adjustment process may seem illogical, it really makes sense if you ponder it. Consider accounts receivable, for example. Where do they come from? From selling to customers on a credit basis (i.e., customers pay some time after they purchase whatever they purchase). Now answer this question: What doesn't a company have when it sells on credit that it would have had if it had sold for cash instead? The answer, of course, is *cash!* Credit sales are considered revenue under accrual accounting, and are therefore used in the calculation of net income. But remember, we are trying to determine the amount of cash generated by operating activities. Any increase in accounts receivable must be deducted from net income because such an increase represents the credit sales that have not been collected as of the end of the year. Accounts receivable decrease when customers pay the cash they owe, so a decrease in accounts receivable is a source of cash.

Exhibit 11-9
Current Assets and Current Liabilities Sections of Balance Sheets for Sanguine Company for 1996 and 1995

SANGUINE COMPANY
Partial Balance Sheets
December 31, 1996, and December 31, 1995
Current Assets and Current Liabilities Only
(in thousands)

	1996	1995	Increase/(Decrease)
Current Assets:			
Cash	$ 2,800	$ 2,420	$ 380
Accounts Receivable	2,925	3,112	(187)
Merchandise Inventory	970	866	104
Prepaid Expenses	250	200	50
Total Current Assets	$ 6,945	$ 6,598	$ 347
Current Liabilities:			
Accounts Payable	$ 2,020	$ 1,816	$ 204
Notes Payable	3,400	2,700	700
Total Current Liabilities	$ 5,420	$ 4,516	$ 904

Note: In this exhibit, parentheses are used to indicate decreases in an item.

Now think about accounts payable. Where do they come from? They are created when a company buys merchandise inventory on a credit basis (it pays some time after the purchase). Now answer this question: What does a company have when it buys on credit that it would not have if it paid cash? The answer, of course, is *cash!* Therefore, an increase in accounts payable is considered a source of cash. Accounts payable decrease as the company pays the cash it owes, so a decrease in accounts payable is a use of cash.

After we include the adjustments for the changes in the current asset and current liability items, the operating activities section of Sanguine's statement of cash flows looks like Exhibit 11-10.

Exhibit 11-10

Partial Statement of Cash Flows for Sanguine Company: Operating Activities Section

SANGUINE COMPANY
Partial Statement of Cash Flows
For the Year Ended December 31, 1996
(in thousands)

Cash flows from Operating Activities:		
Net Income		$ 449
Adjustments to Reconcile Net Income		
to Net Cash Provided by Operating Activities:		
Depreciation Expense	$ 231	
Decrease in Accounts Receivable	187	
Increase in Merchandise Inventory	(104)	
Increase in Prepaid Expense	(50)	
Increase in Accounts Payable	204	
Increase in Notes Payable	700	1,168
Net Cash Provided by Operating Activities		$1,617

Notice that in this section of the statement of cash flows parentheses indicate adjustments to net income that must be subtracted. Other adjustments are added to net income to determine the cash provided by operating activities.

We have now determined that Sanguine Company generated a positive cash flow of $1,617,000 through its operating activities during 1996. Since cash increased during 1996 by only $380,000 there must have been cash outflow in one or both of the other types of activities (investing and financing). We will look first at investing activities.

Determining Cash Flow from Investing Activities

Determining cash flow from investing activities is done by analyzing the long-term asset section of the balance sheet. Sanguine Company calls this section "Plant and Equipment." We have duplicated that section from the company's comparative balance sheets in Exhibit 11-11, and we have added a column that indicates how much each item changed from the end of 1995 to the end of 1996.

SANGUINE COMPANY
Partial Balance Sheets
December 31, 1996, and December 31, 1995
Plant and Equipment Only
(in thousands)

	1996		1995		Increase/ (Decrease)
Plant and Equipment:					
Buildings	$9,654		$8,029		$1,625
LESS: Accumulated Depreciation	(4,597)		(4,417)		$ 180
Buildings, Net		$ 5,057		$ 3,612	$1,445
Equipment	$3,359		$2,984		$ 375
LESS: Accumulated Depreciation	(1,955)		(1,904)		$ 51
Equipment, Net		1,404		1,080	$ 324
Total Plant and Equipment		$ 6,461		$ 4,692	$1,769

Exhibit 11-11
Long-Term Asset Section of Balance Sheets for Sanguine Company for 1996 and 1995

We already know from the additional information provided about the company's activities earlier in the chapter that Sanguine purchased a building for $1,625,000 and equipment for $375,000 during 1996. But even if these details had not been disclosed, the amounts could have been determined by noting the increase in each asset account. We also know how much depreciation expense was recognized for 1996 from the company's income statement, as given in Exhibit 11-6 ($180,000 on buildings + $51,000 on equipment). In addition, we know Sanguine paid cash for the full $2,000,000 plant and equip-

The company that is having this building built undertook a tremendous investment that would show on its statement of cash flows as an outflow of cash under investing activities. That cash had to come from somewhere. Assuming that the company either sold stock or obtained loans to raise the cash, the financing would be shown on the statement of cash flows as an inflow of cash under financing activities. The construction company doing the work is generating cash inflows which will be reflected in its net income shown in the operating activities section of the statement of cash flows.

Lionel Deleuingne/Stock Boston

ment purchase, and this certainly qualifies as a cash outflow under the investing activities section of the statement of cash flows. Since there are no other items listed in the long-term asset (Plant and Equipment) section of Sanguine's balance sheets, we know that the purchase of the building and equipment is the only item that will be in this section of the statement. After including the investing activities section, Sanguine Company's statement of cash flows is shaping up as shown in Exhibit 11-12.

SANGUINE COMPANY
Partial Statement of Cash Flows
For the Year Ended December 31, 1996
(in thousands)

Cash Flows from Operating Activities:

Net Income		$ 449
Adjustments to Reconcile Net Income to		
Net Cash Provided by Operating Activities:		
Depreciation Expense	$ 231	
Decrease in Accounts Receivable	187	
Increase in Merchandise Inventory	(104)	
Increase in Prepaid Expense	(50)	
Increase in Accounts Payable	204	
Increase in Notes Payable	700	1,168
Net Cash Provided by Operating Activities		$ 1,617
Cash Flows from Investing Activities:		
Purchase of Building	$(1,625)	
Purchase of Equipment	(375)	
Net Cash Used by Investing Activities		$(2,000)

If we combine the cash provided by operating activities and the cash used by investing activities, we arrive at a net cash outflow for 1996 of $383,000 ($1,617,000 inflow – $2,000,000 outflow). This means there must have been cash inflow from the third broad activity (financing), because we know that overall cash increased by $380,000 during 1996.

Determining Cash Flow from Financing Activities

Determining cash flow from financing activities is done by analyzing the long-term liabilities and stockholders' equity sections of the balance sheet. We have duplicated those sections from Sanguine Company's comparative balance sheets in Exhibit 11-13, and have provided a column that shows how much each item changed from the end of 1995 to the end of 1996.

The $900,000 cash inflow ($500,000 in long-term debt + $400,000 from the sale of additional shares of common stock) is fairly straightforward, and can

SANGUINE COMPANY
Partial Balance Sheets
December 31, 1996, and December 31, 1995
Long-Term Liabilities and Stockholders' Equity Only
(in thousands)

	1996	1995	Increase/ (Decrease)
Long-Term Liabilities	$ 2,500	$ 2,000	$ 500
Stockholders' Equity:			
Common Stock, No Par Value	3,400	3,000	$ 400
Retained Earnings	2,086	1,774	$ 312

be determined simply by looking at the change in those two items on Sanguine's comparative balance sheets (Exhibit 11-13). In addition, there was a cash outflow in the form of cash dividends during 1996 of $137,000. We know the amount because it was the other bit of additional information provided earlier in the chapter. But if we didn't already know the amount of dividends, we could determine it from Sanguine's balance sheets and income statement (Exhibits 11-5 and 11-6) as follows.

We know the balance in retained earnings at the end of 1996 after the dividends were paid ($2,086,000). We also know the retained earnings balance at the end of 1995 ($1,774,000) and the net income for 1996 ($449,000). Net income is this period's addition to retained earnings. Therefore:

Retained Earnings at 12/31/95	$ 1,774,000
PLUS: 1996 Net Income	449,000
LESS: Dividends Paid During 1996	?
Equals Retained Earnings at 12/31/96	$ 2,086,000

The unknown amount of dividends must be $137,000. This calculation is based on the relationships we already know from the statement of retained earnings:

RE (Beginning) + Net Income − Dividends = RE (Ending)

With this piece of information in hand, we are now prepared to present Sanguine Company's full statement of cash flows for the year ended December 31, 1996. If we have considered everything we should have, the cash provided by operating activities combined with the cash used by investing activities and the cash provided by financing activities should be equal to the change in cash from the end of 1995 to the end of 1996. The completed statement is shown in Exhibit 11-14 on page 360.

SANGUINE COMPANY
Statement of Cash Flows
for the Year Ended December 31, 1996
(in thousands)

Cash Flows from Operating Activities:

Net Income		$ 449
Adjustments to Reconcile Net Income		
to Net Cash Provided by Operating Activities:		
Depreciation Expense	$ 231	
Decrease in Accounts Receivable	187	
Increase in Merchandise Inventory	(104)	
Increase in Prepaid Expense	(50)	
Increase in Accounts Payable	204	
Increase in Notes Payable	700	1,168
Net Cash Provided by Operating Activities		$ 1,617

Cash Flows From Investing Activities:

Purchase of Building	$(1,625)	
Purchase of Equipment	(375)	
Net Cash Used by Investing Activities		$(2,000)

Cash Flows from Financing Activities:

Proceeds from Long-Term Loan	$ 500	
Proceeds from Sale of Common Stock	400	
Payment of Cash Dividends	(137)	
Net Cash Provided by Financing Activities		$ 763
Net Increase in Cash During 1996		$ 380

Exhibit 11-14
Complete Statement of Cash Flows for Sanguine Company

Sanguine Company's statement of cash flows was a fairly simple one to create because there were relatively few things to consider in its construction. As we said earlier, actual statements of cash flows for actual companies can contain some rather exotic items. But whether simple or complex, all statements of cash flows assume the basic format used in the one we did for Sanguine Company.

HOW TO USE THE STATEMENT OF CASH FLOWS

The purpose of the statement of cash flows is to disclose where a company got cash during a specific time period and what it used the cash for. One of the most important things the statement shows is what a company invested in during the period and how that investment was financed. We are talking here about a company's investment in long-lived productive assets that will be used to produce revenues and, eventually, cash. *The things the company invested in during the period are presented in the middle section of the statement (investing activities). How that investment was financed is presented in the top section of the statement (operating activities) and the bottom section of the statement (financing activities).*

To demonstrate this concept, we have extracted the cash flow totals for the three types of activities from Sanguine's statement of cash flows (Exhibit 11-14):

Net Cash Provided by Operating Activities .... $ 1,617,000
Net Cash Used by Investing Activities .... $(2,000,000)
Net Cash Provided by Financing Activities .... $ 763,000

This presentation shows that Sanguine invested $2,000,000 in a building and equipment during 1996. The investment was made to somehow enhance the way the company conducts its business. It may have been intended to upgrade manufacturing facilities, allow entry into new markets, or develop new products. The point is, there had to be a reason to make this investment. We can't assess whether this investment was good or bad because we have no additional information about the company. However, we can determine where the cash to finance this investment came from.

There are only two sources of cash available to Sanguine (or any other company, for that matter). Cash is either generated internally (from profitable operations) or it is obtained from external sources (borrowing or selling stock). You can see by looking at the presentation above that Sanguine generated about 80 percent of the cash required for the investment internally (operating activities). The rest came from outside sources (financing activities). With that in mind, focus on this important concept: *In the long run, all investment (middle section of the statement of cash flows) must be financed through operations (top section of the statement).*

Now you can see why the statement of cash flows is an economic decision maker's most valuable tool in determining how a company is financing its investments. By carefully examining it, users can obtain insights into many aspects of a company's operations. The statement of cash flows, in combination with the three financial statements introduced earlier in this text (income statement, statement of owners' equity, and balance sheet), provides important information upon which economic decision makers rely. In order for this information to be truly useful, however, decision makers must be assured that the statements were prepared under a consistently applied set of guidelines. The set of guidelines and the assurance process are the topics of the next chapter.

SUMMARY

One of the disadvantages of accrual basis accounting is that it takes the financial statement reader's eye off cash. Over the past several decades, economic decision makers' interest in the cash flows of companies has risen. The statement of cash flows was developed to give financial statement users information about the cash flows of companies during a particular period. Information necessary for the development of a statement of cash flows can be found on a company's comparative balance sheets and the income statement of the period.

The statement of cash flows provides information about cash flows used by or provided by three major types of business activities: operating, investing, and financing. Calculation of the cash flows provided by operating activities begins with net income. Adjustments to this figure are made for any revenue items not producing cash this period and expense items not using cash this period. Results of investing activities can be found in the long-term asset section of the balance sheet. Typical transactions that are classified as investing activities are the purchase and sale of property, plant, and equipment. The financing activities section of the statement of cash flows shows what types of external financing the company used to provide funds. Information showing the results of financing activities can be found in the long-term liability section and the owners' equity section of the balance sheet.

The statement of cash flows furnishes valuable information about the cash inflows and outflows of a business during a particular period. It provides an explanation of the changes in cash from the beginning to the end of a period. Therefore, the statement of cash flows can be considered a financial statement analysis tool as well as a financial statement.

Key Terms

direct method The format of a statement of cash flows that provides detail about the individual sources and uses of cash associated with operating activities. (p. 343)

financing activities Business activities, such as the issuance of debt or equity and the payment of dividends, that focus on the external financing of the company. (p. 348)

indirect method The more widely used format of the statement of cash flows. This approach begins with a reconciliation of accrual net income to the cash provided by or used by operating activities. (p. 343)

investing activities Business activities related to long-term assets. Examples are the purchase and sale of property, plant, and equipment. (p. 347)

operating activities Activities that result in cash inflows and outflows generated from the normal course of business. (p. 346)

statement of cash flows A financial statement that provides information about the causes of a change in a company's cash balance from the beginning to the end of a specific period. (p. 342)

working capital The difference between current assets and current liabilities. (p. 342)

REVIEW THE FACTS

A. When did the present format of the statement of cash flows come into existence?

B. What is the main purpose of the statement of cash flows?

C. Name the two methods of preparing the statement of cash flows. Which method is more commonly used by publicly traded companies?

D. What are the three major classifications of activities presented on the statement of cash flows?

E. In what category are the cash flows related to interest and dividends received and interest paid usually reported?

F. Provide examples of an inflow of cash and an outflow of cash for each of the three categories of business activity shown on the statement of cash flows.

G. What is the starting point for calculation of cash flows from operating activities?

H. Where are the items included in operating activities reported in the financial statements?

I. Where are the items included in investing activities reported in the financial statements?

J. Where are the items included in financing activities reported in the financial statements?

K. Which section(s) of the statement of cash flows tell the user how much cash the company used to acquire depreciable assets?

L. Which section(s) of the statement of cash flows tell the user how investments made by the company were financed?

APPLY WHAT YOU HAVE LEARNED

11-10. Presented below is a list of items relating to the concepts discussed in this chapter, followed by definitions of those items in scrambled order:

a. Operating activities   **e.** Financing activities

b. Indirect method   **f.** Working capital

c. Depreciation expense   **g.** Direct method

d. Comparative financial statements   **h.** Investing activities

1. ____ Provides a reconciliation of accrual net income to the cash provided by or used by operating activities.

2. ____ Accounting reports providing information from two or more consecutive periods at once.

3. ____ Activities centered around the actual day-to-day business transactions of a company.

4. ____ Current assets less current liabilities.

5. ____ Business activities related to long-term assets.

6. ____ Provides detail as to the individual sources and uses of cash associated with operating activities.

7. ____ An item that reduces reported net income, but does not require the use of cash.

8. ____ Activities such as the issuance of debt or equity and the payment of dividends.

REQUIRED:

Match the letter next to each item on the list with the appropriate definition. Each letter will be used only once.

11-11. Listed below are the three broad types of activities that can either generate or use cash in any business, followed by descriptions of various items.

a. Operating activities

b. Investing activities

c. Financing activities

1. ____ Payment of dividends.

2. ____ Adjustment for depreciation.

3. ____ Purchase of merchandise inventory.

4. ____ Purchase of vehicles.

5. ____ Repayment of 90-day loans.

6. ___ Issuing capital stock.

7. ___ Payment of wages to employees.

8. ___ Payment of taxes.

9. ___ Cash from sale of property and equipment.

10. ___ Loans to other companies.

11. ___ Adjustments for changes in current asset and current liability items.

12. ___ Cash from selling investments in other companies.

REQUIRED:

Classify each of the items listed above by placing the letter of the appropriate activity category in the space provided.

11-12. Following are the changes in some of Scott Burt Company's assets, liabilities, and equities from December 31, 1995, to December 31, 1996:

1. ___ Accounts payable decreased.

2. ___ Property and equipment increased.

3. ___ Accounts receivable increased.

4. ___ Long-term notes payable decreased.

5. ___ Prepaid expenses decreased.

6. ___ Short-term notes payable increased.

7. ___ Taxes payable decreased.

8. ___ Common stock increased.

9. ___ Wages payable increased.

10. ___ Merchandise inventory decreased.

REQUIRED:

Burt is in the process of preparing the operating activities section of its statement of cash flows for 1996. Some of the items above will be included and others will not. Place the letter "S" in the space next to each item that should be considered a source of cash in the operating activities section and place the letter "U" in the space next to each item that should be considered a use of cash in the operating activities section. Place the letter "N" next to any item not included in the operating activities section.

11-13. Presented below are partial comparative balance sheets of Reggie Company at December 31, 1996 and 1995:

REGGIE COMPANY
Partial Balance Sheets
December 31, 1996, and December 31, 1995
Current Assets and Current Liabilities Only
(in thousands)

	1996	1995	Increase/ (Decrease)
Current Assets:			
Cash	$ 3,400	$ 2,920	$ 480
Accounts Receivable	1,825	2,212	(387)
Merchandise Inventory	1,170	966	204
Prepaid Expenses	240	270	(30)
Total Current Assets	$ 6,635	$ 6,368	$ 267
Current Liabilities:			
Accounts Payable	$ 2,321	$ 1,740	$ 581
Notes Payable	3,100	3,300	(200)
Total Current Liabilities	$ 5,421	$ 5,040	$ 381

Additional Information: Net income for 1996 was $406,000. Included in the operating expenses for the year was depreciation expense of $175,000.

REQUIRED:

Prepare the operating activities section of Reggie Company's statement of cash flows for 1996.

11-14. Presented below are partial comparative balance sheets of Halifax Company at December 31, 1996 and 1995:

HALIFAX COMPANY
Partial Balance Sheets
December 31, 1996, and December 31, 1995
Current Assets and Current Liabilities Only
(in thousands)

	1996	1995	Increase/ (Decrease)
Current Assets:			
Cash	$ 2,110	$ 2,650	$ (540)
Accounts Receivable	1,254	977	277
Merchandise Inventory	730	856	(126)
Prepaid Expenses	127	114	13
Total Current Assets	$ 4,221	$ 4,597	$ (376)
Current Liabilities:			
Accounts Payable	$ 1,054	$ 1,330	$ (276)
Notes Payable	2,100	1,750	350
Total Current Liabilities	$ 3,154	$ 3,080	$ 74

Additional Information: Net income for 1996 was $86,900. Included in the operating expenses for the year was depreciation expense of $102,000.

REQUIRED:

Prepare the operating activities section of Halifax Company's statement of cash flows for 1996.

11-15. Presented below is Montrose Company's statement of cash flows for the year ended December 31, 1995:

MONTROSE COMPANY
Statement of Cash Flows
For the Year Ended December 31, 1995
(in thousands)

Cash Flows from Operating Activities:		
Net Income		$ 389
Adjustments to Reconcile Net Income		
to Net Cash Provided by Operating Activities:		
Depreciation Expense	$ 131	
Increase in Accounts Receivable	(287)	
Increase in Merchandise Inventory	(104)	
Increase in Prepaid Expense	(70)	
Decrease in Accounts Payable	(304)	
Increase in Notes Payable	300	(334)
Net Cash Provided by Operating Activities		$ 55
Cash Flows from Investing Activities:		
Purchase of Building	$(1,255)	
Purchase of Equipment	(304)	
Net Cash Used by Investing Activities		$(1,559)
Cash Flows from Financing Activities:		
Proceeds from Long-Term Loan	$ 800	
Proceeds from Sale of Common Stock	300	
Payment of Cash Dividends	(100)	
Net Cash Provided by Financing Activities		$ 1,000
Net Decrease in Cash During 1995		$(504)

REQUIRED:

Respond to the following questions:
a. For which of the three broad types of activities did Montrose use the majority of its cash during 1995?

b. What does your answer to the previous question tell you about Montrose Company?

c. From which of the three broad types of activities did Montrose obtain the majority of its cash during 1995?

d. Is the activity you identified in the previous requirement an appropriate source of cash in the long run? Explain your reasoning.

11-16. Presented below is Hendrick Company's statement of cash flows for the year ended December 31, 1996:

HENDRICK COMPANY
Statement of Cash Flows
For the Year Ended December 31, 1996
(in thousands)

Cash Flows from Operating Activities:		
Net Income		$ 1,608
Adjustments to Reconcile Net Income		
to Net Cash Provided by Operating Activities:		
Depreciation Expense	$ 218	
Increase in Accounts Receivable	(341)	
Decrease in Merchandise Inventory	81	
Increase in Prepaid Expense	(100)	
Increase in Accounts Payable	104	
Increase in Notes Payable	50	12
Net Cash Provided by Operating Activities		$ 1,620
Cash Flows from Investing Activities:		
Purchase of Building	$(1,000)	
Purchase of Equipment	(200)	
Net Cash Used by Investing Activities		$(1,200)
Cash Flows from Financing Activities:		
Repayment of Long-Term Loan	$ (350)	
Proceeds from Sale of Common Stock	350	
Payment of Cash Dividends	(100)	
Net Cash Used by Financing Activities		$ (100)
Net Increase in Cash During 1996		$ 320

REQUIRED:

Respond to the following questions:
  a. For which of the three types of activities did Hendrick use the majority of its cash during 1996?

  b. What does your answer to the previous question tell you about Hendrick Company?

  c. From which of the three types of activities did Hendrick obtain the majority of its cash during 1996?

  d. Is the activity you identified in the previous requirement an appropriate source of cash in the long run? Explain your reasoning.

11-17. Use the balance sheets, income statement and the additional information provided below to complete this problem.

HOGLE COMPANY
Balance Sheets
at December 31, 1996, and December 31, 1995
(in thousands)

	1996	1996	1995	1995
ASSETS:				
Current Assets:				
Cash		$ 1,618		$ 1,220
Accounts Receivable		1,925		2,112
Merchandise Inventory		1,070		966
Prepaid Expenses		188		149
Total Current Assets		$ 4,801		$ 4,447
Plant and Equipment:				
Buildings	$4,818		$3,292	
LESS: Accumulated Depreciation	(361)		(300)	
Buildings, Net		$ 4,457		$ 2,992
Equipment	$1,434		$1,145	
LESS: Accumulated Depreciation	(141)		(100)	
Equipment, Net		1,293		1,045
Total Plant and Equipment		$ 5,750		$ 4,037
Total Assets		$10,551		$ 8,484
LIABILITIES:				
Current Liabilities:				
Accounts Payable		$ 1,818		$ 1,686
Notes Payable		900		1,100
Total Current Liabilities		$ 2,718		$ 2,786
Long-Term Liabilities		2,500		2,000
Total Liabilities		$ 5,218		$ 4,786
STOCKHOLDERS' EQUITY:				
Common Stock, No Par Value		$ 3,390		$ 2,041
Retained Earnings		1,943		1,657
Total Stockholders' Equity		$ 5,333		$ 3,698
Total Liabilities and				
Stockholders' Equity		$10,551		$ 8,484

HOGLE COMPANY
Income Statement
For the Year Ending December 31, 1996
(in thousands)

Net Sales		$11,228
LESS: Cost of Goods Sold		7,751
Gross Profit on Sales		$ 3,477
LESS: Operating Expenses:		
Depreciation—Buildings and Equipment	$ 102	
Other Selling and Administrative	2,667	
Total Expenses		(2,769)
Operating Income		$ 708
LESS: Interest Expense		(168)
Income Before Taxes		$ 540
Income Taxes		(114)
Net Income		$ 426

Additional Information: There were no sales of plant and equipment during the year, and the company paid dividends to stockholders during the year of $140,000.

REQUIRED:

a. Prepare Hogle Company's statement of cash flows for the year ended December 31, 1996.

b. In which of the three categories of activities did Hogle use the majority of its cash during 1996?

c. What does your answer to the previous question tell you about Hogle Company?

d. From which of the three types of activities did Hogle obtain the majority of its cash during 1996?

e. Is the activity you identified in the previous requirement an appropriate source of cash in the long run? Explain your reasoning.

11-18. Use the balance sheets, income statement, and the additional information below to complete this problem.

PAT BECK COMPANY
Balance Sheets
at December 31, 1996, and December 31, 1995
(in thousands)

	1996		1995	
ASSETS:				
Current Assets:				
Cash		$ 529		$ 660
Accounts Receivable		1,006		1,011
Merchandise Inventory		396		452
Prepaid Expenses		38		62
Total Current Assets		$ 1,969		$ 2,185
Plant and Equipment:				
Buildings	$2,000		$1,681	
LESS: Accumulated Depreciation	(176)		(146)	
Buildings, Net		$ 1,824		$ 1,535
Equipment	$ 809		$ 609	
LESS: Accumulated Depreciation	(76)		(61)	
Equipment, Net		733		548
Total Plant and Equipment		$ 2,557		$ 2,083
Total Assets		$ 4,526		$ 4,268
LIABILITIES:				
Current Liabilities:				
Accounts Payable		$ 726		$ 809
Notes Payable		750		600
Total Current Liabilities		$ 1,476		$ 1,409
Long-Term Liabilities		1,500		1,200
Total Liabilities		$ 2,976		$ 2,609
STOCKHOLDERS' EQUITY:				
Common Stock, No Par Value		$ 1,300		$ 1,000
Retained Earnings		250		659
Total Stockholders' Equity		$ 1,550		$ 1,659
Total Liabilities and				
Stockholders' Equity		$ 4,526		$ 4,268

PAT BECK COMPANY
Income Statement
For the Year Ended December 31, 1996
(in thousands)

Sales		$ 6,391
LESS: Cost of Goods Sold		4,474
Gross Profit on Sales		$ 1,917
LESS: Operating Expenses:		
Depreciation—Buildings and Equipment	$ 45	
Other Selling and Administrative	2,066	
Total Expenses		(2,111)
Operating Income		$ (194)
LESS: Interest Expense		(145)
Income Before Taxes		$ (339)
Income Taxes		-0-
Net Loss		$ (339)

Additional Information: There were no sales of plant and equipment during the year, and the company paid dividends to stockholders during the year of $70,000.

REQUIRED:

a. Prepare Beck Company's statement of cash flows for the year ended December 31, 1996.

b. In which of the three broad activities did Beck use the majority of its cash during 1996?

c. What does your answer to the previous question tell you about Beck Company?

d. In which of the three broad activities did Beck obtain the majority of its cash during 1996?

e. Is the activity you identified in the previous requirement an appropriate source of cash in the long run? Explain your reasoning.

f. Prepare Beck Company's statement of retained earnings for 1996.

11-19. Presented below are the totals from the main three sections of Arlene Job and Company's most recent statement of cash flows:

Net Cash Provided by Operating Activities..................	$ 1,812,000
Net Cash Used by Investing Activities..........................	$(1,280,000)
Net Cash Used by Financing Activities.........................	$(153,000)

REQUIRED:

a. What do these totals tell you about Job and Company?

b. What additional information would you want to see before you analyze Job and Company's ability to generate positive cash flow in the future?

c. Did Job and Company have a net income or loss for the period? What additional information would you want before trying to predict the company's net income for next period?

11-20. Presented below are the totals from the main three sections of Kay Coleman and Company's most recent statement of cash flows:

Net Cash Used by Operating Activities	$(835,000)
Net Cash Used by Investing Activities..........................	$(1,280,000)
Net Cash Provided by Financing Activities..................	$ 2,153,000

REQUIRED:

a. What do these totals tell you about Coleman and Company?

b. What additional information would you want to see before you analyze Coleman and Company's ability to generate positive cash flow in the future?

c. Did Coleman and Company have a net income or loss for the period? What additional information would you want before trying to predict the company's net income for next period?

11-21. Presented below are the totals from the main three sections of Carl Faulkner and Company's most recent statement of cash flows:

Net Cash Used by Operating Activities	$(1,409,000)
Net Cash Provided by Investing Activities	$ 1,980,000
Net Cash Used by Financing Activities........................	$(303,000)

REQUIRED:

a. What do these totals tell you about Faulkner and Company?

b. What additional information would you want to see before you analyze Faulkner and Company's ability to generate positive cash flow in the future?

11-22. Remember, tools are developed to solve problems. This chapter is titled "Tools of the Trade, Part III The Statement of Cash Flows: Bringing the Focus Back to Cash."

REQUIRED:

a. Explain in your own words what caused the focus of financial statements to shift to something other than cash.

b. Describe how the statement of cash flows serves as a tool to bring the focus of economic decision makers back to cash.

12

Generally Accepted Accounting Principles and Forms of Outside Assurance on Financial Statements

Economic decision makers rely on the information provided in financial statements. For this information to be truly useful, external decision makers must be assured that the statements were prepared under a consistently applied set of guidelines. The guidelines are called generally accepted accounting principles (GAAP), and the assurance is provided through the audit process.

In Chapter 7, we discussed two very different approaches to the measurement of revenues and expenses: cash basis accounting and accrual basis accounting. We stressed that each of them has advantages and disadvantages in relation to the other. Further, we stated that neither of them is "correct" in the sense of being in accordance with some natural law of accounting and finance. However, we also pointed out that the use of different measurement bases makes valid comparisons across companies impossible.

In your study of Chapter 11, you learned about the statement of cash flows, a financial statement designed to bring the focus of accrual accounting back to cash. The statement of cash flows is actually a form of financial statement analysis (a subject we will cover in more depth in Chapter 14). The whole purpose of financial statement analysis is for economic decision makers to draw conclusions based on comparisons. These comparisons may be of accounting information for a single company over multiple years, or the decision maker may compare companies to one another or to industry averages.

The necessary premises of valid financial statement analysis are comparability and consistency of the accounting information. Most large companies use the accrual basis of measurement for external reporting purposes, so everything is fine, right? *Wrong!* Even within the boundaries of accrual accounting, there are many different ideas about how to measure and value items. Just a few of those variations were noted in Chapters 8 and 9 when we discussed depreciation and inventory cost flow methods. In response to the problems of comparability and consistency caused by these variations, a system of rules and standards has been developed for presenting financial information in financial statements.

In this chapter, we will explore how the accounting profession has responded to the needs of financial statement users for consistent and comparable information.

After completing your work on this chapter, you should be able to do the following:

1. Explain what generally accepted accounting principles (GAAP) are and why they are important to economic decision makers.
2. Describe the development of GAAP since the early 1900s.
3. Describe the purpose of the Securities and Exchange Commission (SEC) and its role in establishing accounting standards.
4. Describe the process used by the Financial Accounting Standards Board to create accounting standards.
5. Explain the five basic assumptions under which GAAP operate.
6. List and define the four basic principles of GAAP.
7. Describe in your own words the three modifying conventions under which it is allowable to modify GAAP.
8. Explain what an audit is and what it is not.
9. Compare and contrast the levels of assurance provided by an audit, a review, and a compilation.

GENERALLY ACCEPTED ACCOUNTING PRINCIPLES

In its *Statement of Financial Accounting Concepts #1*, the Financial Accounting Standards Board stated that a particular problem exists for those decision makers who

lack the authority to prescribe the financial information they want from an enterprise and therefore must use the information that management communicates to them. (paragraph 28)

The decision makers referred to by the FASB are the external financial statement users we have discussed throughout this book. They are not involved in the day-to-day operation of a company and do not know what accounting methods and assumptions were used in preparing the financial statements they receive. If they are to have confidence in those financial statements, they must have assurance that the statements possess certain qualitative characteristics.

We reviewed the qualitative characteristics of useful accounting information in Chapter 3. One of those characteristics, you will recall, is *comparability*. We stated that economic decision making involves the evaluation of alternatives (often companies). In order to be useful for that evaluation, the accounting information for one company must be comparable to the accounting information for the other company or companies. Without some assurance that the measurement criteria used by the companies is the same, any comparison among them is meaningless.

Another characteristic of useful accounting information we discussed in Chapter 3 is *consistency*. Consistency means that events and transactions are treated the same way over time. For example, if Cathie Barker Company treats events and transactions in a certain way in 1995, but in a completely different way in 1996, an external decision maker would find it difficult to evaluate Barker's 1995 and 1996 financial statements relative to each other.

The need for comparability between and among financial statements, coupled with the need for consistent treatment of transactions and events from year to year, led to the development of what has come to be known as generally accepted accounting principles.

Generally accepted accounting principles (GAAP) can be broadly defined as a set of standards (rules) adopted by the accounting profession to be used in preparing accounting information for external economic decision makers. "Generally accepted," by the way, does not mean "universally accepted." In fact, many of the standards we will discuss have provoked debate and criticism.

generally accepted accounting principles (GAAP) Guidelines for presentation of financial accounting information designed to serve external decision makers' need for consistent and comparable information.

Who Is Bound by GAAP?

We have stated several times that economic decision makers can be broadly classified as either external or internal to an entity. External decision makers make decisions *about* the company, and the information they use to do so is limited to what the enterprise provides to them. Internal decision makers, on the other hand, make decisions *for* the company, and have access to a greater amount of accounting and financial information pertaining to the enterprise.

Generally accepted accounting principles were developed over time to provide assurance to the external users that the information they have at their disposal in a given decision situation was prepared in accordance with some well-defined set of rules and guidelines. For this reason, GAAP applies to the information prepared for use by external parties (financial accounting information), but *not* to the information prepared for use by internal parties (management accounting information). This is an important distinction, so make certain you grasp it. You must be aware which information is prepared under the guidelines of GAAP and which is not.

It may surprise you to learn that only some companies must adhere to GAAP even in the preparation of their financial accounting information. In fact, the only companies required by law to follow GAAP are those whose stock is traded on one of the national or regional stock exchanges and those that have bonds listed on one of the major bond exchanges. These companies are regulated by the Securities and Exchange Commission. Companies not subject to SEC regulation may use whatever accounting procedures they desire, unless, of course, the external users are in a position to demand that GAAP be followed.

For instance, banks and other lending institutions are accustomed to seeing financial results prepared under GAAP rules and often require all companies wishing to borrow funds from them to adhere to those rules. Once again, the logic is fairly easy to follow. Suppose Friendly Bank is deciding whether to lend money to either the Karen Amundsen Company or the Alan Bailey Company. Amundsen is required by the SEC to follow GAAP, but Bailey is not. How can the loan committee at the bank compare these alternative investment options if the two companies use vastly different approaches to measuring and reporting the results of their business activities? The answer is obvious: They can't. Therefore, Bailey Company is, for all practical purposes, forced to adopt GAAP procedures, even though it is not legally required to do so.

Another factor that causes companies to adopt GAAP even when not required by law to do so is the audit, which is discussed later in this chapter. Virtually all companies that are audited end up following GAAP.

DISCUSSION QUESTIONS

12-1. Why do you think a company would be opposed to adopting GAAP?

The History of GAAP

Prior to 1900, the economy of the United States was relatively unsophisticated, and accounting for that economy was equally unsophisticated. Most businesses were family-owned and operated, and the accounting reports generated were mostly for internal use. Only banks and other lending institutions were in a position to dictate the form of external reports, and there was little uniformity in what they required.

By the turn of the century, however, the U.S. economy was undergoing significant change. The emergence of large corporations with absentee ownership created a demand for greater disclosure and more uniformity in accounting reports. In 1903, the United States Steel Corporation became the first American company to publish financial statements accompanied by an auditor's report. Clearly, the time had come for the establishment of a generally accepted set of accounting rules and guidelines.

The first development in the establishment of GAAP was a recommendation in 1917 by the Federal Trade Commission (FTC) that the accounting profession be regulated by the federal government and that accounting rules be set by the government. Quite naturally, the accounting profession was alarmed by this prospect and took immediate steps to demonstrate its ability to regulate itself. At that time, The American Institute of Accountants (AIA) was a relatively young (formed in 1887) and loosely organized professional association. The threat of regulation by the federal government, however, forced the AIA to get serious about setting standards for the practice of accounting. It appointed a committee to study the situation and develop accounting standards for all AIA members to follow. The committee took its work seriously and convinced government officials that the accounting profession was capable of governing itself. The threat of a government-established uniform code of accounting receded, at least for the time being.

The second major event affecting the development of GAAP was the Great Depression. After the stock market crash of 1929, pressure began to mount again for federal regulation of the accounting profession. The origins of modern GAAP can be traced directly to this period.

Widespread fraud and various degrees of corruption existed throughout the securities market in the 1920s. There is little question that inadequate disclosure of important information in the financial statement presentations of the day was at least partially responsible for the ease with which investors were defrauded. Inadequate disclosure also contributed to the stock market crash of 1929 and the Great Depression that followed it. A report by the House Committee on Interstate and Foreign Commerce described the situation this way:

> During the post-war decade [1919–1929] some 50 billions of new securities were floated in the United States. Fully half or $25,000,000,000 worth of securities floated during this period have been proved to be worthless. These cold figures spell tragedy in the lives of thousands of individuals who invested their life savings, accumulated after years of effort, in these worthless securities. The flotation of such a mass of essentially fraudulent securities was made possible because of the complete abandonment by many

underwriters and dealers in securities of those standards of fair, honest, and prudent dealing that should be basic to the encouragement of investment in any enterprise.

(Report No. 85, 73rd Congress 1st Session, p. 2)

Since securities dealers proved incapable of voluntary fairness, honesty, and prudence, Congress was determined to legislate these qualities. The event that actually precipitated congressional action was probably the bankruptcy of Kreuger & Toll, Inc. Our account of that event is based on Dale and Tonya Flesher's article "Ivar Kreuger's Contribution to U.S. Financial Reporting," in the July 1986 issue of *The Accounting Review*, Vol. LXI, No. 3.

A tremendous number of companies and individuals were utterly destroyed financially by the stock market crash of 1929 and the Great Depression that followed. The lack of consistently applied accounting standards is acknowledged to be at least partially responsible for these events.

Bettmann

Ivar Kreuger built an international financial empire based on secrecy. He managed to convince investors, his corporate directors, and the few accountants Kreuger & Toll employed that complete secrecy was crucial to corporate success. No one but Kreuger knew the details of any aspects of Kreuger & Toll's operation. Whenever Kreuger found it necessary to produce financial statements, he prepared them himself, without regard for any company records. Company accountants were then directed to make the company's records correspond to the financial statements Kreuger had created.

Kreuger & Toll securities were very popular, not only because of their high dividend rates (over 20 percent annually), but also because they were issued in small denominations so that even small investors could take part. Kreuger & Toll securities seemed like a "sure thing." As Flesher and Flesher explain:

E ven after the stock market crash in 1929, Kreuger & Toll securities sold well. At that time, Kreuger & Toll securities were listed on more stock exchanges and were more widely held than any other security in the world. The company at no time suspended dividend or interest payments. Of course, there is no reason why the onset of the Depression would have any effect on dividend payments since dividends had never been based on profits. Instead, Kreuger was operating a gigantic pyramid scheme where new financing had to be obtained constantly to pay interest and dividends on outstanding securities. High dividend payments were necessary to ensure the continued sale of new securities. And the continued sale of new securities was necessary to make the dividend payments. It was a never-ending cycle. Eventually, the pyramid was bound to topple.

(Flesher and Flesher, "Ivar Kreuger's Contribution," p. 424)

The Great Depression inevitably eroded the base of Kreuger's pyramid scheme. The legitimate portions of the empire became less profitable, and as money became scarce, investors had no more funds to give. On March 12, 1932, Kreuger, apparently convinced that the end of his empire was certain, took his own life.

On the date of Kreuger's death, Kreuger & Toll stock was selling for $5 per share. Within days, the stock lost half its value; within weeks, it was selling for only 5 cents per share. Kreuger's dishonesty caused tragedy in the lives of thousands of innocent investors, who lost hundreds of millions of dollars.

When the U.S. Senate considered enacting securities laws in 1933, the Kreuger case was uppermost in the senators' minds. They focused on the fact that Kreuger & Toll was so successful at defrauding so many people because Ivar Kreuger had had to answer to no one. It seemed abundantly clear that government regulation of the securities markets was needed to put an end to the secret manipulations and dishonesty that Kreuger & Toll exemplified. The creation of the Securities and Exchange Commission (SEC) in 1934 was one of the federal government's responses to this need.

The Securities and Exchange Commission (SEC)

The Securities and Exchange Commission was mentioned briefly in Chapter 5, where we described its influence on the trading of stocks and bonds. The SEC is a federal agency created by Congress. Its five members, called commissioners, are appointed by the president of the United States and confirmed by the Senate. Commissioners serve five-year staggered terms, meaning one commissioner's term expires each year. One of the members is designated by the president to serve as chairperson of the Commission. The president has the authority to remove a person from the position of chairperson, but not to remove members from the Commission itself—an arrangement stipulated by Congress to lessen political pressures on the Commission. Also, members appointed by one president cannot be removed by a new president. Each of the five commissioners has an equal vote in all matters before the Commission, and no more than three can be members of the same political party.

At the time of its creation, the SEC was given explicit authority by Congress to prescribe for publicly traded companies:

$t$he items or details to be shown in the balance sheet and earning statement, and the methods to be followed in the preparation of accounts, in the appraisal or valuation of assets and liabilities, in the determination of depreciation and depletion, ... and in the preparation...of consolidated balance sheets or income accounts.

(Securities Act of 1933, Section19)

This mandate was actually twofold. The SEC was given the authority to establish (1) the rules, standards, and procedures used to account for transactions and events; and (2) the form and content of published financial reporting.

Many thought the creation of the SEC meant that the debate over who would establish accounting rules and standards was resolved in favor of the government. Not so. In 1938, the SEC decided, by a vote of 3 to 2, to allow the accounting profession to establish standards of accounting, so long as there was "substantial authoritative support" for those standards (ASR 4, subparagraph 101). The Commission viewed its own principal objective to be in the area of adequate disclosure in financial reporting.

The decision to leave the setting of accounting standards up to the accounting profession was a profoundly important one, because had the SEC decided differently, U.S. accounting standards today would very likely be a set of rules established by the federal government. Instead, for over 50 years, accounting standards have been the product of a series of professional committees and boards, beginning with the Committee on Accounting Procedure.

DISCUSSION QUESTIONS

12-2. What are the pros and cons of having accounting rules established by the federal government?

12-3. What are the pros and cons of having accounting rules established by the accounting profession?

Committee on Accounting Procedure (CAP) In operation from 1930 to 1959, this committee issued pronouncements called Accounting Research Bulletins (ARBs).

Accounting Research Bulletins (ARBs) The pronouncements issued by the Committee on Accounting Procedure.

The Committee on Accounting Procedure (CAP)

Formed in 1930, the **Committee on Accounting Procedure (CAP)** was revitalized and enlarged in 1938 after the decision by the SEC to leave standard setting to the accounting profession. The CAP issued pronouncements called **Accounting Research Bulletins (ARBs)**, but these addressed only very specific accounting topics. The Committee was criticized for failing to establish any kind of conceptual framework for its bulletins. Between 1938 and 1959, when the committee was disbanded, 51 ARBs were issued. While the bulletins were often ambiguous and the CAP lacked any authority to enforce its recommendations, these documents did achieve a measure of general acceptance among members of the American Institute of Accountants (AIA). Thus, they constituted the first step toward development of the standards in existence today.

The Accounting Principles Board (APB)

Accounting Principles Board (APB) The standards-setting organization that was the immediate predecessor of the Financial Accounting Standards Board.

In 1959, the American Institute of Certified Public Accountants (AICPA), which had evolved from the AIA, dissolved the Committee on Accounting Procedure and replaced it with the **Accounting Principles Board (APB)**. The major reason for this action was the feeling that the CAP was too concerned with practice issues and lacked the structure to conduct research into how a conceptual framework might be created. The APB's charter provided for a research division.

APB Opinions The pronouncements issued by the Accounting Principles Board.

Unfortunately, research in this important area never materialized. Like the CAP, the APB failed to establish a conceptual framework of accounting from which to approach the standards-setting process. During its existence, it issued 31 pronouncements, called **APB Opinions**, but critics complained that these addressed only what accounting practice *was*, not what it *should be*. By the late 1960s, the AICPA was actively studying ways to improve the standards-setting process. Oddly enough, the Institute came to the conclusion that it could best support the process of development of accounting standards by relinquishing control over that process. Both the CAP and the APB had been created by the Institute. The AICPA now realized that an independent standards-setting body was needed. Creation of that body, the Financial Accounting Standards Board, in 1973 is the most recent major event in the historical development of GAAP. (See Exhibit 12-1.)

Exhibit 12-1
GAAP: A Historical Perspective

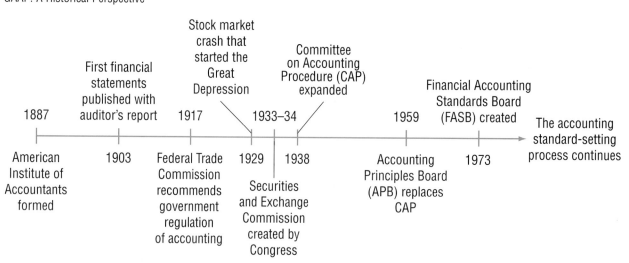

Financial Accounting Standards Board (FASB)

The express mission of the **Financial Accounting Standards Board (FASB)** is

to establish and improve standards of financial accounting and reporting for the guidance and education of the public, including issuers, auditors, and users of financial information.

(Robert S. Kay and D. Gerald Searfoss, eds.,
Handbook of Accounting and Auditing, 2nd ed.
[Boston: Warren, Gorham & Lamont, 1989], p. 46-8)

There are several key differences between the FASB and the two earlier standard-setting bodies, and these differences have allowed the FASB to attain a much higher degree of acceptance in both the accounting profession and the business community.

■ *The FASB is an independent body and its members work for it full-time.* Both the CAP and APB were organizations of professional accounting groups of their time (the AIA and the AICPA), and their members were volunteers who continued in their primary occupations while serving as members. Upon appointment to the FASB, members are required to resign from their present employment and devote themselves to the Board full-time. Members serve five-year terms and are eligible for reappointment for one consecutive term.

■ *The FASB is smaller in size than its predecessors.* The CAP was composed of 22 members, the APB of 21. In both instances, the size of the organization, coupled with the volunteer status of the members, made organizing meetings extremely difficult. When meetings were held, it was almost impossible to obtain agreement on issues because of the number of people involved. The FASB, in contrast, has just seven members, all of whom work only for the Board. While it is still not easy to get members to agree on difficult issues, it is certainly easier than it was with the unwieldy CAP or APB.

■ *The FASB's members are not all accountants.* Both the CAP and APB were composed of practicing accountants. Members of the FASB come from diverse employment backgrounds, though they are required to have knowledge of accounting, finance, and business in general. This diversity gives the FASB a broader perspective in discerning the public interest in matters of financial accounting and reporting.

■ *Early on, the FASB established a conceptual framework of accounting from which to approach the process of setting standards.* We have referred to this conceptual framework repeatedly throughout this text. All our discussions of the primary and secondary characteristics of useful accounting information are based on it. While not everyone agrees with the concepts established by the FASB, most concede that the framework has changed the emphasis in setting standards from one of *what is* to one of *what should be.*

12-4. Why do you think it is significant that the FASB is independent of the AICPA?

12-5. If FASB members are not required to be accountants, from what other professional backgrounds are members likely to be drawn?

12-6. How do you think a conceptual framework shifts the standards-setting process from *what is* to *what should be*?

The Standards-Setting Process Today

From its inception, the FASB has employed a due process approach to setting standards. The CAP and, to a lesser extent, the APB established accounting standards without much input from those who would be affected by the standards. This approach, while efficient, breeds discontent and resentment. The FASB takes a different approach. From the time an issue that may require a new (or revised) standard is identified to the time a standard is set, there is ample opportunity for interested parties to make known their feelings on the matter.

12-7. In what ways does a due process approach to setting standards lessen discontent and resentment?

Under the guidance of the FASB, setting standards is a ten-step circular process emphasizing due process:

1. Identifying issues
2. Setting an agenda
3. Appointing a task force
4. Creating a discussion memorandum
5. Holding public hearings

6. Inviting comment letters
7. Deliberating
8. Writing an exposure draft
9. Issuing a Statement of Financial Accounting Standards
10. Conducting a postenactment review

STEP 1 *Identifying issues.*

Accounting issues and problems are identified either by the FASB itself or by other interested parties. Issues considered over the years have been raised by public accounting firms, the AICPA, business organizations, the U.S. Congress, and many others. Some of the issues brought to the Board's attention are fairly simple, others are very complex. While the FASB has no set rules for determining whether an identified issue requires its attention, the Board attempts to treat seriously all issues raised by interested parties.

STEP 2 *Setting an agenda.*

Choosing agenda items is a critical step in the process. Obviously, not all issues raised make it past this step. In considering an issue, the FASB takes account of its own resources, the perceived urgency of the matter, and any interrelationship with other projects already under consideration.

STEP 3 *Appointing a task force.*

Once an item is placed on the agenda, a task force is appointed to see the project through to its conclusion—which may either be the creation of a new standard or the dropping of the project after some investigation of the issue. Task forces usually include FASB members as well as outside experts in the area or areas affected by the issue at hand. When making appointments to these task forces, the FASB attempts to choose members with a diversity of views on the agenda item. The object is to obtain as many different perspectives as possible.

STEP 4 *Creating a discussion memorandum.*

The task force appointed in Step 3 prepares a discussion memorandum, which defines the problem, explains the issues, and describes the scope of the project. This document also includes several alternative solutions, but no recommendations are offered at this point in the process. Instead, all interested parties are invited to respond to the memorandum issued.

STEP 5 *Holding public hearings.*

While it is not mandatory, the Board always holds open public hearings on major projects it is considering. These hearings are announced in the financial press, and anyone interested may attend and make an oral presentation of his or her views.

STEP 6 *Inviting comment letters.*

Those unable to attend the public hearings to discuss the issues involved in a particular project are invited to write comment letters. Every letter is considered by the Board.

STEP 7 *Deliberating.*

Once all interested parties have had an opportunity to express their views, either through public hearings or comment letters, the Board deliberates on whether or not to move on to Step 8. Also considered in the deliberation process are recommendations from the Board's technical staff and the task force appointed in Step 3.

STEP 8 *Writing an exposure draft.*

Any project that reaches this step will very likely result in a new standard under GAAP. In fact, the FASB's exposure draft is intended to be as close to a final pronouncement as possible. Still, the proposed standard is exposed to public comment for at least 60 days, and often undergoes significant modification as a result of comments received at this stage.

STEP 9 *Issuing a Statement of Financial Accounting Standards.*

After a proposed standard has gone through the first eight steps of the process, the FASB members must vote on whether or not to put it in place. If a majority of the seven members approve the new rule, it becomes a part of GAAP. The new rule is then issued as a **Statement of Financial Accounting Standards (SFAS)** by the FASB.

STEP 10 *Conducting a postenactment review.*

This is the step that makes GAAP standards setting a circular process. The FASB has recognized that financial accounting and reporting are dynamic areas, and that therefore the rules governing them must be constantly reconsidered and refined or amended. So at the end of the standards-setting process, the standard passed by the Board becomes eligible for consideration as an issue or problem and the process may begin again with Step 1.

Beginning with the Committee on Accounting Procedure, continuing with the Accounting Principles Board, and finally with the Financial Accounting Standards Board, there have been well over 200 official pronouncements establishing standards that constitute generally accepted accounting principles. (See Exhibit 12-2.) Most of these standards address very narrow issues dealing with how specific events or items should be treated. Woven throughout these pronouncements, however, are several underlying assumptions, principles, and modifying conventions that provide a context for the specific applications. An

Statement of Financial Accounting Standards (SFAS) The official name of a pronouncement issued by FASB as part of GAAP.

Exhibit 12-2
The Development of GAAP

WHEN	WHO	WHAT
1938–1959	Committee on Accounting Procedure (CAP)	Accounting Research Bulletins (ARBs)
1959–1973	Accounting Principles Board (APB)	APB Opinions
1973–present	Financial Accounting Standards Board (FASB)	Statements of Financial Accounting Standards (SFAS)

understanding of these concepts is essential to anyone attempting to use financial information prepared under the various provisions of GAAP.

In the next section, we will discuss the five basic assumptions underlying generally accepted accounting principles. Then, in the following section, we will describe the four basic principles of accounting under GAAP. This will be followed by a section considering the modifying conventions to GAAP.

Basic Assumptions of GAAP

There are five basic assumptions underlying GAAP. Whenever economic decision makers look at financial reports prepared under GAAP, they can be assured the reports were prepared based on the separate entity, going concern, monetary unit, stable dollar, and time period assumptions. We will discuss each in turn.

Separate Entity

separate entity assumption
The assumption that economic activity can be identified with a particular economic entity and that the results of activities for each entity will be recorded separately.

The **separate entity assumption** is that economic activity can be identified with a particular economic entity. Economic entities may be individuals, proprietorships, partnerships, corporations, or even a division of a business. The separate entity assumption maintains that the activities of any economic entity can be separately identified, and therefore, results of those activities can be separately identified as well.

Reports of economic activity (financial accounting information) prepared under GAAP must identify the economic entity and include only items related to that entity. For example, the revenues and expenses reported in the income statement of General Motors are the revenues and expenses of General Motors and no other economic entity (including its owners and officers). The same holds true for the assets, liabilities and equities reported in General Motors's balance sheet.

Going Concern

going concern assumption
Unless there is persuasive evidence to the contrary, it is assumed that businesses will continue to operate indefinitely.

The **going concern assumption** is that unless there is persuasive evidence to the contrary, it is assumed that businesses will continue to operate indefinitely. The implications of this assumption are *enormous*. Without the going concern assumption, accrual accounting would not be possible. For example, revenue is recognized under accrual accounting when it is earned, not when the cash associated with the revenue is received. Unless it can be assumed the company owing the money will be around long enough to pay it, recognition before the cash is received would be inappropriate. The going concern assumption allows financial statement users to rely on a balance sheet that reports accounts receivable.

The going concern assumption is equally critical to expense recognition. For example, without an assumption that the business will continue to operate, it would be inappropriate to allocate the costs of assets to future periods. Thus, the going concern assumption is crucial for the acceptance of depreciation as an appropriate approach to expense recognition.

Monetary Unit

The **monetary unit assumption** holds that all economic transactions and events can be measured using some monetary unit. It is assumed that quantitative data expressed in some monetary unit are the most useful way to measure and communicate economic information. In the United States, we use the dollar; in the United Kingdom, they use the pound; and in Japan, they use the yen. Whatever the currency, financial accounting information prepared under GAAP uses monetary units as the basis for measurement.

Measuring results of business activities in monetary units seems like a good approach, but it has some limitations. Suppose a multimillion-dollar corporation suddenly loses its chief executive officer (CEO). Several candidates are being considered to fill the position: Donald Trump, Ross Perot, Hillary Clinton, Lee Iaccoca, and you. Will the replacement of the CEO be an important business activity? Certainly! Will the choice among the candidates impact the company? Certainly! In fact, if you were named CEO, the company would be impacted adversely that very day (no offense intended). Can that immediate impact be measured in monetary units? No. But the monetary unit assumption embraces the notion that the monetary unit will be accepted as our basis of measurement despite its limitations.

DISCUSSION QUESTIONS

12-8. Besides the situation described in the text, identify two other results of business activity that cannot be measured in monetary units.

(*Hint:* Think about things a company "has.")

Stable Dollar

The **stable dollar assumption** is that the value of the dollar does not change over time. This assumption allows inflation and deflation to be ignored in financial reports prepared under GAAP. Under the stable dollar assumption, dollars used to measure assets in 1963 and dollars used to measure assets in 1993 are combined without any adjustment for changing prices during that 30-year period.

Have you ever found something several years old that still had a price tag on it and been amazed by how much lower the price for an article like that was back then? Think about what kinds of differences could occur over 30 years—the financial reports of major U.S. companies include items measured in dollars from the 1960s, 1970s, 1980s, and 1990s. Based on the stable dollar assumption, these "different dollars" are all combined without regard for the impact of inflation.

Time Period

time period assumption
The assumption that the economic activities of an entity can be traced to some specific time period and results of those activities can be reported for any arbitrary time period chosen.

The **time period assumption** is that the economic activities of an entity can be traced to some specific time period. The actual results of business activity cannot be precisely measured until the company ceases operations and makes a complete tally of all economic impacts. But accounting information is demanded by both internal and external decision makers in the interim, so companies issue reports that show how profitable they have been for some arbitrary time period (income statement) and their financial position at the end of that time period (balance sheet). The time period assumption holds that the economic events and transactions of that time period can be measured with some degree of reliability.

Business activity is impacted by demands of customers, actions by competitors, changes in economic forces, and other factors. In most cases, the activity is not dictated by the calendar. With that in mind, it *may* seem arbitrary to report results of business activities in time periods determined by the calendar. But economic decision makers' need for comparable information has created a strong tradition in the United States that accounting information be made available on a quarterly (every three months) basis as well as annually. The time period assumption allows users to feel confident that the results of business activity can be reasonably measured in these standardized time periods.

BASIC PRINCIPLES OF ACCOUNTING UNDER GAAP

There are four basic principles pertaining to how transactions and events are to be measured under GAAP. Obviously, how these things are measured dictates how they are reported in financial statements. When economic decision makers look at financial reports prepared under GAAP, they can be assured that the reports were prepared based on the principles of historical cost, revenue recognition, expense recognition, and full discosure.

Historical Cost

historical cost principle
Balance sheet items are generally reported at their cost, not their value.

The **historical cost principle** requires that in most cases items on the balance sheet be reported at their cost—what was paid for them—not their current value. Contrary to popular belief, accounting does not deal with value or worth. Rather, accounting standards focus on reporting results of activities in as objective a manner as possible. Cost is an objective measure based on an actual transaction—value is not.

Many people feel a balance sheet should show how much a company's assets are worth, not how much they cost. We agree it would be desirable to show the current value of the items on the balance sheet; this information would be very relevant in a variety of decision-making settings. However, the current value of an asset is not always a reliable item of information—particularly, since verifiability is such a difficult issue. If we turned to appraisers for the current value of, say, a building, there would be some variation in their estimates. The historical cost of assets may not be as relevant as current value, but at least it is a reliable information item. It is verifiable, neutral, and representationally faithful.

The accounting profession has experimented with ways to make the balance sheet items more reflective of their current values, but every experiment has exposed the subjective nature of the valuation process and has caused a return to the historical cost principle. So, balance sheets prepared under GAAP disclose the cost of assets, not what they are worth.

DISCUSSION QUESTIONS

12-9. Assume you are asked to establish guidelines for the reporting of the current value of items presented on balance sheets. Describe the guidelines or restrictions you would create to ensure the maximum level of comparability possible among current values reported by companies.

Revenue Recognition and Expense Recognition

revenue recognition principle Revenue is recognized when it is earned, rather than when the cash associated with revenue is received.

The **revenue recognition principle** states that revenue is recognized when it is earned, rather than when the cash associated with the revenue is collected. The **expense recognition principle** holds that expenses are to be matched to the same income statement period as the revenues they helped generate, rather than when the cash associated with the expenses is paid.

expense recognition principle Expenses must be matched to the same income statement period as the revenues they helped generate.

These two principles are discussed together here, first, because they are closely related, and second, because we have already discussed them in depth in Chapter 7 when we presented accrual basis accounting. The accounting profession has adopted accrual accounting as GAAP. While accrual accounting has some weaknesses, the accounting profession has decided the accrual method of revenue and expense recognition is superior to any alternative recognition basis. Keep in mind, however, that "generally accepted" is not synonymous with "universally accepted." The accrual basis is not the "correct" method of accounting. Rather, it is the method most of the accounting profession has accepted as the best way to measure reality.

Full Disclosure

full disclosure principle The financial statements prepared by a company must provide users with the information they need to make economic decisions.

The **full disclosure principle** ensures that the financial statements prepared by a company provide users with the information they need to make economic decisions. Actually, *adequate* disclosure is probably a more appropriate name for this principle because financial reports prepared under GAAP do not have to disclose *everything*. Rather, they must disclose an adequate amount of information to be useful to economic decision makers. Whenever accounting reports are prepared, accountants are faced with the dilemma of providing sufficient information for the users' needs without including so much detail that the statements become cumbersome.

The key to deciding what information should be included is determining whether the inclusion or exclusion of an item will make a difference to the user. This is a very difficult judgment in many instances because the needs of different users are different, and often conflicting. Essentially, the intent is to present enough information to ensure that the reasonably prudent user will not only not be misled, but will also be able to draw reasonable conclusions from the information provided.

Information required under the full disclosure principle may be disclosed in a variety of places besides in the financial statements themselves. Information is also included in the notes to the financial statements and in supplementary schedules, both of which provide additional detail about items included in the main body of the financial statements.

Modifying Conventions to GAAP

The standards established as GAAP would be unworkable if they were so rigid that they never allowed for special circumstances. There are three basic situations in which GAAP may be modified. In other words, these are circumstances under which companies are allowed to "bend the rules."

Materiality

materiality The modifying convention that allows departure from GAAP if the treatment of an item is not significant enough to influence the judgment of a reasonable person.

The **materiality** convention allows for GAAP to be modified if the treatment of the item is not significant enough to matter. An item is material if its inclusion or exclusion would influence the judgment of a reasonable person. If an item is deemed to be immaterial, it need not be treated according to GAAP. As an example, assume a company purchased a wastebasket for $10 and estimated its useful life to be ten years. Accrual accounting takes the position that the wastebasket should be recorded as an asset and depreciated using some systematic and rational allocation method over its ten-year life. But the cost of record keeping for a small item like this far outweighs any benefit derived from depreciating it. No reasonable person is going to be misled by expensing the wastebasket (recording the entire $10 as an expense at the time of purchase).

Materiality is a relative concept: What is material for one company may not be for another. For example, General Motors has sales revenue of well over $100 billion per year. Including a $10,000 sale in the wrong income statement period would not be material for users of GM's financial statements. For Sam Balderas Used Car Sales, which averages about $100,000 in sales each year, including a $10,000 sale in the wrong income statement period would be a material error. There are no hard-and-fast rules about what is material, so evaluating materiality requires a tremendous amount of judgment.

Industry Peculiarities

industry peculiarity A circumstance in which the characteristics of activity in a particular industry cause adherence to a particular GAAP rule to result in misleading information.

An **industry peculiarity** is a situation in which the characteristics of activity in a particular industry make adherence to a particular GAAP rule result in misleading information. Certain industries have, over time, developed treatments of these peculiar circumstances that fairly present the results of the activity, but do not follow GAAP. When this is the case, businesses throughout the entire industry use accounting methods other than those prescribed by GAAP. Because all companies in that industry treat the item in the same manner, for one company to do otherwise would produce financial statements that could not be compared to those of other companies in the industry. Instances in which industry peculiarities call for a departure from GAAP are not common. However, as a reader of financial statements, you should be aware that there are circumstances which allow the presentation of financial information that appears to be in violation of basic principles and assumptions of GAAP.

For example, in the agriculture industry, crops are often reported on the balance sheet at market value. This may appear to be a violation of GAAP's historical cost principle, but this industry-wide deviation from GAAP actually enhances the comparability, and therefore, the usefulness of the information. Other industries, such as banking and public utilities, have characteristics that would cause strict adherence to GAAP guidelines to actually misrepresent the results of the business activities. These characteristics, or industry peculiarities, result in approved departures from GAAP.

Conservatism

conservatism In a situation where two approaches to valuation or measurement are allowed under GAAP and the choice is unclear, the treatment least likely to overstate assets or income, or understate liabilities, is to be selected.

Conservatism provides a guideline in difficult valuation or measurement situations. If more than one choice of presentation or valuation method meets GAAP guidelines, conservatism suggests that the alternative least likely to overstate financial position or earnings should be selected. In other words, when the choice between accounting treatments is not clear, the one least likely to overstate assets or income, or understate liabilities, should be selected. However, conservatism in no way justifies the *intentional* understating of a company's assets or income.

DISCUSSION QUESTIONS

12-10. Describe two different situations in which a company's management would wish to understate the assets or income of the business.

We have explored the basic assumptions and principles upon which generally accepted accounting principles are founded. We have also cited the situations in which GAAP rules may be modified. So now you have an understanding of the basic guidelines companies follow in recording results of their business activities and preparing financial statements. The purpose of generally accepted accounting principles is to assure external users that the financial statements they are reading were prepared according to a consistently applied set of standards. But exactly how do these external decision makers know that GAAP guidelines were followed? Do they have to rely on management's word-of honor?

FORMS OF OUTSIDE ASSURANCE ON FINANCIAL STATEMENTS

Common sense dictates that external decision makers cannot rely solely on the integrity of a company's management, for it is usually in management's best interests to present financial statements that reflect as favorably as possible on the company's performance. Obviously, there is a need for some assurance from outside the company as to the fairness of the financial statement presentation. We will now explore how this assurance is obtained.

History of the Audit

"Audit" derives from the Latin word "*audire*," meaning "to hear." "Hearing" does not seem to fit our modern usage of the term, but the derivation can be found in historical accounting practices. Auditing, as we know it, goes back at least to thirteenth-century England, to an accounting practice described by A.C. Littleton in his book *Accounting Evolution to 1900*:

> Since the issue was usually one of honest discharge of fiscal responsibility, the purpose of these audits would be to test the proper administration of that responsibility. To accomplish this purpose, the facts in the case would need to be laid before persons who would recognize error or omission when present. In the early days this usually involved "hearing the accounts" for few men could read and very few could write; the word "audit" itself means to hear. (p. 262)

In the United States, the practice of auditing didn't really begin until after 1900, when the emergence of large corporations with absentee ownership created a need for an independent review of a company's financial statements. To meet that need, the profession of auditing developed.

Earlier in the chapter, we mentioned that the first company to publish financial statements accompanied by a statement from an independent auditor was United States Steel. That audit opinion, issued by Price Waterhouse & Co. in 1903 (Exhibit 12-3), is much more strongly worded than the opinions issued today. In fact, the audit opinion Price Waterhouse & Co. would have issued had this audit been for the year 1993 instead of 1903 would be significantly different, as you will learn as we explore of the audit process.

We have examined the books of the U.S. Steel Corporation and its Subsidiary Companies for the year ending December 31, 1902, and certify that the Balance Sheet at that date and the Relative Income Account are correctly prepared therefrom.

We have satisfied ourselves that during the year only actual additions and extensions have been charged to Property Account; that ample provision has been made for Depreciation and Extinguishment, and that the item of "Deferred Charges" represents expenditures reasonably and properly carried forward to operations of subsequent years.

We are satisfied that the valuation of the inventories of stocks on hand as certified by the responsible officials have been carefully and accurately made at approximate cost; also that the cost of material and labor on contracts in progress has been carefully ascertained, and that the profit taken on these contracts is fair and reasonable.

Full provision has been made for bad and doubtful accounts receivable and for all ascertainable liabilities.

We have verified cash and securities by actual inspection or by certificates from the Depositories, and are of opinion that the Stocks and Bonds are fully worth the value at which they are stated in the Balance Sheet.

And we certify that in our opinion the Balance Sheet is properly drawn up so as to show the true financial position of the Corporation and its Subsidiary Companies, and that the Relative Income Account is a fair and correct statement of the net earnings for the fiscal year ending at that date.

DISCUSSION QUESTIONS

12-11. In the audit report shown in Exhibit 12-3, to what do the words "Relative Income Account" refer? Explain how you arrived at your answer.

What Exactly Is an Audit?

Perhaps the best way to approach this subject is to talk about what an audit is not! An audit is *not* the preparation of the financial statements. The client company is responsible for doing that. A company may hire an outside accountant to prepare the statements, but this is not the audit. In fact, the auditor has no authority to change anything in the statements without the consent of the client. An audit is *also* not an examination of all the records to make sure that the financial statements are accurate. Read that sentence again. Does it surprise you? It does many people, because they think that is exactly what an audit is.

audit Examination by an independent CPA of enough of a company's records to determine whether the financial statements have been prepared in accordance with GAAP.

An **audit** consists of examining *enough* of the company's records to determine whether the financial statements have been prepared in accordance with GAAP. To examine all records would be incredibly expensive—so expensive, in fact, that companies could not afford it.

DISCUSSION QUESTIONS

12-12. Describe how you would decide *which* and *how many* records to examine in order to determine whether a company's financial statements were prepared in accordance with GAAP.

Auditing standards require that auditors have an extensive knowledge of the economy, the relevant industry, and the client's business. Auditors must make inquiries of company personnel and conduct numerous analytical and audit procedures. When they complete an audit, auditors make no claim as to the accuracy of the financial statements they have audited. What they try to achieve is *reasonable assurance* that there are no *material misstatements* in those financial statements. "Reasonable assurance" means what a rational person would consider sufficient. "Material misstatement," you will infer from our discussion of materiality earlier in the chapter, means that there are no misstatements significant enough to influence the judgment of a reasonable person.

Who Performs Audits?

generally accepted auditing standards (GAAS) A set of standards (rules) governing the behavior of CPAs with regard to the performance of audits.

Individuals who are qualified as certified public accountants (CPAs) are the only ones approved to perform independent audits of American businesses, but not all CPAs are auditors. Auditing is a highly specialized function governed by a set of standards called **generally accepted auditing standards (GAAS)**. The pronouncements detailing the procedures that must be followed by CPAs during audits are called Statements on Auditing Standards (SAS). Even though auditing standards are established in much the same way GAAP standards are, do not confuse GAAS with GAAP.

Auditors walk a curious kind of tightrope in our society. Lawyers have one responsibility, and that is to represent their clients (who pay them to fulfill that responsibility). Doctors have one responsibility, and that is to care for their patients (who pay them to fulfill that responsibility). Auditors, on the other hand, have a dual responsibility: They are responsible to their clients (who pay them), but they also have a responsibility to all those who use the audited financial statements. They are expected to remain independent of the entity they are auditing and objective in their assessment of the presentation in the financial statements. It is a difficult balancing act, and auditors' performance of it has been subjected to a tremendous amount of criticism in recent years. In fact, there has been a renewed call for direct government regulation of the accounting profession, particularly in the area of auditing. The performance of auditors in the events leading up to the savings and loan crisis of the 1980s is a particularly sore point with critics, although just how much blame for the S&L debacle can be attributed to auditors is debatable.

DISCUSSION QUESTIONS

12-13. What potential problems do you think can arise from the auditor's dual responsibility?

Remember, since 1934, the Securities and Exchange Commission has had the statutory authority to regulate accounting. Currently, the SEC delegates that authority to the FASB, and only intervenes in the development of standards when it strongly objects to FASB's actions. Whether the SEC will become more involved in the standard-setting process is uncertain. The accounting profession, eager to remain self-governing, is making a great effort to demonstrate it has the ability to police itself.

The Audit Opinion

opinion An auditor's judgment as to the fairness of the financial statement presentation.

At the conclusion of an audit, the auditor issues an **opinion** as to the fairness (*not* the accuracy) of the financial statement presentation. There are several different opinions that can be rendered under GAAS, depending on the findings of the audit:

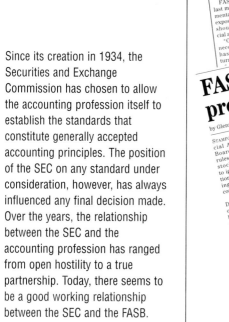

Since its creation in 1934, the Securities and Exchange Commission has chosen to allow the accounting profession itself to establish the standards that constitute generally accepted accounting principles. The position of the SEC on any standard under consideration, however, has always influenced any final decision made. Over the years, the relationship between the SEC and the accounting profession has ranged from open hostility to a true partnership. Today, there seems to be a good working relationship between the SEC and the FASB.

Courtesy of Accounting Today.

unqualified opinion States that the auditors find the financial statements to be fairly presented in accordance with GAAP. Also called a "clean" opinion.

■ **Unqualified opinion.** This is what all companies being audited hope to receive, and most do. It is also called (unofficially) a "clean" opinion. In most instances, an unqualified opinion will be stated, word for word, like the example shown in Exhibit 12-4 on page 400. The only thing changed will be the name of the company being audited, the name of the auditor, and the dates.

In addition to the unqualified or clean opinion, there are four types of modified audit reports. We are not going to present examples of these because their wording differs under different circumstances. The modified audit reports are:

qualified opinion The opinion issued when the departure from GAAP affects no more than one of the financial statements.

■ **Qualified opinion.** Not long ago this form of modification was fairly common, but recent changes in GAAS have greatly reduced the number of instances where a qualified opinion is appropriate. A qualified audit report asserts that the financial statements are presented fairly in accordance with GAAP "except for" a specific financial statement item or account balance. This exception does not cause a pervasive departure from GAAP throughout the statements.

disclaimer An audit report stating that the auditor is unable to render an opinion on the financial statements.

adverse opinion An audit opinion given when the financial statements contain pervasive departures from GAAP.

modification not affecting opinion A comment added to an unqualified audit opinion addressing any matter the auditor feels is important to the understanding of the financial statements.

■ **Disclaimer**. This audit report states that the auditor is unable to render an opinion on the financial statements. The auditor may issue a disclaimer when a material uncertainty exists that keeps the auditor from being able to conclude whether the statements are presented fairly. A disclaimer is also issued when a significant restriction was placed on the auditor as to what audit procedures could be performed.

■ **Adverse opinion**. This modification, known informally as the "kiss of death" report, is used when there are departures from GAAP so pervasive that in the opinion of the auditor the financial statements are *not* presented fairly in accordance with GAAP. In this case, a reasonable person cannot rely on the financial statements.

■ **Modification not affecting opinion**. The auditor may comment on any other matter she or he feels is important to the understanding of the financial statements. There are various circumstances that might lead to this type of modification. The important point is that the auditor is still issuing an unqualified or "clean" opinion when this type of modification is used.

Exhibit 12-4
Standard Unqualified Audit Opinion

Board of Directors
Rosita Corporation
Clemson, South Carolina

We have audited the accompanying balance sheets of Rosita Corporation as of December 31, 1996 and 1995 and the related statements of income, retained earnings, and cash flows for the years then ended. These financial statements are the responsibility of the Corporation's management. Our responsibility is to express an opinion on these financial statements based on our audits.

We conducted our audits in accordance with generally accepted auditing standards. Those standards require that we plan and perform the audit to obtain reasonable assurance about whether the financial statements are free of material misstatement. An audit includes examining, on a test basis, evidence supporting the amounts and disclosures in the financial statements. An audit also includes assessing the accounting principles used and significant estimates made by management, as well as evaluating the overall financial statement presentation. We believe that our audits provide a reasonable basis for our opinion.

In our opinion, the financial statements referred to above present fairly, in all material respects, the financial position of Rosita Corporation as of December 31, 1996 and 1995, and the results of its operations and its cash flows for the years then ended in conformity with generally accepted accounting principles.

February 12, 1997

Jones and Price, CPAs
Jones and Price, CPAs

Many people believe that the audit opinion should be the first thing examined by an external financial statement user. If users understand what it is and what it is not, the audit and the resulting audit opinion can certainly be of great benefit to the external user. However, sometimes external users are willing to accept a level of assurance somewhat lower than that provided by audited financial statements, which are extremely expensive to produce. In these circumstances, they still desire some assurance that the financial statements are reliable and conform to GAAP. In response to this need, the accounting profession has developed the review of financial statements.

The Review

review Inquiries of company personnel and analytical procedures performed by an independent CPA sufficient to provide negative assurance against serious GAAP problems.

There are important distinctions between reviewed financial statements and audited financial statements, but unfortunately, many people do not understand them. Perhaps the best way to distinguish between the review and the audit is to look at the standard review statement issued by an accountant. An example is provided in Exhibit 12-5. Read it carefully. Then compare the review statement to the audit opinion presented in Exhibit 12-4. A careful comparison should prove illuminating.

While a **review** offers substantially less assurance to external users than an audit does, it at least provides what is known as *negative assurance*—meaning it tells the user that the accountant is *not aware of* any serious GAAP problems.

Exhibit 12-5
Standard Review Report

Board of Directors
Havershott Company
Mesa, Arizona

We have reviewed the accompanying balance sheet of Havershott Company as of December 31, 1996, and the related statements of income, retained earnings, and cash flows for the year then ended, in accordance with standards established by the American Institute of Certified Public Accountants. All information included in these financial statements is the representation of the management of Havershott Company.

A review consists principally of inquiries of company personnel and analytical procedures applied to financial data. It is substantially less in scope than an examination in accordance with generally accepted auditing standards, the objective of which is the expression of an opinion regarding the financial statements taken as a whole. Accordingly, we do not express such an opinion.

Based on our review, we are not aware of any material modifications that should be made to the accompanying financial statements in order for them to be in conformity with generally accepted accounting principles.

February 18, 1997

Jones and Doran, CPAs
Jones and Doran, CPAs

Reviews cost a great deal less than complete audits and are useful in a variety of settings. For example, many publicly traded companies obtain a review report for their interim (quarterly) statements. Many private corporations obtain a review report for banking requirements, for bonding requirements, and for other outside parties needing independently prepared financial statements. The North American Securities Administrators Association allows reviewed financial statements instead of audited statements when stock is issued to the public by small corporations meeting specific criteria. These small corporations, which are not SEC-regulated, file a Form U-7 (Small Corporate Offering Registration Form), and are then allowed to raise up to $1 million from the public every 12 months.

Reviews of financial statements are performed following guidelines in the pronouncements known as Statements on Standards for Accounting and Review Services (SSARS). A senior technical committee of the AICPA, known as the Accounting and Review Services Committee (ARSC), has issued seven SSARS since their work began in 1978.

The CPA conducting a review is required by SSARS to have both a knowledge of the accounting principles and practices for the client's industry and an in-depth understanding of the client's business. She must perform analytical procedures, such as ratio analysis, and then further investigate any information that appears questionable based on her analysis. The CPA also conducts interviews with the owners and requires them to submit a representation letter that confirms, among other things, that they have provided complete and accurate information to the CPA.

The Compilation

compilation Preparation by a CPA of a company's financial statements from records provided by the company, with no assurance that the information presented in the statements complies with GAAP.

Before we end this chapter, there is one other type of service we need to discuss—the **compilation**. We have chosen to include a discussion of this service because compilations are often confused with the other services offered by CPAs. Unlike the audit and the review, the compilation is not intended to provide *any* assurance that the financial statements are presented fairly in accordance with GAAP. Perhaps the best way to illustrate the nature of this service is to present the standard compilation report. You will find an example of one in Exhibit 12-6. Take the time to compare it to both the audit report in Exhibit 12-4 and the review report in Exhibit 12-5.

Businesses generally hire accountants to compile financial statements because their own employees lack either the necessary skills or the time to prepare the statements. In most cases, the accountant is not an employee of the company and is therefore considered independent. However, compilations can be conducted by accountants who are not independent of the business issuing financial statements. In fact, CPA's performing compilations for a company may be on the board of directors, own stock in the company, be married to the president of the company, or be associated with the company in any other way. The compilation report is the only CPA-prepared statement that can be issued by a CPA who is not independent of the client. In this situation, the absence of independence is disclosed in the report.

Board of Directors
Wooster Company
Miami, Florida

We have compiled the accompanying balance sheet of Wooster Company as of
December 31, 1996, and the related statements of income, retained earnings, and
cash flows for the year then ended in accordance with standards established by the
American Institute of Certified Public Accountants.

A compilation is limited to presenting in the form of financial statements information
that is the representation of management. We have not audited or reviewed the
accompanying financial statements and, accordingly, do not express an opinion or any
other form of assurance on them.

February 19, 1997

Werner and Price, CPAs
Werner and Price, CPAs

Exhibit 12-6
Standard Compilation Report

In preparing the financial statements, the independent accountant provides no assurance as to conformity with GAAP. If, however, the CPA knows of a departure from GAAP measurement, she must include that disclosure in the compilation report. For example, if Pete's Shoe Store has decided to calculate its revenues based on estimated future sales, the compilation report would include an additional paragraph telling of this departure from GAAP measurement.

All additional disclosures required by GAAP (i.e., the notes to the financial statements) can be omitted from a compilation. The compilation report simply includes an additional paragraph telling the reader that management has chosen to omit notes and supplemental disclosures. In fact, SSARS do not require that the CPA make any inquiries of the owners *unless* the information appears questionable. For example, if Pete's Shoe Store showed no inventory at the end of the month, the CPA should make additional inquiries of Pete, since it would seem questionable that not one pair of shoes was on the shelf (in inventory).

Compilations are professional services. Standards require that the CPA who renders this service have a knowledge of accounting principles and practices in the client's industry, along with a general understanding of the client's business.

Exhibit 12-7 on page 404 provides a snapshot comparison of the differences among audits, reviews, and compilations. As a user of financial information, be sure to properly interpret whether the statements have been audited, reviewed, or compiled. Of the forms of outside assurance discussed in the chapter, only the unqualified audit opinion states that the financial statements being audited are (in the opinion of the auditor) "in conformity with generally accepted accounting principles."

Exhibit 12-7

Comparison of Services Performed by CPAs

	Audit	Review	Compilation
1. What assurance is provided by the report?	Fair presentation in accordance with GAAP	Limited assurance as to GAAP	No assurance as to GAAP
2. What level of knowledge about the client's industry must the CPA have?	Extensive	General	General
3. What level of knowledge about the client's business must the CPA have?	Extensive	Thorough	General
4. What pronouncements regulate how the report is prepared?	SAS	SSARS	SSARS
5. What inquiries must the CPA make?	Inquiry, analytical procedures, and extensive audit procedures required	Inquiry and analytical procedures required, plus additional procedures if information is questionable	No inquiries required unless information supplied by client is questionable

Generally accepted accounting principles were developed to establish comparability among the financial statements of different companies. These principles are also intended to maintain consistency in the way companies account for events and transactions from year to year. The audit and, to a lesser extent, the review were developed as mechanisms to provide assurance to external parties that the financial statements they use to make economic decisions have been prepared in accordance with established standards.

Now that we have discussed generally accepted accounting principles and the forms of outside assurance, we can look more deeply into the financial accounting information available to external decision makers. Two major forms of financial reporting are the annual report and Form 10-K, both of which will be discussed in the next chapter.

SUMMARY

In order to be useful in the economic decision-making process, financial statements of different companies must be comparable. The accounting methods and procedures used by a company must also be consistent from period to period if performance over time is to be reasonably monitored. In response to the need for comparable and consistent financial information, generally accepted accounting principles (GAAP) have been developed over time.

GAAP is a set of standards addressing both very broad issues and very specific applications.

The Securities and Exchange Commission (SEC) has the legal authority to regulate accounting practice. However, it has delegated that authority to bodies closely tied to the accounting profession. Currently, the organization principally responsible for establishing GAAP in the United States is the Financial Accounting Standards Board (FASB), which was created in 1973. Prior to that time, accounting standards were established by the Accounting Principles Board (APB) and, before that, the Committee on Accounting Procedure (CAP). The standards set by these bodies have come about in response to needs expressed by various interested parties. The FASB, more so than its predecessors, emphasizes a "due process" approach, whereby all parties affected by the standards have an opportunity to express their opinions on proposed standards.

The standards making up GAAP were developed based on five basic assumptions—separate entity, going concern, monetary unit, stable dollar, and time period—and four basic principles—historical cost, revenue and expense recognition, and full disclosure. These items serve as a conceptual foundation for the creation of guidelines to regulate accounting practice. GAAP guidelines are meant to apply to a wide range of companies and a variety of situations. They would not be usable if they did not allow for modifications under certain circumstances. Three basic modifying conventions—materiality, industry peculiarities, and conservatism—identify situations in which GAAP rules may be modified.

The primary beneficiaries of generally accepted accounting principles are the external users of financial statements. These economic decision makers require some form of outside assurance that the financial statements have been prepared according to GAAP.

The most stringent form of outside assurance is the audit. An audit consists of the examination by an independent party of enough of a company's records to determine whether the company's financial statements have been prepared in accordance with GAAP. At the conclusion of the audit, the auditor issues a statement—called the audit opinion—as to the company's compliance with GAAP.

A less expensive alternative to the audit is the review. A review is much narrower in scope than an audit and the independent CPA conducting the review does not express an opinion as to whether the financial statements under review were prepared according to GAAP. Instead, the CPA states that nothing came to light that would indicate a major violation of GAAP. This is known as *negative assurance*.

A third service provided by CPAs, the compilation, consists of an accountant actually preparing a company's financial statements from records provided by the company. The compilation provides no assurance whatsoever that the accounting information presented in the financial statements complies with GAAP.

Key Terms

Accounting Principles Board (APB) The standards-setting organization that was the immediate predecessor of the Financial Accounting Standards Board. (p. 384)

Accounting Research Bulletins (ARBs) The pronouncements issued by the Committee on Accounting Procedure. (p. 383)

adverse opinion An audit opinion given when the financial statements contain pervasive departures from GAAP. (p. 400)

APB Opinions The pronouncements issued by the Accounting Principles Board. (p. 384)

audit Examination by an independent CPA of enough of a company's records to determine whether the financial statements have been prepared in accordance with GAAP. (p. 397)

Committee on Accounting Procedure (CAP) In operation from 1930 to 1959, this committee issued pronouncements called Accounting Research Bulletins (ARBs). (p. 383)

compilation Preparation by a CPA of a company's financial statements from records provided by the company, with no assurance that the information presented in the statements complies with GAAP. (p. 402)

conservatism In a situation where two approaches to valuation or measurement are allowed under GAAP and the choice is unclear, the treatment least likely to overstate assets or income, or understate liabilities, is to be selected. (p. 394)

disclaimer An audit report stating that the auditor is unable to render an opinion on the financial statements. (p. 400)

expense recognition principle Expenses must be matched to the same income statement period as the revenues they helped generate. (p. 392)

Financial Accounting Standards Board (FASB) The organization that is principally responsible for establishing accounting guidelines and rules in the United States at the present time. (p. 385)

full disclosure principle The financial statements prepared by a company must provide users with the information they need to make economic decisions. (p. 392)

generally accepted accounting principles (GAAP) Guidelines for presentation of financial accounting information designed to serve external decision makers' need for consistent and comparable information. (p. 378)

generally accepted auditing standards (GAAS) A set of standards (rules) governing the behavior of CPAs with regard to the performance of audits. (p. 397)

going concern assumption Unless there is persuasive evidence to the contrary, it is assumed that businesses will continue to operate indefinitely. (p. 389)

historical cost principle Balance sheet items are generally reported at their cost, not their value. (p. 391)

industry peculiarity A circumstance in which the characteristics of activity in a particular industry cause adherence to a particular GAAP rule to result in misleading information. (p. 394)

materiality The modifying convention that allows departure from GAAP if the treatment of an item is not significant enough to influence the judgment of a reasonable person. (p. 393)

modification not affecting opinion A comment added to an unqualified audit opinion addressing any matter the auditor feels is important to the understanding of the financial statements. (p. 400)

monetary unit assumption The assumption that all economic transactions and events can be measured using some monetary unit. (p. 390)

opinion An auditor's judgment as to the fairness of the financial statement presentation. (p. 398)

qualified opinion The opinion issued when the departure from GAAP affects no more than one of the financial statements. (p. 399)

revenue recognition principle Revenue is recognized when it is earned, rather than when the cash associated with revenue is received. (p. 392)

review Inquiries of company personnel and analytical procedures performed by an independent CPA sufficient to provide negative assurance against serious GAAP problems. (p. 401)

separate entity assumption The assumption that economic activity can be identified with a particular economic entity and that the results of activities for each entity will be recorded separately. (p. 389)

stable dollar assumption The assumption that allows financial statements to ignore the fact that the value of the dollar changes over time. (p. 390)

Statement of Financial Accounting Standards (SFAS) The official name of a pronouncement issued by FASB as part of GAAP. (p. 388)

time period assumption The assumption that the economic activities of an entity can be traced to some specific time period and results of those activities can be reported for any arbitrary time period chosen. (p. 391)

unqualified opinion States that the auditors find the financial statements to be fairly presented in accordance with GAAP. Also called a "clean" opinion. (p. 399)

Review the Facts

A. Explain how the characteristics of comparability and consistency affect economic decision making.

B. Broadly define GAAP.

C. Which companies must adhere to GAAP?

D. Explain why companies may adopt GAAP even if they are not required by law to do so.

E. Explain the role of the SEC in the regulation of accounting practice.

F. What is the name and abbreviation for the current accounting standards-setting group?

G. List four differences between the FASB and its predecessors.

H. Describe the ten-step process used by FASB to set standards.

I. Explain the five basic assumptions under which GAAP operate.

J. Describe the four basic principles pertaining to how transactions and events are to be measured under GAAP.

K. Identify three situations in which it is allowable to modify GAAP.

L. Name two things an audit is *not*.

M. Explain "reasonable assurance" and "material misstatements."

N. Who can perform independent audits?

O. By what standards are auditors governed?

P. Describe an auditor's dual responsibility.

Q. Name and describe the five types of audit report that can be issued.

R. What type of assurance is offered by a review?

S. Describe a compilation.

APPLY WHAT YOU HAVE LEARNED

12-14. Presented below are some items related to the issue of outside assurance discussed in this chapter, followed by the definitions of those items in scrambled order.

a. Audit

b. Review

c. Compilation

d. Unqualified opinion

e. Qualified opinion

f. Disclaimer

g. Adverse opinion

h. Modification not affecting opinion

1. ___ Caused by a material uncertainty the auditor does not feel can be adequately communicated, or by the placing of a significant restriction on the auditor as to what records may be examined.

2. ___ The process of examining a company's records to determine whether the financial statements have been prepared in accordance with GAAP standards.

3. ___ Rendered when there are departures from GAAP so pervasive that a reasonable person cannot rely on the financial statements.

4. ___ Provides what is known as negative assurance.

5. ___ A comment made by an auditor in her or his report deemed to be important to the understanding of the financial statements. The opinion rendered, however, is still unqualified.

6. ___ Unofficially referred to as a "clean" opinion.

7. ___ A service provided by an accountant in which the financial statements are prepared, but no assurance is offered as to their conformity to GAAP.

8. ___ Issued when there is a nonpervasive departure from GAAP.

Match the letter next to each item with the appropriate definition. Each letter will be used only once.

12-15. Presented below is a list of the assumptions, principles, and modifying conventions of GAAP as discussed in this chapter. Descriptions relating to those items are listed below in scrambled order.

a. Separate entity   **g.** Revenue recognition
b. Going concern   **h.** Expense recognition
c. Monetary unit   **i.** Full disclosure
d. Stable dollar   **j.** Materiality
e. Time period   **k.** Industry peculiarities
f. Historical cost   **l.** Conservatism

1. ____ Balance sheet items are not shown at their current value.

2. ____ Economic transactions and events can be expressed using some valuation of money.

3. ____ Amounts earned are recorded and reported when there is a legal claim to the cash associated with the earnings.

4. ____ Inflation and deflation are ignored in financial reports.

5. ____ When in doubt, choose the accounting alternative least likely to overstate assets or income.

6. ____ Economic activity can be identified with a particular economic entity.

7. ____ Financial statements must provide users with the information they need to make economic decisions.

8. ____ Unless there is persuasive evidence otherwise, businesses are assumed to operate indefinitely.

9. ____ Not all items are significant enough to influence the judgment of a reasonable person.

10. ____ Economic activities can be traced to a specific income statement period.

11. ____ Adherence to GAAP would be misleading because of a characteristic of the company's type of business activities.

12. ____ Economic sacrifices are recognized in the same income statement period as the revenues they generate.

REQUIRED:

Match the letter next to each item on the list with the appropriate description. Each letter will be used only once.

12-16. Consider each of the following independent situations:

1. Monolith, Inc., is applying for a loan at the Stevens Bank and Trust and must provide the bank with current financial statements. Since the corporation has only $44,000 of assets, the accountant has decided to list the $200,000 house owned by the president of the company as an asset on Monolith's balance sheet.

2. Upper management of Mike Burbidge and Company has a problem. They have been analyzing the financial statements prepared by the corporate controller for the year ended December 31, 1995. The income statement shows a net income of $375,000 for the year; management had predicted net income of only about $50,000 for 1995. Now it looks as if 1996 will be the bad year, and management would like to "smooth" earnings somewhat by showing some of 1995's net income in 1996. To do this, they have decided to count all the December 1995 sales as January 1996 sales. This will lower the 1995 net income to $172,000. That way, the company can still report a net income for 1995 that is much better than expected, and have a head start on 1996.

3. Jan Ruttenburr, Inc., purchased a building in December 1995 for a cash price of $250,000. Management has decided to count the entire cost of the building as an expense in 1995 because it was a bad year (a $1,800,000 loss) and another $250,000 expense won't make that much difference.

4. A product liability lawsuit was filed against Betty Jo Clardy Company just as 1996 was drawing to a close. The company has decided not to make any mention of the litigation in its annual report to the stockholders. Although the outcome of the suit looks bleak, it is not certain the company will lose and management feels it would only make the stockholders nervous if they knew about it.

5. Lehi Mills and Company has owned a building for 25 years. The building originally cost $75,000 to construct and has an estimated useful life of 30 years with no residual value. The straight-line depreciation method has been used, so the building now has a book value of only $12,500. Last month, Pam Bowden Company offered Mills $450,000 for the building, so Mr. Mills (owner and president of Mills and Company) has decided to list the building on this year's balance sheet at $450,000.

6. DeLoy Fillerup is really proud of himself. He has straightened out the accounting procedures at Hometown Gas and Electric, Inc. Before he became the corporation's accountant, the procedures violated GAAP. Now, with the changes DeLoy made, the company follows each and every GAAP guideline to the last detail. Just one problem—Hometown Gas and Electric is the only public utility company adhering to every GAAP guideline.

7. Ratliff Textiles, Inc., purchased a new stitching machine and set up its records to depreciate the asset over five years. Mr. Ratliff is uneasy about using the five-year life the company normally uses for machines of this type. His business instinct tells him that new technology is just around the corner (probably within the next three years), so he thinks a three-year life might be more realistic. The general manager has convinced him to use the five-year life anyway, because it will result in lower depreciation expense each year.

REQUIRED:

For each of the situations in the problem, identify the GAAP assumptions, principles, and/or modifying conventions violated. Explain your reasoning.

12-17. There are ten steps in the standards-setting process used by the Financial Accounting Standards Board. They are:

1. Identifying issues
2. Setting an agenda
3. Appointing a task force
4. Creating a discussion memorandum
5. Holding public hearings
6. Inviting comment letters
7. Deliberating
8. Writing an exposure draft
9. Issuing a Statement of Financial Accounting Standards
10. Conducting a postenactment review

REQUIRED:

a. Explain in your own words what happens in each of the ten steps of the standards-setting process.
b. What is meant by a "due process approach" to setting accounting standards and why has this approach made the FASB more successful than previous standards-setting bodies?

12-18. The Committee on Accounting Procedure (CAP) and the Accounting Principles Board (APB) were the two bodies responsible for setting accounting standards prior to the creation of the FASB in 1973. The chapter identified four key differences between the FASB and the two earlier standards-setting groups:

1. The FASB is independent and its members work full time.
2. The FASB is smaller.
3. The FASB includes nonaccountants as members.
4. The FASB established a conceptual framework of accounting.

REQUIRED:

Explain in your own words what each difference means and why it has made the FASB more successful than either the CAP or the APB.

12-19. Generally accepted accounting principles have been developed over time to aid in comparability among the financial statements of different companies. They are also intended to maintain consistency in the way a firm accounts for transactions and events from period to period.

An audit is intended to provide some assurance to external parties that the financial statements they examine are reasonably presented.

REQUIRED:

a. What determines whether a company in the United States is required to prepare its financial statements according to GAAP?

b. Why are some companies forced to adhere to GAAP even though they are not required by law to do so?

c. Identify a specific decision made by an external decision maker, and explain:

   (1) Why comparability of the accounting information used is important and how GAAP supports comparability.

   (2) Why consistency of the accounting information used is important and how GAAP supports consistency.

12-20. Compare and contrast the audit, the review, and the compilation by discussing the following:

1. The procedures involved in each.
2. The degree of assurance each provides to external financial statement users.
3. As a business owner, the factors you would consider when choosing between presenting audited or reviewed financial statements to a potential investor.

12-21. Listed below are several items described in the text as having contributed to the development of GAAP. For each item, describe in your own words the role it played.

a. Federal Trade Commission
b. American Institute of Certified Public Accountants (formerly American Institute of Accountants)
c. The stock market crash of 1929 and the resulting Great Depression
d. Securities and Exchange Commission
e. Committee on Accounting Procedure
f. Accounting Principles Board
g. Financial Accounting Standards Board

12-22. Included with the purchase of this text was a copy of the 1994 Rockwell annual report. On page 27 of the annual report is the audit opinion expressed by the accounting firm of Deloitte and Touche. In this chapter, you were shown the audit opinion expressed by Price Waterhouse and Company on the 1902 U.S. Steel financial statements (Exhibit 12-3 on page 396).

Read these two audit opinions carefully and then compare them in terms of the following issues, citing specific phrases from the two opinions to support your findings:

a. The division of responsibility for the financial statements between management of the company and the independent auditor.
b. How the audit was actually conducted.
c. The level of assurance provided to external parties.

13

Financial Reporting: The Annual Report and Form 10-K

The four financial statements we have presented thus far contain only a part of the information resulting from the overall process of financial reporting. Two principal groups who rely on the results of financial reporting are stockholders (owners) and regulators (in particular, the SEC). The most comprehensive financial report to stockholders is the company's annual report. Publicly held corporations are required to file a variety of documents with the SEC, the most comprehensive of which is the Form 10-K.

financial reporting Financial disclosures provided to economic decision makers that include both quantitative (numerical) information and qualitative (descriptive) information.

T hus far, we have focused on the accounting information found in financial statements. We have explored the construction and use of the income statement, statement of owners' equity, balance sheet, and the statement of cash flows. These statements are important sources of information about the results of business activities and the financial position of companies. However, financial statements do not provide all the information needed by economic decision makers.

The increasing complexity of business, the continuing refinement of accounting practices, and the effects of government rules and regulations have given rise to additional types of financial disclosure. *Financial reporting* is a more comprehensive term than *financial statements*. **Financial reporting** includes both quantitative information and descriptive information.

> A lthough financial reporting and financial statements have essentially the same objectives, some useful information is better provided by financial statements and some is better provided, or can only be provided, by means of financial reporting other than financial statements.
>
> —SFAC 1, FASB, 1978, para. 5

As the quotation suggests, financial statements are an important part of financial reporting, but they are only a part. Other types of reporting have evolved to provide information that it would be awkward or impossible to include in financial statements.

The two major consumers of corporate financial reports in America today are shareholders and regulators. Indeed, these are the two groups to whom corporate America must regularly answer. Their demands for extensive information from companies have shaped the development of financial reporting over the past hundred years. In this chapter, we examine two important components of financial reporting: the annual report, which was developed to meet the demands of stockholders; and Form 10-K, which is prescribed by the Securities and Exchange Commission (SEC).

annual report The most comprehensive presentation of financial reporting a company provides to its stockholders. Contains financial statements and other information designed to assist economic decision makers.

The most comprehensive presentation of financial reporting to stockholders, the **annual report**, contains not only a company's financial statements but also other information designed to assist economic decision makers to predict the future and timing of cash flows. We will take an in-depth look at the items presented in the annual report in the first part of this chapter, using Rockwell's annual report as our example.

Form 10-K A report filed annually with the Securities and Exchange Commission by publicly traded companies. Includes detailed financial information and descriptive information that is generally beyond what is found in the annual report.

The major regulatory agency to which American corporations that sell their stocks or bonds to the public must respond is the Securities and Exchange Commission. The most widely used report required by the SEC is the **Form 10-K**, a comprehensive annual report that includes financial statements as well as an array of additional financial and nonfinancial information.

After completing your work on this chapter, you should be able to do the following:

1. Describe in your own words the difference between financial statements and financial reporting.
2. Explain the basic purpose of the SEC's Integrated Disclosure System.
3. Identify and describe the items required by the SEC to be disclosed in the annual report and explain how they are used by economic decision makers.
4. Distinguish between primary and fully diluted earnings per share.
5. Describe three information items found in the annual report that are not required by the SEC and explain why they are useful to decision makers.
6. Explain the purpose of Form 10-K, and describe how the information provided in the form differs from that furnished in the annual report.
7. Gather information about companies and obtain annual reports.
8. Explain the purpose of the Special Committee on Financial Reporting and the approach it took to meet its goal.
9. Outline the four major areas in which the Special Committee made recommendations.

EVOLUTION OF THE ANNUAL REPORT

In 1901, a number of small steel companies combined to become the mammoth United States Steel Corporation. At their first annual meeting in 1902, the stockholders of the newly created corporation voted to require management to provide them with a report of the company's performance each year and its financial position at the end of each year. In 1903, U.S. Steel distributed an annual report to the stockholders. This was the first annual report issued by a U.S. company.

Before long, other companies began distributing annual reports to their stockholders, and by 1920 such reports had become quite common. The annual report was originally intended to be used only by stockholders. When U.S. Steel was organized, the owners realized they could not possibly maintain day-to-day involvement in the management of this huge new company. That is why they voted to require the annual report. Its purpose was to communicate information to the absentee owners (stockholders) about the status of their investment. As we shall see when we look at the various elements of the annual report, all communications in it are addressed specifically to the stockholders.

Before long, however, other external parties became interested in companies' annual reports. Remember, external parties do not have the authority to prescribe what kind of financial information they receive from a company; they must rely on what the company chooses to provide. The annual report has become one of the primary sources of financial information available to creditors, suppliers, customers, and other external economic decision makers.

Annual reports issued by U.S. companies in the early years of the twentieth century contained highly condensed financial statements that provided little detail about the company's operations. Apparently, management's stinginess with information was intentional. Donald Jones offers this excerpt from one annual report of the early 1900s:

> The settled plan of the directors has been to withhold all information from stockholders and others that is not called for by the stockholders in a body. So far no request for information has been made in the manner prescribed by the directors....
>
> (Donald Jones, "Management Freedom in Annual Reports," *Financial Executive* [August, 1971],Vol. 39, No. 8, p. 24.)

As the century progressed, companies began to furnish more and more detail about the items contained in their financial statements. Some of these changes in reporting practices were voluntary efforts to provide better information to statement users. Others resulted from the demands of regulatory authorities, primarily the SEC. (The events leading up to the formation of the SEC were discussed in Chapter 12.)

Early annual reports were just that—annual reports. There was nothing flashy or innovative about them. In recent years, however, many large corporations have gone to great lengths to produce annual reports that also serve as public relations and advertising publications. One year, McDonald's Corporation designed the cover of its annual report to resemble a french fry box; the actual report inside was in the form of a newspaper. The GE Capital Services 1993 annual report is triangular when closed, but is designed to stand as a pyramid.

Teri Stratford

SEC Disclosure Regulations

There was an expressed commitment by the SEC in the early years of its existence to create only a very limited number of simple regulations. However, as time passed, the regulations established by the Commission turned out to be quite numerous and anything but simple. You will be delighted to learn that we are only going to mention two of the multitude of SEC regulations—Regulation S-X and Regulation S-K, which deal specifically with disclosure requirements.

Regulation S-X prescribes the rules for the form and content of financial statements filed as part of Form 10-K, the primary document required of publicly traded companies under the SEC's disclosure guidelines. This was one of the first regulations established by the Commission and has been revised and amended many times over the years. In its present form the regulation contains 12 articles (sections) and is 95 pages long (in very tiny print).

Regulation S-K specifies the content of the nonfinancial statement portions of Form 10-K. This regulation was also among the first established by the SEC and, like Regulation S-X, it has been revised and amended many times over the years. In its present form, it contains 10 subparts (sections) and is 93 pages long (again, in very tiny print).

Regulation S-X Prescribes the rules for the form and content of financial statements in the Form 10-K that must be filed with the Securities and Exchange Commission by publicly traded companies.

Regulation S-K Specifies the content of the nonfinancial statement portions of the Form 10-K that must be filed with the Securities and Exchange Commission by publicly traded companies.

The SEC's Integrated Disclosure System

Integrated Disclosure System A system of reporting developed by the Securities and Exchange Commission that has eliminated much of the duplication between the information disclosed in Form 10-K and that disclosed in the annual report.

Between September 1980 and March 1982, the SEC made substantial revisions in the disclosure requirements covered by Regulations S-X and S-K. These improvements resulted in the SEC's **Integrated Disclosure System**, whose primary objectives are:

> (1) to simplify and improve the quality of disclosures provided to investors and other users of financial information, (2) to reduce the costs involved by implementing a single disclosure system, and (3) to encourage the combination of shareholder communications with official SEC filings.
>
> (Fred Skousen, *An Introduction to the SEC*, [Cincinnati: South-Western Publishing Company, 1991], p. 46)

The Integrated Disclosure System has been successful in reducing the duplication between the information disclosed in Form 10-K and that disclosed in the annual report to stockholders. Most annual reports issued nowadays follow these guidelines.

First we will take a detailed look at one company's annual report, and then we will examine what kind of additional information is made available in the same company's Form 10-K.

ITEMS IN THE ANNUAL REPORT REQUIRED BY THE SEC

Skousen summarizes the major disclosures that the SEC requires in the annual report to shareholders:

A. Audited financial statements: balance sheets for two years and income and cash flow statements for three years.

B. Five-year selected financial data.

C. Management's discussion and analysis of financial condition and results of operations.

D. Brief description of the business.

E. Three-year financial information about: industry segments, foreign and domestic operations, and export sales.

F. Identification of directors and executive officers, with the principal occupation and employer of each.

G. The principal market in which the securities of the firm are traded; high and low market prices of the company's common stock for each quarter of the two most recent fiscal years and dividends paid on common stock during those years.

H. Offer to provide a free copy of the 10-K report to shareholders upon written request, unless the annual report complies with Form 10-K disclosure requirements.

Now, using the 1994 annual report of Rockwell International as an example, let's locate and discuss each of these items.

A. Audited financial statements: balance sheets for two years and income and cash flow statements for three years. Rockwell provides these statements on pages 28–30 of its annual report. In addition to the statements required, Rockwell includes a statement of owners' equity, in the form of the Statement of Consolidated Shareowners' Equity on page 31. Notice that the title of each of Rockwell's financial statements indicates the statement is consolidated. **Consolidated financial statements** present information about the results of activities and the financial position of a parent company and its subsidiaries as if they were one enterprise with several branches or divisions. When one corporation owns enough of the voting stock of another corporation to control its activities, the investing company is called the **parent company**. The corporation whose stock is owned by the parent company is called a **subsidiary**. So Rockwell's consolidated financial statements include information about its subsidiaries' activities as well as about its own.

Look at Rockwell's income statement. The basic format should be familiar to you by now. What may be new is the section called "Earning per Common Share." GAAP requires that the disclosures in this section be presented on the face of the income statement. **Earnings per share (EPS)** is perhaps the most widely used measure of a company's earnings performance. It is popular because it shows how much of a company's total earnings is attributable to each share of common stock. In its simplest form, EPS is calculated as follows:

$$\text{Earnings per share} = \frac{\text{Net income}}{\text{Average number of shares of common stock outstanding}}$$

Primary earnings per share is the most basic of the presentations in this section of the income statement. It is calculated as shown above. Using the information provided on Rockwell's income statement, we can see how the primary earnings per share figures were determined.

1994	1993
$\dfrac{\$634.1}{220.5 \text{ Shares}} = \$2.87$	$\dfrac{\$561.9}{219.8 \text{ Shares}} = \$2.55$

Notice that in addition to the EPS based on net income, Rockwell shows additional primary earnings per share figures for 1992: figures for the cumulative effect of a change in accounting principle, and the income before that item. Disclosure of these additional EPS figures is also required by GAAP.

Below the primary EPS figures shown on the face of the income statement, Rockwell presents information about fully diluted earnings per share. These figures are required because Rockwell has issued some type of security that could, at the discretion of the investor or because of market forces, be converted to common stock. These are known as **convertible securities**. For example, convertible bonds are debt instruments that may be turned into shares of common stock. Also, companies may issue preferred stock that is convertible into shares of common stock. If a corporation has issued *any* type

---

consolidated financial statements Financial statements that include the results of operations and the financial position of the parent company and its subsidiary companies as if they were one enterprise with several branches or divisions.

parent company A company that owns a majority of another company's voting stock.

subsidiary A company that has a majority of its voting stock owned by another company.

earnings per share (EPS) A calculation indicating how much of a company's total earnings is attributable to each share of common stock.

primary earnings per share The most basic presentation of EPS. Divides earnings figures for the period by the average number of shares of common stock outstanding.

convertible securities Debt or equity securities that can be converted into shares of the company's common stock.

fully diluted earnings per share A more stringent EPS calculation than primary earnings per share. This calculation includes the potential impact of convertible securities in the denominator of the EPS calculation.

of convertible securities, it is always possible that it will have to issue more shares of common stock to meet conversion requirements. Whenever shares of stock outstanding are increased, the earnings attributable to each share decrease. Hence, converting other securities to common stock will decrease (or dilute) EPS.

Fully diluted earnings per share figures reflect the results of a "what if" scenario. The calculations involved are complex, but the major point is that convertible securities are assumed to be converted into shares of common stock. As you can see, Rockwell reports the average number of shares outstanding for both primary and fully diluted EPS, and in each year the number of shares is higher for fully diluted EPS. The same income figures are used for both EPS calculations, so with the additional shares assumed to be outstanding, fully diluted EPS figures would have to be smaller than those reported as primary EPS.

Although EPS figures are widely used by financial analysts, stockbrokers, and other economic decision makers, they have serious limitations. The biggest drawback of heavy reliance on per share figures is that it diverts attention from the company's overall performance. Since EPS can be increased simply by reducing the number of shares outstanding, any company can manipulate EPS figures by going into the secondary stock market and buying back shares of its own stock. Another limitation is that since EPS is based on the number of shares outstanding, we cannot reliably compare the performance of companies with differing amounts of outstanding stock.

DISCUSSION QUESTIONS

13-1. Does Rockwell present a multistep or a single-step income statement in its annual report?

13-2. Rockwell's 1993 sales figure of $10,840,000,000 indicates results of business activity for what calendar months?

Suppose that during 1994 Rockwell had repurchased 50 million shares of its own common stock so the average shares outstanding were 170.5 million for primary earnings per share and 174.5 million for fully diluted earnings per share. Primary earnings per share would then be $3.72 and fully diluted earnings per share would be $3.63.

13-3. Do the recalculated EPS figures mean Rockwell performed better in 1994? Explain your reasoning.

13-4. What information would the recalculated EPS figures convey to you if you were a Rockwell common stockholder?

We have said that it is important for management to present in the annual report all the information necessary for external decision makers to reasonably assess the financial well-being of the firm. It is impossible to provide all the crucial details within the confines of the financial statements themselves, so at the bottom of each of Rockwell's financial statements you will find the following phrase:

See Notes to Financial Statements

This phrase signifies that the financial statements are merely summaries of the results of operations and the company's financial position. The classified balance sheet and the detailed income statement contain a lot of information, but there are many things they do not disclose. **Notes to the financial statements** (sometimes called **footnotes**) are included in the annual report to provide additional detail and explanation of the amounts in the financial statements. In effect, the notes un-summarize the presentation in the statements themselves.

Users of financial statements should always read the accompanying notes. Often it is there, rather than on the face of the financial statements, that specific information required by the SEC or GAAP is disclosed. It is not uncommon for an annual report to contain 10 to 15 pages of notes along with the set of financial statements. Rockwell's notes to the financial statements are found on pages 32–40 of its annual report.

notes to the financial statements Provide additional detail and explanation of the amounts on the face of the financial statements; an important part of financial statement disclosure.

footnotes Another name for the notes to the financial statements.

DISCUSSION QUESTIONS

13-5. Current GAAP rules require Rockwell to show the cumulative effect of the change in accounting principle on the 1992 income statement net of tax. What is the reasoning behind this requirement?

13-6. The cumulative effect of a change in accounting principle shown on Rockwell's 1992 income statement ($1,519,000,000), is the "net of tax" amount. What was the total impact of this change before considering any tax effects?

The accounting profession considers the notes to the financial statements to be an integral part of the financial statements. Therefore, when an auditor expresses an opinion on the financial statements, that opinion applies to the accompanying notes as well. The audit report of the Rockwell financial statements is shown on page 27 of the annual report.

13-7. What type of audit opinion did Deloitte & Touche express on Rockwell International's financial statements?

B. Five-year selected financial data. Highlights of the specific financial data items required by the SEC are:

■ Net sales or operating revenues.
■ Income (loss) from continuing operations, in total and per common share.
■ Total assets.
■ Long-term obligations.
■ Cash dividends declared per common share.
■ Additional items believed to enhance understanding and highlight trends in financial condition and results of operations.

Rockwell presents these required disclosures on page 41 of the annual report. From this single page of information, economic decision makers can get an overall view of the company's progress in the preceding five years.

DISCUSSION QUESTIONS

13-8. How would you characterize Rockwell's performance and financial position over the last five years? Cite at least two examples of figures from page 41 of the company's annual report to support your conclusion.

13-9. Describe Rockwell's dividend policy. Is it reasonable given the net income figures presented? Explain.

management discussion and analysis (MD&A)
A required narrative in the annual report focusing on the company's financial condition, changes in financial condition, and results of operations.

C. Management's discussion and analysis of financial condition and results of operations. The **management discussion and analysis (MD&A)** section of annual reports is of increasing interest to consumers of financial reports. This section is a factual narrative of the company's financial condition, changes in financial condition, and results of operations. The SEC offers broad guidelines for the preparation of the MD&A. Generally, disclosure in this section should include discussions of:

■ The company's liquidity, capital resources, and results of operations.
■ Significant events or uncertainties and any favorable or unfavorable trends.
■ The effects of inflation and changing prices.
■ Causes of any material changes in the financial statements.

Management may also project future activities or results of operations for the firm, but this is optional.

Some companies structure the MD&A section of their annual reports under the three broad headings identified by the SEC: Liquidity, Capital Resources, and Results of Operations. Rockwell's MD&A presentation, however, does not follow that format. Instead, it discusses a variety of topics indicated by headings in blue print. The discussion begins on page 22 and spans five pages of the annual report.

DISCUSSION QUESTIONS

13-10. How much additional expense resulting from "environmental issues" can you expect to be reported by Rockwell in future periods?

13-11. How much did Rockwell lose as a result of earthquake damage in 1994? Based on the MD&A, how much would you expect the company to lose in future years as a result of earthquake damage?

D. Brief description of the business. The SEC requires that this section include information about:

■ The principal products and/or services the company produces.
■ Sources and availability of raw materials needed by the operation.
■ Status of any new products under development.

While the SEC requires only a *brief* description of the business covering the three points listed above, this is one area in which companies rarely skimp on coverage. In fact, this section of many annual reports looks like an advertising brochure. In a very real sense, it *is* advertising. Remember, not only present stockholders receive the annual report; potential investors, creditors, suppliers, and customers also rely on this source of information. Rockwell International meets the SEC's requirements with the extensive description of its business presented on pages 6–19 of its annual report.

13-12. Without reading a word, what can you learn about Rockwell by looking at the photos on pages 6–11 of its annual report?

E. Three-year financial information about: industry segments, foreign and domestic operations, and export sales. With the expansion and diversification of American corporations in recent years, economic decision makers require information about the various types of business activities in which companies are involved. An economic decision maker needs to consider not only the overall profitability and financial health of a corporation. It is also important to examine to what degree the firm is involved in various types of activity. The SEC requirement that three years' worth of financial information be presented on industry segments, foreign and domestic operations, and export sales helps companies meet these informational needs.

The financial information about industry segments (also called *line-of-business information*) lets users of the annual report know to what degree the corporation is involved in various industries. Readers can determine how much of a company's earnings resulted from activities in each industry. Information about how much of the company's resources are committed to activities in each industry is also provided.

Some corporations' operations are centered on two or three key types of business; other, more highly diversified corporations have operations in a dozen or more different industries. Users of the line-of-business information assess the appropriateness of the corporation's degree of diversification. Opinions about the potential of the company's operations in the various industrial sectors will vary. It is up to users of this detailed information to draw their own conclusions.

Rockwell provides sales and earnings information by business segment for the last five years on page 23 of its annual report. Descriptions of recent activities within each business segment are included on pages 12–19. Additional financial information about the four major lines of business (electronics, aerospace, automotive, graphic systems) is included in item 22 of the Notes to the Financial Statements on page 39.

13-13. According to the information on page 23 of Rockwell's annual report, the electronics division has been responsible for more sales than any other business segment each year since 1990. Which business segment provided Rockwell with the most sales in the mid-1980s? Explain where in the annual report you found this information.

13-14. Of the four distinct lines of business in which Rockwell International operates, which one do you think has the greatest potential for growth over the next five years? Why?

13-15. Which of the four industries in which Rockwell operates would you consider to be the riskiest? Why?

Most major American corporations today operate in other countries as well as in the United States. In other words, they have both foreign and domestic operations. It is important for economic decision makers to know what proportions of a company's business activities take place in various countries so that they can assess both the risk and the potential inherent in the operations in each location. Some foreign countries face political conflicts or economic crises. Others are expected to experience widespread economic growth in the near future. Clearly, then, information about the location of a corporation's activities is crucial for decision makers assessing the future profitability of a company.

Rockwell's information about its foreign and domestic operations is provided in item 22 of the Notes to the Financial Statements on pages 39–40. The corporation conducts activities in five geographic areas. Operations within the United States (domestic operations) account for the majority of sales and earnings. Most of Rockwell's assets are also committed to its U.S. operations.

Notice that the total sales figures shown on page 40 correspond to those indicated on Rockwell's income statement. For example, the $10,840 million shown as 1993 sales can be traced to the first line of the income statement on page 28. In addition to the sales figures for each geographic area, an amount identified as "eliminations" is also reported in item 22. This figure represents the amount of sales that were made by one Rockwell business segment to another. To prevent overstatement of revenues, companies are not allowed to include results of transactions within the corporate entity in the sales figures they show on their income statements. However, in the table on page 40 of Rockwell's annual report, the sales figures for each geographic area *do* include sales to other Rockwell operations. Eliminations reconcile these total sales figures with those reported on the income statement.

Information about the assets of each geographic segment of Rockwell's operations is also shown on page 40 of its annual report. Note that for each geographic area, there are two asset amounts. Those under the heading "Segments" are assets specifically involved with the primary business activities of the facilities in that area. Those identified as "Corporate" are assets that support the operations, most often in an administrative capacity. For example, the corporate assets in the U.S. area would include Rockwell's corporate headquarters. Assets designated as "Segments" and those shown as "Corporate" total each year to account for Rockwell's total asset figure shown on its balance sheet on page 29.

In addition to information about a company's foreign and domestic operations, the SEC requires disclosure of three-year financial information concerning the export sales of the corporation. These sales are the result of U. S. operations selling products in other countries. Rockwell provides this information in a single sentence below the first table on page 40 of its annual report.

DISCUSSION QUESTIONS

13-16. How would readers of the annual report use information about the level of export sales to evaluate a company as a potential investment?

F. Identification of directors and executive officers, with the principal occupation and employer of each. This is one of the SEC's most specific requirements. Companies have flexibility as to presentation, so long as they provide the required information. Rockwell's executive officers are identified on page 43. The members of Rockwell's Board of Directors are identified on page 42. Notice that Rockwell follows the common practice described in an earlier chapter— Donald Beall is the chairman of the board as well as the chief executive officer.

DISCUSSION QUESTIONS

13-17. Why do you think the SEC requires that information about corporate board members' current employers be provided in the annual report?

13-18. What potential problems has Rockwell created by having Donald Beall serve as both chairman of its board of directors and company CEO?

G. The principal market in which the securities of the firm are traded;
high and low market prices of the company's common stock for each quarter
of the two most recent fiscal years and dividends paid on common stock dur-
ing those years. This is another highly specific item of disclosure required
by the SEC. Rockwell International meets the first part of this requirement by
offering the information, on page 44 of its annual report, that the company's
common stock is traded in 6 different countries on a total of 13 stock
exchanges. Rockwell certainly *is* an international company.

The SEC requires the disclosure of specific market price and dividend information, but does not specify the amount of attention to be given to each item nor
the manner in which the information is to be conveyed. Both types of information are found on page 1 of Rockwell's annual report. The market price information is presented in a table, while the dividend information is shown graphically.

DISCUSSION QUESTIONS

13-19. Why do you think Rockwell chose to present market
price and dividend information on page 1 of its
annual report?

H. Offer to provide a free copy of the 10-K report to shareholders upon
written request, unless the annual report complies with Form 10-K disclo-
sure requirements. The requirements for disclosures made in Form 10-K are
somewhat more detailed than those for disclosures made in the annual report.
For this reason, most companies provide the 10-K to their shareholders and
others, but only if requested.

DISCUSSION QUESTIONS

13-20. In the Rockwell annual report, where did you find
the information needed to request a copy of the
company's Form 10-K?

Now that we have examined the portions of Rockwell's annual report required by the SEC, let's see what other information the company chose to provide.

ITEMS IN THE ANNUAL REPORT NOT REQUIRED BY THE SEC

Companies often include information in their annual reports that is not specifically required by the SEC. Typical items in this category are three that appear in Rockwell's annual report: the letter to the stockholders, the management report, and a section on the company's corporate citizenship.

Letter to the Stockholders

letter to the stockholders
An item often included in annual reports to allow management to express its assessment of the company's performance, position, and prospects for the future.

The purpose of the **letter to the stockholders** is to express, in narrative form, the corporate officers' assessment of the company's performance for the year, its financial position at year-end, and its prospects for the future. This letter should not be viewed as an objective assessment because it is generally the intent of the officers to portray the company's performance for the year in the best possible light. If the company has had a successful year, the letter to the stockholders is relatively easy to write. But, if it has had a poor year, the letter's emphasis will usually be on future prospects.

Take the time now to read the entire Letter to Shareowners included in Rockwell's annual report, noting the very optimistic tone.

The Management Report

management report
A statement addressing how responsibility for the annual report information was divided between the company's management and the company's auditors.

The **management report** addresses the division of responsibility for information in the annual report between the company's management and its independent auditor. It usually appears adjacent to the independent auditor's report because both reports clarify this division of responsibility.

Years ago, it became obvious that many readers of annual reports were confused as to who was responsible for what. There was nothing in either the annual report itself or the audit opinion that expressly stated whether it was management or the auditors who prepared the financial statements and other information included in the report. In response to the problems caused by this confusion, the accounting profession rephrased the standard audit opinion so that the first paragraph now reads:

> We have audited the accompanying balance sheet of [company name] as of [date] and the related statements of income, stockholders' equity and cash flows for the period ended [date]. *These financial statements are the responsibility of the Company's management. Our responsibility is to express an opinion on these financial statements based on our audits.*
>
> (Emphasis added.)

Thus, readers of the audit opinion are now aware that management is responsible for *preparing* the financial statements, and auditors are responsible for *examining* and *verifying* them as to their conformity to GAAP.

In addition, most annual reports now include a report from management detailing its responsibilities associated with preparing the financial statements and other information in the report. The wording of the management report is not as standard as that of the report of the independent auditor, but generally it includes the following items:

- A statement that management is responsible for the preparation, integrity, and objectivity of the financial statements and other financial information presented in the report.
- A statement that the financial statements were prepared in accordance with generally accepted accounting principles.
- An acknowledgment that certain estimates and judgments were required in the preparation of the financial statements.

Corporate Citizenship

Just what is corporate citizenship? Rockwell International uses that title for the section of its annual report that tells the shareholder what a nice, responsible company it is. No regulatory body requires, or even suggests, such a section, but most companies spend at least a page or two describing their contributions of time and money to worthwhile causes.

The demand for this information relates to our discussion of business and social responsibility back in Chapter 1. Many contemporary investors only want to supply funds to corporations that act responsibly. For instance, corporate executives have been pressured in recent years to commit corporate funds to environmentally responsible activities. Increasing interest in environmental issues by the investment community may soon lead to a situation in which management's failure to make a real commitment in this direction will affect the company's bottom line.

Most companies include a section in their annual report detailing their commitment to good corporate citizenship. Many large companies in the U.S., however, do not limit their publicity efforts in the area of social responsibility to what is contained in the annual report. The Lamp is a quarterly publication provided by Exxon to its stockholders and other interested parties. This publication, produced at significant cost, further outlines the company's efforts to be a good corporate citizen.

Teri Stratford/Courtesy of Exxon Corporation.

You may recall that several years ago pressure from environmentally aware consumers and investors resulted in the near-extinction of Styrofoam from the fast-food industry. This was one of the earliest clear-cut results of this type of pressure. Many corporations took up the environmental cause as a sign of their commitment to socially responsible behavior. McDonald's Corporation has been touting its environmentally sound activities ever since abandoning Styrofoam containers. Its Environmental Affairs Office provides information about the company's policies and activities, and brochures containing examples of McDonald's socially responsible corporate behavior (see Exhibit 13-1) are made available to consumers in most McDonald's restaurants.

Socially responsible corporate behavior is not limited to environmental issues. Annual reports provide information about a variety of corporate activities, ranging from donations to local Boys' and Girls' Clubs to employee blood donation drives. Corporations often highlight their policies on hiring ethnic minorities and women. Employee benefits (e.g., day-care and health club facilities) are also favorite points to mention. The "Corporate Citizenship" section of Rockwell's annual report points up the company's charitable contributions, environmental responsibility, and efforts to cultivate ethical behavior among its employees.

We stated at the outset of this chapter that the annual report is one of the most comprehensive forms of financial reporting available to external economic decision makers. It provides a tremendous amount of useful information to these external parties as they evaluate a company's financial performance and position. However, sometimes decision makers desire information beyond what is offered in the annual report. In that case, the next step may be to explore the disclosures filed with the SEC, the most common of which is Form 10-K.

Our rainforest policy. 5

Tropical rainforests play an important role in the Earth's ecology. And their destruction threatens the delicate environmental balance of our planet.

For the record: NOWHERE IN THE WORLD DOES McDONALD'S® PURCHASE BEEF RAISED ON RAINFOREST (OR RECENTLY DEFORESTED RAINFOREST) LAND.

In fact, McDonald's has a strict corporate policy against using rainforest beef.

" . . . it is McDonald's policy to use only locally produced and processed beef in every country where we have restaurants. In those isolated areas where domestic beef is not available, it is imported from approved McDonald's suppliers from other countries. In all cases, however, McDonald's does not, has not, and will not permit the destruction of tropical rainforests for our beef supply . . . This policy is strictly enforced and closely monitored. Any McDonald's supplier who is found to deviate from this policy or cannot prove compliance with it will be immediately discontinued."

In the U.S., we use only 100% pure U.S. domestic beef. In Canada, we use only 100% pure Canadian beef. And in Europe, we use only European Economic Community grown and approved beef.

McDonald's will continue to monitor its beef suppliers and adopt policies and practices aimed at protecting the global environment on which we all depend.

Printed on Recycled Paper

FOR MORE INFORMATION WRITE:
McDonald's Environmental Affairs,
McDonald's Corporation, Oak Brook, Illinois 60521.   ©1990 McDonald's Corporation

Exhibit 13-1
McDonald's Brochure

BUILDING THE FORM 10-K

Rockwell's Form 10-K is a 46-page document that has a much different "personality" than its annual report. Gone are the glossy pages and color photos. Exhibit 13-2, on page 432, shows the cover of Rockwell's Form 10-K—note the stark contrast to the cover of the company's annual report. But a reader browsing through the Form 10-K will quickly realize that some of the information is the same as that given in the annual report. This is not surprising. After all, the SEC regulates disclosures in both documents.

Rather than demanding duplication of information already in annual reports or other documents, the SEC's Integrated Disclosure System encourages "incorporation by reference" in Form 10-K. The SEC suggests that corporations submit a copy of their annual report or other useful documents with their Form 10-K. If the information required by Form 10-K is identical to that included in another submitted document, the corporation need only direct the reader to specific pages of that document. An example of how incorporating by reference reduces duplication of information is provided in the excerpt from a Form 10-K shown in Exhibit 13-3 on page 433.

Exhibit 13-2 Cover of Rockwell International's 1994 Form 10-K

SECURITIES AND EXCHANGE COMMISSION
Washington, D.C. 20549

FORM 10-K

ANNUAL REPORT PURSUANT TO SECTION 13 OR 15(d) OF
THE SECURITIES EXCHANGE ACT OF 1934

For the fiscal year ended September 30, 1994, Commission file number 1-1035

Rockwell International Corporation
(Exact name of registrant as specified in its charter)

Delaware
(State or other jurisdiction of
incorporation or organization)

95-1054708
(I.R.S. Employer
Identification No.)

**2201 Seal Beach Boulevard,
Seal Beach, California**
(Address of principal executive offices)

90740-8250
(Zip Code)

Registrant's telephone number, including area code: (412) 565-4090 (Office of the Secretary)

SECURITIES REGISTERED PURSUANT
TO SECTION 12(b) OF THE ACT:

Title of each class	Name of each exchange on which registered
$4.75 Convertible Preferred Stock, Series A	New York and Boston Stock Exchanges
$1.35 Convertible Preferred Stock, Series B	New York Stock Exchange
Common Stock, $1 Par Value	New York, Boston, Chicago, Pacific, Philadelphia, Basel, Frankfurt, Geneva, Lausanne, London, Tokyo, Toronto and Zurich Stock Exchanges
8⅞% Notes due September 15, 1999	New York Stock Exchange
8⅜% Notes due February 15, 2001	New York Stock Exchange
6¾% Notes due September 15, 2002	New York Stock Exchange

SECURITIES REGISTERED PURSUANT
TO SECTION 12(g) OF THE ACT:
Class A Common Stock, $1 par Value
(Title of Class)

Indicate by check mark whether the registrant (1) has filed all reports required to be filed by Section 13 or 15(d) of the Securities Exchange Act of 1934 during the preceding 12 months (or for such shorter period that the registrant was required to file such reports), and (2) has been subject to such filing requirements for the past 90 days. Yes ✓ No ____

Indicate by check mark if disclosure of delinquent filers pursuant to Item 405 of Regulations S-K is not contained herein, and will not be contained, to the best of registrant's knowledge, in definitive proxy or information statements incorporated by reference in Part III of this Form 10-K or any amendment to this form 10-K. [✓]

The aggregate market value of registrant's voting stock held by non-affiliates of registrant at November 30, 1994, was approximately $7.2 billion.

181,360,245 shares of registrant's Common Stock, par value $1 per share, and 36,477, 298 shares of registrant's Class A Common Stock, par value $1 per share, were outstanding on November 30, 1994.

DOCUMENTS INCORPORATED BY REFERENCE

Proxy Statement for the Annual Meeting of Shareowners of registrant to be held on February 1, 1995. Certain information therein is incorporated by reference into Part III hereof.

Exhibit 13-3
Examples of Incorporating by
Reference in a Form 10-K

ITEM 5. MARKET FOR THE COMPANY'S COMMON EQUITY AND
RELATED STOCKHOLDER MATTERS

The stock information appearing on page 2 of the Company's Annual Report to
Shareholders, included in this Form 10-K—Annual Report as Exhibit 13, is incorporated herein by reference.

ITEM 6. SELECTED FINANCIAL DATA

The selected financial data for the five years ended July 31, 1988, which
appears on page 6 of the Company's Annual Report to Shareholders, included
in this Form 10-K—Annual Report, as Exhibit 13, is incorporated herein by
reference.

ITEM 7. MANAGEMENT'S DISCUSSION AND ANALYSIS OF FINANCIAL
CONDITION AND RESULTS OF OPERATIONS

Management's discussion of financial condition and results of operations which
appears on pages 7 and 8 of the Company's Annual Report to Shareholders,
included in this Form 10-K—Annual Report, as Exhibit 13, is incorporated herein
by reference.

DISCUSSION QUESTIONS

**13-22. What document did Rockwell submit with its Form
10-K to reduce duplication of effort?**

The SEC's Integrated Disclosure System has had a significant effect on annual
reports. As Fred Skousen points out in *An Introduction to the SEC,*

> With the encouragement of the SEC requirements allowing for
> incorporation by reference, the Form 10-Ks of companies are
> becoming much smaller and the information in annual reports to
> shareholders is expanding.

(p. 99)

What exactly does the SEC want companies to disclose in Form 10-K that
isn't contained in their annual reports? The outline of the content of Form 10-
K shown in Exhibit 13-4 on page 434 provides some answers.

Part I

    Item 1.   Business
    Item 2.   Properties
    Item 3.   Legal Proceedings
    Item 4.   Submission of Matters to a Vote of Security Holders

Part II

    Item 5.   Market for the Company's Common Equity and Related Stockholder Matters
    Item 6.   Selected Financial Data
    Item 7.   Management's Discussion and Analysis of Financial Condition and Results of Operations
    Item 8.   Financial Statements and Supplementary Data
    Item 9.   Changes in and Disagreements with Accountants on Accounting and Financial Disclosure

Part III

    Item 10.   Directors and Executive Officers of the Company
    Item 11.   Executive Compensation
    Item 12.   Security Ownership of Certain Beneficial Owners and Management
    Item 13.   Certain Relationships and Related Transactions

Part IV

    Item 14.   Exhibits, Financial Statement Schedules and Reports on Form 8-K

Exhibit 13-4
Outline of Contents of Form 10-K

Note that many of the items required on the form overlap the information companies must provide in the annual report. The difference is that the level of detail required for the Form 10-K is often much greater. Some economic decision makers find the annual report sufficient for their needs; others require the greater specificity of Form 10-K.

It was not the SEC's intent in devising the Integrated Disclosure System to eliminate the need for either of these two forms of financial reporting. The Commission views the annual report and the Form 10-K as having different audiences and meeting different needs. Each serves an important function, as explained in the following statement from the Commission itself:

> Disclosure requirements in annual reports evolved in the context of shareholders making voting decisions. The Form 10-K has traditionally confirmed information previously delivered to investors and other users making economic decisions about the company and, as a result, has been more detailed. The Commission recognizes that the information content in Form 10-K not only was originally formulated for a specialized use, but that within those groups which have utilized the Form there are different constituencies. Those constituencies which have been the most frequent users of Form 10-K information are institutional investors, professional security analysts and sophisticated individual investors. The Commission believes that it continues to be appropriate to focus primarily on these frequent user constituencies in formulating Form 10-K requirements, but that such a focus would

not be appropriate in formulating requirements for the annual report to security holders.

(FRR .23, para. 102.01a)

Although some consumers of information need to see Form 10-K, you—at least for now—will probably find the information in corporate annual reports sufficient for your decision-making needs. So, how do you get a company's annual report information when you need it?

HOW TO GET AN ANNUAL REPORT

Annual reports are prepared to communicate important information from the corporation to its owners (shareholders). Thus, if you own shares of stock in a corporation, you will automatically receive a copy of its annual report.

How should you go about getting an annual report if you are *not* a shareholder? You might first try one of the fundamental sources of information: the library. In this section, we will introduce you to some basic information sources available in most libraries.

If you wish to get annual report *information* and don't care that it is not in the form of a glossy-paged booklet, you can use computerized information sources. Many libraries today provide computers with CD-ROM capabilities. Data on the CDs are accessed in much the same way as the files on a traditional computer disk, though a CD holds much more data. Among the most popular CD-ROM products offering company information are:

- *Infotrac*: Contains company profiles, investment reports and article citations.
- *Proquest*: This is the CD-ROM version of ABI/Inform, the premier source of business articles. Contains citations and the full text of articles, including photos and graphical images.
- *Moody's*: Provides full-text annual reports of U.S. and international operations.

In years past, the annual report was about the only source of information about companies and industries. Recent advances in technology, however, have greatly increased the amount and type of information available about both companies and the industries in which they operate. More and more libraries are equipped with computer systems that provide access to an almost limitless variety of data.

Richard Pasley/Stock Boston

On-line systems that access databases are another type of widely used information source. In these systems, the amount of data is not restricted to what can be contained on a CD, so the user can obtain much more extensive information. The computer terminal sorts through a vast amount of data and retrieves whatever the user requests. Among the most widely used databases containing company information are:

■ *DIALOG*: Provides access to over 400 databases, covering a wide range of topics, not all of which are business-related. Available information includes annual reports and articles (both full-text and citations).
■ *LEXIS/NEXIS*: Contains full text of all SEC-required filings (e.g., Form 10-K) as well as various business articles and newsletters.

Computerized sources of company information are likely to expand in availability and coverage. However, they may not meet your information needs. What if you want to receive a copy of a corporation's actual annual report? Just ask! We mean it! Corporations are well aware that investors provide them with much of the capital they need to operate, so most freely offer information to potential investors (see Exhibit 13-5).

Exhibit 13-5
Information-Capital Flow Between Companies and Investors

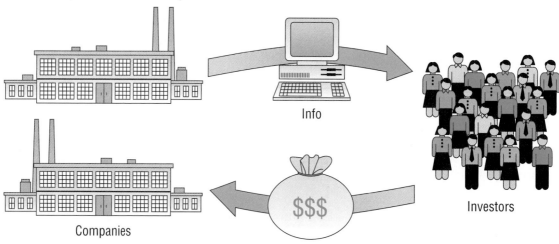

Info

$$$

Companies

Investors

You may think that if you don't qualify as a potential investor, companies won't want to be bothered with your request for an annual report. Think again! Corporations know that public image can be a crucial factor in a company's success or failure. Generally, requests for annual reports are gladly received, and corporations will promptly send along the information.

How do you contact a company to request its annual report? If all you know is the name of the company, you can find the address, phone number, and fax number in any one of several business directories that list companies alphabetically and provide basic information about each. One or more of the following business directories should be available at your library:

- *Ward's Business Directory of U.S. Private and Public Companies*
- *All-In-One Business Contactbook*
- *Million Dollar Directory*
- *Standard and Poor's Register of Corporations*

Exhibit 13-6 shows the entry for Rockwell International found in the *All-In-One Business Contactbook*. Notice that a separate phone number is listed for Investor Relations/Services. Even if a separate number is not provided, most companies have an office that serves as a public relations link to the investors and others interested in the company. Employees in these offices are generally very courteous and will gladly give you the information you need.

Exhibit 13-6
Rockwell International Entry in
All-In-One Business Contactbook

Main Phone: (617) 878-6100
Fax: x366
Description: Subsidiary. *SIC Code(s)*: 6022.

ROCKWELL GRAPHIC SYSTEMS
700 Oakmont Lane
Westmont, IL 60559
Main Phone: (708) 850-5600
Fax: (708) 850-6310
Telex: 190156
Annual Sales: $1,200 million.
Description: Division. *Activities:* Newspaper and commercial web printing presses. *SIC Code(s):* 3555.

ROCKWELL INTERNATIONAL CORP.
2230 E. Imperial Highway
El Segundo, CA 90245
Main Phone: (213) 647-5000
Personnel: (213) 647-5271
Investor Relations/Svcs: (213) 647-5386
Fax: (213) 647-5030
Alternate Fax: (213) 647-5220
Telex: 62831807
Annual Sales: $11,946 million.
Description: Public. *Industry Sector:* Manufacturing. *SIC Code(s):* 3761, 3679, 3714.

ROCKWELL INTERNATIONAL CORP. AUTOMOTIVE OPERATIONS
2135 W. Maple Road
Troy, MI 48084
Main Phone: (313) 435-1000
Fax: (313) 435-1968
Description: Division. *SIC Code(s):* 3714, 3089.

ROCKWELL INTERNATIONAL CORP. AVIONICS GROUP
400 Collins N.E.
Cedar Rapids, IA 52498
Main Phone: (319) 395-1000
Fax: (319) 435-3282
Description: Division. *SIC Code(s):* 3812

ROCKWELL INTERNATIONAL CORP. DULUTH
1800 Satellite Blvd.
Duluth, GA 31036
Main Phone: (404) 476-6300
Marketing Communications: (404) 497-5269
Annual Sales: $155 million.
Description: Division. *Activities:* Tactical missiles. *SIC Code(s):* 3825

ROCKWELL INTERNATIONAL CORP. GENERAL AVIATION DIV.
P.O. Box 1060

Rockwell's entry in *Ward's Business Directory of U.S. Private and Public Companies* shows only the main phone number of corporate headquarters, but does include other information items of interest. Take a close look at Exhibit 13-7 on page 438. The ticker symbol (ROK) is the abbreviation assigned to the company's stock. As indicated in the entry, Rockwell's stock is listed on the New York Stock Exchange (NYSE). With this information, you can easily find current stock price information in *The Wall Street Journal*, other business publications, or major newspapers.

SIC(s): 3714 Motor Vehicle Parts & Accessories.
Description: Manufacturing: Sunroofs.

H. Rockwell and Son
164 Troy St.   (717) 673-5148
Canton, PA 17724
Sales: $5.5 million
Employees: 20   **Type**: Private
Founded: 1852
SIC(s): 5999 Miscellaneous Retail Stores Nec; 5191 Farm Supplies.
Officer(s): J.H. Rockwell, *Partner*; J.H. Rockwell, *CFO*; Philip Rockwell, *Dir. of Mktg*; David Rockwell, *Dir of Systems*.

Rockwell International Corp.
2230 E. Imperial Hwy.   (310) 647-5000
El Segundo, CA 90245
Sales: $12,378.7 million   **FY End**: 9-30
Employees: 101,923   **Type**: Public
Ticker Symbol: ROK   **Exchange**: NYSE
Founded: 1928   **Import/Export**
SIC(s): 3761 Guided Missiles & Space Vehicles; 3679 Electronic Components Nec; 3714 Motor Vehicle Parts & Accessories.
Description: Manufacturing: Advanced technology for aerospace, electronic, automotive and graphic industries.
Officer(s): Donald R. Beall, *CEO & Chm Bd;* Robert A. dePalma, *VP of Fin;* Robert H. Murphy, *Senior VP of Human Resources.*

Rockwell International Corp.
Aerospace Operations
2230 E. Imperial Hwy.   (310) 647-5000
El Segundo, CA 90245
Employees: 37,500   **Type**: Division
Founded: 1961

Immediate Parent: Rockwell International Corp.
SIC(s): 3761 Guided Missiles & Space Vehicles; 3764 Space Propulsion Units & Parts; 3721 Aircraft; 3663 Radio & T.V. Communications Equipment
Description: Manufacturing: Space vehicles, rockets, missiles and propulsion units, advanced military aircraft and space satellites.
Officer(s): Sam F. Iacobellis, *President*; W.M. Barnes, *Senior VP & CFO.*

Rockwell International Corp.
Automotive Operations
2135 W. Maple Rd.   (313) 435-1000
Troy, MI 48084
Sales: $2,560.0 million   **FY End**: 9-30
Employees: 18,848   **Type**: Division
Founded: 1909
Immediate Parent: Rockwell International Corp.
SIC(s): 3714 Motor Vehicle Parts & Accessories.
Description: Manufacturing: Automobile parts.
Officer(s): Arthur P. Ronan, *President*; Bill Fabrizio, *VP of Fin*; H.L. Booth, *VP of Sales*; Sam Valanju, *Dir of Systems*; R.A. Jackson, *VP of Human Resources.*

Rockwell International Corp.
Autonetics Marine and Aircraft
P.O. Box 4921   (714) 762-2913
Anaheim, CA 92803
Sales: $40.0 million   **FY End**: 9-30
Employees: 310   **Type**: Division
Immediate Parent: Rockwell International Corp.
SIC(s): 3812 Search & Navigation Equipment

Exhibit 13-7

Rockwell International Entry in *Ward's Business Directory of U.S. Private and Public Companies*

13-23. Why doesn't the company listed after Rockwell International Corporation in Exhibit 13-7 have a ticker symbol? What about the company listed before Rockwell?

Business directories such as the ones described in this section offer you the information necessary to contact companies and request annual reports. But what if you want additional information about a company?

GATHERING ADDITIONAL INFORMATION ABOUT A COMPANY

What if you want more information about a company than can be found in its annual report? Suppose you want to learn when Rockwell was incorporated and in what state, how the business was started, how it grew into the company it is today, and what the company has been up to lately. These are just a few of the things you might want to know if:

1. You were considering Rockwell stocks or bonds as an investment.
2. Your company was deciding whether to buy products from one of the Rockwell companies.
3. Your company was deciding whether to sell products to one of the Rockwell companies.
4. You were considering whether to interview for a job with one of the Rockwell companies.

Does that last one surprise you? It shouldn't. Throughout this text, we have talked about "economic decision makers," and you may have gotten the impression that this term applies only to people who make high-powered financial decisions. But *you* are an economic decision maker. In a very short time, you will be going through the job interview process, and if deciding which companies to apply to for employment isn't a financial decision, we don't know what is! Think of the advantage you would have in a job interview if you possessed some background information on the company. Not only would you be able to ask more relevant questions, but the interviewer would almost certainly be impressed that you were ambitious enough to "do your homework."

Finding detailed information about companies is not difficult. Again, libraries generally have a wide variety of resources available. Many of these contain in-depth analyses of companies' financial results. Others provide detailed comparisons of a company's financial results with those of other companies. At this point, assume you want only basic information about the background of the company and its recent activities. There are a number of sources for that kind of information.

Hoover's Handbook of American Business offers two pages of information on each of the companies it profiles. Most of the information it provides about Rockwell (Exhibit 13-8 on pages 440-441) is not available in the company's annual report, and a good deal of it would be useful to you if you were interviewing for any sort of position with Rockwell. The background details provided in the sections titled "Overview" and "When" are particularly relevant to potential employees.

ROCKWELL INTERNATIONAL CORP.

OVERVIEW

The space shuttle or the B-1 bomber might look more exciting on the cover of the annual report, but Rockwell CEO Don Beall knows that printing presses and fax machines add a little wind beneath his company's wings too. Based in Seal Beach, California, Rockwell International is NASA's largest contractor and a major defense supplier, but it continues to work to increase its presence in commercial sectors.

Rockwell is the world's #1 maker of fax and data modems and is the world leader in web offset press equipment for commercial and newspaper printing. The company also makes industrial automation products, including programmable controllers and worker-machine interface devices, and is a leading supplier of components for light and heavy vehicles.

Rockwell's largest customer is still the US government (39% of sales). The company builds the space shuttle orbiter, provides support and modification for the B-1B, makes defense electronics systems, and is designing the power system for Space Station *Freedom*.

While Rockwell's sales have dipped slightly because of government cutbacks, its profits have risen thanks to strong performances from its industrial automation, telecommunications, and automotive businesses.

WHEN

Rockwell International is the legacy of 2 early 20th-century entrepreneurs: Willard Rockwell and Clement Melville Keys.

Willard Rockwell gained control of Wisconsin Parts Company, an Oshkosh maker of automotive axles, in 1919. He went on to acquire a number of industrial manufacturers, merging them in 1953 to create Rockwell Spring & Axle. Renamed Rockwell-Standard (1958), by 1967 this company led the world in the production of mechanical automotive parts.

In 1928 Keys founded North American Aviation (NAA) as a holding company for his aviation interests. General Motors bought North American in 1934 and installed James Kindelberger as its president. In 1935 the company moved from Dundalk, Maryland, to Inglewood, California, where it built military training planes. North American built over 15,000 AT-6 trainers during WWII and produced the B-25 bomber (1940) and the P-51 fighter (1940). By the end of WWII, the company had built nearly 43,000 aircraft, more than any other US manufacturer.

North American's sales plunged at the end of WWII. In 1948 GM took its subsidiary public; Kindelberger revitalized the company, opening new factories in Downey, California (1948), and Columbus, Ohio (1950). Major products included the F-86 (1948), a highly successful jet fighter of the Korean War, and its successor the F-100 (1953), America's first production supersonic aircraft. The company also produced the X-15 rocket plane (1959) and the XB-70 bomber (1964).

In the 1960s North American built rocket engines and spacecraft for the Apollo program. In 1967 the company merged with Rockwell Standard, creating North American Rockwell (changed to current name in 1973).

Rockwell won the prime contracts for the B-1 bomber (1970) and the space shuttle orbiter (1972). In 1973 Rockwell bought Collins Radio, which would form the backbone of its avionics segment. The company ventured into consumer goods briefly, buying Admiral in 1974 and selling it in 1979.

Rockwell invested its B-1 proceeds in industrial electronics, acquiring Allen-Bradley for $1.7 billion in 1985. Facing declining defense-related revenues as B-1 production ended, Don Beall, who had become CEO in 1988, spent billions on plant modernization and R&D for Rockwell's electronics and graphics segments. In 1989 Rockwell sold its Measurement & Flow Control Division and bought Baker Perkins, a UK-based printing machinery company. In 1991 it sold its fiber optic transmission equipment unit to Alcatel Alsthom.

In 1993 it bought a computer-chip–making plant from Western Digital for $115 million and also acquired industrial automation supplier Sprecher + Schuh for $105 million.

In 1994 Rockwell signed a deal to sell its automotive plastics unit to Plastics Acquisition, a subsidiary of Cambridge Industries. Also in 1994 Rockwell signed an agreement with software developer Zexel USA to provide the hardware for an in-vehicle navigation system for Oldsmobiles.

NYSE symbol: ROK
Fiscal year ends: September 30

WHO

Chairman and CEO: Donald R. Beall, age 55, $1,715,000 pay
EVP and COO: Kent M. Black, age 54, $926,491 pay
EVP and Deputy Chairman for Major Programs: Sam F. Iacobellis, age 64, $809,667 pay
EVP and COO, Automotive and Industrial Automation: Don H. Davis, Jr., age 53, $646,468 pay (prior to promotion)
SVP, General Counsel, and Secretary: Charles H. Harff, age 64, $660,000 pay
SVP Finance and Planning and CFO: W. Michael Barnes, age 51
SVP Organization and Human Resources: Robert H. Murphy, age 55
Auditors: Deloitte & Touche

WHERE

HQ: Rockwell International Corporation, 2201 Seal Beach Blvd., Seal Beach, CA 90740-8250
Phone: 310-797-3311
Fax: 310-797-5690 (Public Relations)

Rockwell operates manufacturing and R&D facilities around the world.

	1993 Sales		1993 Operating Income	
	$ mil.	% of total	$ mil.	% of total
North America	8,801	81	972	90
Europe	1,408	13	67	6
Asia/Pacific	435	4	24	2
South America	196	2	27	2
Total	**10,840**	**100**	**1,090**	**100**

WHAT

	1993 Sales		1993 Operating Income	
	$ mil.	% of total	$ mil.	% of total
Electronics	4,666	43	598	55
Aerospace	3,006	28	369	34
Automotive	2,536	23	126	11
Graphics	632	6	(3)	—
Total	**10,840**	**100**	**1,090**	**100**

Electronics
Avionics
Defense electronics
Industrial automation
Telecommunications
Aerospace
B-1B support
National Aero-Space Plane (NASP)
Propulsion system for Atlas and Delta rockets
Space shuttle orbiter and main engines

Automotive
Heavy vehicles systems/components (antilock braking sytems, clutches, axles, transmissions)
Light vehicles systems/components (door components, suspension systems, sunroofs, wheels)
Graphics
Web offset presses for newspaper and commercial presses

KEY COMPETITORS

Alcatel Alsthom
AlliedSignal
AM International
Apple
Baldwin Technology
Boeing
Borg-Warner Automotive
British Aerospace
Cummins Engine
Dana
Eaton
FlightSafety
General Dynamics
Harris
Hayes Microcomputer
Hitachi
Honeywell
IBM
Intel
Lockheed
Loral
Martin Marietta
Matsushita
McDonnell Douglas
Motorola
Northrup
Grumman
Orbital Sciences
Raytheon
Rolls-Royce
Siemens
Texas Instruments
Textron
Thiokol
Thomson SA
Unisys
United Technologies
U.S. Robotics
Westinghouse
Zoom Telephonics

HOW MUCH

	9-Year Growth	1984	1985	1986	1987	1988	1989	1990	1991	1992	1993
Sales ($ mil.)	1.7%	9,322	11,338	12,296	12,123	11,946	12,518	12,379	11,927	10,910	10,840
Net income ($ mil.)	1.4%	497	595	611	635	812	735	624	601	483	562
Income as % of sales	—	5.3%	5.3%	5.0%	5.2%	6.8%	5.9%	5.0%	5.0%	4.4%	5.2%
Earnings per share ($)	5.5%	1.55	1.91	1.98	2.23	3.01	2.84	2.53	2.54	2.14	2.51
Stock price—high ($)	—	16.38	20.34	23.81	30.13	23.50	27.13	28.75	29.25	29.38	38.50
Stock price—low ($)	—	11.19	14.56	15.28	14.25	16.13	19.75	20.50	22.75	22.25	27.88
Stock price—close ($)	10.8%	14.78	17.41	22.09	19.00	21.75	23.75	27.75	27.38	29.00	37.13
P/E—high	—	11	11	12	14	8	10	11	12	14	15
P/E—low	—	7	8	8	6	5	7	8	9	10	11
Dividends per share ($)	8.5%	0.46	0.52	0.58	0.65	0.71	0.75	0.80	0.86	0.92	0.96
Book value per share ($)	5.5%	8.25	9.99	10.70	11.85	13.20	15.91	17.51	18.50	12.55	13.35
Employees	(3.5%)	105,757	123,266	121,194	116,418	112,160	108,715	101,923	87,004	78,685	77,028

1993 Year-end:
Debt ratio: 25.8%
Return on equity: 19.6%
Cash (mil.): $773
Current ratio: 1.65
Long-term debt (mil.): $1,028
No. of shares (mil.): 224
Dividends:
1993 average yield: 2.6%
1993 payout: 37.6%
Market value (mil.): $8,169

Stock Price History
High/Low 1984-93

13-24. Pretend you are interviewing for a job with Rockwell. Specify what type of position you would be seeking. Then identify items of information in Exhibit 13-8 that would be particularly beneficial for you to know before you go into the interview.

Background information is certainly useful, but at times it is important to know what the company has been up to lately. An easy-to-use source of recent news about companies is *Standard and Poor's Corporation Records*. This publication, which comes in six loose-leaf sections and is updated quarterly, contains various types of information. Some quarterly updates include quarterly financial data about the company; other entries highlight the company's recent activities. Exhibit 13-9 shows a recent entry for Rockwell International.

Exhibit 13-9
Rockwell International Entry in *Standard and Poor's Corporation Records*

ROCKWELL INTL. CORP.

Elects Director—Sept. 7, 1994, Rockwell International Corp. (ROK) announced that Judith L. Estrin was elected to its board of directors, increasing the board to 14 members.

To Relocate Shuttle Orbitor Manufacturing Activities—Sept. 8, 1994, Rockwell International Corp. (ROK) announced that it will relocate its Space Systems Division's (SSD) shuttle manufacturing activities to its Orbiter Modification Center in Palmdale, Calif., from its plant in Downey, Calif.

ROK said the move will include the organizations responsible for producing Shuttle modification kits, mission kits and major orbiter components and will involve approximately 300 positions.

Engineering, subcontract management, business management and prototype/advanced manufacturing will remain in Downey.

Vice President Dies—Sept. 9, 1994, Rockwell International Corp. (ROK) Scott L. Holden, vice president and associate general counsel, died.

Sells Plant to Subsidiary of Quixote Corp.—September 14, 1994, Quixote Corp. (QUIX) announced that its Disc Manufacturing Inc. subsidiary acquired a 218,000-square-foot manufacturing facility in Anaheim, Calif., from Rockwell International Corp. (ROK).

QUIX said the acquisition is part of the subsidiary's $65,000,000 program to double manufacturing capacity to about 200,000,000 units by year-end 1997. QUIX said the subsidiary plans to spend about $16,000,000 in fiscal 1995 to upgrade the plant and add equipment.

QUIX said Disc Manufacturing expects to begin moving into the new facility by year-end 1994 and to fully occupy the plant by June 1995, after which its current Anaheim facility will be vacated.

Acquires ICOM Inc.—Oct. 21, 1994, Rockwell International Corp. (ROK) reported that it acquired ICOM Inc., a privately held supplier in the automation software industry.

ROK said it will merge ICOM with ROK's Allen-Bradley Co. Inc. subsidiary to form an automation software unit.

Reliance Electric Co. Considering Tender Offer by Subsidiary—Oct. 21, 1994, Reliance Electric Co. (REE) announced that its board is "carefully considering" an offer by a subsidiary of Rockwell International Corp. (ROK) to acquire all stock of REE, including the offer's implications for REE's planned acquisition by General Signal Corp. (GSX).

REE said it urged shareholders not to act on the ROK offer until they hear from REE. ROK announced on October 21 that its subsidiary began a tender offer for all REE stock at $30 per share for Cl. A common and an equivalent price for convertible shares.

Another commonly used information source is *Moody's Industrial Manual*. It offers extensive company histories and more detailed financial information than can be found in *Hoover's Handbook of American Business* and *Standard and Poor's Corporation Records*.

All of the information sources we have discussed are fairly easy to find and use. Which you choose to consult will depend on the purpose of your information search.

THE FUTURE OF THE ANNUAL REPORT

Now that we've examined the information in corporate annual reports and Form 10-Ks, shown you how to get an annual report, and explored ways to gather additional information about a company, you should have a good understanding of the kind of information companies currently provide through financial reporting. We have seen that the corporate annual report is the cornerstone of financial reporting. You know how it evolved and what it looks like today. But what about tomorrow? There are indications that the form and content of the annual report may undergo significant change as we enter the twenty-first century.

Longstanding concerns about the relevance and usefulness of business reporting spurred the American Institute of Certified Public Accountants to form the **Special Committee on Financial Reporting** in 1991. This 14-member group, comprising leaders in public accounting, industry, and academia, was charged with reviewing the current state of financial reporting and making recommendations for changes in the nature and extent of information that management provides to those making lending or investing decisions. In addition, the AICPA's Special Committee was asked to examine the auditor's level of involvement with the various types of information and to recommend changes in that area where necessary.

Recognizing that its recommendations would be useful only if they answered the real needs of users of financial reporting information, the Committee conducted an unprecedented in-depth study to discover those needs. Over 200 books and articles on information users' needs were identified, abstracts of each were entered into a database, and the search for answers began. Soon a disconcerting fact emerged: Those who wrote about users' information needs were just about everybody but actual users! Exhibit 13-10 on page 444 shows the groups responsible for authoring the numerous articles and books in the Committee's database. Note the preponderance of academics, auditors, and standard setters.

Special Committee on Financial Reporting Formed by the AICPA to investigate the information needs of users of financial reports. The Committee has proposed a new model of business reporting.

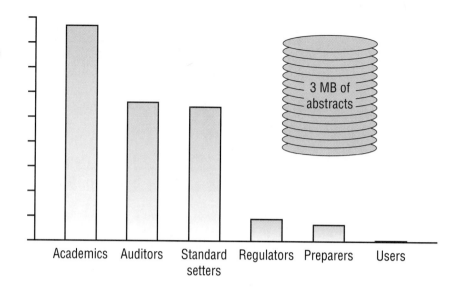

3 MB of
abstracts

Academics   Auditors   Standard   Regulators   Preparers   Users
setters

DISCUSSION QUESTIONS

13-25. Why do you think users of financial reports rarely write about their information needs?

Because the Committee was determined to get a true picture of information users' needs, it changed its approach and went directly to the users themselves. The Committee formed two focus groups, one consisting of investors and another of creditors, and met with them several times to discuss key issues. Thousands of analysts' reports were studied to determine the types of information these users considered important. The Committee also examined policy documents from user groups such as the Association for Investment Management and Research and Robert Morris Associates.

After the information gathered from the users was compiled, the Committee drew certain conclusions. To validate those conclusions, it commissioned Lou Harris Associates to conduct a large random telephone survey of users. The results of this survey of 600 equity investors and 600 creditors confirmed the Committee's conclusions and helped it fine-tune its recommendations.

One final factor the Committee considered before issuing its recommendations was the cost of providing the information items desired by users in relation to the benefits of doing so. The recommendations were then incorporated into a proposed model of business reporting that was published in late 1994. Suggested changes focus on four major areas: types of information, financial statements, auditing, and facilitating change.

Improving the Types of Information

The Special Committee concluded that the financial information companies now offer is useful but not sufficient. In addition to the financial statement disclosures currently provided, users want the operating data and performance measurements that management uses to manage the business (i.e., market share, percentage of defects, revenue per worker). They would also like to see management's analysis of the changes in these indicators.

The Committee recommended that forward-looking information become a key component of business reporting. The Committee's model includes: (a) opportunities and risks; (b) management's plans, including key success factors; and (c) comparison of actual business performance with previously disclosed forward-looking information. The SEC already requires disclosures about opportunities and risks in the management discussion and analysis section of the annual reports. The new model goes further in proposing that the discussion of these topics be made a separate element of the report, and it provides a framework for the disclosure.

Users want more background information about companies than they are now receiving. The SEC currently requires companies to furnish a description of the scope of their businesses and properties in the annual report. The new model retains this disclosure requirement and suggests adding background information on (1) broad objectives and strategies and (2) the impact of industry structure on the company.

In addition to suggesting improvements and additions in other types of information, the Committee also provided recommendations to enhance the primary form of financial information—the financial statements.

Enhancing Financial Statements

The Special Committee concluded that "Users generally are comfortable with the framework provided by financial statements, and standard setters should retain their basic form and content. However, several areas in financial statements should be enhanced to meet users' needs for information." Indeed, the

Committee's proposed model includes a number of changes in financial statement presentation.

The most pervasive change suggested by the Committee is in distinguishing between the effects of core and noncore activities. *Core activities* are described by the Committee as usual, typical, and recurring transactions or events. *Noncore activities* are unusual or nonrecurring transactions or events.

The separation of core and noncore activities appears to be the same as the separation of recurring and nonrecurring events presented earlier in this text—with some minor differences, it is. The real difference in the Committee's model is the extent to which the separation is carried throughout the financial statements. Companies would not only distinguish between *results* of core and noncore activities on the face of the income statement, but would also distinguish between *earnings per share information* related to core activities and EPS related to noncore activities. The separation would extend to the balance sheet and statement of cash flows as well: The balance sheet would show noncore assets and liabilities separate from core assets and liabilities; the statement of cash flows would show core and noncore cash flows separately.

The second important change in financial statement presentation recommended by the Committee is in the area of segment reporting. As we saw in going through Rockwell's annual report, there is already a requirement for disclosure about a company's business segments. The new model suggests that companies present a broader array of information at the segment level. The Committee explains the usefulness of these additional disclosures as follows:

> Multisegment companies operate diverse businesses that are subject to different opportunities and risks. Many users view business segments as the engines that generate future earnings or cash flows and, thereby, drive returns on investments. Segment information provides additional insight into the opportunities and risks of investments and sharpens predictions. For a company with more than one business segment, most types of information specified by the model apply to the business segment level. Because of its predictive value, improving segment reporting is of the highest priority.

As the quotation above indicates, the Committee definitely focused on the usefulness of the information provided. Other changes to the financial reporting process suggested by the Committee are also aimed at making the financial information more useful to the users of the information. Economic decision makers want assurance that the information they receive is reliable and fairly presents the company's position. For this reason, although auditing was not a major focus of its work, the Committee did investigate the auditor's role in the changing environment of financial reporting.

Improving Auditing

The Committee's report points out that if additional types of information are going to be provided in financial reports, it follows that those who provide assurance as to the fairness of information presentation—namely, the auditors—must be prepared to deal with the changes. This may require both new auditing standards and new training for auditors, for if financial reports change, it stands to reason that the activities necessary to provide assurance about the information they contain will also surely change.

Given the wide range of additional information suggested by the new model, the Committee recommended that the relationship between the auditor and the client become more flexible. That is, some companies may want only their financial statements audited, while others may decide to provide assurance on other elements of the report. Regulators, users, and the companies themselves must consider the costs of assurance when deciding what information items should be audited.

Improved auditor involvement would surely enhance the usefulness of the information provided. Indeed, work in this area is underway. The newly formed AICPA Special Committee on Assurance Services has begun to investigate the changing role of the auditor in the changing environment of business reporting. Auditing is not the only profession that will be affected if the changes recommended by the Special Committee on Financial Reporting are adopted. The Committee identified several other groups that also must be ready to face the challenges of change.

Facilitating Change

Even if the Committee's model is not adopted, one thing is certain—changes will occur! Environmental, technological, and societal changes will inevitably force changes in business, and hence in business reporting.

One of the groups sure to be affected by these changes is standard setters. Since the needs of users of financial reporting information will certainly change over time, standard setters should be prepared to adopt a longer-term view of issues. To ensure that standard setters are attentive to the needs of information users, the Committee recommends adding users to standard-setting boards, advisory councils, and task forces. Additionally, it suggests that standard setters sponsor research about users' decision-making processes.

In today's litigious environment, forward-looking information that fails to perfectly predict future outcomes may result in lawsuits by disgruntled investors. To encourage companies that want to provide this kind of useful information but fear unreasonable lawsuits if they do so, the Committee suggests that lawmakers, regulators, and standard setters take action to protect information providers from groundless legal claims. Certainly, legitimate claims should still be pursued, but companies must be protected from unwarranted claims arising from the types of information users are requesting.

Diverse business reporting practices among nations have impaired economic decision makers' ability to compare companies. The weak international standards presently in place have been ineffective in meeting users' needs. The Committee urges U.S. standard setters and regulators to set the pace in developing international reporting standards that are both uniform and useful. Here again, the new model may be helpful:

> Focusing on the information needs of users, rather than choosing from among existing standards and practices of countries participating in the standard-setting process, offers a promising new approach. Users' needs for the types of information in the Committee's model of business reporting may not differ fundamentally depending on the country in which the user is located. If similar, those information needs offer a common framework that standard setters and regulators from all countries can look to in setting international standards.

The Special Committee on Financial Reporting has no authority to establish standards of financial reporting or to change any of the disclosure requirements related to annual reports. Its recommendations, however, have provided a valuable service by bringing to light the issue of information users' needs.

As this book is written, the Committee's new model has only been out a few months, but already it has sparked an interesting debate. You have a vested interest in the type and quality of financial reporting because in a very short time you will be using the information contained in these reports to make economic decisions. We invite you, therefore, to take an active interest in the fate of the new model in particular and in the future development of financial reporting in general.

SUMMARY

The financial statements we explored in earlier chapters (income statement, balance sheet, statement of owners' equity, and statement of cash flows) are important sources of information, but they do not provide all the information needed by economic decision makers. Financial statements are only a part of financial reporting, which includes not only quantitative information but descriptive information, as well.

Two major consumers of corporate financial reports are stockholders and government regulators, most notably the Securities and Exchange Commission (SEC). The most comprehensive presentation of financial reporting to stockholders is the annual report. The SEC has specific disclosure requirements for information provided in the annual report. Using Rockwell's annual report as an example, each of these items was examined.

In addition to the items required by the SEC, many companies include in their annual reports such items as a letter to the stockholders from the company officers, a management report detailing the division of responsibility between management and the independent auditor, and a description of the company's corporate citizenship and charitable activities.

Publicly traded companies are required to file a Form 10-K annually with the SEC. Specific disclosure requirements are detailed in Regulation S-X, which prescribes the rules for the form and content of the financial statements included in the 10-K, and Regulation S-K, which specifies the content of the nonfinancial statement portions of the 10-K. The SEC's Integrated Disclosure System encourages companies to eliminate duplication between the annual report and Form 10-K through "incorporation by reference."

Gathering information about publicly traded companies is not difficult. Libraries have a variety of sources for financial, descriptive, and background information on these companies. Additionally, the company's annual report may have the information you need. Most companies will gladly send you a copy of their annual report on request.

Business reporting is likely to undergo significant changes in the near future since information users are demanding more types of information and requesting better presentation of the information now being provided. The AICPA's Special Committee on Financial Reporting recently proposed a model that recommends significant changes in the content and presentation of financial reporting information.

Key Terms

annual report The most comprehensive presentation of financial reporting a company provides to its stockholders. Contains financial statements and other information designed to assist economic decision makers. (p. 415)

consolidated financial statements Financial statements that include the results of operations and the financial position of the parent company and its subsidiary companies as if they were one enterprise with several branches or divisions. (p. 419)

convertible securities Debt or equity securities that can be converted into shares of the company's common stock. (p. 419)

earnings per share (EPS) A calculation indicating how much of a company's total earnings is attributable to each share of common stock. (p. 419)

financial reporting Financial disclosures provided to economic decision makers that include both quantitative (numerical) information and qualitative (descriptive) information. (p. 415)

footnotes Another name for the notes to the financial statements. (p. 421)

Form 10-K A report filed annually with the Securities and Exchange Commission by publicly traded companies. Includes detailed financial information and descriptive information that is generally beyond what is found in the annual report. (p. 415)

fully diluted earnings per share
A more stringent EPS calculation than primary earnings per share. This calculation includes the potential impact of convertible securities in the denominator of the EPS calculation. (p. 420)

Integrated Disclosure System A system of reporting developed by the Securities and Exchange Commission that has eliminated much of the duplication between the information disclosed in Form 10-K and that disclosed in the annual report. (p. 418)

letter to the stockholders An item often included in annual reports to allow management to express its assessment of the company's performance, position, and prospects for the future. (p. 428)

management discussion and analysis (MD&A) A required narrative in the annual report focusing on the company's financial condition, changes in financial condition, and results of operations. (p. 422)

management report A statement addressing how responsibility for the annual report information was divided between the company's management and the company's auditors. (p. 428)

notes to the financial statements Provide additional detail and expla-nation of the amounts on the face of the financial statements; an important part of financial statement disclosure. (p. 421)

parent company A company that owns a majority of another company's voting stock. (p. 419)

primary earnings per share The most basic presentation of EPS. Divides earnings figures for the period by the average number of shares of common stock outstanding. (p. 419)

Regulation S-K Specifies the content of the nonfinancial statement portions of the Form 10-K that must be filed with the Securities and Exchange Commission by publicly traded companies. (p. 417)

Regulation S-X Prescribes the rules for the form and content of financial statements in the Form 10-K that must be filed with the Securities and Exchange Commission by publicly traded companies. (p. 417)

Special Committee on Financial Reporting Formed by the AICPA to investigate the information needs of users of financial reports. The Committee has proposed a new model of business reporting. (p. 443)

subsidiary A company that has a majority of its voting stock owned by another company. (p. 419)

REVIEW THE FACTS

A. Distinguish between financial reporting and financial statements.

B. Identify the two major documents created as a result of the financial reporting process.

C. What is the primary purpose of the SEC's Integrated Disclosure System?

D. Explain the earnings per share calculation, and distinguish between primary and fully diluted earnings per share.

E. What is the purpose of the notes to the financial statements?

F. Identify the items that should be discussed in the MD&A section of the annual report.

G. Why is the brief description of the business often more detailed than required?

H. Identify three items not required by the SEC, but commonly found in corporate annual reports; describe what can be learned from each.

I. Explain the concept of "incorporating by reference."

J. According to the SEC, who are the primary users of the Form 10-K?

K. Why are corporations generally cooperative when individuals request their annual reports?

L. How can learning about a company before interviewing for a job there be helpful?

M. Describe the major changes suggested by the Special Committee on Financial Reporting.

APPLY WHAT YOU HAVE LEARNED

13-27. Listed below are the items required by the SEC to be included in the annual report, along with some items not required but normally included:

1. ___ Audited financial statements.

2. ___ The principal market in which the securities of the firm are traded.

3. ___ Industry segment disclosures for the last three fiscal years.

4. ___ The management report.

5. ___ Offer to provide a free copy of Form 10-K to shareholders upon written request, unless the annual report complies with Form 10-K disclosure requirements.

6. ___ Report on corporate citizenship.

7. ___ Management's discussion and analysis of financial condition and results of operations.

8. ___ Five-year selected financial data.

9. ___ Brief description of the business.

10. ___ Letter to the stockholders.

11. ___ Identification of directors and executive officers, with the principal occupation and employer of each.

12. ___ High and low market prices of the company's common stock for each quarter of the two most recent fiscal years and dividends paid on common stock during those years.

REQUIRED

Identify each of the items as either required (R) or optional (O).

13-28. Presented below are some of the items discussed in this chapter, followed by the definitions of those items in scrambled order.

a. Financial reporting   **e.** SEC Integrated Disclosure System

b. Financial statements   **f.** Annual report

c. Regulation S-X   **g.** SEC Form 10-K

d. Regulation S-K   **h.** Notes to financial statements

1. ____ One of its objectives is to simplify and improve the quality of disclosures provided to investors and other users of financial information.

2. ____ Includes not only quantitative information but also descriptive information.

3. ____ Intended to provide important information that should be considered by financial statement users.

4. ____ Specifies the content of the nonfinancial statement portions of the SEC's Form 10-K.

5. ____ Its content was originally formulated for specialized use by institutional investors, professional security analysts, and sophisticated individual investors.

6. ____ As presented in the annual report, there are balance sheets for two years and statements of income, cash flows, and stockholders' equity for three years.

7. ____ Originally intended to be used only by stockholders.

8. ____ Prescribes the rules of the form and content of financial statements filed with the SEC.

REQUIRED

Match the letter next to each item on the list with the appropriate definition. Each letter will be used only once.

13-29. This problem deals with information contained in Rockwell's 1994 annual report, which was included with your purchase of this text.

a. Identify the specific numbers on Rockwell's income statements and statements of shareowners' equity that show the articulation of these two statements.

b. Identify the specific numbers on Rockwell's balance sheets and statements of shareowners' equity that show the articulation of these two statements.

c. Rockwell's statement of cash flows shows "cash at beginning of year" and "cash at end of year" for 1992, 1993, and 1994. Of these six numbers, how many can be tied directly to figures presented on the balance sheets? Why is this the case?

13-30. This problem deals with information contained in Sara Lee Corporation's 1994 annual report, which is reproduced in the appendix at the end of this book.

a. Identify the specific numbers on Sara Lee's income statements and statements of common stockholders' equity that show the articulation of these two statements.

b. Identify the specific numbers on Sara Lee's balance sheets and statements of common stockholders' equity that show the articulation of these two statements.

13-31. This problem deals with information contained in Sara Lee Corporation's 1994 annual report, which is reproduced in the appendix at the end of this book.

a. Sara Lee's statement of cash flows shows "cash and cash equivalents at beginning of year" and "cash and cash equivalents at end of year" for 1992, 1993, and 1994. Of these six numbers, how many can be tied directly to figures presented on the balance sheets? Why is this the case?

b. Sara Lee's statement of cash flows reveals that cash and cash equivalents decreased by $136,000,000 from July 3, 1993, to July 2, 1994. Explain in your own words:

   (1) What caused cash and cash equivalents to decrease during the 1994 fiscal year? Include in your answer an analysis of the three broad activities (operating, investing, and financing).

   (2) How you might react to the decrease if you

      (a) owned Sara Lee common stock.

      (b) were considering the purchase of Sara Lee common stock.

      (c) were one of Sara Lee's long-term creditors.

      (d) were one of Sara Lee's short-term creditors.

13-32. This problem deals with information contained in Rockwell's 1994 annual report, which was included with your purchase of this text.

a. The ending balance of owners' equity for one period should be the beginning balance for the next period. Is the ending balance of Rockwell's 1992 total shareowners' equity ($2,778,000,000) the beginning balance for 1993? Show figures to support your conclusion.

b. The three net income (loss) figures shown on Rockwell's income statements are:

1992	1993	1994
$(1,036.0)	$561.9	$634.1

The figures for net income in the five-year review match the 1993 and 1994 income statement figures, but not that of 1992. Explain why this is so.

c. The level of Rockwell's export sales has risen over the last three years. Has the proportion of its total U.S. sales that result from exports also risen? What about the proportion of the corporation's total sales that result from export sales? Provide calculations to support your conclusions.

13-33. As Rockwell's new CEO, you have decided to make a bold move. Instead of continuing operations in all four segments (electronics, aerospace, automotive, graphic systems), you have decided to concentrate the corporation's efforts on three of these lines of business. Use information from Rockwell's 1994 annual report to do the following:

a. Identify which line of business you would discontinue. Cite specific reasons for your choice.

b. Determine to which of the remaining segments you would allocate the resources that had been planned for use in the eliminated line of business. You may choose to give the newly available resources to one, two, or all three of the remaining operations. Provide specific reasons for your decisions.

13-34. Rockwell International has operations in several foreign countries. The company's annual report shows financial information for four geographic areas outside the United States: Canada, Europe, Asia-Pacific, and Latin America.

a. Of the four geographic areas listed above, which do you think offers the greatest potential for expanding Rockwell's operations? Explain your reasoning.

b. Which of the foreign geographic areas in which Rockwell operates do you consider to be the riskiest? Why?

c. Regardless of your answers to parts a and b of this problem, decide which of the four areas of foreign operations Rockwell should discontinue. Provide information from Rockwell's annual report to support your conclusion.

13-35. This problem deals with the *Consolidated Balance Sheets* found in Sara Lee Corporation's 1994 annual report, reproduced in the appendix of this book.

a. To what does the term "Capital surplus" refer?

b. As of July 3, 1993, what were the corporation's total liabilities?

c. As of July 3, 1993, what was the corporation's total stockholders' equity?

d. Using figures as of July 3, 1993, show that Sara Lee's balance sheet depicts the accounting equation.

13-36. This problem deals with information contained in Sara Lee Corporation's 1994 annual report, which is reproduced in the appendix of this book.

a. What type of audit opinion did the Sara Lee financial statements receive?

b. Does Sara Lee present a multistep or a single-step income statement in its annual report? How can you tell?

13-37. This problem deals with information contained in Sara Lee Corporation's 1994 annual report, which is reproduced in the appendix of this book.

a. How would you characterize the level of sales achieved by Sara Lee over the last eleven years?

b. Look at the three net income figures shown on Sara Lee's income statements in relation to the total revenue shown:

1992	1993	1994
$761 and $13,243	$704 and $14,580	$199 and $15,536

What explanation can you find in the annual report for the relatively low net income figure for 1994?

13-38. This problem deals with information contained in Sara Lee Corporation's 1994 annual report, which is reproduced in the appendix of this book.

a. Describe the dividend policy of Sara Lee as it relates to both preferred stock and common stock.

b. Sara Lee paid dividends in 1994 of $332 million. Net income for 1994 was $199 million. Explain how this was possible.

13-39. This problem deals with information contained in Sara Lee Corporation's 1994 annual report, which is reproduced in the appendix of this book.

a. What characteristics of Sara Lee does the "Special Report" included in the annual report (pages 6 and 7) convey?

b. If you had not yet examined the financial statements of Sara Lee presented in the annual report, what impression of the company's performance during 1994 would you get by reading the letter to the stockholders? Cite at least two specific phrases from the letter to support your conclusion.

13-40. This problem deals with information contained in Sara Lee Corporation's 1994 annual report, which is reproduced in the appendix of this book, and Rockwell International's 1994 annual report, which was included with the purchase of this text.

    The Securities and Exchange Commission requires that the following items be included in the annual report:

1. Audited financial statements: balance sheets for two years and income and cash flow statements for three years.

        Rockwell _____   Sara Lee _____

2. Five-year selected financial data.

        Rockwell _____   Sara Lee _____

3. Management's discussion and analysis of financial condition and results of operations.

        Rockwell _____   Sara Lee _____

4. Brief description of the business.

        Rockwell _____   Sara Lee _____

5. Industry segment disclosures for the last three fiscal years.

        Rockwell _____   Sara Lee _____

6. Identification of directors and executive officers, with the principal occupation and employer of each.

        Rockwell _____   Sara Lee _____

7. The principal market in which the securities of the firm are traded.

        Rockwell _____   Sara Lee _____

8. Range of market prices of the company's common stock for each quarter of the two most recent fiscal years and dividends paid on common stock during those years.

        Rockwell _____   Sara Lee _____

9. Offer to provide a free copy of the 10-K report to shareholders upon written request, unless the annual report complies with Form 10-K disclosure requirements.

        Rockwell _____   Sara Lee _____

a. Locate these required items in both the Rockwell and Sara Lee annual reports. After noting the location of each of the items in each report, number them 1 through 9 to indicate the order of presentation in each report.

b. If you found a difference in the order of presentation, comment briefly on why you think the two companies chose to present the required items as they did.

c. Do you think readers of annual reports would be better served if the SEC required a specific order of presentation for the items? Explain your reasoning.

13-41. This problem deals with information contained in Sara Lee Corporation's 1994 annual report, which is reproduced in the appendix of this book, and Rockwell International's 1994 annual report, which was included with the purchase of this text.

The chapter discussed the following items usually found in the annual report even though they are not required by the Securities and Exchange Commission:

1. Letter to the stockholders

2. The management report

3. Corporate citizenship

REQUIRED:

a. Look through the two annual reports and see if you can locate these three items. If an item is found in only one of the reports, comment briefly on its contents. If an item is included in both reports, compare the presentations.

b. Are any other nonrequired items included in either of the two annual reports? If so, comment briefly on why you think these items are included.

14

Financial Statement Analysis

Financial statement information is a basic ingredient in economic decision making. Financial statement analysis is the process of looking beyond the face of the financial statements to gather additional information and insight. Ratio analysis is a technique which focuses on the relationships between and among financial statement items. When used properly, ratio analysis offers valuable additional information to economic decision makers.

F inancial reporting is an essential source of information for economic decision makers, and financial statements are a central component of financial reporting. In Chapter 13, we explored the information provided in the annual report and the SEC's Form 10-K. Gathering and reading this kind of information, however, is but the first step in making the information helpful in the decision-making process. Financial statement information only becomes truly useful when it is analyzed.

financial statement analysis The process of looking beyond the face of the financial statements to gather more information.

Financial statement analysis is the process of looking beyond the face of the financial statements to gather even more information. This analysis, which is used to gain additional insight into companies, can take many different forms. In fact, you already performed one type of financial statement analysis when you looked at Rockwell's five-year financial data to see if items increased or decreased over time and drew conclusions based on that finding as part of your work on Chapter 13. Your study of the statement of cash flows in Chapter 11 was also a type of financial statement analysis, for the statement of cash flows is a full-blown financial statement devoted to analyzing what caused the change in cash from one period to the next.

ratio analysis A technique for analyzing the relationship between two items from a company's financial statements for a given period.

In this chapter, we will explore another form of financial statement analysis—ratio analysis—and show you how to use its results in proper combination with other information to make economic decisions. **Ratio analysis** is a technique for analyzing the relationship between two items from a company's financial statements for a given period. These items may be on the same financial statement, or they may come from different financial statements. The ratios discussed in this chapter are based on items from the balance sheet and the income statement.

After completing your work on this chapter, you should be able to do the following:

1. Identify the three major categories of users of financial statement analysis and describe the objectives of each.
2. Gather information to evaluate general economic conditions and outlooks.
3. Describe the ways in which political climate and political events can affect business.
4. Locate sources of information about specific industries.
5. Describe the purpose of ratio analysis and explain the three primary characteristics it helps users evaluate.
6. Calculate financial ratios designed to measure a company's profitability, liquidity, and solvency.
7. Explain the purpose of the Standard Industrial Classification system and specify what an SIC code indicates.
8. Evaluate a company's ratios using a comparison to industry averages.
9. Use ratio values from consecutive time periods to evaluate the profitability, liquidity, and solvency of a business.
10. State in your own words the limitations of ratio analysis.

WHO PERFORMS FINANCIAL STATEMENT ANALYSIS AND WHY?

Several different types of economic decision makers perform financial statement analysis, and because their objectives vary, their perspectives on the results of that analysis will differ. Our focus in this chapter will be on three types of economic decision makers:

1. Creditors (short-term and long-term)
2. Equity investors (present and potential)
3. Company management

Certainly other parties—such as independent auditors, government agencies, and prospective employees—are interested in analyzing a company's financial statements, but we will concentrate on these three important categories of users. First, we will examine their objectives, and later in this chapter, we will see how ratio analysis meets their informational needs.

Objectives of Creditors

short-term creditors Creditors who lend money, expecting repayment within one year. Together with long-term creditors, one of the three major categories of financial statement users.

trade creditors Short-term creditors who sell goods and services to companies in the normal course of business.

Creditors lend money to a company on either a short-term or a long-term basis. There are two major types of **short-term creditors**. One group, called **trade creditors**, provides goods and services to a business and expects payment within whatever time period is customary in the industry (usually between 30 and 60 days). Trade creditors do not normally receive interest. Since the credit they extend to a company is essentially an interest-free loan, their primary objective in analyzing a company's financial statements is to determine whether that company pays its bills on time and will be able to pay promptly in the future.

The other type of short-term creditor is the *lending institution* offering commercial loans to support the day-to-day operations of a business. In this situation, described in Chapter 5, a company borrows money from a bank and signs a short-term note. Unlike trade creditors, banks charge interest. The objectives of these two groups of short-term creditors, however, are very similar. Both want to be assured of receiving prompt payments from the company.

long-term creditors Banks, corporate bondholders, and any others who lend money for extended periods of time, often up to 40 years. Together with short-term creditors, one of the three major categories of financial statement users.

Long-term creditors are also interested in receiving prompt payments, but their perspective is somewhat different. These creditors—generally banks and corporate bondholders—lend money to companies for relatively long periods of time. Therefore, in analyzing a company's financial statements, their principal objectives are to determine whether the company will be able to make its periodic interest payments and to repay the loan when required.

When we explore the information resulting from ratio analysis later in the chapter, we will see how it is used by both short-term and long-term creditors. However, creditors are only one of the users of this information.

Objectives of Equity Investors

equity investors Those who purchase an ownership interest in a company. One of the three major categories of financial statement users.

Equity investors, the second category of users of financial statement analysis, are those who purchase an ownership interest in a company. In the corporate form of business, these are the people or institutions that purchase shares of common stock. Those who buy (or are considering buying) shares of a company's common stock desire a return on their investment. You will recall from our discussion in Chapter 5 that return on investment for an equity investor has two components:

1. *Dividends*: the distribution of earnings from a corporation to its owners (stockholders).

2. *Stock appreciation*: the increase in the selling price of a share of stock in the secondary stock market between the time it is purchased and the time it is sold.

When analyzing a company's financial statements, then, equity investors (present and potential) want to determine if the company will be able to distribute dividends in the future and if its stock will rise in value. Both of these future activities depend on the company's ability to generate income in the future. Cash dividends can only be paid if a company has sufficient cash as well as sufficient retained earnings, both of which depend on future generation of earnings. Further, generation of earnings is widely considered to be the single most important factor impacting a company's stock appreciation over time.

Both creditors and equity investors are *external decision makers* who use ratio analysis. However, ratio analysis is also a useful tool for *internal decision makers*, namely, a company's management.

Objectives of Management

management The people responsible for a company's day-to-day operation. One of the three major categories of financial statement users.

Management is responsible for a company's day-to-day operation. Because managers are internal decision makers, their objectives in performing financial statement analysis are somewhat different from those of external parties such as creditors and equity investors.

In the context of this chapter, management has two major objectives in analyzing its company's financial statements. The first is to put those statements in the best possible light before presenting them to important external parties. This is a natural and legitimate objective, since a company's relationship with creditors and stockholders is vital. However, management's natural desire to analyze the company's financial statements with a view toward favorably impressing external parties can lead to managing the financial statements rather than managing the business.

DISCUSSION QUESTIONS

14-1. What do you think the phrase "managing the financial statements rather than managing the business" means?

Management's second objective in analyzing the company's financial statements is to monitor the overall performance of the business. The company's financial statements, of course, provide managers with important information for making business decisions, but because managers are internal parties, they also have access to additional, internally-generated information. At times, in fact, management accounting information is the primary focus of managers when they are evaluating the performance of their company. Later you may explore the use of this internally-generated information, but for now our discussion in this chapter is limited to publicly available financial accounting information.

Now that you understand the basic objectives of the three primary users of financial statement analysis, we can explore important factors that affect company performance and should be considered by anyone undertaking financial statement analysis.

Gathering Background Information— An Important First Step

In Chapter 13, we discussed how to find background information on companies. Anyone who wants to do a thorough analysis of a company's financial statements should consult the sources suggested in Chapter 13 and gather enough background information on the company to put its financial statement information in proper context.

Since businesses do not operate in a vacuum, it is also important to gather background information about a company's environment. The Financial Accounting Standards Board warns that external factors can greatly impact a company's performance:

> Those who use financial information for business and economic decisions need to combine information provided by financial reporting with pertinent information from other sources, for example, information about general economic conditions or expectations, political events and political climate, or industry outlook.
>
> (FASB, Statement of Concepts #1, para. 22)

Because ratio analysis is based on financial statement information, conclusions drawn from its results should also consider the three factors mentioned in the FASB statement: general economic conditions, political events and political climate, and industry outlook.

General Economic Conditions and Expectations

The general economic environment in which a company operates affects its business activity and therefore its financial results. For a company producing goods bought by the general public, bright economic conditions generally enhance sales. For a company manufacturing and selling equipment to other companies, an economy that encourages business growth is an important factor. So general economic conditions and expectations is the first factor to consider when evaluating the performance and overall financial position of a business.

The health of the American economy is a topic that receives widespread news coverage. Popular business periodicals such as *Business Week* and *Fortune* inform their readers about current economic conditions. Statistical data on measures of economic health (e.g., gross national product, producer price index) are available in such books as *The Economic Indicators Handbook*. The U.S. Department of Commerce, in a monthly publication called the *Survey of Current Business*, provides data from dozens of general economic indicators as well as business cycle indicators.

Economic decision makers not only evaluate past performance of businesses: they also attempt to predict future performance. Business periodicals are good sources for information about anticipated changes in economic conditions. Business analysts, economists, and politicians often voice their views on television, on radio, and in print. Remember, though, all of these "expert" predictions of the future of the American economy are, at best, educated guesses. Use this information carefully!

Although general economic conditions certainly affect a company's performance, a company's poor performance should not be excused because the economy is in a recession. Neither should a company's exceptional performance be dismissed as simply the product of a healthy economy. Economic conditions provide *one context* within which we evaluate the results of business activity. Other external factors must also be considered.

Political Events and Political Climate

Politics is the second external factor mentioned by the FASB. "Political events" and "political climate" are closely related terms. The difference is that an event is an action that has already taken place, whereas a climate is a situation that can lead to an action.

Both Republicans and Democrats take credit whenever the general economy improves and blame each other whenever it declines. That is the nature of politics. The truth is that both improvement and decline in the general economy result from many interrelated and complex factors. Indeed, the factors affecting

The Republican majority in Congress promises to bring many significant changes to the federal government and is sure to have a tremendous impact on the general economy. Here, Newt Gingrich, the first Republican Speaker of the House in 40 years, outlines some of those planned changes for the media.

John Duricka/AP/Wide World Photos

the general economy are so complicated and intertwined that the usual "we did it—they did it" political arguments are simplistic and misleading. Still, there is no question that what goes on in politics, both domestic and foreign, has a significant influence on the general economy as well as on the world of business.

The congressional election of 1994 is a perfect example of how political events can impact the economy. On November 8, 1994, the Republicans captured control of both the United States Senate and House of Representatives for the first time in 40 years. The new Republican majority is promising to redefine the role of the federal government and reshape congressional legislation to carry out its economic-social agenda. Whether you think these changes bode well or ill for the United States will depend on your political philosophy. There is, however, one thing on which liberals and conservatives agree: The actions taken by Congress (and the president) on such matters as the amount of government regulation, income taxes, health care, and welfare reform will have an enormous impact on the general economy. And we know that changes in the general economy will impact business activity.

The collapse of the Soviet Union, the reunification of Germany, and other world political events that marked the end of the Cold War have had strong repercussions in the U.S. economy. Reduced purchases by the Pentagon of items used for national defense, for example, have forced companies like Motorola, Lockheed, and Rockwell International (whose annual report we scrutinized in Chapter 13) to make major adjustments in their businesses. These foreign political events have shaken up the entire defense industry, and that has had a ripple effect on many other industries and the communities that depend on them.

Very few people anticipated the collapse of the Soviet Union's influence on world events. The tearing down of the Berlin Wall was symbolic of the demise of communism in Eastern Europe. What upheaval in world politics awaits us as we enter the 21st century is anybody's guess. One thing is for sure: the world political climate will exert tremendous influence on the world economy.

Piel/Gamma-Liaison, Inc.

One important indicator of political climate is how business is perceived by the general public. As we discussed in Chapter 1, some people see the world of business as an arena of greed and exploitation, while others view it as an exciting field of action rich with creative opportunities. How the general public perceives "big business" can impact business activity and business prosperity.

For example, over the last 20 years or so, companies' positions on certain social and environmental issues have become important to the general public. A few decades ago, most businesses would not have considered the environmental impact of a business decision. Today, because of the changed political climate, even a company not legally obligated to do so will often look for alternatives that reduce air or water pollution. Why? Because environmentally sound business decisions are "politically correct," and therefore wise business decisions.

You will recall from our discussion of Rockwell International's annual report in Chapter 13 that it contained a section titled "Corporate Citizenship" in which the company discussed its commitment to the environment and described its charitable and philanthropic activities. This type of item is becoming almost the rule in annual reports by U.S. companies to their stockholders.

We raise the subject of social responsibility in business again here because a growing number of people have resolved to invest their money only in companies that have a genuine commitment to responsible behavior. This trend has generated a broader sense of social responsibility in American corporations.

Suppose you decide to invest your money solely in socially responsible companies. Where can you learn about a company's real behavior in this area? Don't expect to find that information in the company's annual report or in any other company-produced publication. We have read literally thousands of annual reports over the years and have yet to see one that stated the company's mission is to plunder the environment, exploit its workers, or gouge its customers. They all say pretty much the same thing: We are splendid corporate citizens sincerely committed to our customers, our employees, the environment, and the future of the world!

Where, then, can you find accurate, objective information about a company's corporate citizenship? Your library most likely has publications intended to give you this information, but the evaluations you read will reflect the writer's views of corporate social responsibility, which may not coincide with your own. We suggest that instead of naively accepting such appraisals, you prepare yourself to evaluate the evaluators by reading a book entitled *Socially Responsible Investing: How to Invest with Your Conscience* by Alan J. Miller (New York Institute of Finance, 1991). Miller's book is an excellent place to start your research because besides providing an evenhanded and thoughtful treatment of conscience-driven investment, it contains references to hundreds of other publications on the same subject.

Thus far we've explored the impact of both economic and political conditions on business activity. In addition to considering these factors when using financial information, the FASB also warns us to consider the outlook for the industry in which the company operates.

Industry Outlook

The third factor to consider when using financial information is the industry in which a company operates, for industry affiliation may define the company's prospects for future growth. As Roy Taub, vice president of Standard and Poor's, once pointed out:

> The industry is the environment in which the company operates and it defines both the opportunities the company may seize and the challenges it must face.

(S&P, 1983, p. 2)

Industry opportunities and *challenges*, then, are key considerations in evaluating a company's outlook. For example, a company in an industry that is facing an overall decline in demand may be powerless to take any action to encourage its own future growth. As we mentioned earlier, cuts in the federal defense budget have resulted in reduced demand for such items as military aircraft and tanks, impacting the entire industry producing these goods. Certainly, this type of industry-wide effect touches all companies within the industry.

Government action is not the only force that produces industry-wide effects. Technological change often spurs spectacular growth within an industry. The field of telecommunications, for instance, has undergone a revolution in the past decade. Just a short time ago, the fax machine was an expensive luxury—a form of communication reserved for "big business." Today, not only do most small businesses own a fax machine, but many individuals have one as well. Indeed, public fax machines are becoming as common as public telephones.

Often a technological change that opens the doors of opportunity in one industry closes them in another. For example, the development of personal computers has virtually wiped out opportunities for expansion among companies producing typewriters. So when considering a company's outlook for the future, it is important to learn what lies ahead for the entire industry.

DISCUSSION QUESTIONS

14-2. Changes in society, family structures, and the way people behave and interact has changed dramatically since the 1970s. Cite two examples of such changes, identify industries the changes have affected, and describe how they impacted those industries.

Not only does a company's industry affiliation impact the opportunities it faces, but it may also define the challenges ahead. For example, a few decades ago, companies did not have to consider the environmental impact of their actions. Certainly, some corporations made an effort to minimize the pollution caused by their operations, but most did not pay any attention to how their operations affected the environment. After the establishment of the Environmental Protection Agency, however, many companies were forced to spend significant amounts of money to comply with EPA regulations. These regulations hit some industries harder than others. For example, when the EPA banned the use of DDT as a pesticide, companies that manufactured this product either converted to the production of other products or went out of business. The impact of this ban was felt in agriculture as well, as farmers who had depended on DDT as their primary pesticide were forced to switch to less effective, sometimes more expensive, products.

The flipside of government regulation is deregulation. This action has an impact on all companies operating within the deregulated industry. For example, when the federal government deregulated the commercial airline industry in the early 1980s, all airline companies were affected, and many did not survive.

Prior to deregulation, airfares were standard since they were set by the federal government. All airlines flying passengers from one specific destination to another specific destination charged the same fare. Companies competed on amenities—in-flight movies, food, drink, and the like—not price. The govern-

Some airlines, such as People Express, did not survive the deregulation of the airline industry. Others that either went out of business or merged with other airlines include Eastern Airlines, Brannif Airlines, and Western Airlines. Even many of those that have survived are finding the skies to be less than friendly. Between the years 1992 and 1994 Delta Airlines, for example, had net losses totaling well over $1 billion dollars.

Eric Sanders/Gamma-Liaison, Inc.

ment also required airlines to operate unprofitable flights for the convenience of customers in underpopulated or out-of-the way areas. Fares of profitable flights were set high enough to offset the companies' losses from these unprofitable flights.

Then came deregulation—and competition. Forced to make every flight profitable, airlines canceled many routes and began scrambling madly to attract customers. The result was a price war that forced several legendary carriers like Pan Am out of business. Deregulation was seen by newer "upstart" companies as an opportunity, but even they often found themselves up against serious challenges. Some of the most enterprising upstarts, like People Express, folded.

So, business opportunities and challenges may be interrelated, and they are frequently a direct result of membership in a particular industry. The American economy encompasses a wide range of industries with greatly varying prospects. You, as an economic decision maker, need to consider a company's industry if you are to gain an accurate picture of that company's prospects.

DISCUSSION QUESTIONS

14-3. Identify two industries and describe their similarities and differences.

14-4. If you were offered an upper-level management position in two companies—one from each of the industries you identified in your response to Question 14-3—which would you take? Why?

14-5. If you had $2,000 to invest and your only options were the common stock of two companies—one from each of the industries you identified in your response to Question 14-3—which would you choose? Explain your reasoning.

Where do you look for information about a particular industry? Several sources are available. *Standard and Poor's Industry Surveys* is composed of a number of sections with various types of information. One section offers recent articles about each industry written by professional business analysts or drawn from business publications. Another good source is the *U.S. Industrial Outlook*, which offers background information and projections for the 10 fastest- and 10 slowest-growing industries, 40 service industries, and over 150 manufacturing industries. This book includes references to sources that contain more detailed information about each industry. For a short overview of an industry, you might try *Inside U.S. Business: A Concise Encyclopedia of Leading Industries*, which includes several pages of information about each industry, arranged alphabetically.

Heeding the warning of the FASB, we have explored the importance of background information and suggested how you can gather data on general economic conditions and expectations, political climate and events, and industry outlook. The impact of each of these factors on a company's past performance and its prospects should be considered when doing any type of financial statement analysis, for these impacts provide the context within which financial information should be evaluated.

Now we turn to the heart of this chapter—ratio analysis.

RATIO ANALYSIS: CALCULATING THE RATIOS

Before we compute any ratios, you need to understand that the absolute numbers resulting from the calculations are of little value in themselves. It is the *analysis* and *interpretation* of the numbers—the art of ratio analysis—that produces the desired information. To be truly useful to economic decision makers, a company's ratios need to be compared to other information, such as the ratio values for industry averages or the company's ratios in past years. So after introducing all of the ratios in this section of the chapter, we will make these comparisons and interpret the findings in the next.

Ratio analysis, as we explained at the beginning of the chapter, is a method of analyzing the relationship between two items from a company's financial statements for a given period. You will recall that we said important relationships may exist between two items on the same financial statement or between two items from different financial statements. All the ratios we present here are based on information from the balance sheet and the income statement. Some use items from the same financial statement, while others use one item from each statement.

As we introduce each ratio, we will explore what information it offers and show how it is calculated. The 14 ratios we have selected for presentation are representative ratios only. There are many more ratios than these. The reason we chose these particular 14 is that they are the ratios found in the *Almanac of Business and Industrial Financial Ratios*, which we will use later in the chapter to compare Rockwell's ratios to industry averages.

One other thing needs to be mentioned before we begin computing and comparing ratios: There is a lack of consistency among analysts in the way they calculate various ratios. Even when the *name* of the ratio is the same from one analyst to the next, the *financial statement items* the two analysts used to calculate that ratio may have been different. This inconsistency often makes it very difficult to compare ratios calculated by different analysts or financial publications. Descriptions of the ratios in this chapter are consistent with those provided in the *Almanac of Business and Industrial Financial Ratios,* a widely used source of financial ratio data, but by no means the only one. Computations of each ratio will be illustrated using the Rockwell Corporation financial statements presented in the company's 1994 annual report. Be certain you understand how we determined which figures from Rockwell's balance sheet and income statement to use for each ratio.

A variety of ratios are computed by decision makers analyzing financial statements. These ratios are used to glean information about a company's past performance and current financial position that will help the decision maker predict future results of business activity. The 14 ratios presented in this chapter are used to measure either profitability, liquidity, or solvency—three characteristics important to those assessing a company's well-being. As each characteristic is described, we will discuss which users are most interested in it and why it is of concern to them.

Measuring Profitability

profitability The ease with which a company generates income.

profitability ratios A set of ratios developed to predict a firm's ability to generate sufficient profits (and ultimately cash) to fulfill its obligations.

Profitability is the ease with which a company generates income. If a company generates a high level of income very easily, it is said to have high profitability. All companies must maintain at least a minimum level of profitability in order to meet their obligations, such as servicing long-term debt and paying dividends to stockholders. **Profitability ratios** are used to measure a firm's past performance and to help predict its future profitability level. Present and potential stockholders, and long-term creditors, therefore, use these ratios to evaluate investments. Similarly, managers use them to monitor and evaluate their own companies' performance.

Profitability ratios must be utilized carefully. Managers have two potential reasons to boost these ratios and make the company appear very profitable. First, they may want to make the company's financial results look more appealing to external decision makers. Second, their own compensation may be directly tied to these profitability ratios, for often managers receive bonuses based on the level of profitability achieved by the company.

Stockholders and creditors also want the company to be profitable, right? Well, yes. But profitability ratios are based on short-term results (usually one year) and the only way to boost them is to attain the highest possible profit for any given year. That doesn't sound so bad, does it? However:

A PREOCCUPATION WITH SHORT-TERM PROFITS IS DETRIMENTAL TO THE LONG-TERM VALUE OF A BUSINESS!

Stockholders and creditors, then, should generally take a longer-term view of the company's health than can be measured by profitability alone.

As you look at the profitability ratios in this section, focus both on what they are supposed to reveal about a company and on how they might encourage shortsighted behavior by management. It is quite common for managers to slant business decisions toward what will make the ratios "look better" to the decision makers using their company's financial statements.

14-6. Give an example of a management decision that would be made differently depending on whether the decision is considering the short-term or long-term well-being of the company. Explain the impact of the two different perspectives on the outcome of the decision.

return on assets ratio
A profitability ratio that measures the return earned on a company's investment in assets.

Return on Assets Ratio The **return on assets ratio** (sometimes called the *return on total assets*) measures how efficiently a company's assets are being used to produce profits. After all, the reason companies invest in assets is to produce revenue and ultimately profit (net income). Delta Airlines, for example, invests in aircraft and other assets for the express purpose of producing income. Delta's creditors (particularly long-term), stockholders, and management are all interested in knowing how efficiently the aircraft and other assets are being used to produce the company's income. The return on assets ratio is one approach to measuring that efficiency. It is computed as follows:

$$\text{Return on assets} = \frac{\text{Net income before taxes}}{\text{Total assets}}$$

The numerator comes from the income statement and represents the total return (pretax) on the company's assets. The denominator is drawn from the balance sheet, and indicates the company's level of investment in assets. We calculate Rockwell's return on assets for 1994:

$$\frac{\$1,021.3}{\$9,860.8} = .10357 \text{ or } 10.4\%$$

If a company has a low return on its assets, how would it determine the cause of the problem and improve the situation? The answer to that question lies in the next two profitability ratios we will examine, because they are actually the two components of the return on assets ratio.

profit margin before income tax ratio
A profitability ratio that measures the earnings produced from a given level of revenues by comparing net income before income tax to the revenue figure.

Profit Margin Before Income Tax Ratio The **profit margin before income tax ratio** has the same numerator as the return on assets ratio. The denominator for this ratio is total sales for the period. By comparing net income to sales, we can determine the amount of income produced by a given level of revenue. In other words, we can compare the amount of inflows (revenues) to what is left of those inflows after all the outflows (expenses) have been considered. We calculate the profit margin before income tax as follows:

$$\text{Profit margin before income tax} = \frac{\text{Net income before taxes}}{\text{Sales}}$$

Both components of the profit margin before tax are drawn from the income statement. This ratio indicates the contribution of sales to the overall profitability of the company—that is, it shows how much net income is generated from a dollar of sales. Rockwell's profit margin before income taxes for 1994 is:

$$\frac{\$\ 1,021.3}{\$11,123.3} = .0918 \text{ or } 9.2\%$$

DISCUSSION QUESTIONS

14-7. **What situations might cause a company to have a low profit margin before income tax?**

Profit margin before income tax is just one component of the return on assets ratio; the second component—total asset turnover—is equally important.

total asset turnover ratio
A profitability ratio that indicates the amount of revenues produced for a given level of assets used.

Total Asset Turnover Ratio   The **total asset turnover ratio** shows the amount of sales produced for a given level of assets used. The purpose of this ratio is similar to that of the return on total assets ratio. However, total asset turnover indicates how effectively the company uses its total assets to generate *sales* rather than net income. Total asset turnover has the same denominator as the return on assets ratio, but the numerator is total sales for the period. We calculate total asset turnover as follows:

$$\text{Total asset turnover} = \frac{\text{Sales}}{\text{Total assets}}$$

The numerator is drawn from the income statement and the denominator from the balance sheet. We calculate the total asset turnover ratio for Rockwell in 1994 as:

$$\frac{\$11,123.3}{\$\ 9,860.8} = 1.128 \text{ or } 1.13 \text{ times}$$

By comparing the sales figure for the period to the total assets used to produce the revenue, we can determine the amount of revenue produced by a given level of asset investment. Our calculation indicates that Rockwell produced 1.13 times as many dollars in sales as it had invested in assets.

Now that we have explored both components of the return on assets ratio, let's look closer at the relationship among the three ratios:

$$\begin{array}{ccc} \text{Return on} \\ \text{assets} \end{array} = \begin{array}{c} \text{Profit margin} \\ \text{before income tax} \end{array} \times \begin{array}{c} \text{Total asset} \\ \text{turnover} \end{array}$$

$$\frac{\text{Net income}}{\text{before taxes}}{\text{Total assets}} = \frac{\text{Net income}}{\text{before taxes}}{\text{Sales}} \times \frac{\text{Sales}}{\text{Total assets}}$$

If a company's return on assets is low, both its profit margin before income tax and its total asset turnover should be investigated—separately—to determine the source of the problem. After each component is analyzed, the company will be in a position to focus on areas needing improvement.

Rather than relying on any single measure of profitability, wise financial statement users turn to several different ratios. We will explore three more profitability ratios.

Profit Margin After Income Tax Ratio As its name suggests, this ratio is only slightly different from the profit margin measure already discussed. The **profit margin after income tax ratio** indicates the amount of *after-tax* net income generated by a dollar of sales. This is a subtle difference, but it may be important in some analyses. The profit margin after income tax is calculated as follows:

profit margin after income tax ratio A profitability ratio that measures the earnings produced from a given level of revenues by comparing net income after income tax to the revenue figure.

$$\text{Profit margin after income tax} = \frac{\text{Net income after taxes}}{\text{Sales}}$$

Both components of this ratio are drawn from the income statement. The calculation of Rockwell's profit margin after income tax for 1994 is:

$$\frac{\$ \quad 634.1}{\$11,123.3} = .057 \text{ or } 5.7\%$$

Whether computing profit margin before or after taxes, the result is a useful measure of profitability. As Dennis E. Logue suggests in the *Handbook of Modern Finance*:

The profit margin percentage measures a firm's ability to (1) obtain higher prices for its products relative to competitors and (2) control the level of operating costs, or expenses, relative to revenues generated. By holding down costs, a firm increases the profits from a given amount of revenue and thereby improves its profit margin percentage.

Just as profit margin after tax is very similar to profit margin before tax, the final two profitability ratios we will examine are very similar to one another.

return on equity ratio
A profitability ratio that measures the after-tax net income generated from a given level of investment by a company's owners.

Return on Equity Ratio   The **return on equity ratio** demonstrates profitability by comparing a company's after-tax net income to the amount of investment by the company's owners. Equity—in this case, shareholders' equity—is the owners' claim to the assets of the business. Return on equity indicates how much after-tax income was generated for a given level of equity. The return on equity ratio is calculated as follows:

$$\text{Return on equity} = \frac{\text{Net income after taxes}}{\text{Equity}}$$

The numerator of this ratio is drawn from the income statement and the denominator is taken from the balance sheet. The calculation of Rockwell's return on equity for 1994 is:

$$\frac{\$\ 634.1}{\$3,355.6} = .189 \text{ or } 18.9\%$$

The final profitability ratio we will examine is only slightly different from the return on equity ratio.

return before interest on equity ratio A profitability ratio that measures the level of earnings (before the cost of borrowing) generated from a given level of equity.

Return Before Interest on Equity Ratio   As its name suggests, the **return before interest on equity ratio** considers the earnings of the company before interest expense. To calculate net income before interest, we add the interest expense of the period to the after-tax net income. This addition of interest expense to the numerator is the only difference between return before interest on equity and return on equity. The denominator, total shareholders' equity, remains the same. So:

$$\text{Return before interest on equity} = \frac{\text{Net income after taxes} + \text{Interest expense}}{\text{Equity}}$$

The calculation of Rockwell's return before interest on equity for 1994 is:

$$\frac{\$\ 634.1 + \$\ 96.6}{\$3,355.6} = .218 \text{ or } 21.8\%$$

By the nature of the calculation, as long as a company has at least some interest expense, its return before interest on equity will be higher than its return on equity.

Measuring Liquidity

liquidity The ease with which an item, such as an asset, can be converted to cash. The liquidity of a firm refers to the company's ability to generate sufficient cash to meet its short-term obligations.

An asset's **liquidity** describes the ease with which it can be converted to cash. A company's liquidity refers to its ability to generate the cash needed to meet its short-term obligations. Clearly, all economic decision makers must consider a firm's liquidity, for if a company cannot meet its current obligations, it may not be around long enough to be profitable in the long run. Short-term creditors and company's management, however, tend to be the information users who pay most careful attention to liquidity.

liquidity ratios A set of ratios developed to measure a firm's ability to generate sufficient cash in the short run to retire short-term liabilities.

Over time many ratios have been developed specifically to measure liquidity. The five **liquidity ratios** we have chosen to discuss take different approaches to evaluating a firm's ability to generate sufficient cash to meet its short-term obligations. Several of them consider current assets and current liabilities. Recall that a current asset is one that is either already cash or is expected to become cash within one year, and a current liability is any obligation that must be paid within one year. If we are interested in liquidity, certainly we would expect to find helpful information in these two balance sheet categories.

current ratio A liquidity ratio that measures a company's ability to meet short-term obligations by comparing current assets to current liabilities.

Current Ratio The **current ratio** is probably the most widely used measure of a company's liquidity. It compares current assets to current liabilities, offering a measure of the company's ability to meet its short-term financial obligations with cash generated from current assets. The current ratio is calculated as follows:

$$\text{Current ratio} = \frac{\text{Current assets}}{\text{Current liabilities}}$$

This ratio indicates the amount of current assets for each dollar of current liabilities. The 1994 current ratio for Rockwell International is:

$$\frac{\$4,927.8}{\$3,019.8} = 1.63$$

This figure indicates that Rockwell had $1.63 of current assets for every $1.00 of current liabilities at the end of 1994.

Many experts believe that companies should maintain a ratio of $2.00 of current assets to every $1.00 of current liabilities because of the uncertain nature of some of the current assets. For example, some accounts receivable may not be collected, and some inventory may not be salable. There are companies that exceed this recommendation and maintain *more* than twice as many current assets as current liabilities. However, many companies have found that a current ratio lower than 2:1 is adequate. You will learn how to interpret Rockwell's current ratio of 1.63 later in this chapter.

DISCUSSION QUESTIONS

14-10. If Rockwell must borrow money to retire current liabilities, it will have to pay interest on the borrowed funds. What effect (if any) will the additional interest expense have on the following ratios:

a. Profit margin before income tax?
b. Profit margin after income tax?
c. Return on assets?
d. Return on equity?
e. Total asset turnover?

Quick Ratio   The **quick ratio**, which is sometimes called the **acid test ratio**, is similar to the current ratio. It is a more stringent test of liquidity, however, because it considers only current assets that are highly liquid (quickly convertible into cash) in the numerator. Some variation exists as to what assets are included in the quick ratio calculation because the definition of "highly liquid" is very subjective. We will calculate the quick ratio as:

$$\text{Quick ratio} = \frac{\text{Cash} + \text{Accounts receivable} + \text{Notes receivable}}{\text{Current liabilities}}$$

In the numerator of our equation, cash is obviously liquid. We also assume accounts receivable and notes receivable will be quickly converted to cash. However, if a company knows that any account receivable or note receivable will not be quickly converted, it should not include that item in the calculation of this ratio. The denominator of the quick ratio is identical to the one used for the current ratio.

DISCUSSION QUESTIONS

14-11. Besides the three assets—cash, accounts receivable, and notes receivable—considered in our version of the quick ratio, what other current assets might a company have?

The 1994 quick ratio for Rockwell International is:

$$\frac{\$\,628.3 + \$2,267.2}{\$3,019.8} = .959$$

This figure suggests that Rockwell has $.96 of quick assets for each $1.00 of current liabilities. Note that Rockwell's quick ratio (.959) is lower than its current ratio (1.63). That is as it should be because assets that are not highly liquid have been removed from the numerator, while the denominator has remained untouched. Some experts believe that a company should maintain a ratio of $1.00 of quick assets to every $1.00 of current liabilities. As our calculation shows, Rockwell's quick ratio is a bit lower than that. Again, however, the absolute number is not very meaningful. Later in the chapter we will see how to interpret results of the quick ratio calculation.

14-12. How would holding an excessive amount of inventory affect the following ratios:

a. Profit margin before income tax?
b. Profit margin after income tax?
c. Return on assets?
d. Return on equity?
e. Current ratio?
f. Quick ratio?
g. Total asset turnover?

The liquidity ratios we have examined thus far have focused on the proportion of current assets to current liabilities. The next liquidity ratio considers the difference between current assets and current liabilities.

working capital The difference between current assets and current liabilities.

net sales to working capital ratio A ratio used to measure the level of sales generated from a given level of working capital.

Net Sales to Working Capital Ratio   Recall that liquidity refers to a company's ability to generate sufficient cash to meet its short-term obligations. Our discussion of the current ratio suggested that to maintain their liquidity, companies should have more current assets than current liabilities. The difference between current assets and current liabilities is called **working capital**. Some decision makers use working capital to evaluate a company's liquidity. The **net sales to working capital ratio** goes one step further: It indicates the level of sales generated for a given level of working capital, and it is calculated as follows:

$$\text{Net sales to working capital} = \frac{\text{Sales}}{\text{Current assets} - \text{Current liabilities}}$$

This ratio indicates the amount of sales generated for each $1.00 of working capital. The 1994 net sales to working capital ratio for Rockwell International is:

$$\frac{\$11,123.3}{\$4,927.8 - \$3,019.8} = 5.83$$

This figure suggests that in 1994 Rockwell generated $5.83 in sales for every $1.00 of working capital it had at the end of 1994.

The net sales to working capital ratio is not the only liquidity ratio to focus on the generation of sales. Receivables turnover does, as well.

receivables turnover ratio A liquidity ratio that measures how quickly a company collects its accounts receivable.

Receivables Turnover Ratio   The **receivables turnover ratio** measures the liquidity of accounts receivable. Accounts receivable is the amount a company is owed by its customers, and it is often a sizable current asset. Companies need to convert accounts receivable to cash as quickly as possible because they represent interest-free loans to customers. Most companies routinely sell to their customers on a credit basis. Virtually all of Rockwell's sales, for example, are credit sales. If its customers don't pay in a timely manner, before long Rockwell will be unable to pay its own bills.

The receivables turnover ratio indicates how quickly a company collects its receivables. The calculation for receivables turnover is:

$$\text{Receivables turnover} = \frac{\text{Sales}}{\text{Accounts receivable}}$$

The sales figure is drawn from the income statement and accounts receivable is found on the balance sheet. The 1994 receivables turnover ratio for Rockwell International is:

$$\frac{\$11,123.3}{\$\ 2,267.2} = 4.9 \text{ times}$$

This means that Rockwell turns its receivables over an average of 4.9 times per year. A higher number would indicate that Rockwell is turning over its receivables more often, suggesting that the company is collecting cash from its credit customers more quickly. A lower number would suggest that it is collecting payment from customers more slowly.

The information that Rockwell turns over its accounts receivable 4.9 times per year becomes easier to interpret if we extend it to determine the average collection period for Rockwell's accounts receivable. We can do that by dividing the receivables turnover into 365 (the number of days in a year). This will tell us the average time it takes Rockwell to collect its receivables:

$$\frac{365}{4.9} = 74.49 \text{ days}$$

Our calculation shows that it takes Rockwell an average of 74.49 days from the time it makes a credit sale to collect cash from the customer. Is that good or bad? Once again, there is no way to tell from the absolute number. This figure only becomes meaningful when it is compared to Rockwell's results for other years and/or the average for the industry in which Rockwell operates. Later on in the chapter, when we compare Rockwell's ratios to those presented in the *Almanac of Business and Industrial Financial Ratios*, we will use the 4.9 figure because the *Almanac* presents industry averages on receivables turnover rather than average collection period of receivables.

The final liquidity ratio we present is very similar in nature to the receivables turnover.

inventory turnover ratio
A liquidity ratio that indicates how long a company holds its inventory.

Inventory Turnover Ratio Like the receivables turnover ratio, the **inventory turnover ratio** is a measure of the liquidity of one specific asset—in this case, inventory. This ratio indicates the number of times total merchandise inventory is purchased and sold during a period. The calculation of inventory turnover is as follows:

$$\text{Inventory turnover} = \frac{\text{Cost of sales}}{\text{Inventory}}$$

The cost of sales figure, an expense, is drawn from the income statement, and inventory, an asset, is found on the balance sheet. The 1994 inventory turnover ratio for Rockwell International is:

$$\frac{\$8,675.2}{\$1,532.8} = 5.66 \text{ times}$$

This means Rockwell turns its inventory over an average of 5.66 times per year. A higher number would indicate that Rockwell is turning over its inventory more often, suggesting that the company is requiring a lower investment in inventory to support its sales.

The information that Rockwell turns over its inventory 5.66 times per year becomes easier to interpret if we extend it to determine the average number of days Rockwell holds its inventory. We can do that by dividing the inventory turnover into 365 (the number of days in a year). This will tell us the average time Rockwell holds inventory between its purchase and its sale.

$$\frac{365}{5.66} = 64.49 \text{ days}$$

Our calculation shows that, on average, 64.49 days pass between the time Rockwell purchases inventory and the time it sells that inventory. Is that good or bad? As was the case with receivables turnover, there is no way to tell from the absolute number. This figure only becomes useful when it is compared to Rockwell's results for other years and/or the average for the industry in which Rockwell operates. Later on in the chapter, when we compare Rockwell's ratios to industry averages, we will use the 5.66 because the *Almanac* presents data on inventory turnover ratios rather than the average days inventory is held.

Measuring Solvency

Solvency is the third important characteristic that decision makers use as an indication of companies' financial well-being.

solvency A company's ability to meet the obligations created by its long-term debt.

solvency ratios A set of ratios developed to measure a firm's ability to meet its long-term debt obligations.

Solvency is a company's ability to meet the obligations created by its long-term debt. Obligations resulting from debt include both paying back the amount borrowed and paying interest on the debt. A set of **solvency ratios** has been developed to measure firms' solvency. Some of these ratios focus on the overall level of debt a company carries, while others measure a company's ability to make interest payments. A solvency ratio focusing on ability to make interest payments is similar in purpose to a liquidity ratio.

Solvency ratios are of most interest to stockholders, long-term creditors, and, of course, company management. There are numerous solvency ratios; we will look at three of the ones most widely used.

debt ratio A solvency ratio that indicates what proportion of a company's assets is financed by debt.

Debt Ratio The **debt ratio** measures what proportion of a company's assets is financed by debt. All of a company's assets are claimed by either creditors or the owners. This can be demonstrated by looking once again at the accounting (business) equation:

$$\text{Assets} = \text{Liabilities} + \text{Owners' Equity}$$
$$100\% = \text{Some } \% + \text{Some } \%$$

Calculation of the debt ratio illustrates the percentage of assets that are supported by debt financing. Creditors and stockholders watch the debt ratio from their individual perspectives, and tend to get nervous if they perceive it to be out of balance. The format of the debt ratio may vary somewhat. We will calculate it as follows:

$$\text{Debt ratio} = \frac{\text{Total liabilities}}{\text{Total assets}}$$

Both of the items necessary to calculate the debt ratio can be found on the balance sheet. Rockwell's 1994 debt ratio is:

$$\frac{\$6{,}505.2}{\$9{,}860.8} = .6597 \text{ or } 65.97\%$$

This would indicate that 65.97 percent of Rockwell's assets are supported by debt, leaving 34.03 percent of the company's assets to be claimed by the shareholders. There is no hard-and-fast rule concerning what amount of a company's assets should be financed through debt and what amount should be supported by equity. A company's debt ratio must be evaluated in light of the industry in which the company operates, how mature the company is (new businesses tend to have more debt relative to equity), and management's philosophy concerning the proper balance between debt financing and equity financing.

DISCUSSION QUESTIONS

14-13. How did we determine Rockwell's 1994 total liabilities were $6,505.2 million? Provide a calculation to support your answer.

The debt ratio indicates the relationship between the amount of liabilities and the assets held by a company. The next solvency ratio we will examine considers a company's liabilities in relation to stockholders' equity.

net worth The difference between assets and liabilities. More commonly called owners' equity.

total liabilities to net worth ratio A solvency ratio indicating the relationship between creditors' claims to a company's assets and the owners' claim to those assets.

Total Liabilities to Net Worth Ratio   **Net worth** is a term you may not know. It refers to the difference between assets and liabilities. In other words, net worth is owners' equity. In a corporate setting, net worth refers to total shareholders' equity. The **total liabilities to net worth ratio** is a solvency ratio indicating the relationship between creditors' claims to the company's assets (liabilities) and owners' claims to those assets (net worth). It is very similar to the debt ratio. In fact, the total liabilities to net worth ratio and the debt ratio offer the same information presented in different ways.

Look back at Rockwell's debt ratio for a minute. We determined it to be 65.97 percent. We know that if 65.97 percent of Rockwell's assets are financed by debt, the remaining 34.03 percent must be financed by equity. A quick glance at those two percentages will tell you that the debt percentage is nearly twice the equity percentage. That is precisely what the total liabilities to net worth (equity) ratio is going to tell us—how much debt a company has in relation to its equity. For Rockwell, that should turn out to be about $2 of debt for every $1 of equity. Let's check and see.

As is obvious from its name, the total liabilities to net worth ratio is calculated as:

$$\text{Total liabilities to net worth} = \frac{\text{Total liabilities}}{\text{Net worth}}$$

Both of the items necessary to calculate the total liabilities to net worth ratio can be found on the balance sheet. The numerator is the same as for the debt ratio. Rockwell's 1994 total liabilities to net worth ratio is:

$$\frac{\$6,505.2}{\$3,355.6} = 1.94$$

Well, what do you know about that! Rockwell has $1.94 of debt for every $1 of equity—the proportion we expected as a result of our analysis of Rockwell's debt ratio.

Both the debt ratio and total liabilities to net worth ratio focus on the overall debt load carried by a company. The last solvency ratio we will examine indicates a company's ability to meet the obligations associated with its debt load.

Coverage Ratio The **coverage ratio**, also called the **times interest earned ratio**, indicates a company's ability to make its periodic interest payments. It compares the amount of income available for interest payments to the interest requirements. Creditors use this ratio to assess the risk associated with lending money to a business. The formula used to calculate this ratio is:

> **coverage ratio** A solvency ratio that provides an indication of a company's ability to make its periodic interest payments.
>
> **times interest earned ratio** Another name for the coverage ratio.

$$\text{Coverage ratio} = \frac{\text{Earnings before interest expense and income taxes}}{\text{Interest expense}}$$

The numerator consists of earnings before interest and tax expense because this figure represents the amount of earnings available for periodic interest payments. Like the denominator—interest expense—it is found on the income statement. Rockwell's 1994 coverage ratio is:

$$\frac{\$1,117.9}{\$\ \ \ 96.6} = 11.57$$

Some experts feel a coverage ratio of at least 4 provides an appropriate degree of safety for creditors. This means a company's earnings before interest and taxes should be at least four times as great as its interest expense. Rockwell's figure far exceeds that level.

In order to arrive at a valid assessment of a company's solvency, financial statement users should evaluate ratios that indicate the level of debt carried by the company (e.g., debt ratio and total liabilities to net worth) as well as those indicating the company's ability to meet its obligations associated with the debt (e.g., coverage ratio). In fact, when evaluating any of the three characteristics indicative of a company's well-being, more than one approach should be considered.

Exhibit 14-1 summarizes the calculations and purpose of the profitability, liquidity, and solvency ratios discussed in this chapter.

Exhibit 14-1 Summary of Key Ratios

Ratio	Calculation	Purpose of Ratio
Profitability Ratios		
1. Return on Assets	$\dfrac{\text{Net income before taxes}}{\text{Total assets}}$	Measures the return earned on investment in assets.
2. Profit Margin Before Income Tax	$\dfrac{\text{Net income before taxes}}{\text{Sales}}$	Measures the pretax earnings produced from a given level of revenues.
3. Total Asset Turnover	$\dfrac{\text{Sales}}{\text{Total assets}}$	Indicates the firm's ability to generate revenues from a given level of assets.
4. Profit Margin After Income Tax	$\dfrac{\text{Net income after taxes}}{\text{Sales}}$	Measures the amount of after-tax net income generated by a dollar of sales.
5. Return on Equity	$\dfrac{\text{Net income after taxes}}{\text{Equity}}$	Measures the after-tax income generated from a given level of equity.
6. Return Before Interest on Equity	$\dfrac{\text{Net income after taxes} + \text{Interest expense}}{\text{Equity}}$	Measures the return on equity before the cost of borrowing.
Liquidity Ratios		
7. Current Ratio	$\dfrac{\text{Current assets}}{\text{Current liabilities}}$	Indicates a company's ability to meet short-term obligations.
8. Quick Ratio	$\dfrac{\text{Cash} + \text{Accounts receivable} + \text{Notes receivable}}{\text{Current liabilities}}$	Measures short-term liquidity more stringently than the current ratio does.
9. Net Sales to Working Capital	$\dfrac{\text{Sales}}{\text{Current assets} - \text{Current liabilities}}$	Measures the level of sales generated from a given level of working capital.
10. Receivables Turnover	$\dfrac{\text{Sales}}{\text{Accounts receivable}}$	Indicates how quickly a company collects its receivables.
11. Inventory Turnover	$\dfrac{\text{Cost of sales}}{\text{Inventory}}$	Indicates how long a company holds its inventory.
Solvency Ratios		
12. Debt Ratio	$\dfrac{\text{Total liabilities}}{\text{Total assets}}$	Measures the proportion of assets financed by debt.
13. Total Liabilities to Net Worth	$\dfrac{\text{Total liabilities}}{\text{Net worth}}$	Directly compares the amount of debt financing to the amount of equity financing.
14. Coverage Ratio	$\dfrac{\text{Earnings before interest expense and income taxes}}{\text{Interest expense}}$	Indicates a company's ability to make its periodic interest payments.

14-14. Assume you had to decide to invest in one of two companies with no information other than values of four of their financial ratios. Which four would you want to know? Explain the reasons for your choices.

14-15. Martino Company and Patco Corporation are in the same line of business. However, Martino uses straight-line depreciation, whereas Patco uses an accelerated depreciation method. If this is the *only* difference in the business activity of the two companies, how should their financial ratios compare at the end of their first year of operations? Explain the effect of the difference in depreciation methods on each of the 14 ratios described in this chapter.

RATIO ANALYSIS: USING THE RATIOS

We have calculated 14 ratios based on the financial statements included in Rockwell's 1994 annual report. What now? How do we use these ratios to evaluate the profitability, liquidity, and solvency of the business?

We stated several times throughout the previous section that the ratios we were calculating were of little value in and of themselves. We said that to be really useful, they had to be compared, either to Rockwell's same ratios for other years, or to the same ratios computed for the industry in which Rockwell operates. This is the kind of interpretation we meant earlier when we referred to the "art of ratio analysis."

In this section of the chapter, we will first do the industry comparison, and then the company analysis. Before we can proceed to the industry comparison, however, you need to understand the system developed to classify companies into industry groupings.

Standard Industrial Classification System

In Chapter 13, we made reference to a variety of publications you can use to find information about different industries and companies. All of these publications list companies alphabetically, but many of them also group firms by their industry affiliation. In other words, you may find lists in which companies are grouped or identified according to the industry in which they operate. The most widely accepted method for indicating the various industries is known as the *Standard Industrial Classification (SIC)* system. This system uses four-digit SIC codes to specify the industry in which a company operates.

The SIC codes were developed by a multiagency Technical Committee on Industrial Classification, under the sponsorship of the federal Office of Management and Budget, and they have attained broad acceptance in financial publications. Even the Internal Revenue Service (IRS) uses a slightly modified version of these codes for the filing of corporate income tax returns.

To use the SIC codes properly, you need to be familiar with how the SIC system works. Each of the four digits of an SIC code has a specific meaning.

The first two digits indicate the major industrial division into which a company has been classified. The SIC separates American industry into 11 major divisions, as shown in Exhibit 14-2. In fact, we can broadly identify a company just by looking at the first digit of its SIC code. If the first digit is a 0, the company's major business pursuit is agriculture, forestry, or fishing. If the first digit is a 1, the company is being classified as a member of either the mining division or the construction division.

Exhibit 14-2

The 11 Major Industrial Divisions of the SIC System

01 to 09	Agriculture, Forestry, and Fishing
10 to 14	Mining
15 to 17	Construction
20 to 39	Manufacturing
40 to 49	Transportation, Communications, Electric, Gas, and Sanitary Services
50 to 51	Wholesale Trade
52 to 59	Retail Trade
60 to 67	Finance, Insurance, and Real Estate
70 to 89	Services
91 to 97	Public Administration
99	Nonclassifiable Establishments

Let's take a closer look at the manufacturing division, indicated by digits 20 to 39. Any company whose SIC code has a 2 or a 3 as its first digit is classified as a manufacturer. That's a pretty broad category if you think about all the different products manufactured in the United States. However, we can figure out what group the company belongs to by checking the second digit of its SIC code.

The 11 major industrial divisions are further broken down into more specific groups. Exhibit 14-3 on page 484 lists the 82 major groups indicated by the first two digits of the SIC code. Consider a company that has an SIC code with 37 as the first two digits. We know immediately that the company is a manufacturer because the first digit is a 3. Under the SIC code classifications, a 7 as the second digit further classifies this company into Group 37, manufacturers of transportation equipment. So, any company whose SIC code has 37 as the first two digits is a company that manufactures transportation equipment.

Exhibit 14-3   The 82 Major Groups in the SIC System

Industrial Division A. Agriculture, Forestry, and Fishing

   Major Group 01. Agricultural production—crops
   Major Group 02. Agriculture production livestock and animal specialties
   Major Group 07. Agricultural services
   Major Group 08. Forestry
   Major Group 09. Fishing, hunting, and trapping

Industrial Division B. Mining

   Major Group 10. Metal mining
   Major Group 12. Coal mining
   Major Group 13. Oil and gas extraction
   Major Group 14. Mining and quarrying of nonmetallic minerals, except fuels

Industrial Division C. Construction

   Major Group 15. Building construction—general contractors and operative builders
   Major Group 16. Heavy construction other than building construction—contractors
   Major Group 17. Construction—special trade contractors

Industrial Division D. Manufacturing

   Major Group 20. Food and kindred products
   Major Group 21. Tobacco products
   Major Group 22. Textile mill products
   Major Group 23. Apparel and other finished products made from fabrics and similar materials
   Major Group 24. Lumber and wood products, except furniture
   Major Group 25. Furniture and fixtures
   Major Group 26. Paper and allied products
   Major Group 27. Printing, publishing, and allied industries
   Major Group 28. Chemicals and allied products
   Major Group 29. Petroleum refining and related industries
   Major Group 30. Rubber and miscellaneous plastics products
   Major Group 31. Leather and leather products
   Major Group 32. Stone, clay, glass, and concrete products
   Major Group 33. Primary metal industries
   Major Group 34. Fabricated metal products, except machinery and transportation equipment
   Major Group 35. Industrial and commercial machinery and computer equipment
   Major Group 36. Electronic and other electrical equipment and components, except computer equipment
   Major Group 37. Transportation equipment
   Major Group 38. Measuring, analyzing, and controlling instruments; photographic, medical and optical goods; watches and clocks
   Major Group 39. Miscellaneous manufacturing industries

Industrial Division E. Transportation, Communications, Electric, Gas, and Sanitary Services

   Major Group 40. Railroad transportation
   Major Group 41. Local and suburban transit and interurban highway passenger transportation
   Major Group 42. Motor freight transportation and warehousing
   Major Group 43. United States Postal Service
   Major Group 44. Water transportation
   Major Group 45. Transportation by air
   Major Group 46. Pipelines, except natural gas
   Major Group 47. Transportation services
   Major Group 48. Communications

Major Group 49. Electric, gas, and sanitary services

Industrial Division F. Wholesale Trade

Major Group 50. Wholesale trade—durable goods

Major Group 51. Wholesale trade—nondurable goods

Industrial Division G. Retail Trade

Major Group 52. Building materials, hardware, garden supply, and mobile home dealers

Major Group 53. General merchandise stores

Major Group 54. Food stores

Major Group 55. Automotive dealers and gasoline service stations

Major Group 56. Apparel and accessory stores

Major Group 57. Home furniture, furnishings, and equipment stores

Major Group 58. Eating and drinking places

Major Group 59. Miscellaneous retail

Industrial Division H. Finance, Insurance, and Real Estate

Major Group 60. Depository institutions

Major Group 61. Nondepository credit institutions

Major Group 62. Security and commodity brokers, dealers, exchanges, and services

Major Group 63. Insurance carriers

Major Group 64. Insurance agents, brokers, and service

Major Group 65. Real estate

Major Group 67. Holding and other investment offices

Industrial Division I. Services

Major Group 70. Hotels, rooming houses, camps, and other lodging places

Major Group 72. Personal services

Major Group 73. Business services

Major Group 75. Automotive repair, services, and parking

Major Group 76. Miscellaneous repair services

Major Group 78. Motion pictures

Major Group 79. Amusement and recreation services

Major Group 80. Health services

Major Group 81. Legal services

Major Group 82. Educational services

Major Group 83. Social services

Major Group 84. Museums, art galleries, and botanical and zoological gardens

Major Group 86. Membership organizations

Major Group 87. Engineering, accounting, research, management, and related services

Major Group 88. Private households

Major Group 89. Miscellaneous services

Industrial Division J. Public Administration

Major Group 91. Executive, legislative, and general government, except finance

Major Group 92. Justice, public order, and safety

Major Group 93. Public finance, taxation, and monetary policy

Major Group 94. Administration of human resource programs

Major Group 95. Administration of environmental quality and housing programs

Major Group 96. Administration of economic programs

Major Group 97. National security and international affairs

Industrial Division K. Nonclassifiable Establishments

Major Group 99. Nonclassifiable establishments

If you think about the many different forms of transportation, you will realize that the information provided by the second digit of the SIC code is not detailed enough to specify the industry in which the company operates. It is the third and fourth digits of the code that tell us the specific type of transportation equipment our company manufactures.

Assume our company has a complete four-digit SIC code of 3715. The last two digits—15—tell us precisely what type of transportation equipment this company manufactures. Exhibit 14-4 is an excerpt from the *Standard Industrial Classification Manual*, which provides a numerical listing of each SIC code and the specific type of operation it indicates. Note that 3700 is not a specific code, but rather the category heading for all classifications of transportation equipment. Within the 3700s, the third digit of each code offers specific information. For instance, SIC code 3710 refers to Motor Vehicles and Equipment—a subheading of 3700 that includes all SIC codes from 3711 to 3716. Companies are generally not classified into categories ending in 0 unless information is not yet available to allow proper classification.

Exhibit 14-4

Excerpt from Standard Industrial Classification Manual

3700	**TRANSPORTATION EQUIPMENT**
3710	**Motor Vehicles and Equipment**
3711	Motor vehicles and car bodies
3713	Truck and bus bodies
3714	Motor vehicle parts and accessories
3715	Truck trailers
3716	Motor homes
3720	**Aircraft and Parts**
3721	Aircraft
3724	Aircraft engines and engine parts
3728	Aircraft parts and equipment, nec
3730	**Ship and Boat Building and Repairing**
3731	Ship building and repairing
3732	Boat building and repairing
3740	**Railroad Equipment**
3743	Railroad equipment
3750	**Motorcycles, Bicycles, and Parts**
3751	Motorcycles, bicycles, and parts
3760	**Guided Missiles, Space Vehicles, Parts**
3761	Guided missiles and space vehicles
3764	Space propulsion units and parts
3769	Space vehicle equipment, nec
3790	**Miscellaneous Transportation Equipment**
3792	Travel trailers and campers
3795	Tanks and tank components
3799	Transportation equipment, nec

Since our company's SIC code is 3715, we can tell from the information in Exhibit 14-4 that it manufactures truck trailers. If the company's SIC code had been 3795, we would know that it manufactures tanks and tank components. Notice several categories use the term "nec" in their titles. This abbreviation indicates these categories include operations of the type described and other closely related types "not elsewhere classified." Even with approximately 900 four-digit SIC code categories, the system may not have a classification which clearly identifies a company's activities.

Now that you have a basic understanding of the most widely accepted classification system for identifying business activities, we can proceed to gather the information we need to evaluate the ratios we calculated for Rockwell.

Industry Comparisons

Now we can begin to gather even more information from the computations performed earlier in this chapter. We are going to compare the absolute numbers calculated as the ratio values for Rockwell to values for industry averages. There are several sources of information about industry averages. We will, as mentioned earlier, use data gathered from the *Almanac of Business and Industrial Financial Ratios*. For your information, you can also obtain industry averages from two other widely used sources: *Robert Morris Associates' Annual Statement Studies* and *Dun & Bradstreet's Industry Norms and Key Business Ratios*.

Whatever source you use, your first step in making an industry comparison is to determine the industry affiliation of the company being analyzed. That is, you need to determine which SIC code properly identifies the activities of the company. Several business directories mentioned in Chapter 13 provide SIC codes for companies:

■ *Ward's Business Directory of U.S. Private and Public Companies*
■ *All-In-One Business Contactbook*
■ *Million Dollar Directory*
■ *Standard and Poor's Register of Corporations*

In checking these sources for Rockwell's SIC code, we find some confusing information: The *Million Dollar Directory* lists 6 different codes for Rockwell, *Standard and Poor's* suggests that Rockwell has 19 SIC codes, while *Ward's Business Directory* and the *All-In-One Business Contactbook* agree that Rockwell has only 3 SIC codes! How can this be? Recall that Rockwell is a diversified company, meaning it operates in more than one industry. Diversification adds a special challenge to classifying companies by SIC code.

No single SIC code can properly indicate *all* the operations of a diversified company. However, for purposes of industry comparisons, we need to identify a code that indicates the *primary* activities of the business. As a first step in that direction, let's examine the three codes listed by both *Ward's Business Directory* and the *All-In-One Business Contactbook*:

■ 3761—Guided Missiles and Space Vehicles
■ 3679—Electronic Components, NEC
■ 3714—Motor Vehicle Parts and Accessories

As you recall from your exploration of Rockwell's annual report, the company is indeed involved in activities that would fall into each of these three categories. Our task is to determine which one of the classifications best identifies Rockwell's operations. The company's annual report provides information to help us make this determination.

Rockwell had sales in 1994 of over $11 billion. These sales resulted from the operation of four distinctly different business segments. On page 23 of the annual report, Rockwell presents segment information. Using the sales totals in that presentation, we can determine which of the four segments we should consider Rockwell's predominate business activity:

	Sales	Percent
Electronics	$ 5,015	45.1%
Aerospace	2,627	23.6%
Automotive	2,826	25.4%
Graphic Systems	655	5.9%
Total	$11,123	100.0%

Since Rockwell did nearly twice as much business in electronics as it did in any of the other three segments, we determine that it should be considered an electronics manufacturing company. Reviewing the three SIC codes listed for Rockwell by *Ward's* and *All-In-One*, we find that one, 3679, relates to electronics. So, based on the sales data from the annual report, we conclude that SIC code 3679 is a reasonable classification for Rockwell.

Now we can look in the *Almanac of Business and Industrial Financial Ratios* for the data to make an industry comparison of Rockwell's ratios. Data in the *Almanac* is compiled from approximately 3.7 million corporate federal income tax returns. Gathering data from the Internal Revenue Service (IRS) rather than other publicly available sources of financial information has two distinct advantages: (1) information on *all* active corporations is included (other sources include only large, or publicly held corporations); (2) because of substantial penalties for misreporting, corporate data submitted to the IRS is more reliable than that from other sources.

The IRS uses industry groupings which closely follow the SIC codes. However, the IRS classifications are not as specific as the four-digit SIC codes. Generally, a single IRS classification covers several SIC codes. The *Almanac* provides an easy-to-use table of correspondence to identify the IRS classification which properly identifies each SIC code. For our example, Rockwell's SIC code, 3679, corresponds to the IRS industry group 3670. This IRS group includes SIC codes from 3671 to 3679, as well as a few others.

Information provided in the *Almanac* for each industry is four pages, consisting of two tables. Table I provides an analysis of all companies in the particular industry, regardless of whether they had any net income for the year. Table II provides the same information items as Table I, but it considers only companies that showed a net income for the year. Exhibit 14-5 is a portion of Table II for IRS classification 3670.

Exhibit 14-5

Page from *Almanac* showing Table II for Industry 3670

Table II
Corporations with Net Income

Manufacturing
3670

Electronic Components and Accessories

Money Amounts and Size of Assets in Thousands of Dollars

	Total	Zero Assets	Under 100	100 to 250	251 to 500	501 to 1,000	1,001 to 5,000	5,001 to 10,000	10,001 to 25,000	25,001 to 50,000	50,001 to 100,000	100,001 to 250,000	250,001 and over
Number of Enterprises 1	7058	286	1676	990	1378	864	1276	202	195	70	51	38	32

Selected Financial Ratios (Times to 1)

		Total	Zero Assets	Under 100	100 to 250	251 to 500	501 to 1,000	1,001 to 5,000	5,001 to 10,000	10,001 to 25,000	25,001 to 50,000	50,001 to 100,000	100,001 to 250,000	250,001 and over
Current Ratio	24	1.6	•	1.7	0.8	2.7	3.7	2.0	2.2	2.3	2.3	2.2	2.2	1.5
Quick Ratio	25	1.0	•	1.0	0.6	1.8	2.6	1.1	1.2	1.3	1.3	1.2	1.3	0.9
Net Sales to Working Capital	26	4.9	•	15.5	•	4.5	3.9	6.0	4.5	3.9	3.6	3.8	3.5	5.3
Coverage Ratio	27	4.5	•	6.0	3.3	9.0	5.7	4.7	6.7	7.7	7.4	5.2	5.9	3.9
Total Asset Turnover	28	1.1	•	3.7	3.8	2.4	2.0	2.1	1.8	1.5	1.4	1.3	1.2	1.0
Inventory Turnover	29	3.8	•	4.2	4.7	6.1	7.1	4.8	3.5	3.6	3.6	4.6	3.8	3.6
Receivables Turnover	30	5.0	•	•	8.7	8.1	8.9	7.2	5.7	5.6	5.3	6.2	4.3	4.5
Total Liabilities to Net Worth	31	1.2	•	•	•	0.7	0.5	1.2	1.0	0.7	0.8	1.0	0.9	1.4

Selected Financial Factors (in Percentages)

		Total	Zero Assets	Under 100	100 to 250	251 to 500	501 to 1,000	1,001 to 5,000	5,001 to 10,000	10,001 to 25,000	25,001 to 50,000	50,001 to 100,000	100,001 to 250,000	250,001 and over
Debt Ratio	32	55.1	•	•	•	40.2	34.8	54.3	48.8	41.9	45.1	50.3	48.1	57.5
Return on Assets	33	11.9	•	•	29.7	17.0	14.2	14.6	18.9	15.4	14.6	12.8	15.8	10.3
Return on Equity	34	14.8	•	•	•	23.4	16.2	21.7	24.4	18.1	17.8	15.7	18.6	12.2
Return Before Interest on Equity	35	26.5	•	•	•	28.3	21.8	32.0	•	26.5	26.5	25.8	30.4	24.3
Profit Margin, Before Income Tax	36	8.3	22.5	11.5	5.4	6.3	5.9	5.5	9.0	9.0	9.0	7.8	11.5	8.1
Profit Margin, After Income Tax	37	6.0	16.3	10.7	5.3	5.9	5.3	4.7	7.0	7.1	7.0	5.9	8.4	5.5

Source: Leo Troy, Almanac of Business and Industrial Financial Ratios © 1994. Reprinted by permission of Prentice Hall, Inc., Englewood Cliffs, New Jersey.

Looking down the left-hand column of the exhibit, you will see the 14 key financial ratios we presented earlier in this chapter. They are not in the same order as we covered them, but that won't bother us. The fact that they are numbered from 24 to 37 will not bother us either. As we said earlier, there is more to the *Almanac*'s Table II than we have reproduced here. We did not include items 1 through 23 because we are interested only in the ratios (items 24 to 37).

Also included in the portion of Table II reproduced in Exhibit 14-5 are 13 columns of data. Looking at the column headings, we discover that the first column ("Total") provides averages for all companies in the industry. The other columns provide averages for companies of different size within the industry. As we compare Rockwell's ratios to industry averages, we will be interested in the first column and the last column—the first because we want to see how Rockwell compares with the entire industry, and the last because Rockwell is comparable in size to companies with total assets exceeding $250 million.

Finally, look at Exhibit 14-6. The list of ratios and the two columns of averages were drawn directly from the *Almanac*. The last column shows the 14 key ratios as we calculated them in this chapter. Now at last, we can begin to analyze Rockwell's ratios in a context that can give us some insight into how the company compares with its industry.

Exhibit 14-6
Key Ratio Comparisons: Total Industry, Companies with Assets Exceeding $250 Million, and Rockwell International

Ratio		Total Industry	250,001 and Over	Rockwell International
Current Ratio	24	1.6	1.5	1.63
Quick Ratio	25	1.0	0.9	.959
Net Sales to Working Capital	26	4.9	5.3	5.83
Coverage Ratio	27	4.5	3.9	11.57
Total Asset Turnover	28	1.1	1.0	1.13
Inventory Turnover	29	3.8	3.6	5.66
Receivables Turnover	30	5.0	4.5	4.9
Total Liabilities to Net Worth	31	1.2	1.4	1.94
Debt Ratio	32	55.1	57.5	65.97
Return on Assets	33	11.9	10.3	10.4
Return on Equity	34	14.8	12.2	18.9
Return Before Interest on Equity	35	26.5	24.3	21.8
Profit Margin, Before Income Tax	36	8.3	8.1	9.2
Profit Margin, After Income Tax	37	6.0	5.5	5.7

Note that in most instances there isn't a great deal of difference between the averages given in Exhibit 14-6 for the entire industry and those for companies with assets over $250 million. In those cases where there is a significant difference, we think more weight should be given to large-company averages. As you can see from the exhibit, many of the ratios we calculated in the chapter for Rockwell are very close to *both* the overall industry averages and the averages for companies with assets over $250 million. However, a few of the figures merit further analysis.

Coverage Ratio (#27)   The coverage ratio is intended to measure a company's ability to make its periodic interest payments. The prevailing view is that a firm's earnings before interest and taxes should be about four times its interest expense. Rockwell's coverage ratio is much higher than the averages both for the entire industry and for the companies with assets over $250 million—so much higher, in fact, that we think it wise to go back and recalculate the ratio to see if we did it correctly. The calculation, you recall, is:

$$\text{Coverage ratio} = \frac{\text{Earnings before interest expense and income taxes}}{\text{Interest expense}}$$

Rockwell's 1994 coverage ratio is:

$$\frac{\$1,117.9}{\$\quad 96.6} = 11.57$$

We *did* calculate correctly the first time: Rockwell's ratio really is that much higher than the industry averages. We went through the recalculation to point out something very important to you: Whenever you find a company's ratio to be this much different from the average for the industry, it's a good idea to recheck your arithmetic.

So, what does Rockwell's very high coverage ratio mean? It means that this company will certainly have no difficulty making its periodic interest payments. This is a very important piece of information for both long-term creditors and investors.

DISCUSSION QUESTIONS

14-6. Assume that Rockwell had a coverage ratio of 1.57 instead of 11.57. Assume further that you own some of Rockwell's corporate bonds. Would you be concerned? Explain your reasoning.

Inventory Turnover (#29)   The inventory turnover ratio is intended to measure how long a company holds its inventory. It costs a great deal of money to hold inventory, so companies are anxious to keep their inventory levels low. Frequent inventory turnover indicates either that the company is producing high-quality products in great demand or that management is proficient at monitoring inventory levels. A high inventory turnover ratio signals that a company is able to generate sales with a relatively low investment in inventory.

It may seem to you that there is not much difference between Rockwell's inventory turnover of 5.66 and the other two figures shown in Exhibit 14-6. As we said when we introduced this ratio, the import of inventory turnover ratio values only becomes clear when they are extended to the average inventory holding period:

Industry	$250 Million and Over	Rockwell
$\frac{365}{3.8} = 96$ days	$\frac{365}{3.6} = 101$ days	$\frac{365}{5.66} = 64.49$ days

These calculations show that Rockwell holds its inventory more than a month less than other electronics companies. Given the very high cost of holding inventory, this is a very significant difference. It indicates that Rockwell is handling its inventory investment more efficiently than other companies in its industry.

DISCUSSION QUESTIONS

14-17. Which of the following do you think would be interested in Rockwell's inventory turnover ratio:

 a. Trade creditors?
 b. Other short-term creditors (banks)?
 c. Long-term creditors?
 d. Stockholders?

 Explain your reasoning.

Total Liabilities to Net Worth (#31)   This ratio compares the amount of debt financing directly to the amount of equity financing. The electronics industry average is $1.20 of debt for every $1.00 of equity. The average for electronics companies with assets over $250 million is $1.40 of debt for every $1.00 of equity. Rockwell has $1.94 of debt for each $1.00 of equity investment. This is a significant difference.

Should economic decision makers be concerned about Rockwell's solvency? Recall that solvency refers to a company's ability to meet its obligations arising from long-term debt. Periodic interest payments are the obligations that will be the first to arise. Will Rockwell have any problem meeting the periodic interest payments associated with its debt load? Not if the company's coverage ratio is any indication!

Debt Ratio (#32) This ratio measures the proportion of assets financed by debt. Since Rockwell's total liabilities to net worth ratio was higher than the ratio for other companies in its industry, we would expect its debt ratio also to be higher, because these two ratios really measure the same thing.

To see more clearly what the debt ratio reveals, consider the following:

Total Industry

Assets	=	Liabilities	+	Owners' Equity
100%	=	55.1%	+	44.9%

Companies with Assets over $250 Million

Assets	=	Liabilities	+	Owners' Equity
100%	=	57.5%	+	42.5%

Rockwell

Assets	=	Liabilities	+	Owners' Equity
100%	=	65.97%	+	34.03%

From this comparison, it is obvious that Rockwell has financed a significantly higher proportion of its assets through debt than have other companies in its industry. Whether this situation is cause for concern is impossible for us to say. It is entirely dependent on the perspective of those actually analyzing Rockwell's financial statements.

DISCUSSION QUESTIONS

14-18. Which of the following might be concerned about Rockwell's higher-than-average total liabilities to net worth ratio and debt ratio:

a. Trade creditors?
b. Other short-term creditors (banks)?
c. Long-term creditors?
d. Stockholders?

Explain the reason for their concern.

At least two other ratios in Exhibit 14-6 may warrant further analysis: Rockwell's return on equity ratio (#34) and return before interest on equity ratio (#35) are somewhat different from averages of both the entire industry and companies of comparable asset size.

Compare Rockwell's return on equity ratio (#34) and its return before interest on equity ratio (#35) to averages for both the entire industry and companies in the industry having assets over $250 million.

14-19. Are Rockwell's return on equity and return before interest on equity ratios better or worse than those for the entire industry and for companies of comparable asset size? Explain your reasoning.

14-20. Since the return on equity ratio and the return before interest on equity ratio are so closely related, what conclusion can you draw from the fact that on one of these ratios Rockwell performs above the averages, while on the other it performs below the averages?

14-21. Which of the following do you think would be interested in Rockwell's return on equity ratio and its return before interest on equity ratio:

    a. Trade creditors?
    b. Other short-term creditors (banks)?
    c. Long-term creditors?
    d. Stockholders?
    e. Management?

    Explain your reasoning.

Overall, we think Rockwell compares favorably with both the entire electronics industry and with companies in the industry having assets over $250 million. We must also keep in mind that both Exhibits 14-5 and 14-6 are based on Table II of the *Almanac*, which includes only companies with a net income. Had we done a comparison of Rockwell's ratios to the ratios presented in Table I of the *Almanac*, the results would have been much more impressive.

In short, the results of our industry comparison suggest that Rockwell is a very solid company compared to other electronics firms. Our analysis will not be complete, however, until we compare Rockwell's 1994 ratios to the company's same ratios for other years. This will allow us to assess Rockwell's performance over time.

Company Analysis

Exhibit 14-7 presents an analysis of Rockwell's financial results for the years 1990 through 1994. Calculations of the 14 key ratios are based on information from Rockwell's 1994 annual report. Most of the necessary information was gathered from the five-year selected financial data on page 41 of the report. Since the five-year selected financial data offer no detail on Rockwell's current assets, we were not able to calculate the quick ratio, receivables turnover, or inventory turnover for the years 1990, 1991, and 1992. These ratios can be calculated for 1993 and 1994 because the necessary information on current assets is included in the balance sheet presentation on page 29 of Rockwell's annual report.

Exhibit 14-7
Ratio Analysis of Rockwell's
Financial Results, 1990–1994

	1990	1991	1992	1993	1994
Current ratio (#24)	1.24	1.45	1.55	1.68	1.63
Quick ratio (#25)	*	*	*	1.01	.96
Net sales to working capital (#26)	12.62	7.62	6.32	5.42	5.83
Coverage ratio (#27)	8.29	8.58	8.25	9.68	11.57
Total asset turnover (#28)	1.22	1.22	1.12	1.12	1.13
Inventory turnover (#29)	*	*	*	5.97	5.66
Receivables turnover (#30)	*	*	*	4.90	4.90
Total liabilities to net worth (#31)	1.30	1.22	2.50	2.28	1.94
Debt ratio (#32)	43.45	54.95	71.45	69.50	65.97
Return on assets (#33)	10.90	10.90	8.00	9.30	10.40
Return on equity (#34)	14.90	14.20	17.40	19.00	18.90
Return before interest on equity (#35)	25.10	24.20	28.00	30.60	21.80
Profit margin before tax (#36)	8.50	8.60	7.10	8.30	9.20
Profit margin after tax (#37)	5.00	5.00	4.40	5.20	5.70

*The data needed to calculate these ratios are not available in Rockwell's 1994 annual report.

DISCUSSION QUESTIONS

14-22. Where do you think you could find the details on Rockwell's current assets needed to provide the ratio values missing from Exhibit 14-7?

Different users would zero in on different parts of the analysis in Exhibit 14-7, depending on their individual perspective. Short-term creditors, for example, would probably be most interested in the liquidity ratios. Long-term creditors and stockholders would probably focus on the solvency ratios, but they would certainly also pay attention to the profitability ratios. Rockwell's management, of course, would be interested in all of these ratios.

Our five-year analysis of Rockwell's ratios can be used to accomplish a couple of things, both of which grow out of the industry comparisons we did earlier. First, we can analyze the Rockwell ratios that were about the same as those for the entire electronics industry and those for companies with assets over $250 million. We want to see if those 1994 Rockwell ratios are representative of the company's performance over the five-year period. Of the 14 ratios in our industry analysis, there were 8 for which Rockwell's results were about the same as the industry averages. Rockwell's five-year results for those ratios are presented in Exhibit 14-8.

Exhibit 14-8
Rockwell's Ratios That Were
Comparable to Industry Averages

	1990	1991	1992	1993	1994
Current ratio (#24)	1.24	1.45	1.55	1.68	1.63
Quick ratio (#25)	*	*	*	1.01	.96
Net sales to working capital (#26) ...	12.62	7.62	6.32	5.42	5.83
Total asset turnover (#28)	1.22	1.22	1.12	1.12	1.13
Receivables turnover (#30)	*	*	*	4.90	4.90
Return on assets (#33)	10.90	10.90	8.00	9.30	10.40
Profit margin before tax (#36)	8.50	8.60	7.10	8.30	9.20
Profit margin after tax (#37)	5.00	5.00	4.40	5.20	5.70

*The data needed to calculate these ratios are not available in Rockwell's 1994 annual report.

As the presentation in Exhibit 14-8 indicates, these ratios are fairly consistent over the five year period. One exception is the net sales to working capital ratio (#26) for 1990, which is very high relative to the other four years. Since our purpose is to determine if Rockwell's 1994 results are representative of recent company performance, one unusually high ratio in 1990 does not warrant further investigation. We are satisfied that Rockwell's 1994 results for these eight ratios are representative of the company's performance in recent years.

The second group of ratio values from Exhibit 14-6 that we will examine more closely consists of the six ratios for which Rockwell's 1994 results were significantly different from those of the entire electronics industry and those for companies of comparable asset size. Rockwell's five-year results for those ratios are presented in Exhibit 14-9.

Exhibit 14-9
Ratios for Which Rockwell's
1994 Results Were Significantly
Different from Industry Averages

	1990	1991	1992	1993	1994
Coverage ratio (#27)	8.29	8.58	8.25	9.68	11.57
Inventory turnover (#29)	*	*	*	5.97	5.66
Total liabilities to net worth (#31)	1.30	1.22	2.50	2.28	1.94
Debt ratio (#32)	43.45	54.95	71.45	69.50	65.97
Return on equity (#34)	14.90	14.20	17.40	19.00	18.90
Return before interest on equity (#35)	25.10	24.20	28.00	30.60	21.80

*The data needed to calculate this ratio are not available in Rockwell's 1994 annual report.

The analysis presented in Exhibit 14-9 reveals some interesting information about Rockwell. The coverage ratio (#27) increased fairly steadily over the five-year period. Remember that many experts recommend a coverage ratio of at least 4. Rockwell's coverage ratio is at least twice that in all the years of the analysis. This should be viewed as a positive. The other five ratios in this analysis are directly or indirectly tied to the amount of Rockwell's debt load.

Of particular interest to us is the debt ratio over the five years. Clearly, the proportion of Rockwell's assets financed by borrowing increased from 1990 to 1992. Then, as you can see, that proportion declined in 1993 and 1994. Once again, it is helpful to look at this ratio in the context of the balance sheet equation:

1990				
Assets	=	Liabilities	+	Owners' Equity
100%	=	43.45%	+	56.55%

1992				
Assets	=	Liabilities	+	Owners' Equity
100%	=	71.45%	+	28.55%

1994				
Assets	=	Liabilities	+	Owners' Equity
100%	=	65.97%	+	34.03%

DISCUSSION QUESTIONS

14-23. What concerns do you think the following categories of financial statement users might have about the relative proportion of assets financed by debt and equity:

   a. Long-term creditors?
   b. Stockholders?

Based on Rockwell's financial data over the last five years, we can conclude that the company has been reducing its overall debt load since 1992. This is evident from the trend seen in both the debt ratio and the total liabilities to net worth ratio. Even at the peak of the company's level of debt financing (1992), Rockwell's coverage ratio suggests that making periodic interest payments was not a problem. This is an example that illustrates the principle that no conclusion should be drawn based on a single ratio value.

The ratios in this chapter and others you will work with in the future are interrelated. Any conclusions drawn from ratio analysis must consider the company's overall financial position and performance rather than one aspect alone. Moreover, as we pointed out in the section on gathering background information, you cannot make full use of financial information unless you consider such external factors as general economic conditions and expectations, political events and political climate, and industry outlook.

LIMITATIONS OF RATIO ANALYSIS

Ratio analysis is a splendid tool for gathering additional information about a company, but it does have its limitations:

1. *Attempting to predict the future using past results is problematic at best.* Changes in the general economy, in the economy of the particular industry being studied, and in management are just some of the uncertainties that can cause past results to be an unreliable predictor of the future.

2. *The financial statements used as the basis of the ratios are based on historical cost.* In a time of changing prices, this makes comparison between years difficult.

3. *Figures from the balance sheet (i.e., assets, liabilities) used in the calculation of the ratios are year-end numbers.* Since most businesses have their fiscal year-end when business is slow, the balances in such accounts as receivables, payables, and inventory at year-end may not be representative of the rest of the year. Some analysts suggest using averages (i.e., average current assets for the year). However, even when this approach is taken, the problem is not eliminated, for averages are typically based on year-end numbers from two consecutive years.

4. *Comparing the ratios of a company in one industry with those of a company in another industry is difficult because industry peculiarities will cause the ratios to differ.* Even comparison of companies within an industry may not be reasonable at times because different companies use different accounting methods (e.g., depreciation methods).

5. *There are no hard-and-fast rules telling the analyst what numbers to use to calculate the ratios.* We discussed this problem when we presented the quick ratio and the debt ratio. Lack of uniformity concerning what is to be included in the calculation of ratios makes comparison extremely difficult.

Perhaps the greatest single limitation of ratio analysis is that people tend to place too much reliance on the ratios. Financial ratios should not be viewed as a magical checklist in the evaluation process. Ratio analysis is only a fraction of the information decision makers should consider when making credit, investment, and similar types of decisions.

SUMMARY

In response to the need to reduce uncertainty in the decision-making process, several analytical techniques have been developed to assist economic decision makers as they evaluate financial statement information. Three major categories of financial statement users are creditors (short-term and long-term), equity investors (present and potential), and company management. Because their objectives vary, their perspectives on the results of financial statement analysis will differ.

Three external factors—general economic conditions and expectations, political events and political climate, and industry outlook—impact business performance and should be considered when evaluating results of any type of financial statement analysis.

One very important method of financial statement analysis is ratio analysis, a technique for analyzing the relationship between two items from a company's financial statements for a given period. Ratios are computed by dividing the dollar amount of one item from the financial statements by the dollar amount of the other item from the statements.

A great many ratios have been developed over time to help economic decision makers assess a company's financial health. Since not all ratios are relevant in a given decision situation, care must be taken to select appropriate ratios to analyze. It also must be understood that ratio values, in and of themselves, have very little meaning. They only become meaningful when compared to other relevant information, such as industry averages or the company's ratio values from other years.

Financial ratios can be broadly classified as profitability ratios, liquidity ratios, and solvency ratios. Profitability ratios attempt to measure the ease with which companies generate income. Liquidity ratios are designed to measure a company's ability to generate positive cash flow in the short run to pay off short-term liabilities. Solvency ratios are intended to measure a company's ability to meet the obligations created by its long-term debt.

Each of the profitability, liquidity, and solvency ratios is capable of providing valuable information for both internal decision makers and external decision makers. Ratio analysis, however, has its limitations. Too much reliance on the financial statements and the ratios derived from them is dangerous and potentially disastrous to decision makers. Ratio analysis is a tool. As with the other tools we have discussed throughout this book, it must be used wisely and in the proper context.

Key Terms

acid test ratio Another name for the quick ratio. (p. 475)

coverage ratio A solvency ratio that provides an indication of a company's ability to make its periodic interest payments. (p. 480)

current ratio A liquidity ratio that measures a company's ability to meet short-term obligations by comparing current assets to current liabilities. (p. 474)

debt ratio A solvency ratio that indicates what proportion of a company's assets is financed by debt. (p. 478)

equity investors Those who purchase an ownership interest in a company. One of the three major categories of financial statement users. (p. 460)

financial statement analysis The process of looking beyond the face of the financial statements to gather more information. (p. 459)

inventory turnover ratio A liquidity ratio that indicates how long a company holds its inventory. (p. 477)

liquidity The ease with which an item, such as an asset, can be converted to cash. The liquidity of a firm refers to the company's ability to generate sufficient cash to meet its short-term obligations. (p. 473)

liquidity ratios A set of ratios developed to measure a firm's ability to generate sufficient cash in the short run to retire short-term liabilities. (p. 474)

long-term creditors Banks, corporate bondholders, and any others who lend money for extended periods of time, often up to 40 years. Together with short-term creditors, one of the three major categories of financial statement users. (p. 460)

management The people responsible for a company's day-to-day operation. One of the three major categories of financial statement users. (p. 461)

net sales to working capital ratio A ratio used to measure the level of sales generated from a given level of working capital. (p. 476)

net worth The difference between assets and liabilities. More commonly called *owners' equity*. (p. 479)

profit margin after income tax ratio A profitability ratio that measures the earnings produced from a given level of revenues by comparing net income after income tax to the revenue figure. (p. 472)

profit margin before income tax ratio A profitability ratio that measures the earnings produced from a given level of revenues by comparing net income before income tax to the revenue figure. (p. 470)

profitability The ease with which a company generates income. (p. 469)

profitability ratios A set of ratios developed to predict a firm's ability to generate sufficient profits (and ultimately cash) to fulfill its obligations. (p. 469)

quick ratio A liquidity ratio that is similar to the current ratio, but a more stringent test of liquidity, because only current assets considered to be highly liquid (quickly converted to cash) are included in the calculation. Also called the acid test ratio. (p. 475)

ratio analysis A technique for analyzing the relationship between two items from a company's financial statements for a given period. (p. 459)

receivables turnover ratio A liquidity ratio that measures how quickly a company collects its accounts receivable. (p. 476)

return before interest on equity ratio A profitability ratio that measures the level of earnings (before the cost of borrowing) generated from a given level of equity. (p. 473)

return on assets ratio A profitability ratio that measures the return earned on a company's investment in assets. (p. 470)

return on equity ratio A profitability ratio that measures the after-tax net income generated from a given level of investment by a company's owners. (p. 473)

short-term creditors Creditors who lend money, expecting repayment within one year. Together with long-term creditors, one of the three major categories of financial statement users. (p. 460)

solvency A company's ability to meet the obligations created by its long-term debt. (p. 478)

solvency ratios A set of ratios developed to measure a firm's ability to meet its long-term debt obligations. (p. 478)

times interest earned ratio Another name for the coverage ratio. (p. 480)

total asset turnover ratio A profitability ratio that indicates the amount of revenues produced for a given level of assets used. (p. 471)

total liabilities to net worth ratio A solvency ratio indicating the relationship between creditors' claims to a company's assets and the owners' claim to those assets. (p. 479)

trade creditors Short-term creditors who sell goods and services to companies in the normal course of business. (p. 460)

working capital The difference between current assets and current liabilities. (p. 476)

REVIEW THE FACTS

A. What is the purpose of financial statement analysis?

B. List the three financial statement user groups discussed in the chapter and describe what each group hopes to learn from financial statement analysis.

C. Describe the three types of external factors the Financial Accounting Standards Board (FASB) warns users of financial information to consider, and explain how each factor can impact a company's performance.

D. From which financial statements are components of the ratios discussed in the chapter drawn?

E. What is profitability?

F. List the six profitability ratios discussed in the chapter. For each one, describe the calculation used and the purpose of the ratio.

G. What are the two component ratios of the return on assets?

H. What is liquidity?

I. List the five liquidity ratios discussed in the chapter. For each one, describe the calculation used and the purpose of the ratio.

J. What is the difference between the current ratio and the quick ratio? What is the purpose in examining both?

K. What is solvency?

L. List the three solvency ratios discussed in the chapter. For each one, describe the calculation used and the purpose of the ratio.

M. How are the debt ratio and total liabilities to net worth related?

N. What information can be gathered from calculating a company's coverage ratio?

O. Briefly describe the purpose and meaning of SIC codes.

P. Describe what additional information can be gleaned from an industry comparison of a company's ratios.

Q. What is the purpose of conducting a comparison among a company's ratio values from several recent years?

R. Describe the six limitations of ratio analysis discussed in the chapter.

APPLY WHAT YOU HAVE LEARNED

14-24. Listed below are some items relating to the concepts presented in this chapter, followed by definitions of those items in scrambled order:

a. Financial statement analysis

b. Ratio analysis

c. Short-term creditors

d. Long-term creditors

e. Stockholders

f. Management

g. Profitability

h. Profitability ratios

i. Liquidity

j. Liquidity ratios

k. Solvency

l. Solvency ratios

m. Standard Industrial Classification

1. ____ Designed to measure a firm's ability to generate sufficient cash to meet its short-term obligations.

2. ____ A method for analyzing the relationship between two items from a company's financial statements for a given period.

3. ____ Designed to measure the ease with which a company generates income.

4. ____ Focus on interest payments and the overall debt load a company carries.

5. ____ A system of four-digit codes to indicate a company's industry.

6. ____ Looking beyond the face of the financial statements to gather additional information.

7. ____ Those who own an equity interest in a corporation.

8. ____ The ease with which an item, such as an asset, can be converted into cash.

9. ____ Trade creditors and lending institutions such as banks.

10. ____ A company's ability to meet the obligations created by its long-term debt.

11. ____ Bondholders and lending institutions such as banks.

12. ____ The ease with which companies generate income.

13. ____ Responsible for a company's day-to-day operations.

REQUIRED:

Match the letter next to each item on the list with the appropriate definition. Each letter will be used only once.

14-25. Listed below are all the ratios discussed in this chapter, followed by explanations of what the ratios are designed to measure in scrambled order.

a. Return on assets

b. Profit margin before income tax

c. Profit margin after income tax

d. Total asset turnover

e. Current ratio

f. Quick ratio

g. Net sales to working capital

h. Debt ratio

i. Coverage ratio

j. Return on equity

k. Return before interest on equity

l. Receivables turnover

m. Inventory turnover

n. Total liabilities to net worth

1. ____ Most common ratio used to measure a company's ability to meet short-term obligations.
2. ____ Measures a company's ability to make periodic interest payments.
3. ____ Measures the return earned on investment in assets.
4. ____ A more stringent test of short-term liquidity than the current ratio.
5. ____ Measures the pretax earnings produced from a given level of revenues.
6. ____ Measures the amount of after-tax net income generated by a dollar of sales.
7. ____ Measures the level of sales a company generated using its working capital.
8. ____ Indicates the proportion of assets financed by debt.
9. ____ Measures a company's ability to generate revenues from a given level of assets.
10. ____ Compares the amount of debt financing with the amount of equity financing.
11. ____ Measures how much after-tax income was generated for a given level of equity investment.
12. ____ Indicates how long a company holds its inventory.
13. ____ Measures the return on equity before the cost of borrowing.
14. ____ Measures how quickly a company collects amounts owed to it by its customers.

REQUIRED:

Match the letter next to each item on the list with the appropriate explanation. Each letter will be used only once.

14-26. Listed below are all the ratios discussed in this chapter.

1. ___ Return on assets
2. ___ Debt ratio
3. ___ Profit margin before income tax
4. ___ Quick ratio
5. ___ Total asset turnover
6. ___ Current ratio
7. ___ Net sales to working capital
8. ___ Coverage ratio
9. ___ Return on equity
10. ___ Receivables turnover
11. ___ Return before interest on equity
12. ___ Inventory turnover
13. ___ Total liabilities to net worth
14. ___ Profit margin after income tax

REQUIRED:

Identify each of the 14 ratios as a profitability ratio, a liquidity ratio, or a solvency ratio by responding "P," "L," or "S" for each item.

14-27. Presented below are partial comparative balance sheets of Reggie Company at December 31, 1996 and 1995:

REGGIE COMPANY
Partial Balance Sheets
December 31, 1996, and December 31, 1995
Current Assets and Current Liabilities Only
(in thousands)

	1996	1995
Current Assets:		
Cash	$ 3,400	$ 2,920
Accounts Receivable	1,825	2,212
Merchandise Inventory	1,170	966
Prepaid Expenses	240	270
Total Current Assets	$ 6,635	$ 6,368
Current Liabilities:		
Accounts Payable	$ 2,321	$ 1,740
Notes Payable	3,100	3,300
Total Current Liabilities	$ 5,421	$ 5,040

REQUIRED:

a. Calculate Reggie's current ratios for 1996 and 1995.

b. Calculate Reggie's quick ratios for 1996 and 1995.

c. Which financial statement users are most interested in these two sets of ratios? Explain why the ratios are considered important to these users.

d. Assume that the average company in Reggie's industry has a current ratio of 2:1 and a quick ratio of 1.25:1. If you were evaluating Reggie's liquidity, what could you learn by comparing Reggie's ratios to the industry averages?

14-28. Presented below are partial comparative balance sheets of Halifax Company at December 31, 1996 and 1995:

HALIFAX COMPANY
Partial Balance Sheets
December 31, 1996, and December 31, 1995
Current Assets and Current Liabilities Only
(in thousands)

	1996	1995
Current Assets:		
Cash	$ 2,110	$ 2,650
Accounts Receivable	1,254	977
Merchandise Inventory	730	856
Prepaid Expenses	127	114
Total Current Assets	$ 4,221	$ 4,597
Current Liabilities:		
Accounts Payable	$ 1,054	$ 1,330
Notes Payable	2,100	1,750
Total Current Liabilities	$ 3,154	$ 3,080

REQUIRED:

a. Calculate Halifax's current ratios for 1996 and 1995.

b. Calculate Halifax's quick ratios for 1996 and 1995.

c. Which financial statement users are most interested in these two sets of ratios? Explain why the ratios are considered important to these users.

d. Assume that the average company in Halifax's industry has a current ratio of 2.5:1 and a quick ratio of 1:1. If you were evaluating Halifax's liquidity, what could you learn by comparing Halifax's ratios to those of the industry averages?

e. What, if anything, could you determine by comparing Halifax's current ratio and quick ratio for 1995 with the same ratios for 1996? Explain your reasoning.

14-29. A five-year comparative analysis of George Souval Company's current ratio and quick ratio looks like this:

	1990	1991	1992	1993	1994
Current ratio	1.24	1.95	2.55	3.68	4.13
Quick ratio	1.20	1.06	.96	.77	.51

REQUIRED:

a. What does this analysis tell you about the overall liquidity of Souval Company over the five-year period?

b. What does this analysis tell you about what has happened to the composition of Souval's current assets over the five-year period?

14-30. A five-year comparative analysis of Dale Simon Company's current ratio and quick ratio looks like this:

	1990	1991	1992	1993	1994
Current ratio	4.24	3.95	2.95	2.68	1.93
Quick ratio	.51	.86	1.03	1.33	1.68

REQUIRED:

a. What does this analysis tell you about the overall liquidity of Simon Company over the five-year period?

b. What does this analysis tell you about what has happened to the composition of Simon's current assets over the five-year period?

14-31. A five-year comparative analysis of Margene "Muggsey" Morgan Company's profit margin before tax and profit margin after tax looks like this:

	1990	1991	1992	1993	1994
Profit margin before tax	3.68	4.61	6.88	7.96	9.87
Profit margin after tax	2.22	2.95	4.41	5.27	7.09

REQUIRED:

a. What does this analysis indicate about Morgan's performance over the five-year period?

b. Which of the following would be interested in this analysis? Include in your answer a brief discussion of how you think each of them would interpret this analysis.

   (1) Trade creditors

   (2) Long-term creditors

   (3) Stockholders

14-32. A five-year comparative analysis of Colleen Gailey Company's profit margin before tax and profit margin after tax looks like this:

	1990	1991	1992	1993	1994
Profit margin before tax	11.28	9.16	8.48	7.01	5.78
Profit margin after tax	9.33	8.59	6.14	5.72	3.89

REQUIRED:

a. What does this analysis indicate about Gailey's performance over the five-year period?

b. Which of the following would be interested in this analysis? Include in your answer a brief discussion of how you think each of them would interpret this analysis.

    (1) Trade creditors

    (2) Long-term creditors

    (3) Stockholders

14-33. A five-year comparative analysis of Sybel Kauffman Company's total liabilities to net worth ratio and debt ratio looks like this:

	1990	1991	1992	1993	1994
Total liabilities to net worth	2.75	2.50	2.25	1.50	1.00
Debt ratio	73.33	71.43	69.23	60.00	50.00

REQUIRED:

a. What does this analysis indicate about Kauffman's capital structure over the five-year period?

b. Which of the following would be interested in this analysis? Include in your answer a brief discussion of how you think each of them would interpret this analysis.

    (1) Trade creditors

    (2) Long-term creditors

    (3) Stockholders

14-34. A five-year comparative analysis of Peggy Beezley Company's total liabilities to net worth ratio and debt ratio looks like this:

	1990	1991	1992	1993	1994
Total liabilities to net worth	1.50	1.15	2.65	2.25	1.90
Debt ratio	60.00	53.49	72.60	69.23	65.52

REQUIRED:

a. What does this analysis indicate about Beezley's capital structure over the five-year period?

b. Which of the following would be interested in this analysis? Include in your answer a brief discussion of how you think each of them would interpret this analysis.

   (1) Trade creditors

   (2) Long-term creditors

   (3) Stockholders

14-35. Presented on page 509 are the comparative balance sheets for Hogle Company at December 31, 1996 and 1995. Also included is Hogle's income statement for the year ended December 31, 1996.

REQUIRED:

Calculate the following ratios for 1996:

   (1) Return on assets

   (2) Profit margin before income tax

   (3) Total asset turnover

   (4) Profit margin after income tax

   (5) Return on equity

   (6) Return before interest on equity

   (7) Current ratio

   (8) Quick ratio

   (9) Net sales to working capital

  (10) Receivables turnover

  (11) Inventory turnover

  (12) Debt ratio

  (13) Total liabilities to net worth

  (14) Coverage ratio

HOGLE COMPANY
Balance Sheets
December 31, 1996 and December 31, 1995
(in thousands)

ASSETS:	1996	1995
Current Assets:		
Cash	$ 1,618	$ 1,220
Accounts Receivable	1,925	2,112
Merchandise Inventory	1,070	966
Prepaid Expenses	188	149
Total Current Assets	$ 4,801	$ 4,447
Plant and Equipment:		
Buildings, Net	$ 4,457	$ 2,992
Equipment, Net	1,293	1,045
Total Plant and Equipment	$ 5,750	$ 4,037
Total Assets	$10,551	$ 8,484
LIABILITIES:		
Current Liabilities:		
Accounts Payable	$ 1,818	$ 1,686
Notes Payable	900	1,100
Total Current Liabilities	$ 2,718	$ 2,786
Long-Term Liabilities	2,500	2,000
Total Liabilities	$ 5,218	$ 4,786
STOCKHOLDERS' EQUITY:		
Common Stock, No Par Value	$ 3,390	$ 2,041
Retained Earnings	1,943	1,657
Total Stockholders' Equity	$ 5,333	$ 3,698
Total Liabilities and Stockholders' Equity	$10,551	$ 8,484

HOGLE COMPANY
Income Statement
For the Year Ended December 31, 1996
(in thousands)

Sales Revenue		$11,228
LESS: Cost of Goods Sold		7,751
Gross Profit on Sales		$ 3,477
LESS: Operating Expenses:		
Depreciation—Buildings and Equipment	$ 102	
Other Selling and Administrative	2,667	
Total Expenses		(2,769)
Income Before Interest and Taxes		$ 708
LESS: Interest Expense		(168)
Income Before Taxes		$ 540
Income Taxes		(114)
Net Income		$ 426

14-36. Presented on page 511 are the comparative balance sheets for Brandywine Company at December 31, 1996 and 1995 and the income statements for the years ended December 31, 1996 and 1995.

REQUIRED:

a. Calculate the following ratios for 1996 and 1995:

   (1) Return on assets

   (2) Profit margin before income tax

   (3) Total asset turnover

   (4) Profit margin after income tax

   (5) Return on equity

   (6) Return before interest on equity

   (7) Current ratio

   (8) Quick ratio

   (9) Net sales to working capital

   (10) Receivables turnover

   (11) Inventory turnover

   (12) Debt ratio

   (13) Total liabilities to net worth

   (14) Coverage ratio

b. Using the ratios you calculated in the previous requirement, complete the following comparison of Brandywine's ratios to those of its entire industry and companies of comparable asset size for 1996.

	Total Industry	Assets Between $5 Million and $10 Million	Brandywine
Current ratio	1.46	1.95	
Quick ratio	.93	1.11	
Net sales to working capital	6.42	5.78	
Coverage ratio	5.63	5.16	
Total asset turnover	1.76	1.42	
Inventory turnover	5.73	5.47	
Receivables turnover	7.83	6.54	
Total liabilities to net worth	1.94	1.93	
Debt ratio	65.99	65.87	
Return on assets	9.30	10.40	
Return on equity	6.12	5.85	
Return before interest on equity	8.92	9.73	
Profit margin before tax	6.27	5.88	
Profit margin after tax	4.99	4.61	

(Requirement c. is on page 512.)

BRANDYWINE COMPANY
Balance Sheets
December 31, 1996 and December 31, 1995
(in thousands)

ASSETS:	1996	1995
Current Assets:		
Cash	$ 1,292	$ 980
Accounts Receivable	1,068	1,112
Merchandise Inventory	970	906
Prepaid Expenses	88	109
Total Current Assets	$ 3,418	$ 3,107
Plant and Equipment:		
Buildings, Net	$ 3,457	$ 2,442
Equipment, Net	993	945
Total Plant and Equipment	$ 4,450	$ 3,387
Total Assets	$ 7,868	$ 6,494
LIABILITIES:		
Current Liabilities:		
Accounts Payable	$ 998	$ 786
Notes Payable	600	500
Total Current Liabilities	$ 1,598	$ 1,286
Long-Term Liabilities	837	467
Total Liabilities	$ 2,435	$ 1,753
STOCKHOLDERS' EQUITY:		
Common Stock, No Par Value	$ 2,490	$ 2,000
Retained Earnings	2,943	2,741
Total Stockholders' Equity	$ 5,433	$ 4,741
Total Liabilities and Stockholders' Equity	$ 7,868	$ 6,494

BRANDYWINE COMPANY
Income Statements
For the Years Ended December 31, 1996 and 1995
(in thousands)

	1996	1995
Sales Revenue	$ 9,228	$ 8,765
LESS: Cost of Goods Sold	6,751	6,097
Gross Profit on Sales	$ 2,477	$ 2,668
LESS: Operating Expenses:		
Depreciation—Buildings and Equipment	$ 80	$ 56
Other Selling and Administrative	1,667	1,442
Total Expenses	$ (1,747)	$(1,498)
Income Before Interest and Taxes	$ 730	$ 1,170
LESS: Interest Expense	(98)	(89)
Income Before Taxes	$ 632	$ 1,081
Income Taxes	(190)	(357)
Net Income	$ 442	$ 724

c. Analyze the industry comparison you completed in the previous requirement as follows:

   (1) Identify any ratios you think *do not* warrant further analysis. Be sure to explain why any particular ratio is *not* going to be analyzed further.

   (2) For those ratios you felt deserved further analysis, assess whether Brandywine's ratios are better or worse relative to both the entire industry and companies of comparable asset size.

14-37. Presented below is a comparison of Eastwood Company's ratios for the years 1992 through 1996.

	1992	1993	1994	1995	1996
Current ratio	1.77	1.91	2.93	2.41	3.12
Quick ratio	1.40	1.26	1.08	.94	.79
Net sales to working capital	10.33	9.89	9.43	7.67	5.19
Coverage ratio	6.90	6.91	5.76	5.24	3.49
Total asset turnover	1.46	1.40	1.17	1.08	.99
Inventory turnover	8.88	8.24	8.11	6.46	4.45
Receivables turnover	8.93	7.41	6.52	5.87	5.34
Total liabilities to net worth	.96	1.22	1.97	2.21	2.54
Debt ratio	48.97	54.95	66.33	68.85	71.75
Return on assets	9.28	8.44	8.20	7.68	6.21
Return on equity	8.31	8.06	7.22	6.38	4.77
Return before interest on equity	9.98	9.56	8.80	8.43	5.71
Profit margin before tax	10.00	9.45	8.27	7.78	4.12
Profit margin after tax	8.66	7.90	7.14	6.52	2.28

REQUIRED:

Analyze the five-year company comparison as follows:

  a. Identify any ratios you think *do not* warrant further analysis. Be sure to explain why any particular ratio is *not* going to be analyzed further.

  b. For each ratio you felt deserved further analysis, assess whether it has improved or gotten worse over the five-year period.

  c. Based on your analysis of the five-year company comparison, comment briefly on the trend of Eastwood Company's performance over the five-year period.

Applications 14-38 through 14-42 are based on the following comparative financial statements of Ross Atkinson and Company:

ROSS ATKINSON and COMPANY
Balance Sheets
December 31, 1996 and December 31, 1995
(in thousands)

ASSETS:		1996		1995
Current Assets:				
Cash		$ 2,240		$ 1,936
Accounts Receivable		2,340		2,490
Merchandise Inventory		776		693
Prepaid Expenses		200		160
Total Current Assets		$ 5,556		$ 5,279
Plant and Equipment:				
Buildings	$ 7,723		$ 6,423	
LESS:Accumulated Depreciation	(3,677)		(3,534)	
Buildings, Net		$ 4,046		$ 2,889
Equipment	$ 2,687		$ 2,387	
LESS:Accumulated Depreciation	(1,564)		(1,523)	
Equipment, Net		1,123		864
Total Plant and Equipment		$ 5,169		$ 3,753
Total Assets		$10,725		$ 9,032
LIABILITIES:				
Current Liabilities:				
Accounts Payable		$ 1,616		$ 1,080
Notes Payable		2,720		2,920
Total Current Liabilities		$ 4,336		$ 4,000
Long-Term Liabilities		2,000		1,600
Total Liabilities		$ 6,336		$ 5,600
STOCKHOLDERS' EQUITY:				
Common Stock, No Par Value		$ 3,000		$ 2,400
Retained Earnings		1,389		1,032
Total Stockholders' Equity		$ 4,389		$ 3,432
Total Liabilities and Stockholders' Equity		$10,725		$ 9,032

ROSS ATKINSON and COMPANY
Income Statements
For the Years Ended December 31, 1996 and 1995
(in thousands)

		1996		1995
Sales Revenue		$14,745		$12,908
LESS: Cost of Goods Sold		10,213		8,761
Gross Profit on Sales		$ 4,532		$ 4,147
LESS: Operating Expenses:				
Advertising and Sales Commissions	$ 1,022		$ 546	
General and Administrative	2,721		2,451	
Total Expenses		(3,743)		(2,997)
Income Before Interest and Taxes		$ 789		$ 1,150
LESS: Interest Expense		(172)		(137)
Income Before Taxes		$ 617		$ 1,013
LESS: Income Taxes		(123)		(355)
Net Income		$ 494		$ 658

14-38. REQUIRED:

Using the Atkinson and Company financial statements, calculate the following ratios for 1996 and 1995:

  (1) Return on assets

  (2) Profit margin before income tax

  (3) Total asset turnover

  (4) Profit margin after income tax

  (5) Return on equity

  (6) Return before interest on equity

  (7) Current ratio

  (8) Quick ratio

  (9) Net sales to working capital

  (10) Receivables turnover

  (11) Inventory turnover

  (12) Debt ratio

  (13) Total liabilities to net worth

  (14) Coverage ratio

14-39. Presented below is a partially completed comparison of Atkinson's ratios to those of its entire industry and companies of comparable asset size for 1996.

	Total Industry	Assets Between $10 Million and $25 Million	Atkinson
Current ratio	2.24	1.95	
Quick ratio	1.33	1.31	
Net sales to working capital	7.22	9.38	
Coverage ratio	5.43	3.16	
Total asset turnover	1.76	1.42	
Inventory turnover	5.78	5.77	
Receivables turnover	7.83	6.54	
Total liabilities to net worth	2.28	1.94	
Debt ratio	69.51	65.99	
Return on assets	9.30	10.40	
Return on equity	16.12	15.85	
Return before interest on equity	11.11	11.73	
Profit margin before tax	6.67	3.88	
Profit margin after tax	4.49	2.61	

REQUIRED:

a. Complete the industry comparison by calculating each of Atkinson and Company's ratios for 1996 and recording them in the space provided. (*Note*: If you have completed Application 14-38, you have already done the calculations. Just use the ratios you have already calculated.)

b. Analyze the industry comparison you completed in the previous requirement as follows:

    (1) Identify any ratios you think *do not* warrant further analysis. Be sure to explain why any particular ratio is *not* going to be analyzed further.

    (2) For those ratios you felt deserved further analysis, assess whether Atkinson's ratios are better or worse relative to both the entire industry and companies of comparable asset size.

    (3) Based on your analysis of the industry comparison, comment briefly on how you think Atkinson and Company compares to other companies in its industry.

14-40. Presented below is a partially completed comparison of Atkinson's ratios for the years 1992 through 1996.

	1992	1993	1994	1995	1996
Current ratio	2.07	2.62	1.79		
Quick ratio	1.00	1.09	1.01		
Net sales to working capital	9.33	8.41	9.97		
Coverage ratio	6.31	5.44	4.48		
Total asset turnover	1.11	1.86	1.34		
Inventory turnover	10.88	11.37	11.81		
Receivables turnover	4.80	4.99	5.10		
Total liabilities to net worth	1.22	1.65	1.61		
Debt ratio	54.95	62.26	61.69		
Return on assets	5.22	6.11	5.34		
Return on equity	10.98	11.62	11.05		
Return before interest on equity	14.48	13.77	15.43		
Profit margin before tax	4.68	4.12	4.44		
Profit margin after tax	3.06	3.16	3.31		

REQUIRED:

a. Complete the five-year company comparison by calculating each of Atkinson's ratios for 1995 and 1996 and recording them in the space provided. (*Note:* If you have completed Application 14-38 you have already done the calculations. Just use the ratios you have already calculated.)

b. Analyze the five-year company comparison you completed in the previous requirement as follows:

(1) Identify any ratios you think *do not* warrant further analysis. Be sure to explain why any particular ratio is *not* going to be analyzed further.

(2) For each ratio you felt deserved further analysis, assess whether it has improved or gotten worse over the five-year period.

(3) Based on your analysis of the five-year company comparison, comment briefly on the trend of Atkinson and Company's performance over the five-year period.

14-41. This chapter focused on ratio analysis performed on the income statement and the balance sheet. For this reason, the financial statements for Ross Atkinson and Company did not include a statement of cash flows. In order to assess the company's overall performance in 1996, however, you should also look at its statement of cash flows.

REQUIRED:

a. Using the 1995 and 1996 comparative balance sheets and the income statement for 1996, prepare Atkinson's 1996 statement of cash flows.

b. Which of the three broad activities (operating, investing, and financing) provided Atkinson with the majority of its cash during 1996?

c. Briefly discuss whether the activity you identified in the previous requirement is an appropriate source of cash in the long run.

d. In which of the three broad activities (operating, investing, and financing) did Atkinson use most of its cash during 1996?

e. Briefly discuss what your answer to the previous requirement reveals about Atkinson.

14-42. This chapter focused on ratio analysis performed on the income statement and the balance sheet. For this reason, the financial statements for Ross Atkinson and Company did not include a statement of stockholders' equity. In order to assess the company's overall performance in 1996, however, you should also look at the company's statement of stockholders' equity.

REQUIRED:

a. Using the 1995 and 1996 comparative balance sheets and the income statement for 1996, prepare Atkinson's 1996 statement of stockholders' equity.

b. Briefly discuss how the statement of stockholders' equity demonstrates articulation among Atkinson's financial statements.

Applications 14-43 through 14-45 use the financial information from Sara Lee Corporation's 1994 annual report, which was reprinted in the appendix.

14-43. REQUIRED:

Using the Sara Lee Corporation financial statements, calculate the following ratios for 1993 and 1994. (Assume minority interest is part of stockholders' equity.)

(1) Return on assets

(2) Profit margin before income tax

(3) Total asset turnover

(4) Profit margin after income tax

(5) Return on equity

(6) Return before interest on equity

(7) Current ratio

(8) Quick ratio

(9) Net sales to working capital

(10) Receivables turnover

(11) Inventory turnover

(12) Debt ratio

(13) Total liabilities to net worth

(14) Coverage ratio

14-44. REQUIRED:

a. Using the Sara Lee financial statements and the eleven-year financial summary, complete the following five-year company ratio analysis. If you find it impossible to calculate a particular ratio, put an asterisk (*) where the ratio would go. (*Note:* if you have completed Application 14-43, you have already calculated the ratios for 1993 and 1994. Just use the ratios you have already calculated.) (Assume minority interest is part of stockholders' equity.)

	1990	1991	1992	1993	1994
Current ratio					
Quick ratio					
Net sales to working capital					
Coverage ratio					
Total asset turnover					
Inventory turnover					
Receivables turnover					
Total liabilities to net worth					
Debt ratio					
Return on assets					
Return on equity					
Return before interest on equity					
Profit margin before tax					
Profit margin after tax					

b. Analyze the five-year company comparison you completed in the previous requirement as follows:

(1) Identify any ratios you think *do not* warrant further analysis. Be sure to explain why any particular ratio is *not* going to be analyzed further.

(2) For each ratio you felt deserved further analysis, assess whether it has improved or gotten worse over the five-year period.

(3) Based on your analysis of the five-year company comparison, comment briefly on the trend of Sara Lee's performance over the five-year period.

14-45. This application requires a visit to the library. It also requires that your library have the 1994 *Almanac of Business and Industrial Financial Ratios*.

REQUIRED:

a. Go to the library to consult the 1994 *Almanac of Business and Industrial Financial Ratios*. In the *Almanac* find the tables pertaining to Sara Lee's industry. (Use SIC code 2050.)

b. Using the information from Table I ("Corporations with and without Net Income") and the financial statements from Sara Lee's annual report, complete the following industry comparison. (*Note*: If you have completed Application 14-43 or 14-44, you have already done the 1994 calculations for Sara Lee. Just use the ratios you have already calculated.)

	Total Industry	Companies of Comparable Asset Size	Sara Lee
Current ratio			
Quick ratio			
Net sales to working capital			
Coverage ratio			
Total asset turnover			
Inventory turnover			
Receivables turnover			
Total liabilities to net worth			
Debt ratio			
Return on assets			
Return on equity			
Return before interest on equity			
Profit margin before tax			
Profit margin after tax			

d. Analyze the industry comparison you completed in the previous requirement as follows:

   (1) Identify any ratios you think *do not* warrant further analysis. Be sure to explain why any particular ratio is *not* going to be analyzed further.

   (2) For each ratio you felt deserved further analysis, assess whether Sara Lee's ratios are better or worse relative to both the entire industry and companies of comparable asset size.

   (3) Based on your analysis of the industry comparison, comment briefly on how you think Sara Lee compares to other companies in its industry.

14-46. Listed below are the 11 numerical divisions of the Standard Industrial Classification system, followed by the various industries in scrambled order.

a. 01 to 09	**g.** 52 to 59
b. 10 to 14	**h.** 60 to 67
c. 15 to 17	**i.** 70 to 89
d. 20 to 39	**j.** 91 to 97
e. 40 to 49	**k.** 99
f. 50 to 51	

1. ___ Wholesale Trade
2. ___ Construction
3. ___ Public Administration
4. ___ Services
5. ___ Agriculture, Forestry, and Fishing
6. ___ Nonclassifiable Establishments
7. ___ Manufacturing
8. ___ Retail Trade
9. ___ Mining
10. ___ Finance, Insurance, and Real Estate
11. ___ Transportation, Communications, Electric, Gas, and Sanitary Services

REQUIRED:

Match the letter next to each item on the list with the appropriate industry.

14-47. The chapter discussed several limitations of ratio analysis. They were:

(1) Using past results to predict future performance.
(2) Using historical cost as a basis for ratios.
(3) Using year-end balances as either the numerator or denominator for many ratios.
(4) Industry peculiarities.
(5) Lack of uniformity in defining the numerators and denominators used in calculating ratios.
(6) Giving too much credence to ratio analysis.

REQUIRED:

Explain in your own words why each of the six items listed above limit the usefulness of ratio analysis.

Sara Lee Corporation

Annual Report
1994

FINANCIAL HIGHLIGHTS

(in millions except per share data)	Years ended		
	July 2, 1994[1]	July 3, 1993[3]	Change
Results of operations			
Net sales	$15,536	$14,580	6.6%
Net income before restructuring and effect of accounting change	729	704	3.5
Net income after restructuring and effect of accounting change	199	704	(71.8)
Net income per common share before restructuring and effect of accounting change	1.47	1.40	5.0
Net income per common share after restructuring and effect of accounting change	.37	1.40	(73.6)
Average shares outstanding	480	485	(1.1)
Other information			
Capital expenditures	$ 628	$ 728	(13.8)%
Depreciation and amortization	568	522	8.8
Total advertising and promotion expense	1,498	1,455	3.0
Long-term debt	1,496	1,164	28.5
Common stockholders' equity	3,326	3,551	(6.3)
Dividends per common share	.63	.56	11.6
Total-debt-to-total-capital	38.9%	34.9%	
Return on average common stockholders' equity	5.1%[2]	19.6%	

[1] See Notes to Financial Statements regarding the restructuring of the corporation's worldwide
operations and the effect of the change in the method of accounting for income taxes.
[2] Adjusting net income to exclude the effects of the restructuring and the accounting change results
in a return on average common stockholders' equity of 20.5%.
[3] 53-week year.

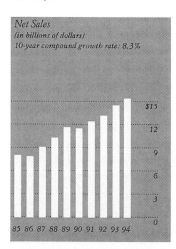

Net Sales
(in billions of dollars)
10-year compound growth rate: 8.3%

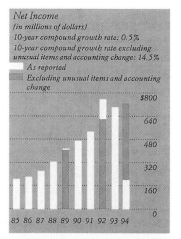

Net Income
(in millions of dollars)
10-year compound growth rate: 0.5%
10-year compound growth rate excluding
unusual items and accounting change: 14.5%
▢ As reported
▢ Excluding unusual items and accounting change

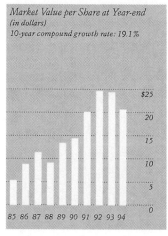

Market Value per Share at Year-end
(in dollars)
10-year compound growth rate: 19.1%

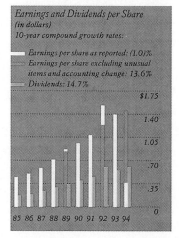

Earnings and Dividends per Share
(in dollars)
10-year compound growth rates:
▢ Earnings per share as reported: (1.0)%
Earnings per share excluding unusual
items and accounting change: 13.6%
▢ Dividends: 14.7%

While fiscal 1994 was certainly a successful year, with sales and operating earnings reaching record levels, it was not a year of "business as usual" at Sara Lee Corporation. In fact, there were several events that made 1994 a notable year.

We reported record financial results, but for the first time in almost two decades, our per share earnings increase failed to meet our internal targets. This shortfall from our plan largely reflected significant weaknesses in our European hosiery and knit products operations. Most of the remaining businesses at Sara Lee reported quite excellent results.

These European Personal Products operations were subjected to aggressive redirection throughout all of fiscal 1994. Many of these realignments were completed by year-end, with particular emphasis on comprehensive management changes and fresh product strategies. In addition, plans were announced to reduce excess capacity over the next few years and to provide for more cost-effective manufacturing and sourcing for these operations. The current fiscal year will, in my judgment, see a major recovery for our hosiery and knit products businesses in Europe.

The second extraordinary event of last year was our decision to undertake a worldwide restructuring program— a program whose primary purpose is to make our worldwide Personal Products businesses more competitive. We have done this at a time when Sara Lee is strong and producing record results. The restructuring program is aimed at

assuring that our Personal Products businesses will continue to produce a high level of future profitability.

Finally, 1994 was notable for key management changes. Our most senior operating officers, Paul Fulton and Cor Boonstra, retired during the year. Both of them have made important and lasting contributions to the development of Sara Lee Corporation. During the year, they were replaced by Steve McMillan and Don Franceschini, who currently serve as executive vice presidents and directors of the corporation.

During his 20 years with Sara Lee, Steve has been highly successful in assuming numerous key operating assignments in the United States and Europe. Don is the former head of Playtex Apparel, with 30 years of world-wide business experience in the branded packaged consumer apparel business, and an impressive record of superior results in that industry. I would encourage you to read their letters in this annual report.

These unusual events of last year, coupled with free trade and other issues within our business environment, have caused Sara Lee management to give careful thought to the broad direction of our company. As such, we have made some subtle, but important, adjustments

to our mission, strategies and financial goals, which we shall pursue in the years ahead. As you may know, our ability and willingness to change have been salient characteristics of Sara Lee for many years. Let me relate our current thoughts with regard to these new directives.

Our commitment to a decentralized operating structure and an entrepreneurial management culture has been tightened by emphasizing in the clearest manner possible that each Sara Lee manager has accountability, responsibility and authority for his or her own profit center. Simply put, we must resist the forces that attempt to make us act like a large company. Our decentralized and entrepreneurial management structure is, and must remain, the most defining managerial attribute of Sara Lee Corporation.

In our second strategy, we have expanded our commitment to our individual consumers and our trade customers by directing our efforts to ensure total satisfaction with our products and services. In this regard, we will diligently balance consumer value with strong brand equity support. Additionally, we shall provide a broader range of new products that offer unique and improved benefits to meet consumer expectations. We are determined to be the industry leader in providing consumer and customer satisfaction.

In our pursuit of global expansion, Sara Lee's third strategy, we shall continue to extend the geographic reach of selected businesses in new and current markets. We have many opportunities to do just that. It is imperative, however, that this expansion be pursued with a clear emphasis on high-return businesses. In today's perilously competitive market-place, with the advent of free trade and free markets, growth must come by way of ventures that rely on strong brands and marketing, and on avoiding the risks inherent in high capital outlays.

Our strong resolve to improve returns, our fourth strategy, is reflected in several ways. We have emphasized this attention to higher returns by adding a return on capital measure; we have increased our return on equity target by two percentage points to 22%; and we have established a materially increased return on investment goal for our Personal Products businesses.

Sara Lee's mission statement has been modified, as well, to incorporate a greater orientation toward brand building — and toward doing so profitably. We at Sara Lee shall always focus our energies on the activity of building brands, for that activity is the principal means we shall employ to the end of creating stockholder value.

Sara Lee has now begun its 1995 fiscal year. As we do that, it is my judgment that the business positions we hold in our marketplaces can be characterized as preeminent in almost every case. We are acutely aware of the challenges and opportunities inherent in being the leader. It is those branded, leadership positions and a committed management team that will take us to another year of record results in 1995.

CORPORATE STRATEGIES

Entrepreneurial Management
We shall employ a decentralized management structure which divides the company into distinct profit centers managed by individuals to whom we delegate a high degree of accountability, responsibility and authority. This structure is designed to produce a highly motivated, results-oriented management.

Consumer and Customer Satisfaction
In each of our product categories we shall be the leader in satisfying our consumers and our trade customers.

Global Expansion
We shall pursue profitable growth by extending the geographic reach of our businesses while continuing to aggressively build our brands in existing markets.

Improved Returns
We shall raise the corporation's return on capital and return on equity, with a particular focus on improving returns in the Personal Products business.

John H. Bryan
Chairman of the Board
and Chief Executive Officer
August 25, 1994

Fiscal 1994 was a year of significant progress and accomplishment for the Packaged Meats and Bakery, Coffee and Grocery, and Household and Personal Care lines of business. Each of these major business groups enjoyed good profit growth, exceeded its plan and posted record profits and returns.

We began the year with a strong cost reduction effort in each business, consistent with our continuing program to improve returns. This effort contributed to significant increases in returns on sales and returns on investment in each business.

Even with a strong focus on returns, we have continued to build our brands. For example, in our Packaged Meats and Bakery business, we increased market shares in essentially every major product category in which we compete. Our continuing ability to improve the returns in our business has provided the funds to invest in new growth opportunities around the world.

Despite a pattern of increasing green coffee prices throughout the year, our Coffee and Grocery business had record returns. We continued to develop our positions in Central Europe and expanded in Scandinavia by increasing our interest in the Norwegian coffee company Friele. In addition, we continued to build our *Pickwick* tea position and enjoyed strong sales growth from our Douwe Egberts and Superior coffee systems organizations that market to restaurants.

The addition of four European processed meats brands, acquired in fiscal 1993, yielded positive results for Sara Lee Meats in fiscal 1994. We continued our expansion outside the United States by acquiring an interest in Kir Alimentos, a leading processed meats company in Mexico. Sara Lee Meats' stable of outstanding brands, including

Hillshire Farm, Jimmy Dean, Ball Park and *Bryan,* produced market share increases in most major categories.

Sara Lee Bakery enjoyed a successful year, driven by very strong growth in the U.S. retail business. *Sara Lee* continues to be the leading frozen baked goods brand in the United States, the United Kingdom and Australia. Propelled by the excellent performance of its core products and new product successes, such as *Sara Lee* Cream Pie and Crumb Coffee Cake, U.S. retail unit volume increased significantly in fiscal 1994.

Sara Lee Bakery is further developing growth opportunities by expanding in Mexico and the Pacific Rim and by introducing a line of fresh baked goods. After only two years in the Mexican market, *Sara Lee* is the best-selling frozen food brand, and in the Asia-Pacific region, Sara Lee Bakery continues to explore new growth opportunities. Fresh baked goods were successfully introduced under the *Sara Lee* brand in California in fiscal 1994.

PYA/Monarch, Sara Lee's foodservice distribution business, posted excellent results in fiscal 1994, with increased sales as well as unit volume growth of 7%. Furthermore, we achieved the highest return on investment in PYA/Monarch's history.

Our decentralized approach to managing our businesses—placing responsibility and authority in the hands of local management—contributed to the further global expansion of our

Household and Personal Care businesses. The acquisition of the *Duschdas, Badedas, Williams* and *Fissan* brands from SmithKline Beecham added significantly to the size and scale of our businesses in key European markets. The performance of these brands exceeded our plans and contributed to a further concentration of the Household and Personal Care business around core categories. Smaller acquisitions in the United States, Greece and China should fuel growth in these markets in fiscal 1995.

Our direct selling operation continued to offer exciting growth prospects as we expanded our business in the Philippines, South Africa, Indonesia and Mexico, and developed a plan for China. In fiscal 1995, direct selling will be one of our fastest-growing businesses.

The strengths and strategies that produced such positive results in fiscal 1994 provide powerful momentum as we enter 1995. We have leading brands and a talented, experienced management team that focuses intensely on meeting its goals. Because of these strengths, we are enthusiastic and have a high degree of confidence that we will generate good results again next year.

C. Steven McMillan
Executive Vice President

Operating results for Sara Lee Personal Products were mixed in fiscal 1994. Strong performances were recorded by U.S. knit products, and worldwide intimates and accessories. Worldwide hosiery and European knit products posted weak results, and plans are in place to improve those businesses.

In North America, very strong performance from our $2 billion knit products business was achieved through double-digit volume growth. The *Hanes* and *Hanes Her Way* megabrand continues to lead the mass-merchandise channels. The exceptional efficiency developed over the years, through investment in vertical integration and state-of-the-art equipment, will continue to provide knit products with a competitive advantage.

Additionally, innovation that delivers preferred products with value to consumers is well under way in our lower-margin fleece business. These improvements, combined with continued strong performance in men's and boys', and women's and girls' underwear, will provide exceptional growth for our knit products business.

In our $1.2 billion North American hosiery business, casual fashion trends led to reduced sales of sheer hosiery and increased sales of opaque legwear and socks. A shift in product mix and deep-discounting practices also put severe pressure on brand values and profitability. Overall results for North American hosiery are expected to improve in fiscal 1995.

Intimates and Accessories, led by the *Playtex, Bali* and *Coach* brands, achieved solid growth in fiscal 1994. Unit volumes for our North American foundations business grew sharply. These businesses should continue their double-digit growth in profitability.

Simply stated, failed market strategies, management issues and deep retail discounting in Europe primarily accounted for the overall performance shortfall in Personal Products. The decline in hosiery sales in a highly competitive and weakened economic environment led to erosion of profit margins. Expensive new product initiatives targeted to expand hosiery sales in a declining market, executional issues in knit products and the high cost of manufacturing in Europe also impacted profit performance.

Sara Lee is the largest hosiery company in Europe, with sales of $735 million and leading positions in France, Germany, the United Kingdom and Italy by virtue of the *Dim, Bellinda, Nur Die, Pretty Polly* and *Filodoro* brands. Knit products—a $200 million business in Europe—includes our *Abanderado* and *Princesa* brands in Spain, which hold the number-one positions in men's and women's underwear, respectively. The *Dim* label leads the men's and women's underwear market in France, while the *Liabel* brand leads in men's underwear in Italy. The *Hanes* brand is a small but growing player in European activewear.

Contrary to the performance issues in hosiery and knit products, European intimate apparel, led by the *Playtex, Dim* and *Wonderbra* brands, posted strong double-digit operating profit growth and achieved a solid unit volume increase for the fiscal year.

Our three European businesses—hosiery, knitwear and intimates—provide us with leading market positions and a substantial competitive edge as we enter fiscal 1995. We have a compre-hensive plan under way in Europe that included a number of key management changes made in the latter half of the fiscal year. We also have implemented new marketing initiatives and will introduce innovative products that provide higher gross margins.

In June 1994, Sara Lee undertook a major restructuring program to reduce costs, eliminate excess capacity and improve sourcing and distribution activities in Personal Products. The vast majority of the $732 million pretax charge relates to the Personal Products business. The program is expected to produce annual savings reaching approximately $250 million in fiscal 1998. Again, the majority of the savings will come from Personal Products. The program will dramatically improve profit performance and enable Personal Products to capitalize on its most recent investments, balance capacity and achieve low-cost producer status.

In closing, 1994 results for several Personal Products businesses were unacceptable, but numerous actions were taken to return these operations to strong, double-digit profit growth in fiscal 1995. We are confident that a sharp focus on higher returns, aggressive advertising and the power of Sara Lee's leading brands will enable us to achieve our goals in fiscal 1995.

Donald J. Franceschini
Executive Vice President

While other companies have seen the strength of their brands eroded in recent years by private-label competition, we at Sara Lee Corporation have held fast to the proposition that the best way to build value for stockholders is to build the value of our brands.

"We're in the business of brands, and we instinctively resist private-label opportunities," states Steve McMillan, executive vice president. "Otherwise, we'd be a supplier today who could be replaced tomorrow. Given a choice between building brands and building plants, we'll invest in our brands every time."

Sara Lee's faith in brands is reinforced by marketplace realities. Despite media reports to the contrary, research shows that sales of private-label products have been flat or have actually shrunk as a percentage of the U.S. market in recent years. One study put domestic private-label sales at 14.7% in 1992, down slightly from a peak of 15.3% a decade ago.

Meanwhile, brand loyalty is on the upswing. Fully 74% of consumers polled by the market research firm Yankelovich Partners in 1993 said they are reluctant to switch brands once they find one they like, up from 71% in 1991. And the Washington, D.C.-based Grocery Manufacturers of America points out that 81 of the 100 best-selling products in U.S. supermarkets are national brands. The comparable figure for drug stores is an even higher 92 out of 100.

Sara Lee's managers recognize two keys to enhancing brand value. The first is to maintain a consistent level of quality that consumers come to rely on and trust. The second is to communicate clearly the benefits that differentiate our brands from competing products.

"A brand is a communications device," says McMillan, who has responsibility for Sara Lee's Packaged Meats and Bakery, Coffee and Grocery, and Household and Personal Care lines of business. "It says to a consumer, 'Here's what you should expect and here's what you're going to get.' Consumers, in fact, create brands."

Executive Vice President Don Franceschini concurs, noting that only "consistent delivery of value to the consumer can ensure that the expectation is in sync with the product benefits."

Franceschini, who oversees Sara Lee Personal Products, believes a brand must have a clearly defined marketplace position—one reinforced by the sum total of its attributes. These include its look, feel, packaging, merchandising in stores and advertising in the media. "A brand should be so consistent in its presentation that no matter where in the world you find it, you know it when you see it," Franceschini contends.

Senior Vice President Jack Ward, who manages Sara Lee Knit Products in North and South America, speaks of this clearly defined market position in terms of a *unique selling proposition.* "There must be a clear image in the consumer's mind of what a brand can do and how it differs from others."

"A brand doesn't truly exist until it exists in the mind of the consumer," asserts Lew Frankfort, senior vice president responsible for Sara Lee's intimate apparel, accessories and Champion activewear businesses. "It then takes on a life all its own. It is a powerful symbol, an attitude, a perception of quality."

Brand acceptance is a barometer of consumer confidence, according to John Bryan, Sara Lee's chairman and chief executive officer. "The value consumers attach to a brand is borne of the confidence they have that the brand will perform as intended," says Bryan. "Only brands enjoy this level of trust with consumers. Manufacturers of branded products have been able to provide exceptionally high quality on a scale unimagined by private-label concerns."

Because this confidence can be maintained only through consumer satisfaction, Sara Lee focuses its efforts on making sure our brands deliver on a commitment to quality. According to Paul Lustig, president and chief executive officer of Sara Lee Bakery worldwide, "We have an ongoing challenge to always live up to the expectations inherent in our name. Satisfying our customers isn't even enough," Lustig believes. "What we need to do is *delight* our customers each and every time they purchase."

Sara Lee's commitment to investing in brands is most evident in the success we have enjoyed in creating *megabrands*: those brands with an image so powerful that the consumer gives them "permission" to cross into an ever-expanding range of product categories. According to Lucien Nessim, senior vice president responsible for Sara Lee Personal Products in Europe, "Once consumers believe a brand stands for quality in one product category, they are likely to believe it will stand for the same quality in another category. It's our job as marketers to fully leverage the potential found in a strong brand name."

An excellent example of megabranding is the explosive growth of the

Hanes brand, associated 10 years ago primarily with men's underwear. Today, the *Hanes* and *Hanes Her Way* megabrand—a family of products ranging from men's and women's underwear and activewear to socks, knit accessories, bras and casual shoes—has annual sales volume of $1.8 billion. Revenues for this megabrand have grown six-fold in the past decade.

The success of the *Hanes* and *Hanes Her Way* brands is a classic case of a line of products with a clear and consistent position—department store quality at discount store prices. It's no accident that this megabrand is supported by an aggressive marketing budget that has more than doubled over the past five years and has produced the creative campaign, "Wait'll We Get Our *Hanes* On You." Our uniform approach to packaging further reinforces the impression that consumers can expect the same, consistent standard of quality from any *Hanes* or *Hanes Her Way* product they buy.

Other Sara Lee megabrands include *Hillshire Farm,* the national leader in the smoked sausage category, and the *Sara Lee* brand, which has been using its strong franchise in frozen baked goods to move into the deli meat category. This is eloquent testimony to an important megabrand phenomenon: advertising aimed at promoting a single product stimulates sales of an entire family of products.

Understanding the equity a brand name has in the minds of consumers is vital to megabrand-building. For instance, Sara Lee Bakery discovered that consumers made an extraordinarily

positive association between the *Sara Lee* brand and pies, even though the company didn't advertise its pies and was, in fact, a distant number-two competitor in the category. Armed with this information, the Bakery expanded its line of pies. The products were launched with new packaging and a significant advertising budget, and went on to achieve a 70% volume increase over the last two years.

Research also suggested that the equity of the *Coach* brand, Sara Lee's line of quality leather goods, could be extended from accessories to apparel. After a test with unisex leather coats, Coach introduced a highly successful line of men's and women's coats in several distribution channels. Coach invests a significant portion of its sales dollars in consumer research, a major factor in its outstanding performance, according to Frankfort. Growth in sales and operating earnings has exceeded 35% a year on a compounded basis since Sara Lee acquired Coach in 1985.

Sara Lee has discovered that brands tend to travel well. While private-label products may perform in certain neighborhoods or markets, they haven't proven capable of spanning the globe like branded products.

"We take seriously the concept of 'thinking globally, but acting locally,'" states Frank Meysman, senior vice president responsible for Coffee and Grocery, and Household and Personal Care. "To us, it means delivering the same consistent quality inherent in a given brand, but meeting the market by responding to local needs and tastes."

Hanes knitwear products, for example, are successful in Europe, Australia and Japan. *Sara Lee* frozen baked goods are leaders in both the United Kingdom and Australia as well as in the United States. The familiar *Kiwi* shoe polish tin can be found in more than 100 countries. And *Douwe Egberts* coffee has developed a true pan-European presence, bolstered by its consistent graphic identity and unified advertising. According to an annual study by *Financial World* magazine, the value of the *Douwe Egberts* brand rose 16% in 1993—the largest increase in the coffee category and one of the largest among 290 brands surveyed.

"We believe that our brands have just begun to tap their global growth potential," says Bryan. "Our executives have searched for new opportunities in Asia, the most populous of the world's continents, and found the Chinese, in particular, exceptionally brand-conscious. The prospect of more than a billion brand-loyal consumers, who could create an economy bigger than that of the United States within one generation, should give pause to those who doubt the continued vitality of brands."

A food industry analyst said recently that if a major brand applies itself, it "will win any battle" with private-label products. Like others bullish on brands, he believes brand marketers have little to fear. If a brand meets consumers' demands for quality, consistency and performance, and communicates these benefits effectively, the battle is over before it even begins.

Sara Lee Packaged Meats and Bakery recorded strong financial results in fiscal 1994, with increased sales and profits in each of its major businesses—Packaged Meats, Bakery and Foodservice. Sales for the year rose 6% to $5.5 billion, and operating income increased 19% to $340 million before the restructuring charge.

Packaged Meats and Bakery
1994 Worldwide Sales (dollar share)

■ *United States*
▨ *Western/Central Europe*
Asia-Pacific/Latin America
Other

2% 1%
7%
90%

SARA LEE PACKAGED MEATS

Strong brand equity and responsive product development enabled Sara Lee to maintain a leading position in the $20 billion U.S. packaged meats industry during fiscal 1994. Sara Lee Packaged Meats posted a unit volume increase of 2%, excluding acquisitions, and retained the number-one position in the supermarket channel.

Business and Strategic Overview

Broadening its line of "better-for-you" and convenience products, enhancing brand equity and continuing its commitment to quality, customer satisfaction and efficiency are key strategies for Sara Lee Packaged Meats.

Sara Lee continued to have a significant presence in U.S. meat categories. During fiscal 1994, the company accelerated efforts to develop and market reduced-fat processed meat products and supported those introductions with significant increases in advertising.

National brands, including *Hillshire Farm, Jimmy Dean* and *Ball Park,* and regional brands, such as *Kahn's* and *Bryan,* enjoyed the number-one or number-two positions in the hot dog, smoked sausage, breakfast sausage, luncheon meat, corn dog, cocktail link and breakfast sandwich categories during fiscal 1994.

The *Hillshire Farm* megabrand continued to lead the smoked sausage category, capitalizing on the introduction of reduced-fat versions of popular products. New television advertising to strengthen the *Hillshire Farm* brand's

position in core categories debuted in late fiscal 1994.

Jimmy Dean Foods, the national leader in the U.S. breakfast sausage category, developed new convenience products and made improvements in existing breakfast sausage and sandwich items to enhance consumer satisfaction with taste and appearance. Other initiatives included a comprehensive package redesign.

Hygrade Food Products extended its growing *Ball Park* brand through new products and segmentation. Sara Lee will continue to leverage the *Ball Park* brand in fiscal 1995 with "better-for-you" and convenience variations.

Bil Mar's *Mr. Turkey* line continued to capitalize upon the popularity of low-fat turkey products, such as turkey hot dogs and luncheon meats. A more contemporary package design for *Mr. Turkey* products was completed in fiscal 1994.

Bryan Foods, a leader in Southern markets, maintained strong positions in key categories, such as luncheon meats, hot dogs and smoked sausage, while implementing low-cost production initiatives.

Bessin Corporation, a kosher processed meats company acquired in fiscal 1993, focused on improving manufacturing efficiency for its line of premium-priced kosher meats. Bessin's products include hot dogs and bagel dogs sold under the *Best's Kosher* and *Sinai 48* brands.

The company continued to extend the presence of the *Sara Lee* brand in premium meats sold at supermarket deli counters. *Sara Lee* branded deli sales

reached record levels in fiscal 1994.

Outside the United States, Sara Lee's strategic emphasis is to improve returns and market shares in new regions. The corporation entered the European market through the establishment of Sara Lee Processed Meats (Europe) B.V. in fiscal 1993 and the Mexican market through a joint venture with Kir Alimentos, that country's second-largest packaged meats company, in fiscal 1994.

To boost profit margins throughout Sara Lee's meats businesses, operating efficiencies, including reconfiguration of manufacturing processes and cost containment, were implemented.

Major New Products

The "better-for-you" and convenience categories dominated product development during fiscal 1994.

Sara Lee introduced 97% fat-free hot dogs under the *Ball Park 97, Bryan Juicy 'N Lean* and *Kahn's Extra Lean* labels in early fiscal 1995. Additionally, *Ball Park Lite* and *Ball Park Beef Lite* hot dogs were reformulated to be lower in fat.

Hillshire Farm began national distribution of low-fat, regular-sliced luncheon meats in fiscal 1994. The product is available in eight varieties that are at least 97% fat-free. *Hillshire Farm* Lite Smoked Sausage and Lite Polska Kielbasa also were reformulated to be lower in fat.

Jimmy Dean Foods brought three varieties of single-serve *Meal-Sized Sandwiches* breakfast products to the convenience market in fiscal 1994, while

Sara Lee Packaged Meats and Bakery	As reported		Excluding restructuring					
(dollars in millions)	5-year compound growth rate	1994	5-year compound growth rate	1994	1993	1992	1991	1990
Sales	(1.6)%	$5,472	(1.6)%	$5,472	$5,148	$4,703	$5,124	$4,959
Operating income	2.8	318	4.2	340	287	264	229	208
Capital expenditures	(10.1)	108	(10.1)	108	99	96	102	135
Depreciation and amortization	5.2	108	5.2	108	99	97	93	87
Return on investment*		40.5%		43.1%	37.6%	31.8%	25.3%	23.4%

*Measures return on average net operating assets.

Hillshire Farm introduced *Lit'l Cheddy Hots* cocktail links.

Global Opportunities

While the packaged meats industry in many global markets traditionally has been fragmented and largely unbranded, Sara Lee has extended and leveraged its expertise to build successful brands outside the United States.

Sara Lee Processed Meats (Europe) B.V. markets products under the *Stegeman* brand in the Netherlands, *Dacor* in Belgium, *Argal* in Spain and *Nobre* in Portugal. This business is growing profitably through cost-containment programs and improved procurement, manufacturing, product development and marketing activities.

In 1994, Sara Lee entered into a joint venture with Kir Alimentos, Mexico's second-largest packaged meats company and a leading manufacturer of hot dogs, luncheon meat, sausage and ham under the *Kir* and *Duby* brands. This transaction will greatly facilitate the manufacturing and marketing of the corporation's products and brands in the Mexican market.

Sara Lee will consider further global expansion in markets where it can establish a strong presence while achieving acceptable margins and returns.

SARA LEE BAKERY

Customer service, consumer satisfaction and a commitment to core products brought Sara Lee Bakery strong results for 1994, with increased sales, profits and margins. Unit volumes, excluding acquisitions, rose 4%.

Business and Strategic Overview

Sara Lee Bakery sells frozen baked products through retail, foodservice, bakery-deli and direct channels. Products are sold in North America, Europe and the Asia-Pacific region.

Through innovative product development, and quality and service initiatives, strong growth was achieved in the $10.5 billion U.S. frozen baked goods industry in fiscal 1994.

To maximize returns and drive growth in highly competitive markets, Sara Lee Bakery is leveraging brand equity, emphasizing high-margin core

products and enhancing service and consumer satisfaction.

Sara Lee's number-one position rose to a 21% dollar share in the U.S. retail channel of the frozen baked goods market. Popular new products and an aggressive advertising campaign fueled demand in core categories, such as pies, cheesecakes, pound cakes and Danish. These high-margin products are instrumental in achieving superior returns.

The power of the *Sara Lee* brand is being leveraged to expand the business into new, yet related, categories. An outstanding example is Sara Lee Bakery's line of cream pies, introduced in late fiscal 1993. Only one year later, Sara Lee held a number-two position in this category, achieving half the share of the market leader and significantly boosting its share of the total retail pie market.

Another key strategy is to explore growth potential outside the conventional frozen baked goods industry. A new line of fresh baked breakfast goods— *Sara Lee* bagels, English muffins and crumpets—is being distributed in California by International Baking Company, a business acquired in fiscal 1993.

Sara Lee's foodservice and bakery-deli businesses are capitalizing on increased demand for premium baked goods in restaurants, institutional settings and delicatessens, while concentrating on high-margin products, such as cakes, muffins, bagels and Danish. Sara Lee Bakery's network of direct outlet stores continues to post strong sales.

Sara Lee Packaged Meats and Bakery   Fiscal 1994 Highlights

■ *Sara Lee Packaged Meats maintained its number-one position in the supermarket channel and launched numerous reduced-fat products.*

■ *Popular products and an aggressive advertising campaign pushed Sara Lee Bakery's number-one position to a 21% dollar share of the U.S. retail channel of the frozen baked goods market.*

■ *Sara Lee Foodservice posted increased sales and profits and continued programs to enhance product ordering and delivery.*

In its commitment to customer service and consumer-defined standards of quality, Sara Lee incorporates sensory data—consumer perceptions about taste, appearance and value—into product development and marketing. This enhances new product success and assures continuous improvement.

European and Asia-Pacific operations recorded unit volume increases in fiscal 1994. Principal European markets are the United Kingdom, France, Germany, Norway and Denmark. Expansion plans target Holland and Greece. Markets served by Sara Lee Australia include Hong Kong, Singapore, New Zealand, Malaysia, Taiwan, Korea, the Philippines, Indonesia and Thailand.

Major New Products

Consumer preferences and opportunities to leverage brand equity are the primary inspiration for new Sara Lee Bakery products.

Sara Lee Crumb Coffee Cake, introduced in fiscal 1994, was well received by consumers. National distribution of the *Sara Lee* Cream Pie line began in fiscal 1994. A new fruit cobbler line enjoyed brisk sales in the foodservice category.

Sara Lee Gourmet and Toaster-Size English Muffins, Authentic Deli-Style Bagels and Traditional British Crumpets, all fresh bakery products, debuted in California in fiscal 1994.

In the foodservice and bakery-deli sectors, a reformulated pumpkin pie that is shelf-stable for up to three days

was introduced in fiscal 1994. The pie, which is shipped frozen, offers the benefit of table or deli-case display.

Global Opportunities

Increased distribution of Sara Lee Bakery products will be facilitated by joint ventures in which production and distribution expertise can be applied in local regions.

Sara Lee Bakery is entering new markets around the world by developing strategies tailored to regional economies and consumer preferences. Market knowledge and distribution access, gained through local partnerships, establish a strong presence for the *Sara Lee* brand in retail channels. Modular manufacturing plants that offer efficient, regional production are a means of delivering products even more quickly and economically in some markets.

Expansion of the production capabilities of Sara Lee's operations in the United Kingdom presents an opportunity to increase distribution in Europe. The United Kingdom is Sara Lee's largest international franchise in terms of product sales, with an 18% market share, double that of the closest branded competitor. To address heavy competition from private-label products in the United Kingdom, Sara Lee is pricing products aggressively and managing production costs carefully.

Additional opportunities for growth lie in Australia, where Sara Lee has a 40% market share.

The corporation's position in the

Mexican frozen dessert market grew significantly in fiscal 1994, establishing Sara Lee as number one in frozen desserts in Mexico.

Sara Lee Bakery products in Mexico are distributed through a partnership with a major Mexican baked goods company. This venture combines Sara Lee's manufacturing capability with a local distribution network, setting the stage for successful new product introductions.

SARA LEE FOODSERVICE

PYA/Monarch, Sara Lee's foodservice distribution business, posted positive results for fiscal 1994, with increased sales, unit volumes and operating income.

The nation's fifth-largest foodservice company and the leader in the Southeast United States, PYA/Monarch distributes dry, refrigerated and frozen foods, paper products, equipment and supplies to institutional and commercial foodservice customers. The business serves individual customers in the Southern United States and restaurant chains throughout the South, Midwest and East.

Growth strategies include sales force expansion to develop a larger base of individual customers, and service enhancements to increase restaurant chain accounts. Information processing technology is being implemented to facilitate customer ordering, expedite product delivery and improve inventory management.

Sara Lee Coffee and Grocery reported solid financial results for fiscal 1994, with operating income of $299 million before the restructuring charge, up 2%, and sales of $2.1 billion, an increase of 2%. Unit volumes were flat for European retail and out-of-home roasted coffee, the largest product segment.

Coffee and Grocery 1994 Worldwide Sales (dollar share)

■ United States
▨ Western/Central Europe
　Asia-Pacific/Latin America
　Other

2% 1%
14%
83%

COFFEE

Strong brand equity, continued emphasis on innovative product development and marketing, cost containment and successful management of fluctuating green coffee prices yielded positive results for Sara Lee's coffee business in fiscal 1994.

Business and Strategic Overview

Support for its strong brand franchises, experienced inventory management and responsive retail pricing enabled Sara Lee to maintain its profitable position in the $10 billion Western and Central European roasted coffee market.

The flagship *Douwe Egberts* brand and a collection of other leading coffee brands, including *Maison du Café, Marcilla* and *Merrild,* enjoy significant brand equity and consumer loyalty. In the Netherlands, Belgium and Hungary, Sara Lee holds number-one positions in retail roasted coffee, with number-two shares in Denmark, France and the Czech Republic, and a leading position in Spain.

Green coffee cost increases during fiscal 1994 began with a tightening of supply but were influenced subsequently by economic and social conditions in many producing nations, as well as by investment fund participation in the commodity markets. Sara Lee's response has been to carefully protect profits.

Overall positions were maintained in major markets, with only slight changes in market share. Gains in market share were recorded in Denmark, the United

Kingdom and the Czech Republic, while there were small declines in the Netherlands, Belgium and France. Market shares in Spain and Australia were stable.

Sara Lee's retail coffee operations continued to emphasize product development and retailing tailored to specific regions. These products are supported by centralized marketing and advertising functions in line with a "family branding" approach that has been introduced gradually throughout Sara Lee's European coffee markets. Unified packaging and graphics, and a coordinated communications strategy, recognize national preferences while yielding operational efficiencies.

In the Netherlands, where Sara Lee is the leading coffee roaster with a 73% share, consumer loyalty led to strong sales for the full range of *Douwe Egberts* products. Building on the *Aroma Rood* core brand, Sara Lee has introduced a number of successful extensions, such as the *Boncafé, Piazza* and *Cafuego* brands. It also markets a moderately priced coffee blend in the Netherlands under the *Kanis & Gunnink* brand, which, driven by competitive pricing, gained market share in fiscal 1994.

Sara Lee maintains a 54% share of the Belgian roasted coffee market with its traditional line of *Douwe Egberts* products and the *Jacqmotte* and *Chat Noir* varieties.

In Denmark, where Sara Lee sells the *Merrild* brand, market share increased to 30%, despite competitive

retail conditions.

In France, Sara Lee posted a fiscal 1994 market share of 15%. Considerable growth has been achieved by a premium sub-brand under the *Maison du Café* label, which now ranks second in the premium segment of the French market.

The *Marcilla* and *Soley* brands in Spain together held a 21% share at fiscal year-end. The *Marcilla* brand underwent a package redesign as part of the final phase of the "family branding" strategy in fiscal 1994.

In the developing Central European economies of Hungary and the Czech Republic, Sara Lee maintained solid market positions. Sara Lee holds a 42% share in Hungary and a 33% share in the Czech Republic.

Strong sales were posted again for roasted and ground coffee under the *Harris* brand, with a 25% market share in Australia. The *Moccona* brand maintained its leading position in the instant coffee segment.

Sara Lee is one of the world's largest suppliers in the out-of-home coffee market. Douwe Egberts Coffee Systems in Europe and Superior Coffee and Foods in the United States serve this growing market.

Sara Lee's success in the out-of-home coffee market results from delivery of consistently high quality at reasonable cost, with comprehensive equipment, supply and service support for customers of virtually any size.

Sara Lee Coffee and Grocery	As reported			Excluding restructuring						
(dollars in millions)	5-year compound growth rate	1994		5-year compound growth rate	1994	1993	1992	1991	1990	
Sales	2.9%	$2,090		2.9%	$2,090	$2,058	$1,919	$1,938	$1,834	
Operating income	12.8	274		14.8	299	292	254	245	199	
Capital expenditures	7.1	69		7.1	69	87	73	77	72	
Depreciation and amortization	7.7	74		7.7	74	80	68	61	66	
Return on investment*		86.4%			93.6%	70.8%	64.7%	58.7%	48.9%	

*Measures return on average net operating assets.

Major New Products

New product development enables Sara Lee to capitalize on changing tastes and lifestyle trends.

Responding to consumer demand for high-quality espresso products, Sara Lee introduced *Piazza D'Oro* coffee in the Dutch retail and out-of-home markets. In France, a decaffeinated version of the *Maison du Café L'Or* premium blend was launched.

In the Netherlands, Sara Lee introduced the *Douwe Egberts Grand Café* assortment of flavored instant coffees, offering Cappuccino, Amaretto, Café Vienna and Irish Coffee varieties.

Sara Lee launched the *Piazza* brand in the out-of-home market in Portugal and premium blend *Superior Metropolitan* coffee in the U.S. out-of-home market.

Global Opportunities

Continued success for Sara Lee's coffee business will be driven by development of new national and regional brands, expansion of the out-of-home segment and strategic acquisitions.

Already one of Sara Lee's most global businesses, reaching consumers in Europe, North America and Australia, the coffee business will continue to expand into new markets.

Sara Lee evaluates acquisitions that provide access to new markets or strengthen the company's competitive position. In early fiscal 1994, Sara Lee significantly increased its interest in the Norwegian coffee company Friele, which holds a 27% share in the Norwegian roasted coffee market. Per capita, Norway is among the world's largest coffee-consuming nations.

Sara Lee entered the coffee system market in Mexico in fiscal 1994.

TEA

Supported by aggressive advertising and innovative product extensions, Sara Lee's *Pickwick* brand continues to grow in the stable, $2.6 billion European tea market.

Pickwick traditional, herbal and fruit teas hold the number-one position in the Netherlands and the number-two position in Belgium. Particularly strong fiscal year 1994 sales were posted in

Denmark, Germany and Hungary.

Pickwick Cocktails tea, single-serving packets with a mixture of three fruit tastes, was introduced in the Netherlands in fiscal 1994, as was *Pickwick* Ice Tea Lemon in cans and one-liter bottles. New herbal varieties of *Pickwick* tea, featuring fruit pieces and natural aromas, were introduced in Germany.

Russia represents a growth opportunity, as high-quality tea from the West is in great demand. Significant exports of *Pickwick* black and fruit-flavored teas to Russia began in early fiscal 1994. The brand is now in distribution in every major Russian city.

GROCERY

Sara Lee markets nuts under the *Duyvis* brand in the Netherlands, the *Duyvis* and *Felix* brands in Belgium, and the *Duyvis Bénénuts* brand in France. Rice is sold under the Dutch *Lassie* brand.

New product introductions were the emphasis of Sara Lee's nuts business during fiscal 1994. In the Netherlands, new *Tijgernootjes* and *Duyvis* Pinda's Speciaal nut products were supported by aggressive advertising.

More contemporary packaging was introduced for Sara Lee's *Lassie* rice. The century-old brand holds the leading share of the Dutch market, which remained stable during the year.

Sara Lee Coffee and Grocery   Fiscal 1994 Highlights

- *Despite rising green coffee prices, Sara Lee Coffee and Grocery improved returns and maintained margins and overall positions in European coffee markets.*

- *Pursuing global expansion, Sara Lee entered Mexico's coffee system market and increased its interest in the Norwegian coffee company Friele.*

- *New product varieties and effective advertising sustained the popularity of the Pickwick tea brand in major European markets.*

Sara Lee Personal Products—intimates and accessories, knit products and hosiery—reported a 6% increase in sales and a 7% decline in operating income before the restructuring charge. U.S. knit products and worldwide intimates were strong performers. Worldwide hosiery and European knitwear had declining sales and profits.

Personal Products 1994 Worldwide Sales
(dollar share)

■ United States
■ Western/Central Europe
  Asia-Pacific/Latin America
  Other   3%

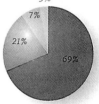

SARA LEE INTIMATES

Sara Lee Intimates leveraged the strength of its global brands in fiscal 1994, posting strong growth in sales and profits. Unit volume, excluding acquisitions, increased 11% as Sara Lee brought product and marketing innovation to *Playtex, Bali, Hanes Her Way* and *Dim* products, created new core product lines and pursued undeveloped category niches.

Business and Strategic Overview

To maintain its profitable growth, Sara Lee Intimates is expanding its capacity and distribution, and broadening its consumer base by adding new products to its popular lines of bras, panties and shapewear. Capital expenditures will double in the next fiscal year to increase capacity and improve manufacturing efficiency.

Sara Lee, which has a 22% share of the U.S. bra market, will build on the equity of its brands in all channels of distribution by continuing to market products that provide function, fit, comfort and value. Marketing expenditures will increase in fiscal 1995 to produce advertising and promotions that update brand images and strengthen sales.

During fiscal 1994, the *Playtex* brand, distributed in mass-merchandise outlets and department stores throughout North America, Europe and the Pacific Rim, produced solid results. Playtex built on the successful 1993 launch of *Playtex Secrets* bras and panty slimmers by extending the brand into light control

garments, tripling *Playtex Secrets* sales. Playtex also had its most successful style launch in recent history with the introduction of the *Eighteen Hour Comfort Strap* bra with cushioned straps for full-figured women.

In Europe, new *Playtex Caresse* cotton/Lycra panties were successfully introduced in fiscal 1994. Playtex's U.S. marketing program, which will include new print and television advertising in fiscal 1995, distinguishes the brand by focusing on traditional fit and comfort with contemporary styling.

In fiscal 1994, the *Bali* brand increased its strong position in department stores with the introduction of *Bali* daywear panties and the addition of two new styles to the *Satin Tracings* collection of stretch underwire bras.

Hanes Her Way bras and control panties held their number-one positions in the U.S. mass-merchandise market in fiscal 1994. Sara Lee introduced value-priced products that borrow from the *Bali* brand's popular styling and colors and are tailored to younger consumers. Sales of *Just My Size* bras and panty slimmers for full-figured women grew significantly through updated styles and enhanced distribution.

Canadelle, the leading producer of bras and panties in Canada, improved its leading market position by updating products under the *Wonderbra, Daisyfresh* and *Playtex* brands. Canadelle also introduced the *Hanes Her Way* brand into the Canadian market.

In Mexico, where the *Playtex* brand

leads the higher-priced market segment, three new *Hanes Her Way* bra and panty collections were introduced.

In Europe, the *Dim* brand continued its evolution as a megabrand and showed moderate unit volume growth in the midst of a lingering recession. In addition to introducing several new styles, Dim redesigned its packaging and advertising to reestablish the brand's prominence and make product attributes clearer to consumers.

Major New Products

In both the United States and Europe, new styles and colors, as well as features that emphasize fit and comfort, are being added to core product lines.

Playtex will further revitalize its *Eighteen Hour* brand in fiscal 1995 by introducing the *Comfort Stretch* seamless bra for full-figured women. Two new *Playtex Secrets* lines—*Cotton Elegance* and *Satin Bouquet* bras and panty slimmers with revolutionary spot-control technology—will be launched in department stores in late fiscal 1995.

Bali will build on its successful *Satin Tracings* launch of fiscal 1993 by introducing the *Cotton Tracings* line of stretch cotton bras. Bali also will introduce the *Smooth Compliments* collection of lightly lined bras with stretch padding, and *Illusions* shapewear with the proprietary control technology used in *Playtex Secrets* products.

Sara Lee will continue to freshen styles and broaden distribution of *Hanes Her Way* and *Just My Size* products in

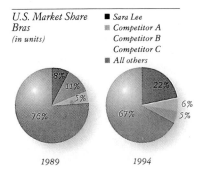

*U.S. Market Share
Bras
(in units)*

■ *Sara Lee*
▨ *Competitor A*
Competitor B
Competitor C
▨ *All others*

1989   1994

mass-merchandise outlets, supporting them with improved packaging and point-of-sale materials.

The *Wonderbra* push-up bra's unprecedented success in the United Kingdom served as a springboard for the product's launch in U.S. department stores, where its cleavage-enhancing properties were promoted with striking point-of-sale displays. The product will be in full U.S. distribution in early fiscal 1995, and Sara Lee plans to develop an expanded line of figure-enhancing products under the *Wonderbra* name.

In fiscal 1995, Dim, number one in bra sales in France, will introduce the cotton-lined *Soutien Up* push-up bra and will relaunch *Rosy* bras, panties and lingerie, targeting sophisticated consumers.

Global Opportunities

Throughout the United States, Canada, Mexico and Europe, Sara Lee Intimates is focusing on product innovation to build brand equity and improve market share.

In Canada, the strength of the *Playtex, Wonderbra* and *Daisyfresh* brands is being leveraged in all distribution channels. In Mexico, where the *Playtex* brand is a market leader, the potential for growth is strong as more consumers look for quality branded products, such as *Hanes Her Way* bras.

In the fragmented European bra market, Sara Lee is well-positioned to strengthen its *Playtex* and *Dim* brands.

In addition, there are plans to continue growth in South Africa and Australia through brands such as *Playtex, Hanes Her Way* and *Formfit.*

SARA LEE ACCESSORIES

In fiscal 1994, Coach strengthened its position as an international marketer of high-quality handbags, business cases, business accessories and small leather goods. Increased sales in existing retail channels and expanded distribution drove the brand's growth globally. New products, including the *Madison Collection* of tailored day-into-evening handbags, broadened the brand's appeal.

In fiscal 1995, Coach will continue its growth through new product introduc-

tions, such as the *Sonoma Collection,* which features relaxed styling in suede and textured leathers. Coach will expand its presence in underdeveloped U.S. markets and will open 16 new stores worldwide, including the first free-standing Coach store in Japan.

Mark Cross, a premium leather goods company acquired in fiscal 1993, will enhance its product line and open nine new freestanding stores.

In fiscal 1994, Aris Isotoner, which manufactures men's and women's gloves, slippers and knitwear, focused on revital-izing the *Isotoner* brand and strengthening its market leadership position. The *Isotoner* slipper line was expanded with several new styles and fabrics, and a Teflon-coated umbrella that repels water was introduced.

Aris now markets only leather gloves, *Aris Leathers by Isotoner,* while its line of knit hats, scarves and gloves are being sold under the *Isotoner* brand. All packaging for *Aris* and *Isotoner* products was redesigned in fiscal 1994, and upcoming advertising will use the theme "*Isotoner* Keeps You in Comfort." In fiscal 1995, Aris Isotoner will expand its presence in Europe, where it markets gloves, slippers and umbrellas under the *Isotoner* brand.

SARA LEE KNIT PRODUCTS

Sara Lee's U.S. knit products business posted strong results for fiscal 1994, bolstered by both the underwear and activewear segments. European knit products reported lower results due to heavy competition and a continuing

---

Sara Lee Personal Products   Fiscal 1994 Highlights

■ *A restructuring plan, announced in June 1994, began addressing overcapacity and low returns in portions of the worldwide hosiery and knitwear businesses.*

■ *Bolstered by the success of product innovations by Dim, Playtex, Bali and Hanes Her Way, Sara Lee Intimates posted healthy unit volume increases.*

■ *Value-added products, strong brands and powerful marketing programs, such as Sara Lee's partnership with the Olympics, yielded positive results for Sara Lee Knit Products.*

Sara Lee Personal Products	As reported		Excluding restructuring					
(dollars in millions)	5-year compound growth rate	1994	5-year compound growth rate	1994	1993	1992	1991	1990
Sales	18.9%	$6,449	18.9%	$6,449	$6,098	$5,398	$4,000	$3,620
Operating income (loss)	NM	(71)	14.3	559	602	582	459	403
Capital expenditures	11.9	408	11.9	408	485	271	253	310
Depreciation and amortization	28.3	289	28.3	289	265	232	164	134
Return on investment*		NM		20.8%	26.4%	27.8%	25.5%	27.3%

*Measures return on average net operating assets.

recession. Combining results from all geographic regions, Sara Lee Knit Products reported a worldwide unit volume increase of 8%.

Business and Strategic Overview

Sara Lee is positioning its global knit products business for improved profitability and growth through value-added product offerings and cost-effective manufacturing and sourcing. It also is leveraging strong brands, such as *Hanes, Hanes Her Way, Champion* and *Dim,* to drive new product success and enter new markets.

During fiscal 1994, challenging market conditions, overcapacity and low returns necessitated a restructuring program providing for plant closings and realignments in certain U.S. retail fleece categories and in European underwear and activewear. These adjustments, part of Sara Lee's worldwide initiative announced in June 1994, are expected to produce significant savings over the next several years.

In the United States, Sara Lee Knit Products is taking advantage of the strength of the *Hanes* and *Hanes Her Way* megabrand to market new and innovative product line extensions. Product sales for this megabrand in fiscal 1994 totaled $1.8 billion. The *Hanes* brand maintained its solid number-two position, with a 31% share of the $2 billion U.S. men's and boys' underwear market.

In the $1.4 billion U.S. women's and girls' panties category, *Hanes Her Way* and other Sara Lee brands significantly

increased their leading position to 27% of the market. The girls' panties business, driven by product improvements and new licensing agreements, moved into the number-one spot for the first time.

Sara Lee Knit Products' activewear line includes T-shirts, fleecewear and jersey products sold to screenprint and retail channels. Screenprint unit volumes increased strongly in fiscal 1994. Retail jersey sustained good market share growth during the fiscal year, as did *Team Hanes* T-shirts. In line with its strategy of emphasizing higher-margin, value-added products, Sara Lee is expanding license agreements and strengthening its *Team Hanes* program, which markets licensed college and professional sportswear.

Champion Products is concentrating on its collegiate and professional athletic core products, as well as licensed apparel, including replicas of professional team uniforms. Champion exited its Spring City private-label business in early fiscal 1995.

The equity of the *Champion* brand is being strengthened in fiscal 1995 through improved distribution, enhanced in-store merchandising and product-focused advertising.

Sara Lee continues to capitalize on its unique partnership agreement with the Olympic Games, combining Games sponsorship, product licensing and U.S. Team outfitting. Virtually all licensed T-shirts and fleece products related to the 1994 and 1996 Olympic Games and marketed in the United States will be

Hanes or *Champion* products. In addition, Sara Lee has the rights to use the USA Olympic Rings and Atlanta Games logos on most *Hanes, Hanes Her Way* and *Champion* products, marketing materials, advertising, packaging and promotions.

In Europe, knit products market shares improved slightly, and Sara Lee maintained leading men's underwear positions in France, Italy and Spain. Recessionary conditions and heavy competition led to disappointing sales and profits, however. The strategic focus is to restore margins for underwear and activewear through internal cost reductions and increased sales of higher-margin, value-added products with improved quality. Among initiatives to lower costs is the centralization of research and development and material sourcing.

Retail distribution of *Hanes* activewear, currently in France, the United Kingdom, Germany and the Benelux countries, will be expanded in fiscal 1995. This line of primarily screenprint products is enhancing quality to drive sales. *Champion* products are targeted for relaunch in France and expansion in Italy, supported by aggressive marketing.

Major New Products

Product development in Sara Lee's knit products business emphasizes value-added product lines and extensions, expansion into related categories where new product entries can leverage the strong megabrands, and further development of licensing agreements.

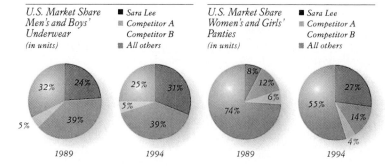

U.S. Market Share
Men's and Boys'
Underwear
(in units)

- Sara Lee
- Competitor A
- Competitor B
- All others

1989 — 32%, 24%, 39%, 5%

1994 — 25%, 31%, 5%, 39%

U.S. Market Share
Women's and Girls'
Panties
(in units)

- Sara Lee
- Competitor A
- Competitor B
- All others

1989 — 8%, 12%, 6%, 74%

1994 — 55%, 27%, 14%, 4%

Hanes Cool Comfort briefs for men, a cotton mesh product that offers exceptional comfort, was distributed nationally in fiscal 1994. Test marketing of a *Hanes Cool Comfort* T-shirt begins in fiscal 1995. *Hanes* boxer briefs entered selected markets in early fiscal 1995.

Hanes Her Way nylon panties, launched in the mass-merchandise market in late fiscal 1993, continued to enjoy strong sales. The girls' underwear segment introduced several additional—and popular—licensed products in fiscal 1994, including underwear with graphics based on three film, toy and television properties: *The Lion King, Barbie* and *The Flintstones.*

In an example of effective mega-branding, Sara Lee began distributing a line of *Hanes Her Way* casual leather and canvas shoes in the mass-merchandise market in late fiscal 1994.

Premium quality *Hanes Signature Collection* adult activewear was launched in fiscal 1994.

In fiscal 1995, Champion will introduce new athletic team uniform replicas and an expanded T-shirt line that includes pocket-Ts and shirts featuring the *Champion* script in a striking new graphic treatment.

In Europe, a long-term license has been secured to distribute a line of *Cacharel* men's briefs and T-shirts in Spain, Italy and France. In Spain, several line extensions of the corporation's leading underwear brands—*Abanderado* for men and *Princesa* for women—are being introduced.

Global Opportunities

Sara Lee knit products will grow worldwide by pursuing markets in developing nations, leveraging the equity of strong Sara Lee brands, such as *Hanes* and *Hanes Her Way,* and capitalizing on the global trend toward more casual lifestyles.

Europe's knit products markets, though suffering from excess capacity and recessionary pressures, remain a growth opportunity as Sara Lee consolidates fragmented markets and pursues cost-effective manufacturing and sourcing.

The knit products business is positioned for growth in Mexico and South America, where Sara Lee has established new marketing organizations. Sales will be driven by the strength and popularity of the *Hanes* and *Hanes Her Way* brands, as well as the *Rinbros* brand, which holds the leading position in men's and boys' underwear in Mexico. Expansion is planned as Sara Lee Knit Products capitalizes on its strong relationships with major U.S.-based retailers opening new outlets in Latin America.

Sara Lee continues to build business in its core knit products categories in Australia with *Stubbies* casual clothing and *King Gee* workwear, as well as with *Hanes* and *Champion* products in Japan.

Further expansion in Asia-Pacific markets is being achieved through Intercon Garments and Upxon, Inc., apparel companies acquired in late fiscal 1993. Intercon and Upxon market knit products throughout the

Philippines and Japan, respectively.

SARA LEE HOSIERY

Sales and earnings for Sara Lee's hosiery businesses in the United States and Europe were down from the previous year, the result of a continued decline in the global sheer hosiery market. Changing fashions and casual lifestyle trends remained prominent factors, and European operations battled a lingering recession. Worldwide sheer hosiery unit volumes dropped 6%, excluding acquisitions.

Business and Strategic Overview

To improve the profitability of its hosiery business, Sara Lee is emphasizing its value-added product offerings, improving quality and durability, bringing production capacity in line with market needs and reinforcing the equity of major brands.

Through the power of its *Hanes* and *L'eggs* brands, Sara Lee maintained its leading share of the $2.7 billion U.S. sheer hosiery market in fiscal 1994. The *Hanes* brand leads the department- and specialty-store channels with a 60% dollar share. The *L'eggs* brand has a 56% dollar share of the food, drug and mass-merchandise market.

In Europe, Sara Lee gained share in many of its markets, maintaining the number-one positions in France, the United Kingdom and Germany through such well-known brands as *Dim, Pretty Polly, Elbeo, Nur Die* and *Bellinda.*

As part of the worldwide restructur-

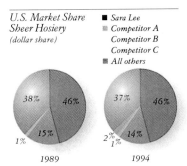

U.S. Market Share
Sheer Hosiery
(dollar share)

■ *Sara Lee*
▨ *Competitor A*
Competitor B
Competitor C
▨ *All others*

1989

1994

ing of Sara Lee's Personal Products business announced in June 1994, sheer hosiery capacity in all major markets is being adjusted to match market demand. Concurrently, capacity for more casual products, such as tights, opaques and trouser socks, is being increased. These changes will enable Sara Lee to better capitalize on demand in all legwear categories, while maintaining leading market shares.

Sara Lee will continue to build brand equity through increased advertising support and strategic package and display redesigns. In addition, an extensive public awareness campaign designed to convey messages about the quality, comfort and functionality of sheer hosiery products is under way. In advertising, quality improvements and features that enhance appearance are being emphasized at all price points.

L'eggs has begun reengineering product displays, simplifying the purchase decision with quicker access to information regarding fit, appearance, comfort and specific product features.

In Europe, the *Dim* brand has undergone an entire packaging and advertising redesign aimed at reestablishing the dominance of this strong megabrand and more clearly communicating product attributes.

Major New Products

Product development in both the United States and Europe is focusing on value-added products to drive sales in the sheer hosiery business and capitalize on emerging trends in casual legwear.

In the United States, 15 products were either launched during the latter half of fiscal 1994 or will be introduced in early fiscal 1995.

Hanes introductions included two products offering waist-to-toe figure control: *Smooth Illusions* hosiery, which combines body contouring with a sheer appearance, and the more moderately priced *Profiles* brand. Other successful introductions were *Silk Reflections Soft Touch* microfiber hosiery and the *Silk Reflections Plus* product for full-figured women. During fiscal 1995, Hanes will feature a new line of casual legwear for younger women through its *E.G. Smith* designer label.

In fiscal 1994, *L'eggs New Sheer Energy* hosiery, with enhanced comfort and fit, was introduced nationally. L'eggs also introduced sheer and casual legwear under the *Hanes Her Way* brand, *Color Me Natural* hosiery for African-American women, and a new toning and shaping product, *Sheer Energy Shapers*.

Control-top, microfiber and ultra-

sheer features are the focus of new or improved hosiery in Europe as well. The Filodoro Group, a leading Italian hosiery manufacturer acquired in fiscal 1993, will expand product offerings in the children's category and begin distribution of its *Philippe Matignon* brand in France.

Global Opportunities

Long-term profitability for Sara Lee's hosiery business will be fueled by progressive new product development, as well as initiatives and acquisitions that open new markets.

Fiscal 1994 acquisitions included The South African Hosiery Company (Pty.) Ltd., which markets products under several brand names in South Africa, and Peri Shoji Co., Ltd., which further established Sara Lee hosiery in Japan. Sara Lee acquired a majority ownership position in Shanghai Vocal Enterprise Ltd., a Chinese hosiery company, early in fiscal 1995.

Geographic expansion continued in the Americas, with the *Hanes* and *L'eggs* brands going into full distribution in Canada during fiscal 1994. In addition, the *L'eggs* brand and designer collection of *Donna Karan* hosiery were introduced in Mexico and Japan.

Sara Lee Household and Personal Care reported strong results for fiscal 1994. Sales totaled $1.5 billion, up 20%. Operating profit was $166 million before the restructuring charge, up 31%. Operations benefited from growth in core product sales and the acquisition of SmithKline Beecham's personal care division.

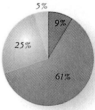

*Household and Personal Care
1994 Worldwide Sales (dollar share)*

- ■ United States
- ▨ Western/Central Europe
- Asia-Pacific/Latin America
- Other

HOUSEHOLD AND PERSONAL CARE

Sara Lee's Household and Personal Care business has a foundation for sustained global growth with regional and international branded products marketed in more than 120 countries.

Business and Strategic Overview

Strategically, Sara Lee is focusing on core products, containing costs, improving efficiencies and capitalizing on its worldwide reach to penetrate new markets.

In the primary core categories of shoe care, body care, insecticides and baby care, acquisitions provided additional products, economies of scale and entry into new markets. Product innovation and brand extensions strengthened market positions, and significant increases in advertising reinforced brand equity.

Sara Lee's shoe care business, principally consisting of sales under the *Kiwi* brand in 113 countries, strengthened its global position through product development and strategic partnerships. Joint ventures in China and India in fiscal 1994 are providing access to these exciting new markets.

In the body care category, the July 1993 acquisition of the European bath and body care businesses of SmithKline Beecham gave Sara Lee powerful branded product lines in key markets, extending the reach of its personal care business and sharpening manufacturing and operating efficiencies.

The established equity of *Duschdas*

and *Badedas* bath and shower products was of principal value in the SmithKline acquisition. The *Duschdas* brand is number one in its category in Germany, and *Badedas* products are marketed throughout Europe. Sara Lee also gained a strong position in the men's toiletries market through the addition of the *Williams* brand in France and *Brylcreem* products in the United Kingdom.

Vapona and *Catch* insecticides maintained market share despite unseasonably cold summer weather in fiscal 1994. The *Ridsect* line in Malaysia posted strong sales and was extended into Thailand and Hong Kong.

In the baby care category, which includes baby wipes, powder, lotion and shampoo, the *Zwitsal* brand continued to be the leader in several European markets. A strategic focus for the *Zwitsal* line is growth in Asia-Pacific countries that have a high demand for baby care products. In fiscal 1994, *Zwitsal* products were introduced in Malaysia, Thailand, Hong Kong, China, Taiwan, Malawi and Kenya.

The baby care line was expanded during the fiscal year through the acquisition of the *Fissan* and *Proderm* brands. The *Fissan* line of baby shampoo, soap and powder holds strong positions in Italy and Germany. The *Proderm* brand, with its range of baby shampoo, oil and wipes, maintained strong positions in Greece.

Ambi-Pur air fresheners, *Zendium* and *Prodent* oral care products, and

Biotex and *Neutral* detergents also are important products for Sara Lee; all maintained good market positions in fiscal 1994.

Sara Lee sustained solid performance in the furniture care business with its *Endust* and *Behold* brands, acquired in fiscal 1993. The *Endust* brand is one of North America's leading dusting and cleaning products, and *Behold* polish is a major value-priced line in furniture care.

Major New Products

Opportunities to add value to core categories and reach new markets will drive product development.

In fiscal 1994, Sara Lee introduced the *Tana* Pen Stick, a water-based shoe cream in an innovative dispenser-applicator, marketed in France, Belgium, the Netherlands, Germany, Austria and Switzerland. A similar product, *Kiwi Prodes* polish, was introduced in Japan.

Growth of the *Duschdas* brand was strengthened by the new *Duschdas* 2-in-1 Sport shower gel/moisturizer. Sara Lee introduced a similar product, *Sanex* 2-in-1 gel. The well-established *Sanex* brand is marketed in several European and Asia-Pacific countries. Sara Lee also successfully launched a new line of *Sanex* shampoo in normal, dry and anti-dandruff formulas.

An electrical diffuser insecticide was introduced in Belgium, France, the Netherlands, Spain and Portugal under a variety of regional brand names.

Sara Lee Household and Personal Care	As reported		Excluding restructuring						
(dollars in millions)	5-year compound growth rate	1994	5-year compound growth rate	1994	1993	1992	1991	1990
Sales	3.6%	$1,530	3.6%	$1,530	$1,279	$1,227	$1,319	$1,196
Operating income	(3.6)	111	4.5	166	126	107	152	128
Capital expenditures	0.0	41	0.0	41	42	44	54	41
Depreciation and amortization	8.2	71	8.2	71	55	53	55	47
Return on investment*		31.4%		43.3%	37.5%	29.6%	35.7%	31.5%

*Measures return on average net operating assets.

Sara Lee launched the *Ambi-Pur* Parfum d'Interieur electrical diffuser air freshener in the Netherlands, Spain, Italy, Portugal and Greece.

Biotex Compact pre-wash laundry detergent was introduced in fiscal 1994, boosting market share for the *Biotex* brand in the Dutch market.

Global Opportunities

Sara Lee will achieve long-term success in the Household and Personal Care business by developing successful products and lines and expanding them into emerging markets.

In addition to strengthening its presence in several European markets, Sara Lee fortified its position in the Asia-Pacific region with the introduction of its brands in Malaysia, Hong Kong and Thailand in fiscal 1994.

Joint ventures and acquisitions set the stage for entry into other key markets during fiscal 1994. A joint venture with China's largest shoe care manufacturer, Golden Rooster, provided an entree into the Chinese market. Sara Lee's *Kiwi* brand will gain access to the Indian market through a joint venture in that nation. Also, Sara Lee's acquisition of Kiwi Brands (Pty.) Ltd., completed in fiscal 1994, will strengthen Sara Lee's presence in shoe, bath and body care products in South Africa.

Sara Lee is building a foundation for the Household and Personal Care line of business in Central and Eastern Europe. It expanded a marketing unit in Hungary during the fiscal year and made preparations for an expansion program targeting the Czech Republic.

DIRECT SELLING

Sara Lee's direct selling business continues to grow through penetration of new markets, expansion of product lines and strategic acquisitions.

Direct selling distributes a wide range of cosmetics, fragrances, toiletries, personal products and jewelry through a network of independent sales representatives. With direct selling divisions in Mexico, Indonesia, the Philippines and South Africa, Sara Lee is well-positioned to develop opportunities in this $70 billion global market.

House of Fuller, Sara Lee's direct selling division in Mexico since 1968, posted record sales for the fiscal year, attributable in part to a significant sales force expansion. House of Sara Lee, in Indonesia and the Philippines, became number two in those markets after less than two years of operation.

In fiscal 1994, Sara Lee purchased Avroy Shlain Cosmetics (Pty.) Ltd., the number-one direct selling organization in South Africa.

The ongoing strategic emphasis for the direct selling business is to build on the strength of the corporation's global branded portfolio and production capability in developing nations where access to retail stores is limited. Expansion programs will focus on Southeast Asia, Latin America and Africa.

Sara Lee Household and Personal Care   Fiscal 1994 Highlights

- *Sara Lee's acquisition of the SmithKline Beecham bath and body care business included strong branded products in key European markets.*

- *The Household and Personal Care business' global reach was extended through joint ventures, opening markets in China and India.*

- *Sara Lee's direct selling division posted record sales in Mexico and acquired the number-one direct selling organization in South Africa.*

Sara Lee Corporation achieved record sales and earnings from operations in fiscal 1994, but this year clearly presented more challenges than we have faced in recent periods. Measuring the company's performance against our financial goals, excluding the impact of the restructuring charge and accounting change from net income, we met two of our targets, falling short of the third.

For the first time in nine years, we did not meet our 8% real earnings per share growth goal, as inflation-adjusted earnings rose only 2.9%. Including our strong performance in prior years, however, we are pleased to report 8.2% and 9.9% real earnings per share growth over the past 5- and 10-year periods, respectively, surpassing our 8% growth goal in both time periods. We are committed to achieving this aggressive growth goal in the future.

Return on equity was 20.5%, slightly above our 20% return on equity goal. We recognize that return on equity is an important measure of management's ability to invest stockholder funds wisely and have, in fact, increased our return on equity goal to 22% beginning in fiscal 1995.

Our third financial goal is to maintain a total-debt-to-total-capital ratio of no more than 40% over time. We ended fiscal 1994 with a 38.9% leverage ratio, below our 40% target.

Of considerable significance, Sara Lee announced a worldwide program to improve productivity and returns and to lower costs. The plan, resulting in an after-tax fourth quarter charge of $495 million, will enhance future growth and profitability, primarily in our Personal Products operations.

The charge included severance related to a reduction of our global workforce, and also involved the closing, consolidation and realignment of worldwide production and distribution facilities. This program will begin lowering costs in fiscal 1995, with annual savings expected to reach approximately

$250 million in fiscal 1998.

While Sara Lee's stock continues to provide superior returns over the long term, stockholder wealth fell in 1994 due to a lower stock price. This decrease was in line with declines in stock prices for many consumer products companies over the last 12 months.

The graph "Increase in Stockholder Value" shows the compound average annual return (assuming reinvestment of dividends) to Sara Lee stockholders relative to alternative investments such as the S&P 500 Index and U.S. Treasury Bills. Our 5- and 10-year compound average annual stockholder returns were 12.3% and 22.8%, respectively—above returns from both the S&P 500 and Treasury Bills in each time period.

We recognize that a prosperous company must invest in its businesses to ensure a strong future. In 1994, Sara Lee spent $628 million on capital expenditures to add capacity and improve returns. After two years of capital outlays above $600 million, we anticipate lower spending in 1995 as capital needs moderate and we focus on improving returns in several of our more capital-intensive operations.

To ensure that our brands retain their strong equity with consumers, we spent a record $1.5 billion in media and promotion in fiscal 1994.

We also enhanced our worldwide market positions through acquisitions, investing $412 million in cash in 1994.

Consistent with our strategy of building strong personal care positions worldwide, we acquired SmithKline Beecham's European soap, shampoo and toiletries businesses. This acquisition gave us strong brands in key markets and important production and distribution synergies.

In recognition of the positive social, political and economic developments in South Africa, Sara Lee reentered that market through the acquisition of Kiwi Brands (Pty.) Ltd.

and its subsidiaries. Kiwi produces and markets shoe care products. Subsidiaries include The South African Hosiery Company (Pty.) Ltd., that country's largest sheer hosiery company; Playtex, a producer and distributor of intimate apparel items; and Avroy Shlain Cosmetics (Pty.) Ltd., a direct marketer of personal care products. With sales of approximately $130 million, these businesses establish Sara Lee as one of the largest multinationals in South Africa.

We acquired a position in Kir Alimentos, a leading processed meats company in Mexico with the number-two market position. Mexico's growing marketplace represents a significant opportunity for Sara Lee.

Looking to fiscal 1995, we expect earnings growth to exceed last year's modest increase despite higher interest rates and rising commodity costs for some of our products. Opportunities exist to enhance the equity of our leading brands in key product categories around the world. These strong, growing positions, combined with programs to lower costs and improve productivity, will keep Sara Lee Corporation in the forefront of vital, profitable, U.S.-based multinationals, responsive to today's rapidly changing markets.

Michael E. Murphy
Vice Chairman and
Chief Financial and
Administrative Officer

FINANCIAL GOALS

Sara Lee Corporation strives to achieve three key financial goals:

- *real (inflation-adjusted) growth in earnings per share of 8% per year over time*
- *a return on equity of at least 20% (raised to 22% beginning in fiscal 1995)*
- *a total-debt-to-total-capital ratio of no more than 40% over time*

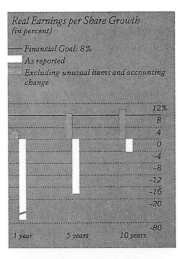

Real Earnings per Share Growth (in percent)

- Financial Goal: 8%
- As reported
- Excluding unusual items and accounting change

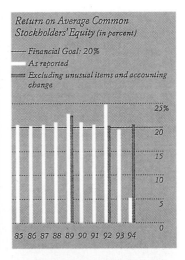

Return on Average Common Stockholders' Equity (in percent)

- Financial Goal: 20%
- As reported
- Excluding unusual items and accounting change

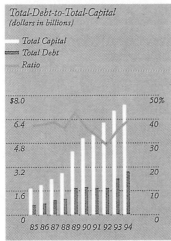

Total-Debt-to-Total-Capital (dollars in billions)

- Total Capital
- Total Debt
- Ratio

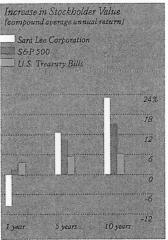

Increase in Stockholder Value (compound average annual return)

- Sara Lee Corporation
- S&P 500
- U.S. Treasury Bills

FINANCIAL SUMMARY

(dollars in millions except per share data)	Years ended	
	July 2, 1994[1]	July 3, 1993[2]
Results of operations		
Net sales	$15,536	$14,580
Operating income	632	1,307
Income before income taxes	389	1,082
Net income	199	704
Effective tax rate	39.9%	34.9%
Financial position		
Total assets	$11,665	$10,862
Long-term debt	1,496	1,164
Redeemable preferred stock	331	357
Common stockholders' equity	3,326	3,551
Return on average common stockholders' equity	5.1%	19.6%
Per common share[5]		
Net income—primary	$ .37	$ 1.40
Average shares outstanding (in millions)	480	485
Net income—fully diluted	.36	1.37
Average shares outstanding (in millions)	498	504
Dividends[6]	.63	.56
Book value at year-end	6.92	7.31
Market value at year-end	20.63	24.25
Other information		
Capital expenditures	$ 628	$ 728
Depreciation and amortization	568	522
Media advertising expense	371	392
Total advertising and promotion expense	1,498	1,455
Common stockholders of record	95,600	88,100
Number of employees	145,900	138,000

[1]In 1994, a restructuring provision reduced operating income and income before income taxes by $732 and net income by $495. In addition, in 1994, the cumulative effect of adopting a mandated change in the method of accounting for income taxes reduced net income by $35.

[2]53-week year.

[3]Fiscal 1992 income before income taxes includes a $412 gain on sale of business offset by a $190 restructuring provision. These transactions increased net income by $140.

[4]Fiscal 1989 income before income taxes includes an $87 gain on sales of businesses offset by a $55 restructuring provision. These transactions increased net income by $11.

[5]Restated for the 2-for-1 stock splits in fiscal 1993, 1990, 1987 and 1984.

[6]Fiscal 1992 includes a $.12 special dividend.

The Notes to Financial Statements should be read in conjunction with the Financial Summary.

	June 27, 1992[3]	June 29, 1991	June 30, 1990	July 1, 1989[4]	July 2, 1988[2]	June 27, 1987	June 28, 1986	June 29, 1985	June 30, 1984
					Years ended				
	$13,243	$12,381	$11,606	$11,718	$10,424	$9,155	$7,938	$8,117	$7,000
	1,207	1,085	938	847	753	632	514	474	414
	1,174	830	713	639	513	448	356	345	314
	761	535	470	410	325	267	223	206	188
	35.2%	35.5%	34.1%	35.8%	36.7%	40.4%	37.2%	40.3%	40.1%
	$ 9,989	$ 8,122	$ 7,636	$ 6,523	$ 5,012	$4,192	$3,503	$3,216	$2,822
	1,389	1,399	1,524	1,488	893	633	634	464	359
	351	344	338	182	225	75	75	75	75
	3,382	2,550	2,292	1,915	1,575	1,416	1,155	991	957
	24.7%	20.6%	20.9%	22.7%	21.1%	20.5%	20.4%	20.5%	19.4%
	$ 1.54	$ 1.08	$ .96	$ .88	$ .71	$ .59	$ .51	$ .45	$ .41
	476	464	460	454	447	447	433	443	453
	1.50	1.05	.93	.87	.71	.59	.50	.45	.41
	497	485	480	456	447	447	434	444	454
	.61	.46	.41	.35	.29	.24	.20	.18	.16
	7.05	5.48	4.97	4.21	3.56	3.20	2.70	2.32	2.16
	24.81	20.19	14.56	13.47	9.22	11.63	8.91	5.39	3.60
	$ 509	$ 522	$ 595	$ 541	$ 449	$ 287	$ 222	$ 247	$ 155
	472	394	351	280	251	202	165	153	136
	325	288	313	303	253	203	195	202	177
	1,294	1,067	1,013	925	801	637	587	594	513
	75,400	69,400	64,800	56,500	52,400	50,000	44,900	42,600	40,500
	128,000	113,400	107,800	101,800	85,700	92,400	87,000	92,800	90,900

This Financial Review discusses the corporation's results of operations and financial position. The discussion should be read in conjunction with the Review of Operations and the Consolidated Financial Statements and related notes.

Results of Operations

Net sales increased 6.6% to $15.5 billion in 1994, from $14.6 billion in 1993 and $13.2 billion in 1992. The increase in 1994 was principally attributable to business acquisitions and unit volume growth, offset in part by the weakening of foreign currencies relative to the U.S. dollar. The increase in 1993 resulted principally from business acquisitions, net of dispositions, unit volume growth and the strengthening of foreign currencies relative to the U.S. dollar. Excluding the effects of foreign currencies and acquisitions and dispositions, sales dollars increased 3% in 1994 and 5% in 1993.

The gross profit margin was 37.6% in 1994, compared with 38.0% in 1993 and 37.3% in 1992. The decrease in 1994 was attributable to margin declines in European hosiery and knit products businesses, offset in part by improved margins in the Household and Personal Care and Packaged Meats and Bakery operations. The improvement in 1993 was attributable to increased operating efficiencies resulting from business restructuring, tighter cost controls and benefits resulting from capital expenditures.

Operating income, which is pretax earnings before interest and corporate expenses, decreased 51.6% to $632 million, from $1,307 million in 1993, while the 1993 operating income reflected an 8.2% increase over the $1,207 million in 1992.

On June 6, 1994, the corporation announced a restructuring of its worldwide operations which will result in the closure of 94 manufacturing and distribution facilities and the severance of 9,900 employees. This restructuring

reduced 1994 operating income, net income and primary earnings per share by $732 million, $495 million and $1.03, respectively. The 1994 operating income includes charges for restructuring as follows: Personal Products— $630 million; Household and Personal Care—$55 million; Coffee and Grocery—$25 million; and Packaged Meats and Bakery—$22 million.

Of the total pretax charge for restructuring, $289 million relates to anticipated losses associated with the disposal of land, buildings and improvements, and machinery and equipment; $112 million relates to anticipated expenditures to close and dispose of the idle facilities; $239 million relates to anticipated payments to severed employees; $33 million relates to the recognition of pension benefits associated with the severed employee group; and $59 million primarily relates to losses associated with the disposal of certain businesses. As of July 2, 1994, no material actions contemplated in the restructuring plan have taken place.

Restructuring actions are expected to be substantially completed by 1996, and the corporation expects to fund the costs of the plan from internal sources and available borrowing capacity.

The corporation expects the restructuring plan to begin lowering operating costs in 1995 and to generate increasing savings in subsequent years, growing to an annual savings of approximately $250 million in 1998. Savings from the planned actions will be used for both business-building initiatives and profit improvement.

Excluding the effects of the restructuring charge, acquisitions and fluctuations in foreign exchange rates, operating income in 1994 was virtually unchanged from 1993 and increased by approximately 2% in 1993. In 1994, operating income in the Packaged Foods segment increased 2.3% and Packaged Consumer Products segment decreased 94.5%.

Excluding the restructuring charge, operating income in the Packaged Foods segment increased 10.5% while the Packaged Consumer Products segment was virtually unchanged from 1993 results. The increase in the Packaged Foods segment is primarily attributable to higher unit volumes, operating efficiencies, cost controls and business acquisitions, offset in part by the weakening of foreign currencies relative to the U.S. dollar. The flat results in the Packaged Consumer Products segment were primarily attributable to weak performances in the European hosiery and knit products operations and the weakening of foreign currencies relative to the U.S. dollar, offset by the impact of business acquisitions and strong U.S. knit products and worldwide intimates results.

Net interest expense was $145 million in 1994, compared with $82 million in 1993 and $94 million in 1992. The increase in 1994 was a result of increased financing needs for acquisitions and capital expenditures. The reduction in 1993 was primarily a result of lower short-term interest rates and the temporary refinancing of maturing long-term debt with short-term notes payable.

Unallocated corporate expenses are costs not directly attributable to specific segment operations. Unallocated corporate expenses were $98 million in 1994 and $143 million in 1993. The reduction in 1994 was primarily attributable to lower administrative expenses and costs related to hedging foreign currency movements. Unallocated corporate expenses, excluding the impact of unusual items, were $161 million in 1992. The unusual items recognized in 1992 consisted of a $412 million gain from the sale of the corporation's over-the-counter pharmaceutical business, offset in part by a $190 million provision primarily related to restructuring the Packaged Foods segment. The restructuring consisted primarily of the sale of assets, consolidation and reconfiguration of facilities and certain employee costs.

The effective tax rate was 39.9% in 1994, 34.9% in 1993 and 35.2% in 1992. Excluding the impact of unusual items in 1994 and 1992, the effective tax rates were 35.0% and 34.8%, respectively.

In fiscal 1994, the corporation adopted Statement of Financial Accounting Standards No. 109, "Accounting for Income Taxes." The cumulative effect of this mandated accounting change was a one-time charge of $35 million, or $.07 per share.

In 1994, net income decreased 71.8% to $199 million and primary earnings per share decreased 73.6% to $.37. Excluding the effects of the restructuring charge and the cumulative effect of the accounting change, net income and primary earnings per share in 1994 increased 3.5% and 5.0%, respectively. After giving effect to the two-for-one stock split, which became effective December 1, 1992, primary earnings per share in 1993 decreased 9.1% to $1.40 from $1.54 in 1992. Excluding the unusual items reported in 1992, net income and primary earnings per share increased 13.5% and 12.9%, respectively, in 1993.

During 1994, the corporation acquired several companies for an aggregate purchase price of $412 million in cash. The principal acquisitions were the European personal care businesses of SmithKline Beecham (Household and Personal Care), Kiwi Brands (Pty.) Ltd. and subsidiaries (Household and Personal Care and Personal Products) and Maglificio Bellia S.p.A. (Personal Products).

During 1993, the corporation acquired several companies for an aggregate purchase price of $352 million in cash and the issuance of common stock having a market value of $69 million. The principal acquisitions were BP Nutrition's Consumer Food Group (Packaged Meats and Bakery) and the

Filodoro Group (Personal Products). During 1992, the corporation acquired Playtex Apparel, Inc. (Personal Products), Pretty Polly Limited (Personal Products) and several small companies for a total purchase price of $657 million and the issuance of common stock with a market value of $167 million. Also during 1992, the corporation acquired a minority position and an option to acquire the remaining shares of Playtex FP Group Incorporated for $40 million and the issuance of common stock with a market value of $23 million.

These transactions are discussed in greater detail in the Acquisitions and Divestments Note to the financial statements on page 46. Sales and operating income of businesses sold are summarized in the Industry Segment Information Note to the financial statements on page 53.

During the past three years, the general rate of inflation has averaged 2.4%. Additionally, approximately 39% of the corporation's inventories are valued on the last-in, first-out basis. As a result, much of the current cost of production is reflected in operating results and not retained as a component of inventory.

Financial Position

Cash provided by operations in 1994 of $839 million was comparable to that provided in 1993 and lower than the $976 million generated in 1992. Net cash generated from operating activities in 1994 was adversely impacted by lower gross margins and increased levels of inventory and trade accounts receivable. The reduction in 1993 versus 1992 resulted from expenditures made in restructuring the corporation's domestic Packaged Foods and foreign Packaged Consumer Products segments, offset in part by improved gross margins and operating profits.

Net cash used in investment activities was $937 million in 1994, $967

million in 1993 and $381 million in 1992. During 1994, capital expenditures of $628 million decreased from the record level of $728 million in 1993. A significant portion of these expenditures was for the reduction of manufacturing and distribution costs, and for expansion of capacity to meet internal growth.

During 1992, expenditures to acquire plant and equipment and businesses were largely offset by approximately $800 million of proceeds received from the sale of the corporation's over-the-counter pharmaceutical business. Capital expenditures are anticipated to decline to between $500 million and $550 million in 1995. The planned level of capital expenditures is needed primarily to complete manufacturing and distribution cost reduction initiatives for the Personal Products businesses and to increase capacity in the Intimates businesses. The 1995 expenditures will be funded from internal sources and available borrowing capacity. The corporation retains substantial flexibility to adjust its spending levels in order to act upon other opportunities, such as business acquisitions.

During 1994, cash of $42 million was used in financing activities. In 1994, a domestic subsidiary of the corporation issued $200 million of equity securities, the proceeds of which were used to purchase shares of the corporation's common stock. During 1993, cash of $248 million was provided from financing activities, primarily through the utilization of available short-term debt capacity. As of July 2, 1994, the total-debt-to-total-capital ratio increased to 38.9% from 34.9% at July 3, 1993. The current capital structure is within the corporation's objective of maintaining a total-debt-to-total-capital ratio of no more than 40% over time and provides sufficient financial flexibility to pursue business opportunities.

MANAGEMENT'S REPORT ON FINANCIAL INFORMATION

Management of Sara Lee Corporation is responsible for the preparation and integrity of the financial information included in this annual report. The financial statements have been prepared in accordance with generally accepted accounting principles and, where required, reflect our best estimates and judgments.

It is the corporation's policy to maintain a control-conscious environment through an effective system of internal accounting controls supported by formal policies and procedures communicated throughout the corporation. These controls are adequate to provide reasonable assurance that assets are safeguarded against loss or unauthorized use and to produce the records necessary for the preparation of financial information. There are limits inherent in all systems of internal control based on the recognition that the costs of such systems should be related to the benefits to be derived. We believe the corporation's systems provide this appropriate balance.

The control environment is complemented by the corporation's internal auditors, who perform extensive audits and evaluate the adequacy of and the adherence to these controls, policies and procedures. In addition, the corporation's independent public accountants have developed an understanding of our accounting and financial controls, and have conducted such tests as they consider necessary to support their report below.

The board of directors pursues its oversight role for the financial statements through the Audit Committee, which is composed solely of outside directors. The Audit Committee meets regularly with management, the corporate internal auditors and Arthur Andersen LLP, jointly and separately, to receive reports on management's process of implementation and administration of internal accounting controls, as well as auditing and financial reporting matters. Both Arthur Andersen LLP and the internal auditors have unrestricted access to the Audit Committee.

The corporation maintains high standards in selecting, training and developing personnel to help ensure that management's objectives of maintaining strong, effective internal controls and unbiased, uniform reporting standards are attained. We believe it is essential for the corporation to conduct its business affairs in accordance with the highest ethical standards as expressed in Sara Lee Corporation's Code of Conduct.

John H. Bryan
Chairman of the Board and
Chief Executive Officer

Michael E. Murphy
Vice Chairman and
Chief Financial and
Administrative Officer

REPORT OF INDEPENDENT PUBLIC ACCOUNTANTS

To the Board of Directors
and Stockholders,
Sara Lee Corporation:

We have audited the accompanying consolidated balance sheets of SARA LEE CORPORATION (a Maryland corporation) AND SUBSIDIARIES as of July 2, 1994, July 3, 1993 and June 27, 1992, and the related consolidated statements of income, common stockholders' equity, and cash flows for each of the three years in the period ended July 2, 1994. These consolidated financial statements are the responsibility of the Corporation's management. Our responsibility is to express an opinion on these consolidated financial statements based on our audits.

We conducted our audits in accordance with generally accepted auditing standards. Those standards require that we plan and perform the audit to obtain reasonable assurance about whether the consolidated financial statements are free of material misstatement. An audit includes examining, on a test basis, evidence supporting the amounts and disclosures in the consolidated financial statements. An audit also includes assessing the accounting principles used and significant estimates made by management, as well as evaluating the overall consolidated financial statement presentation. We believe that our audits provide a reasonable basis for our opinion.

In our opinion, the consolidated financial statements referred to above present fairly, in all material respects, the financial position of Sara Lee Corporation and Subsidiaries as of July 2, 1994, July 3, 1993 and June 27, 1992, and the results of their operations and their cash flows for each of the three years in the period ended July 2, 1994 in conformity with generally accepted accounting principles.

As explained in the Notes to Financial Statements, the Corporation adopted the requirements of Statement of Financial Accounting Standards No. 109, "Accounting for Income Taxes," effective July 4, 1993.

Arthur Andersen LLP
Chicago, Illinois,
August 1, 1994.

CONSOLIDATED STATEMENTS OF INCOME

(in millions except per share data)	Years ended		
	July 2, 1994	July 3, 1993	June 27, 1992
Net sales	$15,536	$14,580	$13,243
Cost of sales	9,700	9,039	8,306
Selling, general and administrative expenses	4,570	4,377	3,891
Interest expense	188	162	172
Interest income	(43)	(80)	(78)
Unusual items			
Gain on sale of a business	—	—	(412)
Restructuring provision	732	—	190
	15,147	13,498	12,069
Income before income taxes	389	1,082	1,174
Income taxes	155	378	413
Net income before accounting change	234	704	761
Cumulative effect of accounting change	(35)	—	—
Net income	199	704	761
Preferred dividends, net of tax	(24)	(26)	(29)
Net income available for common stockholders	$ 175	$ 678	$ 732
Net income per common share–primary			
Before cumulative effect of accounting change	$ .44	$ 1.40	$ 1.54
Cumulative effect of accounting change	(.07)	—	—
	$ .37	$ 1.40	$ 1.54
Average shares outstanding	480	485	476
Net income per common share–fully diluted			
Before cumulative effect of accounting change	$ .43	$ 1.37	$ 1.50
Cumulative effect of accounting change	(.07)	—	—
	$ .36	$ 1.37	$ 1.50
Average shares outstanding	498	504	497

The accompanying Notes to Financial Statements are an integral part of these statements.

CONSOLIDATED BALANCE SHEETS

(dollars in millions except share data)

	July 2, 1994	July 3, 1993	June 27, 1992
Cash and equivalents	$ 189	$ 325	$ 198
Trade accounts receivable, less allowances of $164 in 1994 and $154 in 1993 and 1992	1,472	1,171	1,180
Inventories			
Finished goods	1,603	1,413	1,311
Work in process	361	322	325
Materials and supplies	603	545	524
	2,567	2,280	2,160
Other current assets	241	200	157
Total current assets	4,469	3,976	3,695
Investments in associated companies	142	205	186
Trademarks and other assets	492	518	580
Property			
Land	131	129	108
Buildings and improvements	1,746	1,570	1,476
Machinery and equipment	3,077	2,804	2,594
Construction in progress	283	339	231
	5,237	4,842	4,409
Accumulated depreciation	2,337	1,964	1,836
Property, net	2,900	2,878	2,573
Intangible assets, net	3,662	3,285	2,955
	$11,665	$10,862	$9,989

The accompanying Notes to Financial Statements are an integral part of these balance sheets.

	July 2, 1994	July 3, 1993	June 27, 1992
Notes payable	$ 1,281	$ 843	$ 154
Accounts payable	1,253	1,151	1,110
Accrued liabilities			
Payroll and employee benefits	668	429	408
Advertising and promotion	313	282	214
Taxes other than payroll and income	206	179	182
Income taxes	13	50	4
Other	1,103	909	991
Current maturities of long-term debt	82	426	237
Total current liabilities	4,919	4,269	3,300
Long-term debt	1,496	1,164	1,389
Deferred income taxes	290	512	488
Other liabilities	783	705	776
Minority interest in subsidiaries	520	304	303
Preferred stock (authorized 13,500,000 shares; no par value)			
Convertible adjustable: Issued and outstanding—607,000 shares			
in 1993 and 1992; redeemable at $50 per share	—	30	30
Auction: Issued and outstanding—3,000 shares; redeemable at			
$100,000 per share	300	300	300
ESOP convertible: Issued and outstanding—4,678,857 shares in 1994,			
4,755,217 shares in 1993 and 4,792,736 shares in 1992	339	345	348
Unearned deferred compensation	(308)	(318)	(327)
Common stockholders' equity			
Common stock: (authorized 600,000,000 shares; $1.33 1/3 par value)			
Issued and outstanding—480,765,240 shares in 1994,			
485,378,368 shares in 1993 and 239,862,390 shares in 1992	641	647	320
Capital surplus	76	66	306
Retained earnings	2,799	3,056	2,649
Translation adjustments	(170)	(194)	126
Unearned restricted stock issued for future services	(20)	(24)	(19)
Total common stockholders' equity	3,326	3,551	3,382
	$11,665	$10,862	$9,989

CONSOLIDATED STATEMENTS OF COMMON STOCKHOLDERS' EQUITY

(dollars in millions except per share data)	Total	Common Stock	Capital Surplus	Retained Earnings	Translation Adjustments	Unearned Restricted Stock
Balances at June 29, 1991	$2,550	$310	$ 68	$2,208	$ (12)	$(24)
Net income	761	—	—	761	—	—
Cash dividends						
Common ($.6125 per share)	(290)	—	—	(290)	—	—
Convertible adjustable preferred ($2.75 per share)	(2)	—	—	(2)	—	—
Auction preferred ($3,824.33 per share)	(11)	—	—	(11)	—	—
ESOP convertible preferred ($5.4375 per share)	(26)	—	—	(26)	—	—
Stock issuances						
Business acquisitions	190	6	184	—	—	—
Stock option and benefit plans	51	4	47	—	—	—
Restricted stock, less amortization of $6	6	—	2	—	—	4
Translation adjustments	138	—	—	—	138	—
ESOP tax benefit	10	—	—	10	—	—
Other	5	—	5	(1)	—	1
Balances at June 27, 1992	3,382	320	306	2,649	126	(19)
Net income	704	—	—	704	—	—
Cash dividends						
Common ($.56 per share)	(270)	—	—	(270)	—	—
Convertible adjustable preferred ($2.75 per share)	(2)	—	—	(2)	—	—
Auction preferred ($2,860.33 per share)	(8)	—	—	(8)	—	—
ESOP convertible preferred ($5.4375 per share)	(26)	—	—	(26)	—	—
Two-for-one stock split	—	322	(322)	—	—	—
Stock issuances						
Business acquisitions	69	3	66	—	—	—
Stock option and benefit plans	66	6	60	—	—	—
Restricted stock, less amortization of $4	4	—	8	—	—	(4)
Reacquired shares	(77)	(4)	(73)	—	—	—
Translation adjustments	(320)	—	—	—	(320)	—
ESOP tax benefit	10	—	—	10	—	—
Other	19	—	21	(1)	—	(1)
Balances at July 3, 1993	3,551	647	66	3,056	(194)	(24)
Net income	199	—	—	199	—	—
Cash dividends						
Common ($.625 per share)	(298)	—	—	(298)	—	—
Auction preferred ($2,732.33 per share)	(8)	—	—	(8)	—	—
ESOP convertible preferred ($5.4375 per share)	(26)	—	—	(26)	—	—
Stock issuances						
Stock option and benefit plans	69	6	63	—	—	—
Restricted stock, less amortization of $4	4	—	2	—	—	2
Reacquired shares	(224)	(12)	(82)	(130)	—	—
Translation adjustments	24	—	—	—	24	—
ESOP tax benefit	10	—	—	10	—	—
Other	25	—	27	(4)	—	2
Balances at July 2, 1994	$3,326	$641	$ 76	$2,799	$(170)	$(20)

The accompanying Notes to Financial Statements are an integral part of these statements.

CONSOLIDATED STATEMENTS OF CASH FLOWS

(dollars in millions)

	Years ended		
	July 2, 1994	July 3, 1993	June 27, 1992
Operating activities			
Net income	$ 199	$ 704	$ 761
Adjustments for noncash charges included in net income			
Depreciation and amortization of intangibles	568	522	472
Unusual items, net	732	—	(222)
Cumulative effect of accounting change	35	—	—
(Decrease) increase in deferred taxes	(222)	27	48
Other noncash credits, net	(109)	(117)	(93)
Changes in current assets and liabilities, net of businesses acquired and sold			
(Increase) decrease in trade accounts receivable	(162)	57	(118)
(Increase) in inventories	(224)	(124)	(288)
(Increase) decrease in other current assets	(29)	(40)	11
Increase (decrease) in accounts payable	20	(10)	160
Increase (decrease) in accrued liabilities	31	(169)	245
Net cash from operating activities	839	850	976
Investment activities			
Purchases of property and equipment	(628)	(728)	(509)
Acquisitions of businesses	(412)	(352)	(657)
Returns from (investments in) associated companies	48	5	(60)
Dispositions of businesses	—	31	805
Sales of property	49	51	34
Other	6	26	6
Net cash used in investment activities	(937)	(967)	(381)
Financing activities			
Issuances of common stock	69	66	51
Purchases of common stock	(224)	(77)	—
Redemption of preferred stock	(30)	—	—
Issuance of equity securities by subsidiary	200	—	—
Borrowings of long-term debt	385	256	64
Repayments of long-term debt	(438)	(300)	(86)
Short-term borrowings (repayments), net	328	609	(232)
Payments of dividends	(332)	(306)	(329)
Net cash from (used in) financing activities	(42)	248	(532)
Effect of changes in foreign exchange rates on cash	4	(4)	10
Increase (decrease) in cash and equivalents	(136)	127	73
Cash and equivalents at beginning of year	325	198	125
Cash and equivalents at end of year	$ 189	$ 325	$ 198

The accompanying Notes to Financial Statements are an integral part of these statements.

Summary of Significant Accounting Policies

Consolidation

The consolidated financial statements include all majority-owned subsidiaries. All significant intercompany transactions of consolidated subsidiaries are eliminated. Acquisitions recorded as purchases are included in the income statement from the date of acquisition.

Investments in associated companies

Investments in associated companies consist of minority positions in several companies whose activities are similar to those of the corporation's operating divisions. The equity method of accounting is used when the corporation's ownership exceeds 20% and it exercises significant influence over the investee. Other minority positions are recorded at cost.

Fiscal year

The corporation's fiscal year ends on the Saturday closest to June 30. Fiscal 1994 and 1992 were 52-week years, while 1993 was a 53-week year. Unless otherwise stated, references to years relate to fiscal years.

Intangible assets

The excess of cost over the fair market value of tangible net assets and trademarks of acquired businesses are amortized on a straight-line basis over the periods of expected benefit, which range from 10 years to 40 years. Accumulated amortization of intangible assets amounted to $572 at July 2, 1994, $457 at July 3, 1993 and $366 at June 27, 1992.

Subsequent to its acquisition, the corporation continually evaluates whether later events and circumstances have occurred that indicate the remaining estimated useful life of an intangible asset may warrant revision or that the remaining balance of an intangible asset may not be recoverable. When factors indicate that an intangible asset should be evaluated for possible impairment, the corporation uses an estimate of the related business' undiscounted future cash flows over the remaining life of the asset in measuring whether the intangible asset is recoverable.

Inventory valuation

Inventories are valued at the lower of cost (in 1994, approximately 39% at last-in, first-out [LIFO] and the remainder at first-in, first-out [FIFO]) or market. Inventories recorded at LIFO were approximately $24 at July 2, 1994, $38 at July 3, 1993 and $35 at June 27, 1992, lower than if they had been valued at FIFO. Inventory cost includes material and conversion costs. The corporation enters into forward foreign exchange contracts to hedge its exposure to currency fluctuations on certain inventory purchases. Gains and losses on these contracts are deferred and included in the cost of the inventory.

Property

Property is stated at cost, and depreciation is computed using principally the straight-line method at annual rates of 2% to 20% for buildings and improvements, and 4% to 33% for machinery and equipment. Additions and improvements that substantially extend the useful life of a particular asset and interest costs incurred during the construction period of major properties are capitalized. Repair and maintenance costs are charged to expense. Upon sale, the cost and related accumulated depreciation are removed from the accounts.

Foreign operations

Foreign-currency-denominated assets and liabilities are translated into U.S. dollars at the exchange rates existing at the balance sheet date. Translation adjustments resulting from fluctuations in exchange rates, and gains and losses on forward exchange contracts and currency swaps used to hedge long-term foreign investments, are recorded as a separate component of common stockholders' equity. Income and expense items are translated at the average exchange rates during the respective periods.

Net income per common share

Primary net income per common share is based on the average number of common shares outstanding and common share equivalents and net income reduced for preferred dividends, net of the tax benefits related to the ESOP convertible preferred stock dividends. The fully diluted net income per share calculation assumes conversion of the ESOP convertible preferred stock into common stock and further adjusts net income for the additional ESOP compensation expense, net of tax benefits, resulting from the assumed replacement of the ESOP convertible preferred stock dividends with common stock dividends.

Income taxes

Income taxes are provided on the income reported in the financial statements, regardless of when such taxes are payable. U.S. income taxes are provided on undistributed earnings of foreign subsidiaries that are intended to be remitted to the corporation. If the permanently reinvested earnings of foreign subsidiaries were remitted, the U.S. income taxes due under current tax law would not be material.

Advertising

During 1994, the American Institute of Certified Public Accountants issued Statement of Position 93-7, "Reporting on Advertising Costs," which will be effective for the corporation's fiscal 1995 statements. The statement primarily requires that the cost of advertising be expensed no later than the first time the advertising takes place. The impact of adopting this statement is not expected to have a material impact upon the corporation's results of operations or financial position.

Common Stock

Under the corporation's stock option plans, executive employees may be granted options to purchase common stock at the market value on the date of grant. Under the corporation's non-qualified stock option plans, an active employee will receive a replacement stock option equal to the number of shares surrendered upon a stock-for-stock exercise. The exercise price of the replacement option will be 100% of the market value at the date of exercise of the original option and will remain exercisable for the remaining term of the original option.

At July 2, 1994, 7,809,751 common shares were available for granting; options had been granted on 13,018,410 shares at prices ranging from $5.38 to $31.94 per share. During 1994, options on 3,707,564 shares were granted at prices ranging from $20.63 to $27.81; options for 2,321,765 shares were exercised at prices ranging from $3.56 to $25.63; and options for 880,163 shares expired or were canceled. Options exercisable at year-end were: 1994—9,548,858; 1993—10,425,115; and 1992—3,911,336.

Employees may purchase up to twenty-five thousand dollars market value of common stock annually at 85% of the market value. At July 2, 1994, 2,173,225 shares of common stock were available for issuance under this stock purchase plan.

The corporation has a restricted stock plan that provides for awards of common stock to executive employees, subject to forfeiture if employment terminates prior to the end of prescribed periods. The market value of shares awarded under the plan is recorded as unearned compensation. The unearned amount is amortized to compensation expense over the periods the restrictions lapse.

Effective December 1, 1992, the corporation declared a two-for-one stock split in the form of a 100% stock dividend.

Changes in outstanding common shares for the past three years were:

		1994	1993	1992
Beginning balances		485,378,368	239,862,390	232,683,861
Stock issuances	Business acquisitions	—	1,924,411	4,334,226
	Stock option and benefit plans	4,413,148	4,276,753	2,803,939
	Restricted stock plan	87,000	238,700	58,000
	Two-for-one stock split	—	241,988,568	—
Stock purchased/retired		(9,098,100)	(2,922,000)	—
Other		(15,176)	9,546	(17,636)
Ending balances		480,765,240	485,378,368	239,862,390

Preferred Stock

The corporation redeemed its cumulative convertible adjustable preferred stock on July 26, 1993 for $30. Quarterly dividends were based on the higher of yields of selected U.S. government securities or a minimum annual rate of 5.5%.

Six series of 500 shares each of nonvoting auction preferred stock are outstanding. Dividends are cumulative and are determined every 49 days through specific auction procedures.

The convertible preferred stock sold to the corporation's Employee Stock Ownership Plan (ESOP) is redeemable at the option of the corporation at any time after December 15, 2001. Each share is currently convertible into four shares of the corporation's common stock and is entitled to 5.133 votes. This stock has a 7.5% annual dividend rate, payable semiannually, and has a liquidation value of $72.50 plus accrued but unpaid dividends. The purchase of the preferred stock by the ESOP was funded with notes guaranteed by the corporation. The loan is included in long-term debt and is offset in the corporation's Consolidated Balance Sheets under the caption Unearned Deferred Compensation. Each year, the corporation makes contributions that, with the dividends on the preferred stock held by the ESOP, will be used to pay loan interest and principal. Shares are allocated to participants based upon the ratio of the current year's debt service to the sum of the total principal and interest payments

over the life of the loan. Plan expense is recognized in accordance with methods prescribed by the FASB.

ESOP-related expenses amounted to $11 in 1994, $11 in 1993 and $10 in 1992. Payments to the ESOP were $38 in 1994, $35 in 1993 and $32 in 1992. Principal and interest payments by the ESOP amounted to $11 and $27 in 1994, $7 and $28 in 1993, and $4 and $28 in 1992.

The fair value of the auction preferred stock approximated its carrying value as of July 2, 1994 and July 3, 1993. The fair value of the ESOP preferred stock was $443 and $530 at July 2, 1994 and July 3, 1993, respectively.

The corporation has a Preferred Stock Purchase Rights Plan. The Rights are exercisable 10 days after certain events involving the acquisition of 20% or more of the corporation's outstanding common stock or the commencement of a tender or exchange offer for at least 25% of the common stock. Upon the occurrence of such an event, each Right, unless redeemed by the board of directors, entitles the holder to receive common stock equal to twice the exercise price of the Right. The exercise price is $140 multiplied by the number of preferred shares held. There are 3,000,000 shares of preferred stock reserved for issuance upon exercise of the Rights.

Minority Interest in Subsidiaries

A domestic subsidiary of the corporation issued $200 of preferred equity securities in 1994. No gain or loss was recognized as a result of the transaction and the corporation owned substantially all of the voting equity of the subsidiary, both before and after the transaction. The securities issued by the subsidiary provide the holder a rate of return based upon a specified inter-bank borrowing

rate, are redeemable in 1996, and may be called at any time by the subsidiary. The subsidiary has the option of redeeming the securities with either cash, debt or equity of the corporation. The subsidiary used the cash proceeds received to purchase the common stock of the corporation on the open market.

A wholly owned foreign subsidiary of the corporation issued preferred equity

securities in fiscal 1990 and 1991 totaling $295. The securities provide a rate of return based upon specified inter-bank borrowing rates. The securities are redeemable in 1997 in exchange for common shares of the issuer, which may then be put to the corporation for preferred stock. The subsidiary may call the securities at any time.

Acquisitions and Divestments

During 1994, the corporation acquired several companies for an aggregate purchase price of $412 in cash. The principal acquisitions were the European personal care businesses of SmithKline Beecham; Kiwi Brands (Pty.) Ltd. and subsidiaries, a group of South African companies that manufacture and market personal care products and hosiery; and Maglificio Bellia S.p.A., a manufacturer and marketer of intimate apparel in Italy.

During 1993, the corporation acquired several companies for an aggregate purchase price of $352 in cash and the issuance of 1,924,411 shares of common stock having a market value of $69. The principal acquisitions were

BP Nutrition's Consumer Food Group, a manufacturer and marketer of packaged meat products in Europe, and the Filodoro Group, a manufacturer and marketer of hosiery in Italy.

During 1992, the corporation acquired several companies for an aggregate purchase price of $657 in cash and the issuance of 3,875,622 shares of common stock having a market value of $167. The principal acquisitions were Playtex Apparel, Inc., an international manufacturer and distributor of intimate apparel products, and Pretty Polly Limited, a manufacturer and marketer of hosiery in the United Kingdom. During the year, the corporation also acquired a minority position in Playtex FP Group

Incorporated, a manufacturer and marketer of personal care products, for $40 in cash and the issuance of 458,604 shares of common stock having a market value of $23. During 1994, the corporation disposed of substantially all of its investment in Playtex FP Group.

During 1992, the corporation sold businesses for proceeds of $805. The most significant disposition was the corporation's European-based, over-the-counter pharmaceutical business, Nicholas. The corporation made several divestments in 1993, which did not have a material effect on operating results or financial position.

Commitments and Contingencies

The corporation enters into interest rate swap agreements to manage interest rate fluctuations and lower its cost of borrowing. The differential to be paid or received on these agreements is accrued as interest rates change and is recognized over the lives of the respective agreements. The terms of swap agreements, which effectively converted short-term variable-rate debt into fixed-rate debt at the respective year-end, are shown below:

	1994	1993	1992
Aggregate notional principal	*$150*	*$161*	*$13*
Weighted average interest rate	8.8%	8.8%	8.1%
Weighted average maturity in years	.4	1.3	1.4

The corporation enters into forward foreign exchange contracts to hedge the foreign currency exposure of its net investments in European subsidiaries, intercompany loans and firm commitments. The corporation primarily sells European currencies and purchases U.S. dollars to hedge these foreign currency positions. As of July 2, 1994, the U.S. dollar equivalent of the primary foreign currencies sold forward was $242 French francs, $174 German marks, $151 Italian lira and $104 British pounds. These contracts have maturity dates that are generally less than one year. Similar arrangements were in place in prior years.

The corporation utilizes currency swaps to hedge the currency exposure of certain net investments in foreign operations and intercompany loans. The terms of the currency swaps, which effectively converted U.S. dollar- and Swiss franc-denominated debt into Dutch guilder-denominated debt, and hedged certain French franc-denominated intercompany loans at the respective year-end, are shown below:

	1994	1993	1992
Aggregate notional principal	*$546*	*$563*	*$922*
Weighted average interest rate	6.7%	5.8%	6.5%
Weighted average maturity in years	1.2	1.9	1.8

A large number of major international financial institutions are counterparties to the interest rate swaps, currency swaps and forward exchange contracts. The corporation continually monitors its positions and the credit ratings of its counterparties and, by policy, limits the amount of agreements or contracts it enters into with any one party. While the corporation may be exposed to credit losses in the event of nonperformance by these counterparties, it does not anticipate losses, because of the control procedures mentioned.

The fair market value of the corporation's interest rate swaps, currency swaps and forward exchange contracts approximated their carrying value in the financial statements as of July 2, 1994 and July 3, 1993. Fair value is estimated based upon the amount that the corporation would receive or pay to terminate the agreements as of the reporting date, utilizing quoted prices for comparable contracts and discounted cash flows.

The corporation had third-party guarantees outstanding, aggregating approximately $28 at July 2, 1994, $22 at July 3, 1993 and $24 at June 27, 1992. These guarantees relate primarily to financial arrangements to support various suppliers of the corporation, and are secured by the inventory and fixed assets of suppliers.

Trade accounts receivable due from highly leveraged customers were $52 at July 2, 1994, $41 at July 3, 1993 and $48 at June 27, 1992. The financial position of these businesses has been considered in determining allowances for doubtful accounts.

Rental expense under operating leases amounted to approximately $207 in 1994, $182 in 1993 and $175 in 1992. Future minimum annual fixed rentals required during the years ending in 1995 through 1999 under noncancelable operating leases having an original term of more than one year are $100, $72, $58, $49 and $39, respectively. The aggregate obligation subsequent to 1999 is $106.

The corporation is contingently liable for long-term leases on properties operated by others. The minimum annual rentals under these leases average approximately $6 for the years ending in 1995-1999, $2 in 2000-2004 and $1 in 2005-2009.

The corporation is a party to several pending legal proceedings and claims, and environmental actions by governmental agencies. Although the outcome of such items cannot be determined with certainty, the corporation's general counsel and management are of the opinion that the final outcome should not have a material effect on the corporation's results of operations or financial position.

NOTES TO FINANCIAL STATEMENTS
(dollars in millions except per share data)

Credit Facilities

The corporation has numerous credit facilities available, including revolving credit agreements totaling $1,900 that have an average annual fee of .1%. These agreements support commercial paper borrowings. Because of their short maturity, the fair value of notes payable approximates carrying value. Selected data on the corporation's short-term obligations follow:

	1994	1993	1992
Maximum period-end borrowings	$1,998	$1,484	$1,024
Average borrowings during the year	1,833	1,067	753
Weighted average interest rate during the year	4.2%	5.3%	6.2%
Weighted average interest rate at year-end	5.0	5.0	12.0

Long-Term Debt

		Interest Rate Range	Maturity	1994	1993	1992
U.S. dollar obligations:	ESOP debt	8.176%	2004	$ 323	$ 334	$ 341
	Eurodollar bonds			—	150	150
	Notes and debentures	4.40-9.70	1995-2016	876	548	476
	Revenue bonds	2.50-4.40	2001-2019	23	25	28
	Zero coupon notes	10.00-14.25	2014-2015	12	11	10
	Various other obligations			8	17	25
				1,242	1,085	1,030
Foreign currency obligations:	Swiss franc	4.75	1998	96	223	243
	Dutch guilder	6.50-8.625	1995-1998	123	177	203
	Various other obligations			117	105	150
				336	505	596
Total long-term debt				1,578	1,590	1,626
Less current maturities				82	426	237
				$1,496	$1,164	$1,389

The ESOP debt is guaranteed by the corporation.

The zero coupon notes are net of unamortized discounts of $112 in 1994, $113 in 1993 and $114 in 1992. Principal payments of $19 and $105 are due in 2014 and 2015, respectively.

Payments required on long-term debt during the years ending in 1995 through 1999 are $82, $93, $121, $253 and $81, respectively.

The corporation made cash interest payments of $203, $161 and $171 in 1994, 1993 and 1992, respectively.

The estimated fair value of the corporation's long-term debt, including current maturities, was $1,549 at July 2, 1994 and $1,645 at July 3, 1993.

The fair value of the corporation's long-term debt, including the current portion, is estimated using discounted cash flows based on the corporation's current incremental borrowing rates for similar types of borrowing arrangements.

Unusual Items

In the fourth quarter of 1994, the corporation provided for the costs of restructuring its worldwide operations. This restructuring provision reduced 1994 income before income taxes, net income and net income per common share by $732, $495 and $1.03, respectively. Of the total pretax charge, $289 relates to anticipated losses associated

A-36

with the disposal of land, buildings and improvements, and machinery and equipment; $112 relates to anticipated expenditures to close and dispose of the idle facilities; $239 relates to anticipated payments to severed employees; $33 relates to the recognition of pension benefits associated with the severed employee group; and $59 primarily relates to losses associated with the disposal of certain businesses. As of July 2, 1994, no material actions con-templated in the restructuring plan have taken place. Restructuring actions are expected to be substantially completed by 1996.

In 1992, the corporation sold its European-based over-the-counter phar-maceutical business, Nicholas, for a pretax gain of approximately $412 (equivalent to $.56 per share). Also in 1992, the board of directors approved a series of plans primarily related to the Packaged Foods segment designed to improve operating margins through the elimination of excess capacity and the disposition of operations that did not meet strategic goals. The restructuring consisted primarily of the sale of assets, consolidation and reconfiguration of facilities, and certain employee costs. The provision for this restructuring was $190. Together, these 1992 unusual items resulted in a net pretax gain of $222, or $.30 per share.

Retirement Plans

The corporation has noncontributory defined benefit plans covering certain of its domestic employees. The benefits under these plans are primarily based on years of service and compensation levels. The plans are funded in conformity with the requirements of applicable government regulations. The plans' assets consist principally of marketable equity securities, corporate and govern-ment debt securities and real estate.

The corporation's foreign subsidiar-ies have plans for employees consistent with local practices.

The corporation also sponsors defined contribution pension plans at several of its subsidiaries. Contributions are deter-mined as a percent of each covered employee's salary.

Certain employees are covered by union-sponsored, collectively bargained, multi-employer pension plans. Contri-butions are determined in accordance with the provisions of negotiated labor contracts and generally are based on the number of hours worked.

The annual pension expense for all plans was:

	1994	1993	1992
Defined benefit plans	$ 31	$ 30	$ 8
Defined contribution plans	11	13	13
Multi-employer plans	4	4	4
Total pension expense	$ 46	$ 47	$ 25

The increase in pension expense from 1992 to 1993 resulted from an increase in the benefits provided under certain foreign plans, the use of a lower discount rate in determining plan obligations and the impact of acquisitions.

The components of the defined benefit plan expenses were:

	1994	1993	1992
Benefits earned by employees	$ 52	$ 50	$ 41
Interest on projected benefit obligations	92	90	73
Actual investment return on plan assets	(99)	(131)	(108)
Net amortization and deferral	(14)	21	2
Net pension expense	$ 31	$ 30	$ 8

NOTES TO FINANCIAL STATEMENTS
(dollars in millions except per share data)

The status of defined benefit plans at the respective year-end was:

	1994	1993	1992
Fair market value of plan assets	**$1,420**	**$1,284**	**$1,244**
Actuarial present value of benefits for services rendered:			
Accumulated benefits based on salaries to date			
Vested	1,144	989	877
Nonvested	38	42	38
Additional benefits based on estimated future salary levels	217	222	218
Projected benefit obligations	1,399	1,253	1,133
Excess of plan assets over projected benefit obligations	21	31	111
Unamortized net transitional asset	(26)	(33)	(48)
Unrecognized net gain	(8)	(62)	(71)
Unrecognized prior service cost	88	89	75
Prepaid pension liability recognized on the Consolidated Balance Sheets	$ 75	$ 25	$ 67

Weighted average rates used in determining pension expense and related obligations for defined benefit plans were:

	1994	1993	1992
Discount rate	7.5%	7.6%	7.9%
Rate of compensation increase	5.2	5.3	5.8
Long-term rate of return on plan assets	8.3	8.8	8.8

Effective July 4, 1993, the corporation adopted Statement of Financial Accounting Standards No. 106, "Employers' Accounting for Postretirement Benefits Other than Pensions," (SFAS 106) for its domestic retiree benefit plans. Under SFAS 106, the corporation accrues the estimated cost of retiree health care and life insurance benefits during the employees' active service periods. The corporation's previous method of accounting for postretirement benefits other than pensions was similar to that required by SFAS 106, and as of the start of fiscal 1994, the accumulated benefit obligation for domestic employees had been accrued.

The corporation provides health care and life insurance benefits to certain domestic retired employees, their covered dependents and beneficiaries. Generally, employees who have attained age 55 and who have rendered 10 years of service are eligible for these postretirement benefits. Certain retirees are required to contribute to plans in order to maintain coverage. The domestic postretirement benefit expense was $15 in 1994, $18 in 1993 and $14 in 1992. The components of the 1994 expense were:

	1994
Benefits earned by employees	$ 4
Interest on accumulated benefit obligations	11
Net postretirement benefit expense	$ 15

The status of domestic postretirement
benefit plans at July 2, 1994 was:

	1994
Actuarial present value of benefits for services rendered:	
Retirees	$ 87
Fully eligible active plan participants	19
Other active participants	48
Accumulated benefit obligations	154
Fair market value of plan assets	2
Accumulated benefit obligations in excess of plan assets	152
Unrecognized net transitional asset	15
Unrecognized net loss	(4)
Unrecognized prior service cost	(1)
Postretirement benefit obligations recognized on Consolidated Balance Sheet	$162

The discount rate used to determine the 1994 accumulated postretirement benefit obligations was 7.75%. The assumed health care cost trend rate was 15% in 1994 decreasing to 7% in 2002 and beyond. Increasing the health care cost trend by one percentage point would have increased the 1994 postretirement benefit obligations by approximately 8% and the annual plan expense by approximately 12%.

Employees outside the United States are covered principally by government-sponsored plans, and the cost of company-provided plans is not material. The corporation is required to adopt SFAS 106 for its plans outside the United States in 1996.

Income Taxes

Effective July 4, 1993, the corporation adopted Statement of Financial Accounting Standards No. 109, "Accounting for Income Taxes," (SFAS 109). The cumulative effect as of July 4, 1993, of adopting SFAS 109, was a one-time charge of $35, or $.07 per share, primarily due to adjusting deferred taxes from historical to current rates. Financial statements for years prior to 1994 have not been restated to reflect the adoption of this standard. The effect of this new standard on 1994 income tax expense, exclusive of the cumulative effect adjustment, is not material.

The provisions for income taxes computed by applying the U.S. statutory rate to income before taxes as reconciled to the actual provisions were:

	1994		1993		1992	
	Amount	Percent	Amount	Percent	Amount	Percent
Income before provision for income taxes						
United States	$ 218	56.0%	$ 615	56.8%	$ 283	24.1%
Foreign	171	44.0	467	43.2	891	75.9
	$ 389	100.0%	$1,082	100.0%	$1,174	100.0%
Taxes at U.S. statutory rates	$ 136	35.0%	$ 368	34.0%	$ 399	34.0%
State taxes, net of federal benefit	24	6.2	22	2.0	17	1.4
Difference between U.S. and foreign rates	(34)	(8.8)	(31)	(2.8)	(28)	(2.4)
Nondeductible amortization	46	11.7	44	4.0	37	3.2
Other, net	(17)	(4.2)	(25)	(2.3)	(12)	(1.0)
Taxes at effective worldwide tax rates	$ 155	39.9%	$ 378	34.9%	$ 413	35.2%

NOTES TO FINANCIAL STATEMENTS
(dollars in millions except per share data)

Current and deferred tax provisions were:

	1994		1993		1992	
	Current	Deferred	Current	Deferred	Current	Deferred
United States	$200	$(144)	$175	$(7)	$ 98	$24
Foreign	143	(61)	159	17	238	27
State	34	(17)	33	1	21	5
	$377	$(222)	$367	$11	$357	$56

Following are the components of the deferred tax provisions occurring as a result of transactions being reported in different years for financial and tax reporting:

	1994	1993	1992
Depreciation	$ 22	$ 1	$ 8
Unremitted earnings of foreign subsidiaries	—	20	14
Inventory valuation methods	2	(1)	(4)
Restructuring reserves	(230)	—	—
Other, net	(16)	(9)	38
	$(222)	$ 11	$ 56
Cash payments for income taxes	$ 295	$304	$381

The deferred tax (assets) liabilities as of July 2, 1994, were:

	1994
Deferred tax (assets):	
Pension, postretirement and other employee benefits	$ (4)
Net operating loss and other tax carryforwards	(15)
Restructuring reserves	(230)
Reserves not deductible until paid	(243)
Deferred tax liabilities:	
Property, plant and equipment	230
Other	62
Net deferred tax (assets)	$(200)

Industry Segment Information

The corporation's business segments are described in the Review of Operations on pages 8 through 31.

| | Packaged Foods | | Packaged Consumer Products | | | | |
	Packaged Meats and Bakery	Coffee and Grocery	Personal Products	Household and Personal Care	Corporate	Inter-segment	Total
1994							
Sales[1]	$5,472	$2,090	$6,449	$1,530	$ —	$(5)	$15,536
Pretax income (loss)[2]	318	274	(71)	111	(243)[3]	—	389
Assets	1,662	1,776	6,535	1,335	357[5]	—	11,665
Depreciation and amortization	108	74	289	71	26	—	568
Capital expenditures	108	69	408	41	2	—	628
1993							
Sales[1]	$5,148	$2,058	$6,098	$1,279	$ —	$(3)	$14,580
Pretax income	287	292	602	126	(225)[3]	—	1,082
Assets	1,560	1,629	6,209	859	605[5]	—	10,862
Depreciation and amortization	99	80	265	55	23	—	522
Capital expenditures	99	87	485	42	15	—	728
1992							
Sales[1]	$4,703	$1,919	$5,398	$1,227	$ —	$(4)	$13,243
Pretax income	264	254	582	107	(33)[3,4]	—	1,174
Assets	1,253	1,851	5,395	970	520[5]	—	9,989
Depreciation and amortization	97	68	232	53	22	—	472
Capital expenditures	96	73	271	44	25	—	509

[1] Includes sales between segments. Such sales are at transfer prices that are equivalent to market value.

[2] Includes provisions for restructuring reported in the 1994 Consolidated Statement of Income, as follows: Packaged Meats and Bakery $22; Coffee and Grocery $25; Personal Products $630; and Household and Personal Care $55.

[3] Includes net interest expense of $145 in 1994, $82 in 1993 and $94 in 1992 incurred primarily in the United States to finance and support consolidated operations.

[4] Includes unusual items reported in the 1992 Consolidated Statement of Income. The gain of $412 relates to the Packaged Consumer Products segment. Restructuring charges of $126 and $64 are related to Packaged Foods and Packaged Consumer Products, respectively.

[5] Principally cash and equivalents and investments in associated companies and certain fixed assets.

Included in sales and operating income in the Industry Segment Information are the following sales and pretax income (loss) applicable to businesses sold prior to July 2, 1994:

| | 1994 | | 1993 | | 1992 | |
	Sales	Pretax income	Sales	Pretax income	Sales	Pretax income
Packaged Meats and Bakery	—	—	$88	$(1)	$160	$(6)
Household and Personal Care	—	—	8	—	55	3

Geographic Area Information

	United States	Western/ Central Europe	Asia-Pacific/ Latin America	Other	Corporate	Inter-area	Total
1994							
Sales[1]	$9,782	$4,433	$1,006	$348	$ —	$(33)	$15,536
Pretax income[2]	330	193	65	44	(243)[3]	—	389
Assets[6]	5,558	4,459	984	307	357[5]	—	11,665
1993							
Sales[1]	$9,423	$4,114	$ 801	$257	$ —	$(15)	$14,580
Pretax income	763	422	94	28	(225)[3]	—	1,082
Assets[6]	5,364	3,880	858	155	605[5]	—	10,862
1992							
Sales[1]	$8,736	$3,605	$ 655	$265	$ —	$(18)	$13,243
Pretax income	697	418	65	27	(33)[3,4]	—	1,174
Assets[6]	4,731	4,053	597	88	520[5]	—	9,989

[1] Includes sales between geographic areas. Such sales are at transfer prices that are equivalent to market value.

[2] Includes provisions for restructuring reported in the 1994 Consolidated Statement of Income, as follows: United States $483; Western/Central Europe $200; Asia-Pacific/Latin America $42; and Other $7.

[3] Includes net interest expense of $145 in 1994, $82 in 1993 and $94 in 1992 incurred primarily in the United States to finance and support consolidated operations.

[4] Includes the unusual items reported in the 1992 Consolidated Statement of Income. The gain of $412 relates to operating activities outside the United States, and substantially all restructuring charges of $190 relate to operating activities within the United States.

[5] Principally cash and equivalents and investments in associated companies and certain fixed assets.

[6] The tangible net assets of foreign operations included in the accompanying Consolidated Balance Sheets were $594 at July 2, 1994, $651 at July 3, 1993 and $863 at June 27, 1992.

Quarterly Financial Data (unaudited)

	First	Second	Third	Fourth
			Quarter	
1994				
Net sales	$3,796	$4,010	$3,664	$4,066
Gross profit	1,412	1,533	1,388	1,503
Net income (loss)	120[1]	236	152	(309)[2]
Per common share—Net income (loss)	.24[1]	.48	.30	(.65)[2]
Cash dividends declared	.145	.16	.16	.16
Market price—high	26.63	28.25	26.00	23.75
—low	21.00	23.38	21.00	20.13
1993				
Net sales	$3,583	$3,840	$3,308	$3,849
Gross profit	1,355	1,493	1,259	1,434
Net income	142	220	152	190
Per common share[5]—Net income	.28	.44	.30	.38
Cash dividends declared	.125	.145	.145	.145
Market price—high	29.19	32.44	31.88	28.13
—low	24.75	27.63	27.00	23.25
1992				
Net sales	$3,107	$3,594	$3,143	$3,399
Gross profit	1,098	1,316	1,195	1,328
Net income	263[3]	190	138	170
Per common share[5]—Net income	.55[3]	.38	.27	.34
Cash dividends declared	.118	.245[4]	.125	.125
Market price—high	22.88	28.38	29.07	26.63
—low	20.13	20.63	24.50	23.32

[1] Includes cumulative effect of accounting change of $35.
[2] Includes provision for restructuring of $495.
[3] Includes nonrecurring net gain of $140.
[4] Includes $.12 special dividend.
[5] Restated for the 2-for-1 stock split in December 1992.

BOARD OF DIRECTORS

CORPORATE OFFICERS

Seated from left:
Paul A. Allaire
John H. Bryan
Newton N. Minow
Joan D. Manley
Richard L. Thomas

Standing from left:
Baron G. Kraijenhoff
Duane L. Burnham
James L. Ketelsen
Donald J. Franceschini
Willie D. Davis
Charles W. Coker
Rozanne L. Ridgway
Sir Arvi H. Parbo
Vernon E. Jordan, Jr.
Allen F. Jacobson
C. Steven McMillan
Michael E. Murphy

Not pictured:
Frans H. J. J. Andriessen

In 1994, Sara Lee Corporation continued its long-standing commitment to women in a number of ways. By supporting women in sports, Sara Lee helped celebrate a spirit of competition and achievement that extended from a junior high basketball team in New England to Olympic athletes in Lillehammer.

As is the case in hundreds of cities across the United States, funding for girls' sports programs isn't easy to come by in Montpelier, Vermont. State monies are scarce and local businesses are inundated with pleas to sponsor everything from Little League baseball teams to soccer clubs.

So when the Central Vermont Cyclones, a stand-out Amateur Athletic Union (AAU) basketball team of 13- and 14-year-old girls, were invited to play at the Junior Olympic competition in New Orleans in July, the cost of plane fares and hotel rooms threatened to keep the team in New England.

But the Cyclones' spirits rose when Champion Jogbra, a division of Sara Lee Corporation, learned of the team's financial straits and came to its aid. The Vermont-based manufacturer and marketer of sports bras and women's athletic wear sponsored the Cyclones' trip to New Orleans and outfitted the players in *Jogbra* apparel.

Recognizing the fact that 85 percent of Sara Lee's consumers are women, and that funding for their sports programs still lags that for men, the corporation and its divisions have supported women's sports through the years by sponsoring programs for players of all ages. That commitment culminated with Sara Lee's partnership with the 1994 Winter Olympic Games in Lillehammer and the 1996 Summer Games in Atlanta. Separately, L'eggs sponsored the U.S. Figure Skating Team until the Winter Games, and Champion is sponsoring the U.S. Volleyball Team until the Summer Games begin.

Lending Olympic Support

While the Olympic partnership offers Sara Lee an unprecedented opportunity to promote its *Champion, Hanes, L'eggs* and *Playtex* brands, an Olympic sponsorship also means the corporation can help bring even more prominence to the value of athletics—especially for women. At the 1994 Winter Games, a record number of women competed in more than 60 events, and at the 1996 Summer Games, women will compete in 270 events.

Olympic dreams inspire many players who competed in the Junior Olympic basketball tournament in New Orleans. Teams that clinch a place at nationals often compete under the watchful eye of college recruiters. They follow the careers of the promising players, some of whom will one day be part of the U.S. Olympic Team. Indeed, some 70 percent of the women who play for the U.S. Basketball Team get their start on community teams like the Central Vermont Cyclones.

Head coach Doug Bresette said he was proud of the way the Cyclones performed in the Junior Olympics, particularly against the big-city players. "We received many compliments on our tenacity. Some of the teams we played were ranked in the top 10 in the country, and our team was thrilled to compete on this national level. Not one of them will ever forget the experience."

Lessons for Life

Most athletes and coaches acknowledge—though not easily at times—that winning isn't everything. Simply being part of a team has helped set the lives of millions of children on a steady course. And for those who persevere—learning what

Champion Jogbra sponsored the Central Vermont Cyclones, whose winning season earned them a spot in July at the Junior Olympics, held in New Orleans.

The Cyclones' team members are honor students as well as athletes, and each participates in at least two other sports.

"bone-tired" feels like after a long practice and discovering self-discipline—these early lessons pay off later in life.

The lifelong value of sports and physical activity for children, particularly girls, is well-documented. Women who were active in sports and recreational activities as girls feel greater confidence, self-esteem and pride than those who were not. High school girls who spend more time participating in sports also tend to have higher grades and are more likely to graduate from high school and attend college.

And it's not just traditional activities like jogging and aerobics that attract active women once they're out of school. In fact, while participation in these "entry-level" sports declined between 1984 and 1990, there was an increase in the number of women who preferred more competitive sports such as basketball, golf, soccer, downhill skiing and backpacking.

Donna Lopiano, executive director of the Women's Sports Foundation, says that while boys traditionally have developed their self-esteem through sports, which provide valuable role models, the same has not been true for girls. "By putting money into the Olympics, corporations and organizations are investing in role models for girls, too," she says. Funding sports can have even more far-reaching benefits when the programs are at a grassroots level and enjoyed by girls of varying abilities. "A little money makes a big difference in a youth program," Lopiano says.

Sara Lee Corporation has sponsored many women's sports programs in the last decade, the most prominent being the NCAA Woman of the Year Award, which was part of a $6 million sponsorship of NCAA women's programs from 1991 to 1993. The winners of the award, a women's sports equivalent of the prestigious Heisman Trophy, each received $15,000 for women's athletic programs at their respective colleges after demonstrating outstanding athletic, academic and community service achievements.

Programs at Work

Sara Lee also sponsors the Sara Lee Classic with the Ladies Professional Golf Association (LPGA). The annual tournament, which began in 1988, raises money for Vanderbilt Children's Hospital in Nashville and the Tennessee Special Olympics. The Sara Lee Classic also supports the LPGA Foundation, which started the Junior Golf Program for inner-city children and young people across the country, and maintains an academic scholarship program for junior golfers.

In 1993, Champion Jogbra sponsored the Susan G. Komen Foundation's Race for the Cure series. More than 125,000 walkers and runners took part in races around the country to help raise money for breast cancer education, treatment and research. The series funded mammogram screenings for low-income women in the dozens of communities where the races were held.

Most recently, the Sara Lee Foundation granted funds to the Women's Law Project of the Legal Assistance Foundation of Chicago. The organization won an important victory for students in Chicago Public Schools by lobbying for girls' soccer teams.

For many years, the school district had offered soccer as a sanctioned sport only to boys in public high schools. At the few schools that did have soccer clubs for girls, coaches were unpaid, the teams had to raise money themselves to pay for insurance and there were no championship tournaments organized by the school district.

The Women's Law Project joined forces with young women and coaches throughout Chicago and launched a successful campaign to make girls' soccer a sanctioned, funded varsity sport.

Since the 1972 passage of Title IX, which stipulated equal funding for men's and women's athletic programs in high schools and colleges, the number of girls and women competing has increased seven-fold.

Difficult to measure is the positive impact on the lives of thousands of young women who have found personal and professional fulfillment—and a stronger sense of themselves—through the simple opportunity to use their athletic talents. Sara Lee remains committed to fostering the desires and skills of these young women.

Corporate Information

The corporation's annual report to stockholders and proxy statement together contain substantially all the information presented in the Form 10-K report filed with the Securities and Exchange Commission. Individuals interested in receiving the Form 10-K, quarterly reports or other printed corporate literature should write to the Investor Relations and Corporate Affairs Department at the corporate headquarters address or call (312) 558-4947.

Investor Inquiries

Securities analysts, portfolio managers and representatives of financial institutions seeking information about the corporation should contact Lynn L. McHugh, director—investor relations, at the corporate headquarters or call (312) 558-4966.

Stockholder Inquiries

Stockholders with inquiries relating to stockholder records, stock transfers, change of ownership, change of address and dividend payments should write to Norma L. Quigley, manager—shareholder services, at the corporate headquarters or call (312) 558-8662.

Stock Listing

Sara Lee Corporation's common stock is listed under the symbol SLE on the New York, Chicago and Pacific stock exchanges. The stock also is traded in London and Amsterdam, on the Swiss stock exchanges in Zurich, Geneva and Basel, and on the Paris Bourse. Options are traded on the American Stock Exchange. The corporation's daily trading activity, stock price and dividend information are in the financial sections of most major newspapers.

Return on Owning Sara Lee Corporation Stock

After adjustment for stock splits, a single share of Sara Lee Corporation common stock purchased on June 30, 1984 at its $3.59 price was worth $28.02 on June 30, 1994, assuming the reinvestment of dividends and before consideration of taxes. This is an increase of 680%, or a compound annual growth rate of 22.8% over the 10-year period. After adjusting for the impact of inflation over the past 10 years, the same initial investment would have grown to $20.16. This is an increase of 461%, or a compound annual real growth rate of 18.8%.

Dividends

Sara Lee Corporation's quarterly dividends on common stock are paid on or about the first day of January, April, July and October. The corporation has paid 194 consecutive quarterly dividends.

Dividend Reinvestment

All stockholders are invited to participate in the corporation's automatic dividend reinvestment program. The program gives stockholders a convenient and economical way to reinvest their dividends in Sara Lee Corporation stock and/or invest additional cash amounts free of brokerage or service charges. For further information, write to: Sara Lee Corporation, Dividend Reinvestment Plan, Three First National Plaza, Chicago, Illinois 60602-4260.

Annual Meeting

The corporation's 1994 annual meeting of stockholders will be held Thursday, October 27, 1994 at 10 a.m. at the Arthur Rubloff Auditorium of the Art Institute of Chicago, Columbus Drive between Monroe and Jackson Streets, Chicago, Illinois.

Italicized brand names used throughout this report are trademarks of Sara Lee Corporation and its subsidiaries.

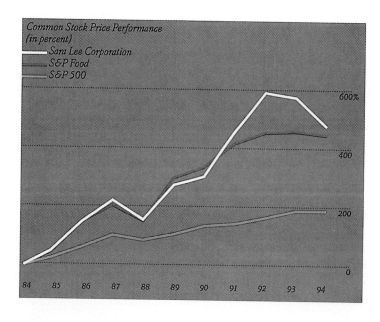

Common Stock Price Performance (in percent)
— Sara Lee Corporation
— S&P Food
— S&P 500

Glossary

accelerated depreciation methods   Those methods that record more depreciation expense in the early years of an asset's life and less in the later years. (p. 232)

account form   A common format of the balance sheet, in which assets are placed on the left side of the page and liabilities and owners' equity on the right side. (p. 95)

accounting elements   The categories under which the results of all accounting transactions can be classified. (p. 93)

accounting equation   Assets = Liabilities + Owners' Equity. Also called the business equation. (p. 95)

accounting information   Raw data concerning transactions that have been transformed into financial numbers that can be used by economic decision makers. (p. 72)

Accounting Principles Board (APB)   The standards-setting organization that was the immediate predecessor of the Financial Accounting Standards Board. (p. 384)

Accounting Research Bulletins (ARBs)   The pronouncements issued by the Committee on Accounting Procedure. (p. 383)

accrual basis accounting   A method of accounting in which revenues are recognized when they are earned, regardless of when the associated cash is collected. The expenses incurred in generating the revenue are recognized when the benefit is derived rather than when the associated cash is paid. (p. 199)

accruals   Adjustments made to record items that should be included on the income statement, but have not yet been recorded. (p. 207)

accrue   As used in accounting, to come into being as a legally enforceable claim. (p. 199)

accrued expenses   Expenses appropriately recognized under accrual accounting in one income statement period although the associated cash will be paid in a later income statement period. (p. 207)

accrued revenues   Revenues appropriately recognized under accrual accounting in one income statement period although the associated cash will be received in a later income statement period. (p. 207)

accumulated depreciation   The total amount of cost that has been systematically converted to expense since a long-lived asset was first purchased. (p. 212)

acid test ratio   Another name for the quick ratio. (p. 475)

additional paid-in capital   The amount in excess of the stock's par value received by the corporation when par value stock is issued. (p. 103)

adjustments   Changes made in recorded amounts of revenues and expenses in order to follow the guidelines of accrual accounting. (p. 206)

adverse opinion   An audit opinion given when the financial statements contain pervasive departures from GAAP. (p. 400)

annual report   The most comprehensive presentation of financial reporting a company provides to its stockholders. Contains financial statements and other information designed to assist economic decision makers. (p. 415)

APB Opinions The pronouncements issued by the Accounting Principles Board. (p. 384)

articles of incorporation An application for a charter allowing the operation of a corporation. (p. 98)

articulation The relationships (links) among the financial statements. (p. 173)

assets An accounting element that is one of the three components of a balance sheet. Assets are probable future economic benefits controlled by an entity as a result of previous transactions or events—that is, what a company has. (p. 93)

audit Examination by an independent CPA of enough of a company's records to determine whether the financial statements have been prepared in accordance with GAAP. (p. 397)

authorized shares The maximum number of shares of stock a corporation has been given permission to issue under its corporate charter. (p. 101)

average cost method The inventory cost flow method that assigns an average cost to the units of inventory on hand at the time of each sale. (p. 289)

balance sheet A financial statement providing information about an entity's present condition. Reports what a company possesses (assets) and who has claim to those possessions (liabilities and owners' equity). (p. 92)

beginning inventory The amount of merchandise inventory (units or dollars) on hand at the beginning of the income statement period. (p. 266)

bond An interest-bearing debt instrument that allows corporations to borrow large amounts of funds for long periods of time and creates a liability for the borrower. (p. 128)

book inventory The amount of ending inventory (units and dollars) resulting from transactions recorded by a perpetual inventory system. (p. 277)

book value The original cost of a long-lived asset less its accumulated depreciation. This item is often shown on the balance sheet. (p. 212)

business Depending on the context, the area of commerce or trade, an individual company, or the process of producing and distributing goods and services. (p. 4)

business equation Assets = Liabilities + Owners' Equity. Also called the accounting equation. (p. 95)

business segment A portion of the business for which assets, results of operations, and activities can be separately identified. (p. 321)

bylaws The basic rules by which a corporation is operated. (p. 99)

capital A factor of production that includes the buildings, machinery, and tools used to produce goods and services. Also, sometimes used to refer to the money used to buy those items. (p. 4)

capitalism A type of market economy. The economic system in place in the United States. (p. 5)

cash basis accounting A basis of accounting in which cash is the sole criterion used in measuring revenue and expense for a given income statement period. Revenue is recognized when the associated cash is received, and expense is recognized when the associated cash is paid. (p. 195)

cash flow The movement of cash in and out of a company. (p. 68)

character ethics Another name for virtues ethics. Sometimes called classical ethics. (p. 51)

chief executive officer (CEO) The person responsible for all activities of the corporation. This person is usually also the president. (p. 100)

classified balance sheet A balance sheet showing assets and liabilities categorized into current and long-term items. (p. 312)

cognitive dissonance The hesitation that sets in after an alternative has been chosen, but before it has been implemented. In common language, having "second thoughts." (p. 45)

collateral Something of value that will be forfeited if a borrower fails to make payments as agreed. (p. 126)

commercial borrowing The process that businesses go through to obtain financing. (p. 122)

Committee on Accounting Procedure (CAP) In operation from 1930 to 1959, this committee issued pronouncements called Accounting Research Bulletins (ARBs). (p. 383)

common stock   A share of ownership in a corporation. Each share represents one vote in the election of the board of directors and other pertinent corporate matters. (p. 102)

communism   A type of a planned economy, characterized by dictatorial government control. (p. 5)

comparability   One of the two secondary qualitative characteristics of useful accounting information. It means reports generated for one entity may be usefully compared with the reports generated for other entities. (p. 78)

comparative financial statements   Financial statements showing results from two or more consecutive periods. (p. 328)

compilation   Preparation by a CPA of a company's financial statements from records provided by the company, with no assurance that the information presented in the statements complies with GAAP. (p. 402)

conservatism   In a situation where two approaches to valuation or measurement are allowed under GAAP and the choice is unclear, the treatment least likely to overstate assets or income, or understate liabilities, is to be selected. (p. 394)

consistency   One of the two secondary qualitative characteristics of useful accounting information. It means an entity consistently uses the same accounting methods and procedures from period to period. (p. 78)

consolidated financial statements   Financial statements that include the results of operations and the financial position of the parent company and its subsidiary companies as if they were one enterprise with several branches or divisions. (p. 419)

consumer borrowing   Loans obtained by individuals to buy homes, cars, or other personal property. (p. 122)

contract rate   Another name for nominal interest rate. (p. 129)

contributed capital   Total amount invested in a corporation by its shareholders. Also called paid-in capital. (p. 102)

controller   The person in charge of all accounting functions of a corporation. (p. 100)

convertible securities   Debt or equity securities that can be converted into shares of the company's common stock. (p. 419)

corporate charter   A legal contract between a corporation and the state in which it is incorporated. (p. 98)

corporation   One of the three forms of business organization. The only one that is legally considered to be an entity separate from its owners. (p. 16)

cost/benefit analysis   Deals with the trade-off between the rewards of selecting a given alternative and the sacrifices required to obtain those rewards. (p. 40)

cost of goods sold   The cost of the product sold as the primary business activity of a company. (p. 155) The cost of the merchandise inventory no longer on hand, and assumed sold during the period. (p. 266)

cost of sales   Another name for cost of goods sold. (p. 155, p. 266)

coupon rate   Another name for nominal interest rate. (p. 129)

coverage ratio   A solvency ratio that provides an indication of a company's ability to make its periodic interest payments. (p. 480)

creative decision making   Allowing, even forcing, oneself to consider more than just the obvious alternatives in a decision situation. (p. 44)

cumulative effect of a change in accounting principle   Results of adopting a new accounting standard or changing from one acceptable method of accounting to another. One of the nonrecurring items shown net of tax on the income statement. (p. 326)

current assets   Assets that are either cash or will become cash within one year. (p. 312)

current liabilities   Liabilities that must be paid within one year. (p. 314)

current ratio   A liquidity ratio that measures a company's ability to meet short-term obligations by comparing current assets to current liabilities. (p. 474)

data   The raw results of transactions and events. Data are of little use to decision makers because they do not differentiate among transactions of relatively different importance. (p. 72)

date of declaration The date upon which a corporation announces plans to distribute a dividend. At this point, the corporation becomes legally obligated to make the distribution: A liability is created. (p. 171)

date of payment The date a corporate dividend is actually paid. The payment date is generally announced on the date of declaration. (p. 171)

date of record Owners of the shares of stock on this day are the ones who will receive the dividend announced on the date of declaration. (p. 171)

debt financing Acquiring funds for business operations by borrowing. Debt financing is one type of external financing. (p. 121)

debt ratio A solvency ratio that indicates what proportion of a company's assets is financed by debt. (p. 478)

decision making The process of identifying alternative courses of action and selecting an appropriate alternative in a given decision situation. (p. 38)

defaulting Failing to repay a loan as agreed. (p. 124)

deferrals Situations in which cash is either received or paid, but the income statement effect is delayed until some later period. Deferred revenues are recorded as liabilities, and deferred expenses are recorded as assets. (p. 207)

deferred expenses Expenses created when cash is paid before any benefit is received. Because the benefit to be derived is in the future, the item is recorded as an asset. Later, when the benefit is received from the item, it will be recognized as an expense. (p. 208)

deferred revenues Revenues created when cash is received before the revenue is earned. Because the cash received has not yet been earned, an obligation is created and a liability is recorded. Later, when the cash is deemed to have been earned, it will be recognized as a revenue. (p. 207)

depreciable amount Another name for depreciable base. (p. 205)

depreciable base The total amount of depreciation expense that is allowed to be claimed for an

asset during its useful life. The depreciable base is the cost of the asset less its residual value. (p. 205)

depreciation The systematic and rational conversion of a long-lived asset's cost from asset to expense in the income statement periods benefited. (p. 204)

depreciation expense The amount of cost associated with a long-lived asset converted to expense in a given income statement period. (p. 205)

direct method The format of a statement of cash flows that provides detail about the individual sources and uses of cash associated with operating activities. (p. 343)

disclaimer An audit opinion stating that the auditor is unable to render an opinion on the financial statements. (p. 400)

discontinued operations The disposal of a business segment. One of the nonrecurring items shown net of tax on the income statement. (p. 321)

discount If a bond's selling price is below its par value, the bond is being sold at a discount. (p. 132)

dividends A distribution of earnings from a corporation to its owners. Dividends are most commonly distributed in the form of cash. (p. 102)

double-declining-balance method An accelerated depreciation method in which depreciation expense is twice the straight-line percentage multiplied by the book value of the asset. (p. 235)

double taxation The tax imposed on the after-tax profits of a corporation that have been distributed to the stockholders in the form of dividends. (p. 17)

drawings Distributions to the owners of proprietorships and partnerships. Also called withdrawals. (p. 165)

earned equity The total amount a company has earned since its beginning, less any amounts distributed to the owner(s). In a corporation, this is called retained earnings. (p. 94)

earnings Another name for net income. (p. 153)

earnings per share (EPS) A calculation indicating how much of a company's total earnings is attributable to each share of common stock. (p. 419)

economic decision making Generally, the process of making decisions involving money; here, decision making that takes place in the course of business transactions. (p. 65)

effective interest rate The rate of interest actually earned by a bondholder. This amount will be different from the nominal interest rate if the bond is bought at a discount or premium. Also called yield rate or market interest rate. (p. 129)

ending inventory The amount of inventory (in units or dollars) still on hand at the end of an accounting period. (p. 266)

entrepreneurs People willing to accept the opportunities and risks of starting and running businesses. (p. 4)

entrepreneurship The factor of production that brings the other three factors—natural resources, labor, and capital—together to form a business. (p. 4)

equity An accounting element that is one of the three components of a balance sheet. Equity is the residual interest in the assets of an entity that remains after deducting liabilities. (p. 94)

equity financing Acquiring funds for business operations by giving up ownership interest in the company. For a corporation, this means issuing capital stock. Equity financing is one type of external financing. (p. 121)

equity investors Those who purchase an ownership interest in a company. One of the three major categories of financial statement users. (p. 460)

ethics A system of standards of conduct and moral judgment. (p. 51)

expense recognition principle Expenses must be matched to the same income statement period as the revenues they helped generate. (p. 392)

expenses An accounting element representing the outflow of assets resulting from an entity's ongoing major or central operations. These are the sacrifices required to attain the rewards (revenues) of doing business. (p. 153)

exports Goods that are produced in one country and sold in another country. (p. 23)

external decision makers Economic decision makers outside a company who make decisions about the company. The accounting information they use to make those decisions is limited to what the company provides them. (p. 66)

external financing Acquiring funds from outside the company. Equity and debt financing are the two major types of external financing. (p. 121)

extraordinary item A gain or loss that is both unusual in nature and infrequent in occurrence. One of the nonrecurring items shown net of tax on the income statement. (p. 323)

extrinsic reward Any reward that comes from outside the decision maker. The money earned for fulfilling job responsibilities is an example of an extrinsic reward. (p. 40)

face value Another name for par value of a bond. (p. 129)

factors of production The four major items needed to support economic activity: natural resources, labor, capital, and entrepreneurship. (p. 4)

feedback value A primary characteristic of relevance. To be useful, accounting must provide decision makers with information that allows them to assess the progress of an investment. (p. 76)

FIFO (first in, first out) The inventory flow concept based on the assumption that the first units of inventory purchased are the first ones sold. (p. 269)

financial accounting The branch of accounting developed to meet the informational needs of external decision makers. (p. 68)

Financial Accounting Standards Board (FASB) The organization that is principally responsible for establishing accounting guidelines and rules in the United States at the present time. (p. 74, p. 385)

financial reporting Financial disclosures provided to economic decision makers that include both quantitative (numerical) information and qualitative (descriptive) information. (p. 415)

financial statement analysis The process of looking beyond the face of the financial statements to gather more information. (p. 459)

financing activities Business activities such as the issuance of debt or equity and the payment of dividends, that focus on the external financing of the company. (p. 348)

footnotes Another name for the notes to the financial statements. (p. 421)

Form 10-K A report filed annually with the Securities and Exchange Commission by publicly traded companies. Includes detailed financial information and descriptive information that is generally beyond what is found in the annual report. (p. 415)

full disclosure principle The financial statements prepared by a company must provide users with the information they need to make economic decisions. (p. 392)

fully diluted earnings per share A more stringent EPS calculation than primary earnings per share. This calculation includes the potential impact of convertible securities in the denominator of the EPS calculation. (p. 420)

gains Net inflows resulting from peripheral activities of a company. An example is the sale of an asset for more than its book value. (p. 241)

generally accepted accounting principles (GAAP) Guidelines for presentation of financial accounting information designed to serve external decision makers' need for consistent and comparable information. (p. 378)

generally accepted auditing standards (GAAS) A set of standards (rules) governing the behavior of CPAs with regard to the performance of audits. (p. 397)

going concern assumption Unless there is persuasive evidence to the contrary, it is assumed that businesses will continue to operate indefinitely. (p. 389)

goods available for sale The total amount of merchandise inventory a company has available to sell in a given income statement period. (p. 266)

gross margin An item shown on a multistep income statement, calculated as: Sales – Cost of Goods Sold. (p. 157)

gross profit The excess of benefit received over the sacrifice made to complete a sale. Gross profit considers only the cost of the item sold; it does not consider the other costs of operations. (p. 8) Another name for gross margin. (p. 157)

group decision making Two or more persons working together to solve a problem. (p. 54)

historical cost principle Balance sheet items are generally reported at their cost, not their value. (p. 391)

human resource factor Equivalent to labor. One of the factors of production. (p. 4)

hybrid companies Those companies involved in more than one type of activity (manufacturing, merchandising, service). (p. 22)

imports Goods that are produced outside the country in which they are sold. (p. 23)

income from operations Another name for operating income, shown on the multistep income statement. (p. 157)

income statement A financial statement providing information about an entity's past performance. Its purpose is to measure the results of the entity's operations for some specific time period. (p. 152)

incorporators Individuals who make application to form a corporation. (p. 98)

indenture The legal agreement made between a bond issuer and a bondholder that states repayment terms and other details. (p. 129)

indirect method The more widely used format of the statement of cash flows. This approach begins with a reconciliation of accrual net income to the cash provided by or used by operating activities. (p. 343)

individual decision making One person working alone to solve a problem. (p. 54)

industry peculiarity A circumstance in which the characteristics of activity in a particular industry cause adherence to a particular GAAP rule to result in misleading information. (p. 394)

information Data that have been transformed so that they are useful in the decision-making process. (p. 72)

Integrated Disclosure System A system of reporting developed by the Securities and Exchange Commission that has eliminated much of the duplication between the information disclosed in Form 10-K and that disclosed in the annual report. (p. 418)

interest The cost to the borrower of using someone else's money. Also, what can be earned by lending money to someone else. (p. 124)

internal decision makers Economic decision makers within a company who make decisions for the company. They have access to much or all of the accounting information generated within the company. (p. 66)

internal financing Providing funds for the operation of a company through the earnings process of that company. (p. 121)

intrinsic reward Any reward that comes from within the decision maker. The sense of satisfaction that comes from doing a job well is an example of an intrinsic reward. (p. 40)

intuitive style A style of processing information in which decisions are based on hunches after considering the big picture and brainstorming to find possible solutions. (p. 42)

inventory Another term for merchandise inventory. (p. 265)

inventory turnover ratio A liquidity ratio that indicates how long a company holds its inventory. (p. 477)

investing activities Business activities related to long-term assets. Examples are the purchase and sale of property, plant, and equipment. (p. 347)

investment bankers Intermediaries between the corporation issuing stock and the investors who ultimately purchase the shares. Also called underwriters. (p. 109)

investments by owners That part of owners' equity generated by the receipt of cash (or other assets) from the owners. (p. 94)

issued shares Stock that has been distributed to the owners of the corporation in exchange for cash or other assets. (p. 101)

labor The mental and physical efforts of all workers performing tasks required to produce and sell goods and services. This factor of production is also called the human resource factor. (p. 4)

letter to the stockholders An item often included in annual reports to allow management to express its assessment of the company's performance, position, and prospects for the future. (p. 428)

liabilities An accounting element that is one of the three components of a balance sheet. Liabilities are probable future sacrifices of assets arising from present obligations of an entity as a result of past transactions or events—that is, what a company owes. (p. 93)

LIFO (last in, first out) The inventory flow concept based on the assumption that the last units of inventory purchased are the first ones sold. (p. 270)

liquidity An item's "nearness to cash." (p. 313) The ease with which an item, such as an asset, can be converted to cash. The liquidity of a firm refers to the company's ability to generate sufficient cash to meet its short-term obligations. (p. 473)

liquidity ratios A set of ratios developed to measure a firm's ability to generate sufficient cash in the short run to retire short-term liabilities. (p. 474)

long-term assets Assets that are expected to benefit the company for longer than one year. (p. 313)

long-term creditors Banks, corporate bondholders, and any others who lend money for extended periods of time, often up to 40 years. Together with short-term creditors, one of the three major categories of financial statement users. (p. 460)

long-term financing Any financing in which repayment extends beyond five years. This type of financing supports the long-range goals of the company. (p. 122)

long-term liabilities Amounts that are not due for repayment until at least one year from now. (p. 314)

losses Net outflows resulting from peripheral activities of a company. An example is the sale of an asset for less than its book value. (p. 241)

management The people responsible for a company's day-to-day operation. One of the three major categories of financial statement users. (p. 461)

management accounting The branch of accounting developed to meet the informational needs of internal decision makers. (p. 68)

management discussion and analysis (MD&A) A required narrative in the annual report focusing on the company's financial condition, changes in financial condition, and results of operations. (p. 422)

management report A statement addressing the division of responsibility for the annual report information between the company's management and the company's auditors. (p. 428)

manufacturing The business activity that converts purchased raw materials into some tangible, physical product. (p. 19)

market economy A type of economy in which all or most of the factors of production are privately owned and that relies on competition in the marketplace to determine the most efficient way to allocate the economy's resources. (p. 5)

market interest rate Another name for the effective interest rate. (p. 130)

market price Another name for the selling price of a bond. (p. 130)

matching Relating the expenses to the revenues of a particular income statement period. Once it is determined in which period a revenue should be recognized, the expenses that helped to generate the revenue are matched to that same period. (p. 202)

materiality The modifying convention that allows departure from GAAP if the treatment of an item is not significant enough to influence the judgment of a reasonable person. (p. 393)

mercenary society A society based on mutual distrust in which members must be constantly on their guard against being taken advantage of by others. (p. 10)

merchandise inventory The physical units (goods) a company buys to resell as part of its business operation. (p. 265)

merchandising The business activity involving the selling of finished goods produced by other businesses. (p. 19)

modification not affecting opinion A comment added to an unqualified audit opinion addressing any matter the auditor feels is important to the understanding of the financial statements. (p. 400)

monetary unit assumption The assumption that all economic transactions and events can be measured using some monetary unit. (p. 390)

mortgage A document that states the agreement between a lender and a borrower who has secured the loan by offering something of value as collateral. (p. 126)

multistep income statement An income statement format that highlights gross margin and operating income. (p. 157)

natural resources Land and the materials that come from the land, such as timber, mineral deposits, oil deposits, and water. One of the factors of production. (p. 4)

net cash flow The difference between cash inflows and cash outflows; it can be either positive or negative. (p. 68)

net earnings Another name for net income. (p. 153)

net income The amount of profit that remains after all costs have been considered. The net reward of doing business for a specific time period. (p. 8, p. 153)

net loss The difference between revenues and expenses of a period in which expenses are greater than revenues. (p. 153)

net of tax The proper presentation format for nonrecurring items shown below income from continuing operations on the income statement. (p. 320)

net profit Actual profit; equivalent to net income. (p. 8)

net sales to working capital ratio A ratio used to measure the level of sales generated for a given level of working capital. (p. 476)

net worth The difference between assets and liabilities. More commonly called *owners' equity*. (p. 479)

neutrality A primary characteristic of reliability. To be useful, accounting information must be free of bias. (p. 76)

no-par stock Stock that has no par value assigned to it. (p. 104)

nominal interest rate The interest rate set by the issuers of bonds, stated as a percentage of the par value of the bonds. Also called the contract rate or coupon rate, or stated rate. (p. 129)

nonrecurring item Results of activities that cannot be expected to occur again, and therefore should not be used to predict future performance. (p. 317)

nonroutine decisions Decisions that must be made in new and unfamiliar circumstances. (p. 41)

note payable An agreement between a lender and borrower that creates a liability for the borrower. (p. 125)

notes to the financial statements Providing additional detail and explanation of the amounts on the face of the financial statements; an important part of financial statement disclosure. (p. 421)

operating activities Activities that result in cash inflows and outflows generated from the normal course of business. (p. 346)

operating income Income produced by the major business activity of the company. An item shown on the multistep income statement. (p. 157)

opinion An auditor's judgment as to the fairness of the financial statement presentation. (p. 398)

opportunity cost The benefit or benefits forgone by not selecting a particular alternative. Once an alternative is selected in a decision situation, the benefits of all rejected alternatives become part of the opportunity cost of the alternative selected. (p. 39)

outstanding shares Shares of stock actually held by shareholders. The number may be different than that for issued shares because a corporation may reacquire its own stock (treasury stock). (p. 101)

owners' equity The owners' residual interest in the assets of a company after consideration of its liabilities. (p. 95)

paid-in capital The portion of stockholders' equity representing amounts invested by the owners of the corporation. Consists of common stock, preferred stock, and amounts received in excess of the par values of those stocks. Also called contributed capital. (p. 102)

par value (for bonds) The amount that must be paid back upon maturity of a bond. Also called face value. (p. 129)

par value (for stocks) An arbitrary amount assigned to each share of stock by the incorporators at the time of incorporation. (p.102)

par value stock Stock with a par value printed on the stock certificate (see par value). (p. 102)

parent company A company that owns a majority of another company's voting stock. (p. 419)

partnership A business form similar to a proprietorship, but having two or more owners. (p. 14)

period Length of time (usually a month, quarter, or year) for which activity is being reported on an income statement. (p. 154)

periodic inventory system An inventory system in which all inventory and cost of goods sold calculations are done at the end of the income statement period. (p. 275)

perpetual inventory system An inventory system in which both the physical count of inventory units and the cost classification (asset or expense) are updated whenever there is a transaction involving inventory. (p. 275)

personal values The system of beliefs that guides an individual in determining what is right and what is wrong in the decision-making process. (p. 49)

planned economy An economy in which a strong, centralized government controls all or most of the natural resources, labor, and capital used to produce goods and services. (p. 5)

predictive value A primary characteristic of relevance. To be useful, accounting must provide information to decision makers that can be used to predict the future and timing of cash flows. (p. 76)

preferred (preference) stock A share of ownership in a corporation that has preference over common stock as to dividends and as to assets upon liquidation of the corporation. Usually nonvoting stock. (p. 105)

premium If a bond's selling price is above its par value, the bond is being sold at a premium. (p. 132)

primary earnings per share   The most basic presentation of EPS. Divides earnings figures for the period by the average number of shares of common stock outstanding. (p. 419)

primary stock market   The business activity involved in the initial issue of stock from a corporation. (p.109)

principal   In the case of notes and mortgages, the amount of funds actually borrowed. (p. 127)

profit   The excess of benefit over sacrifice. See gross profit and net profit. A less formal name for net income. (p. 8, p. 153)

profitability   The ease with which a company generates income. (p. 469)

profitability ratios   A set of ratios developed to predict a firm's ability to generate sufficient profits (and ultimately cash) to fulfill its obligations. (p. 469)

profit margin after income tax ratio   A profitability ratio that measures the earnings produced from a given level of revenues by comparing net income after income tax to the revenue figure. (p. 472)

profit margin before income tax ratio   A profitability ratio that measures the earnings produced from a given level of revenues by comparing net income before income tax to the revenue figure. (p. 470)

profit motive   The motivational factor that drives a person to do something when the benefit derived from doing it is greater than the sacrifice required to do it. (p. 7)

proprietorship   A business that is owned by one individual. (p. 12)

prospectus   A description of an upcoming bond issue that is provided as information for potential investors. (p. 132)

purchases   The amount of merchandise inventory bought during the income statement period. (p. 266)

qualified opinion   The opinion issued when the departure from GAAP affects no more than one of the financial statements. (p. 399)

qualitative characteristics   These are characteristics upon which an assessment of the usefulness of accounting information can be based.

They include the primary characteristics of relevance (predictive value, feedback value, and timeliness) and reliability (verifiability, representational faithfulness, and neutrality), and the secondary characteristics of comparability and consistency. (p. 75)

quandary ethics   Another name for rules ethics. Sometimes called modern ethics. (p. 52)

quick ratio   A liquidity ratio that is similar to the current ratio, but a more stringent test of liquidity, because only current assets considered to be highly liquid (quickly converted to cash) are included in the calculation. Also called the acid test ratio. (p. 475)

quotas   Quantity limitation placed on imported goods. (p. 25)

ratio analysis   A technique for analyzing the relationship between two items from a company's financial statements for a given period. (p. 459)

reasoned decision making   An approach to decision making in which the decision maker attempts to consider all aspects of a situation before deciding on a course of action. (p. 43)

receivables turnover ratio   A liquidity ratio that measures how quickly a company collects its accounts receivable. (p. 476)

recognition   The process of recording an event in your records and reporting it on your financial statements. (p. 194)

Regulation S-K   Specifies the content of the non-financial statement portions of the Form 10-K that must be filed with the Securities and Exchange Commission by publicly traded companies. (p. 417)

Regulation S-X   Prescribes the rules for the form and content of financial statements in the Form 10-K that must be filed with the Securities and Exchange Commission by publicly traded companies. (p. 417)

relevance   One of the two primary qualitative characteristics of useful accounting information. It means the information must have a bearing on a particular decision situation. (p. 75)

reliability   One of the two primary qualitative characteristics of useful accounting information. It means the information must be reasonably accurate. (p. 75)

report form The vertical format of a balance sheet in which assets, liabilities, and owners' equity are shown one after another down the page. (p. 96)

representational faithfulness A primary characteristic of reliability. To be useful, accounting information must reasonably report what actually happened. (p. 76)

residual value The estimated value of an asset when it has reached the end of its useful life. Also called salvage or scrap value. (p. 205)

retail merchandiser A company that buys its product from a wholesaler or manufacturer and then sells the product to the end consumer. (p. 19)

retained earnings Earnings reinvested in a corporation. Equal to the total profits of the corporation since it was organized less amounts distributed to the stockholders in the form of dividends. (p. 102)

return before interest on equity ratio A profitability ratio that measures the level of earnings (before the cost of borrowing) generated from a given level of equity. (p. 473)

return on assets ratio A profitability ratio that measures the return earned on the company's investment in assets. (p. 470)

return on equity ratio A profitability ratio that measures the after-tax net income generated from a given level of investment by a company's owners. (p. 473)

revenue recognition principle Revenue is recognized when it is earned, rather than when the cash associated with revenue is received. (p. 392)

revenues An accounting element representing the inflows of assets as a result of an entity's ongoing major or central operations. These are the rewards of doing business. (p. 152)

review Inquiries of company personnel and analytical procedures performed by an independent CPA sufficient to provide negative assurance against serious GAAP problems. (p. 401)

reward The benefit or benefits attained by selecting an alternative in a decision situation. (p. 38)

risk The probability that an alternative selected in a decision situation will yield unsatisfactory results. (p. 41)

routine decisions Recurring decision situations in which an appropriate solution need be found only once. That decision becomes the rule, or standard, and whenever the situation recurs, the rule is implemented. (p. 41)

rules ethics A system of ethics in which the rules of conduct come from outside the individual. When a situation occurs, the individual determines the appropriate rule of conduct and applies it to the decision required by the situation. Also called quandary ethics. (p. 52)

sacrifice Something given up in order to attain a desired reward. (p. 38)

sales Another term for sales revenue. (p. 157)

sales revenue The revenue generated from the sale of a tangible product as a major business activity. (p. 157)

salvage value Another name for residual value. (p. 205)

scrap value Another name for salvage or residual value. (p. 205)

secondary stock market The business activity focusing on trades of stock among investors subsequent to the initial issue. (p. 109)

secretary The person who maintains the minutes of meetings of the board of directors and stockholders of a corporation. This person may also represent the corporation in legal proceedings. (p. 100)

Securities and Exchange Commission (SEC) The government agency empowered to regulate the buying and selling of stocks and bonds. (p. 109)

selling price The amount received when bonds are issued or sold. This amount is affected by the difference between the nominal interest rate and the market rate. Selling price is usually stated as a percentage of the bond's par value. (p. 130)

separate entity assumption The assumption that economic activity can be identified with a particular economic entity and that the results of activities for each entity will be recorded separately. (p. 389)

service   A business activity that does not deal with tangible products, but rather provides some sort of service as its major operation. (p. 21)

shareholders   The owners of a corporation. Also called stockholders. (p. 99)

short-term creditors   Creditors who lend money, expecting repayment within one year. Together with long-term creditors, one of the three major categories of financial statement users. (p. 460)

short-term financing   Financing secured to support an operation's day-to-day activities. Repayment is usually required within five years. (p. 122)

single-step income statement   A format of the income statement that gathers all revenues into "total revenues" and all expenses into "total expenses." Net income is calculated as a subtraction of total expenses from total revenues. (p. 156)

socialism   A type of planned economy in which a government chosen by the people controls the resources of the society. (p. 5)

sole proprietorship   Equivalent to a proprietorship. (p. 12)

solvency   A company's ability to meet the obligations created by its long-term debt. (p. 478)

solvency ratios   A set of ratios developed to measure a firm's ability to meet its long-term debt obligations. (p. 478)

Special Committee on Financial Reporting   Formed by the AICPA to investigate the information needs of users of financial reports. The Committee has proposed a new model of business reporting. (p. 443)

stable dollar assumption   The assumption that allows financial statements to ignore the fact that the value of the dollar changes over time. (p. 390)

stakeholder   Anyone who is affected by the way a company conducts its business. (p. 11)

stated rate   Another name for nominal interest rate. (p. 129)

statement of cash flows   A financial statement that provides information about the causes of a change in a company's cash balance from the beginning to the end of a specific period. (p. 342)

statement of earnings   Another name for the income statement. (p. 154)

Statement of Financial Accounting Standards (SFAS)   The official name of a pronouncement issued by FASB as part of GAAP. (p. 388)

statement of financial condition   Another name for the balance sheet. (p. 95)

statement of financial position   Another name for the balance sheet. (p. 95)

statement of owners' equity   The financial statement that reports activity in the capital accounts of proprietorships and partnerships and in the stockholders' equity accounts of corporations. The statement of owners' equity serves as a bridge between the income statement and the balance sheet. (p. 160)

statement of results of operations   The formal name of the income statement. (p. 154)

statement of retained earnings   A corporate financial statement that shows the changes in retained earnings during a particular period. (p. 170)

stock certificate   Document providing evidence of ownership of shares in a corporation. (p. 100)

stock exchange   An organization that brings together buyers and sellers of stock. (p. 108)

stockholder   A person who owns shares of stock in a corporation. (p. 17)

stockholders' equity   The corporate form of owners' equity. Stockholders' equity is divided into contributed capital and retained earnings. (p. 102)

stock market   A general term referring to activities in the secondary stock market. (p. 108)

stock offering   The process of announcing the issue of shares of stock. (p. 109)

straight-line depreciation   One of several acceptable methods of calculating periodic depreciation. The depreciable base of an asset is divided by its estimated useful life. The result is the amount of depreciation expense to be recognized in each year of the item's estimated useful life: (Cost – residual value)/N = annual depreciation expense. (p. 206)

subsidiary   A company that has a majority of its voting stock owned by another company. (p. 419)

sympathetic society   A society in which all affairs are conducted with the love of others in mind. (p. 10)

syndicate   A group of underwriters working together to get a large bond issue sold to the public. (p. 131)

systematic style   A style of processing information in which decisions are made after breaking a problem down into parts and methodically approaching each part. (p. 42)

tariffs   Taxes that raise the price of imported products so they cost about the same as products produced within the country. (p. 25)

timeliness   A primary characteristic of relevance. To be useful, accounting information must be provided in time to influence a particular decision. (p. 75)

time period assumption   The assumption that the economic activities of an entity can be traced to some specific time period and results of those activities can be reported for any arbitrary time period chosen. (p. 391)

times interest earned ratio   Another name for the coverage ratio. (p. 480)

title   Proof of legal ownership of an item. (p. 200)

total asset turnover ratio   A profitability ratio that indicates the amount of revenues produced for a given level of assets used. (p. 471)

total liabilities to net worth ratio   A solvency ratio indicating the relationship between creditors' claims to a company's assets and the owners' claim to those assets. (p. 479)

trade creditors   Short-term creditors who sell goods and services to companies in the normal course of business. (p. 460)

translation   The conversion of the currency of one country into its equivalent in another country's currency. (p. 23)

treasurer   The person in charge of managing the cash of a corporation. (p.100)

treasury stock   Corporate stock that has been issued and then reacquired by the corporation. (p. 101)

uncertainty   A lack of complete information about the future. The greater the degree of uncertainty, the greater the risk of selecting unacceptable alternatives. (p. 41)

underwriters   Professionals in the field of investment banking. Also called investment bankers. (p. 109)

unqualified opinion   States that the auditors find the financial statements to be fairly presented in accordance with GAAP. Also called a "clean" opinion. (p. 399)

verifiability   A primary characteristic of reliability. Information is considered verifiable if several individuals, working independently, would arrive at similar conclusions using the same data. (p. 76)

virtues ethics   A system of ethics in which the individual decides what kind of person he or she desires to be, thereby establishing a code of conduct that can be applied to any situation. Also called character ethics. (p. 51)

wholesale merchandiser   A company that buys its product from the manufacturer (or another wholesaler) and then sells the product to a retail merchandiser. (p. 19)

withdrawals   Another name for drawings. (p. 165)

working capital   The difference between current assets and current liabilities. (p. 342, p. 476)

yield rate   Another name for the effective interest rate. (p. 130)

Index